PENGUIN BOOKS

THREE THOUSAND STITCHES

Sudha Murty was born in 1950, in Shiggaon, North Karnataka. Author, philanthropist, educator, public speaker and engineer, she completed her master's in computer science from IISc, Bangalore. She is the founder of the Infosys Foundation and the chairperson of the Murty Trust. A bestselling author, with more than 300 titles to her acclaim, some of her most famous books include *Three Thousand Stitches*, *Dollar Bahu* and *Wise and Otherwise*. She writes in English and Kannada, and her books have been translated into all major Indian languages and have sold over 60 lakh copies around the country.

Over the years, Sudha Murty has been recognized with many prestigious awards, including the Padma Bhushan and the Padma Shri from the Government of India in 2023 and 2006, respectively; Bal Sahitya Puraskar in 2023; the R.K. Narayan Award for Literature in 2006; the Lal Bahadur Shastri National Award in 2020; and Lokmanya Tilak and Mahatma awards in 2024. She was also awarded the Rajyotsava and Attimabbe Award for excellence in Kannada literature from the Government of Karnataka in 2000 and 2012. Sudha Murty has received nineteen honorary doctorates from various universities across India. Currently, she is also serving as the President-nominated member of Parliament in the Rajya Sabha.

THREE THOUSAND STITCHES

Ordinary People, Extraordinary Lives

Sudha Murty

PENGUIN BOOKS

An imprint of Penguin Random House

PENGUIN BOOKS

Penguin Books is an imprint of the Penguin Random House group of companies whose addresses can be found at global.penguinrandomhouse.com

Published by Penguin Random House India Pvt. Ltd
4th Floor, Capital Tower 1, MG Road,
Gurugram 122 002, Haryana, India

First published in Penguin Books by Penguin Random House India 2017
This edition published in 2025

ISBN 9780143440055

Typeset in Dante MT Std by Manipal Digital Systems, Manipal
Printed at Thomson Press India Ltd, New Delhi

www.penguin.co.in

Contents

To T.J.S. George,
who gave me my first break to write in English

Preface

I often get letters from students and parents telling me how beneficial my books have been for them and their children. I want to thank them and all those who have exposed me to different facets of life, filling my pot of learning with knowledge and experience. This includes the young men and women who have shown me how they put aside their bitter experiences to move forward in life with joy and hope.

There are some who feel that most of my writing is fiction, but my life has unmistakably proven to be stranger than that.

Fifteen years ago, renowned journalist T.J.S. George asked me to write a weekly column for the *New Indian Express*. I was hesitant at first—all because I was educated in a Kannada-medium school till the tenth grade. It was only natural then that I was more comfortable with Kannada than English. George said to me, 'A language is but a vehicle. It's the person inside who's weaving the story that's more important. You are a storyteller. So just get on with your story and the language will fall into place.'

And so began my journey in English. I am what I am today as an English author because of George. He gave me the title of my first book, *Wise and Otherwise,* and wrote the foreword too. His foresight and encouragement catapulted me from a hesitant writer to a widely read author.

I often dream about the world being filled with many Georges who will come forward to support such writers and encourage them to experiment and explore their potential.

I want to thank my young and bright editor, Shrutkeerti Khurana, and also Udayan Mitra and Meru Gokhale for bringing out this book.

1

Three Thousand Stitches

We set up the Infosys Foundation in 1996. Unfortunately, I knew precious little of how things worked in a non-profit organization. I knew more about software, management, programming and tackling software bugs. Examinations, mark sheets and deadlines occupied most of my days. The concept behind the foundation was that it must make a difference to the common man—*bahujan hitaya, bahujan sukhaya*—it must provide compassionate aid regardless of caste, creed, language or religion.

As we pondered over the issues before us—malnutrition, education, rural development, self-sufficiency, access to medicine, cultural activities and the revival of the arts, among others—there was one issue that occupied my uppermost thoughts—the devadasi tradition that was pervasive throughout India.

The word devadasi means 'servant of the Lord'. Traditionally, devadasis were musicians and dancers who practised their craft in temples to please the gods. They had a high status in society. We can see the evidence of it in the caves of Badami, as well as in stories like that of the devadasi Vinapodi, who was very dear to the ruling king of the Chalukya dynasty between the sixth and seventh century in northern Karnataka. The king donated enormous sums of money to temples. However, as time went by, the temples were destroyed and the tradition of the devadasis fell into the wrong hands. Young girls were initially dedicated to the worship and service of a deity or a temple in good faith, but eventually, the word devadasi became synonymous with sex worker. Some were born into the life, while others were 'sacrificed' to the temples by their parents due to various reasons, or simply because they caught a hair infection like the ringworm of the scalp, assumed to be indicative that the girl was destined to be a devadasi.

As I thought about their plight, I recalled my visit to the Yellamma Gudda (or Renuka temple) in the Belgaum district of Karnataka years ago. I remembered their green saris and bangles, the smears of yellow *bhandara* (a coarse turmeric powder) and their thick, long hair as they entered the temple with goddess masks, coconuts, neem leaves and a *kalash* (a metal pot). 'Why can't I tackle this problem?' I wondered. I didn't realize then that I was choosing one of the most difficult tasks for our very first project.

With innocence and bubbling enthusiasm, I chose a place in northern Karnataka where the practice was rampant and prostitution was carried on in the name of religion. My plan was to talk to the devadasis and write down their concerns to help me understand their predicament, followed by organizing a few discussions targeted towards solving their problems within a few months.

On my first day in the district, I armed myself with a notebook and pen and set out. I dressed simply, with no jewellery or bindi. I wore a pair of jeans, T-shirt and a cap. After some time, I found a group of devadasis sitting below a tree near a temple. They were chatting and removing lice from each other's hair.

Without thinking, I went up to them, interrupting their conversation. '*Namaskaram*, Amma. I've come here to help you. Tell me your problems and I'll write them down.'

They must have been discussing something important because the women gave me a dirty look. They lobbed questions at me with increasing ferocity.

'Who are you? Did we invite you here?'

'Have you come to write about us? In that case, we don't want to talk to you.'

'Are you an officer? Or a minister? If we tell you our problems, how will you solve them?'

'Go away. Go back to where you came from.'

I did not move. In fact, I persisted. 'I want to help you. Please listen to me. Are you aware that there is a dangerous illness called AIDS that you could be exposed to? There is no cure for . . .'

'Just go,' one of them snapped. I glanced at their faces. They were furious.

But I did not leave. 'Maybe they need a little convincing,' I thought.

Without warning, one of them stood up, took off her chappal and threw it at me. 'Can't you understand simple Kannada? Just get lost.'

Insulted and humiliated, I felt my tears threatening to spill over. I turned back and fled.

Upon returning home, with the insult fresh on my mind, I told myself, 'I won't go there again.'

However, a few days later, it occurred to me that the women were probably upset about something else and that maybe I had simply chosen the wrong time and date to visit them.

So after another week, I went there again. This visit took place during the tomato harvest. The devadasi women were happily distributing small, oval-shaped bright red tomatoes to each other from the baskets kept near them. I approached them and smiled pleasantly. 'Hello, I've come to meet you again! Please hear me out. I really, really want to help you.'

They laughed at me. 'We don't need your help. But would you like to buy some tomatoes?'

'No, I am not very fond of tomatoes.'

'What kind of a woman are you? Who doesn't like tomatoes?'

I attempted to engage them once more, 'Have you heard of AIDS? You must know that the government is spending a lot of money on increasing awareness about it.'

'Are you a government agent? Or maybe you belong to a political party. How much commission are you getting to do this? Come on, tell us! We don't even have a proper hospital in this area and here you are, trying to educate us about a scary disease. We don't need your help. Our goddess will help us in difficult times.'

I stood dumbfounded, struggling to find words.

One of the women said decisively, 'This lady must be a journalist. That's why she has a pen and paper. She'll write about us and make money by exploiting us.' Upon hearing this, the others started throwing tomatoes at me.

This time, my emotions overpowered me and I started to cry. Sobbing, I fled from there once again.

I was in despair. 'Why should I work on this project? Why do they keep insulting me? Where else do the beneficiaries humiliate the person working for their well-being? I am not a good fit for this field. Yes, I should resign and go back to my academic career. The foundation can choose a different trustee.'

When I reached home, I sat down to compose a resignation letter.

My father came down the stairs and seeing me busy with my head bent close to the paper, he asked, 'What are you writing so frantically?'

I narrated the entire episode to him.

To my amazement, rather than sympathizing with me, my father chuckled and said, 'I didn't know that you were so impractical.'

I stared at him in anger.

He took an ice cream from the fridge and forced me to sit down and eat it. 'It'll cool your head,' he said and smiled. After a few minutes, he said, 'Please remember. Prostitution has existed in society since ancient times and has become an integral part of life. It is one of the root problems of all civilizations. Many kings and saints have tried to eliminate it but no law or punishment has been successful in bringing it down to zero. Not one nation in the world is free of this. Then how can you change the entire system by yourself? You're just an ordinary woman! What you should do is reduce your expectations and lower your goal. For instance, try to help ten devadasis leave their profession. Rehabilitate them and show them what it means to lead a normal life. This will guarantee that their children will not follow in their footsteps. Make that your aim, and the day you accomplish it, I will feel very proud knowing that I gave birth to a daughter who helped ten helpless women make the most difficult transition from being sex workers to independent women.'

'But they threw chappals and tomatoes at me, Kaka,' I whined petulantly. I always called my father 'Kaka'.

'Actually, you got a promotion today—from chappals to tomatoes. If you pursue this and go there a third time, maybe you'll get something even better!' His joke brought a reluctant smile to my face.

'They won't even talk to me. Then how can I work for them?'

'Look at yourself,' my father said, dragging me in front of the nearest mirror. 'You are casually dressed in a T-shirt, a pair of jeans and a cap. This may be your style, but the common man and a rural Indian woman like the devadasi will never connect or identify with you. If you wear a sari, a *mangalsutra*, put on a bindi and tie your hair, I'm sure that they will receive you much better than before. I'll also come with you. An old man like me will be of great help to you in such an adventure.'

I protested, 'I don't want to alter my appearance for their sake. I don't believe in such superficial changes.'

'Well, if you want to change them, then you have to change yourself first. Change your attitude. Of course, it's your decision in the end.'

He left me in front of the mirror and walked away.

My parents had never thrust their choices or beliefs on me or any of my siblings, whether it was about education, profession or marriage. They always gave their advice and helped us if we wanted, but I made all the choices.

For a few days, I was confused. I thought about the skills needed for social work. There was no glamour or money in this profession and I could not behave like an executive in a corporate house. I required language skills, of which English may not be needed at all! I should be able to sit down on the floor and eat the local food, no matter where I travelled for work. I had to listen patiently, and most of all, I should love the work I did. What would give me higher satisfaction—keeping my external appearance the way it was or the work that I would do?

After some introspection, I decided to change my appearance and concentrate completely on the work.

Before my next visit, I pulled my hair back, tied it and adorned it with flowers. I wore a two-hundred-rupee sari, a big bindi, a mangalsutra and glass bangles. I transformed myself into the 'bharatiya nari', the stereotypical traditional Indian woman, and took my father along with me to meet the devadasis.

This time, when we went there, upon seeing my aged father, they said, 'Namaste.'

My father introduced me. 'This is my daughter and she is a teacher. She has come here on a holiday. I told her how difficult your lives are. Your children are the reason for your existence and you want to educate them irrespective of what happens to your health, am I right?'

They replied in unison, 'Yes, sir!'

'Since my daughter is a teacher, she can guide you with your children's education and help them find better jobs. She'll give you information about some scholarships which you may not be aware of and help your kids with it so that your financial burden may be reduced. Is that okay with you? If not, it's all right. She'll go to some other village and try to help the people there. Please don't feel pressured. Think about it and get back to us. We'll be back in ten minutes.'

Grasping my hand tightly, he pulled me a short distance away.

'Why did you say all that?' I asked. 'You should have first told them about things like the dangers of AIDS.'

'Don't be foolish. We will tell them about it some other time. If you start with something negative, then nobody will like it. The first introduction should always be positive and bring real hope to the beneficiary. And just like I've promised them, you must help their children get scholarships first. Work on AIDS later.'

'And why did you tell them I'm a teacher, Kaka?' I demanded. 'You could have said I was a social worker.'

My father offered a calm rebuttal. 'They consider teaching to be one of the most respectable jobs and you are a professor, aren't you?'

I nodded reluctantly, still unsure of his strategy.

When we went back, the women were ready to listen. They called me *akka* or 'elder sister' in Kannada.

So I started working with them to help their children secure the promised scholarships. Some of these children even started going to college within a year. Only after this happened did I bring up the subject of AIDS, and this time, they heard me out. Months went by. It took me almost three years to establish a relationship with them. I was their darling akka and eventually, they trusted me enough to share their heart-touching stories and the trials they had endured.

Innocent girls had been sold into the trade by their husbands, brothers, fathers, boyfriends, uncles or other relatives. Some entered the sex trade on their own hoping to earn some money for their families and help future generations escape poverty. Still others were lured into it with the promise of a real job, only to find themselves tricked to work as sex workers. Hearing their stories, there were moments when I couldn't hide my tears, yet they were the ones who held my hand and consoled me! Each story was different but the end was the same—they all suffered at the hands of a society that exploited them and filled them with guilt and shame as a final insult.

I realized that simply donating money would not bolster their confidence or build their self-esteem. The best solution

I could think of was to unite them towards a common goal by helping them build their own organization. The state government of Karnataka had many good policies that encouraged housing, marriage schemes and scholarships, but if we started an association or a union exclusively for the devadasis, they could address each other's problems. In time, they would become bold and independent, learning to organize themselves in the process.

Thus, an organization for the devadasis was formed. I believe that God cannot be present everywhere at once and, in return, he sends people to do his work. Abhay Kumar, a kind-hearted and idealistic young man from Delhi, joined us unexpectedly. He wanted to work with me and so I decided to give him the toughest job in order to test his passion for social work. I told Abhay, 'If you work with the devadasis for eight months and survive, I'll think about absorbing you into the project full-time.'

As promised, he did not show up for eight months, and then one day, he confidently strolled into my office, a little thinner, but grinning from ear to ear.

I said, 'Abhay, now you know how hard social work is. It takes extreme commitment and persistence to keep going. You can go back to Delhi with the satisfaction of having made a difference to so many lives. You are a good human being and I'm sure that this little experience will stay with you and help you later.'

He smiled and replied in impeccable Kannada, 'Who said that I wanted to go back to Delhi? I've decided to stay in Karnataka and complete this project.'

'Abhay, this is serious work. You are young and that's a great disadvantage in this line of work and . . .' My voice faded away. I didn't know what else to say!

'Don't worry about that, ma'am! You gave me the best job I could possibly have. I thought that you might give me a desk job. I never imagined that you'd give me fieldwork, that too, the privilege of working with the devadasis. This past year has made me realize their agony and unbearable hardships. Knowing that, how can I ever work anywhere apart from here?'

I was astonished at such sincerity and compassion in one so young. I offered him a stipend to help with his expenses but he stopped me with a show of his hand, 'I don't need that much. I already have a scooter and a few sets of clothes. I just need two meals a day, a roof over my head and a little money for petrol. That's it.'

I gazed at him fondly and knew that I was seeing a man who had found his purpose in life. He bid goodbye and left my office with determined strides.

Obviously, Abhay became the project lead, and I supported him wholeheartedly, taking care to converse with him regularly about the project's progress.

One day, I met with the devadasis and inquired about the welfare of their children.

'Our greatest difficulty is supporting our children's education,' they said. 'Most of the time, we can't afford their school fees and then we have to go back to what we know to get quick money.'

'We will take care of all your children's educational expenses irrespective of which class they are in. But that means that you must not continue being a devadasi, no matter what,' I replied firmly.

The women agreed without hesitation. They had come to trust Abhay and me and knew that we would keep our word.

Hundreds of children were enrolled in the project—some went on to do professional courses while others went on to complete their primary, middle or high school classes. We held camps on AIDS awareness and prevention and sponsored street art and plays to educate the women and children on various medical issues—including the simple fact that infected hair is not an indication that one must become a devadasi. Rather, it is a simple curable disease that causes the hair to stick together and become matted over time. The women got themselves treated and some of them even had their heads shaved.

Eventually, we were able to get them loans by becoming their guarantors. Often, the women would tell me, 'Akka, please help us get a loan. If we can't repay it, then it is as good as cheating you and you know that we'll never do that.' By this time I knew in my heart that a rich man might cheat me but our devadasis never would. They had great faith in me and I in them.

On the other hand, life became more dangerous for Abhay and me. We received death threats from pimps, local goons and others through phone calls, letters and messages. I was scared more for Abhay than myself. Though I asked for police protection, Abhay flatly refused and said, 'Our devadasis will protect me. Don't worry about me.'

A few weeks later, some pimps threw acid on three devadasis who had left their profession for good. But we all still refused to give up. The plastic surgery the victims underwent helped to bring back their confidence. They would not be intimidated. Our strength came from these women who were collectively trying to leave this hated profession. Though the government supplemented their income, many also started rearing goats, cows and buffaloes.

Over time, we established small schools that offered night classes which the devadasis could attend. It was an uphill battle that took years of effort from everybody involved. After twelve years, some of the women met me to discuss a particular issue.

'Akka, we want to start a bank, but we are afraid to do it on our own.'

'What do you think happens in a bank?' I asked.

'Well, you need a lot of money to start a bank or even have an account. You must wear expensive clothes. We've seen that bankers usually wear suits and ties and sit in air-conditioned offices, but we don't have money for such things, Akka.'

After they brought this problem to our attention, Abhay and I sat down with the women and explained the basics of banking to them. A few professionals were consulted, and under their guidance, they started a bank of their own, with the exception of a few legal and administrative services that we provided. However, we insisted that the bank employees and shareholders should be restricted only to the devadasi community. So finally, the women were able to save money through fixed deposits and obtain low-interest loans. All profits had to be shared with the bank members. Eventually, the bank grew and the women themselves became its directors and took over its running.

Less than three years later, the bank had Rs 80 lakh in deposits and provided employment to former devadasis, but its most important achievement was that almost 3000 women were out of the devadasi system.

On their third anniversary, I received a letter from the bank.

We are very happy to share that three years have passed since the bank was started. Now, the bank is of sound financial health and none of us practise or make any money through the devadasi tradition. We have each paid a hundred rupees and have three lakhs saved for a big celebration. We have rented out a hall and arranged lunch for everyone. Please come and join us for our big day. Akka, you are very dear to us and we want you to be our chief guest for the occasion. You have travelled hundreds of times at your own cost and spent endless money for our sake even though we are strangers. This time, we want to book a round-trip air-conditioned Volvo bus ticket, a good hotel and an all-expenses-paid trip for you. Our money has been earned legally, ethically and morally. We are sure that you won't refuse our humble and earnest request.

Tears welled up in my eyes. Seventeen years ago, chappals were my reward, but now, they wanted to pay for my travel to the best of their ability. I knew how much the comfort of an air-conditioned Volvo bus and a hotel meant to them.

I decided to attend the function at my expense.

On the day of the function, I found that there were no politicians or garlands or long speeches as was typical. It was a simple event. At first, some women sang a song of agony written by the devadasis. Then another group came and described their experiences on their journey to independence. Their children, many of whom had become doctors, nurses, lawyers, clerks, government employees, teachers, railway employees and bank officers, came and thanked their mothers and the organization for supporting their education.

And then it was my turn to speak.

I stood there, and my words suddenly failed me. My mind went blank, and then, distantly, I remembered my father's words: 'I will feel very proud knowing that I gave birth to a daughter who helped ten helpless women make the most difficult transition from being sex workers to independent women.'

I am usually a spontaneous speaker but on that day, I was too choked with emotion. I didn't know where to begin. For the first time in my life, I felt that the day I meet God, I will be able to stand up straight and say confidently, 'You've given me a lot in this lifetime, and I hope that I have returned at least something. I've served 3000 of your children in the best way I could, relieving them of the meaningless and cruel devadasi system. Your children are your flowers and I am returning them to you.'

Then my eyes fell on the women. They were so eager to listen to me. They wanted to hear what I had to say. Abhay was there too, looking overwhelmed by everything they had done for us.

I quoted a Sanskrit *shloka* my grandfather had taught me when I was six years old: 'O God, I don't need a kingdom nor do I desire to be an emperor. I don't want rebirth or the golden vessels or heaven. I don't need anything from you. O Lord, if you want to give me something, then give me a soft heart and hard hands, so that I can wipe the tears of others.'

Silently, I came back to my chair. I didn't know what the women must be thinking or feeling at that moment.

An old devadasi climbed up on to the stage and stood there proudly. With a firm voice, she said, 'We want to give our akka a special gift. It is an embroidered bedspread and each of us has stitched some portion of it. So there are three thousand stitches. It may not look beautiful but we all wanted to be present in this bedspread.' Then she looked straight at me and continued, 'This is from our hearts to yours. This will keep you cool in the summer and warm in the winter—just like our affection towards you. You were by our side during our difficult times, and we want to be with you too.'

It is the best gift I have ever received.

2

How to Beat the Boys

Recently, when I visited the US, I had to speak to a crowd of both students and highly successful people. I always prefer interacting with the audience, so I opened the floor to questions.

After several questions were asked, a middle-aged man stood to speak. 'Ma'am, you are very confident and clear in communicating your thoughts. You are absolutely at ease while talking to us . . . '

I was direct. 'Please don't praise me. Ask me your question.'

'I think you must have studied abroad or done your MBA from a university in the West. Is that what gives you such confidence?' he asked.

Without wasting a second, I replied, 'It comes from my B.V.B.'

He seemed puzzled. 'What do you mean—my B.V.B.?'

I smiled. 'I'm talking about the Basappa Veerappa Bhoomaraddi College of Engineering and Technology in Hubli, a medium-sized town in the state of Karnataka in

India. I have never studied outside of India. The only reason I stand here before you is because of that college.'

In a lighter vein, I continued, 'I'm sure that the young people in the software industry who are present here today will appreciate the contribution of Infosys to India and to the US. Infosys has made Bengaluru, Karnataka and India proud. Had I not been in B.V.B., I would not have become an engineer. If I wasn't an engineer, then I wouldn't have been able to support my husband. And if my husband didn't have his family's backing, he may or may not have had the chance to establish Infosys at all! In that case, all of you wouldn't have gathered here today to hear me speak.'

Everyone clapped and laughed, but I really meant what I said. After the session got over and the crowd left, I felt tired and chose to sit alone on a couch nearby.

My mind went back to 1968. I was a seventeen-year-old girl with an abundance of courage, confidence and the dream to become an engineer. I came from an educated, though middle-class, conservative Brahmin family. My father was a professor of obstetrics and gynaecology in Karnataka Medical College at Hubli, while my mother was a schoolteacher before she got married.

I finished my pre-university exams with excellent marks and told my family that I wanted to pursue engineering. I had always been fascinated with science, even more so with its application. Engineering was one of those branches of science that would allow me to utilize my creativity, especially in design. But it was as if I had dropped a bomb inside our house.

The immediate reaction was of shock. Engineering was clearly an all-male domain and hence considered a taboo for girls in those days. There was no questioning the status quo, wherein girls were expected to be in the company of other female students in a medical or science college. The idea of a woman entering the engineering field had possibly never popped up in anyone's mind. It was akin to expecting pigs to fly.

I was my grandmother's favourite granddaughter, but even she looked at me with disdain and said, 'If you go ahead and do this, no man from north Karnataka will marry you. Who wants to marry a woman engineer? I am so disappointed in you.' My grandmother never thought that I would do anything she disapproved of. However, she also didn't know that in the city of Mysore, across the river of Tungabhadra, lived a man named Narayana Murthy who would later want to marry me.

My grandfather, a history teacher and my first guru to teach me reading and writing, only mildly opposed it. 'My child, you are wonderful at history. Why can't you do something in this field? You could be a great scholar one day. Don't chase a dry subject like engineering.'

My mother, who was extremely proficient in mathematics, said, 'You are good in maths. Why don't you complete your post-graduation in mathematics and get a job as a professor? You can easily work in a college after you get married instead of being a hard-core engineer struggling to balance family and work.'

My father, a liberal man who believed in education for women, thought for a moment and said, 'I think that you should pursue medicine. You are excellent with people and languages. To tell you the truth, I don't know much about engineering. We don't have a single engineer in our family. It is a male-dominated industry and you may not find another girl in your class. What if you have to spend four years without a real friend to talk to? Think about it. However, the decision is yours and I will support you.'

Many of my aunts also thought that no one would marry me if I chose engineering. This would possibly entail that I marry somebody from another community, an absolutely unheard of thing in those days.

However, I didn't care. As a student of history, I had read Hiuen Tsang's book *Si-Yu-Ki*. Before Tsang's travel to India, everybody discouraged him from making the journey on foot, but he refused to listen and decided to go. In time, he became famous for his seventeen-year-long journey to India. Taking courage from Tsang, I told my family, 'I want to do engineering. Come what may, I am ready for the consequences of my actions.'

I filled out the application form for B.V.B. College of Engineering and Technology, submitted it and soon received the news that I had been selected to the college on the basis of my marks. I was ecstatic, but little did I know that the college staff was discomfited by this development.

The principal at the time was B.C. Khanapure, who happened to know my father. They both met at a barber shop one day and the principal expressed his genuine anguish at what he perceived to be an awkward situation. He told my father, 'Doctor Sahib, I know that your daughter is very intelligent and that she has been given admission only because of merit, but I'm afraid we have some problems. She will be the only girl in college. It is going to be difficult for her. First, we don't have a ladies' toilet on campus. We don't have a ladies' room for her to relax either. Second, our boys are young with raging hormones and I am sure that they will trouble her. They may not do anything in front of the staff but they will definitely do something later. They may not cooperate with her or help her because they are not used to talking to girls. As a father of four daughters, I am concerned about yours too. Can you tell her to change her mind for her own sake?'

My father replied, 'I agree with you, Professor Sahib. I know you mean well, but my daughter is hell-bent on pursuing engineering. Frankly, she's not doing anything wrong. So I have decided to let her pursue it.'

'In that case, Doctor Sahib, I have a small request. Please ask her to wear a sari to college as it is a man's world out there and the sari will be an appropriate dress for the environment she will be in. She should not talk to the boys unnecessarily because that will give rise to rumours and that's never good for a girl in our society. Also, tell her to avoid going to the college canteen and spending time there with the boys.'

My father came back and told me about this conversation. I readily agreed to all of the requests since I had no intention of changing my mind.

Eventually, I would become friendly with some of the boys, but I always knew where to draw the line. The truth is that it were these same boys who would teach me some of life's lessons later, such as the value of keeping a sense of perspective, the importance of taking it easy every now and then and being a good sport. Many of the boys, who are now older gentlemen, are like my brothers even after fifty years! Finally, it was the lack of ladies' toilets on campus that made me understand the difficulty faced by many women in India due to the insufficiency or sheer absence of toilets. Eventually, this would lead me to build more than 13,000 toilets in Karnataka alone!

Meanwhile, my mother chose an auspicious day for me to pay the tuition fee. It was a Thursday and happened to be the end of the month. My mother nagged me to pay the fee of Rs 400 that day although my father only had Rs 300 left. He told her, 'Wait for a few days. I will get my salary and then Sudha can pay her fees.'

My mother refused to budge. 'Our daughter is going to college. It is a big deal. We must pay the fees today—it will be good for her studies.'

While they were still going back and forth, my father's assistant, Dr S.S. Hiremath, came along with his father-in-law, Patil, who was the headman of the Baad village near Shiggaon, the town where I was born. Patil curiously asked what was going on and my father explained the situation to him. He then took out his wallet and gave my father a hundred rupees. He said, 'Doctor Sahib, please accept this money. I want to gift it to this girl who is doing something path-breaking. I have seen parents take loans and sell their houses or farms to pay their sons' fees so that they can become engineers. In fact, sometimes, they don't even know whether their child will study properly or not. Look at your daughter. She desperately wants to do this and I think she is right.'

'No, Mr Patil,' my father refused. 'I can't take such an expensive gift. I will accept this as a loan and return it to you next month after I receive my salary.'

Patil continued as though he hadn't heard my father, 'The most important thing is for your daughter to do her best and complete her course and become a model for other girls.' Then he turned to me and said, 'Sudha, promise me that you will always be ethical, impartial and hard-working and that you will bring a good name to your family and society.'

I nodded meekly, suddenly humbled.

My first day of college arrived a month later. I wore a white sari for the first time, touched the feet of all the elders at home and prayed to Goddess Saraswati who had been very kind to me. I then made my way to the college.

As soon as I reached, the principal called me and gave me a key. He said, 'Here, Ms Kulkarni, take this. This is the key of a tiny room in the corner of the electrical engineering department on the second floor. You can use this room whenever you want.'

I thanked him profusely, took the key and immediately went to see the room. I opened the door excitedly, but alas! The room had two broken desks and there was no sign of a toilet. It was so dusty that I could not even consider entering it. Seeing me there, a cleaner came running with a broom in his hand. Without looking at me, he said, 'I'm so sorry. Principal Sahib told me yesterday that a girl student was going to join the college today, but I thought that he was joking. So I didn't clean the room. Anyway, I will do it right now.'

After he had finished cleaning, I still felt that the room was dusty. Calmly, I told him, 'Leave the broom here and give me a wet cloth, please. I will clean the room myself.'

After cleaning the room to my satisfaction, I brushed off the dust on my clothes and went to class.

When I entered the room on the ground floor, there were 149 pairs of eyes staring at me as though I were some kind of an exotic animal. It was true though. I was the one hundred and fiftieth animal in this zoo! I knew that some of them wanted to whistle but I kept a straight face and looked around for a place to sit. The first bench was empty. As I was about to sit there, I saw that someone had spilt blue ink right in the middle of the seat. This was obviously meant for me. I felt tears threatening to spill over, but I blinked them away. Making use of the newspaper in my hand, I wiped the seat clean and sat on a corner of the bench.

I could hear the boys whispering behind me. One grumbled, 'Why the hell did you put ink on the seat? Now she may go and complain to the principal.'

Another boy replied, 'How can she prove that I have done it? There are 149 of us here.'

Despite feeling hurt, I did not go to the principal to complain. He had already warned my father that if I complained, these boys might persist in troubling me further and I may eventually have to leave the college. So, I decided to keep quiet no matter how much these boys tried to harass me.

The truth was that I was afraid of being so troubled by the boys' activities that I would quit engineering altogether. I thought of ways to stay strong—physically and mentally. It would be my *tapas*, or penance. In that instant, I resolved that for the next four years, I would neither miss any class nor ask anyone for help with class notes. In an effort to teach myself self-restraint and self-control, I decided that until I completed my engineering degree, I would wear only white saris, refrain from sweets, sleep on a mat and take baths with cold water. I aimed to become self-sufficient; I would be my best friend and my worst enemy. I didn't know then that such a quote already existed in the Bhagavad Gita where Krishna says, '*Atma aiva hi atmano bandhu aatma aiva ripu atmanah*'.

We really don't need such penance to do well in our studies, but I was young and determined and wanted to do all I could to survive engineering.

I had good teachers who were considerate and sought to look out for me in class. They would occasionally ask, 'Ms Kulkarni, is everything okay with you?'

Even our college principal, Professor Khanapure, went out of his way to inquire about my welfare and if any boys were troubling me.

However, I can't say the same about my classmates.

One day, they brought a small bunch of flowers and stuck it in my plaited hair without my knowledge when the teacher was not around. I heard someone shout from the back—'Ms Flowerpot!' I quietly ran my fingers through my hair, found the flowers and threw them away. I did not say anything.

At times, they would throw paper airplanes at my back. Unfolding the papers, I would find comments such as, 'A woman's place is in the kitchen or in medical science or as a professor, definitely not in an engineering college.'

Others would read, 'We really pity you. Why are you performing penance like Goddess Parvati? At least Parvati had a reason for it. She wanted to marry Shiva. Who is your Shiva?' I would keep the paper planes and refrain from replying.

There was a famous student-friendly activity in our college known as 'fishpond'. Rather than an actual fishpond, it was a fish bowl that carried a collection of anonymous notes, or the 'fish'. Anybody from the college could write a comment or an opinion that would be read out later on our annual college day. All the students would eagerly wait to hear what funny and witty remarks had been selected that year. The designated host would stand on the stage in the college quadrangle and read the notes out loud. Every year, most of the notes were about me. I was often the target of Kannada limericks, one of which I can still remember vividly:

Avva avva genasa,
Kari seeri udisa,
Gandana manege kalisa.

This literally translates to:

> Mom Mom, there is a sweet potato,
> Please give me a black sari and send me to my
>   husband's house,
> This is because I'm always wearing a white sari.

Some of the romantic north Indian boys would modify the lyrics of songs from movies like *Teesri Kasam*:

> *Sajan re jhoot math bolo*
> *Sudha ke pass jaana hai*
> *Na haathi hai na ghoda hai*
> *Vahan paidal jaana hai.*

This can be translated as:

> Dear, come on, don't lie
> I want to go to Sudha
> I neither have an elephant nor a horse
> But I will go walking (to her).

All the boys would then sneak a glance at me to see my reaction, but I would simply hold back my tears and try my hardest to smile.

I knew that my classmates were acting out for a reason. It was not that they wanted to bully or harass me with deliberate intention as is the norm these days. It was just that they were unprepared—both mentally and physically—to deal with a person of the opposite sex studying with them. Our conservative society discouraged the mingling of boys and girls even as friends, and so, I was as interesting as an alien to them. My mind justified the reason for the boys' behaviour and helped me cope. And yet, the remarks, the pranks and the sarcasm continued to hurt.

My only outlet in college was my actual education. I enjoyed the engineering subjects and did very well in my exams. I found that I performed better than the boys, even in hard-core engineering subjects such as smithy, filing, carpentry and welding. The boys wore blue overalls and I wore a blue apron over my sari. I knew that I looked quite funny, but it was a small price to pay for the education I was getting.

When the exam results were announced, everyone else knew my marks before I did. Almost every semester, my classmates and seniors would make a singular effort to find out my marks and display them on the notice board for everyone to see. I had absolutely no privacy.

Over the course of my studies, I realized that the belief 'engineering is a man's domain' is a complete myth. Not only was I just as capable as them, I also scored higher than all my classmates. This gave me additional confidence and I continued to not miss a single day or a single class. I persisted in studying hard, determined to top the subsequent examinations. In time, I became unfazed that my marks were displayed on the notice board. On the contrary, I was proud that I was beating all the boys at their own game as I kept bagging the first rank in the university.

My ability to be self-sufficient made me strong and the boys eventually started to respect me, became dependent on me for surveys and drawings and asked me for the answers of the assignments. I began to make friends and even today, my good friends include Ramesh Jangal from the civil department, my lab partner Sunil Kulkarni, and Fakeer Gowda, M.M. Kulkarni, Hire Gowda, Anand Uthuri, Gajanan Thakur, Prakash Padaki, H.P. Sudarshan and Ramesh Lodaya.

I will never forget my teachers: L.J. Noronha from the electrical engineering department, Yoga Narasimha, a gifted teacher from Bengaluru, Prof. Mallapur from the chemistry department, Prof. Kulkarni from hydraulics and many more. Between my classes, I also spent much time in the library and the librarian became very fond of me over time, eventually giving me extra books.

I also spoke frequently to the gardener about the trees that should be planted in front of the college, and during my four years there, I had him plant coconut trees. Whenever I go to B.V.B. now, I look at the coconut trees and fondly remember my golden days on the campus.

The four years passed quickly and the day came when I finally had to leave. I felt sad. I had come as a scared teenager and was leaving as a confident and bright young engineer! College had taught me the resilience to face any situation, the flexibility to adjust as needed, the importance of building good and healthy relationships with others, sharing notes with classmates and collaborating with others instead of staying by myself. Thus, when I speak of friends, I don't usually think of women but rather of men because I really grew up with them. When I later entered the corporate world, it was again dominated by men. It was only natural for my colleague or friend to be a man and only sometimes would there be women, whom I have got to know over many years.

College is not just a building made up of walls, benches and desks. It is much more intangible than that. The right education should make you a confident person and that is what B.V.B. did for me.

I later completed my master's programme from the Indian Institute of Science, Bengaluru. Yet, B.V.B. continues to have a special place in my heart.

When my father passed away due to old age, I decided to do something in his memory. He had allowed me to go ahead and become an engineer, despite all the odds and the grievances he had heard from our family and society. Thus, I built a lecture hall in his memory in our college campus.

Whenever I go abroad to deliver a speech, at least five people of different ages come and tell me that they are from B.V.B, too. I connect with them immediately and can't help but smile and ask, 'Which year did you graduate? Who were your teachers? How many girls studied in your class?'

Now, whenever I go back to the college, it is like a celebration, like a daughter coming home. Towards the end of the visit, I almost always stand alone in the inner quadrangle of the stage. My memories take me back to the numerous occasions when I received awards for academic excellence. I then spend a few minutes in front of the notice board and walk up to the small room on the second floor of the electrical engineering department that was 'Kulkarni's Room', but no longer dusty now. I remember the bench on which I sat and prepared for my exams. My heart feels a familiar ache when I recall some of my teachers and classmates who are no longer in this world today.

And then, as I walk down the stairs, I come across groups of girls—chatting away happily and wearing jeans, skirts or traditional salwar kameezes. There are almost as many girls as there are boys in the college. When they see me, they lovingly surround me for autographs. In the midst of the crowd and the signings, I think of my parents and my journey of fifty years and my eyes get misty.

May God bless our college, B.V.B!

3

Food for Thought

Rekha is a very dear friend and our families have known each other for generations. Since I hadn't seen her for a long time, I decided to visit her. I picked up the phone and dialled her number.

Her father, Rao, who is like a father to me, picked up the phone. 'Hello?'

We exchanged greetings and I said, 'Uncle, I am coming to your house for lunch tomorrow.'

Her father, a botanist, was very happy. 'Please do. Tomorrow is a Sunday and we can relax a little bit. Don't run off quickly!' he replied.

In a city such as Bengaluru, going from Jayanagar to Malleswaram on a weekday usually takes a minimum of two hours. Travelling on a Sunday is much easier because it takes only half the time. When I reached her home the next day, I could smell that lunch was almost ready, and yet the aromas wafting in from the kitchen indicated to me that the day's menu would somehow be different. None of the typical Karnataka dishes were laid out on the table, and the cuisine was, in fact, quite bland for my taste.

'I may wear a simple sari but I am a foodie, Rekha! Is the lunch specially arranged so that I don't come again?' I joked, as one can with an old friend who will not misunderstand and take offence.

Rekha's father laughed heartily. 'Well,' he sighed. 'Today is my mother's *shraddha* or death anniversary. On this day, we always prepare a meal from indigenous vegetables.'

'What do you mean by indigenous?' I was perplexed. 'Aren't all the vegetables available in our country indigenous, except perhaps ones like cauliflower, cabbage and potato?'

'Oh my God! You have just begun a wrong topic on a wrong day with the wrong person!' exclaimed Rekha in mock dismay. 'After lunch, I think I should just leave you with my father and join you both later in the evening. This will take at least four hours of your time.'

I knew that Rekha's father was a botanist, but it was then that I realized that he was passionate about this subject. Though I had known him for a really long time, I had never seen this facet of his personality before. Probably, he had been too busy during his working years while we had been too busy playing and fooling around.

'Is this really true, Uncle?' I asked.

He nodded.

Since I come from a farmer's family on my paternal side, I have always had a fascination for vegetables. I knew vaguely about the things we could grow, the seasons to grow them in and the ones that we could not grow, including the reasons why.

However, whenever I broached the subject with friends interested in agriculture and farming, I never really received a proper answer. Finally, here was a man more than willing to share his knowledge with me! I couldn't resist.

'You know, Rekha,' I said, 'it is difficult to get knowledgeable people to spend time explaining their subject matter to others. Today, Google is like my grandmother. I log on to the website any time I require an explanation of something I don't understand or want to learn about.'

'Right now, you are logging on to an encyclopaedia,' Rekha smiled and glanced at her father affectionately.

The conversation drifted to other subjects as we ate lunch. The meal constituted of rice, sambar without chillies, daal with black pepper and not chillies, gorikayi (cluster beans), methi saag, cucumber raita and rice payasam. It was accompanied by udin vada with black pepper. There was pickle and some plain yogurt on the side too. After we had eaten this lunch well-suited for someone recovering in a hospital, Rekha's father said, 'Come, let's go to the garden.'

Rekha's family owned an old house in the corner of a street. Her grandfather had been in the British railways and was lucky enough to buy the corner plot at a low price and had built a small home with a large garden there. In a city like Bengaluru, filled with apartments and small spaces, the garden was something of a privilege and a luxury.

Uncle and I walked to the garden while Rekha took a nap. He settled himself on a bench, while I looked around. It was a miniature forest with a large kitchen garden of carrots, okra, fenugreek and spinach—each segregated neatly into sections. A few sugar canes shone brightly in front of us while a dwarf papaya tree heavy with fruit stood in a corner. On the other end was a line of maize as well as flowering trees such as the *parijata* (the Indian coral tree), and roses of varying colours.

'Uncle and Aunty must be spending a lot of time here making this place beautiful,' I thought. 'All the trees and plants seem healthy—almost as if they are happy to be here!'

'Do you think that all the vegetables we have around us are from India? Or are they from other countries?' he asked out of the blue.

I felt as if I was back in school in front of my teacher. But I wasn't scared. Even if I gave him a wrong answer, it wasn't going to affect my progress report. 'Of course, Uncle! India has the largest population of vegetarians. So, in time, we have learnt to make different kinds of vegetarian dishes. Even people who eat meat avoid it during traditional events such as festivals, weddings, death anniversaries and the month of *Shravana*.'

'I agree with your assessment of everything, except that most vegetables are grown in India. The truth is that the majority of our vegetables are not ours at all. They have come from different countries.'

I stared at him in disbelief.

He pointed to a tomato plant—a creeper with multiple fruits, tied to a firm bamboo stick. 'Look at this! Is this an Indian vegetable?'

I thought of tomato soup, tomato rasam, tomato bhat (tomato-flavoured rice), sandwiches and chutney.

'Of course it is. We use it every single day. It is an integral part of Indian cuisine.'

Uncle smiled. 'Well, the tomato did not originate in India, but in Mexico. It made its way to Europe in 1554. Since nobody ate tomatoes over there at the time, they became ornamental plants because of the beautiful deep-red colour. At some point, there was a belief in Europe that it was good for curing infertility, while some thought that it was poisonous. The contradicting perspectives made it difficult for this fruit to be incorporated into their diet for a long time. Its lack of value must have been a real push for initiating Spain's tomato festival, where millions of tomatoes are used every year to this day. A story goes that one business-savvy European surrounded his tomato plants with a sturdy, thick fence to show his neighbours that the fruits were not poisonous, but rather valuable and thus desirable. Gradually, the fruits reached India and began to be used as a commercial crop, thanks to its tempting colour and taste. It must have come to us during the reign of the British. But today, we cannot think of cooking without tomatoes.'

'Wow!' I thought. Out loud, I said, 'Uncle, tell me about an essential item that is used in our cooking but isn't ours.'

'Come on, try and guess. We simply cannot cook without this particular vegetable.'

I closed my eyes and thought of sambar, that essential south Indian dish and the mutter paneer typical of the north Indian cuisine. It took me a while to think of a common ingredient—the chilli. I brushed my thought away. 'No, there's no way that the chilli can be an imported vegetable. There can be no Indian food without it,' I thought.

Uncle looked at me. 'You are right. It is the chilli!' he exclaimed almost as if he had read my mind.

'How did you know?'

'Because people never fail to be shocked when they think of the possibility that chilli could be from another country. I can see it clearly on their faces when the wheels turn inside their head.'

My disbelief was obvious. How could we cook without chillies? It is as important as salt in Indian cooking.

'There are many stories and multiple theories about chillies,' Uncle said. 'When Vasco da Gama came to India, he came from Portugal via Brazil and brought many seeds with him. Later, Marco Polo and the British came to India. Thus, many more plant seeds arrived. The truth is that what we call "indigenous" isn't really ours. Think of chillies, capsicum, corn, groundnut, cashews, beans, potato, papaya, pineapple, custard apple, guava and sapodilla—they are all from South America. Over time, we indigenized them and learnt how to cook them. Some say that the chilli came from the country of the same name, while some others say it came from Mexico. According to a theory, black pepper was the ingredient traditionally used in India to make our food hot and spicy. Some scholars believe that the sole goal of the East India Company was to acquire a monopoly over India's pepper trade, which later ended in India's colonization. But when we began using chillies, we found that it tasted better than black pepper.

To give you an example, we refer to black pepper as *kalu menasu* in Kannada. We gave a similar name to the chilli and called it *menasin kai*. In Hindi, it is frequently referred to as *mirchi*. In the war between black pepper and chilli, the former lost and chilli established itself as the new prince and continues to rule the Indian food industry even today. north Karnataka is famous for its red chillies now.'

'That much I do know, Uncle!' I closed my eyes and had a vision of my younger days. 'I remember seeing acres and acres of red chilli plants during my childhood. The harvest used to take place during the Diwali season. I remember that the Badgi district was dedicated to the sale of chillies. I had gone with my uncle one day and was amazed by the mountains of red chillies I saw there.'

'Oh yes, you are right! Those red chillies are bright red in colour but they aren't really hot or spicy. On the contrary, chillies that grow in the state of Andhra Pradesh in the area of Guntur are extremely spicy. They are a little rounded in shape, not as deep red in colour and are called Guntur chillies. A good cook uses a combination of different kinds of chillies to make the dish delicious and attractive. Now that's what I call indigenous.'

'There were also two other kinds of chillies in our farm—one was a chilli called Gandhar or Ravana chilli that grows upside down and the other one, of course, was capsicum.'

Uncle nodded. 'Capsicum in India is nothing but green or red bell peppers in the West. But if you eat one tiny Ravana chilli, you will have to sit in the bathroom with your backside in pain and drink many bottles of water for a long,

long time! Or you will have to eat five hundred grams of candies, sweets or chocolates.'

We both laughed.

Hearing the laughter, Rekha's mother came and joined us. 'Are you folks joking about today's menu? I'm sorry that there wasn't much variety. When I heard that you were coming for lunch, I told Uncle to inform you that today's food was going to be bland and that you could come another Sunday, but he said that you are like family and wouldn't mind at all,' she said to me.

That sparked my interest. 'Tell me the reason for the bland food, Aunty!'

'We have a method to the madness, I guess. During death anniversaries, we do not use vegetables or spices that have come from other countries. Hence, we use ingredients like fenugreek, black pepper and cucumber, among others. Our ancestors were scared of using new vegetables and named these imports Vishwamitra *srishti*.'

This was the first time that I had heard of such a thing. 'What does that mean?'

Aunty settled into a makeshift chair under the guava tree. 'The story goes that there was a king called Trishanku who wanted to go to heaven along with his physical body. With his strong penance and powers, the sage Vishwamitra was able to send him to heaven, but the gods pushed him back because they were worried that it would set a precedent for people to come in with their physical bodies. That was not to be allowed. Vishwamitra tried to push Trishanku upwards but the gods pushed him down, like a game of tug of war. In the end, Vishwamitra created a new world for Trishanku and called it Trishanku Swarga. He even created vegetables that belonged neither to the earth nor heaven. So vegetables like eggplant and cauliflower are the creations of Vishwamitra, which must not be used at a time such as a dear one's death anniversary.'

Silence fell between us and I pondered over Aunty's story. After a few minutes, I saw Rekha coming towards us with some bananas and oranges and a box of what seemed to be dessert.

'Come,' she said to me, 'have something. The banana is from our garden and the dessert is made from home-grown ingredients too! You must be . . .'

Uncle interrupted, 'Do you know that we make so many desserts in India that aren't original to our country?'

'Appa, tell her the story of the guava and the banana. I really like that one,' Rekha said. She smiled as she handed me a banana.

Uncle grinned, pleased to impart some more knowledge. 'The seeds of guava came from Goa,' he said. 'So some people say that's how it was named. In Kannada, we call it *perala hannu* because we believe that it originated in Peru, South America. Let me tell you a story.

'Durvasa was a famed short-tempered sage in our ancient epics. He cursed anyone who dared to rouse his anger. The sage was married to a woman named Kandali. One day, she said to him, "O sage, people are terribly afraid of you while I have lived with you for such a long time. Don't you think I deserve a great boon from you?"

'Though Durvasa was upset at her words, he did not curse her. He thought seriously about what she had said and decided that she was right. "I will give you a boon. But only one. So think carefully," he said.

'After some thought, she replied, "Create a fruit for me that is unique and blessed with beautiful colours. The tree should grow not in heaven but on earth. It should have the ability to grow easily everywhere in our country. It must give fruits in bunches and for the whole year. The fruit must not have any seeds and must not create a mess when we eat it. When it is not ripe, we should be able to use it as a vegetable and once it is ripe, we should use it while performing pujas. We must be able to use all parts of the tree."

'Durvasa was surprised and impressed at the number of specifications his wife was giving him. He was used to giving curses in anger and then figuring out their solutions once he had calmed down, but this seemingly simple request was a test of his intelligence. "No wonder women are cleverer. Men like me get upset quickly and act before fully thinking of the consequences," he thought.

'The sage prayed to Goddess Saraswati to give him the knowledge with which he could satisfy his wife's demand. After a few minutes, he realized that he would be able to fulfil his wife's desire. Thus he created the banana tree, which is found all over India today. Every part of the tree—the leaf, the bark, the stem, the flowers and its fruits are used daily. Raw banana can be cooked while the ripe banana can be eaten easily by peeling off its skin. It is also an essential part of worship to the gods. The fruit is seedless and presents itself as a bunch. A mature tree lives for a year and smaller saplings are found around it.

'Kandali was ecstatic and named the plant *kandari*. She announced, "Whoever eats this fruit will not get upset, despite the fact that it was created by my short-tempered husband."

'Over a period of time, people started using the banana extensively and loved it. Slowly the name kandari changed to *kadali* and the banana came to be known as kadali *phala* in Sanskrit.' Uncle took a deep breath at the end of his story.

I smiled, amused at the story that seemed to result from fertile imagination. I had a strong urge to grab a banana and took one from the plate in front of me. 'You may have given me bland food today,' I said, 'but I really want some dessert.'

Rekha opened the box. It was filled with different varieties of sweets. I saw gulab jamuns, jhangri (a deep-fried flour-based dessert) and gulkhand (a rose petal-based preserve). I can't resist gulab jamuns, so I immediately picked one up and popped it into my drooling mouth. It was soft and sweet. 'What a dessert!' I remarked, amazed at how delicious it was! 'Nobody can beat us when it comes to Indian desserts. I don't know how people can live in other countries without gulab jamuns.'

'Wait a minute, don't make such sweeping statements,' said Rekha. 'Gulab jamun is not from India.'

'Yeah, right,' I said, not convinced at all. Before she could stop me, I grabbed another gulab jamun and gulped it down.

'I'm serious. A language scholar once came to speak in our college. He told us that apart from English, we use multiple Persian, Arabic and Portuguese words that we aren't even aware of. Gulab jamun is a Persian word and is a dish prepared in Iran. It became popular in India during the Mughal reign because the court language was Persian. The same is true for jhangri, which is a kind of ornament worn on the wrist and the jhangri design resembles it.'

'You will now tell me that even gulkhand is from somewhere else!' I complained loudly.

She grinned, 'You aren't wrong! Gulkhand is a Persian word too—*gul* is nothing but rose and *khand* means sweet. Gul, in fact, originates from the word *gulab* (rose).'

My brain was thoroughly exhausted with all this information. When I saw the oranges, I said with pride, 'I will not call this an orange now, but its Kannada name *narangi*.'

Uncle cleared his throat. 'Narangi is an Indian word but it does not originate in Karnataka. It is made up of two words—*naar* (orange or colour of the sun) and *rangi* (colour).'

The conversation was leaving me feeling truly lost.

'When people stay in one place for some time,' he continued, 'they will unknowingly absorb the culture around them, including their food and language. At times, we adopt the changes into our local cuisine and make it our own. That's exactly what happened with the foods we have discussed.'

I glanced at my watch. It was time for me to leave. I thanked them profusely, especially Uncle, for enlightening me in a way that even Google could not.

There was a huge traffic jam despite it being a Sunday evening as I set out for home, but I wasn't bored on the way. In fact, I was happy to recollect Uncle's words and perhaps, as a result, suddenly remembered an incident.

My mother had two sisters. Though all three sisters were married to men from the same state, their husbands' jobs were in different areas—one lived in south Karnataka in the old Mysore state, my parents lived in Maharashtra and the third stayed in the flatlands in a remote corner of Karnataka.

After their husbands retired, the three sisters lived in Hubli in the same area. It was fun to meet my cousins every day and eat meals together. We celebrated festivals as a family and the food was cooked in one house, though everybody brought home-cooked desserts from their own houses.

During one particular Diwali, we had a host of delicacies. My mother made puri and shrikhand (a popular dish in Maharashtra made from strained yogurt and sugar). My aunt from Mysore made kishmish kheer and a rice-based main course called bisi bele anna, while the other aunt made groundnut-based sweets such as jaggery-based sticky chikki and ball-shaped laddus.

As children, my cousins and I had plenty of fun eating them but in the car, I realized for the first time that all the sisters had absorbed something from the area that they had lived in. Despite their physical proximity, the food in each household was so diverse. I couldn't help but wonder how exciting the food really must be in the different regions of India.

I thought of paneer pizzas, cheese dosas and the Indian 'Chinese' food. They must have originated the same way.

Who really said that India is a country? It is a continent—culturally vibrant, diverse in food and yet, distinctly Indian at heart.

4

Three Handfuls of Water

When I was young, I lived with my grandparents in a tiny village in Karnataka.

My grandmother, Krishnakka, was a good-looking lady. But I rarely saw her dress well, unless there was a festival or an important event.

When I came back from school one day, I found her just about to open a big wooden box containing her silk saris and a few dear possessions. Since she rarely opened this particular box, it always carried an air of fascination for me. I'd always drop whatever I was doing to join her. This time was no different. I dropped my bag and ran to her. I peeped inside and saw a silver kumkum *bharani* (a box used to keep the red powder used for social or religious purposes), a small mirror with a silver handle, a broken, yet useful ivory comb and a few silver vessels.

'My father gave these to me on my wedding,' said my grandmother with pride in her voice. Her father had been gone a long time.

I took the kumkum box in my hand and stared at it. It was a round-shaped box that looked like a miniature pagoda.

I removed the cover and opened it without a second thought. There were three parts to it—the first one contained honeybee wax, the second was a small round mirror and at the bottom was a space to keep the kumkum. I was fascinated. 'Avva,' I began, a little hesitant. 'Out of all your gifts, I love the kumkum bharani the most. Will you please give this to me when I grow up?'

'I have thirteen grandchildren. Each of them must get something. But I will keep this for you,' she smiled as she replied candidly.

Later, she sat unhurriedly in front of a full-length mirror, brushed her hair, wore a nose ring and a nine-yard green Banarasi sari with a yellow blouse. She put on a big bindi and pretty pearl earrings, and decorated her hands with green glass bangles and two gold ones. Then she circled her bun with flowers. She perfectly fit the image of an elderly woman from north Karnataka.

'Avva, there is no festival today. Why are you dressed up like this? Are you going somewhere?' I asked.

'I am going out for lunch and you are going to come with me. Get ready quickly.'

When I paused for a few moments, she added, 'Don't worry about your afternoon class. Your teacher is also coming there.'

In the village school, this kind of adjustment was not unusual. Sometimes, we got a day off in the middle of the week and it was compensated for on a Sunday. Things were more fluid and life was simple, and I was but a bud flowering in this forest of my own.

I didn't need to be told a second time. I was happy at the thought of attending a lunch party and ran to change my clothes. Even in those days, I never took more than a few minutes to get ready.

Avva wasn't usually a talkative person, but she was in a good mood that day. As my grandfather wasn't inclined to accompany her for such functions, she told her husband, 'I am going out for lunch to Indira's house today. I have kept your meal covered with a plantain leaf. Please have it as soon as possible.'

My grandfather, whom I affectionately called Shiggaon Kaka, nodded and continued reading the newspaper.

Within minutes, we stepped out and started walking towards Indira Ajji's house.

'What's the occasion?' I asked.

'My friend Indira has come back from Varanasi and has invited all of us for lunch. It is a wonderful celebration called Kashi Samaradhane.'

'What is that? If Indira Ajji has returned from a visit, then why do we have to celebrate it? Isn't it like going to Hubli or Gadag and coming back? We don't have any party or celebration then!'

Avva sighed. 'There is a lot of difference between going to Kashi and going to Hubli. Kashi is one of the most sacred places on earth. The river Ganga flows there. It is believed that Lord Vishwanath, the Lord of the universe, resides there and gives boons to everyone. It is his favourite place on the planet. There are eighty ghats to bathe in there. Thousands of Sanskrit scholars live in the city. The sari that I am wearing today is known as a Banarasi sari. If you get such a sari as a wedding gift, it is considered to be very lucky as it is from the holy land of Kashi.'

I wasn't fully convinced. 'Still, why is such a lunch organized?' I persisted, despite my desperate desire to eat the goodies at the celebration anyway.

'It is not easy to go to Kashi, no matter how rich or devoted you are. Going there and coming back is an arduous journey. You have to switch many trains and buses. First, people there speak a different language called Hindi. Second, we don't have any relatives to lean on or direct us. Third, it is so cold during winter that you can't even submerge your feet in the freezing river. Fourth, in the summer, the heat makes the ground so flaming hot that you can't walk barefoot for the pujas. Fifth, if the locals there find out that we are outsiders, then more often than not, they try to cheat us. There are stories of people going to Kashi without ever coming back. So when someone returns, we consider them blessed. That's why they give us a feast and we exchange gifts.'

'What are you going to give, Avva?' I was curious.

Avva opened the bag that she was carrying. There was a nice cotton sari inside, along with plenty of fruits and flowers.

'And what will she give us?'

'We will get a Kashi thread and some water from the Ganga, both of which are precious. Wear the thread on your wrist or your neck every day and God will protect you from difficulties.'

That was good news indeed. I needed all the protection I could get for my upcoming examinations.

'You are lucky to get it at such a young age,' Avva said, as she incorrectly interpreted the reason for my smile.

'What does the Kashi thread look like?'

'Well, it is a simple knotted black thread. Kashi is protected by Bhairavnath, who is a great and loyal servant of Lord Shiva. If you go to Kashi and don't see the Kaal Bhairav temple, your yatra or journey is considered incomplete. You will get a Kashi thread from there, which you have to wear for Bhairavnath to protect you. Since the Kashi trip is difficult, he will accompany you in his invisible form until you reach home safely. Then he runs back to assist the next devotee,' finished my grandmother.

'Hmm,' I thought. 'What if he has to help more than one person home?'

Before I could ask, Avva answered, 'I know what you are going to ask me now. Bhairavnath can multiply himself as many times as he wants to.'

So instead, I asked, 'What is the use of the water from the Ganga?'

'Silly girl, how can I ever describe the use of the holy water?' She patted my head affectionately. 'The Ganga is the life of our country. Everybody wants to drink the holy water, but it isn't possible for people like us who live in south India. So we keep a few spoons of *Gangajal*, the holy water from the Ganga, for whoever is in the last days of their life so that they can go to heaven.'

'Avva,' I asked, 'if Kashi is so important and you believe in it so much, then Kaka and you must go there. I will also come with you.'

Avva turned thoughtful. 'I have never ventured out of Karnataka,' she said. 'You know that Kaka and I avoid eating anything when we travel. It takes at least ten days to go to Kashi. And it's better to travel in a group because we don't know the local language. It is difficult to form such a group here, and we are also getting old. We don't want to fall sick on the way and burden the group. So going to Kashi will most likely remain a dream for me. But I am happy that Indira has gone there with her cousins. At least I can visit her and listen to her stories.'

At the time, I didn't understand why my grandmother had such devotion for this holy land.

Soon, we reached Indira Ajji's house. The whole atmosphere was festive. Stumps of banana trees and mango leaves were tied to the sides of the gate. There were plenty of flower decorations all over the place. An intricate rangoli design was drawn on the floor at the entrance. I immediately spotted my classmates running here and there with glee. My teacher was offering home-made drinks to all the children. On one side lay fifty pots containing Gangajal. All the pots had black threads tied around the neck. They were piled up on a table decorated with flowers. A single banana leaf was laid out nearby with all the dishes, though there was no one sitting there. My mind raced to count the number of desserts on the leaf.

Avva and I entered the main room. Since my grandmother was the oldest person there and quite popular too, people seemed to be happy to see her. Avva turned to Indira, 'You are so lucky to have visited Kashi, bathed in the river Ganga and seen Lord Vishwanath in all his glory.'

Indira Ajji smiled gently and invited both of us to sit down. People were gathered around her to hear more about her trip.

Somebody asked, 'What did you think of the famous Annapoorna temple?'

'It was beautiful,' she replied. 'It is located before Lord Vishwanath's temple and is the only temple where Shiva is believed to ask for alms and food from his wife with his begging bowl. He is said to appear in the temple only on a few special days.'

As people started asking more questions, I became bored.

Slowly, I nudged my grandmother. When she turned to look at me, I pointed to the banana leaf and asked, 'Avva, why is nobody sitting for lunch there? I am hungry. Can I go eat the food?'

'Don't even think about it! That food is for Bhairavnath. He has much work to do and has to make the trip back soon. But you can pray to him if you want.'

I didn't see anyone sitting there but remembered that he was supposed to be invisible. So I joined my hands together and prayed facing the leaf.

A short while later, we all had a delicious lunch.

On our way back, my grandmother remarked, 'Isn't it wonderful to hear that Indira took three handfuls of water from the river Ganga and saluted the rising sun? It must be such a beautiful sight. Sometimes, I also wish to do the same. I have convinced myself that the rivulet in our garden is also another form of the Ganga and if I worship her, it is as good as worshipping the river in Kashi.'

It was evening by the time we reached home and from a distance, I could see my grandfather sitting in the verandah. Kaka was my good friend and I ran to tell him about the day.

Just as I approached him, he smiled and asked, 'Did your grandmother tell you about what you must leave behind in Kashi?'

'What are you talking about, Kaka?'

'In the olden days, the journey to Kashi took months and not days. Today, we have trains and roads but then people had to walk and cross forests and face dangers on their way. Many did not make it back to their homes. Emperor Akbar abolished the jizya tax for entry into Varanasi whereas Aurangzeb reintroduced it. Hence the journey to Kashi was expensive. If someone made it to Kashi successfully, they would make an unusual vow—to give up whatever they loved the most after taking three handfuls of water, keeping Lord Sun as a witness. A word given to the Ganga in such a way is considered unbreakable and one is obliged to fulfil it.'

I was fascinated and waited as Kaka took a deep breath.

'There are certain rules that you must follow.'

'What rules?'

'One cannot give up eating rice, wheat flour, milk, lentils, ghee or jaggery. One can give up eating one vegetable and one fruit that freely grows around their hometown or area and a dessert that they love. So if you love jalebis, you can vow to abstain from it, but you can't give up something that you don't like, such as bitter gourd. Whenever you see what you have given up, it will remind you of Kashi.'

'That is quite tough, Kaka!'

My grandfather continued as if he hadn't heard me, 'If a husband and wife go together, they can choose to give up the same things. That is easy as it means that they won't have to cook separately. But if a husband and wife visit individually and choose to abstain from different things, then both of them must leave whatever the other has, too.'

Avva, meanwhile, reached the verandah.

'That sounds too complicated!' I thought. Out loud, I asked, 'Is it very hard to leave what you like, Kaka?'

'It depends on the individual. If you decide to fulfil your vow with your heart and soul, then the desire for the object goes away with time and that way of life simply becomes a habit.'

'What will you leave if you go to Kashi?' I asked mischievously.

'I love your Avva and that's why I will never go to Kashi!' he replied with a twinkle in his eye.

Though Avva was old, she suddenly became shy and quickly walked in.

In a more serious tone, he added, 'It is not up to us to go there. It is Lord Vishwanath's wish. He will call us when it's our time.'

Years flew by and seasons went past. Avva died without ever going to Kashi. She passed away on the day she always wanted to—the day of Bhishmastami or the day Bhishma died. It is believed that the gates of heaven are open on this day. I was in Pune then and by the time I reached Hubli, I could only see her ashes and her picture on the wall. My memory of Avva remained that of an active, cheerful, helpful and affectionate woman.

Based on Avva's last instructions, my aunt gave me the kumkum box and I preserved it like a treasure in an old chest, but did not use it as often as she did because by then, sticker bindis had invaded the Indian market.

As time went by, I started reading extensively and became completely fascinated with Buddhism. Buddha's compassionate heart moved me in ways that I cannot express and I understood why he had taken the famous middle path. Buddhism is represented by a wheel and two deer. Sarnath, the place that had played a big role in Buddha's life and was the place of his first sermon, was a deer park located only a few kilometres away from Varanasi. I realized then that the city got its name from the rivers Varuna and Assi that both join the river Ganga at this location. It is believed to be a sacred land since time immemorial.

In 629 AD, when the Chinese traveller Hiuen Tsang visited India, he described Varanasi in great detail along with a description of its temples, rivulets and the richness of the surroundings. I felt an increasing desire to go to Kashi and yet, it somehow became low on my list of priorities because of work and routine.

During the festival of Diwali in 1995, I received a gift in the form of a book called *Banaras: City of Light* by Diana L. Eck.

I kept it aside, intending to read it after the wonderful madness of the festival was over.

That year, our family decided to celebrate with a traditional *aarti*. I went to my bedroom and opened the old chest. I began rummaging through it to find the silver plate for the puja. Suddenly, I saw the kumkum box. It was a strong reminder of Avva and I forgot about the plate. Gently, I took out the box and recalled the way she used to wear her kumkum. I saw her dressing up for Kashi Samaradhane and remembered how we had walked for the lunch together. Oh, how I used to pester her to give me the treasured kumkum bharani! She believed wholeheartedly in the holiness of Kashi but never visited the city or regretted the miss! I thought to myself, 'Going to Kashi is not tough now. Moreover, I have Diana's book with me. It will help me understand the city better before I go. Maybe I should do it for the sake of my grandmother . . .'

'Are you meditating in there?' my mom called out, cutting my thoughts short. 'Everyone is waiting.'

I found the silver plate quickly and gave it to my mother along with the kumkum bharani.

'Good, this is my mother's precious possession. It will be as if her spirit is with us during the prayers today,' she said.

Once the festive season had ended, I began reading Diana's book—a masterpiece in itself. It was, in fact, the author's PhD thesis at Harvard. She, a foreigner, had come to India and stayed here for years studying about the religious places in our country. And here I was, doing nothing! I felt ashamed of myself. The book inspired me to get to Kashi as soon as I could, if only to satisfy my childhood curiosity and my grandmother's desire.

In February 1996, I managed to find my way there all by myself. I stayed in a hotel and had the darshan of Lord Vishwanath, whose temple was in a corner of the city. He was worshipped using the three-leaved Bilva (Lord Shiva's tree) *patras* and constantly bathed by his devotees who gathered there. There were security gunmen, a barbed wire fence and the Gyanvapi mosque near the temple. The different image of the place I had in my mind disappointed me a little, but I was amazed by the faith of the people of varied ages who had come from all over the country.

Once that was done, I went to see the Manikarnika ghat, where dead bodies are cremated every day and almost endlessly. The strong belief that dying in Kashi is a gateway to heaven has not changed even with the increase in literacy and the changing culture. I visited some more ghats and was taken aback by the amount of dirt in this holy city. I also visited the Banaras Hindu University that was established single-handedly by Madan Mohan Malaviya, and beautiful museums depicting Hindustani ragas through enchanting paintings.

I walked to numerous temples, small and big, including the temples of Annapoorna Devi, Bhairavnath and the famous Hanuman temple named Sankat Mochan, where the monkeys outnumbered the devotees. Though plenty of black threads were being sold around me, I didn't buy any because I had grown out of the belief.

The holy Ganga water was abundant and up for sale in different volumes, shapes and sizes. Even today, the water is considered holy.

In the small lanes of Kashi, I wandered around, aimless and happy in the moment. The beautiful views and the pretty saris caught my eye. What a gorgeous invention the sari is—a rare combination of the cloth-tying method of the Greeks, the Romans and our own. Whenever I travel abroad, I come across people who are fascinated with the border, the richness, the zari and the pallu, which automatically bestows a royal appearance to whoever wears it.

Kashi boasts of unique Banarasi saris which have changed over the years but still remain attractive. I planned to buy a few saris for myself—a pastel-coloured one, a bright one suitable for evening wear and a dark green sari like the one Avva had. The sellers called out to me and the other passers-by. I absolutely loved shopping for saris. But then I changed my mind. 'What was the hurry? I will shop tomorrow after I have seen more,' I thought. So I went about doing some window shopping.

Then I went back to the ghats and finally reached the busy Dashashwamedh ghat. The crowd was preparing for the evening aarti. I glanced at the tourists—they seemed to come not just from different states but also from different countries. They were smiling and taking pictures of their surroundings. The dirt, the small lanes and the claustrophobic closeness of it all did not seem to bother them. The sadhus were in half-meditation and most of the devotees were preparing for their dip in the water. I was tempted. 'Why can't I bathe in the

Ganga too? Maybe I can also offer three handfuls of water to the Ganga and complete my Kashi experience.'

I looked around and the dirt suddenly gave me second thoughts. I didn't want to take a dip there. As if it was meant to be, I remembered an old friend Ajay who lived near the Gai ghat. Maybe I could ask him if there was a cleaner and less crowded spot more suitable for me.

So I located a landline nearby and phoned him. It was obvious that Ajay was upset because I hadn't informed him of my visit. He gave me strict instructions to remain where I was and within a few minutes, he arrived on his scooter.

'Why are you staying in a hotel when you have a friend in the same city? You must move to my home immediately,' he insisted.

I agreed. I had no reason to refuse his warm hospitality.

I shifted to his haveli. Three families lived in the mansion. Each family had a separate kitchen and lived in their own sections of the huge home. Ajay's side of the home had a view of the Ganga with the evening lights shining brightly as far as I could see.

His wife, Nishi, entertained me with delicious Kashi sweets, sumptuous food and paan. Later, he took me to a Hindustani music concert and spoke about the great musicians of Kashi such as Bismillah Khan and Ravi Shankar and how the city was also a place for music lovers. The city, though dirty, was thriving with life and culture.

At dawn, I found myself at the Gai ghat ready for the dip. I sat alone on the steps and then immersed myself in the water till my shoulder blades. The coldness took me by surprise and it took a few minutes for my body to adjust to this new temperature.

I took some water in my palms and my mind instantly went back to Avva. There she was—wearing the green sari and the yellow blouse, looking at me with love and telling me about the three handfuls of water from the Ganga. I saw Kaka sitting on the verandah during sunset, telling me how it was Lord Vishwanath who decided when an individual visited Kashi. How my old grandparents had loved the city and the river Ganga! Tears sprang to my eyes. I was blessed to have grandparents who were content and had such strong beliefs.

'It is so easy to visit Kashi now,' I thought. 'I took a flight from Bengaluru to Delhi and then to Varanasi and reached in a mere five hours.' Now, there was no Kashi Samaradhane or the customary distribution of the holy water or the black thread. Nobody had the time or the inclination.

I looked at the rising sun and was brought back to the present moment. I took the first handful of water and said to myself, 'O Ganga, with the sun as the witness, I give this water on behalf of my grandparents. May their souls rest in peace and be happy wherever they are right now.'

I felt relieved and knew that I had fulfilled my grandparents' desire even though they had never told me to do so.

Then I cupped some more water and said out loud, 'O Ganga, with the sun as the witness, you are the lifeline of our country. You have seen the rise and fall of many kingdoms on your banks. I am grateful and proud to belong to this land.

May you continue to flourish. There is nothing that I can give you but this handful of water.'

With the third handful, I remembered my grandfather's words, 'Give up what you love the most.'

'What should I detach myself from?' I wondered. I loved life, colours, shapes, nature, music, art forms, reading and shopping, especially for saris. My selection of earthy colours was popular and I loved observing the changes in sari designs over the years. 'Well, if the city of Kashi demands what I love the most, then with the sun as the witness, I give up all kinds of shopping from this day on, except for essentials like food, medicine, travel, books and music. I will do so until the day I am no longer in this world,' I said and completed the ritual.

Slowly, I released the water from my palms back to the Ganga.

Somewhere out there, it felt like my grandfather had just smiled. A few minutes later, I waded out of the water and sat on the steps with a towel wrapped around me.

So there would be no more appreciation of my sari choices and none of my friends would call me for wedding shopping. I was worried if I would be able to stick to my vow since I had planned to buy saris that day in Kashi. I wondered if I had chosen to give up shopping on the spur of the moment or if it was pre-planned somehow. To this day, I don't know.

I got up, changed my clothes, took out the kumkum powder from Avva's bharani and put a bit on my forehead.

That was twenty years ago.

The truth is that the vow turned out to be a gateway to freedom. The desire to acquire has vanished over time. Once a year, a few known friends and sisters gave me saris of their choice and I continued to wear them happily for a long time but as the years flew by, I lost interest in that too, and requested them not to gift me anything.

That last handful of water had changed my life forever.

5

Cattle Class

Last year, I was at the Heathrow International Airport in London about to board a flight. Usually, I wear a sari even when I am abroad, but I prefer wearing a salwar kameez while travelling. So there I was—a senior citizen dressed in typical Indian apparel at the terminal gate.

Since the boarding hadn't started, I sat down and began to observe my surroundings. The flight was bound for Bengaluru and so I could hear people around me chatting in Kannada. I saw many old married couples of my age— they were most likely coming back from the US or UK after helping their children either through childbirth or a new home. I saw some British business executives talking to each other about India's progress. Some teenagers were busy with the gadgets in their hands while the younger children were crying or running about the gate.

After a few minutes, the boarding announcement was made and I joined the queue. The woman in front of me was a well-groomed lady in an Indo-Western silk outfit, a Gucci handbag and high heels. Every single strand of her hair was in place and a friend stood next to her in an expensive silk sari, pearl necklace, matching earrings and delicate diamond bangles.

I looked at the vending machine nearby and wondered if I should leave the queue to get some water.

Suddenly, the woman in front of me turned sideways and looked at me with what seemed like pity in her eyes. Extending her hand, she asked, 'May I see your boarding pass, please?'

I was about to hand over my pass to her, but since she didn't seem like an airline employee, I asked, 'Why?'

'Well, this line is meant for business class travellers only,' she said confidently and pointed her finger towards the economy class queue. 'You should go and stand there,' she said.

I was about to tell her that I had a business class ticket but on second thoughts, held back. I wanted to know why she had thought that I wasn't worthy of being in the business class. So I repeated, 'Why should I stand there?'

She sighed. 'Let me explain. There is a big difference in the price of an economy and a business class ticket. The latter costs almost two and a half times more than . . .'

'I think it is three times more,' her friend interrupted.

'Exactly,' said the woman. 'So there are certain privileges that are associated with a business class ticket.'

'Really?' I decided to be mischievous and pretended not to know. 'What kind of privileges are you talking about?'

She seemed annoyed. 'We are allowed to bring two bags but you can only take one. We can board the flight from another, less-crowded queue. We are given better meals and seats. We can extend the seats and lie down flat on them. We always have television screens and there are four washrooms for a small number of passengers.'

Her friend added, 'A priority check-in facility is available for our bags, which means they will come first upon arrival and we get more frequent flyer miles for the same flight.'

'Now that you know the difference, you can go to the economy line,' insisted the woman.

'But I don't want to go there.' I was firm.

The lady turned to her friend. 'It is hard to argue with these cattle-class people. Let the staff come and instruct her where to go. She isn't going to listen to us.'

I didn't get angry. The word 'cattle class' was like a blast from the past and reminded me of another incident.

One day, I had gone to an upscale dinner party in my home city of Bengaluru. Plenty of local celebrities and socialites were in attendance. I was speaking to some guests in Kannada, when a man came to me and said very slowly and clearly in English, 'May I introduce myself? I am . . .'

It was obvious that he thought that I might have a problem understanding the language.

I smiled. 'You can speak to me in English.'

'Oh,' he said, slightly flabbergasted. 'I'm sorry. I thought you weren't comfortable with English because I heard you speaking in Kannada.'

'There's nothing shameful in knowing one's native language. It is, in fact, my right and my privilege. I only speak in English when somebody can't understand Kannada.'

The line in front of me at the airport began moving forward and I came out of my reverie. The two women ahead were whispering among themselves, 'Now she will be sent to the other line. It is so long now! We tried to tell her but she refused to listen to us.'

When it was my turn to show my boarding pass to the attendant, I saw them stop and wait a short distance away, waiting to see what would happen. The attendant took my boarding pass and said brightly, 'Welcome back! We met last week, didn't we?'

'Yes,' I replied.

She smiled and moved on to the next traveller.

I walked a few steps ahead of the women intending to let this go, but then I changed my mind and came back. 'Please tell me—what made you think that I couldn't afford a business class ticket? Even if I didn't have one, was it really your prerogative to tell me where I should stand? Did I ask you for help?'

The women stared at me in silence.

'You refer to the term "cattle class". Class does not mean possession of a huge amount of money,' I continued, unable to stop myself from giving them a piece of my mind. 'There are plenty of wrong ways to earn money in this world. You may be rich enough to buy comfort and luxuries, but the same money doesn't define class or give you the ability to purchase it. Mother Teresa was a classy woman. So is Manjul Bhargava, a great mathematician of Indian origin. The concept that you automatically gain class by acquiring money is an outdated thought process.'

I left without waiting for a reply.

Approximately eight hours later, I reached my destination. It was a weekday and I rushed to office as soon as I could only to learn that my day was going to be spent in multiple meetings. A few hours later, I requested my program director to handle the last meeting of the day by herself as I was already starting to feel tired and jet lagged.

'I am really sorry, but your presence is essential for that discussion,' she replied. 'Our meeting is with the organization's CEO and she is keen to meet you in person. She has been following up with me for a few months now and though I have communicated our decision, she feels that a discussion with you will change the outcome. I have already informed her that the decision will not be reversed irrespective of whom she meets, but she refuses to take me at my word. I urge you to meet her and close this chapter.'

I wasn't new to this situation and reluctantly agreed.

Time went by quickly and soon, I had to go in for the last meeting of the day. Just then, I received an emergency call.

'Go ahead with the meeting,' I said to the program director. 'I will join you later.'

When I entered the conference room after fifteen minutes, I saw the same women from the airport in the middle of a presentation. To my surprise, they were simply dressed—one was wearing a simple khadi sari while the other wore an unglamorous salwar kameez. The clothes were a reminder of the stereotype that is still rampant today. Just like one is expected to wear the finest of silks for a wedding, social workers must present themselves in a plain and uninteresting manner. When they saw me, there was an awkward pause that lasted for only a few seconds before one of them acknowledged my presence and continued the presentation as if nothing had happened.

'My coffee estate is in this village. All the estate workers' children go to a government school nearby. Many are sharp and intelligent but the school has no facilities. The building doesn't even have a roof or clean drinking water. There are no benches, toilets or library. You can see children in the school . . .'

'But no teachers,' I completed the sentence.

She nodded and smiled. 'We request the foundation to be generous and provide the school with proper facilities, including an auditorium, so that the poor kids can enjoy the essentials of a big school.'

My program director opened her mouth to say something, but I signalled her to stop.

'How many children are there in the school?' I asked.

'Around 250.'

'How many of them are the children of the estate workers?'

'All of them. My father got the school sanctioned when he was the MLA,' she said proudly.

'Our foundation helps those who don't have any godfathers or godmothers. Think of the homeless man on the road or the daily-wage worker. Most of them have no one they can run to in times of crisis. We help the children of such people. The estate workers help your business prosper and in return, you can afford to help them. In fact, it is your duty to do so. Helping them also helps you in the long run, but it is the foundation's internal policy to work for the disadvantaged in projects where all the benefits go directly and solely to the underprivileged alone. Maybe this concept is beyond the understanding of the cattle class.'

Both the women looked at each other, unsure of how to respond.

I looked at my program director and said, 'Hey, I want to tell you a story.'

I could see from her face that she was feeling awkward. A story in the middle of a serious meeting?

I began, 'George Bernard Shaw was a great thinker of his times. One day, a dinner was arranged at a British club in his honour. The rules of the club mandated that the men wear a suit and a tie. It was probably the definition of class in those days.

'Bernard Shaw, being who he was, walked into the club in his usual casual attire. The doorman looked at him and said very politely, "Sorry, sir, I cannot allow you to enter the premises."

'"Why not?"

'"You aren't following the dress code of the club, sir."

'"Well, today's dinner is in my honour, so it is my words that matter, not what I wear," replied Bernard, perfectly reasonable in his explanation.

'"Sir, whatever it may be, I can't allow you inside in these clothes."

'Shaw tried to convince the doorman but he wouldn't budge from his stance. So he walked all the way back to his house, changed into appropriate clothes and entered the club.

'A short while later, the room was full, with people sitting in anticipation of his speech. He stood up to address the audience, but first removed his coat and tie and placed it on a chair. "I am not going to talk today," he announced.

'There were surprised murmurs in the audience. Those who knew him personally asked him about the reason for his out-of-character behaviour.

'Shaw narrated the incident that happened a while ago and said, "When I wore a coat and tie, I was allowed to come inside. My mind is in no way affected by the clothes I wear. This means that to all of you who patronize the club, the clothes are more important than my brain. So let the coat and the tie take my place instead."

'Saying thus, he walked out of the room.'

I stood up. 'The meeting is over,' I said. We exchanged cursory goodbyes and I walked back to my room.

My program director followed me, 'Your decision regarding the school was right. But what was that other story all about? And why now? What is this cattle-class business? I didn't understand a thing!'

I smiled at her obvious confusion. 'Only the cattle-class folks will understand what happened back there. You don't worry about it.'

6

A Life Unwritten

It was the year 1943. My father was a young medical doctor posted in a small dispensary in a village known as Chandagad, located on the border of the two states of Maharashtra and Karnataka. It rained continuously for eight months there and the only activity during the remaining four months was tree cutting. It was a lesser-known and thinly populated village surrounded by a thick and enormous forest. Since British officers came to hunt in the jungle, a small clinic was set up there for their convenience. None of the villagers went there because they preferred using the local medicines and plants. So there was nobody in the clinic except my father.

Within a week of his transfer there, my father started getting bored. He was uprooted from the lively city of Pune to this slow and silent village where there seemed to be no people at all! He had no contact with the outside world—his only companion was the calendar on the wall. Sometimes, he would go for a walk outside but when he heard the roar of the tigers in the jungle nearby, he would get scared and walk back to the clinic as fast as he could. It was no wonder then that he was too afraid to step out at night because of the snakes that were often seen slithering on the ground.

One winter morning, he heard heavy breathing outside his main door and bravely decided to peep through the window. He saw a tigress stretching and yawning in the verandah with her cubs by her side. Paralysed with fear, my father did not open the door the entire day. On another day, he opened the window only to find snakes hanging from the roof in front of his house—almost like ropes.

My father wondered if he was transferred to the village as a form of punishment for something he may have done. But there was nothing that he could do to change the situation.

One night, he finished an early dinner and began reading a book in the light of a kerosene lamp. It was raining heavily outside.

Suddenly, he heard a knock on the door. 'Who could it be?' he wondered.

When he opened it, he saw four men wrapped in woollen rugs with sticks in their hands. They said to him in Marathi, 'Doctor Sahib, take your bag and come with us immediately.'

My father barely understood their rustic Marathi. He protested. 'But the clinic is closed and look at the time!'

The men were in no mood to listen—they pushed him and loudly demanded that he accompany them. Quietly, my father picked up his bag and followed them like a lamb to the bullock cart waiting for them. The pouring rain and the moonless night disoriented him and while he didn't know where they were taking him, he sensed that the drive might take some time.

Using all the courage he had left, he asked, 'Where are you taking me?'

There was no reply.

It was a few hours before they reached their destination and the bullock cart came to a complete halt. In the light of a kerosene lamp, somebody escorted them. My father noticed the paddy fields around him and in the middle of it all, he saw a house. The minute he set foot in the house, a female voice said, 'Come, come. The patient is here in this room.'

For the first time since he had come to the village, my father felt that he could finally put his medical expertise to good use. The patient was a young girl, approximately sixteen years old. An old lady was standing near the girl who was obviously in labour. My father turned pale. He went back to the other room and told her family, 'Look, I haven't been trained in delivering a baby and I am a male doctor. You must call someone else.'

But the family refused to listen. 'That's not an option. You must do what needs to be done and we will pay you handsomely,' they insisted. 'The baby may be delivered alive or dead but the girl must be saved.'

My father pleaded with them. 'Please, I am not interested in the money. Let me go now.'

The men came close, shoved him inside the patient's room and locked the door from outside. My father became afraid. He knew he had no choice. He had observed and assisted in a few deliveries under the guidance of his medical college professors, but nothing more. Nervously, he started recalling his limited past experience and theoretical knowledge as his medical instincts kicked in.

There was no table in the room. So he signalled the old lady, who appeared to be deaf and dumb, to help him set up a makeshift table with the sacks of paddy grains around them. Then my father extracted a rubber sheet from his bag and laid it out neatly on top of the sacks.

He asked the girl to lie down on it and instructed the old lady to boil water and sterilize his instruments. By then, the contraction had passed. The girl was sweating profusely and the doctor even more. She looked at him with big innocent, teary eyes and slowly began, 'Don't save me. I don't want to make it through the night.'

'Who are you?'

'I am the daughter of a big zamindar here,' she said in a soft voice. The rain outside made it hard for him to hear her. 'Since there was no high school in our village, my parents let me study in a distant town. There, I fell in love with one of my classmates. At first, I didn't know that I was pregnant, but once I found out, I told the baby's father who immediately ran away. By the time my parents learnt of what had happened, it was too late to do anything. That's why they sent me here to this godforsaken place where nobody would find out.'

She stopped as a strong contraction hit her.

After a few minutes, she said, 'Doctor, I am sure that once the baby is born, my family will kill the child and beat me violently.' Then she grabbed my father's arms as more tears gathered in her eyes, 'Please don't try to save the baby or me. Just leave me alone here and let me die. That's all I want.'

At first, my father didn't know how to respond. Then he said to her as gently as he could, 'I am a doctor and I can't let a patient die when I know that I can do something to save him or her. You mustn't discourage me from doing my duty.'

The girl fell silent.

The labour was hard, scary and long and finally, my father managed to deliver the baby successfully with the assistance of the old lady. The young girl was exhausted and sweaty at the end of the ordeal. She closed her eyes in despair and didn't even ask to see the baby. Hesitantly, she asked, 'Is it a boy or a girl?'

'It's a girl,' replied my father, while trying to check the baby's vitals.

'Oh my God! It's a girl!' she cried. 'Her life will be just like mine—under the cruel pressure of the men in the family. And she doesn't even have a father!' She began sobbing loudly.

But my father was busy with the baby and barely heard her.

Suddenly, the girl realized that something was wrong, 'Doctor, why isn't the baby crying?' When she didn't get a reply, she continued, 'I will be happy if she doesn't survive. She will be spared from a cursed life.'

My father held the baby upside down, gently slapped her and instantly, the baby's strong cries filled the room. When the men outside heard the baby cry, they opened the door and instructed him, 'Doctor, get ready to leave. We will drop you back.'

My father cleaned up his patient, gathered his instruments and packed his bag. The old lady began cleaning the room. He looked at the troubled young girl and said, 'Take the baby and run away from this place if you can find it in your heart to do so. Go to Pune and look for Pune Nursing School. Find a clerk there called Gokhale and tell him that RH has sent you. He will help you get admission in a nursing course. In time, you will become a nurse and lead an independent life, with the ability to take care of your own needs. Raise your daughter with pride. Don't you dare leave her behind or else she will end up suffering like you. That's my most sincere advice for you.'

'But, doctor, how will I go to Pune? I don't even know where it is!'

'Go to the nearest city of Belgaum and then from there, you can take a bus to Pune.'

My father said goodbye to her and came out of the room.

An old man handed him one hundred rupees. 'Doctor, these are your fees for helping the girl with the delivery. I warn you—don't say a word about what happened here today. If you do, I will learn of it and your head will no longer be attached to the rest of your body.'

My father nodded, suddenly overtaken by a sense of calm. 'I'm sorry,' he said. 'I think I forgot my scissors in the room. I will need it tomorrow at the clinic.'

He turned around and went back inside and saw the young girl gazing at the sleeping newborn with tears in her eyes. When the old lady's back was turned towards him, my father handed over the money to the girl. 'This is all I have with me right now,' he said. 'Use it and do what I have told you.'

'Doctor, what is your name?' she asked.

'My name is Dr R.H. Kulkarni, but almost everyone calls me RH. Be brave, child. Goodbye and good luck.'

My father left the room and the house. The return journey was equally rough and he finally reached home at dawn. He was dead tired and soon, sleep took over. The next morning, his mind wandered back to his first patient in the village and his first earning. He became aware of his shortcomings and wished he was better qualified in gynaecology. However, his current shortage of funds made him postpone the dream for another day.

A few months later, he got married and shared his dream of becoming a gynaecologist with his wife.

Time passed quickly. He was transferred to different places in Maharashtra and Karnataka and had four children along the way. By the time he turned forty-two, the couple had carefully saved enough money for further education and my father decided to pursue his desire. So he left his family in Hubli and joined Egmore Medical College in Chennai, and fulfilled his dream of becoming a gynaecologist surgeon. He was one of the few rare male gynaecologists at the time.

He went back to Hubli and started working in Karnataka Medical College as a professor. His sympathetic manner towards the underprivileged and his genuine concern for the women and girls he treated made him quite popular—both as a doctor and as a teacher. The same concern reflected in his liberal attitude towards his daughters and he allowed them to pursue their chosen fields of education, which was unheard of in those days.

My father was an atheist. 'God doesn't reside in a church, mosque or temple,' he would often say. 'I see him in all my patients. If a woman dies during childbirth, then it is the loss of one patient for a doctor but for that child, it is the lifelong loss of a mother. And tell me, who can replace a mother?'

Despite his retirement, my father's love for learning did not diminish and he remained active.

One day, he went for a medical conference to another city. There, he met a young woman in her thirties. She was presenting cases from her experience in the rural areas. My father found her work interesting and went to tell her so after the presentation. 'Doctor, your research is excellent. I am quite impressed by your work,' he said.

'Thank you,' she said.

Just then, someone called out to my father, 'RH, we are waiting for you to grab some lunch. Will you take long?'

The young woman asked, 'What is your name, doctor?'

'Dr R.H. Kulkarni, or RH.'

After a moment of silence, she asked, 'Were you in Chandagad in 1943?'

'Yes.'

'Doctor, I live in a village around forty kilometres away from here. May I request you to come home right now for a brief visit?'

My father was unprepared for such an invitation. Why was she calling him to her house?

'Maybe some other time, doctor,' he replied, hoping to end the matter.

But the woman was persistent, 'You must come. Please. Think of this as a request from someone who has been waiting for you for years now.'

My father was puzzled by her enigmatic answer and still refused, but she pleaded with him. There was something in her eyes—something so desperate—that in the end, he gave in and accompanied her to the village.

On the way to the village, both of them exchanged ideas and she spoke animatedly about her work and her findings. As the two of them approached her residence, my father realized that the house was also a nursing home. He walked in through the front door and saw a lady in her fifties standing in the living room.

The young woman next to him said, 'Ma, this is Dr RH. Is he the one you have been waiting for all these years?'

The woman came forward, bent down and touched her forehead to my father's feet. He felt his feet getting wet from her tears. It was strange. Who were these women? My father didn't know what to do. He quickly bent forward, placed his hands on the older woman's shoulders and pulled her up.

'Doctor, you may not remember me but I can never forget you. Mine must have been your first delivery.'

Still, my father couldn't recognize her.

'A long time ago, you lived in a village on the border of Maharashtra and Karnataka. One night, there was a heavy downpour and you helped me—a young, unmarried girl then—through childbirth. There was no delivery table in the room, so you converted stacks of paddy sacks into a makeshift table. Many hours later, I gave birth to a daughter.'

In a flash, the memories came flooding back and my father recollected that night. 'Of course I remember you!' he said. 'It was the middle of the night and I urged you to go to Pune with your newborn. I think I was as scared as you!'

'You gave me a hundred rupees, which is what my family paid you for the delivery. It was a big amount in those days and still, you handed it all over to me.'

'Yes, my monthly salary was seventy-five rupees then!' added my father with a smile.

'You told me your last name but I couldn't hear it because of the deafening sound of the rain. I took your advice, went to Pune, found your friend Gokhale and became a nurse. It was very, very hard, but I was able to raise my daughter on my own. After such a terrible experience, I wanted my daughter to become a gynaecologist. Luckily, she shared my dream too. Today, she is a doctor and is also married to one and they practise here. At one point, I spent months searching for you but with no luck. Then we heard that you had moved to Karnataka after the reorganization of the state departments in 1956. Meanwhile, Gokhale also passed away and I lost all hope of ever finding you. I prayed to God to give me a chance to meet you and thank you for showing me the right path at the right time.'

My father felt like he was in a Bollywood movie and was enchanted by the unexplained mystery of life. A few kind words and encouragement had changed a young girl's life.

She clasped her hands together, 'We are so grateful to you, doctor. My daughter wanted to call you for the inauguration of the nursing home here and we were very disappointed at not being able to reach you then. Time has passed and now the nursing home is doing very well.'

My father wiped his moist eyes and looked around to see the name of the nursing home. He looked to the right and found himself staring at it—R.H. Diagnostic.

7

No Place Like Home

Infosys Foundation is involved in various types of construction projects like building dharamshalas for poor patients and their caretakers, schools for children in remote areas, houses for the thousands who suffer in calamities such as cyclones and floods, and toilets for both schools and public use in an effort to encourage cleanliness in our country.

From its inception, I wanted the foundation to be independent and have its own office, but during the initial period, we didn't have more than Rs 5000 left in the bank at the end of every financial year, despite the annual funding. Somehow, the will to help others made having our own premises an extremely low priority. Still, the foundation kept short-term fixed deposits and we carefully managed our cash flows to ensure interest, and over the years, we managed to accumulate a sizeable amount.

One day, I learnt of a beautiful plot of land with an old building available for sale in the popular suburb of Jayanagar in Bengaluru. The interest we had saved was just enough to purchase the land. Since the building was not suited for the needs of an office, it was obvious that at some point, we would have to demolish it and build our own. So we decided to leave the land as is until we had saved some more.

The next financial year too, we had less than Rs 5000 in our bank account. Even though we had saved a little interest over the years, the construction cost was higher than the money we had and building our office remained a dream.

Years passed by and finally, in 2002, the foundation was able to accumulate enough interest to begin construction. I was happy. My dream was about to come true. I got the ball rolling, contacted an architect and instructed him to create a simple plan for us.

A few days later, I received an invitation from a Middle Eastern country to speak at a ladies' association there. I decided to accept it because I had some talks scheduled in Dubai and Kuwait soon after. I wanted to complete all my assignments there during one trip and thus save money on the cost of air tickets.

Soon, I was on my way. Like all trips, this one, too, had many meetings and talks lined up. There were also events wherein the who's who of the Indian community in the region was expected to participate. It took courage for most of the people I met to leave their homes behind in India, settle in a foreign country and still hold on to the culture and faith, against many odds. People also spoke about the work we did, or thought we did— sometimes it was factual and sometimes a little exaggerated.

Finally, the day came for my last speaking engagement. It was a good event with lively questions and discussions. When the function drew to a close, I prepared to leave for my hotel.

A few women met me on their way out. 'Ma'am, would you like to buy anything here?' they inquired politely. 'The shopping experience here is quite wonderful. Maybe you'd like some pearls or gold?'

'No,' I replied. 'But is there anything interesting that I can see?'

The women pondered for a moment, shook their heads and said their goodbyes.

Just then, I noticed two women approaching me. One of them said in a low voice, 'Ma'am, we would like to invite you to our small shelter. Will you please consider it?'

'What's there in your shelter?' I asked.

'We want you to see it for yourself. We can tell you about the work we do in various ways, but I don't know which aspect of our work will strike a chord with you.'

My antenna went up. There was something about them and their humble manner that made me curious. I nodded. 'Please give me a few minutes. I will come with you right now,' I said.

I thanked my hosts quickly and left the venue with the women in tow. A short while later, we reached a small house in a residential area. At first glance, it seemed more of an outhouse to me. When we entered, I saw five women there—all in their nightwear. Some of them had swollen eyes and red marks on their cheeks. It was obvious that they were not in the best of health or happy in any way.

Within a few minutes, we were all seated.

'What language should I speak in?' I asked the women who had brought me there.

'Hindi is okay. A little English is also fine.'

The women began telling me their names and the states they were from—one was from Tamil Nadu, two from Andhra Pradesh and one from Kerala.

I exchanged a few pleasantries with them and soon enough, Nazneem, the woman from Andhra Pradesh, started narrating her story, 'Madam, I was a maid in the district of Karimnagar years ago and had three daughters old enough to get married. An agent told me that I would earn much more in the Middle East for the same work I did in India. He told me that I would even get a fifteen-day vacation once a year with free air travel to see my family. I realized that if I worked here for three years, I would save enough to bear the wedding expenses of all my daughters. It was everything I could ask for. Our financial troubles would go away! My husband, who is a vegetable vendor, kept reassuring me that he would look after the girls during my absence. He encouraged me to go as long as I kept in touch regularly. So with my limited savings and by selling all the gold that I had, I paid for my passport, visa, travel fare and the agent's commission.'

Her eyes clouded over as the memories came flooding back. 'When the time came to say goodbye, my heart left heavy and I was afraid. I had never even travelled from Karimnagar to the big city of Hyderabad. Then how would I travel abroad and manage things all alone in a country completely foreign to me? How would I be able to live away from my family?

'The agent assured me, "The family you are going to work for are kind. They are also of the same religion as you. You won't take too much time to adjust. I have already spoken to them. They will treat you as a family member. If you are unhappy, you can come back after a year and not return."

'I felt somewhat relieved and for the first time in my life, I travelled to Hyderabad on my own and then took a flight from the city to come here.'

I interrupted her, 'Were you scared during the flight?'

Nazneem thought for a moment. 'Not really,' she replied. 'In the airplane, I met many women just like me, both young and old, and I felt better knowing that I wasn't alone. Outside the destination airport, we were handed a burka each and were directed to a bus. The heat was unbearable, and it felt like I was almost on fire. Karimnagar is a hot place in India but the level of heat in this country cannot be described. Despite the scorching heat, the bus was not air-conditioned. We were all expecting a luxurious bus, like the one the agent had promised. We dismissed it as an error or a problem with bus availability. In fact, most of us believed that it might rain soon—like it happens in some parts of south India.

'An hour-long ride later, the bus dropped us at a location from where we were taken to different houses for our new jobs.

'The house I was taken to was huge, beautiful and air-conditioned. I was given a tiny room near the kitchen. First, I met the house manager who took my passport and handed me some cleaning supplies and told me something in a language I didn't understand. Thankfully, there was another woman housekeeper from India named Santosh who translated everything for me: "Your work begins right now. Start cleaning the whole house and make it spotless. Madam has no tolerance for dust. Your meal timings are— breakfast at 9 a.m., lunch at 3 p.m. and dinner at 10 p.m. Also, you must wear a burka whenever you go outside the house."

'I took some time to unpack my bags and use the bathroom. Then I went back to search for Santosh. The supplies were good and Santosh taught me how to use them and introduced me to some of the electronic cleaning equipment too.

'Over the next few days, I hardly saw the owner of the house—she was either out of the country or living on a different floor. I always reported to the house manager.

'Santosh and I began to get to know one another. One afternoon, when we had a few minutes alone, she asked me, "Why did you come here? This isn't such a good work environment. We work like donkeys from morning to night with minimal rest and sometimes, we have to endure the wrath of the house manager for no fault of ours. Though we have come for household chores, we always get burdened with extra work. Look at me—I help in the kitchen, bathe all the young children, iron all the clothes and wash all the dishes. Now, they have brought you here to clean the house, but that's not the only work you will be assigned. You may have to do the cook's job when he doesn't show up or run errands as and when needed."

'"It doesn't matter as long as I get a good salary," I replied honestly.

'"That's what I used to think too," said Santosh. There was sadness in her eyes. "We don't get a rupee in our hands. Sometimes, the owner says that the money has been deposited in a bank account or that it has been sent to our family. It's been a year since I came here but I haven't received any payment directly."

"'But our agent said . . .'"

"'It doesn't matter what your agent said or who he is—they are all the same. They have lied to us and lured us into this country and job. We are poor and we fell for the hope they gave us. They know that once we get here, it is difficult to return. The agents know that we are all alone here. In this country, we can't even go out without a man accompanying us. The owners also keep our passports with them, making it impossible to leave this place."

'For the first time since landing there, I became afraid. I didn't know what to do. "Santosh, you have been here for a year. When are you going back? Are you going to quit work or change jobs?"

"'We can't quit or change jobs without the owner's consent. Most of the bosses don't allow it. So I am trying my best to return, but I need money for a one-way ticket and my passport."

"'Do you talk to your family back home?'"

"'Yes, I write letters and hand them over to my agent, but I don't know whether it reaches them. I haven't received even one reply yet. I only get to hear what the agent tells me about my family. I know that they have tried to call me here on the phone, but there are strict instructions against that according to the rules of this house. Madam doesn't want her staff to take personal calls on her landlines.

Moreover, I know that it isn't easy for them to call me here, and I don't want to share my difficulties with them. I hear that a lump sum amount is sent to them every six months. But once I get my ticket, I will go back and never come back here."

'I was slightly relieved to hear that her family was getting some money. "Aren't they supposed to send the money every month?" I asked.

'"The agents are much smarter than us. They keep a salary backlog of at least six months. If I go back to my country and don't return, then they will keep that money. So many people come back for their money and the cycle continues. To someone in our financial position, a six-month salary is a big amount to walk away from."

'"When are you planning to go home?"

'"It depends on the owners. Sometimes, they send the workers home after fifteen months or sometimes after two years. I don't know when they will decide to send me back. I can understand their language now but still pretend not to. I have learnt that Madam is going to India to enjoy the monsoon in Kerala. Since I am from the state and know the local language, she wants me to go with her and look after the children. I will ask her then to allow me to visit my family for a few days and if she does, I won't come back. I have reached a point where I don't even care about the money," said Santosh firmly.

'I could not sleep that night. Had I been duped by the agent? How much money will my family really get? With not many options at my disposal, I decided that the best way forward was to keep a low profile and continue working.

'For the first few weeks, things seemed okay. The staff was usually given leftover food, which was good and I didn't have any complaints related to work. After some time had passed, I started getting extra chores, especially around the time Madam was leaving for a vacation to India. Santosh was going to go with them too and I knew that she wouldn't come back. So I wrote letters to my family and requested her to mail them from India.

'Once Santosh and the family left the country, the house manager instructed me to take on all of Santosh's work as well. Since the owner always entertained guests in his big mansion, there was a lot of cooking and cleaning to be done. There were a total of fourteen children in the house and each child would also frequently bring his or her friends over. I felt trapped—like a bird in a cage. Since the work more than doubled, my efficiency reduced and the house manager became upset and refused to listen to my concerns. She would show me a stick and say, "Don't complain about your work. You are being paid for it. I don't want to hear another word."

'When the unending workload became unbearable during the day, I would sit down and rest for a few minutes. If the house manager found me resting, she would beat me with that same stick. That's when I recalled the marks on Santosh's hand and realized how she had got them. Nobody ever beat me in my home. Though we were poor, we lived with dignity.

'The loneliness and the excess work soon began affecting my health and my ability to work. I longed for my family, my children and my friends. As the days went by, there was nothing but sadness left in my soul.'

I interjected, 'With whom did you share your troubles with, now that Santosh was gone?'

'Nobody,' said Nazneem. 'There was a male gardener who would visit and tend to the lawn and plants outside the house, but I could not speak to him according to the country's rules. I couldn't go out as I only had three nightdresses that I wore day and night. I was not allowed to wear the clothes that I had brought with me. I was only allowed to go shopping with the family, and even then, I had to wear a burka on top of my clothes. So I had no friends or acquaintances to speak to.

'Soon, Madam came back from India, upset and furious. She said to the house manager, "Start keeping a close eye on these Indian women. Santosh never came back after she went home. She cheated me. So for now, don't allow this woman to go home any time soon."

'These words dampened my spirit and I cried in the shadows, wondering when I would see my family again.

'One morning, I overheard a conversation between Madam and the house manager. "Whatever you say, Indian women are the best for household work," she told the manager. "They do their jobs quietly, don't answer back or complain too much."

'The house manager said something unintelligible.

'"Recruit two more," she instructed.

'While I hated the thought of somebody else going through what I had endured, I was at the end of my rope and hoped that this would reduce my workload in the course of time.

'Weeks later, I was down with high fever.'

'Did you go the doctor?' I couldn't contain myself.

'No, the house manager gave me Crocin. We were never taken to the doctor for any reason whatsoever. I had to work despite the fever. A day later, it went up further and I was afraid that my body would give up. Desperate, I approached the manager and asked her to take me to the nearest doctor or hospital.

'She was blunt, "We have multiple house guests today and I really don't have the time."

'I almost broke down. "I can't work today," I said tearfully. "I am in pain and there's a constant throbbing in my head."

'Nonchalantly, she heated up a spoon on the kitchen fire, caught my hand and pressed the hot spoon on my wrist.

'I screamed and she shushed me. "Don't scream. Nobody will come to help you. You are a servant and must behave like one. Go and start working now," she said, her volume matching mine.

'My body started trembling with fear. Was this going to be my fate till I die?

'I don't remember the days ahead with clarity, but the fever came down and my body, at least, felt a little better. But I was dead inside. I had no incentive to wake up in the mornings, but I had no choice. I lived like a robot. When I had time to think, I only thought about returning home to my family.

'One rare day, when there was nobody at home but me, the gardener, Maruti, requested me for a cup of tea. I wore the burka and went to the backyard to give it to him.

'"Please help me get home," I told him as soon as he started sipping the tea. "I don't know anyone here and you know how they treat the helps in this house. My family wouldn't even get to know if something happened to me here. You are like my brother. Please, can you lend me a hand?"

'"Don't even think of running away," he said. I could see that he was afraid. "If the authorities trace you and bring you back, you will suffer unspeakable cruelty. Still, I will try and speak to a few people I know. I will get back to you."

'I touched his feet. It was as if Allah had come to help me through this kind man.

'A month passed before Maruti approached me at a time when we were alone again. It was Eid, a religious holiday, and the family had gone out for the evening. "I met two kind women at an Indian function. I think they may be able to help you," he said.

'"I am so grateful to you. How did you meet them?"

'"The owner once asked me to deliver some flowers to a government official who was attending an Indian wedding ceremony. At the wedding, I was told to wait and that's when I heard about these two women from others. I somehow managed to see them. Since I am a man and free to move about in this country, I was able to meet them a few more times. I told them about your difficulties here. They have told me to inform you that it is risky to leave your work here, but if you decide to do so and go to them, then they will also share the risk with you and try their best to send you back home. I can take you to them. But do it when you go shopping as it will be easier to escape from there."

'I nodded. We decided to wait for the right moment.

'Meanwhile, Maruti gave me a map and the directions to the place I would have to locate when the time came. I memorized everything well so that I could reach there without any confusion. Maruti had already done more than I could have ever imagined and I decided not to involve him further. The punishment for such actions is severe in this country.

'Weeks later, Madam asked me to run an errand. This was my chance.

'I wore a burka, went to the marketplace, bought groceries and handed them to the driver. I told him that I needed to go to the restroom and that I would be back soon. The moment I was out of sight of the driver, I ran! The driver would have taken some time to realize that I was missing. As many women wore the burka, I knew that it would be tough for him to find me. I kept going with my heart beating fast—sometimes I ran and sometimes I walked. Within half an hour, I reached my destination with nothing but the clothes I was wearing. Finally, I was here.'

Nazneem's story ended and she collapsed on the chair, tired from reliving the dark past.

The two women turned to me. 'She came two days ago,' one of them said.

A silence fell in the room. 'No one should have to go through this,' I thought.

Gracy, the woman from Kerala, broke the stillness in the room by sharing her story. She was beautiful and well-spoken. She had also been duped by an agent who had promised her a job to tutor children. And yet, her story was vastly different.

Gracy was an orphan who grew up in a government home for such children. She became a teacher in a convent school and though the salary was enough to get by, it was not enough to achieve her dream of owning a small home. In time, Gracy found a boy she liked but he did not have a steady job or income. Since they didn't have any assets, they made a mutual decision—Gracy would go abroad for tutoring. This would give the couple a chance to earn enough money to purchase a home later and settle down.

When she reached the home she was going to live in, she was quite shocked to find that her employer had four wives and sixteen children—all of whom lived in the huge residence. However, only ten of the boys and girls were old enough to go to pre-school, primary or middle school. Gracy taught the children subjects such as English, mathematics, history, art and craft and manners. For a few years, things seemed all right and she was treated fairly well. She was paid once in six months in bulk and her employer even allowed her a paid vacation to India once a year. The children had also become very fond of her, and she was not mistreated like Nazneem.

As the years passed and the boys reached their mid-teens, their classmates and cousins began frequenting the home. Soon, she became the target of their lecherous stares and she realized for the first time that she was an easy target should they wish to approach her. She became extremely uncomfortable living there. When she tried to share her concerns with one of the employer's wives, she scoffed at her, 'Yes, Gracy, you are so beautiful that many men will desire you. In fact, I won't be surprised if my husband does too!'

From that day on, Gracy became afraid for herself. She began to avoid teaching the older boys and even told the employer that they did not need her help any more, but nobody listened.

'You are paid to teach the children and you must fulfil your responsibility. There's nothing more to say,' said the employer and dismissed her with a wave of his hand.

One day, a friend of the boys came to her room and tried to forcefully kiss her. Due to her presence of mind, she managed to push him out of the room with all her might and didn't mention it to anyone.

The next day, however, she found that one of the boys named Abdul was very upset.

Upon further inquiry, Abdul said, 'My friend is upset for some reason. When I asked him to come home today, he refused and said that it was because of you. Tell me, what have you done?'

Gracy found it hard to share her troubles with a sixteen-year-old, but thought it wise to tell the truth to her ward.

To her astonishment, he laughed. 'You are very attractive,' said Abdul. 'I can't blame my friend for not being able to control himself. If you were ugly like the cook, Fatima, then nobody would want you.'

'Abdul, I am your teacher,' said Gracy very firmly, despite the tremors she was beginning to feel in her body. 'How dare you speak to me like this?'

'I am no longer a child. I am a man now and look at women from a different perspective,' he responded and walked away casually.

'It was then that I realized that the home was a ticking time bomb for me. I was better off living in a rented house in my country than staying under such duress in that residence. Nobody—neither the employer nor his wives—was going to protect me if something were to happen. I was fortunate enough that my passport was with me. And yet, I had no money. But I knew these two kind women here who helped women in such distress.'

'How did you get to know about them?' I asked.

'It was a stroke of luck. Last December, I had attended a Christmas party. It was there that I met them and learnt about their work. Once the time was right, I walked to the shelter, leaving all of my belongings at my employer's home,' she said, staring at the floor.

There was nothing for me to say. I felt ashamed and disgusted at the world today where half of the population does not feel safe.

The two other women—Roja from Tamil Nadu and Neena from Andhra Pradesh—shared their stories with bouts of tears. Their experiences were worse. Each had travelled a different path but both had been raped by their employers.

I couldn't hold back my tears any longer. What a wretched life these women have had! How does one even begin to get over such trauma? It took me a few minutes to compose myself.

I glanced at the two women sitting near me. How did they send these women back?

One of them said, 'Once these women come to the shelter, we go to the Indian embassy and get new passports made for them. It is difficult and at times, we run into problems that cause delays. But the real problem is their departure from here. Legally, we can't keep them in the shelter beyond a certain period of time and we have to buy a one-way ticket for them as soon as we can. And if we have to book it at short notice, we have to almost always pay a high price for it.'

'Who pays for the tickets?'

'We ask around and reach out to everyone we can. The folks in small-paying jobs are high in number but they usually have their own financial problems and other issues. People who do have the money don't really want to support us for a long time. Some would rather buy gold in the souk or hold a party for their friends and families. The rich folks consider this a perennial problem. They are willing to help us for one or two cases but our shelter gets around five women every month. Sooner or later, the donor stops funding the tickets. Sometimes, store owners anonymously buy flight tickets, but everybody is afraid of getting caught some day. Others shrug it off and say that it isn't their problem. They accuse the women of following the path of money. They feel it was their responsibility to verify the agency before coming here. When we began the shelter a few years ago, we pumped in our personal funds. But we aren't rich either and I fear that we won't be able to keep up for long.'

It was a depressing thought. The shelter was a ray of hope for the women caught in difficult circumstances. Where would they go without such a place to run to?

I looked at the clock. It was time to leave for my meeting with a friend. So I said my goodbyes and left the shelter with a heavy heart.

We drove past beautiful homes, wide roads and fancy cars. I felt nothing. All I could think of were the four women and their haunting pasts. Suddenly, I changed my mind.

'Take a U-turn,' I told the driver.

I went back to the shelter and met the two women. I said, 'Infosys Foundation is happy to sponsor one-way tickets for the women in need—be it to their city, village or town. We will take care of the travel cost as long as the shelter has verified them. But you must help them obtain a passport in time and ensure that they are able to board the flight without any hassles.'

The women smiled and agreed.

I smiled back. Finally, I felt like I had lessened some of my burden.

'Tell these women that India is changing,' I told them. 'Gone are the days when people worked for a minuscule salary. In cities, when both the husband and the wife have to go to work, they need a reliable and good housekeeper at home, without which many women choose to quit their jobs. Honesty carries a high price in India now and more and more people are choosing to stay back in the country of their own volition due to the demand in urban areas.'

'The women will be ecstatic to learn of this development,' said one of them. She couldn't stop smiling. 'May God bless the foundation and you for such an invaluable gesture.'

The next day, on my flight back, I couldn't help but think how fortunate we are to live in India. We may not be the richest or the best country in the world, but we have so much freedom. We can switch jobs easily or relocate to a different town or city. If nothing else, most of us have a family that will at least give us a place to stay in times of trouble. We really don't know how lucky we are until we are out of the country.

Out of habit, I began calculating the approximate travel expenses for the women. They had mentioned an average of twenty to twenty-five cases per year. 'This extra annual grant would evaporate my savings for the office building in five years,' I thought, a tad disappointed.

I had to make a choice—build the office or give shelter to these women. I knew, of course, that there really was no choice at all. There was no second-guessing my decision. My conscience and I could still live in a rented three-room space for a few more years.

This happened fifteen years ago.

Last year, we finally moved into our own office and home after twenty years. I named the building 'Neralu'—the shelter.

8

A Powerful Ambassador

I am a storyteller at heart, so it isn't surprising that I fell in love with movies.

When we were children, Bollywood was very different from what it is today. Most movies were in black and white. Then, there were Eastmancolor movies and black and white movies with some songs in colour, until finally, the move was made to colour feature films.

Meena Kumari's tragedies often brought tears to my eyes while Madhubala and Asha Parekh's beautiful song sequences remain etched in my mind. I can't let go of Sadhana and Waheeda Rahman's effortless beauty, while Sanjeev Kumar's powerful acting and Rajesh Khanna's charisma will remain with my generation until we are gone.

I have followed the evolution of Bollywood through the use of technology and also from simple innocent romances to the aggressive and bold portrayal of it today and from classical dances to the drill-team type of dances to breakdance and now, twerking.

Movies were generally taboo in those days and considered a luxury in a village such as mine. We lived in Shiggaon without access to a movie theatre. Besides, there was no electricity in those days. But to our absolute delight, we did get touring talkies in the summer, which were tents set up specifically to screen movies. It was the Lord's answer to our desperation! If we really wanted to see a film, we were accompanied by an adult and our chaperone would decide which movie we would watch. We could only see religious and inspiring movies such as *Sri Krishna Tulabharam*, *Rama Vanavasa* and *Girija Kalyana*. Occasionally, an exception was made and we were allowed to watch a children's movie under adult supervision. We would then go and tell our friends about it. On the big day, my cousins and I would eat early and fill our stomachs so that we wouldn't have to take a break during the movie. We would talk about the film for days on end after the screening. However, the movie-watching days were rare throughout the year.

But nothing stays the same forever. Life changed and I came to the small city of Hubli for my education where there were plenty of movie theatres. And yet, the taboo remained—a teenage girl shouldn't see romantic scenes. So while I happily saw them when I went with my friends, I had to listen to my aunt and close my eyes when I saw the same scenes with her or other senior members of the family.

As the months went past, I became bolder. At the end of every exam season, a bunch of us girls would go together to the movies. We would lie to our families that we were going for a film like *Dashavathara* (about the ten avatars of Lord

Vishnu) and go watch a film of the dreamy hero Rajendra Kumar. All of us had secret crushes on the heroes but we felt awkward sharing this with each other.

When I made it to college, I became what must have been considered 'really bold'. I told my parents, 'I refuse to watch religious films. I have seen enough of them to last me a lifetime. Now, I want to see Rajesh Khanna's movies.'

I lived in a joint family and it was clear that the elders in the family felt astonished and perhaps a little embarrassed at my intensely transparent desire to watch a superstar's movies, especially a hero known for his ridiculous good looks and charm and the ability to drive away all common sense from a girl's mind.

From that day on, my aunt kept a close watch on my grades. The slightest hint of a fall would earn me the comment, 'It is no wonder that your marks are going down. The crappy romantic movies have distracted you and you are no longer able to focus as much as you should.'

Poor Rajesh Khanna was often blamed for my cousins' and my low marks. If only he had known!

Later, I made my way to Bengaluru for my post-graduation. It was heaven! The area known as Majestic boasted of at least thirty movie theatres such as Sangam, Alankar, Kempe Gowda and Majestic, on either side of the road. I frequently managed to watch two movies in one trip.

Once I was left to my own devices in the working ladies' hostel in Pune, there was absolutely no one to stop me and my love for films grew by leaps and bounds. It grew to such an extent that I could study only when movie soundtracks were playing in the background. Many of the students made fun of me.

One day, a few girls gathered at a friend's home.

Someone said to me, 'Movies are a wonderful source of entertainment. But it is like eating dessert every day. It is not good for your health and you will start disliking it at some point.'

'No way,' I protested. 'You can eat different desserts on different days and you'll never reach a point of disliking it. It's the same thing with movies.'

'Easy to say. Not so easy to implement. Are you willing to see a movie every day?'

'Of course I am.' I had no doubt that I could.

My friends were quite thrilled. 'Well, then let's bet on it. If you see 365 movies in 365 days, we will give you one hundred rupees and honour you as Miss Cinema.'

I nodded, quite excited. Thus I began my filmi journey.

Pune was a great city for watching movies. In those days, Nilayam Theatre would screen Raj Kapoor movies—a different one each day. There, I saw all his movies—from the earliest one to the most recent. Once that was done, I switched to the famous director–actor Guru Dutt and watched all his movies in Lakshmi Narayan Theatre. Boredom was nowhere in sight. Just when that was nearing its end, Prabhat Film Company, a pioneer in Marathi movies, began showing their films in Natraj Theatre, which was a stone's throw from my hostel. Some of these were movies from before my time and were those my father had seen when he was a student. So I watched them too—*Manoos*, *Kunku*, *Shejari* and *Ramshastri*, among others. During the days movies were in short supply, I stocked up on English classics at Rahul 70 mm Theatre—*Gone with the Wind*, *To Sir with Love*, *Come September*, *The Ten Commandments*, films featuring Charlie Chaplin, Laurel and Hardy, and other silent movies with subtitles. Occasionally, Deccan Theatre screened Kannada movies too.

At the end of the year, I had successfully watched 365 movies and became such an expert that I could rate any movie that my friends could think of. I even understood the fundamentals for a movie's successful run. Necessary prerequisites consist of a tight story, good music, crisp conversation, excellent script and dialogues, fine acting by the lead roles, appropriate costumes, outstanding direction and careful editing. Then there was the matter of luck which remains undefined to this day. I have encountered films with excellent storylines that have turned out to be box-office flops. So while there is no exact formula for success, too much melodrama and a non-realistic storyline dooms a movie from the start.

My deep interest in films took me to the next level—assessing the acting abilities of the heroes and the skills of the director. Thus I gradually turned into a movie pundit.

Now I am unable to watch as many movies as I would like due to my schedule, yet, I prefer going to a movie theatre, rather than watching it at home.

I also have an interest in visiting countries that aren't considered popular tourist destinations. A few years ago, I added Iran, Poland, Cuba, the Bahamas, Uzbekistan and Iceland to the list. These less visited countries have many advantages.

They are not crowded and have fewer hotel reservations. The flight tickets to these places can be obtained at a short notice and you have the freedom to walk about anywhere you choose. Out of these four countries, the Bahamas was the most exotic of them all, even as I was introduced to the other countries and their specialties—whether it be their markets, vegetables, customs, cuisine, fashion and much more. I enjoy going to farmers' markets to sample the local goodies and always pick up something that I can carry around and eat.

During my visit to Iran, I was utterly fascinated to see yesteryear's Persia, especially since I was aware that we use almost 5000 Persian words in the local language of north Karnataka. The historical connection goes back to the days of the Adil Shahi dynasty. The official language in the court and the military was Persian. So it isn't surprising that many words and nuances of Persian architecture were absorbed by the locals in their language and can still be viewed in Bijapur and Bidar in Karnataka.

In the olden days, trade was an important part of administration and was responsible for bringing revenue into the kingdom. Many trader groups were in existence at that time, which enabled the exchange of goods from China to India and from India to the Western world. This also encouraged the sharing of culture through food, dance, theatre and cloth.

I decided to visit the local market in Shiraz, a prominent city, in an effort to better understand the culture and the type of merchandise and fare. At the market, I noticed a man busy making naans in a small stall and a few people waiting around for their order. The process was fascinating and the naans were ready to be served in a matter of a few minutes. When guests come home in Iran, women do not head to the kitchen and make rotis like we do in India. Instead, the man of the house goes to the naan and roomali roti (another type of thin flatbread) shop and gets them freshly made and in big quantities.

All the cooking made me feel hungry and I approached the man. 'I want to buy two of them,' I said in English.

It was clear that he wasn't too familiar with English, but he understood my request. Soon, he handed me two warm naans on a paper. I noticed him observing my sari and the bindi on my forehead.

Since I didn't know the cost, I offered him a higher denomination currency note so that he could charge me appropriately and return the change.

'Amitabh Bachchan?' he asked.

When I didn't respond, he persisted, 'Salman Khan? Shah Rukh Khan?'

After hearing the names of the famous Bollywood heroes, I realized what he was trying to say. 'Yes,' I replied. 'I am from the same country as them.'

He smiled. 'No money,' he said.

Even when I insisted, he refused. He added, 'India. Bollywood. Very nice. Good dance. Good dress. Good music. Iranian like.'

I understood. Iranians like Bollywood. Since I come from the same land as some of the heroes they like, the man didn't want to take any money from me. He wanted to give them to me as a gift. He probably thought of it as a way of doing something in return for the heroes' countrymen.

'Salaam!' His words broke through my train of thought and he moved on to the next client behind me.

I held those precious naans closely and came back to my room and turned the television on. To my pleasant surprise and amusement, I saw Amitabh Bachchan conversing in Persian with Jaya Bhaduri in the movie *Kabhi Khushi Kabhie Gham*. I had no doubt—Bollywood movies were definitely a rage in this country. The Iranians may not understand the meaning of the songs, but they must like our storylines, the beautiful and flowing silk lehengas, the foot-tapping music, the grandeur of the sets and the acting of the lead characters.

My next visit was to Havana, the capital of Cuba. The city is cut off from Western civilization and remains isolated from most of the world. The local language is Spanish and I couldn't say a single word except 'gracias' or thank you. To my surprise, there didn't seem to be any tourists from India. The weather was warm and there were beautiful sheltered markets that helped us escape the heat. The markets had almost everything possible on sale, including handicrafts, fruits and juices.

So with a glass of coconut water in hand, I wandered through the markets with my sister, who found a bag in a store filled with wooden and leather goods. As I helped her inspect the quality of the bag, she began to negotiate the price—a habit that is part of the Indian DNA, irrespective of one's financial position. Using her hands, the seller indicated the price—fifteen pesos. I noticed a young man standing by watching the interaction with obvious interest. Meanwhile, my sister instantly indicated ten without knowing the true value of the item she was buying. The seller came down to eleven pesos but my sister proudly refused to budge. The woman grinned, agreed and said something in Spanish. I heard the names Madhuri Dixit and Aamir Khan thrown in as the transaction finally took place.

Just when we were about to walk away, the young man on the side finally spoke. 'Do you know why that lady gave you the bag for only ten pesos?' he asked in broken English.

I shook my head.

'She says that she is a big fan of Aamir Khan and Madhuri Dixit. She wants you to tell them that they have fans in Havana and the rest of Cuba.'

I was surprised. 'Can you ask the seller where she sees their movies?'

The seller smiled when she heard the question and said something to the young man.

'She gets the DVDs,' he turned to me and said.

'Are they pirated?' I asked.

'I don't know,' he said. 'I can ask her if you want.'

I decided not to pursue the conversation since we couldn't communicate effectively. While I didn't get all my answers, it was clear that Bollywood enjoyed a big presence internationally, and that I had got a five-peso discount because of it!

I recalled one of my visits to Mumbai where I had met a new-age Indian actor–director and had an animated discussion about movies, of course!

'Bollywood is not just about cinema,' I said. 'If somebody talks about the importance of good values, it may impact one person in the crowd. If someone writes about them, then it may change a few more. But if it is shown in Bollywood through a powerful story, then the impact is much more drastic. As an actor, one must own the responsibility to spread the right messages.'

He agreed with me.

The influence of Bollywood is phenomenal indeed.

My travel adventures also took me to Bukhara, the fifth largest city of Uzbekistan. As I went for an evening stroll, the faint tunes of a familiar song 'Tujh Mein Rab Dikhta Hai' wafted towards me. It was from the movie Rab Ne Bana Di Jodi. Just like the children who couldn't resist following the Pied Piper of Hamelin, my legs directed me towards the source of the music.

Within minutes, I found myself outside a restaurant by a pond—Lyabi House. As I attempted to enter, the doorman stopped me gently with a wave of his hand.

'I'm sorry, but the restaurant is at full capacity today and all our tables are occupied,' he said.

'But that song is mine!' I said, feeling as excited and proud as a six-year-old and pointing inside. 'I am from the country of that music!'

The doorman smiled and stepped aside to let me in.

Hurriedly, I entered the main room and walked right up to the singer, focused on his performance. By now, the music had changed and this time it was 'Tum Hi Ho' from Aashiqui 2. 'I am from India and this song is from my country,' I said to him, the moment he stopped singing.

'Hindustan?' he asked.

I nodded.

'Namaste!' he grinned and nodded his head vigorously, as if to acknowledge what I had just said.

I looked around, and for the first time, I became aware of other people in the restaurant.

We tried to communicate quickly—he in Uzbek and I in Hindi with a spattering of as many Persian words that I could remember. We failed quite miserably.

Then he smiled and his melodious voice filled the air—'Main Shayar To Nahi'. The song must have been quite popular among the locals because suddenly there was a round of applause from the people in the room.

This wasn't about a big achievement such as a space mission or a sports victory, but about running into common people listening to a slice of India in an unknown corner of the world. My whole being felt a rush of mixed emotions—above everything else, a sense of pride that I belonged to a special country.

Even people in a country like England share their love for Bollywood dance. Indian restaurants are popular and are often based on the theme of Bollywood. Iceland also has a restaurant named Gandhi in Reykjavik. There is a statue of late Yash Chopra, a renowned Indian filmmaker, in Interlaken, Switzerland, and a poster of Shah Rukh Khan and Kajol at the entrance of Mount Titlis, a mountain of the Uri Alps.

Bollywood has also contributed to Hollywood's food dishes. There is a drink called Piggy Chops in Milk Bar, West

Hollywood, named after actress Priyanka Chopra, which consists of bananas, almonds, caramel sauce, vanilla ice cream and a splash of ginseng. Mallika Shake, on the other hand, is named after Mallika Sherawat and is a delicious mix of blueberries, blackberries, raspberries and strawberries, topped with chocolate sauce.

Young girls now want to dress like these heroines. I have seen several girls in my friend's boutique asking for dresses like the one Anushka Sharma wore in *Band Baaja Baaraat* or what Madhuri Dixit wore in *Hum Aapke Hain Kaun*.

Before my trip to Uzbekistan, I visited Iceland. I was a south Indian who wasn't used to wearing a sweater at any time of the year. Then how would I wear five layers of clothes? I must be the only crazy one wanting to visit the country, or so I thought. I was pretty sure that I wouldn't run into an Indian there because of the freezing temperatures.

When I finally reached the country for a prearranged tour, I met a nice local guide who greeted me in an accent I could barely understand. 'Do you want to see the locales of the "*Gerua*" song?' he asked.

I didn't understand a word and gazed at him in silence until he felt visibly uncomfortable. So he dug around in his bag and pulled out a DVD of the movie *Dilwale* starring Kajol and Shah Rukh Khan.

'Yes!' I exclaimed, as light dawned on me. I had seen the movie and had wondered where one of the song and dance sequences was shot.

On the way to Black Sand beach, he showed us the video of the song. The black pebbles and the floating icebergs took my breath away and we ended up spending a considerable amount of time there.

'We all love this song. It has made Iceland very popular with your countrymen and enhanced our tourism prospects,' he said.

As we headed back to the hotel, a Spanish fellow traveller next to me added, 'That is very true. We have benefited from Bollywood, too. The "Senorita" song from the movie *Zindagi Na Milegi Dobara* which was shot in Spain has made our country popular. The movie also brought the tomato festival to the limelight!'

I nodded. 'The movie has indeed made Spain a favoured holiday destination for Indians. We fancy the cities of Barcelona and Madrid and the La Tomatino festival. Somebody should consider giving an award to the movie's director Zoya Akhtar for enhancing the country's tourism income.'

I sat back and my mind wandered over the journey of Bollywood from black and white to colour movies, from Prithviraj Kapoor to Ranbir Kapoor, and from the touring talkies that operated for only three months a year to the movie-on-demand access that we have today.

Bollywood has graduated from being a part of the movie industry to becoming a vital partner when it comes to business generation. All in all, it is a great ambassador for our unique country.

9

Rasleela and the Swimming Pool

Harikatha is a traditional art form from the state of Karnataka wherein a narrator or *dasa*, along with a small troupe, goes from village to village and shares stories from the Hindu scriptures and epics. When they visited my village, Shiggaon, the audience eagerly assembled in the temple for an all-night performance. Multiple stories were depicted through dance and to the tunes of tamburas. The enactment was dependent solely on the expertise of the narrator and the dance.

One such evening, I accompanied my cousins to the Harikatha of Gopika Vastra Harana. The Harikatha dasa of this troupe was a well-known promoter named Gopinath who was known to portray stories from the Bhagavata Purana and deeply involve the audience. The stories would usually contain descriptions of Krishna's mischief, his mother's love and the cowherd girls' (or *gopikas'*) adoration.

That day, Gopinath began, 'Everybody, please close your eyes. Today is a warm day in the wondrous city of Vrindavan. Come, walk with me to the banks of the river Yamuna. The water is cold, the lotuses are blooming and the river flows lazily. Once we are there, just look around you. You will see beautiful gopikas sauntering along. What is the colour of their clothes?'

'Red and green!' a young girl said out loud.

'Yellow and orange,' said another.

'Now look at that big beautiful green tree near the river,' said Gopinath. 'The gopikas have changed into their bathing robes and left their dry clothes on the branches of the same tree. It is time for their bath and they get into the water and begin splashing each other. Now let's search for Krishna. Where do you think he is?'

'He's behind the kadamba tree,' someone shouted from the audience.

'He's next to Yashoda!' said another voice.

Gopinath continued, 'Let's approach Krishna. There he is—sitting on the high branch of a tree nearby and wasting his time.'

'Oh, he is such a prankster,' said a young girl from the troupe—one of the gopikas. 'But I like him. He brings a smile to my lips. My mother, however, gets upset because he takes away all the butter from our home.'

Then the troupe took over and the Harikatha continued.

A woman added, 'My mother-in-law has instructed me not to speak to Krishna because he drank all the milk in our house after entering through the back door.'

A voice complained, 'Whenever I take my pot to fetch water, he throws stones at it and breaks it. My husband is quite upset.'

'We must teach him a lesson,' insisted another from the troupe.

'Krishna overheard all of this,' interjected Gopinath, 'and stealthily hid their clothes. Once the gopikas had finished their bath in the river, they walked over to the tree but alas! Their clothes were nowhere to be found! How would they go back home in minimal and wet clothing? Who had stolen their clothes? Just then, they heard melodious tunes that seemed to originate from above them. When they looked up, they saw Krishna holding their clothes in one hand and playing the flute with the other, with his eyes closed. Of course! He must have heard them complaining and decided to take revenge. He wasn't going to return the clothes easily. So they began to plead with him. What did the women say?'

A girl from the audience yelled, 'O Krishna, please give back my sari.'

'And mine too!' shouted another. 'It's my favourite!'

The women began giving descriptions, with their eyes still shut.

'And that black sari with the red border is mine!'

'Oh, please, give me that green and mango-coloured sari!'

Gopinath was happy. 'Ah yes, all of you have seen Krishna now,' he said.

The conversations between Krishna and the gopikas and the audience continued until they raised their hands and surrendered, 'O Krishna! You are a kind-hearted boy and you understand our hearts. Please give us the saris. Otherwise we are left with no choice but to walk home in our wet robes. We are completely dependent on you.'

'Krishna smiled and started throwing down the clothes,' said Gopinath. 'The gopikas wore their saris and after they were well-clothed, Krishna descended from the top and the dancing began.'

The sounds of music and dance filled the air and the night ended on a joyful note. The Harikatha dasa told us to open our eyes. That's when we found out that two and a half hours had passed.

As a young girl, I had a vivid imagination. It was easy to visualize the flow of the river Yamuna, the pink lotuses, the bright and colourful gopikas, Lord Krishna and his naughty but compassionate face, and the music floating from his flute. I was enchanted!

Years later, I went to Vrindavan. To my utter disappointment, the Yamuna was dirty and more of a rivulet than a full-bodied river. The place was now commercialized.

Almost all the priests I observed were directing the devotees to a tree with pieces of cloth tied to it. 'Lord Krishna sat on this tree and threw the clothes down to the gopikas,' they said.

Devotees bowed to the tree and tied a small piece of cloth to it.

The image was not what I had associated with the story. So I closed my eyes and turned away. 'I don't want to see this and ruin my childhood images,' I thought.

I also realized in my adulthood that a story such as this might be considered harassment in the modern world. But the truth is that such a concept did not exist in the olden days. God is considered to be an omnipotent friend—someone who is approachable and whom we can speak to at any time and anyhow we choose. These tales are meant to bring out the human side of the Lord, while retaining the devotion towards him. So he is depicted as a naughty young lad, no more than eight years old, who enjoys spending time with his devotees and teasing them with love and innocence. This is why the women also play along until they completely surrender to the Lord—a gesture of faith after which he gives them whatever they need.

Decades later, I became a grandmother to two little girls—Krishna and Anoushka. When they grew from toddlers to young children, I decided to share some of my childhood stories with them. I thought that they would visualize the scenes just like I had.

One day, when I was playing with them in their residence in London, they asked me for a story. I told them the same tale of Lord Krishna and the gopikas. Since I had their attention, I added the story of *Akshaya Patra* too.

'Draupadi was very hospitable and entertained many guests when she was living in Indraprastha. Unfortunately, due to a turn of events, she had to accompany her husbands on a long exile and felt sad that she could no longer take care of the guests like she used to.

'Her husband, Yudhishthira, prayed to the sun god, Surya, and explained their difficulty in taking care of the guests. So Surya blessed them and handed them a vessel. "This is a special vessel known as Akshaya Patra," he said.

"You can use this to feed as many people as you want. But on one condition . . ."

'"What's that?" asked Yudhishthira.

'"You can't cook any food after the lady of the house has eaten. The vessel can be used again only after the next sunrise."

'Yudhishthira nodded.

'Happily, Draupadi began feeding her visitors with different varieties of food.

'Soon, the news of her pleasing hospitality reached Duryodhana's ears, who felt jealous despite the fact that his cousins were in exile and led a much humbler life than they were used to. A few days later, the short-tempered sage Durvasa arrived at Duryodhana's palace and was treated as an esteemed guest and given all that could be offered.

'Pleased, he blessed Duryodhana. "I am happy with your hospitality towards me and my disciples. Ask me whatever you want and I will fulfil your wish."

'Duryodhana and his evil uncle, Shakuni, had already pre-decided what they would ask for, should Durvasa give them such an opportunity.

'He smiled. "My cousins, the Pandavas, are devout and pious," said Duryodhana, pretending to care for them. "I will be grateful if you could bless them too. If you leave now, you will reach there late in the evening. That is all I want."

'Durvasa agreed and set out with his group.

'On the surface, the request was a simple one and seemed to show the largeness of Duryodhana's heart, but the truth was far from it. Shakuni and Duryodhana knew that by the time Durvasa and his disciples reached the Pandavas' home, Draupadi would have finished her meal and the Pandavas wouldn't be able to feed all of them. This would immediately fuel the sage's wrath, who was then highly likely to curse them.

'After a journey that took many hours, Durvasa reached the Pandavas' abode and said to them, "Your cousin Duryodhana is an excellent host. He has requested me to experience your hospitality too and bless you. My disciples and I will first go for a bath in the river nearby. Please have our food ready for us by the time we return."

'The moment Durvasa left, Yudhishthira rushed into the kitchen and to his dismay, saw Draupadi washing and cleaning the Akshaya Patra. "Draupadi! Durvasa will soon come here with his students for a meal and you have already eaten yours! I don't want to get on his bad side. What should we do?"

'Sunset was fast approaching and Draupadi was at a loss. Unable to think of a solution, her thoughts turned to Krishna, who was as good as a brother to her. Just then, she heard the sound of horses and a chariot pulling up outside the home. She walked towards the entrance but within seconds, Krishna walked in through the open door.

'When he saw Draupadi and the rest of the Pandavas with long faces, he asked, "Why are you all so sad?"

'Yudhishthira explained the situation to him. "Bring the vessel to me," said Krishna.

'With reluctance, Draupadi fetched the Akshaya Patra, "There's nothing there, brother. See for yourself."

'"Sister, you may be a queen but you are definitely not a good cleaner. Look at this—you have left a grain of rice."

'Krishna picked up the grain, ate it and burped rather loudly. "I am happy and my stomach is full. May God bless you," he said and immediately left before the Pandavas could stop him.

'Meanwhile, Durvasa and his students were finishing their bath in the river when they suddenly felt as if they had just had a full meal. Their stomachs felt extremely full and satisfied.

'They looked at each other. "Sir," a student gathered his courage and spoke to Durvasa. "We are feeling full and can't eat any more. Let's skip the visit to the Pandavas' home because we won't be able to eat anything and that might offend them."

'Durvasa smiled and said, "Yes, my children, I understand how you feel. While there is no end to greed in life, hunger is one thing that has its limitation. Once you are full, no matter what you say or do, you just can't force yourself to eat. I will bless the Pandavas from here and we can leave."'

Once the story had ended, both Krishna and Anoushka looked at my face.

'Now that I have told you two stories today, you must think about them and repeat them to me tomorrow!' I said.

The two girls waltzed their way to their room, discussing the last story with each other.

I was happy that I had taught them two important mythological stories in a very simple manner.

The next morning after breakfast, Krishna came and sat next to me. 'Ajji,' she said. 'I have changed a little bit of your story.'

'Tell me then.'

Anoushka also joined us and Krishna began, 'Krishna was a cute little boy who was very naughty. He would frequently visit his friends' homes, open the fridge without permission and eat whatever he wanted to. This upset the mothers and yet everybody was fond of him.'

'He took pizzas, pastas, sandwiches, cheese, butter, yogurt, fruits and everything that caught his fancy,' added Anoushka and giggled.

'Be quiet! I am the one telling the story,' said Krishna. 'It was the Christmas season and all schools were closed. One day, the girls and their mothers decided to meet at the indoor swimming pool. Once they were there, they changed into their swimwear, kept the clothes in the lockers, left the keys on one of the benches in the changing room, showered and jumped into the pool.

'Soon they were in the heated pool splashing around, despite the freezing temperatures outside.

'What they didn't know was that Krishna was also there. He saw the girls from the first floor and opened the window overlooking the pool.

'The girls were talking about him. "Oh, Krishna is so adorable but he troubles me," said one of them. "The other day he ate my cookies but I didn't complain to anyone."

'"Oh, he steals my pencils so often!"

'"Your pencils? He takes my toys!" another girl whined.

'"We must inform the headmistress."

'Krishna heard the comments, went to the changing room, found the locker keys and slipped away.

'After the swim, the girls and the mothers showered and went to gather their clothes from the lockers. But the keys were missing!

'"Who has taken our keys?" they asked the staff.

'"Ma'am, only girls are allowed here at this time of the day. Nobody else can enter."

'"But we are miserable, cold and wet," said one of the mothers. "How will we go home?"

'"My new shoes are also in the locker!" a girl yelled.

'"I have a birthday party to attend after this and my dress is inside the locker! What should I do now?"

'The attendant didn't know what to do. "Give me a few minutes. Let me speak to the manager," she said.

'Suddenly, the tunes from a harmonica floated towards them. They looked towards the source of the beautiful music and saw Krishna on the first floor patio almost right above them. There was a bunch of keys dangling from one of his fingers.

'Once he realized that they had seen him, he stopped playing the harmonica. "Girls, if you complain about me to the headmistress, none of you will get your clothes back."

'"We will sue you!" said a girl.

'"You can sue me all you want, but you can't go anywhere without your clothes. After all, it is snowing outside!"

'"O Krishna, we are very sorry," said the girls in unison.

'"If we wanted to complain, we would have already done so. You are dear to us and we love your pranks! You know that it's the truth. So stop this. We will catch a cold standing here like this. You don't want us to fall sick, do you?" said one of the more logical girls.

'Krishna smiled and threw the keys to the girls. Then they all got dressed and went with Krishna to the nearest café for a hot chocolate.' My granddaughter ended her story.

Anoushka clapped loudly and laughed. She had enjoyed the story!

I nodded to show my appreciation. The truth was that I was completely unprepared for this new variation of the story that seemed to be set in London. The old story made me visualize the river Yamuna, its cold water, the floating lotuses and a flute-playing Krishna but this urban version of the Lord was too hard for me to relate to!

Hesitantly, I turned to Anoushka. What version of the second story would I hear next?

Right on cue, Anoushka started, 'Draupadi was a beautiful and powerful queen. One day, she left the city and decided to stay in a village far away. She drank clear water from the stream, picked organic food directly from the trees and plants and cooked for all the guests who came home. However, the food was insufficient sometimes. She explained this problem to her husband, Yudhishthira, who, in turn, shared the issue with a friend, Surya.

'Surya was very resourceful. He gifted Yudhishthira and Draupadi a special cooker and some additives. He said, "Whenever you make rice in this, add these healthy additives. Two spoons of this cooked rice will be enough for one person. You won't have to cook large quantities or spend hours in search of food. But Draupadi, once you eat, clean the vessel and don't cook in it again that day. This will keep the bacteria away and ensure that the food remains hygienic. So be careful about the way you use it."

'Draupadi nodded. From that day on, she made the special organic rice for her guests.

'One day, her uncle came without informing her, with many people in tow. He said, "Draupadi, I have heard that you make tasty rice. I want to try that today. My group and I will go for a swim first and then come back for the delicious meal."

'Draupadi was upset. First, her uncle hadn't informed her in advance and second, he simply showed up on their doorstep with so many others to feed! Besides, she had already eaten and cleaned the vessel. She was about to give her uncle a piece of her mind but Yudhishthira stopped her. "Uncle has helped us many times, dear wife. Please don't say anything to him. You know how short-tempered he is! Let's not do anything that we will regret later."

'Draupadi was worried. How would she feed so many people now? She immediately called her brother Krishna who was kind, helpful and a strategic thinker. He came to her assistance and asked her to show him the vessel. He took the last grain of rice stuck at the corner of the vessel and ate it.

'"Hmm, the rice is indeed very tasty but I am sure that your uncle and the other guests will not come back for it."

'"Why?" asked Draupadi.

'"They know why," he said with a mysterious smile and left for an appointment.

'Meanwhile, at the swimming pool, each member of the group swallowed a little bit of the chlorine water. Since the chlorine level was high that day, all of them soon began feeling uncomfortable and kept running to the bathroom. Finally, Uncle said to the group, "I think we have all fallen sick and are low on energy at the moment. Let us not go to Draupadi's home for the big meal. It is best to give our stomachs a little break."

'The group murmured in agreement.

'So Uncle called Draupadi on her cell phone and said, "My dear child, please excuse us. We will not be able to eat at your home today. I promise we will come another time."

'Draupadi smiled. As always, her brother had come to her rescue! "You are always welcome here, Uncle, but please let me know in advance next time," she said and hung up.'

I was stumped. The stories had been transformed, and how! After that reinvention, I didn't have the guts to share the story of Draupadi's disrobing in the royal court!

10

A Day in Infosys Foundation

Shoba is one of my school friends. In a small town like Hubli, it is common for close friends to become as comfortable with each other as siblings. As life usually turns out, we walked down different paths and Shoba settled down in Hubli, while I moved to Bengaluru. Her children, like many others in Karnataka, became software engineers and moved to Bengaluru. So Shoba frequented the city to visit her children and often called on me whenever possible.

One day, she phoned my office. Since I was in a meeting, I passed on a message to her that I would call her back later. When I reached out to her in the evening, she asked, 'Why did you take so long to return my call?'

'Shoba, I got time to return my personal calls just a short while ago.'

'I know that you are very busy,' she said, sounding a little concerned. 'But it's so difficult to reach you when I want to—sometimes you are at work or travelling or out for an appointment even during the hours when I think you might be at home. I only wanted to invite you for my grandson's first birthday. It is on Monday and you must come at whatever time is convenient for you.'

'Oh Shoba! It is almost impossible for me to visit you on a working day, especially Monday.'

'Can't you spare one hour for a close friend?' asked Shoba, the way only old friends can do. 'I know that you are the chairperson of a foundation and you must be having visitors all the time asking you for grants, but you can always reschedule or refuse to meet them. They will come again, I'm sure!'

'It isn't that simple,' I replied. 'With the two hours that takes from Jayanagar to your home and back, half my day will be gone. A day at the foundation is filled with many activities, some of which aren't easy to explain. For someone who doesn't work there, it may appear to be the apparent simple task of giving money or grants. If you really want to know what I do, then come and shadow me for a day. Maybe then you will get a glimpse into the complicated nature of social work.'

Enthusiastically, Shoba agreed and a few weeks later, on a Monday, she joined me for a day at the office.

I was happy that she had come. I told her, 'You will only observe and not comment or participate as I go about my day! Is that okay?'

She smiled and nodded.

Meanwhile, I gave my assistant, Asha, a list of people with whom I needed to speak to that morning. Soon, the phone rang. Asha sprang into action and answered the call.

A voice spoke, 'We are from Hubli and know Mrs Sudha Murty very well. I'd like to speak with her.'

'What is your name, madam?'

'Usha. Usha Patil.'

Asha turned to me, 'Usha Patil is on the line. May I connect her to you?'

Usha is a common name in Hubli and so is the last name Patil. I knew at least ten Usha Patils from Hubli—a neighbour, a classmate, a cousin, a cousin's wife, a writer, an acquaintance, a temple priest's daughter and a few more and I wondered who this person was.

Asha seemed to be at a loss, just like me.

I took the phone from Asha. 'Sudha Murty here,' I said.

'I am Usha Patil from Kundgol, a village near Hubli. My son needs a job . . .'

'Do I know you?'

'No, but you are from Hubli. That's why I am sure that you will help someone from there.'

'Usha ji, why did you say that you know me?'

'I do know you through newspapers and television,' she justified. 'But I didn't say that you knew me. Keeping that aside, my son is keen on getting employed soon.'

I was firm. 'I am not responsible for recruiting people at Infosys. Please email the human resources department for this as they have their own procedure.'

'But if you put in a word, they won't refuse your request,' she persisted.

'I'm sorry, Usha ji, but this is a matter of hiring professionals and employees are hired only after interviews and tests. I run the foundation and don't interfere with the process of another department.'

Usha wasn't convinced. She sounded reluctant. 'Then will you give me the details of an appropriate contact?'

'You can send the resume via email,' I replied.

'Please hold on for a moment while I find a pen and take down the email address.'

I didn't have time to wait and gave the phone back to Asha, 'Give her the recruitment email address and from now on, when someone says that they know me well, please also ask if I know them.'

I went and sat down to check my emails.

Leena, my secretary, said, 'Madam, there are 410 emails for you today.'

The number was not unusual. 'Let's separate it based on its category and then start from the bottom.'

Once that was done, we began. The first was an email describing me as if I were some kind of a goddess. 'Leena, just read the last line,' I said.

'The request is for a grant to build a temple,' Leena explained.

The foundation does not help with any religious constructions or restorations unless it is of archaeological importance, as declared by the state or central government. 'Please send our regrets,' I said.

By the time Leena and I moved to the next email, most of the cell phones began chiming in the office indicating that we had received several messages. They were all in response to one that said, 'Infosys Foundation is giving scholarships to all those who apply. Contact the foundation immediately.'

The phones also began ringing.

The news was absolutely untrue. Several years ago, the foundation had offered limited scholarships, but the programme had been terminated based on the exit policy at the end of the specified term. Despite this, we were aware that some people were floating this information on the instant messaging application WhatsApp. As a result, students and parents often inundated us with emails, letters and phone calls.

I asked Asha to reply to each query in the same mode that it was received. I knew it would keep Asha busy for a few hours.

Once that was done, Leena and I opened the second email. A university wanted to confer an honorary doctorate on me.

Leena was thrilled but I wasn't. Soon enough, we read the relevant line, 'Once you receive the doctorate, you will become an alumnus, and we are sure that you will help the university in any way that you can.'

I scratch your back and you scratch mine. 'Please decline the doctorate politely,' I told Leena.

The next request was an invitation to be the chief guest for a college's annual day in Mumbai. While I usually can't go to most of the events that come my way, I make an effort to attend at least a few. Leena told me that the event was only for two hours but the travel time to Mumbai and back would take one and a half days. I considered declining it, but then thought of the students, who I always hold dear.

'If I am going to Mumbai that day for work, I will attend it,' I said.

She checked my diary. 'You are going to be in Mumbai for meetings in the afternoon on that date and there are a few available hours in the morning. Luckily, the venue is close to the airport and you can go there after you land. We can reschedule the flight and you can leave early in the morning from Bengaluru.'

'Tell the college management that I will be there slightly early at 9.30 a.m. and must depart by 11 a.m.'

The shrill ringing of the phone on my desk interrupted our conversation and Asha immediately took the call, 'Hello?'

A few seconds later, she handed me the phone, 'Kasab is on the line.'

I was frightened. At the time, Kasab was a Pakistani militant convicted for the Taj hotel bombing on 26/11 in Mumbai. As far as I knew, he had been executed. But sometimes nothing is as it seems. 'Was he really calling me? And why?'

I told Asha to give me a minute to gather my thoughts and to inform Kasab that I would speak with him.

She spoke to him briefly and turned to me. 'Kasab is very angry. He's saying that he's a patriotic citizen and is asking me why I am addressing him in this manner.'

I was confused. 'What did you say to him, Asha?'

'I called the number from the list you gave me earlier in the morning and told him to hold while I transferred the call to your phone.'

'I never gave you Kasab's number nor did I ask you to call someone by that name. Kasab is dead and gone. Do you even know who he was?'

'I don't know,' she replied casually, least bothered about the affairs of the state.

'Give me the phone.'

I could hear a man fuming on the other end.

'Hello?' I said.

'My grandfather was a freedom fighter and I have served the country as an ex-MLA. I am proud of my heritage. How dare you call me Kasab?'

I sighed. Asha had called Kasabe and mispronounced his name to sound like that of the notorious terrorist. It was an absolute dishonour and an insult to a true patriot.

'I am extremely sorry for the confusion, sir.' I apologized. 'This is Sudha Murty. I told my staff to call you so that I could inform you that I won't be able to come for the wedding as I have to travel on the same day. But I will visit your home on my way to the airport.'

Hearing my voice, Kasabe calmed down. After I disconnected the call, I turned to my assistant, 'Why did you call him Kasab?'

'Madam, there were three phones ringing at the same time. I thought I called him Kasabe, maybe he misheard it. Why will I call him a different name on purpose?'

Meanwhile, the office manager, Krishnamurthy, approached me and said, 'Madam, the payment vouchers are ready.'

Our office is cashless and so are its transactions. This policy turned out to be a boon during the demonetization of currency in 2016 as we were relatively unaffected.

Prashant, the CSR manager, interrupted us, 'Did you promise a matching grant to our employees' non-profit arm during your recent visit to Chandigarh?'

'Yes, I did,' I replied. 'It is a good way to involve them in some of our CSR efforts and will inspire them to pool in money for some of the activities. I have encouraged this in other development centres too, such as Hyderabad, Pune, Mangalore, Thiruvananthapuram, Chennai and Bhubaneswar.'

Prashant's forehead creased with obvious worry. 'We are overshooting the allocated funds for this year. It doesn't match with our plan for the year. Please review our latest budget.'

I understood his concern. Prashant monitored the finances and kept a close eye on the budget.

'We will manage it. It is better to have deserving projects in the pipeline than to worry about the budget. We can request for more money if needed. There are projects that may get delayed or aren't ready yet, so there is no need to worry.'

Since I was once a professor, I often talk like a teacher to everyone in my office. Most of the time, Prashant and Shrutee, the program director, end up being the target of my wisdom-sharing talks because they are responsible for the annual balance sheets and reaching our CSR goals.

Despite my regular interventions, they were often apprehensive when our commitments exceeded the finances in hand.

The next phone call was from the management of the Bannerghatta National Park for a grant update.

During the past summer, we had learnt that the animals there suffered from an acute shortage of drinking water. The authorities had constructed a tub for the tigers to sit in but the water had to be changed every few days to avoid infection and disease. Tigers were difficult to treat when they were unwell and hence, the caretakers were always wary about the water. So I called one of our contractors and instructed him to dig borewells in accessible areas and also construct an overhead water tank. Many tried to dissuade us due to the lack of water in the area but we went ahead anyway. We had to try for the sake of the animals.

The call was to inform us that there was plenty of water in the borewells. The animals would finally get enough good quality water and remain free from diseases as much as possible. I thanked God for this great gesture.

I glanced at Leena. She was still busy sorting the emails into various categories such as travel, pending, appointments, regrets and new initiatives.

Everyone was immersed in their work. At times, I feel like I do not have much to do as most of it is appropriately handled. Only a few new proposals, exceptions or escalations usually come my way.

It was time for Shrutee's appointment with a visitor. She went upstairs to the conference room for the meeting while I began scanning the snail mail kept for me even as the phones kept ringing.

After a few minutes, one of our contractors called for an urgent update. 'Madam,' he said, 'some workers went on holiday a week ago and haven't returned yet. If we have to work with the existing workers alone, the project will be delayed by one month.'

'You can't do this!' I protested. 'I have already invited the chief minister for the inauguration and everything has been planned. You must finish it somehow.'

'Madam, please, then tell me what to do.'

I didn't know what he could do, but kept insisting that he should complete the work faster. After a long discussion, he agreed to hasten his work and delay by only fifteen days. It would be right on time for the inauguration. Experience has taught me that delays happen in most construction works, no matter how good a person is in project management, and hence I allowed some leeway.

Just then, Shrutee requested me to join her for the meeting. 'I have communicated our decision regarding the proposal,' she said. 'But the team wants to meet you. There are three of them. I think it's better to meet them or else they will definitely visit again.'

At Infosys Foundation, we have our own strategies and policies. For instance, we don't approve grants for political parties and no consideration is given to caste, creed or religion during proposal reviews. There is an exit policy, an internal and external audit and a third-party assessment for every project, and we are inclined towards releasing money in instalments.

The project wasn't a good fit for us and hence Shrutee had chosen to decline it.

Here at the foundation, we believe that if we are refusing a proposal, then we must communicate it as soon as possible. *Adinishtura* is better than *antyanishtura*, which means that an initial disappointment is better than a disagreement at the end.

'Okay, I will come,' I said and accompanied her upstairs.

Most people insist on meeting me. A few think that if they put pressure on me directly, I might give in, but they don't know the truth—Shrutee and I are always on the same page.

But I decided to meet the visitors to help Shrutee. Just as I expected, they elaborated on the merits of their proposal for the next thirty minutes. In the end, I said, 'Providing grants is not akin to approving whatever we feel like. Please understand that there are certain systems and processes in place here. Shrutee has communicated the right decision and unfortunately, we will not be able to be a part of this.'

They were upset, but nothing further could be done at this point.

There are times when the company directors forward us letters and requests that come to them. We evaluate them objectively and reject or approve them. I thank the management for never pressuring us or influencing the process.

It was time for lunch. Since my house was nearby, I said to Shoba, 'Let's go eat and come back soon.'

At home, a security guard informed me that my daughter, Akshata, had called.

When I called her back, she threw a flurry of questions at me. 'Where were you yesterday? Are you unwell? Or has something happened there that you aren't telling me? I have been so worried.'

I was surprised by her tone. 'I am right here in Bengaluru. I was attending meetings all day. Why are you worried?'

'When I spoke to the security staff yesterday in the morning, they said that you were in the toilet. When I phoned in the afternoon, they again said that you were in the toilet. It was the same story in the evening and later at night, they said that you were sleeping. This morning, they said that you had left for office. I sent you an email but didn't hear back. Why were you in the restroom all day?'

She sounded anxious.

Calmly, I said, 'Breathe, Akshata! Do some pranayama every day. I had gone for a site visit to check the status of our recently inaugurated toilets. This was followed by other meetings and a panel discussion on how to construct them. I told the security staff that I was going for the toilet project work and maybe he misunderstood it and only remembered the word toilet. Don't be so afraid! As for your email, I haven't seen it yet as it has been a busy day!'

I could hear an immediate sigh of relief.

After hanging up, I went to the main gate and asked the security guard there, 'Didn't I inform all of you that I would be back late because of the toilet project?'

'I wasn't on duty, madam. Yesterday's guard has an ear infection and has taken the day off.'

Well, that explained the guard's inability to hear the day before. But I sure spent a lot of time in the toilet! I smiled to myself and went back inside.

During lunch, my cook and I began making the grocery list. He wanted to know the number of people coming home for dinner and the menu for the night. My mind, however, was still in office matters and it was difficult to make the sudden switch to the domestic conversation. I said, 'Let's talk about it later in the evening. Till then, just make what you can with whatever is available.'

After a quick lunch, Shoba and I returned to the office.

My next appointment was one that had been put off a long time ago. At first, all the three men who came spoke together and I couldn't understand anything. So I asked them to speak one at a time.

'I have received many awards in this area of work,' said the first.

The second one added, 'And I have the political connections to make things happen.'

'Let me first tell you why we have come here and how we will help the urban poor through the drinking water project,' said the third.

'Please allow me to ask you a few questions,' I said gently. 'Have you gone to the proposed area where you intend to work? And if so, what is the distribution of the population and the ratio of the number of males to the number of females?'

The three fell silent.

I changed the line of questioning. 'Where will you get the supply of drinking water from?'

No response.

'Is there an existing system in place that doesn't work? And if so, why not?' I tried again.

With no answers in sight, I gave up. 'Please prepare a well-researched proposal and execution plan with all these answers. After that, we will discuss it at the next internal review. If you give me the details of the location, I will make a personal visit there,' I said. 'It really doesn't matter who is ruling the area politically or who will bestow awards upon us. We specifically target the underprivileged and hope to help them through our efforts and see them smile.'

The three men seemed disappointed, most likely because I hadn't committed any funds for their project.

While I was saying goodbye, there was a knock on the door and Leena came in. 'Madam, you have to reconsider your travel plans. In your absence last week, I received many phone calls from all over the country for project visits in different locations. We have to allocate the site visits between Prashant, Shrutee and you. I need some of your time to block the dates today.'

I glanced at the calendar in the room. 'Fix my tours for the weekends so I can continue with my routine work on weekdays. If I have to visit Delhi, then plan all my project visits around the region, including places like Jammu and Lucknow, at the same time. I want to avoid unnecessary trips as much as possible.'

Leena nodded and went back with a determined glint in her eye. She would figure out the jigsaw puzzle of my travel plans herself.

I made my way to my room. All the emails had been sorted and directed to the appropriate people. I went through the ones left for me and began responding to them.

Next, I switched over to the physical mails. One of my goals is to have a paperless office, but I don't see it happening any time soon. We still receive hard copies of brochures, request letters and invitations.

Since I am an author, I receive many complimentary books too. It is a running joke that the number of authors exceeds the number of readers these days. Some of the writers request for a foreword, others want me to promote their books by stocking them in libraries and schools, and a few want to know my opinion on their books. Some authors send us their original manuscripts and ask us to send it back, which causes unnecessary hassles. The books for libraries are handed over to a selection committee, while the foreword and opinion requests are declined most of the time due to my tight schedule. By evening, our trash bins are usually full.

Then there are letters from my readers to the foundation office. These are a mixed bag—some share their experiences, some criticize certain aspects of my writing while others appreciate it. I take these home to answer during my personal hours.

My task was interrupted by a call from a news channel. The journalist asked me, 'What is your opinion on the current government? What are your thoughts about the demonetization of currency and its execution?'

I declined to comment. I may be good at what I do but I had no expertise in such matters.

I began sifting through the letters, some of which I routed to Leena for a suitable reply. There was a bunch of letters from the families of army martyrs thanking the foundation for our small contribution. Two others caught my attention—one was from the central government and another from the state government. Both were reaching out to the foundation to seek help for some projects. These were added to the agenda for the next week's internal review.

Leena came in to give me an update. 'Madam, I have worked out your travel plans. You will be travelling fifteen days a month for the next three months. Besides losing most of the weekends, you will also miss your distant niece's wedding and your father's death anniversary. Is that okay?'

'That's fine, Leena. Thank you. My father has taught me that work is worship and I know that he would understand if he was here.'

Leena handed over my travel details to Krishnamurthy, who immediately started arranging my tickets and accommodation at the company guesthouses wherever possible. Staying at the guesthouses allows easier coordination of my plans and also allows us to save money that we would otherwise have to spend on hotels.

Minutes later, Shrutee came by. 'I have some good news,' she said. 'The boys whom we supported in the Mathematics Olympiad have got admission in MIT and Caltech. In their media interview, they thanked the foundation profusely and said that our small gift of ten thousand rupees towards their effort pushed them to choose science. There is also an email from Pavagada. The selfless swamiji who works for blind children has written that the midday meal programme has been successful in making the children stay in school. The donation for their music classes has also made them happy. They even received an award recently. He has sent pictures of their bright little faces smiling with pride.'

Once she left, I sat in silence for a few minutes.

The loud ringing of the phone jolted me out of my thoughts. Out of instinct, I picked up the phone but Leena was already on the other extension with the caller. The person was screaming at Leena, 'I deserve more money from the foundation than what they have given me. You are only a secretary. Connect me to your boss and tell them who I am. If you don't, I will go to the media and tell them about the foundation. So be careful before you respond.'

I immediately went to Leena in the next room and took the phone from her.

'Sir, what is the problem?' I asked.

'I requested for two crores for a school but you have given us two lakhs—it is a pittance for the foundation. I want . . . no, I demand an explanation. I am an influential activist and can tarnish the name of the foundation if I want to.'

'Sure. I will give you an explanation. We get more than a hundred genuine applications and around two hundred calls every day. We don't work under any sort of pressure nor do we care to gain any advantage from our grants. There is an established process in place and we have to distribute the grants to the best of our judgement. We do not increase our grants without a review of the progress made. Experience has taught us that the work speaks for itself. Besides, there are trustees who are also involved with the decision-making. We may not be there in the foundation at a future date, but the established processes will continue. I must also tell you that we aren't afraid of the media because we haven't done anything wrong or under wraps.'

The man calmed down and cleared his throat. 'Well, if we do well and clear the review, then will you help us next year?'

'Maybe. We help many organizations and are not afraid of approaching the good ones ourselves. It is the quality of work that attracts us and we do not worry about potential threats or the connections of our beneficiaries.'

I could hear a murmur that vaguely seemed to sound like an apology.

I had had a hard day and was in no mood to let him off the hook. 'Sir, we also have difficult days at the foundation but we try to ensure that it does not affect our relationships with others,' I gave advice that nobody asked me for.

A glance at the clock confirmed that it was almost 5.30 p.m. I was planning to stay back a little longer but Shoba stood up from the chair nearby.

'I think I will leave,' she said.

I walked with her till the main gate to see her off. On the way, she passed the reception, where we had displayed some of our awards.

'Are you proud of all these?' she asked and pointed at the awards.

'In my younger days, I was. As the years passed and my experience grew, I realized that my joy was coming from the work and not from these occasional awards. Today, they don't matter much to me personally but they are important to my organization.'

'Tell me, why do you continue to give your remaining years to this thankless job?' she asked. 'You can sit back, relax, spend time with your grandchildren, go to weddings and birthdays and reduce a little bit of stress from your life.'

'The truth is that I am the luckiest of them all. I love what I do and every day is a holiday for me because of it. Who doesn't love a vacation?' I grinned.

Shoba smiled as she got into the car and nodded. I waved goodbye and went back to work.

11

I Can't, We Can

Recently, I attended a nephew's wedding. It was a wonderful occasion to meet my cousins whom I had spent my childhood with but hadn't met in a long time. The wedding ceremony began and a few cousins and I sat leisurely in a corner.

One of my cousins said, 'I am the president of the laughing club in our community. Come for one of our sessions. We hardly meet any more. This way I will at least get to see you for some time!'

It is common now to see older men and women gather in parks in the morning and attempt to laugh—ha ha ha. I have often wondered how people can make themselves laugh in this manner! I visualized myself attending such an assembly. What would I talk to them about? I was absolutely clueless and so I politely declined.

Another cousin said, 'I am the secretary of the housewives' association in my apartment community. I have already shared with the members that you are my cousin. You must come and address them.'

'But what is the subject matter that you are interested in?'

'You are a wise investor. So give the women tips on how to save and identify high-return investments like you have.'

'I'm not sure I understand. Can you elaborate a little on that?'

'Well, everybody knows how you invested ten thousand rupees in Infosys and made millions in return.'

'I didn't do that for the sake of investment,' I said in a serious tone. 'I gave the seed money to fulfil my husband's dream—a dream that was considered impractical in those days. He is successful now and that's why you are referring to me as a wise millionaire. Had he not been so, you would have called the same move a foolish one. You have it all wrong—I am not the right person to talk about investment. Instead, you can ask me for advice on how to spend money. That will be more suited to my skills!'

People around me laughed.

'I have a special request,' a third cousin said. She began, 'My friend's daughter is a bright student and . . .'

'Is she planning to apply for a job at Infosys?' I interrupted her. 'Because I really can't . . .'

'Have some patience,' she stopped me. 'Let me finish. I thought you would have garnered a lot more patience by now, considering your line of work. The girl wants your guidance. She already has a job offer as well as an admission letter from an American university, and needs to pick one.'

'There's not much guidance I can give. The decision depends on the family's financial position, the girl's ambition and her career plans, along with other social aspects of the family.'

'Come on! Meet her. She really needs your help.'

I was reluctant. But I said, 'Okay, ask her to meet me tomorrow at 9 a.m. She can come to my office.'

The next morning, I met the young petite girl named Jaya. She was shy and quite nervous.

I wanted to make her comfortable, so I told her to sit down and offered her a cup of tea. Then I asked for her mark sheet. Her academic record was outstanding. 'Jaya, what's on your mind?' I did not beat around the bush. 'Where do you see yourself in ten years?'

She was quiet.

I rephrased my question, 'Perhaps you want to be a corporate professional or pursue the academic line? Or maybe something else?'

Still, there was no reply.

'Are you scared of me? Do I look like a monster?' I persisted and smiled.

She smiled back and shook her head. Then she began speaking very softly about her future plans.

I could see that she didn't have any confidence, despite her achievements.

'Jaya, academic excellence is not everything,' I said. 'You must have confidence in yourself. One of the flaws of our education system is that it doesn't really teach us that quality. Our parents, society and the recruitment process concentrate too much on the marks we get. I can give you many examples of people who may not have studied much but have done well for themselves because they believed they could. Confidence doesn't mean that everything will go our way. It simply gives us the ability to accept failures that we will inevitably meet on our path and move forward with hope.'

Without any warning, Jaya started sobbing. Like a toddler. It was heartbreaking.

At first, I was startled. 'Maybe I have given her too strong a dose without knowing her nature,' I thought. In India, most of us excel at giving advice without people asking for it, and I am no exception.

I offered her a tissue and said, 'I am sorry if I have hurt you, Jaya. But I don't know what to tell you. You aren't sharing much with me.'

The girl calmed down and wiped her tears. Her voice was shaking when she spoke, 'No, ma'am, your advice didn't make me cry. The truth is that I feel inferior in front of most people.'

'Why? Anyone in your shoes would be proud of accomplishing so much at your age.'

She paused. Then she said, 'Ma'am, my father was an alcoholic.'

I paused.

She spoke a little more fluently, 'He is now in AA but my younger years were different. He would often get drunk and abuse my mother. She went through so much, and I had no idea what I could do to help her. I grew up scared of my father's temper and in an unhappy and tense atmosphere. Then I thought that the only way I could make a change was to study hard and get a decent job so that I could take my mother and leave. I have a sister too, but my mother doesn't want to leave the family home. She is worried about . . .'

'I think I can understand your mother's concerns. Many in our society still judge women who are separated from their husbands and she's probably concerned about how that might impact her daughters' marriage prospects.'

'You are right, ma'am. She says that I should go abroad and never come back to India. She wants me to get married to a good man irrespective of his caste and creed. Her only condition is that he mustn't drink. But I don't want to run away and leave my mother and sister behind. I want to be here for them. I'm so confused, ma'am. That's the reason why I wanted your advice.'

The word AA was on my mind. 'What is AA?' I asked.

'Alcoholics Anonymous. It is a support group for men and women who are addicted to alcohol. It has taken my father several years to become sober, but the darkness he caused has left a permanent scar on my heart and life. I don't like to share anything personal with him nor do I ask him for advice. I have no respect for him at all.'

'Jaya, I don't know much about AA, but we don't know the circumstances under which he turned to the bottle. He has changed now and it sounds like he is trying hard to be a better man. The best way forward is not to get upset or run away from your problems, but to open a channel of conversation with him. Your father must regret the actions of his past. Is he nice to your mother now?'

'Of course, he has been very good to her since he became sober.'

I sensed that she was feeling better. 'Jaya, go to a counsellor with him and work things out. Having a third party helps in seeing things clearer. You can defer your admission for a year and start working here. After that time has passed, re-evaluate your life by yourself or with the help of a counsellor and you will make the right decision. In a lifespan of many years, you can take time off for a year to figure out what's good for you. It is worth it.'

She smiled and her eyes shone brightly. She thanked me and left.

That day, my thoughts were preoccupied with AA. At the foundation, we are already predisposed to reaching out to people in tough situations. Dharma, on its own, also means protecting someone who needs it, no matter who they are or where they come from. It's pure and simple, and my mind wouldn't rest easy. Besides, we had never worked on this problem before and I had to understand it first. I got some information on AA online but it wasn't sufficient. Multiple questions bounced around in my mind. What was it and how did it really play a role in an alcoholic's life? What challenges does he or she face? Was it hereditary? Does one's financial status or family make a difference? How does counselling help? What is the success rate of de-addiction and where does a person go on from there?

It was clear—I needed first-hand information. I wanted to meet someone to understand the problem a little better. Vaguely, I recalled a friend mentioning in passing many years ago that her son-in-law had been a victim of this. I hadn't been good at keeping in touch and wondered if he would speak to me about it.

I took a chance, picked up the phone and reached out to my friend. I was hesitant. When she came on the line, we chatted for a few minutes and tried to catch up on the time gone by. Finally, I asked her, 'Several years ago, you had told me about your son-in-law, Ramesh, and that he had gone to a de-addiction camp. How is he doing now?'

'With God's grace and with the help of AA, he is sober now and lives a good life.'

'Would he mind if I asked him a few questions about the group? Only if he wants to, of course. I can assure you that it will remain confidential.'

'Sure, I will talk to him about it. I will message you his number if he agrees,' said my friend.

'Thank you!'

Within ten minutes, I received his contact details and immediately called him. The man on the other side of the phone sounded like he was around forty years old.

'Aunty!' said Ramesh, his voice full of warmth. 'I am happy to know that you want to hear about AA. I will share my journey with you and you can write about it too, if you like. It'll be worth it even if one person learns from my mistakes.'

'Why don't you come over for a meal? We can speak leisurely then,' I suggested.

Soon, we decided to meet in my house for lunch.

He was on time and confident in his demeanour. We sat down at the table. There was no need for polite conversation or formalities.

'Tell me about your experience with AA,' I broached the subject without beating around the bush.

'I've read your book titled *The Day I Stopped Drinking Milk*. But if I had to write one, it would be called *The Day I Began Drinking Alcohol*.' He sighed. 'Let me tell you how it all began.

'I belong to a conservative family. As children, we were expected to be home by sunset and were not allowed even tea or coffee! The only liquids I was allowed were milk, water and *teertha* (holy water). I was an excellent student and finished my twelfth grade with outstanding marks.

'A few days later, some of my classmates and I decided to celebrate. We went to a restaurant and ordered a round of drinks. I had never tried alcohol before and it was a close friend, a coffee planter's son from Coorg, who egged me on. "Come on, have a drink! Social drinking is quite acceptable now and it does absolutely no harm. One or two drinks will make you happier than the high you must have got from your top marks! Take this," he said and handed me a peg of whisky with ice cubes.

'Most of us were first-timers. Though the taste of the drink was slightly bitter, we all drank and felt good and relaxed. For some time, I felt that I was floating on air. The music was good and the world around me seemed beautiful and I had a nice buzz. I liked it.

'The evening turned into night and we ordered dinner. Though I was a foodie then, I didn't feel like eating anything. Instead, I quietly went to the bar and took a second peg. Everyone at the table clapped, "You were so cautious first, but look at you now!"

'The night ended on a high note and my friend dropped me home in his car. Since it was late, my parents were already asleep, so I used my key to enter the house and crashed on the bed.

'The next morning, I didn't stir until 7.30 a.m. When I opened my eyes, the sun's rays were shining brightly through the window.

'It was late. I usually woke up at 6 a.m.

'When my mother saw me, she asked, "Are you unwell?"

'I shook my head, but my head was feeling heavy and I had a slight headache.

'"How was the party?"

'"It was fine."

'I headed to the bathroom for a shower and felt slightly better. I went about my routine and at the end of the day, I thought about alcohol. I was fascinated by the high it had brought me.

'A few days later, I wanted to drink again and called my friend. He laughed and said, "No problem, man. Let's have another party."

'This time, it was only the two of us. My friend taught me about the different kinds of alcohol, the qualities and the prices, as I eagerly awaited my peg. We began meeting regularly and without realizing it, I got addicted to alcohol and began yearning for it every day.

'A month later, I got admission in a college in Mumbai and left home. Now I had complete freedom and there was absolutely no one to control me. I began boozing with different classmates. Somehow, I still managed to get decent grades, despite bunking classes—either due to hangovers or because I had slept late the previous night. I even got a good job that paid me well. Unfortunately for me, it also meant that I began drinking more since I could afford more.

'A few years later, I was transferred to Bengaluru. By then, my parents had built another house on the floor upstairs and I told them that I'd like to stay there. I had an arranged marriage and the girl was very nice. But once my wife began living with me, she learnt of my addiction within a few days. Livid, she fought with my poor parents, thinking that they were aware of my alcoholism and had chosen to hide it from her.

'My mother was horrified! She had had no knowledge of my addiction. The only symptom she was aware of was that I had become short-tempered, but she had innocently attributed it to the stress at my workplace. I had, of course, let her think that way. So along with my wife, I got a sermon every day and it greatly annoyed me. She dragged me to temples and gurus. The more they pushed me, the more upset I became. Through it all, my wife continued to believe in me. "You are intelligent," she would say. "You can leave this habit. I know you can control your urges."

'Sometimes her words gave me strength, but I couldn't let go of alcohol.'

I was dumbfounded. This could happen to anyone, especially in this day and age. I stopped him. 'Tell me, how did you find out about AA?'

'Now you must understand my journey, Aunty. Day after day, it became worse and I kept drowning in the problem that I had created. One day, I got a call from my old friend from Coorg. He was visiting Bengaluru with his cousin and invited me to his hotel. I was happy to hear from him and thought that we could have a memorable evening together. When I eventually saw him, I was concerned. The young, handsome boy looked like an old man and a skeleton at that!

"'Shall we order something to drink?" I asked, a few minutes into our meeting.

"'Don't even mention the word alcohol. It is killing me. For a long time, I refused to get married. My parents tried their best to rescue me from this life, but now I have been diagnosed with liver cirrhosis. I can't tell you how much I regret the past! I was born into a good family and grew up in a wonderful place like Coorg where I could have done something meaningful. People always plan a holiday there and I already lived in heaven. I should have become high on nature, but instead I became high on alcohol. I don't have much time left. Don't waste your life, old friend! Learn from me. A man near his death will always tell you the bare truth. This disease is worse than cancer. People will sympathize with you if you have cancer and there are medicines and surgeries that might give you a chance to get back to your old life. But here I am. This is what rock bottom looks like. People look down on me and judge me, even my parents. I thank God that I am not married or I would have ruined another person's life too."

'His words threw me for a loop. How could this have happened to him? This isn't how life is supposed to turn out for people like us.

'I came home and tossed and turned all night. I couldn't stop thinking about him or myself. My life was a mess.

Sometimes, I would skip work because I had drunk too much the previous day. People who were less smart than me were getting promoted and I was being passed over again and again because I wasn't considered reliable enough. Meanwhile, my wife and mother were under our relatives' constant scrutiny because of my condition. It was plain as day—I wasn't that far off from being in the same boat as my friend. The very idea shook me to the core.

'The next morning, there was a call from my friend's hotel. It was his cousin. "Your friend passed away last night," he said. "You were his last visitor."

'I began trembling with shock and fear. It was the lowest point of my life, and I couldn't control my body from shivering. When the shivers stopped, I went to the small cupboard containing all the alcohol, took the bottles and threw them in the trash.

'With the help of my family, I learnt about AA and checked in to the alcohol de-addiction camp. It took a few years for me to become sober and I have been this way ever since. I now dedicate my life to helping others who are in a bad place because of alcoholism. I work with them and show them that there is hope. They can get better.'

He stopped and opened the bag he was carrying. He rummaged in it for a few seconds and took a book out. He handed it to me. 'This is a book on AA and their twelve steps. They include apologizing to those we have hurt, helping others and surrendering to God.'

I took the book from him, eager to read it.

'Aunty, I am ashamed of my past but I am also proud that I could leave it behind me. My wife and mother have played an important role in bringing me back.'

I was amazed to learn so much! He had opened a new door for me.

'Please attend one AA meeting, Aunty!' he said. 'There are two types of meetings—open and closed. Anyone can go for the open ones while the closed gatherings are only for the members. Tomorrow, there is an open session in Electronic City where I am the chairman.'

'Chairman?' I asked out aloud.

'Yes, but not in the regular sense of the word. A chairman here is a mentor who shares his experience, the challenges of his journey and the weak moments too. He also gives input to the members on how to conquer the desire of a few minutes so that the person can survive the urge to drink.'

I said, 'I would like to join you tomorrow. You have shared your story because you know me, but why will other people want to share their darkest moments with me?'

'Once I have the other members' permission to let you in for an open session, then it will not be a problem. Most of them are willing to speak about it because now they recognize the problem and genuinely want to become sober. They don't know how to go about it and that's where AA comes in,' he explained patiently.

'Now that you are a mentor yourself, what about you? Whom do you speak to?'

He smiled and said, 'I continue to have a mentor and visit him weekly. I am human, after all.'

The conversation took a different turn and we spoke about philosophy for some time. When the time came for him to leave, he said, 'See you tomorrow. I will text you the location of the church.'

'Why are you meeting there?' I was curious.

'Aunty, where else can we meet? In a place like Bengaluru, thirty of us cannot fit into an average-sized living room. If we look for places on hire, then the payments have to be budgeted. When we ask people to make an exception or allow us to use their facilities for minimal or no cost, they immediately refuse when they learn of the purpose. We were running out of places to meet and so we approached a church. The management was kind enough to allow us to use a space in their premises.'

I thanked the church authorities in my head for comprehending human nature and allowing sins to be forgiven. It is the essence of life.

'They said we could donate whatever we could afford but insisted that we keep the place clean.'

'Why did they say that? Do people get their drinks there?' I asked innocently.

'Aunty, come on. AA is about not drinking and that's what the whole session is about. A lot of people who drink also smoke. If we consider drug addiction to be one of three brothers, then it is the worst of them all. Alcohol comes next, while smoking is the youngest of the three. The elder brother is usually accompanied by the two younger ones, while the middle brother almost always appears with the youngest. So we keep ashtrays on a table and clean up before we leave.'

'Who funds these meetings? Can Infosys Foundation help?'

'Thanks, Aunty, but AA doesn't take help from anyone on that front,' he replied.

Soon, Ramesh left.

The next day, I reached the venue, a Christian school, at the assigned time. There was a small crowd of both men and women standing outside. The evening was fading away and night was almost upon us.

Suddenly, I felt awkward. At times, being a writer has its negatives. What if someone questioned my presence?

'Why did she come?'

'Is she going to write about us?'

Just then, Ramesh called me inside. He said that he wouldn't be taking the session that day. I entered the room and sat in a corner. It was a regular classroom with tables and benches—there were no DVDs, overhead projector or any fancy equipment.

Within five minutes, the room was full. There were people of different ages and genders, though the number of girls and women was less than the number of men. There were some foreigners too. A group of students entered and announced their presence before retreating to another corner of the room. No one paid any attention to me, but I still felt out of my depth.

A middle-aged person walked in firmly and greeted everyone. Then he sat down in the front, facing us. He opened a book and read out the twelve steps that I had learnt about the day before. I observed some faces looking tense and worried. After that was done, the chairman said, 'Welcome to all fellow members, guests and students. This is an open session. Today, I'd like to share something good. Fellow Bharat, where are you?'

A man in his forties raised his hand.

'Bharat is completing his first birthday here. We will cut the cake at the end of the session.'

Everyone clapped. I didn't understand what was going on. What did the chairman mean by saying it was his first birthday?

'Our guests today may be a little surprised to see this celebration, but the first birthday is a very big deal. It means that Bharat hasn't had alcohol for a year now.'

'So that's what it is,' I thought.

'As the chairman, I will share my experience first. My initiation and drinking began in college under peer pressure. It was cool to drink and I was proud to be in the party crowd. Over the next few years, I became an alcoholic. Still, I was able to land a job, find a good girl and gain appreciation for my work. When I thought the time was right, I asked my girlfriend to marry me, but she refused. She said that I was drunk whenever she met me, irrespective of the time of the day. So I turned to the bottle even more, using my heartbreak as an excuse.

'One day, my parents finally said to me, "Grow up! The girl left you years ago and is now the mother of two children and yet, here you are—still drinking your life away. This has nothing to do with her and everything to do with you—you are an alcoholic. We are ready to help you get your life back on track, but you must realize what you have become."

'I was livid. How dare they label me an alcoholic? I could quit drinking whenever I wanted to. I was the one in control. So I didn't drink for the next two days and thought that I had proved myself. On the third day, my parents wanted to go to a temple nearby and I offered to drive them there. I had a quick shower in the evening, shaved and applied an aftershave lotion. I looked good.

'A short time later, we left for the temple. While driving, my tongue touched my skin briefly and it tasted of the aftershave lotion. I kept licking it and by the time we reached the temple, I was craving for a drink. I dropped my parents, went to the closest bar and stayed there for four hours. Unaware of my actions, my poor parents performed a puja for me at the temple, waited for me, then took an autorickshaw and went back home.

'That was my turning point. It was the day I realized that I couldn't live without booze. So I came to AA and they helped me vocalize what I was. It was here that I found other people like me and I was glad that I wasn't alone in this. Our slogan is "I can't, we can".'

The chairman looked straight at the crowd in front of him, 'If you would like to stay and be with us, please do so. You are always welcome here. People who think that this isn't the place for them, let me tell you that there is a bar on the opposite side of the street. Feel free to leave.'

He paused, waiting for people to exit. One person did, but at a turtle's pace.

Then he said, 'Only an alcoholic can understand another fellow alcoholic. Nobody is going to judge you here. I invite you to share your experience or thoughts.'

By then, the environment felt very informal and I didn't feel awkward any more.

A young lady sitting on one of the benches introduced herself. 'I am Raveena Alcoholic,' she said.

'Hi, Raveena Alcoholic,' responded the other members.

'I come from an affluent family where social drinking was a part of our culture. My parents studied in France and hence frequently discussed wine and its various characteristics. I was introduced to wine at the age of sixteen but the quantity was restricted. The next year, I went to college in Delhi and my parents headed to the Middle East for a financially exciting job opportunity. I stayed back in a residential hostel where I met girls who frequently drank hard liquor such as vodka and whisky. At first, they made fun of me and urged me to try what they were having. So I began experimenting and came to love other drinks too. My parents used to send me a monthly allowance then. Whenever they asked me about my spending, I would conceal my expenses on alcohol. Lying came naturally to me once I started it and I barely felt guilty about it over time.'

'There comes the fourth brother,' I thought.

'Around the time of my graduation, I went to a bar and met a boy. We got along like a house on fire and spent a lot of time learning about each other and our habits. We disclosed our relationship to our parents who approved of the match and we had a lavish wedding. Following the north Indian tradition, there was plenty of wine and liquor on the day of the reception, and the guests drank as much as possible since it was free. After the wedding, my husband and I shifted to Bengaluru. We would sit and drink together every day after he returned from work, but he noticed that I could drink more than him. I needed more than two pegs to get high and I didn't puke afterwards or get a headache immediately either. I thought it was a great quality and that I must push myself further.'

Suddenly, Raveena's voice softened. 'Weeks later, I learnt that I was pregnant and went to a gynaecologist. I didn't tell her about the alcohol. During the third month of pregnancy, I felt very uneasy in the area around my stomach and went to see her again.

'As a part of the routine check-up, she asked me, "Are you drinking alcohol? Perhaps wine?"

'"Wine," I said, concealing the hard liquor I was still downing every now and then.

'"Stop it."

'I tried to but I couldn't control myself. "Doctors are extra careful about these things," I thought. "A sip here and there isn't going to harm the baby."

'So I poured myself some vodka and orange juice the very next day, and continued to drink with my husband.

'Nine months later, a baby boy was born and our families were ecstatic. Everybody celebrated with wine and champagne in our house but it wasn't enough for me.

I needed more. Taking care of a newborn was much more exhausting than I had thought. When the parents had retired for the night to their bedrooms, I went to the mini-bar in the dining room and drank vodka.

'A year passed and my son grew up quickly. I noticed that his milestones were delayed and ran to the doctor. Within a month, it was confirmed—my son was a slow learner and would remain so. The doctor remarked, "I hope you weren't drinking during the pregnancy."

'That hit home. The drinking hadn't harmed me but it had labelled my child "special". He had done nothing to deserve this and yet, he was the one paying for my sins.

'I could not excuse myself and felt like ending my life, but the thought of my son prevented me from taking a step further. If I wasn't around, who would look after him? What does his future hold? My husband and I didn't blame each other, but ourselves. We took strength from each other and decided to quit drinking. It was very hard and we kept failing at our attempts. We ended up drinking in the evenings, just like we used to before.

'Thankfully, we found AA and now that's the time I keep for my meetings. The withdrawal was painful and difficult. Once the evening is past, I am more in control and I return home. My son's face is a stark reminder of why I must never touch a drink again. Why did God make such an addictive thing on earth?' Her voice shook with the emotions that she kept bottled inside her. 'I am scared to have another baby. What if I get another child like my son?'

The chairman stepped in, 'Thank you, Raveena Alcoholic, for sharing your personal story. People come to AA when they reach the lowest point in their lives. That point differs from person to person. We had one teenager who once asked his mother for money to buy alcohol. When she refused to part with it, he pushed her and damaged her leg. In time, she developed a limp. It was an eternal reminder to the son about how he had hurt her and it became his turning point. Once people desperately desire a change in the most honest way possible, they come here because we can help them make it happen.'

Next, a well-dressed middle-aged man in the front row introduced himself. He said, 'I am Harry Alcoholic and belong to a wealthy family. I have no excuse. I got the habit because I enjoyed drinking with my friends. Since my father had his own business, I decided to join him after my graduation and fell in love with one of the secretaries named Maria. She learnt of my weaknesses and about the drinking too. As time passed, we seriously began thinking of marriage.

'"I want you to quit drinking," she told me. "With God's grace and love, you will leave it, I'm sure."

'At first, my parents were hesitant about the match but soon they took to Maria and we had a big fat wedding. Still, I continued to drink. Two years later, my mother and father died in a car crash and I was the only one to inherit all that they had built. I managed the office and Maria managed everything at home, including the finances. We also had a beautiful baby girl and life was wonderful. Yet, my habit continued.

'When Maria spoke to me about it, I didn't heed her words. Every day, I would ask her for money to spend at the bar. One day, she put her foot down, "No, you won't get any more money for this. I decided to marry you in the hope that you would improve and because I loved you. You are the same, despite becoming a father."

'I became so upset that I abused her verbally and told her that the money was mine and that she had no right over it. With tears in her eyes, she handed me some money and I rushed to the bar. The next morning, I felt bad and apologized to her, "I'm so sorry, Maria, I was wrong. I will never do it again."

'But I did. Again and again.

'One day, the same incident repeated itself and Maria refused to give me money. I saw my daughter playing on the side and yelled at Maria with hate, "If you don't give me what I want, I will do something to the baby and then you will regret it."

'I was in complete rage. That's the only reason I said it. I loved my daughter more than my life.

'But Maria turned pale. She probably thought I meant it. She brought out all the money she had and handed it to me. "Take it," she said and walked out of the room with my daughter.

'I took all the money, called a few friends and went to a popular bar that I frequented and whose owner I knew. People would often join me there and praise my gracious nature because I paid for everyone's drinks. But in my heart, I was still mad at Maria. I wanted to show her that I was not a henpecked husband, so I drank more than usual that day. The owner allowed me to crash in a room above the bar because I wasn't in any state to walk or drive.

'When I came home the next morning, there was a note on the fridge. It was a handwritten note from Maria.

I am leaving with my daughter. You will never change. You may have ruined my life, but I don't want my daughter's to be ruined too with a drunk man for a father.

'I looked around the apartment. All their clothes were gone.

'But I knew she would come back. To forget my domestic problems, I began drinking even more. Maria, however, didn't turn up at all. Weeks turned into months and months into years. I didn't know where she was any more.

'Within a few years, I lost everything—my business and my properties.

'Now, the owner of that same popular bar instructed the bouncers not to let me in without money. My friends forgot about me too. It got worse and I began begging at traffic lights. All the money I got went into buying and consuming desi liquor.

'One day, I sat at a traffic signal and thought that I saw Maria in one of the cabs with a child. When I went closer, I realized that it really was her, along with my daughter. Excited, I knocked at the car window. She, however, dismissed me with a wave of her hand. "Never talk to strangers," she said to our daughter. "Look at this dirty man begging here instead of working somewhere."

'She didn't recognize me! Before I could find any words, the light turned green and the car sped away.

'That was the lowest point in my life—I had lost my wife, daughter and what my parents and grandparents had built for me. My family had had a humble beginning. My grandfather had come from Kolar to Bengaluru city as a clerk, worked very hard and saved money to start his own business. It took decades for him to officially reach the "rich" status. His name was Harry and I had been named after him. But look at me! I had squandered away all his wealth and become a beggar. I wanted to commit suicide right there and then.

'I don't remember how but someone took me to an open AA session in a church and for the first time in many years, I felt a ray of hope. I heard people talking about their darkest times. They were people like me who had lost everything and then gone on to build a decent life for themselves. Maybe I could try too. It's been fifteen years since then and I have been sober for a long time. Now I spend my life in service to others like me by bringing them to AA and helping them on their journey.'

The applause in the room was followed by a deafening silence, each of us busy with our own thoughts.

'His daughter must be working now and maybe married too!' I thought. 'His wife is a brave woman. She made the right decision for herself and the child, but what a life they have all led. Everyone has suffered a lifetime because of alcohol addiction.'

I didn't know if alcoholism was a formally recognized medical disease, but AA was a boon for the people it served.

Coffee was served in paper cups for all of us, and a stringed purse and a round medal was circulated. The chairman announced, 'You can contribute only if you are AA members. We don't accept money from others.'

A few contributed and most of the members took the medal, held it close to their heart and prayed.

At last, the chairman invited Bharat to come and cut the cake. 'We have also invited Bharat's family today because he wouldn't have reached this milestone without them,' he said.

With pride, Bharat blew out the lone candle on it and cut the cake. Then he thanked his family profusely along with the people in AA who had given him back his life.

His father then handed him a medal. He was speechless, choked with emotion. After he had composed himself, he said, 'Bharat is my only child and I have celebrated many events with him, including his birthdays and wedding. But today is his real birthday. For a long time, I was ashamed to have a son like him but he has changed and I am a proud father.'

Bharat smiled and patted his father's shoulder and looked at the small gathering with gratitude. 'An alcoholic is an alcoholic forever,' he said. 'I cannot take any medicines with alcoholic content, not even a spoonful of cough syrup when I am unwell. But I am happy with where I am right now and I promise I will continue to celebrate such birthdays every year.'

I glanced at Bharat's wife who stood nearby. It had been no cakewalk for her with the kind of pressure society often forces on Indian women. She had had a troublesome marriage without true companionship and was still standing beside her husband.

A few minutes later, the meeting got over and people started leaving. I also stood up and Ramesh accompanied me to the car waiting outside.

'Does everyone reach sobriety?' I asked Ramesh.

'It depends, Aunty. There are chances of relapsing. That's why we meet regularly to keep our urges in control. Even now, when I see an alcohol ad or a drinking scene in a movie on television, I switch it off. I don't go to any wedding that serves liquor. It is very easy to fall off the wagon. Surrendering to God, which is one of the steps in AA, is very helpful. God doesn't mean a specific religious one. Everyone has a God within themselves. It simply means a higher power. In AA, we have the freedom of choosing our God. It is a great organization and Bengaluru alone has eighty centres. AA operates in 186 countries. Aunty, no wonder our ancestors were intelligent. They told us to keep away from bad habits. It may start as social drinking but unfortunately, some get hooked to it. And once they are hooked, their life becomes miserable. If they had not tried it in the first place, they would not have become alcoholics.'

I sat in the car and thought about the famous Marathi play *Ekach Pyala*, a popular drama of the 1940s, and another one called *Devadas*, which is a play about a man who, as people like to believe, turned to the bottle because he could not marry Paro, the love of his life. But the truth is that he was simply an alcoholic.

In the Marathi play, the protagonist, Sudhakar, and his wife, Sindhu, are a happy couple. One day, an alcoholic friend insists that Sudhakar should drink one sip of alcohol to celebrate an event. He even offers him a peg. Sindhu objects to her husband's drinking, who mocks her, 'O Sindhu, don't worry. Our life's ship will not drown with one peg.'

Unfortunately, her husband likes the taste and in time, becomes a slave to alcohol. The play shows how their life is ruined. The first peg is enough to get you on the journey, if you have a tendency towards alcoholism. Unfortunately, nobody can predict until you try that first glass.

Who says money is the ultimate goal of life? It isn't. You will find out when the time is right.

One of life's goals is the ability to understand human nature and raise a fellow being from rock bottom to becoming a useful member of society. We all lose a few battles in our lives, but we can win the war.

There's always hope.

Scan QR code to access the
Penguin Random House India website

PENGUIN BOOKS

THE OLD MAN AND HIS GOD

Sudha Murty was born in 1950, in Shiggaon, North Karnataka. Author, philanthropist, educator, public speaker and engineer, she completed her master's in computer science from IISc, Bangalore. She is the founder of the Infosys Foundation and the chairperson of the Murty Trust. A bestselling author, with more than 300 titles to her acclaim, some of her most famous books include *Three Thousand Stitches*, *Dollar Bahu* and *Wise and Otherwise*. She writes in English and Kannada, and her books have been translated into all major Indian languages and have sold over 60 lakh copies around the country.

Over the years, Sudha Murty has been recognized with many prestigious awards, including the Padma Bhushan and the Padma Shri from the Government of India in 2023 and 2006, respectively; Bal Sahitya Puraskar in 2023; the R.K. Narayan Award for Literature in 2006; the Lal Bahadur Shastri National Award in 2020; and Lokmanya Tilak and Mahatma awards in 2024. She was also awarded the Rajyotsava and Attimabbe Award for excellence in Kannada literature from the Government of Karnataka in 2000 and 2012. Sudha Murty has received nineteen honorary doctorates from various universities across India. Currently, she is also serving as the President-nominated member of Parliament in the Rajya Sabha.

ALSO BY THE SAME AUTHOR

SUDHA MURTY

THE OLD MAN
AND HIS GOD

*Discovering
the Spirit
of India*

PENGUIN BOOKS

An imprint of Penguin Random House

PENGUIN BOOKS

Penguin Books is an imprint of the Penguin Random House group of companies
whose addresses can be found at global.penguinrandomhouse.com

Published by Penguin Random House India Pvt. Ltd
4th Floor, Capital Tower 1, MG Road,
Gurugram 122 002, Haryana, India

Penguin
Random House
India

First published by Penguin Books India 2006
This edition published in Penguin Books by Penguin Random House India 2025

ISBN 9780144001019

Typeset in Sabon by Mantra Virtual Services, New Delhi
Printed at Thomson Press India Ltd, New Delhi

www.penguin.co.in

MIX
Paper | Supporting
responsible forestry
FSC® C010615

For Infosys Foundation, that has shown me a world beyond, with immense gratitude

Contents

I have now written two collections of my real-life experiences which many say they have enjoyed reading. This is my third. All the experiences mentioned here are real, though the names have been changed in some places. People often ask me how it is that so many interesting things happen only to me. To them I reply that in life's journey we all meet strange people and undergo so many experiences that touch us and sometimes even change us. If you have a sensitive mind and record your observations regularly, you will see your life too is a vast storehouse of stories.

Of course there are some incidents here which happened to me because of the people I met during my work or in my travels. In all the cases I have taken care to take the permission of the people I have written about.

I have often wondered what it is about these experiences that has been appreciated by readers in all corners of the country. I have come to the conclusion that it is because they are told simply and are all true. After all, there is something within all of us that attracts us to the truth. I have tried to hold up a mirror to the lives of the people of our country and attempted to trace that spirit within us which makes us uniquely Indian.

I have dedicated this book to the Infosys Foundation. For many, the foundation is a charitable organization, a branch of a rich company. But for me, it is something closest to my heart. Initially I was a mother to it. I was there from the day it came into existence. Somewhere along the line, it has become the mother and I the child. Holding its hands, I have journeyed many miles, faced praise and criticism. It has been an integral part of my life. We have never abandoned each other.

There are many people who have worked with me in the long journey that a book undergoes from the time it leaves the writer's desk. I would like to thank them all. I want to thank Sudeshna Shome Ghosh of Penguin India, for her efforts, without which the book would not have been published.

The royalty proceeds from this book will go to charity.

November 2005   Sudha Murty
                                                  Bangalore

1

THE OLD MAN AND HIS GOD

A few years back, I was travelling in the Thanjavur district of Tamil Nadu. It was getting dark, and due to a depression over the Bay of Bengal, it was raining heavily. The roads were overflowing with water and my driver stopped the car near a village. 'There is no way we can proceed further in this rain,' said the driver. 'Why don't you look for shelter somewhere nearby rather than sit in the car?'

Stranded in an unknown place among unknown people, I was a bit worried. Nevertheless, I retrieved my umbrella and marched out into the pelting rain. I started walking towards the tiny village, whose name I cannot recall now. There was no electricity and it was a trial walking in the darkness and the rain. In the distance I could just make out the shape of a small temple. I decided it would be an ideal place to take shelter, so I made my way to it. Halfway there, the rain started coming down even more fiercely and the strong wind blew my umbrella away, leaving me completely drenched. I reached the temple soaking wet. As soon as I entered, I heard an elderly person's voice calling out to me. Though I cannot speak Tamil, I could make out the concern in the voice. In the course of my travels, I have come to realize that voices from the heart can be understood irrespective of the language they speak.

I peered into the darkness of the temple and saw an old man of about eighty. Standing next to him was an equally old lady in a traditional nine-yard cotton sari. She said something to him and then approached me with a worn but clean towel in her hand. As I wiped my face and head I noticed that the man was blind. It was obvious from their surroundings that they were very poor. The Shiva temple, where I now stood, was simple with the minimum of ostentation in its decorations. The Shivalinga was bare except for a bilwa leaf on top. The only light came from a single oil lamp. In that flickering light a sense of calm overcame me and I felt myself closer to god than ever before.

In halting Tamil, I asked the man to perform the evening mangalarati, which he did with love and dedication. When he finished, I placed a hundred-rupee note as the dakshina.

He touched the note and pulled away his hand, looking uncomfortable. Politely he said, 'Amma, I can make out that the note is not for ten rupees, the most we usually receive. Whoever you may be, in a temple, your devotion is important, not your money. Even our ancestors have said that a devotee should give as much as he or she can afford to. To me you are a devotee of Shiva, like everyone else who comes here. Please take back this money.'

I was taken aback. I did not know how to react. I looked at the man's wife expecting her to argue with him and urge him to take the money, but she just stood quietly.

Often, in many households, a wife encourages the man's greediness. Here, it was the opposite. She was endorsing her husband's views. So I sat down with them, and with the wind and rain whipping up a frenzy outside, we talked about our lives. I asked them about themselves, their life in the village temple and whether they had anyone to look after them.

Finally I said, 'Both of you are old. You don't have any children to look after your everyday needs. In old age one requires more medicines than groceries. This village is far from any of the towns in the district. Can I suggest something to you?'

At that time, we had started an old-age pension scheme and I thought, looking at their worn-out but clean clothes, they would be the ideal candidates for it.

This time the wife spoke up, 'Please do tell, child.'

'I will send you some money. Keep it in a nationalized bank or post office. The interest on that can be used for your monthly needs. If there is a medical emergency you can use the capital.'

The old man smiled on hearing my words and his face lit up brighter than the lamp.

'You sound much younger than us. You are still foolish. Why do I need money in this great old age? Lord Shiva is also known as Vaidyanathan. He is the Mahavaidya, or great doctor. This village we live in has many kind people. I perform the pooja and they give me rice in return. If either of us is unwell, the local doctor gives us medicines. Our wants are very few. Why would I accept money from an unknown person? If I keep this money in the bank, like you are telling me to, someone will come to know and may harass us. Why should I take on these worries? You are a kind person to offer help to two unknown old people. But we are content; let us live as we always have. We don't need anything more.'

Just then the electricity came back and a bright light lit up the temple. For the first time I saw the couple properly. I could clearly see the peace and happiness on their faces. They were the first people I met who refused help in spite of their obvious need. I did not agree with everything he had just said, but it was clear to me that his contentment had brought him peace. Such an attitude may not let you progress fast, but after a certain period in life it is required. Perhaps this world with its many stresses and strains has much to learn from an old couple in a forgettable corner of India.

FREEDOM OF SPEECH

Alka and I have been friends since the time we were in school and college together. Alka was the star debater of our university. Her arguments, bold, convincing and razor sharp, usually left her opponents floundering. She was called the 'Queen of Speech' by her friends.

Even after college and through our years of marriage and children, we continued to keep in touch. Alka married a mechanical engineer and settled down in Bombay in a beautiful flat on the Worli sea face. Her husband started his own small-scale industry and they were very well off. She had a daughter who got married and went to live in the US. Alka herself went on to become the head of the sociology department in a good college. I always thought of her as having the perfect life.

Once, I had to go to Bombay on some work, and Alka invited me to stay with her. There I met Tulsi, her efficient maid. Tulsi was from the Maharashtra-Karnataka border and spoke the same language as Alka and me. Drought and poverty had forced many families from that region to emigrate to larger cities in search of work. Most ended up as construction workers on daily wages, yet they never lost the hope of being able to save enough money to go back to their villages.

Tulsi too had come to Bombay in search of work, but had settled down here. She had worked in Alka's house for many years and was an asset due to her hardworking nature, punctuality and reliability.

One day, during my visit, Tulsi did not come for work at her usual time. As the clock ticked away, Alka was getting more and more agitated. She had to attend and also speak at an international sociology conference. She had become so used to Tulsi that she could not do anything on her own, though I knew, long back, she used to be a good cook. That is what efficient maids and secretaries do to you at home and in the office.

I was watching her agitation and could not help laughing. This upset her even more. She said, 'It is easy for you to laugh. But you don't know how much I have helped her out in her times of need. How could she do this to me on such a busy day? She knows I have some very important work today. You do not realize the responsibility I have been given in this seminar. You take things too easy. That is why you have remained only a visiting professor.'

I did not get upset at Alka's remarks. After all, we had been friends for long, and had always been very frank with each other. And what she had said was also the truth, which few other people could have said to me.

So instead of laughing, I offered a different solution.

'Alka, why can't we go to Tulsi's house and find out what is causing the delay? There is no point in fuming and increasing your blood pressure.'

I knew Tulsi stayed in a slum just across the road. In a city like Bombay, where rich people stay in beautiful apartments, there are double the number staying in adjoining slums. In fact, these slums have become essential for the survival of the residents of the big apartment blocks. Reluctantly, Alka agreed with my suggestion and we walked across the road to Tulsi's house.

As we approached her house, we heard the sound of voices raised in argument. Some people were quarrelling very loudly. We turned a corner and were surprised to behold the sight of Tulsi berating someone. She was screaming at a man standing quietly near by. Alka whispered to me that it was Raman, Tulsi's husband. His wife was showering the choicest of abuses at him and he was standing with his head bent low. In her extreme agitation, Tulsi was talking in her native dialect. She was so furious I would not have been surprised if she landed a few blows on him as well. Her neighbours were going about their work but were giving sympathetic glances in her direction from time to time. Tulsi finally saw us and calmed down slightly.

'Tulsi, don't use such language. You can solve the problem without bad words. What is the matter? Be cool and tell me what has happened.' I asked her in our language.

By this time Tulsi managed to control her emotions and breaking into tears she replied, 'Amma, with such difficulty I had saved some money and bought a pair of gold bangles and a chain for myself. It was with my own hard-earned money. And do you know what this fellow has done? He has gone and mortgaged them in order to start a paan shop. Is it fair? How can you ask me to be cool? They were my life's savings. I know Alka amma has some important work today but I could not control my anger when he told me this in the morning.'

I stood and consoled her for some time. My work involves talking to many people like her, who are grappling with basic day-to-day survival issues and have nothing to do with the glitz and glamour that many of us take for granted. In any case, being a teacher, I am quite used to giving sermons, whether they are wanted or not.

As we walked back home, Alka was very quiet. I assumed she was worried thinking of all the household work piled up for her. Affectionately I said, 'Don't worry about the cooking and other work. I'll help you now and I am sure Tulsi will be back in the evening. These people talk freely about their feelings and hence forget fast too. I bet by tonight Tulsi will have made up with her husband and may even go off to watch a movie with him.'

By this time we had entered the flat and I made my way to the kitchen to wash the vessels. I am not a very good cook, but I am definitely proficient in washing up. Alka said she would make some tea for us and went to the other corner of the kitchen. To my surprise after a while I heard sounds of sobbing coming from her. She was trying hard to suppress them but the tears were coming down fast.

I walked up to her and laid a hand on her shoulder. The moment I touched her, Alka broke down and started crying openly.

'Alka, please don't be so upset. You should not be so sensitive about what happened to Tulsi . . .'

'I am not worried about Tulsi. I have just realized today that my state is worse than hers.'

I was stunned at her words. She went on, 'It took a great deal of effort for us to buy this flat. You realize how expensive it is, and I gave every paisa from my salary towards the payment. This flat represents my life's savings. But do you know what my husband did? One day, when he was not here, there was a registered letter for him from the bank. I opened it to find that he has mortgaged the flat, which we bought in his name for income tax reasons, to the bank. His business was not doing well and he needed extra money desperately. But he did all this without telling me anything. I was furious. If we lose this flat where shall we go? But we live in "civilized" society, so I could not shout and scream at him. I could not raise my voice and abuse him as the neighbours would then know we were fighting. I have been keeping all this anger inside me for a long time. Tulsi is better off than me. At least she has the freedom to shout at her husband and even hit him if she is angry and then forget about it. I have to live with the hurt festering inside me forever.'

I did not know what to say to her. Helplessly I stared out at the sea from her beautiful balcony. The images I had in my mind about Alka from our schooldays as a bold, confident orator lay ruined. She was nothing but an ordinary, meek, ineffectual woman, unable to stand up to her husband and fight for her rights. To change the subject

I asked her, 'What are you going to speak about at the seminar today?'

Ironically, the answer came, 'Freedom of speech.'

HOREGALLU

Hot summer days remind me of my childhood in a little village. There was a large banyan tree right in the middle of the village, and I would spend many hours playing under it during my holidays. The tree was like a massive umbrella with its branches providing much needed shade and succour. Travellers spent some time sitting under it and catching their breath before going on their way. To make them comfortable there was a 'horegallu' under the tree. Horegallu literally means 'a stone that can bear weight'. It was a large flat stone placed horizontally over two vertical ones, thus making a stone bench on which anyone could sit and rest awhile, chat with a fellow traveller and exchange news of the road. Cool water would be kept in earthern pots near the bench and people could quench their thirst before starting their journeys again. I am sure similar simple arrangements can be found in villages all over the country.

The horegallu in our village holds special memories for me as it is inextricably linked with my grandfather. He was a retired schoolteacher and would spend hours every day sitting under the banyan tree and talking to those resting there. When I would get tired of playing I would sit next to him and observe the people he was speaking to and listen to their conversations. Most of them were villagers taking a break from their work in the fields nearby. They had to walk long distances each day carrying heavy burdens on their heads. Tired out by the heat, they would drink the cool water, wash their faces with it and chat with Grandfather. Their conversation would be about their daily lives and worries.

'Masterji, this summer has been so hot. I have never seen such dry weather.' Or, 'Masterji, it is getting difficult for me to carry these large loads on my head. Thank god for this horegallu. I wish my son would help, but he only wants to go to the city . . .' They spoke about the difficulties they lived with. My grandfather could only listen to them but just talking to him seemed to refresh them for the journey. After some time they would pick up their burdens with some ease and go on their way. The horegallu was an important feature in their lives and as a child I would often not understand why they blessed it so often for being there. After all it was only a stone bench. It was my grandfather who told me, 'Child, a horegallu is essential in any journey. We all carry our burdens according to our situations and capacities. But every once in a while we need to stop, put down that burden and rest. Only then can we be refreshed enough to pick up the load once more. The horegallu gives everyone that opportunity to do so. It helps people regain their strengths.'

Later on in life, I got to see something that reminded me of that stone bench once again. I was working in Bombay. One of my colleagues, Ratna was a senior clerk, middle aged and always smiling. She had done her graduation and been working in the company for nearly twenty-five years. She went about her repetitive, mundane work with an infectious cheerfulness.

Every day, during the lunch hour she would sit with some person in one of the rooms, and they would have long chats. I would often wonder what they talked about. One day, I finally asked her, 'Ratna, what do you talk with each person for the whole lunch hour?'

Ratna smiled and said simply, 'They share their troubles with me.'

'But how can you solve the troubles of so many people? Do you always have an answer for them?'

'No, I only listen.'

'And that is enough? That solves the problem?' I was young and incredulous at such a simplistic outlook. But Ratna answered with the same patience and affection that she must have used with all my colleagues, 'I am not a trained counsellor or an intellectual. No one can solve your problem. You have to do it yourself.'

'Then how do you help them by listening to them?'

'God has given me two ears to listen to others. I hear them out with sympathy and without any judgement. When a person in trouble or under a lot of strain finds an outlet for his worries, it relieves half his burden.'

I thought for sometime and said, 'But don't you ever break the confidence and tell others the secrets you hear, even by mistake?'

'Not even in my dreams. I consider that to be the worst kind of betrayal. I don't think there is a greater sin than betraying someone's confidence. They tell me their worries because they know I will never talk about it or gossip about it to another person. Only when they know their words are secure with me, can they talk to me freely. This way I relieve their burden for a short while till they are ready to pick themselves up and carry on with their journey.'

Her words uncannily echoed my grandfather's, sitting on the stone bench under the banyan tree. Perhaps, in their own small ways, without access to great wealth, both these people were doing some tremendous social service. No one thought of acknowledging their work or rewarding them for it, but they continued to do so, as these small acts of kindness gave them joy. If ever now I happen to pass a horegallu in a village, I remember them and wish there were many more of them in this world.

4

THE WAY YOU LOOK AT IT

A few years ago, I was travelling to a village in Karnataka on some work. I had got delayed and it was getting dark. There were no lights on the road and I was anxious to get to my destination. As we neared the outskirts of the village, the beams of the car's headlights picked out some shrubs on the side of the road. They were thorny shrubs and to my astonishment I saw many women coming out from behind them, shyly covering their heads, each with a tin box in hand. I realized they had gone there to attend to nature's call.

Soon I reached the village headman, Veerappa's house. He was a wealthy man and had arranged an elaborate dinner for me, with many courses including a few different types of sweets. The food was delicious, but my mind was not in enjoying it. I could not get the image of the women skulking out from behind the shrubs out of my mind.

When at last dinner was over, I asked to meet the cook. She was an elderly lady called Sharanamma. She was very shy and talked to me in a low voice. I wanted to know her better, so I said, 'The food was excellent. Can I give you something in return?'

Shyly she replied, 'Amma, I have heard you do a lot of

work for poor people. If possible can you build some public toilets for the women of this village? Life is very difficult for us. Unlike men, we cannot go for our toilet in the day. Like thieves we have to wait till it is dark, then we have to go behind bushes, that too in groups. Whenever a vehicle passes us on the main road and the car's lights fall on us we feel ashamed. And if ever we are unwell and need to go in the middle of the night then heaven help us. This is particularly traumatic for the young girls. We all would be very happy if you could do something about this.'

I was amazed at Sharanamma's sense of responsibility towards her community. I turned to Veerappa and said it was a shame that the headmen of the village had not thought it important that their women should answer nature's call with dignity and in privacy. It is a basic right that should be available to every human being. Finally I told him, 'I am ready to build these toilets for the village if you will maintain them well.' Veerappa, already ashamed after my tirade, readily agreed.

Thus started our foundation's work to build public toilets in the countryside and in key areas in Bangalore. In India people are usually enthusiastic about building temples, mosques and gurudwaras, but no one thinks it important to build something as essential as a toilet. Perhaps because there is no *punya* attached to it.

The toilets that we built in Bangalore were pay-and-use ones. Though many people objected to having to pay, this was one way we could ensure their cleanliness and proper maintenance.

One day, I went to visit the first toilet, near a busy bus-stand in the city. It was an unplanned visit and I stood behind two women as they waited to go in. They looked like working women and regular commuters on one of the buses. Suddenly I heard them mention my name. 'This Sudha Murty is a really mean lady. When she has spent so much money constructing this, why has she made it pay-and-use?' The other one replied. 'You are right. You don't know about her. I have heard from people that she has built many toilets in Bangalore and she is running some trust with the help of toilet money. She must be making a huge profit.'

I was shocked at their words. Even if one tries to do something to improve a city's civic life, people make all kinds of strange comments. For a while I was upset. Then I cooled down and told myself that people may say whatever they like, but I had to do what I had decided on. I know that the public toilets have benefitted many like Sharanamma. What she had perceived to be an act of necessity for the village women, was looked at here by these two women, as a business venture.

After all, life is the way you look at it.

5

A Tale of Two Brothers

Ram and Shyam were identical twins and my students in pre-university and graduate college where they studied for an MCA degree. This meant I taught them for nearly seven years. Obviously, I got to know them and their family quite well in the course of those years. Like many other twins I have known, Ram and Shyam were happy in each other's company and always stayed together in college, sharing homework, lab and class notes. They looked so similar that at times I could not make out which was Ram and which Shyam. 'You should wear something so I can make out one from the other!' I would joke with them. 'I get so confused. What will happen after you get married? Perhaps you should marry identical twins too, then there will be great fun and confusion all around.'

After they completed their MCA degree, they joined a software company. Their father was an industrialist and their mother the principal of a school. They were therefore from an affluent family and owned a large house and a farmhouse. One day, the two young men came to invite me to their wedding. Funnily, they were indeed getting married to two sisters who were also twins!

'It seems like your life story will be like a film script!' I joked again. 'How did you find the twin girls? What are their names?'

'Madam, when we decided to get married we deliberately looked around for twins, as we felt only another pair of twins would be able to understand us and our friendship completely. Their names are Smita and Savita. You must come to our wedding. After all, this was first your idea!'

I did attend the wedding and blessed the two couples wholeheartedly. I felt it must be a great relief for the two sets of parents as well. The two brothers marrying two sisters meant there was not going to be any rivalry between the two couples.

Many months later, out of the blue, Ram and Shyam's mother called me one day. She sounded tired. 'Madam can you come and talk to the children?' she asked wearily.

I could sense there was some problem, and that weekend itself, I went to their house to find out what was the matter. For a while, I was unable to recognize the house, though I was standing right in front of it. Now there were two front doors instead of one and the garden was partitioned into two. I decided I had the wrong address or perhaps they had moved out, but Ram's mother saw me and called out from inside.

I stepped in and immediately sensed an awkwardness and sadness in the air. The house had been partitioned in a bizarre manner. The drawing room was now small, the bedrooms too large and the kitchen in an odd shape. A brick wall ran down the length of the house, from the hall to the kitchen. There was pin drop silence inside. I turned to their mother, 'What happened? Why have you put this wall here?' She told me the sad story.

'Ram and Shyam fought and separated, that is why this wall has come up. Why are you looking so surprised? People change when they grow up. They lose the innocence we saw in them when they were young boys.'

I said, 'Siblings often fight with each other because of their partners, but here they were sisters, so how could they instigate it?'

'We too had the same thoughts when we got them married. For a while things went well. After my husband retired, we decided to divide up the property and give equal shares to the brothers. That's when the trouble started. They both wanted the same house, the same farmhouse. How could we solve such a problem? They were adamant, and we ended up building this wall to separate the two households.'

That old saying is so true, money is one thing which rarely unites and mostly divides people. The quarrel was due to property.

Their mother wanted me to speak to them and advise them as their teacher. But I knew that in money matters there was little the words of their college teacher would change. I tried any way. I said, 'From the time you were conceived you have shared the same space. You shared your mother's womb, you grew up together in this house, sharing your joys and sorrows. You married twins so they would understand your friendship better. You must understand that in life sometimes it is important to compromise and live in peace with loved ones.'

They had no answer to my words and I knew I was talking to deaf ears. I went away, unsuccessful. By the time I reached home, I was late for a dinner appointment with an old friend. He was a colleague of mine and I had known him for many years. Seeing me walk in late, he said, 'You know, punctuality is the sign of a good teacher— not only to the class but elsewhere too.'

I agreed and apologized.

'I am sorry. But which restaurant are we going to now?'

His wife smiled and said, 'We are going to a village thirty kilometers away.'

'Oh, is it in a farmhouse?'

'No, we don't have a farmhouse. The dinner is at a farmer's house.'

I did not understand what they were talking about, so I quietly got into their car. My friend first drove us to the nearest market. There he bought sweets and fruits while his wife got some clothes. Curiously, I asked again, 'Where are we going?'

He coolly replied, 'To my brother's house. He has been asking us to visit him for a long time. I am sure you will like it there.' As far as I knew he did not have any brother or sister. He was the only child of his parents.

'Where has this brother turned up from? Is he a cousin? Or a close friend who is like a brother? Or like in Hindi films, have you suddenly discovered you have a long-lost brother?'

He only chose to smile mysteriously and drove on. Soon we were outside Bangalore and the car was moving fast on the highway. His silence disconcerted me and I wondered if I had asked too many questions and intruded upon his personal life. If we were in America and I had talked so much, he would have told me to shut up and mind my own business. But here in India we cannot resist asking questions about someone's personal life, whether we are interested or not.

Suddenly my friend started talking.

'Fifty-five years ago, I was born in the village we are going to visit. I lost my mother when I was only ten days old. My father had loved her immensely and was broken-hearted but he also had to look after me. I was allergic to cow's milk and with my mother dead I could not drink any milk. I would cry piteously the whole day in hunger. As you know, those days there was no infant formula or powdered milk. I started getting weaker and weaker and hopes for my survival started dwindling. My father was worried but did not know what to do. Help came to him in the form of Seetakka. She was the wife of our servant and had delivered a baby boy only a few days before I was born. Unable to bear my plight, she requested my father, "Anna, if you don't mind, I want to feed this baby my milk along with my son." My father thought for a while, and even though many relatives protested at the arrangement, he agreed and Seetakka saved my life by giving me her milk. She continued to feed me till I developed resistance to cow's milk and other food. I stayed for five years in this village before moving on to other places. But I always remember her and consider her to be a great woman. In fact, I look upon her son Hanuma as my brother. I gave him a part of my share of the property even though my relatives opposed the idea as usual. For them Seetakka was just a servant, but for me she was a large-hearted, simple woman, whose love knew no bounds.

'I am busy in Bangalore now, but I make it a point to visit her son, my brother, at least once a year. After all Seetakka poured her love on us in equal measure without expecting anything in return. We shared the love of the same mother, and that makes us brothers.'

By the time his story ended, we had reached the village and my friend pointed out Hanuma, waiting at the street corner to escort us to his house. All through dinner, watching the love between them, I was remembering the wall between Ram and Shyam's families and wondering at the quirks of destiny, which turned brothers into strangers and the sons of masters and servants into brothers.

Way back in 1974, before Infosys was even a gleam in our eyes, young Narayan Murthy was working as a team member in SESA, a French firm which was building software for handling air cargo at the then newly built Charles De Gaulle Airport in Paris. He was very shy and an idealist.

The money was good, and whatever remained after sending back home to fulfil his various family obligations, he donated to organizations working for the development of our country. His views tended to be leftist and he was an ardent believer in the principles of Marxism. After working in France for a few years, he wanted to come back to India. But unlike the other young Indian engineers, he decided to hitchhike his way back from Paris to Kabul. Carrying his backpack, he took rides in cars and trains, or simply walked when nothing was available. Little did he know when he set out, that this backpack journey would change his destiny, as well as affect many other lives!

One wintry Sunday morning, hitchhiking from an Italian town, he reached Nis, a border town between what was then Yugoslavia and Bulgaria. Once inside the communist block, Murthy realized it was not going to be easy to get rides from passing motorists, so he decided to take a train to Sofia, the capital of Bulgaria. Thus, on reaching Nis, he straightaway walked to the local railway station. His efforts at buying breakfast at the restaurant were not successful since they would not accept the Italian currency he was carrying and the banks were closed. Murthy slept off on the platform till eight p.m., when the Sofia Express arrived at Nis. The train generally stopped there for about two hours to handle the immigration chores. Murthy got on to the train and took his seat. To his delight, the compartment was nearly empty. Being an introvert, he was quite happy to be alone.

As he sat reading a book, a tall, blonde and beautiful girl entered the compartment and settled down in the adjacent seat. Murthy remained buried in his book and did not even bother to exchange a smile. Usually women, anywhere on earth, are talkative, and the girl broke the ice and struck up a conversation with him. When she got to know that he was from India, which then was much in favour of communism and socialism, the conversation naturally veered towards their countries' various policies. Slowly, they began talking about their personal lives as well. The girl explained her situation.

'I am from Sofia. I was sent on a scholarship by the government to Kiev University to do my PhD. There I met a nice young man from East Berlin. We liked each other and decided to get married.' Saying this much, she sighed.

'What was the matter? Why did you not get married?'

Murthy asked sympathetically.

'We did get married and that was the problem. We applied for permission to marry a citizen of another country to our respective governments. They agreed, except that Bulgaria wanted me to complete the term of my bond in my country and my husband was asked to stay back in East Germany for the same period. The result is I travel to East Germany once in six months while my husband comes to Sofia once in six months. This has become extremely frustrating for both of us. We have lost all hopes of leading a normal married life,' she said.

Murthy was touched by this predicament. He said, 'It is an unfair system. Whether it is a communist or a capitalist country, issues like the choice of partner for marriage, or job, and the freedom of expression should not be curtailed . . .'

All this time, a boy was sitting next to the girl. He had tried talking to her but she had not been interested. Murthy and the girl were conversing in French, and the boy had not been able to understand much of what they were talking. After listening to them for a while, the boy disappeared and came back with two burly, fierce-looking gentlemen. Without uttering a word, one of them caught Murthy by his shirt collar and dragged him on to the platform. The other person took the girl away.

Murthy was locked up in a small, dingy room with hardly any ventilation. There was no furniture or heating and only a crude toilet in one corner. He sat down on the floor in a daze. What had happened? Why was he locked up like a criminal? What had happened to the girl?

Gradually he figured it was the discussion on rights and duties of citizens in a communist country that had upset the boy and the cops.

'What will they do to me now? If something happens to me, will my family ever come to know?' he thought desperately. The very thought of his family in Mysore made him go weak with worry. His father was retired and recently struck by paralysis. He had to help his family in getting his three younger sisters married.

Hours passed by. He was not aware whether it was day or night. His wristwatch had been taken away along with his passport and other possessions. He had not eaten anything in over ninety hours. He could hear several trains come and go. After what seemed like an eternity, the door opened and Murthy was dragged on to the platform, put on a train along with a guard and told that his passport would be returned only after he reached Istanbul.

'What was my offence?' Murthy asked the policeman, holding the door of the compartment.

The stone-faced sergeant said, 'Why did you talk against the State? Who was the girl?'

'She was just a traveller like me . . .'

'Then why did she discuss her personal matters with you?' another sergeant immediately raised his voice, not even allowing Murthy to finish his sentence.

'What is wrong in that?' Murthy protested.

'It is against the rules of our country to discuss such issues', the sergeant replied firmly.

Murthy was curious about the girl's fate, 'What happened to her?'

'It is none of your business. We have checked your passport. It is only because you are from India, which is a friendly country, that we are releasing you. Don't try to do anything smart on the way. Just leave our country without any further mischief,' said the first sergeant, forcing him to get in and slamming the door.

The train started moving.

Murthy was tired. He had not eaten or slept in four days. He managed to sit down at a window seat. He was again on a train but things had changed dramatically. Murthy had enjoyed discussing and arguing passionately about the ideals of Karl Marx, Lenin, Mao and Ho Chi Minh sitting at the beautiful roadside cafés of Paris. They were theoretical discussions done on a full stomach. But now, hungry and overwrought after his brush with a communist state, Murthy had to rethink all his ideals. So this was what it was like to live behind the Iron Curtain! The system dealt with ruthless efficiency even a single voice raised against it. It denied basic freedom to its citizens and treated travellers from friendly countries thus. He shuddered to think what might have happened to him if he were from a capitalist country. Watching the countryside go by, Murthy realized the value of freedom. He also realized that the only way to get rid of poverty was not by raising slogans or issuing diktats, but by creating more and more jobs. He vowed then and there to himself that he would generate wealth not only for himself but for many others, legally and ethically. He would see that India was known through the world not for her poverty but for the skills of her young people—

that would be his contribution towards removing India's problems.

Armed with this new resolve, after returning to India he experimented with various jobs at different companies. He started his own small company Softronics for a while and went on to head the software division at Patni Computer Systems. But his greatest desire was to build an export-focussed company, with his values.

Finally, in 1981 he started Infosys.

The communist Murthy, over a period of time, changed to what he refers to now as a socialist capitalist.

The rest is history.

7

An Officegoer's Dilemma

In the numerous software companies setting up office in Bangalore, the issue of corporate social responsibility is being increasingly taken seriously. I was once invited to speak on this to the employees of one such company. Like most other offices this one too resembled a five star hotel, with its marble and granite floors, chandeliers, paintings on the walls, the housekeepers sweeping and mopping incessantly and an extremely polite front office.

I usually follow my talks with a question-answer session. I consider that the litmus test of how well my talk has been received. I have a theory that if people do not ask questions after the lecture, then it must have been either so good that no one has anything more to say, or so bad that no one has understood a single word and hence is quiet!

This time, when the questions were being asked, I thought I saw Shanti among the audience. When she saw me looking at her she waved. As always, I was happy to see her. I have known Shanti ever since she was a student in my college. She is one of those people who seem to have boundless energy, always ready to talk and exchange views. She was also very conscious of her social responsibilities, and I know had contributed a portion of her salary to charity from the time she started working.

When the talk came to an end and everyone started dispersing, I waited for Shanti to come up to me. 'Hello Shanti, how are you?' I was expecting her usual chirpy answer. Instead, I was greeted with a low, sad reply. I was taken aback. 'Shanti, what is the matter? Did you fight with your husband? Don't worry. If husband and wife do not fight then they cannot be called a couple. It is part of the deal. Come on cheer up.' I joked to ease her tension.

In the same low tone Shanti said, 'No Madam, that is not the reason.'

'Then is your project deadline approaching and you have not completed it? Shanti, I have always told you that in the software industry the deadline needs to be kept in mind and therefore project management is very essential. I still vaguely remember that you had got highest marks in that. Are you not practising what you learnt in college?'

'That is not the problem. I have completed my project a little bit ahead of time.'

'Then what is worrying you?'

But Shanti did not want to talk there, instead she took me to her cabin. As we walked I noticed many other employees wishing her. By the time we reached her cabin I felt proud that my student was now the boss. The cabin was very well furnished and Shanti closed the blinds before settling down to talk. We each had a cup of coffee and slowly she started confiding in me.

'Madam, I am very unhappy in this job. To an outsider

it might appear that I have the perfect job. I get an excellent salary, my timings are flexible and the office is very close to my house. I do not have to put up with the stress of rush-hour traffic. I am leading a very good team where each person is committed to the work. But my problem is my boss. She is terrible. She has nothing but harsh words for me. I have not heard a single positive remark from her in the three years I have spent here. If I do a good job, she says someone else could have done it in half the time, and heaven help me if something ever goes wrong and things get delayed. She refuses to understand that sometimes things happen which are beyond my control.

'Suppose I am travelling to Bombay, she will deliberately schedule a meeting at ten-thirty in the morning, even though she knows my flight is supposed to land only at ten. With the traffic it is impossible for me to reach the office in half an hour. By the time I reach she would have finished all the important discussions. I work so hard, sometimes staying back the entire night to complete my work before the deadline, but still she says, "you could have been better." Madam it is impossible to satisfy her.'

'Calm down Shanti. Maybe your boss is the kind of person who is never satisfied with anything, that is her nature and you cannot change that. You have to accept her the way she is. You cannot choose your boss.'

'I really don't feel like working with such a person. At times I feel like quitting. With my experience it would not be difficult to get a better job, but I like this company, my team members and the work I am doing. Why should I leave just for the sake of one person?'

'Have you told your higher managers about the situation?'

'I did. But she is the key person in a number of projects and they don't want to lose her.'

'Give it some time. Perhaps slowly she will understand you and the hard work you are putting in.'

Offering her such words of comfort I left the office. When I did not hear from her again after that I assumed Shanti had solved her problem one way or the other. A couple of years passed and one day I was in Jayanagar market, in Bangalore, buying vegetables.

Long back, Jayanagar was a paradise for all middle-class people. But now, staying here has become a very costly affair. The prices of almost everything have shot up and bargaining is strictly looked down upon. The vegetable sellers are so confident of getting their exorbitant prices that they usually refuse to budge even if one ventures to argue.

That day, I was debating heatedly with the shopkeeper who was asking for Rs 10 for one cucumber. I was actually enjoying the skill with which the man was putting forth his arguments. Neither of us was willing to yield even a paisa to the other person.

Suddenly I heard a voice behind me, 'Good evening Madam. How are you?'

It was Shanti, holding a baby by one hand and a basket of fruits and vegetables in another. She had put on a little bit of weight but I instantly saw the old sparkle back in her eyes.

'Hello Shanti! When did you have the baby?' I asked.

'A year ago.'

'You are looking so cheerful, I am very happy for you Shanti.'

'Madam, now I am happy both at home and at work.'

'That is wonderful. How is your boss? Has she changed?'

Shanti took me aside and said, 'She finally got transferred to another office in the city. My new boss is fantastic. Now I really look forward to going to office. If we ever have a disagreement he immediately talks to me and clears the issue. He is always motivating us by appreciating the effort we are putting in. As a result we have performed much better than expected. If we ever have to stay back late into the night, he too stays late. The teamwork and camaraderie is wonderful now. When I was pregnant he kept telling me to take it easy and work from home if I wanted to, but I insisted on going to office till the day before I delivered the baby.'

'This is great news Shanti. It reminds me of the song *"Man vahi, darpan vahi, na jane sab kuch naya naya . . ."*

'Oh Madam, you are incorrigible.'

Both of us had a hearty laugh standing there in front of the vegetable stall. Then Shanti said, 'Because of our new boss each person is happy working there and feels proud to be part of the team.'

'Yes Shanti, this is something I have learnt over the years—with good attitude you can create a heaven around you, and a good leader can bring about remarkable changes in a team.'

8

THE DESERVING CANDIDATE

A few years back, I was on a selection committee. We were recruiting people for various posts, most of which had a high remuneration. As a result, there was a lot of pressure on us four committee members.

Overnight, I found my popularity had increased many times over. Forgotten relatives dropped by at my house, friends I had lost touch with appeared out of the blue. Religious heads started telling me how important it was to help people from one's community. Ex-students suddenly remembered when Teachers' Day came and sent me cards. Even in the temple I started getting extra helpings of prasad. I was beginning to enjoy the newfound comforts of life!

Unfortunately for these people all four committee members were very honest and we had decided on the day of our first meeting that we would not entertain any requests. Recruitment would be done based solely on merit.

During one of our interview sessions one day, a young girl walked in. Her name was Nandita and she was good looking, smart and well dressed. We asked our first standard question: why do you think you are suitable for this job? The girl replied, 'I have a great deal of confidence. I can handle the pressures of this job well.'

She was speaking with an American accent, so I asked her where she was from. 'I am from Bangalore,' she replied, 'But most of my relatives stay in the US so I go there during all my holidays.'

'Where have you been in the US? We have many clients there.'

'My uncle Ramakrishnan is a very famous Silicon Valley industrialist. My aunt is a correspondent for *New York Times*. My cousin Rohit works in the White House. So I shuttle between New York, Washington and San Francisco.'

'In our work one is required to interact with different kinds of people often.'

'Oh meeting people and talking to them is not a problem, I enjoy that.'

'Have you any experience of that?'

'Yes. I party a lot and meet lots of people.'

'That is not the same as meeting people on business,' I said and we moved on to the technical questions. She answered adequately well and we finished the interview soon after. As she was leaving, Nandita hesitated near the door. Then she turned and asked, 'Can I ask you something?' I always like it when girls ask questions. For too long the definition of a good girl in our society is one who does not question too much and meekly accepts everything. But I like those who dare to break out of this mould and speak their minds. So I told Nandita to go ahead.

She said, 'The salary you are offering for this job is quite less.' I was taken aback. This was not the kind of question or remark I was expecting. I answered, 'It is very good when you compare it with other companies.'

'Oh it is just enough to pay the rent for an apartment and a driver and cook's salary. I am used to these comforts you see.'

'But you said you live with your parents. The company has a bus and we have an excellent canteen.'

'After I start earning I want to live on my own. That is what everyone does nowadays.' And with these words and a pitiful look at me for my ignorance, she left.

As usual I reached home late that evening. My mother admonished me saying, 'You should have remembered that we have to go to Sharayu's granddaughter's birthday. She has already called thrice. Even if it is late go and say a hello. You have to live in society and can't remain engrossed in your work always.'

Like an obedient child I went to Sharayu's house. The usual kind of party was going on. Men were talking about politics and sports. Women were discussing the next party, and since there was an event manager, the children were busy. It was a hot day and trays of cool drinks were doing the rounds. Suddenly I thought I saw a girl who looked a lot like Nandita. She was wearing a sari and was serving drinks to the guests. When I tried looking at her closely she turned away and avoided my eyes.

I was amazed. I went to Sharayu and asked who the pretty girl serving the drinks was. 'Oh that is Nandita. She is a smart and bright girl. Her father owns a canteen in my husband's office. Our office has sponsored her education. She has completed her engineering recently and is searching for a job. She is a quick learner and adjusts well with everybody. We have invited her to help out today. If you are ever having a party, I would strongly recommend asking her father to do the catering.'

I was speechless.

The interviews carried on for the whole of that week. The last candidate to walk in was a boy in his early twenties. He was ordinarily dressed and seemed to be on the quieter side. His answers were all up to the mark and well thought out. I wanted to know more about him as it is always interesting to talk to bright young minds.

'You answered the questions about computer science very well. Since when have you been interested in the area?' Shyly, he said, 'When I was very young.'

'What age?' I was persistent.

'Probably about eight years.'

'Why so early?'

'My mother is a school teacher and often I was alone at home when she was away at work. The best way to pass the time was to attend some classes.'

Somehow I knew that could not be the only reason. He was obviously very bright and his mother must have spent a lot of time channelising his talents in the right direction. I realized this boy will not boast about his background, but I wanted to know more. 'What about your father? What does he do?'

The boy thought for some time. Then he replied, 'Does it matter? You need only look at my capabilities. If you find me suitable please accept me, or reject me if you don't.'

'How much salary are you expecting?'

The boy said a figure which was higher than what we were offering.

'How do you justify such a high salary for your experience?'

'I will justify it by working hard and taking bottomline responsibility. I will ensure that my work is of the highest standards.'

'Do you mind telling me why you want a higher salary?'

'I want to donate a part of it to a trust which helps bright students continue their education if they can't pay the fees.'

I was touched by his answer. After this there was nothing more to ask. When the boy left we were unanimous that we wanted to take him. As we were talking, the clerk who was handing out the travel allowance to those who had come from out of town for the interview, walked in. He said, 'Could you sign for the last candidate? He did not claim his allowance. He said he stayed with his aunt and came to town on some personal work too.'

Now I was amazed at the boy's honesty. I looked closely at his form and at the permanent address. He was the son of a very successful doctor. Obviously money or fame had not robbed him of his honesty and simplicity.

9

THE BUSINESS OF PHILANTHROPY

Sri Hiralal Jain was a successful pharmacist and businessman. He was kind-hearted, unassuming and shy. He had started his career in a pharmaceutical company and had gone on to build his own empire through hard work and honesty.

One day, he came to meet me. We talked about our various projects and initiatives for some time, then he started talking about himself. 'Mrs Murty, God has been exceedingly kind to me. My company is doing well and we are able to launch new products regularly. As a result we have a large range. I have only one son who is studying abroad. I am sure he will complete his studies, join my work and make it even more successful. I am always busy with work and travel and now I feel I have made enough money to last another generation. But there is one gap. I feel I have not done enough to give back to society in any big way. That is why I have come here today with a request.'

I was still not sure where the conversation was leading, and asked him to go on.

'I have learnt a lot about your work with the Infosys Foundation. You help people in the villages and slums. So I want to give you some basic medicines that you can distribute to the poor people. You can appoint a doctor to help you with your work in slums, I will pay his salary and also provide the medicines free.'

I was touched. I said, 'Your proposal is wonderful but we already have some doctors who work part-time on our projects. I will talk to them and tell them to make a list of the medicines they require. I will send you that list every month and come and collect the medicines at an appointed time from your office.'

'No, no, you need not come. I will send them to you. But I have one condition.'

I was worried. I should have known. No one gives a free lunch!

Hiralal Jain said, 'Nobody must come to know of my association with this work. I don't want my name or my company's name to appear anywhere. I want to savour the joy of giving without the publicity. I will remain an unknown donor.'

This was a most unusual request. Normally, most of the people who come with donations are already planning their media statements. They may give the smallest sums of money, but hearing them talk it would seem that they had funded our entire operations.

I agreed readily to his proposal. And so it was decided that every month his head clerk Karim would come with a box of the required medicines. His delivery van came near our office to some retail outlets and our supply would come in that.

I thanked Hiralal Jain and sent up a prayer that 'May his tribe increase'.

So the system fell into place. Initially Hiralal donated Rs 10,000 worth of medicines, which slowly went up to Rs 50,000. He gave us his old Fiat car so the doctors could visit the slums in ease. But we hardly met. Whenever I called him to thank him he would tell me not to waste my time. When I sent him pictures of our medical camps he would call me and say he did not require proof of our work. He had faith in us.

Years went by. Our work got more and more attention and many people started coming up and offering help. One pharmacy store offered to give us as much medicines we wanted every month. But I was reluctant to close the relationship with Hiralal Jain.

One morning I got the news that he had passed away in his sleep. I prayed in silence. A pious soul like that had to go with minimum of fuss and suffering. I went to his office to pay my last respects. Ironically, I realized it was my first visit to his office in so many years. It was simple and decorated spartanly. I noticed a young handsome man in white with red, swollen eyes. The head clerk Karim whispered to me, 'That is Saket Saab. He has just returned from the US.'

I gathered Saket had studied for his MBA in the US and was working there for some years. Now he would come back and take over the business.

Days passed and for two months the old system with Hiralal's company continued. The medicine parcels reached us on time. The third month there was no sign of it. I thought I would wait for a few days and then call. When there was still no sign I dialled Hiralal's office number. A polite voice answered from the other side. I assumed it was the receptionist and wondered what had happened to Karim. I was made to hold the line for some time. Then finally I was told, 'Saket would like to meet you at his office tomorrow morning at nine.'

Since he was the donor it was my duty to respect his wishes. I reached at 8.45 and was taken aback at the changes. Gone was the old spartan look. This was a modern corporate house with a pretty receptionist, fresh flowers in vases, framed paintings on the walls. There was a leather sofa set and the floor was now gleaming granite. A young lady ushered me to an antechamber and offered me some drinks. There was a huge portrait of Hiralal Jain in the hallway. Soon it was nearing nine o'clock, and I started making my way to Saket's office. But I was stopped by the receptionist. 'I am sorry, Saket sir is talking to a business executive and this may take ten more minutes. Please wait.' So I waited. When it was 9.45, I decided it was enough and told her I was leaving. She spoke on the intercom and showed me in finally. When I entered I saw the business executive was still there. Saket looked at him apologetically and excused himself for five minutes. Then he turned to me and came straight to the point.

'I have been going through our old records. My father gave you enormous amounts of money anonymously. I think that was a mistake and a waste of money. I am willing to continue our association but on some new terms. Our company's and my name should appear prominently whenever you hold a camp. You must send someone to pick up the medicines every month. I can give you supplies only from our surplus stock and not what you want. You must address our employees once a year and talk about our donation. After all, philanthropy is key to business promotion.'

By this time, five minutes were over and I got up. Politely I said, 'Thank you but I cannot agree. I cannot find surplus diseases to suit your surplus medicines. I wanted to thank you for the support your father gave us over the years. The conditions were of his choice and we respected that. Now that our association is ending I just want to say, don't mix business and philanthropy. You will not be able to do justice to either. Your father understood that. Perhaps one day you will too.'

I left the office and in the hallway stood and looked at Hiralal Jain's photo for a minute. Silently I said a final goodbye and stepped out.

10

A HELPING HAND

Like many natural disasters of great magnitude, the tsunami waves that struck the shores of our country in December 2004, opened our eyes to the myriad shades of human nature. Through the media, we saw and heard time and again about the devastation wreaked on coastal communities and how aid was pouring in from everywhere. In places which were in the news, the victims were soon inundated by a wave of relief material—saris, dhotis, towels, bed sheets, cooking stoves, vessels, plastic buckets, drinking water, mats, etc. In towns like Nagapattinam, Kadalur, Velankani and Karaikal, one could also see heaps of old and worn-out clothes which no one wanted, lying untouched on either sides of the road.

The relief camps and wedding halls in these places had plenty of volunteers initially, distributing food or ration, giving injections to stop the spread of diseases and helping the injured. Often the victims expressed their dissatisfaction at the food being served as local food habits were being overlooked. Instead they demanded to be allowed to cook their own food. The donor and the benefactor were right in their own ways in this matter.

Our team from the foundation set out first on a fact-finding mission before starting the relief work. For one, we decided to visit the towns in the news later, after they had moved away from the airwaves and the first rush of volunteers had departed. Meanwhile, we went to the smaller, lesser known villages and made a list of the essential articles needed by the people. We discovered that in some towns there was plenty of relief material, but the people had no place to store them and incidents of theft or fights over ownership were becoming common. In other places we realized that the most basic material required for the people to get their lives back together were missing.

Armed with this data we devised the 'tsunami survival kit'. It was a bit like the survival kits I had seen in some stores in the USA, though those were meant for mountaineering accidents. We made some modifications and started assembling our own kit: a huge aluminium trunk with a five-level lock and twenty-five articles that we found were essential for the survivors. While the trunk itself could be used for storage, inside we included things like a tarpaulin, medicines, torch, a small radio, groceries, toiletries, etc. It was a novel idea and our team worked tirelessly in gathering everything.

We purchased most of the items from the source, and the moment the suppliers heard it was for relief work they offered us large discounts and even delivered the material free.

Given the scale of our work, we needed a large area to spread out all the items, assemble the kits and to check if we had put in everything in all the trunks. There were ten of us working on this. My student George Joseph offered us the use of the huge basement of his bungalow, somewhere in the outskirts of Bangalore. We got all the material delivered straight to the basement and started our work in earnest. I was amazed at my team's dedication and professionalism. They assembled nearly a thousand trunks in two days. George too visited us often to ask if we needed anything and made provisions for snacks and tea. The whole process was going smoothly and soon we were ready to start loading the trunks on to the trucks. Now we had a problem. It was difficult to do the loading from our basement workplace and we felt it would be better if we could store them together in a place accessible to a truck. George, as usual, had a solution to our problem. 'Don't worry,' he told me. 'The adjacent plot is empty and I know the owner. The architect comes there once in a while, but if we take permission from his office I am sure they will not have a problem with us storing the trunks there for one night. Nobody will say no to such work.'

The plot was big and a corner one and therefore most convenient for loading the material. We all thought it was a good idea.

The next day, a bright young lady arrived at our basement. Beaming, she introduced herself as a junior architect in the architect's office. 'Lankesh, our main architect is out of station. I came to know through George that you would like to store the trunks on this site. I think it is a nice idea. Not all of us are able to go and help the victims but this way we can do our small bit for them.'

'Thank you. But I hope it will not hinder your work!' I replied.

'No Madam, not at all. Anyway the survey people are coming next week. Please do not hesitate to ask us for any help.'

By the time our work was completed and we shifted everything to the neighbouring plot, it was almost evening. The truck was supposed to come the next morning and all our volunteers were just waiting to go home and rest. They had worked very hard and I felt proud of them. I have learnt that it is better to have ten people who work sincerely than to have hundred people working halfheartedly. I was lucky that all my team members were so hardworking.

Just as we were about to leave a Mercedes drew up in front of us and a man emerged from it, prominently bearing his cellphone and blackberry. He looked smart and was well dressed, but the expression on his face clearly showed his displeasure over some matter.

He approached me and without a word of greeting demanded, 'Who gave you the permission to store your stuff on this plot?'

I realized this was Lankesh, the main architect.

As politely as I could, I answered, 'George told me that he would talk to you and take permission from your office. Yesterday your assistant came and said it was all right. So, I assumed that you were aware of it.'

'No. That is not true. I was travelling and nobody has informed me about this. You may be doing relief work but please understand that you have put your material here without my permission. You should have taken my permission and not my assistant's. I am the architect, and this entire area is my responsibility.'

Surprised at his outburst I said, 'I am sorry for the mistake. Anyway it is a matter of another ten hours. Tomorrow morning the trucks will come and we will load everything on to them.'

'It does not concern me whether it is a matter of a night or a day. I had called the survey people to do their job today. They will come any time. I want you to remove everything.'

'Your assistant told me that they will come only next week. How can I possibly remove so many heavy trunks in such a short time and where can we keep them?' I pleaded.

'I do not know. It is not my problem. Perhaps you can pile them on the roadside. You have not taken my permission. If you had told me earlier, I would have made some space for you.' The man would not budge from his position.

By this time I realized that it was not a matter of us taking permission. He only wanted to show off his power to us. I have met many such people in my work and I knew the futility of arguing with him. But my team members were all young and, by now, boiling over with anger at the man's impudence. They started arguing with him but I stopped them.

'Sorry. I will shift these trunks right now and keep them on the road. We will vacate your plot at the earliest. It means a lot of extra work for us but that is the penalty we will have to pay for incurring your displeasure.'

'Ma'am, if you keep the trunks on the roadside, they

may be stolen or somebody may raise further objections,' Kumar, one of the volunteers, raised his voice in panic.

I smiled and said, 'Don't worry. We will put our banner there and no thief will touch the material. I am sure none of the other neighbours will complain when they know for whom they are meant.'

And it happened just like that. The trunks were kept on the roadside that night and loaded on to the truck the next morning without a hitch. After the trucks left, Kumar came to my office. He was looking dejected and for a while sat with a thoughtful look on his face. Then he said, 'Ma'am, we don't know the victims, they are not related to us in any way. Some of us don't even speak their language. We are doing this only because we want to help in some way. Why can't people understand this? The architect was so rude to you yesterday. Did you not get perturbed? You said you meet people like him often in your work. Tell me Ma'am, why should we do this work if we don't get anything in return except harsh words?'

Just then there was a knock on my door and the security guard I had seen on the plot where we had initially kept the trunks came into the room. I was taken aback and wondered why he had come to my office now that the whole episode was over.

He said, 'Madam, what Lankesh sir did yesterday was wrong. But I am only a poor employee, I could not stand up to him then. After you left yesterday I finished my duty and spent the night guarding the trunks. I did not take your permission for that but I had seen the care with which you had assembled them and how tirelessly you had worked. I too want to do my bit for the people. I don't have much savings so I wanted to give you my one day's salary. Please use it however you think is best.' With these words, he handed me a soiled and sealed envelope and took his leave. I opened it and out dropped a cheque for Rs 160.

I looked at it for some time, then I turned to Kumar and said, 'This cheque is worth Rs 16 lakh to me. You asked why we should continue working? It is for people like these, who open their hearts and put their faith in us.'

11

TRUE SHADES OF NATURE

Working in a disaster relief area opens ones eyes not only to the suffering of the people affected, but also brings out the true character in many people. When the tsunami hit our shores, while most people responded with bravery and generosity, there were plenty of stories of people using it as a publicity gimmick to further their own agendas.

Soon after the rehabilitation work started, it was clear that a massive amount of money was required. Funds started pouring in and almost everyone was seen to be busy with fundraising. Among them happened to be my friend Rekha. Now Rekha is a good person, but talking to her for too long gives me a headache because she refuses to ever come to the point. She lives alone in Bangalore as her husband is in Dubai and daughter is settled in Delhi. She has a lot of energy and often does not know what to do with it!

One day, when I was busy supervising our tsunami relief work in Bangalore, she landed up in my office and started chatting about the effects of the waves. The description carried on for some time, till I got tired and said, 'Yes Rekha I know. I have just spent a few weeks in these areas and have seen for myself the extent of devastation. Did you have some work with me? I am busy with coordinating our relief programme.'

Then she came to the point.

'You know, in the area where I live, there is a youth club. The boys and girls from that club went from door to door collecting money for the victims. They are very keen to hand over the money to you. Will you come and accept it? It would encourage them to do more such work.'

I was happy to hear about this and agreed to go there. After all youngsters need to be appreciated when they take initiative and do such work. But Rekha was still sitting looking hesitant. Finally she said, 'Sudha, the children have ended up spending money from their pockets, going all over the area on their bikes and mopeds . . .'

Immediately I replied, 'In that case Rekha, tell them to deduct that expenditure from the collection before handing it over to me.' Rekha left my office looking happy.

I reached the locality on the appointed day. I was astonished to see that elaborate arrangements had been made for a full-fledged function. There was a well-decorated dais and marquee. A sound system was in place and even the media had been invited. Coffee and biscuits were being served from a table placed in one corner of the field. Soon the function started. There were plenty of people willing to talk and for a long time each person spoke about the tsunami, the devastation, why it had happened etc. People who had never visited the areas tried to speak knowledgeably about the plight of the victims.

Finally, Rekha, who was moderating, handed over a beautifully decorated purse to me. A gang of young people came onto the dais and proceeded to garland me. A mike was thrust at me and I spoke a few words of appreciation and encouragement. Finally it was over and I made my way back to my car. Already, in my mind, I was planning the things I could buy with the contribution. Some milk powder, tarpaulin or fishing nets? I thought it was wonderful how they had collected so much money and handed it over to me out of sheer trust. With such thoughts still on my mind, I opened the purse.

Two pages fell out first. I looked closely and realized it was the expenditure list. There were amounts marked against marquee, video and photo coverage, sound system, flowers, decoration, taxi hire etc. They had collected Rs 10,295 and had spent Rs 10,285. A brand new ten-rupee note fell into my hands from between the pages. That was their final contribution to the relief work!

The next morning there was a photo in the paper of a beaming Rekha handing over the purse to me. I looked at it and added Rs 10 against her name in our list of contributors!

* * *

It is of course not always true that the donors work with their own agendas. Sometimes the beneficiaries too pose problems.

When disaster strikes an area, I have seen that often the actual population of that area almost doubles. Beggars and other people from the surrounding and even far-off places start pouring in, hoping to win some easy bread by joining the refugee camps and standing in the ration queues. When the relief agencies don't coordinate their material well, they end up giving away surplus material to the victims, who then sell it to others. In fact, I have come to realize that our country does not lack relief agencies and donors. What we lack is an efficient system of disbursal.

So at the foundation, we have devised a system. When we take up any relief work, we first do a survey of the area, talk to people and study the depth and nature of the damage. Then we go with only the material that is essential. Before we start disbursing that we make a list of all the people in the area and hand out coupons. The material is handed over when they present the coupons to us at the camp. This way we are sure that the aid reaches the right people and bogus 'victims' cannot take advantage. The system is tedious and time-consuming but we are assured that we are helping the right people.

During our tsunami relief work, we went once to a village where we initially had a meeting with the villagers to discuss their requirements. The next day we came with our material and the queue started forming. Soon we realized we had a problem on our hands. Many people were demanding extra materials and some others were returning time and again for further helpings. We had taken about 15 per cent more than the amount our list indicated but at this rate we would have needed 100 per cent extra.

While I was trying to talk to some people and tell them that things were going wrong, a middle-aged man spoke up from the crowd. 'Yes there are some extra people here today. They too need these things. You are not doing us a favour by giving us all this. They were given to you by other people to hand over to us. It is all ours anyway. And you people come here only because you want some fame saying you have done work. You are doing this for your selfish reasons. Getting all this material is our right and we shall decide how much we want, not you. If you cannot give us, go away. We won't accept anything.'

Many volunteers were very upset to hear this. Some had taken leave without pay to stay in these areas and do the work because they wanted to help. Arguments began and voices started getting raised. But with age I have learnt patience and realized something had to be done before a full-fledged fight broke out.

As calmly as possible I said, 'When we came to your village yesterday you said there are 200 families here. Each one wrote the family's name and number of members. You agreed yesterday that you needed material only for these 200 families. To be on the safer side we have got enough for 230 families. Now you are saying people have come from outside and they too should be given a share. This is a disaster area. We are not entertaining guests and relatives. You have to survive. We cannot do magic and create extra material. If you feel we are helping you out of selfishness, is it not better that we are selfish in this manner rather than hoarding things for ourselves? Please don't try to threaten us. Remember if someone is helping you today, you can be grateful and help someone else in need another time. Today people are queuing up to help you, but after a month the world will forget. If you burn your bridges now you will pay a heavy price. Your behaviour today will determine how the world behaves towards you later.'

The man had no answer. He bowed his head in shame.

12

MADE IN HEAVEN

A t the end of each semester, when the coursework is complete, I do not allow my students to sit and study in the library. Instead, every few days I arrange a debate in the classroom on some topic, where each person has to say something. I do this in order to hone their communication, especially verbal, skills. We all look forward to these debates, which sometimes become so strong and emotional that I have to jump into the fray and remind everyone that it is merely a classroom discussion.

Once, the subject was marriage. The students were discussing various issues that arise during a wedding, like the expenses incurred for the ceremony, the advantages and disadvantages of arranged marriages, how well the two people need to know one another before taking the step, and so on. Some of them said, 'A wedding has always been looked upon as a social occasion in our country. If the families can afford it, why shouldn't they spend as much money as they desire on the preparations and meet other people.' Others said, 'The amount of money spent at a wedding has become a status symbol. It has become a place for exchanging gossip. Parents end up spending their life savings in these ceremonies.' One of them, Sunitha, elaborated further, 'In our country, most bonded labourers have got into a debt trap because of high marriage expenditures. These lavish weddings should be banned.'

I stepped in at this point and told them gently that the expense and the ceremonies don't determine the success of the marriage. Rather, it is the understanding that needs to develop between husband and wife. To prove this, I told them the story of the most successful marriage I have seen so far in my life—that of Yellamma and Madha.

I met them when I happened to be spending a night at a tiny village in the course of my work. I had had a wonderful meal and was enjoying an after-dinner stroll around the village. It was a full-moon night and the quiet and serenity were most welcome to my ears: no noises of phones ringing, cars honking, aeroplanes roaring overhead. Instead leaves on the trees were rustling gently in the breeze, a bird or a dog was calling out now and then into the dark night, which was lit only by the moonlight. Gowramma, the local lady accompanying me, was talking as she walked with me, describing the village's problems of drinking water, procuring pesticides and lack of medical facilities. We were walking towards the large banyan tree, the heart of the village, when I heard someone singing a folk song. I was struck by the beauty and soulfulness of the rendition and asked Gowramma about the singer. She said it must be Madha singing for his wife Yellamma. I immediately asked if I could visit them and we walked to their hut.

Madha and Yellamma were perhaps the poorest people in that village. They had to beg for their meals every day. Yellamma was quite sick and when I reached their hut, she was lying down, while Madha was massaging her feet and singing. It was a rare but touching sight. We started chatting with them, and I asked candidly, 'What problems do you face in this village?'

Yellamma replied, 'We don't have any problems. We do everything together, dividing the work between us. We usually ask each other's opinion. We always tell what is on our minds and if one is wrong the other does not hesitate to correct. If I cannot go out, Madha fetches alms for both of us. We believe that in this journey of life, we should be together in everything. Whether it is some special alms or only a pot of water, we share whatever we earn. We spend the day begging in different parts of the village but are always glad to be with each other at night. We trust each other and are happy with our lives, full of hardships though it is.'

Standing there in front of their ramshackle hut under the bright moonlight, I realized I was listening to great words of wisdom. Yellamma and Madha were the poorest of the poor, uneducated, and had faced great adversities in life, but they had learnt the most valuable lesson: how to live happily with one's partner.

In our society now, marriage is often treated as a security measure, and wedding ceremonies as social events where the status of the couple is on display. It is rare to come across a couple who understand that they are on a journey together, sharing their joys and sorrows. For

Yellamma and Madha marriage was a partnership, not a burden or an object to be flaunted.

13

THE GRATEFUL TENANT

It was a Sunday morning and for once I was eager to attend a function. It is not something I normally look forward to, but this one was special; it was the housewarming ceremony of my friends Ramesh and Sheela's new house.

Ramesh is a professor and Sheela works in a bank. They earn well enough but most of it goes in looking after their large family. In fact, I knew Ramesh had had to spend a large amount on his sister's wedding a few years back. Given this situation, and the fact that with land prices shooting up in Bangalore, it has become difficult for an honest salaried person to buy a house, I knew my friends were very proud and happy to have been able to do so. I too was keen to meet them and be a part of their happiness.

The house was at a new layout in the outskirts of Bangalore. It was simply built and just right for a family of their size. I could see the satisfaction on Ramesh and Sheela's faces. Many of our old friends had also come and we spent a lot of time chatting. We had lunch together and time seemed to fly, there was no time to feel tired or bored. Right after finishing lunch, we were sitting on some chairs laid out in the shade outside the house, and waiting for the paan to arrive. Someone had gone to the nearest market to get it and we knew it would take a while for him to return. We were talking of this and that and I was looking at the house, when I noticed a plaque attached next to the gate. It had the name of the house, Shyamkamal, engraved on polished black granite.

In my experience, people name their houses after their own or children's names. Or it is named after the family deity, like Venkateshwara Nilaya or Raghavendra Prasad or Beereshwara Krupa, etc. Of late more exotic names like Love Nest, Paradise, Seventh Heaven and Sukha Villa, Aishwarya Villa, etc. have been added to the list. (Of course here 'villa' is the French word for 'house' and not the Kannada word meaning 'no'!) Some people with an artistic or literary bent of mind name their houses Megha Dhoot, Nadaswara, Varshini, etc.

But Shyamkamal was not fitting into any of these categories. So I asked, 'Sheela, why is your house called Shyamkamal? I have only heard of the movie *Neelkamal*!'

Sheela and Ramesh exchanged a look. Ramesh said, 'It is a combination of the names of the two people who changed our lives, and the ones we remember and thank each day.'

'What do you mean by that? Who are they?' I asked.

I had known Ramesh and Sheela for many years. His father Madappa was from a village near Dharwad in north Karnataka and Sheela's family was distantly related to Ramesh's. We had been friends from childhood and would go to school and play together. We often ate our meals together and knew each other's relatives quite well. I was quite sure I had never heard of or met anyone called Shyama-Kamal among their relatives.

Ramesh explained, 'Shyamkamal stands for Shyama Rao and Kamala. Do you remember when I was in college in Dharwad, I used to stay with an old couple?'

I thought back to those days of long ago. Of course I remembered. With age, I have discovered it is easier to remember the events of the distant past rather than what happened earlier in the day. In Dharwad, there was an old couple who used to rent their outhouse to college students. Ramesh must have stayed there for six years. But I was still puzzled. Why would he want to name his house after the couple who were after all only his landlords. Ramesh noticed the mystified look on my face, and explained, 'You may not know, Sudha, but those days my family was much against my going to Dharwad for higher studies. They wanted me to stay back in the village and look after the fields. At that time, Shyama Rao supported me wholeheartedly in my decision to study in a bigger town. He was a retired postmaster and my father's friend, and he convinced my father to send me to Dharwad with promises of looking after me. He became more important than my father to me. He gave me a place to stay. My meals used to come from my village in the state government bus every day, but if ever the bus did not come, or I could not go to the bus stand for some reason, his wife, Kamala Bai would share their meal with me. She did not let me go hungry for a single day. And you know how hard up we were, so if I got late in depositing my college fees, Shyama Rao would put aside some money from his meagre pension and help me out.'

'But you used to run errands for them and do odd jobs around their house. In fact we used to call you their Man Friday behind your back,' said Raghav, Ramesh's roommate.

'I won't agree with you Raghav. Think of the old couple. They had no need to do all those things for me. They were not rich but they went out of their way to help me out of my difficulties. Without their help, I do not know where and what I would have been today. I will never forget their generosity. Even after I finished college and was unemployed and despairing, I remember Shyama Rao would speak encouraging words to me and lift my spirits. "Don't feel bad. So what if you have lost the battle, you will win the war", is something he told me often.'

'But why did you name this house after them?' I went back to my first question.

'It was my father's suggestion. You see, he brought me up, his son, because it was his duty, the way I am doing everything possible to bring up my children. But there are some people who do things out of affection, and not duty, and they change your life with their love and generosity. My father said this house should be named after the people who played such an important part in my education. This is a story that my children need to know. I also want them to understand the gratitude I feel towards Shyama Rao and Kamala Bai not through mere words but by my actions.'

Ramesh and his father's gesture moved me immensely.

They reminded me of Dr BR Ambedkar, who decided to call himself Ambedkar after his teacher. It is people like them who reaffirm our faith in humanity and the culture of this ancient country.

14

A FOREIGNER, ALWAYS

Gautam Buddha was born 2,500 years ago as Prince Siddharth in Lumbini, in present-day Nepal. Throughout his lifetime he crisscrossed the subcontinent spreading his message of peace, tolerance and the righteous path. Shravasthi, Rajagraha, Sarnath, Boddh Gaya, Kushinagar are some of the places he visited and which became important centres of Buddhism. Though he imparted most of his teachings in India, in the ensuing centuries, Buddhism spread all over the world. Today, Sri Lanka, Japan, Korea, Thailand are some countries where Buddhism is flourishing. And in the Indian subcontinent too, there are places which retain strong links with Buddhist history.

Nearly twenty-five kilometers from Islamabad, there is a sleepy town called Takshila. At one time, it was the site of the world's oldest university, and an important centre of Buddhist learning. King Ashoka, the great patron of Buddhism, built many viharas here where scholars discussed philosophy and religion for centuries. Hiuen Tsang described the glory and beauty of Takshila in his writings.

Now, all that remains of that bustling university are

the ruins. The Pakistan government has converted part of it into a museum, where one can see splendid works of art including heads of Buddha statues which have been excavated, jewels and panels depicting the life of Buddha. For anyone interested in Buddhism and its history, this museum is a place that has to be seen.

Recently I visited Pakistan for the first time. Though I was there on some other work, I had decided long back that if ever I got the chance to visit Pakistan, I would go to Takshila. I landed in Islamabad with many of the usual preconceived notions about the country in my mind. But soon I saw that women were moving about freely and not always in burqas! The sumptuous meal of channa bhatura, alu paratha and jalebi that our host had prepared for us made us feel more at home. I spent some time shopping for clothes and again, the bazaars and shops were not too different from ours, and we ended up buying the latest bargains. Our taxi driver was humming what turned out to be the latest Hindi film number when I heard him closely. And like in our country, there was a delay in the flight I was to take. So it was not surprising that I found myself feeling quite comfortable.

The next day, I set off for Takshila with a French group. We got a bit delayed in reaching the museum and the curator, perhaps guessing our keen desire to see the exhibits said, 'It is nearing closing time. Why don't you all go in and start looking around, I will explain everything. Your tour organizer can get your tickets meanwhile from the counter.' This seemed like a good idea to all of us and we were soon absorbed in looking at the wonderful articles on display. For me it was additionally moving as I was fulfilling a long-cherished desire. I was seeing parts of our history which I had only read about in books come alive. After a detailed tour, the curator led us outside. There, for the first time, I noticed the ticket window. The rates were Rs 200 for foreigners and Rs 25 for locals. When the organizer handed me my ticket counterfoil I realized I was holding one for Rs 200. Thinking there had been some mistake I went up to the man at the ticket window. 'I understand your reasons for charging more from foreigners as you need all the funds you can get for the upkeep of the museum,' I said. 'But why are you charging me Rs 200? I am from India. This place is as much a part of my heritage as yours.'

The man looked unmoved. In a firm voice he replied, 'You are an Indian and therefore a foreigner.'

The words struck me deeply. I realized, in spite of the similarities in our dress, language, food and even love for Bollywood movies, Partition had divided us forever. It had made us strangers in each other's lands and even in a place like that ancient university town, the Buddha's words of love and tolerance were not enough to bring us together. The Rs 200 ticket brought me crashing back to reality!

15

The Line of Separation

During my trip to Pakistan, I was part of a large group. Each person in the group was keen to visit one place or the other in that country. Some wanted to see Takshila, others Lahore, Islamabad or Karachi. One day, we were having a discussion about this and everyone was voicing his opinion loudly. I noticed only Mrs Roopa Kapoor was sitting quietly. She was a seventy-five-year-old lady from Chennai and did not speak much unless spoken to. So I asked if there was any place she wanted to visit.

Without any hesitation, she said, 'I have to visit Pindi.'

'Where is Pindi? Is it some small town or village? I don't think we will have the time to make a detour like that from our packed itinerary.' Roopa smiled at my ignorance and said, 'I meant Rawalpindi. It is called Pindi for short by those who stay there.' I was intrigued. 'How do you know? Have you ever stayed there?'

'I was born and brought up there,' she replied, and then slowly she told me the story of her life.

She had stayed in Rawalpindi till the age of nineteen, when she got married and settled down in Chennai. Now Chennai was her home and she could speak Tamil and make excellent Tamil dishes like puliyogare and rasam, as well as any natural-born Tamilian. But she had always yearned to come back and see her childhood home if she ever got the chance.

Soon we reached Islamabad and I was surprised to find it surrounded by mountains, as cool as a hill station. Roopa saw my surprise and said, 'Islamabad is a new city. Rawalpindi is a sister city, but it is older. Islamabad was built after the Partition with wide roads, shopping centres and rose gardens. Pindi is only twenty odd kilometers away from Islamabad.' By now the soft-spoken, introverted Mrs Kapoor had become quite garrulous. There was a spark in her eyes and she spoke non-stop. Many of us wanted to see Islamabad first, but she insisted on going on to Rawalpindi.

She needed a companion for the trip and I volunteered to go with her. She was now quite excited, and told me, 'I want to see the house I left fifty-seven years ago.'

'That's a good idea,' I said. Then I remembered the lovely bouquet of flowers I had been presented on landing at Islamabad which I was still carrying. 'I will present this to whoever is staying in your house now.'

She was touched.

As the car left Islamabad airport behind, Mrs Kapoor started pointing out the sights to me like a tour guide. She showed an old building on the left side of the road in a crowded area and said, 'That used to be an electrical goods manufacturing factory. Its owner Kewal Ram Sahani was my father's friend. My friends and I would come to this house for Lakshmi pooja during Diwali.'

I told the driver to slow down a little so that she could

cherish the journey. The car passed Sadar Bazar and looking at an old building with many shops, she said, 'Here my father's cousin Ratan Sethi owned a jewellery shop along with his partner Maqbool Khan. It was known as Khan and Sethi. My wedding jewellery was made here.'

She continued pointing out various buildings, each holding some fond memory for her. But many a times the buildings she was looking for had changed to new skyscrapers and she got disoriented. Suddenly the car stopped. A tyre was punctured, and the driver said it would take him a while to fix it. Roopa Kapoor was restless. She did not want to wait even a minute more than required. So she said, 'You change the tyre. In the meantime I will go and visit some of the old places. We will join you in the next main road. To go to the main road, you take a left turn and the first right turn. You wait for us there.'

She behaved as if she knew every inch of that area and I followed her quietly. We walked into a small lane. She explained, 'I have been here many times with my friends Fatima and Noor. This used to be known as Tailor's Road. My neighbour Mehboob Khan's wife Mehrunnisa Chachi was an expert in designing new embroidery patterns. We used to come and give the designs. Come we will take a short cut . . . that is where my uncle lived.'

By now she was talking more to herself and making her way with ease through the narrow lanes. We went to the next road. There were old houses on the road and she went into the first huge bungalow. She said, 'This was my uncle Motiram Rai's house and the next house was that of Allah Baksh. They were great friends and loved each other. I still remember whenever Allah Baksh Chacha planted a tree in his house, my uncle would plant the same. This mango tree here was planted on a Basant Panchami day. There was so much of joy in both houses. My grandmother prepared kheer and sent me to Allah Baksh's house with a jug full of it. While I was carrying that jug, I bumped into a young man and the hot kheer fell on his feet. I was so scared and embarrassed.'

'Did you know him?'

'Not then but later. I married him!'

She then looked up at the tree and said, 'This has become so old now.'

We walked in through the gate. There was no one around and I was afraid we would be stopped by someone for trespassing. But Roopa was least bothered. It was as if she was in a world of her own. She walked to the back yard while I stood hesitating in the front. A couple walked in and were visibly surprised to see a stranger standing in their garden, that too in a sari. It was also just then that I noticed a board hanging in front of the door. It said 'Dr Salim and Dr Salma: Dentist'.

I started apologizing and explained about Roopa to them. Their faces lost the look of suspicion as soon as I finished my story. Roopa was meanwhile still looking at all the trees and remembering her childhood. The couple welcomed us in courteously. 'Please sit down. Do join us for a cup of tea.' They pulled up two chairs.

By now I was feeling very awkward, disturbing them

in the morning. But Dr Salim said, 'Please sit. We are glad you came. Our grandparents too were from Surat in Gujarat. They emigrated to Pakistan and I was born and brought up here. My parents talk with great nostagia about Surati farsan, parsi dhansak and khakra.'

Just to make conversation I said, 'It must be difficult maintaining such a large bungalow now.'

Dr Salim replied, 'We moved to this house some years back. You see this house happens to resemble the one my parents lived in in Surat, and they made me promise that I would not break it and make apartments as long as I stayed here. Allah has been kind to us and we don't need the money. Our neighbour Allah Baksh's children sold their property long back and now there is a commercial complex.'

By then Roopa had finished wandering in the garden and I formally introduced her to the couple. She asked if she could see the house from the inside. Dr Salim agreed happily. 'After we purchased this house ten years ago we made very few modifications. It is perhaps in the same state as you last saw it,' he said.

I walked in with Roopa. She looked into the main room and said, 'This was where my grandfather used to sit and control the house.' Then she pointed out a coloured glass door and said Allah Baksh's wife had painted it for them. 'That was the window through which she would send dry fruits to my aunt', 'That was where we used to fly kites.' Every brick, every wall held a memory for her. Finally I reminded her that it was time we left. We walked back to the garden and said our goodbyes to the couple. Dr

Salim handed us a packet. 'There is no time for you to eat, but I cannot send two elders away without offering anything. Please take this and if god is willing we will meet again.'

We came out of the house and when we reached the main road the car was there, having followed Roopa's directions. Now she wanted to see her own house.

She told the driver, 'Take a right turn from the Chauraha. I know the way. The first building on the right side is Al-Ameen School for girls and a little further there is a Jesus and Mary convent. A little ahead on the left side, there is a government boys' school. Next to that is the Idgah maidan. Next to that is a lane with five huge bungalows. Each plot is an acre in size. The first one belonged to Kewal Ram. Second to Mia Mehboob Khan and the third one to Sardar Supreet Singh. Fourth one to Rai saheb and the fifth was ours . . .'

She talked on and the driver followed her directions. She was mostly right. Yes the red brick building on the right was Al-Ameen School for girls. The Jesus and Mary convent was now a Loyola College and the government boys' school had become a degree college. But the Idgah maidan was not there. Instead there was a shopping complex. The five beautiful bungalows she described were also missing. Instead there was a mass of shops, hotels, video libraries piled next to each other. Roopa became upset.

'Madam, are you sure it is the same road?', the driver asked politely.

'Of course I am sure. I was born here. I spent nineteen

years here. You were not even born then. How can I make a mistake?'

She told him to stop the car and got off to search. She was sure the house was still there behind the new buildings. She was possessed, as if searching for a lost child, or a precious jewel.

'My house was yellow in colour and there were two storeys. It had an entrance from the right side. From my house I could see the Idgah maidan. Two years back a friend of mine who also stayed here came to see the place and she told me the house was still very much here.'

She turned to me and continued, 'You know, once I had unknowingly walked on the wet cement floor near the entrance of the house and my footmark stayed there forever. My father wanted to keep it as a reminder of me after I got married and went away. I can recognize my house without any trouble.' But there was no house of that description in that area, with the footmark in the entrance. I knew by this time that the house was not there. But Roopa was reluctant to accept it.

We stood in front of the building where she said her house used to be. It was a hotel and a chowkidar was sitting at the entrance.

I asked him, 'How old is this hotel?'

He got up and replied, 'It is only a year old.'

'How long have you been working here?'

'Ever since the old building was demolished and the construction started.'

Roopa was quiet now.

'Was there a two-storeyed yellow building here with

the entrance on the right and footprints along the portico?'

'Yes. There was a building like that but I don't remember the footprints.'

Now I knew that Roopa's house had been demolished to make way for this hotel. I looked at the chowkidar and told him, 'That was my friend's house.'

'Oh please come inside. So what if your house is not there? The hotel stands on the same land. I am sure my owner will be happy to receive you. Have a cup of tea and a samosa.'

I looked at Roopa but she was not listening to our conversation.

She took a handful of soil from the little patch of garden in front of the hotel and said, 'This is my land. This is my soil. My ancestors made this their home. They were born and burnt here. The land, the trees, the air, the water everything was ours. We knew the customs, the culture and the food. One day, some person drew a line and created two nations. And suddenly we became foreigners in our own land. We had to leave and adopt some other place whose language, food and culture were alien to us. A single line made me a stranger to my own land. People who have been uprooted have a special pain which no one else can understand.'

I was quiet. I could only imagine her agony. I held her hand and suddenly realized that the bouquet of flowers I had meant to give to the owners of her old house was lying on the front seat of the car, withering slowly in the December sunshine.

16

A Buddhist on Airport Road

One day, I had to take an auto to get to some place. These days in Bangalore, like other big cities, one is held completely at the mercy of the auto drivers. It is up to them, whether they want to take us or not. And even if we do get one, we have to keep all our fingers crossed till we reach our destination safely. It is rare to find a driver who does not drive his auto like a race car, or has a meter which gives the correct reading.

Anyway, that day I had asked various passing autos but none was ready to take me, so I was standing by the roadside. Suddenly a car stopped a little further ahead and someone rolled down one of the windows and waved at me. Looking carefully, I realized it was my friend Saroja. She was gesturing to me, indicating that I should get into the car. But I was hesitant. I said, 'I'm going towards the airport, it will be too far for you.'

But Saroja was firm, 'Please get in first. This is not a parking area. I too am going towards the airport to my hospital. It will not be out of my way.'

Saroja and I have been friends for a long time now, though our ways of looking at life are completely different. However, we have always maintained a transparency in our views, which has kept the friendship alive. It also helps that Saroja is an open-minded person, and does not hesitate to tell me her opinions. Sometimes we get into arguments, but talking frankly with one another helps to patch things up.

'What are you doing without a car? Why were you waiting for an auto?' Saroja was clearly astonished to see me near an auto stand.

'My drivers are on leave, and I don't like driving on Bangalore's roads these days, so I thought I'll take an auto.'

'You could have taken a taxi!'

'What is wrong in taking an auto? Many people in this city don't own a car.'

'But autos are dangerous.'

'For that matter travelling by road is far more dangerous than travelling by air.'

'That is true, though these days planes never stick to their schedules. I feel sick of travelling.'

'Then you are lucky you don't have to travel too often, given your work at the hospital.'

Saroja and her husband run a small hospital that has been quite successful. Both their sons are married. One stays abroad, while the younger one stays with them with his family. They have a big house, and Saroja is well settled with few worries. Or so I thought!

Without replying to me, Saroja stared outside, frowning.

'What is the matter? You seem unhappy,' I asked.

'To be honest, I am unhappy in the hospital and at home.'

'Why? Everything is so good for you.'

'That is what you think. But at home, my mother-in-law expects me to do everything. She forgets that I am also growing old. My daughter-in-law wants me to look after the grandchildren and manage the home, while she goes out to work. No one understands that as we grow older, we lose the patience to manage everything like we did in our younger days. I am caught between two generations.'

'Saroja, all of us go through this dilemma at this age. We are neither as old-fashioned as our parents, nor as progressive as our sons and daughters-in-law.'

'Besides that my relatives keep bothering me. They come to the hospital for treatment and don't pay us a paisa. I wouldn't have minded that so much but they never even have a word of thanks for us. They behave as if it is their right. If I complain about this to my husband he gets upset.'

'How is your practice?' I tried to change the topic.

'Don't ask me. There is so much competition in Bangalore. It is very difficult to have a private practice and even worse if one's children are not doctors. Often I think it would be better if we just sold the hospital and kept the money in the bank. Nowadays even the patients are so inquisitive. The other day one asked me a dozen questions while I was examining him. They think we can perform miracles with the latest medicines and surgery. If they don't respond to treatment they start complaining that we are exploiting them.'

Saroja was in full flow. 'How is Milind?' I interrupted.

Milind is her son who is a software engineer in the US.

'Oh, life there is not easy. There is so much of retrenchment. He is always under the threat of unemployment. His wife is also working. And there is no domestic help in the US you see, so the children go to a creche. They have not learnt a word of Kannada. I feel sad.'

It was taking us almost half an hour to travel a couple of kilometers, as there were traffic snarls all around. I was scared Saroja would start complaining about the road and the traffic situation as well, so I quickly asked, 'How is your friend Vani?'

'Don't ask me about her. Now that they are doing so well in life, she looks down upon me. How can I continue to be friends with her?'

'How is Vimla?'

Vani and Vimla were Saroja's friends for many years. But now she seemed to have developed problems with both.

'Oh I hardly meet Vimla. She always has either health or financial problems. Who has the time to listen to her complaints?'

Finally I asked the question that was on my mind after hearing her endless worries. 'Saroja, according to you, what is a happy life?'

Saroja looked at me and laughed, probably at my ignorance.

'A perfect life would be one without any worries. Daughters-in-law would be obedient and friendly and mothers-in-law without any expectations from us. Older people would not be demanding and friends would be understanding. Relatives would appreciate our work, and patients would realize that the doctor always tries his or her level best, but are not gods. Everybody would strive for a better life.'

By then we had reached Airport Road and it was time for me to get out of the car. But I wanted to say something to her before that.

'Saroja you are dreaming of utopia. Your dream is an impossible one. If we want to be happy we have to change our attitude and not the world's! The world is full of difficulties and unfulfilled desires just as the earth is full of dust and mud. If you want to keep your feet clean in this muddy world, there are only two solutions. Either cover the entire earth or wear a pair of sandals.'

Saroja interrupted, 'What a great thought. Who told you this?'

By that time I was out of the car and closing the door behind me. I told her, 'I was not fortunate enough to hear these lines from the guru himself as he was born 2,500 years before me. He was the Buddha.'

'When did you become a Buddhist?'

'Just now, in front of you.'

17

SWEET HOSPITALITY

Some years ago, my friend Suman came from the US to stay with me for a month. She had been living abroad for nearly twenty-five years. All her relatives and friends are in Bangalore and Dharwad, and the purpose of her visit was to catch up with all her friends. She had grown-up children who were not interested in visiting India, but she had the freedom to spend as much time as she wanted in her country. She still felt strongly about having her roots in India, perhaps more so because she had been away for so long.

Suman is very conscious of her health, and is always trying to keep her weight under control since she has a history of blood sugar and hypertension in her family. When I went to the US, I stayed with her once and saw her way of living. She diets, exercises, walks and meditates. She spends perhaps up to four hours a day on her fitness regime. When we were in school together she was on the plumper side and used to love eating sweets. Now, she hardly touches them. Knowing her love for them, I can understand the great effort she must be making to abstain from them. Once I asked her how she managed to do it. She replied sadly, 'It is so difficult. But

I practice it. Sometimes I feel like having sweets, which is why we don't keep any in the house.'

When Suman was staying with me, I accompanied her on some of her visits to the houses of friends and relatives. In India, a guest is supposed to be treated like god. Traditionally, the best of everything is put aside for the guest. People will go out of their way to make the guest happy. I have noticed that this is more so in the small towns and villages.

Once, I went with Suman to our friend Jaya's house. Jaya was not keeping well, but had gone to great efforts to prepare many eatables for us. As soon as we arrived, she disappeared into the kitchen and reappeared after a while bearing two tall copper glasses and two plates of sweets. They were all traditional home-made sweets and I could see the copious quantities of ghee and sugar oozing out of them. Jaya was serving us with great warmth and it was getting awkward to say no. In such situations, it is expected that the guest should finish all that has been put on the plate. In fact, it can be perceived to be an insult if food is left uneaten by the guest.

Suman was of course quite upset to see all the sweets being served. She could not afford to abandon her diet. Though it may be easy to stay off the food one has not seen in years, as soon as one is face to face with it, the food becomes irresistible. Temptation and Jaya's coaxing got the better of her and Suman ended up eating all the sweets. By the time we finished those, Jaya arrived bearing a second round of sweets.

'You must drink this payasa,' she said, putting before

us bowls filled to the brim with creamy appali payasa. 'It took me most of the afternoon to prepare this and I made it just for you.'

This time Suman was stronger and refused strictly. Since I was not on a diet, I finished my bowl, enjoying it immensely. It was indeed very good. Jaya was quite upset that Suman had refused the payasa.

'Come on Suman, please have it. We are not as well off as you are now, but I prepared it with a lot of love. You will never get this in the US. Now that you are in India you must forget your diet. Get back to it when you return home.'

By now Suman was in tears. Seeing her state, I told Jaya, 'Don't insist so much. You have made everything with a lot of affection, but let her decide what she wants to eat.'

Jaya was unhappy that I had spoken for Suman. 'If I insist she will have it. This is supposed to be good for health. I knew your grandfather, Suman, and he used to love this payasa. He was a friend of my grandfather's and I remember him well. He was as thin as a stick, even though he used to eat everything, including sweets, and never dieted in his life.'

'That is true. But my grandfather lived in a village and used to work in the paddy fields. He used to walk ten miles a day. That would have burned up all the calories he ate. My grandmother used to walk to the well and fetch water even in her old age. Theirs was a different way of life, our pattern of living has changed completely. Please understand.'

Our visit to Jaya's house ended on a sad note. And as Suman went visiting from house to house, the same story was repeated. At the end of her stay, Suman showed me the reading on the weighing scale. She had put on five kgs. She left India full of worries about how it would affect her health, and not the happy memories she had expected to take back with her.

Her parting words got me thinking. She said, 'People do not understand that hospitality does not mean serving rich food and large helpings. In all the houses I visited, they were upset that I refused to eat so much. For them it was a courtesy, but for me it is like poison. When I went to Delhi, I attended a wedding where they had a separate section with sugar-less food. I thought that was so considerate of the hosts. Nowadays everyone is conscious of one's health and wants to eat healthy food. For me some kinds of food are silent killers and I have to avoid them. I wish my friends had understood this and not taken offence.'

I listened to Suman and felt sad. She was correct. Hospitality means making a person feel at home, allowing her to relax and sharing whatever we have without making anyone uncomfortable. But we seem to have forgotten that. For us hospitality means preparing masses of food and piling up the guest's plate with it. And if she refuses, we get annoyed and jump to conclusions.

As I waved goodbye to Suman, I could only wish that Indian hospitality did not remind her always of a plate of sweets!

18

FRIENDS FOREVER

Radha and Rohini were my students through their college days. They were inseparable friends and I learnt they had studied together since the first year of school. I have rarely seen two friends who were so close to each other. They took all their classes together, attended lab with each other and were horrified when I suggested they take different lab partners as I was in favour of my students changing their lab partners every semester so they could learn to work with different kinds of people.

Of the two Rohini was the quieter one. She was also very talented and could paint and embroider beautifully. In fact often she would stitch similar clothes for herself and Radha and people would think they were sisters. There was such perfect understanding between them that they never felt the need to make other friends. I would see them together and wonder what would happen to their friendship later in life and after they got married. As it turned out, Radha got married first, to Ramesh, a civil engineer, and moved to Delhi. Rohini married Suresh, a mechanical engineer and set up house in Bangalore itself. I would see her once in a while and ask her about Radha. Time passed and both had children.

Meanwhile, I got more involved in my work with the foundation. In the course of that, I was planning to build an orphanage in the outskirts of the city. My funds were limited, so I was looking for someone who would take on the task of building the place at cheaper rates and yet do good work. Cheap is not always the best, is what I found out soon enough.

One day, a man in his late thirties came to meet me. He gave me a wonderful quotation for the work. He had made out a detailed proposal and I was very impressed. So I asked him, 'How will you do all this at the rate you have specified? Won't you be incurring a loss?'

He smiled and replied, 'Madam, this is something I want to do. It is not a business proposition. I am not making any profit on this.'

I was pleased to hear his answer and said, 'It is always good to see young people getting involved in social projects. So are you a philanthropher too?'

Now he grinned widely and answered, 'Actually someone very close to me wanted me to take on this work. I don't know if you remember her but she talks about you very often. Her name is Radha and she is my wife.' Now it all became clear to me. It also explained the name of his construction firm, Radha Constructions.

'Of course I remember Radha. But I thought you were in Delhi? Have you moved here?'

'I left my job and started my own construction company in Delhi. It is doing very well and recently we moved here as I want to expand my work in Bangalore. Since Radha is from Bangalore, she too was keen to come back and stay here for a few years. Soon after we moved she read in the papers about your work and also about this orphanage that you plan to build. She immediately asked me to draft a proposal and meet you with it. You know, it is my belief that Radha has brought me a lot of good luck after our marriage. There was no way I could refuse her.'

I was delighted to hear his story, and especially that he attributed his success to my former student. 'Will you tell her to come and meet me?' I blessed her in my mind, for asking her husband to do this work for us at no profit.

Radha came to meet me the very next day. Of course she looked much older now. I was glad to see the happiness on her face. There is no greater joy for a teacher than to meet an old student who is doing well in life and is satisfied. Invariably, Rohini's name came up in our conversation. 'So do you now dress in similar saris? Are your children as close friends as you two were at their age?'

To my surprise, Radha remained quiet. Then she said, 'I don't know why but Rohini has changed a lot. You know I was so keen to come back to Bangalore because of her too. She was almost like a sister to me. And I know that was the way she felt about me as well. But somehow, things have changed. Our friendship is not the same any more.'

Astonished at her story, I asked Radha to explain further. She said, 'Rohini has changed a lot. Whenever I go to visit her she is very polite, but the warmth is missing. She talks to me like she would to a stranger, and not her oldest friend. I have been trying to work out the reason, but I am still at sea.'

After talking for a while longer, Radha went back home. I felt I should talk to Rohini. Having been their teacher I still thought of them as my students. Teachers tend to be under the illusion that their students will always listen to them! So, I sent word for Rohini. She came to meet me at my office. I was seeing her after many months and was shocked to see her state. There were worry lines on her face, and she looked tired.

I tried talking cheerfully to her, 'So Rohini what have you painted lately? Do you remember how you always used to pester me to give you a sari which you could embroider? Well, Radha gave me a plain sari yesterday. Will you make something on it?'

Quietly Rohini replied, 'No Madam. I have stopped doing all that.'

'What is the matter with you Rohini? You seem to be under a lot of stress. I came to know from Radha that you are no longer friendly with her? Did she do something to hurt you?'

'Not really. You see, now there is a lot of difference in Radha's and my economic situations. Her husband is doing well, whereas we are having a lot of financial problems. I don't think it is possible for people of unequal status to be friends. Now that Radha is rich she pities me.'

'Why do you say so? Did she say anything to you?'

'Whenever she comes she brings expensive toys for my daughter and presents me with silk saris at the least pretext. She knows I cannot reciprocate. Perhaps she looks down at me and I am not comfortable around her. So I have tried to keep a distance between us.'

Now I understood. And Radha was not even aware of all this! I explained quietly to Rohini, 'Come on. You must realize that in a true friendship the status does not matter. It is what you make of the situation. If Radha had given your daughter cheap toys you would have said she is doing so because you are poor. It is not what Radha does, but what your interpretation of it is. You must have read of the friendship between Krishna and Sudama. One was poor and the other a king, yet they kept their friendship alive. Radha gives you what she can afford and you too can try to give her something within your means. It need not be expensive. You are so talented. You can give her some paintings, or make a dress for her child. It is not the price but the thought behind a gift that matters. Don't spoil your friendship of so many years because of an inferiority complex. Give Radha a chance. Shall I tell you an interesting line that I read somewhere once?'

Rohini was sitting quietly listening to me and nodded her head.

'I was born with relatives, but at least I can choose my friends!'

We both burst out laughing. Rohini went home looking much happier and a few days later I received a beautiful sari with intricate thread work done all over it. The card read, 'From Radha and Rohini'.

19

THE PERFECT LIFE

Many years ago, I was heading a project in the company where I was working. My team consisted of mostly married women of similar age and background. We were given one big hall to sit in. I had a cabin with a glass partition, while the others sat outside. During lunch hours the women would sit outside and gossip. They were just loud enough for me to hear them from behind my partition and I would end up listening to the stories of their households.

Most of the women were quite talkative, except for one called Neeta. And while the rest used to usually complain about their husbands and in-laws, Neeta would be the only one who had anything positive to say about her family.

When Neela would grumble about her mother-in-law, Neeta would say, 'My mother-in-law is like my mother.' Then Kusuma would say, 'My sister-in-law is so jealous of me.' And Neeta could be heard saying, 'My sister-in-law is fantastic. We share everything like sisters.' Geeta's husband had a short temper and she would talk about how he got angry about the smallest issues. But Neeta would say she was more short-tempered than her husband, in fact he hardly ever lost his temper.

One day Neeta came to the office wearing a very pretty pink sari. Everyone commented what a lovely sari it was and I asked her, 'Where did you buy it from? Is it your birthday?' Neeta blushed and replied, 'Yes, madam, it is a birthday gift from my husband.'

And so we heard stories of her perfect family everyday. Whereas everyone had the standard complaints of all working women, on how they had to juggle their office work and responsibilities at home, where they got little support from their husbands or in-laws, Neeta would relate how her father-in-law helped out the kids with their homework, and how her husband helped her in the kitchen.

It was the common consensus that Neeta was a lucky person, perhaps even the eighth wonder of the world. Savitri, the poetess, said, 'Neeta's family is better even than the flawed moon—it does not have any defects!'

Those days of laughter and joking passed and slowly the group dissolved and each went their own way. Many years later, I got a call from Neeta. For some time I could not place her but then slowly her stories came back to me. She was Mrs Perfect! She spoke softly into the phone and I thought I heard a trace of anxiety in her voice. She wanted to come and meet me one day and I told her to do so.

The day she stepped into my office I was astonished to see her state. While her friends had progressed from youth to middle age, Neeta seemed to have jumped straight to old age. She was frail and her hair had greyed. We talked for a while about our old team members, but she had no idea where they were now. So I told her. Neela, who used to fight with her mother-in-law and had moved out of the house with her husband, had finally gone back and looked after the old lady in her illness. Kusuma had helped out her 'jealous' sister-in-law when she was in trouble and Geeta's husband had mellowed down with age and was now a pleasant, jovial person to talk to.

Life had gone round like a wheel for most of these people. They had taken on the challenges and responsibilities that came with age and had faced them with courage. Then I asked Neeta, 'So how are you now? You never had the troubles that these people had.'

She looked even sadder at my words and there were tears in her eyes. 'Madam you don't know the problems I am facing.'

'You and problems, Neeta?'

'Yes Madam. I am suffering from depression. I have to go to the psychiatrist.'

'There is nothing wrong with that Neeta. It is good that you are taking a doctor's help to overcome your condition. It is like going to a doctor for any other ailment, there is nothing to worry about there.'

'Madam, I have been depressed for so long that the psychiatrist says if I shared it with someone I know and respect, it might help me. That is why I asked to meet you.'

'I am glad you thought of me Neeta, but why are you so depressed? You had such a wonderful family life.'

'I always had lots of problems. I just could never bring myself to talk about them. My mother-in-law and sister-in-law were worse than Neela's and Kusuma's. My husband always took their side in any argument. I was so miserable. When my friends would talk about their families I always wished I could share my story with them, but my mother had told me never to talk ill of my family in public. She said I should always restrain my emotions and whatever happens at home, should put up a happy face outside it. As a result I would pretend to be happy. For me being frank meant showing my weakness.'

I was stunned by her words. I had always thought being frank was a virtue. I was taught to look around me at all the misery that existed in the world and then compare others' problems with my own. I had counted my blessings when I felt sad and that had kept me going even in my darkest days.

Meanwhile Neeta was still pouring out her heart. 'Do you remember that pink sari I wore one day which everyone commented on and said was so pretty? Even you had asked me where I got it from. I lied that it was a birthday gift from my husband. He has never given me anything on my birthdays. Nobody helped me with my children's homework or in the kitchen. I would struggle all alone trying to do everything. My life was no different from my colleagues', but at least they gave themselves the freedom to talk about it and comment in public. I was too busy trying to show I had a perfect life.'

'Now that you have realized that did not work, forget the past and try to be happy.'

'Nothing comes free. I paid a heavy price trying to keep up the pretence of my life. I suffered from repeated bouts of depression. I tried talking about this with some people but they did not understand and I heard some make nasty comments about me. I hope you understand why I have come to you today and told you the truth.'

I took Neeta's hand in mine and said to her, 'Everyone has secrets. We all have faults that we try to hide. But the problem arises when we don't acknowledge those troubles and faults even to ourselves and pretend to be what we are not. A peacock looks beautiful when it dances but it cannot sing. A cuckoo is dark but has a golden voice. That is why a cuckoo should never dance and a peacock should not try to sing! We can live our lives in happiness only when we acknowledge our difficulties and failures and try to overcome them with our strength of character.'

20

HUNDRED PER CENT FREE

At the Infosys Foundation, we get hundreds of letters every day asking for monetary help for all kinds of purposes—for higher education, a wedding, medical help and so on. Usually we try to verify the genuineness of the claim and then we give sixty to eighty per cent of the total money required by the person. Once I got a letter from someone I had offered to pay a part of the money he required. He said, 'You are very hard-hearted. Why can't you give me the entire amount that I have asked for?' I do so because two incidents in my life taught me that sometimes it is better to let a person struggle. It provides an incentive to strive harder. Anything given away for free loses value and is not treated with the respect it deserves.

A few years back, when I looked out of my office window, I used to see a young boy of about fourteen selling dusters at the traffic light. He was thin as a stick and dressed in rags. I used to compare his state with the smartly-dressed children sitting in school buses, carrying their bags of books and would feel bad at the boy's deprivation. One day, I decided to do something about it and called him up to my office. He walked in looking scared and diffident. I offered him some coffee and biscuits to make him feel at ease. Initially he was feeling too awkward to eat. But slowly, he relaxed and after drinking the coffee answered my questions.

His name was Ravi and his father was a coolie and his mother a housemaid. He studied in a local school and in the morning hours he sold car dusters to earn some money for his education.

I asked, 'How much money do you make every month?'

He said, 'Between thirty to forty rupees a month'

'Can I see your progress card?'

The next day the boy came with his progress card. He was doing well in school and was obviously a bright child. So I said, 'Suppose I gave you fifty rupees a month, then you would not need to sell dusters in the morning. Instead you can use the time to do your homework or learn something else.' The boy was taken aback at the proposition and looked at me uncomprehendingly. So I said, 'Just suppose I am buying all your stock of cloth every month and also giving a few rupees extra. That would mean you are earning Rs 50. Use it to study further. But I will want to see your progress report every three months before giving you the money.' Now he understood and agreeing to my idea he left with great joy written on his face.

Thereafter he came to my office every three months and after showing his card he would leave with the money. His progress report showed he was doing well in school. One day, he asked to speak to me. I was happy to see a smart, confident young boy in front of me. He came straight to the point, 'Madam, now my stipend should be increased to Rs 100 per month.'

'Why do you say so?'

'Madam, two years back each duster was for Rs 2. Now it is Rs 4. So, you should pay me Rs 100 per month.'

I looked at him in surprise. Obviously he looked at the money he got from me each month as his due and did not feel the need to work himself to earn more.

Another incident soon after that convinced me to start my policy of extending only part of the help where money was concerned.

I am very fond of atlases. When I was growing up in a village, it was difficult to get hold of one. So when I started the foundation I decided to start distributing atlases free to school libraries. In them children could see the country and the world and learn the vastness of the planet they lived in. I thought it was the perfect way to open a child's eyes to the immense variety of life on earth. Later, teachers used to come to my office and collect them free for their schools.

Once I was spending some time in the rural parts of Karnataka on work. It was dusk and the cattle were coming back after their day's grazing. There was a pall of dust everywhere and I smelled the wonderful aroma of fresh groundnuts in the air. A man was sitting with a pile of freshly plucked groundnuts in front of the local school gate. It was quite irresistible and I went up to him and asked for a kilo. The man was a farmer selling his product directly to customers passing that way.

He weighed a kilo and gave it to me loose. 'Take this and put it in your bag,' he said. I was not carrying one, so I asked him to get one from somewhere. He thought for a minute then he turned to his assistant and said, 'Run into the school, the classrooms are still open. There will be a big red book there, with thick pages. Tear out one page and get it.' Before I could protest the boy had run into the school. Soon he came holding a colourful page and I was handed my kilo of groundnuts in it. I looked closely at the page and realized it was from one of the atlases I had given to the school some months back! I was shocked.

'Why did you tear the page from this book?' I asked. The man answered, 'Oh some lady gives these book free to the school. The paper is nice and thick, so we use it sometimes for wrapping things.'

Then seeing the shocked look on my face he said placatingly, 'We do it only when we need paper in a hurry, not otherwise.'

I looked down sadly at the pack of groundnuts in my hand. In that dim light, I was sure I could make out the seal of our foundation on it.

21

Two Faces of Poverty

Leela has been working in my office for many years. She sweeps, dusts and mops. She does her work quietly and takes on any extra work without any complaints. Since she was always so quiet and I was usually very busy, I did not know much about her personal life, apart from the fact that her husband had deserted her and she was bringing up three daughters singlehandedly.

One day, she came in to clean my office and after doing her work, stood hesitantly in front of me. It was such an uncharacteristic thing for her to do, that I was surprised. Slowly, she brought out a soiled bundle and put it in front of me. Then she said in a low voice, 'Madam can you lend me twenty thousand rupees?' I was still puzzled and asked, 'What happened Leela? Why do you suddenly need so much money?' She replied, 'My youngest daughter wants to join college and I need the money for that.' While she was explaining I opened the cloth bundle. Inside, there was a pair of worn out gold bangles. 'Why are you giving this to me Leela?' I asked.

'These are the only assets I have. I will do anything to see my daughter studies further. She is very bright. She wants to become an engineer.'

I could make out the pride in her voice when she spoke of the girl. But when has a child not seemed the best and the brightest to her mother? So I told Leela, 'Take back these bangles. I am not a moneylender. I want to meet your daughter and talk to her myself. Ask her to come and meet me with her school marks cards.'

The next day a pretty girl in ordinary but clean clothes was waiting for me in the office. Her face was bright with intelligence and as soon as I entered she stood up politely.

'Madam I am Leelamma's daughter,' she introduced herself. 'My name is Girija. My mother said you wanted to talk to me.'

Then she placed her marks cards in front of me. I was taken aback to see the high marks she had scored consistently. She also had numerous extra-curricular activity certificates. No wonder Leela was so proud of her and wanted to pledge her bangles for her. I looked again at her closely. She was fair and her face was as clear as dew. That seemed strange, as Leela was short and dark. We talked for a few more minutes and I could make out Girija's fondness for her mother and sisters in her words. I sent her back and called Leela.

'Leela, I met your other two daughters when they came to the office some times, but I am very impressed after meeting Girija. There is something about her that sets her apart. You were right, she is very bright. I will help you out with the fees. If she performs well I will give her entire course fees. She has it in her to change her future, if she continues to work hard . . .' I was talking while clearing my desk and only after I had spoken for so long I realized that Leela was standing without saying a word. Finally she said, 'I need to tell you something before you proceed further with your help. Girija is not my child. I have adopted her.' I was amazed. 'When? Why?' I asked.

She sighed. 'It is a long story. Many years ago I was working for a young girl. She was staying by herself. Her parents were in the US and she was supposed to go to them after finishing her studies. I was a cook in the house. The girl was good looking and quite friendly. Often boys and girls would be at her house and there was a lot of fun, music, laughter and partying.

'One day I found the girl looking worried and sad. She would often talk to me so I asked her what the matter was. She confessed that she was pregnant. The boy who was responsible had gone abroad soon after hearing the news and she was left in the lurch. She did not dare tell her parents and it was too late for an abortion.

'What could I do after hearing such a story? I looked after her through her pregnancy, cooking the best foods. She gave birth to a baby girl in a nursing home here. All the while no one but me knew about the situation. Soon after the baby was born she told me to take it and put it in an orphanage. I tried, but holding the tiny baby in my arms I found myself unable to give her away and decided to bring her up. I already had two daughters and my husband had deserted me, but I knew I would always find enough to share with this new soul. That girl is Girija.'

I was dumbstruck by Leela's story and her courage

and generosity. The crushing poverty of her life had not diminished the humanity within her.

Yet not all children are fortunate enough to find a Leela to take care of them. There are others whose stories of cruelty and neglect can amaze even the most cynical of people. One such unfortunate child was Somnath.

Usually I try not to give money to individual parents. Instead, we give it to a hospital where they take care of the needy at nominal rates. Once I made an exception and have regretted it ever since. It started one day when Ramappa came to meet me. He was standing in the reception arguing with my secretary who did not want to let him in without an appointment. Since he was already there I saw no point in turning him away and asked him in. His son, he said, was suffering from cancer and needed urgent surgery. He was a clerk and could in no way afford the Rs 2 lakh needed. I looked at all the papers and medical certificates he had got with him. Then I told him to get some more papers—proof of hospitalization, pathological report, estimation of the operation, his id in the hospital, etc. I also wanted the doctor's name so I could talk to him.

Ramappa thought for a while, then said, 'All right I will bring the papers tomorrow.' But the next day, Ramappa turned up holding a child by the hand. The boy was obviously very sick and it made a pathetic sight. I was furious that he had dragged the child all the way to my office in this condition. 'Why did you get him?' I asked. 'I only wanted to see some papers.'

Ramappa was ready with his reply. 'It would take me

a few days to get all the papers you wanted, so I got the child as proof.'

I felt sorry for Somnath and wrote out a cheque for Rs 25,000. Ramappa said, 'Can you give me a letter that you have given me this money? I can show it to other donors. If they see your name they too will agree to help me.' I could see nothing wrong in writing such a letter and gave it to him. Ramappa thanked me wholeheartedly and went away promising to let me know how the operation went. But there was no news from him and a year passed. We too forgot about Ramappa till the auditors were doing their work and I realized that Ramappa had not called nor sent any other papers or receipts of the operation. I called up the hospital he had mentioned and wanted to know if they had operated on any child called Somnath that year. I was sad to hear that they hadn't. Perhaps Ramappa could not raise all the money, I thought and berated myself for not helping him more or following up on the case.

I decided to go and meet him. I still had the address he had given me. When I found the place, it was locked. It was a big, three-storeyed building in the latest style with plenty of tiles and granite. It was by far the grandest house in the locality. Having come so far I did not want to go without finding out more about Somnath, so I knocked on the next door. An old lady came out and was least taken aback to find a stranger at her door asking questions. She talked freely to me.

'Where are Ramappa and Somnath?' I asked her.

'Somnath died six months ago.'

I was saddened, but not surprised.

The old woman was meanwhile chatting away. 'Somnath's disease came as a boon for Ramappa. He got a letter from some famous lady who gave him 25,000 rupees for the operation. With that he went around to other donors and managed to raise Rs 8 lakh. He used the money to build this new house and also started an auto business. Now he is doing very well in life.'

'But didn't he get Somnath's operation done?'

'Ramappa was no fool to get him operated. He was least bothered about it. In the end, he used to carry him around when he went to collect the money. Poor Somnath suffered a lot and died at home.'

I was dumbstruck. By then a man appeared from inside and told the old woman not to talk. But she replied fiercely, 'Why should I not talk? I saw Somnath from the day he was born. I saw him suffer. God will certainly not forgive Ramappa for what he did to his own son.'

I had got to know enough by then and took my leave. I found myself in tears as I walked to the car. All I could do was thank god there are still people like Leela in this world. They lessen the pain and suffering inflicted by people like Ramappa, of whom unfortunately there are plenty.

22

INDIA, THE HOLY LAND

Maya was a simple young lady who lived in the Tibetan settlement in the outskirts of Mundugod, near Hubli in north Karnataka. She used to teach the Tibetan language to the children in the camp, so they would not forget their roots. She was smart and hard working.

My father was a doctor working in Hubli and he occasionally visited that settlement. If any of the Tibetans wanted further treatment, they would visit my father at the Government Hospital in Hubli. Maya too started visiting my father when she was expecting her first child.

Over the months she became quite friendly with all of us. Whenever she came to the hospital she would pay us a visit too. My mother would invite her for a meal and we would spend some time chatting.

In the beginning, we would be in awe of her and stare at her almost-white skin, dove eyes, the little flat nose and her two long, thin plaits. Slowly we accepted her as a friend and she graduated to become my knitting teacher. Her visits were sessions of knitting, chatting and talking about her life in the camp and back in her country for which she still yearned. Maya would describe her homeland to us with great affection, nostalgia and at times, with tears in her eyes.

'Tibetans are simple people. We are all Buddhists but our Buddhism is of a different kind. It is called Vajrayana. There's been a lot of influence from India, particularly Bengal, in our country and religious practices. Even our script resembles Bengali.'

Her words filled me with a sense of wonder about this exotic land called Tibet and I would pester her to tell me more about that country. One day we started talking about the Dalai Lama.

'What is the meaning of Dalai Lama?' I asked.

'It means "ocean of knowledge". Ours is a unique country where religious heads have ruled for 500 years. We believe in rebirth and that each Dalai Lama is an incarnation of the previous one. The present Dalai Lama is the fourteenth . . . You know, India is the holy land of Buddha. Historically, we have always respected India. There is a nice story about how Buddhism came to Tibet through India . . .'

I could not wait to hear about this!

'Long ago there was a king in Tibet who was kidnapped by his enemies. They demanded a ransom of gold, equal to the weight of the king. When the imprisoned king heard this, he somehow sent word to his son, "Don't waste any gold to get me back. Instead, spend that money to bring good learned Buddhist monks from India. With their help, open many schools and monasteries so that our people can live in peace and gain knowledge".'

Months passed and Maya delivered a baby. After that

our meetings became less frequent. But she succeeded in awakening within me a curiosity about Tibet and a great respect for Buddhism

Recently I got a chance to visit Tibet and memories of Maya filled my mind. I knew I would be seeing a Tibet filled with Chinese but nevertheless I was keen to go. Among the places I wanted to see was a Buddha temple at Yerlong valley which she had described to me.

When I finally reached the valley, it was past midday. There was a cold wind blowing though the sun was shining brightly. The Brahmaputra was flowing like a stream here, nothing like the raging torrent in Assam. Snow-capped mountains circled the valley and there was absolute silence all around.

The monastery at Yerlong is supposed to be a famous pilgrimage spot, but I could see only a handful of people in the entire place. After seeing everything inside I sat down on the steps and observed the serene beauty of the place.

I noticed an old woman accompanied by a young man walking into the monastery. The woman was very old, her face was wrinkled and she walked slowly and weakly. She was wearing the traditional Tibetan dress and her hair was plaited. The young man on the other hand was dressed in the usual modern manner, in tight jeans and a body-hugging t-shirt. The woman started circumambulating the monastery using her stick for support while the man sat down on the steps like me.

When she finished, I realized the old lady was staring at me. Then she said something to the young man in

Tibetan. She looked tired by the end of her ritual and sat down on the steps. She said something to her companion again but he took little notice of her. So she slowly picked up her stick and came towards me. She sat down near me, took my hands and saying something, she gently raised my hands to her eyes and then kissed them. Before I could say anything, she got up and started to walk away. But I noticed she was smiling, as if she had achieved a long-held desire. I realized there was a wetness where her eyes had touched my hand.

Now the young boy reluctantly came up to me and apologised. 'Please forgive my grandmother,' he said. 'She is from a village in the interior part of Tibet. She has never ventured out of her village. This is the first time she has come to Yerlong. I beg your pardon for her behaviour.'

He was talking to me in English with an Indian accent.

'How come you speak English like us?' I asked in surprise.

'My name is KeTsang. I was in India for five years. I studied at Loyola College in Chennai. Now I run a restaurant in Lhasa. People here like Indian food and movies. I accompanied my grandmother for her pilgrimage. She was thanking you.'

'But for what? I have not done anything for her!'

'That is true, but your country has. It has sheltered our Dalai Lama for so many years. He is a living God to us, particularly to the older generation. We all respect the Dalai Lama, but due to political reasons, we cannot express it in public. You might have seen that there isn't a single photo of his in any public place in the whole of

Lhasa. He is the fourteenth, but we have paintings, statues and pictures only up to the thirteenth.'

I still did not understand the old lady's gesture. The grandson explained, 'She said, "I am an old lady and don't know how long I will live. If I don't thank you before I die, I will never attain peace. Let anyone punish me for this, it does not matter. It is a gift that I met an Indian today and was able to thank you for sheltering our Dalai Lama. Yours is truly a compassionate land."'

Her words eerily echoed Maya's from many years back. I could only look down at the wet spot on my hand and smile.

I was once invited to speak on motherhood at a seminar. It was a well-attended seminar and people from different walks of life had gathered. Some were medical practitioners, others were from orphanages, adoption agencies, and NGOs. Religious heads, successful mothers (the definition of which, according to the organizers, were those whose children had done well in life and earned lots of money), young mothers, all were there.

There were numerous stalls selling baby products, books on motherhood, on how to handle adolescents etc. The speakers were good and most of the time they spoke from the heart about their experiences. The media was present in full force, clicking away photos of celebrities. Since this had been organized by the social welfare department, there were many government officials and a big gathering of students too.

When my turn came, I started narrating an incident that I had been witness to many years ago.

Manjula was a cook in a friend, Dr Arati's house. Manjula's husband was a good-for-nothing. She had five children and when she became pregnant for the sixth time, she decided to get it aborted. She also decided to get a tubectomy done.

Dr Arati, however, came up with a different idea. Her sister was rich but childless and wanted to adopt a newborn baby. She was desparately searching for one, so Arati gave a suggestion.

'Manjula, instead of aborting the baby, why don't you deliver it, and irrespective of the gender, my sister will adopt it. She does not even stay in this city so you won't need to see the baby's face ever. She will adopt it legally and help you with the education of your remaining children too. This child, which is now unwanted, will be brought up well with lots of love. Think it over, the decision is yours and I will not insist.'

Manjula thought for a couple of days and finally agreed to the proposal. In a few months she delivered a baby girl. Dr Arati's sister also arrived that day after completing all the formalities. It had been decided that she would take the baby a day after it was born. But when the time came to hand over the child, Manjula refused to give her away. Her breasts were now full of milk and the baby had started feeding. She pressed the baby against her weak body and started crying, 'I agree that I am very poor. Even if I get a handful of rice, I will share that with this baby. But I cannot part with her. She is so tiny and so completely dependent on me. I am breaking my promise but I cannot live without my child. Please pardon me.'

Arati and her sister were naturally upset. They had prepared themselves to welcome this baby to their family. But seeing Manjula weep, they realized that motherhood may not always answer to the logic of agreements.

I concluded my speech saying that many times I have

seen a mother is ready to sacrifice anything for her children. Motherhood is a natural instinct. Our culture glorifies it and a mother is held in great respect, over anybody else. I was rewarded with great applause. I too was satisfied with my speech.

I stepped down from the podium, and saw Meera standing near by. She was blind and taught orphans in a blind school. She was representing her school at the seminar. I knew her fairly well because I visited her school often. I went up to her and said, 'Meera how are you?' She was quiet for a minute. 'I am fine, Madam. Can you do me a favour?'

'Tell me what is it?'

'Ahmed Ismail was supposed to pick me up and drop me to my school. But just now he called up on my cellphone and said that he is stuck in a traffic jam and will take more time. Can you drop me to my school?' Ahmed Ismail was a trustee of the blind school.

Meera's school was on my way to the office and so I agreed immediately. In the car, I noticed she was very quiet and so started the conversation.

'Meera, how was the seminar today? Did you like my lecture?'

I was expecting the usual polite answer, saying it was very good.

But Meera answered, 'I didn't like your lecture. Sorry for being so blunt, but life is not always like that.'

I was taken aback. I wanted to know the reason behind it and asked her, 'Tell me Meera. Why did you say that? What I narrated was a true incident and not a story.

Sometimes truth is stranger than fiction.'

Meera sighed, 'Yes, sometimes truth is stranger than fiction. That is really what I wanted to tell you. Let me tell you another story. There was once a five-year-old girl who was half-blind. Both her parents were labourers. The girl would complain often that she could not see clearly, but they would say that was because she wasn't eating properly and they would take her to the doctor when they managed to collect some money. One day, they finally took her to the doctor. He told them the girl needed an operation which cost a lot of money, else she would go blind slowly. The parents discussed something between themselves and took her to a bus-stand. They gave her a packet of biscuits and told her, "Child, eat the biscuits and we will be back in five minutes."

'For the first time in her life the child had got an entire packet of biscuits for herself. She was overjoyed and sat down to enjoy them. With her half blind eyes she could just make out her mother's torn red sari pallu disappear in the crowd. The day wore on, it started getting colder and she realized that it was getting dark. The packet of biscuits was over long back. She was alone, helpless and scared. She started calling for her parents and searched in vain for them, trying to spot the torn red pallu.'

'What happened after that?'

'The child continued to search for her parents, sleeping wherever she got a place. One day, a kind-hearted man saw her pitiable condition and took her to the blind school. The child could not give any address or name by which they could trace the parents. He requested the matron that in case any parent came forward to claim the child, they could hand her over after examining them. But nobody came looking for her. The child waited for her mother for several years, till one day she gave up all hope.'

I turned to Meera to see she was crying and I realized so was I. Even though I knew the answer in my heart, I asked her, 'Meera, how did you know all these details about that child?'

Through her tears, she replied, 'Because I was that half-blind child. Now, tell me, how could my mother leave me like that? She deceived me with a pack of biscuits. What happened to the motherhood that you spoke so strongly about? Is poverty more powerful than motherhood?'

I did not have any answer for her, but could only hold her hand in my own. I realized that there were as many kinds of mothers as there are people on this earth, and poverty can lead to acts of great desperation.

Even today, if I happen to see a woman on the road wearing a red sari, I think of Meera and her experience of motherhood.

24

VILLAGE ENCOUNTERS

One of my aims, when starting the Infosys Foundation, was to inculcate and spread the joy of reading among as many students and young children in the rural areas as possible. From my own experience of having grown up in a small town, I knew the best way to do this was to help schools and local libraries stock up on good books for children. It was in the course of identifying good government schools and youth clubs in the rural areas of Karnataka, that I happened to meet many young people from the small villages and towns of this state.

Krishna Murthy was a young man of about twenty who I met during my travels. He had recently graduated from a college in Bangalore. His father owned large properties and agricultural lands in the village and was therefore very well off. Krishna Murthy on the other hand, was taken in completely by the charms of city life and was intent on staying on in Bangalore rather than returning to his village as his father wanted. No amount of explaining could budge him. On the request of his father, I told him that life in a big city like Bangalore can be stressful, what with the rising costs of living, the high pollution levels, impossible traffic situation and water and electricity shortages. But young Krishna Murthy was adamant. Finally I told him about Guruprasad.

I met Guruprasad in my Bangalore office.

I had been very busy with my travels and been able to meet him only two months after he first said he wanted to talk to me about our library project. He had been very keen to meet only me. He was about twenty-three or twenty-four years of age and looked like any other young person these days, smartly dressed and equipped with the latest gadgets like cellphone, organizer etc. He was from a village called Kandale in Shimoga district. He had a jolly face and showed a great deal of spirit and enthusiasm. As we talked, I learnt that he had graduated with honours in English from a reputed college in Bangalore. A national level chess player, he was the eldest of two sons. His father was an agriculturist. After discussing his ideas for our library project, our conversation turned to Indian villages and life there.

'How do you spend your time in the village?' I asked him.

'Oh! There are numerous activities to keep me busy. I have a very lucrative mushroom business and everyday I have to work four to five hours on that. We have a big ancestral house. I live there with my parents and other relatives. In my village there is no pollution, though with better connectivity, we get almost all provisions usually available in cities close by. When I am not working at my business or looking after the house, I coach children in chess. We have also formed a youth club where along with my friends, I have started a library. The library has become a meeting point for many young people like me. We exchange ideas there and talk about which new books we should try to procure. I heard about your foundation's work there and came to meet you so we can take some books for our collection. I have been trying to start similar clubs and libraries in the neighbouring villages with the help of like-minded boys and girls.

'Life in our village is clean, healthy and I am happy being there as I am living the life I always wanted to.'

I was curious to know how much he was earning by his mushroom business.

'It depends upon how much you invest. If you invest ten rupees you can easily make forty rupees. It is better than any fluctuating share market. I earn much more than I would in Bangalore. I also don't need to spend enormous amounts of money commuting and paying exorbitant rents. I have a car which helps me a lot in my work. I don't feel inferior when talking to any city person. Nobody ever forced me to stay on in the village. It was my own decision and I am happy I took it.'

Guruprasad's words reminded me of one of Kuvempu's poems

Vasantha vanadali kooguva kogile
Raajana padaviya bayasuvudilla
Hoovina maradali jeenu hulugalu
Morevudu raajana bhayadindalla'
It is not in anticipation of the king's throne,
That in the springs, the cuckoo sings so beautifully
Nor is it out of fear of the king's anger
That the bees hum in the flower gardens

Guruprasad had decided on the course of his life by staying in his village and was happy there. He was doing what he enjoyed without giving in to any pressures but by using his own intelligence.

After hearing the story Krishna Murthy promised to think about staying on in his village. I don't know what he decided eventually and how happy he was with his decision. But till today I am convinced that it is young people like Guruprasad who can bring about change and a breath of fresh air to their villages. The future lies with him and many others like him.

25

May You Be the Mother of a Hundred Children

I was on my way to the railway station. I had the nine o'clock Bangalore-Hubli Kittur Express to catch. Halfway to the station our car stopped. There was a huge traffic jam. There was no way we could move either forward or reverse the car. I sat and watched helplessly as a few two-wheelers scraped past the car through a narrow gap. Finally I asked my driver what the matter was. Traffic jams are not uncommon but this was something unusual. He got out of the car and said the road ahead was blocked by some people holding a communal harmony meet. I now realized it was perhaps impossible to get to the station. The papers had reported about the meeting and had warned that the roads would be blocked for some time. The car was moved into a bylane and seeing there was no way I could try and make my way back home, I decided to join the crowd and listen to the speeches.

From a distance, I could see the dais. There were various religious heads sitting on a row of chairs on the stage. An elderly gentleman stood next to me and commented loudly, 'All this is just a drama. In India, everything is decided on the basis of caste and community. Even our elections are dictated by them. Whoever comes to power thinks only of the betterment of his community. It is easy to give speeches but in practical life they forget everything.'

Just then a middle-aged lady started speaking into the mike. From the way she was speaking, so confidently, it was apparent that she was used to giving speeches and had the gift of the gab. Her analogies were quite convincing. 'When you eat a meal, do you eat only chapattis or rice? No, you also need a vegetable, a dal and some curd. The tastes of the dishes vary, but only when they are put together do you get a wholesome meal. Similarly different communities need to live together in harmony and build a strong country . . .' etc. 'It is a nice speech but who follows all this in real life?' the gentleman next to me commented.

'Why do you say that?' I had to ask finally. He looked at me, surprised at my unexpected question, then answered, 'Because my family has suffered a lot. My son did not get a job as he was not from the right community, my daughter was transferred as her boss wanted to replace her with someone from his own community. It is everywhere. Wherever you go, the first thing people want to know is which caste or religion you belong to.'

The woman was still talking on the podium. 'What is her name?' I asked.

'She is Ambabhavani, a gifted speaker from Tamil Nadu.'

Her name rang a bell somewhere in my mind and

suddenly I was transported away from the jostling crowds and the loud speeches. I was in a time long past with my paternal grandmother, Amba Bai.

Amba Bai was affectionately called Ambakka or Ambakka Aai by everyone in the village. She spent her whole life in one little village, Savalagi, near Bijapur in north Karnataka. Like most other women of her generation she had never stepped into a school. She was married early and spent her life fulfilling the responsibilities of looking after a large family. She was widowed early and I always remember seeing her with a shaven head, wearing a red sari, the pallu covering her head always, as was the tradition in the then orthodox Brahmin society. She lived till she was eighty-nine and in her whole life she knew only the worlds of her ten children, forty grandchildren, her village and the fields.

Since we were farmers she owned large mudhouses with cows, horses and buffaloes. There was a large granary and big trees that cooled the house during the hot summers. There were rows of cacti planted just outside the house. They kept out the mosquitoes, we were told. Ajji (that's what we called Amba Bai) looked after the fields and the farmers with a passion. In fact, I don't recall her ever spending too much time in the kitchen making pickles or sweets like other grandmothers. She would be up early and after her bath spend some time doing her daily puja. She would make some jowar rotis and a vegetable, and then head out to the fields. She would spend time there talking to the farmers about the seeds they had got, the state of the well or the health of their cattle. Her other passion in life was to help the women of the village deliver their babies.

Though I did not realize this till I was a teenager, Ajji was most unlike an orthodox Brahmin widow. She was very much for women's education, family planning and had much to say about the way society treated widows.

Those days there were few facilities available to the villages. There were a handful of medical colleges and not every taluk had a government hospital. In this scenario women who had borne children were the only help to others during childbirth. My grandmother was one of them. She was very proud of the fact that she had delivered ten perfectly healthy children, all of whom survived. And in turn, she would help others during their delivery irrespective of caste or community. She always had a word of advice or a handy tip for the various pregnant women of the village.

I would often hear various such nuggets from her. 'Savitri, be careful. Don't lift heavy articles. Eat well and drink more milk.'

'Peerambi, you have had two miscarriages. Be careful this time. Eat lots of vegetables and fruits. You should be careful but don't sit idle. Pregnancy is not a disease. You should be active. Do some light work. Send your husband Hussain Saab to my house. I will give some sambar powder. My daughter-in-law prepares it very well.'

Of course not everyone appreciated her advising them. One such person was Shakuntala Desai, who had stayed in the city for some time and had gone to school. 'What does Ambakka know about these things?' she would comment loudly, 'Has she ever gone to school or read a medical book? She is not a doctor.'

But Ajji would be least bothered by these comments. She would only laugh and say, 'Let that Shakuntala get pregnant. I will deliver the baby. My four decades of experience is better than any book!'

My father's job took us to various towns to live in, but we always came to Ajji's village during the holidays. They were joyous days and we would enjoy ourselves thoroughly.

Once, when we were at the village, there was a wedding in the neighbouring village. Ajji always refused to attend these social gatherings. That time, I too decided to stay back with her and one night there was only Ajji, me and our helper Dyamappa in that large house.

It was an unusually cold, moonless winter night in December. It was pitch dark outside. Ajji and I were sleeping together. Dyamappa had spread his bed on the front veranda and was fast asleep. For the first time that night, I saw Ajji remove her pallu from her head and the wisps of grey hair on her head. She touched them and said, 'Society has some such cruel customs. Would you believe that I once had thick long plaits hanging down my back? How I loved my hair and what a source of envy it was for the other girls! But the day your grandfather died, no one even asked my permission before chopping off that beautiful hair. I cried as much for my hair as for my husband. No one understood my grief. Tell me, if a wife dies, does the widower keep his head shaved for the rest of his life? No, within no time he is ready to be a groom again and bring home another bride!'

At that age, I could not understand her pain, but now, when I recall her words, I realize how helpless she must have felt.

After sometime she changed her topic. 'Our Peerambi is due anytime. I think it will be tonight. It is a moonless night after all. Peerambi is good and pious, but she is so shy, I am sure she will not say anything to anyone till the pain becomes unbearable. I have been praying for her safe delivery to our family deity Kallolli Venkatesha and also at the Peer Saab Darga in Bijapur. Everyone wants sons, but I do hope there is a girl this time. Daughters care for parents wherever they are. Any woman can do a man's job but a man cannot do a woman's job. After your Ajja's death, am I not looking after the entire farming? Akkavva, always remember women have more patience and common sense. If only men realized that . . .'

Ajji had so many grandchildren she found it hard to remember all their names. So she would call all her granddaughters Akkavva and grandsons Bala.

As Ajji rambled on into the night, there was a knock on the door. Instinctively Ajji said, 'That must be Hussain.' And indeed it was. Ajji covered her head again and forgetting her griefs about widowhood, she asked quickly, 'Is Peerambi in labour?'

'Yes, she has had the pains since this evening.'

'And you are telling me now? You don't understand how precious time is when a woman is in labour. Let us go now. Don't waste any more time.'

She started giving instructions to Hussain and Dyamappa simultaneously.

'Hussain, cut the cactus, take a few sprigs of neem. Dyamappa, you light two big lanterns . . .

'Akkavva, you stay at home. Dyamappa will be with you. I have to hurry now.'

She was gathering some things from her room and putting them into her wooden carry-box. By that time, the huge Dyamappa, with his large white turban on his head and massive moustaches appeared at the door bearing two lanterns. In the pitch darkness he made a terrifying picture and immediately brought to my mind the Ravana in the Ramayana play I had seen recently. There was no way I was going to stay alone in the house with him! I insisted I wanted to go with Ajji.

Ajji was impatient. 'Akkavva, don't be adamant. After all, you are a teenage girl now. You should not see these things. I will leave you at your friend Girija's house.' But like any other teenager, I was adamant and would not budge from my decision.

Finally Ajji gave up. She went to the puja room, said a quick prayer and locked the house behind her. Four of us set off in pitch darkness to Hussain saab's house. Hussain lead first with a lantern, Ajji, with me clutching on to her hand, followed and Dyamappa brought up the rear, carrying the other lantern.

We made our way across the village. Ajji walked with ease while I stumbled beside her. It was cold and I did not know the way. All the time Ajji kept up a constant stream of instructions for Hussain and Dyamappa.

'Hussain, when we reach, fill the large drums with water. Dyamappa will help you. Boil some water. Burn some coal. Put all the chickens and lambs in the shed. See that they don't come wandering around . . .'

Finally we reached Hussain's house. Peerambi's cries of pain could be heard coming from inside.

Hussain and Peerambi lived alone. They were poor farm labourers who worked on daily wages. Their neighbour Mehboob Bi was there, attending to Peerambi. Seeing Ajji she looked relieved. 'Now there is nothing to worry. Ambakka aai has come.'

Ajji washed her feet and hands and went inside the room with her paraphernalia, slamming the doors and windows shut behind her. Outside on the wooden bench, Hussain and Dyamappa sat awaiting further instructions from Ajji. I was curious to find out what would happen next.

Inside, I could hear Ajji speaking affectionately to Peerambi. 'Don't worry. Delivery is not an impossible thing. I have given birth to ten children. Just cooperate and I will help you. Pray to God to give you strength. Don't lose courage . . .' In between, she opened the window partly and told Hussain, 'I want some turmeric powder. I can't search in your house. Get it from Mehboob Bi's house. Dyamappa, give me one more big bowl of boiling water. Hussain, take a new cane tray, clean it with turmeric water and pass it inside. Dyamappa, I want some more burning coal . . .'

The pious gentle Ajji was a dictator now!

The next few hours were punctuated by Peerambi's anguished cries and Ajji's patient, consoling words, while Hussain sat outside tense and Dyamappa nonchalantly smoked a bidi. The night got dark and then it started getting lighter and lighter. The cock, locked in its coop, crowed and with the rising sun we heard the sounds of a baby's crying.

Ajji opened one window pane and announced, 'Hussain, you are blessed with a son. He looks just like your father Mohammed Saab. Peerambi had a tough time but God is kind. Mother and child are both safe and healthy.'

S-l-a-a-m . . . the door shut again. But this time outside we grinned at each other in joy. Hussain knelt down and said a prayer of thanks. Then he jumped up and knocked on the door, wanting to see the baby. It remained shut. Ajji was not entertaining any visitors till she was done.

'Your clothes are dirty,' she shouted from inside. 'First have a bath, wear clean clothes and then come in, otherwise you will infect the baby and mother.'

Hussain rushed to the bathroom, which was just a thatched partition and poured buckets of clean water from the well on himself.

Even after he rushed in, I could hear only Ajji's voice. 'Peerambi, my work is over. I have to rush home. Today is my husband's death ceremony. There are many rituals to be completed. The priests will arrive any time and I have to help them. I will leave now and if you want anything, send word through Hussain.

'Peerambi, to a woman, delivering a baby is like going to the deathbed and waking up again. Be careful. Mehboob Bi, please keep Peerambi's room clean. Don't put any new clothes on the baby. They will hurt him.

Wrap him in an old clean dhoti. Don't kiss the baby on his lips. Don't show the baby to everybody. Don't keep touching him. Boil the drinking water and immerse an iron ladle in that. Peerambi should drink only that water. I will send a pot of home made ghee and soft rice and rasam for Peerambi to eat . . . Now I have to go. Bheemappa is supposed to come and clean the garden today. If I am late, he will run away . . .'

By now she had allowed the window to be opened. I peeped in and saw the tired but joyous face of Peerambi and a tiny, chubby version of Mohammed Saab, Hussain's father, asleep on the cane tray. The neem leaves were hanging, the cactus was kept in a corner and the fragrance of the *lobana* had filled the entire room. Ajji also looked tired and there was sweat on her forehead. But she was cleaning her accessories vigorously in the hot water and wiping them before placing them carefully back in her wooden box.

Just as we were about to leave, Hussain bent down and touched Ajji's feet. In a choked voice he said, 'Ambakka aai, I do not know how to thank you. We are poor and cannot give you anything. But I can thank you sincerely from the bottom of my heart. You are a mother of a hundred children. You have blessed my son by bringing him into this world. He will never stray from the correct path.'

Ajji touched him on his shoulder and raised him. There were tears in her eyes too. She wiped them and said, 'Hussain, God only wants us to help each other in difficult times. Peerambi is after all like another Akkavva to me.'

By now the sun was up and I followed Ajji back home without stumbling. Dyamappa was strolling lazily far behind us. One doubt was worrying me and I had to clear it. 'Ajji, you have given birth only to ten children. Why did Hussain say you are a mother of hundred?'

Ajji smiled and adjusting the pallu that was slipping off her head because of her brisk walk, she said, 'Yes. I have given birth only to ten children but these hands have brought out a hundred children in our village. Akkavva, I will pray that you become the mother of a hundred children, irrespective of the number you yourself give birth to.'

Scan QR code to access the
Penguin Random House India website

PENGUIN BOOKS

THE DAY I STOPPED DRINKING MILK

Sudha Murty was born in 1950, in Shiggaon, North Karnataka. Author, philanthropist, educator, public speaker and engineer, she completed her master's in computer science from IISc, Bangalore. She is the founder of the Infosys Foundation and the chairperson of the Murty Trust. A bestselling author, with more than 300 titles to her acclaim, some of her most famous books include *Three Thousand Stitches*, *Dollar Bahu* and *Wise and Otherwise*. She writes in English and Kannada, and her books have been translated into all major Indian languages and have sold over 60 lakh copies around the country.

Over the years, Sudha Murty has been recognized with many prestigious awards, including the Padma Bhushan and the Padma Shri from the Government of India in 2023 and 2006, respectively; Bal Sahitya Puraskar in 2023; the R.K. Narayan Award for Literature in 2006; the Lal Bahadur Shastri National Award in 2020; and Lokmanya Tilak and Mahatma awards in 2024. She was also awarded the Rajyotsava and Attimabbe Award for excellence in Kannada literature from the Government of Karnataka in 2000 and 2012. Sudha Murty has received nineteen honorary doctorates from various universities across India. Currently, she is also serving as the President-nominated member of Parliament in the Rajya Sabha.

ALSO BY THE SAME AUTHOR

SUDHA MURTY

THE DAY I STOPPED
DRINKING MILK

Life Stories from Here and There

PENGUIN BOOKS

An imprint of Penguin Random House

PENGUIN BOOKS

Penguin Books is an imprint of the Penguin Random House group of companies
whose addresses can be found at global.penguinrandomhouse.com

Published by Penguin Random House India Pvt. Ltd
4th Floor, Capital Tower 1, MG Road,
Gurugram 122 002, Haryana, India

First published by Penguin Books India 2012
This edition published in Penguin Books by Penguin Random House India 2025

59

ISBN 9780143418658

Typeset in Dante MT by Eleven Arts, Delhi
Printed at Thomson Press India Ltd, New Delhi

www.penguin.co.in

To Lakshmi, my new daughter
and Rishi, my new son

Contents

Preface

One may wonder why I am writing about the personal lives of many people who have confided in me about their problems. Isn't it unethical to do so? However, most of the people I have written about requested me to change their names and use their problems as case studies. Some like Vishnu and Portado encouraged me to tell their stories so that others should not become like them. I thank all these people wholeheartedly and am grateful for their strength and kindness that has allowed me to share their stories with you.

This is my fourth book of recollections of my experiences as a teacher, a writer and a social worker. I want to thank my new editor, Shrutkeerti Khurana, whose hard work has made an immense difference to this book. Her constant interaction with me made me think of some stories in a different way and also helped me look at things from a youngster's point of view.

I would also like to thank Udayan Mitra of Penguin Books for convincing me to bring out a new volume of my stories and thoughts.

SUDHA MURTY

1

Bombay to Bangalore

It was the beginning of summer. I was boarding Udyan Express at Gulbarga railway station. My destination was Bangalore. As I boarded the train, I saw that the second-class compartment was jam-packed with people. Though the compartment was reserved, there were many unauthorized people in it. This side of Karnataka is popularly known as Hyderabad Karnataka since the Nizam of Hyderabad once ruled this area. There is scarcity of water here, which makes the land dry, and the farmers cannot grow anything during summer. Hence, many poor farmers and landless labourers from Hyderabad Karnataka immigrate to Bangalore and other big cities during the summer for jobs in construction. They return to their homes in the rainy season to cultivate their lands. This was April, so the train compartment was particularly crowded.

I sat down and was pushed to the corner of the berth. Though it was meant for three people, there were already six of us sitting on it. I looked around and saw students who were eager to come to Bangalore and explore different options to enhance their careers. There were merchants who were talking about what goods to order from Bangalore. Some government officers, though, were criticizing Gulbarga. 'What a place! Staying here is impossible because of the heat. No wonder people call this a punishment transfer!'

The ticket collector came in and started checking people's tickets and reservations. It was difficult to guess who had a ticket and who had a reservation. Some people had tickets but no reservation. This was an overnight train and people needed sleeper berths, but they were limited in number. People who did not have a reserved berth were begging the ticket collector to accommodate them 'somehow'. It was next to impossible for him to listen to everyone.

With his eagle eye, he easily located people who did not have a ticket. People without tickets were pleading, 'Sir, the previous train was cancelled. We had a reservation on that train. It is not our fault. We don't want to pay for this ticket again.' Some were begging him, 'Sir, I was late to the station and there was a big queue. I didn't have time to buy a ticket. So, I got into this compartment.' The collector must have read the Bhagavad Gita thoroughly; he remained calm while listening to their stories and kept issuing new tickets for ticketless passengers.

Suddenly, he looked in my direction and asked, 'What about your ticket?'

'I have already shown my ticket to you,' I said.

'Not you, madam, the girl hiding below your berth. Hey, come out, where is your ticket?'

I realized that someone was sitting below my berth. When the collector yelled at her, the girl came out of hiding. She was thin, dark, scared and looked like she had been crying profusely. She must have been about thirteen or fourteen years old. She had uncombed hair and was dressed in a torn skirt and blouse. She was trembling and folded both her hands.

The collector asked again, 'Who are you? From which station did you get on? Where are you going? I can issue a full ticket for you with a fine.'

The girl did not reply. The collector was getting very angry since he had been dealing with countless ticketless passengers. He took out his anger on this little girl. 'I know all you runaways,' he shouted. 'You take a free ride in trains and cause tremendous problems. You neither reply to my questions nor pay for your ticket. I have to answer to my bosses . . .'

The girl still did not say anything. The people around the girl were not bothered at all and went about their business. Some were counting the money for their ticket and some were getting ready to get down at Wadi Junction, the next stop. People on the top berth were preparing to sleep and others were busy with their dinner. This was something unusual for me, because I had never seen such a situation in my vast experience of social work.

The girl stood quietly as if she had not heard anything. The collector caught hold of her arms and told her to get down at the next station. 'I will hand you over to the police myself. They will put you in an orphanage,' he said. 'It is not my headache. Get down at Wadi.'

The girl did not move. The collector started forcibly pulling her out from the compartment. Suddenly, I had a strange feeling. I stood up and called out to the collector. 'Sir, I will pay for her ticket,' I said. 'It is getting dark. I don't want a young girl on the platform at this time.'

The collector raised his eyebrows and looked at me. He smiled and said, 'Madam, it is very kind of you to offer to buy her a ticket. But I have seen many children like her. They get in at one station, then get off at the next and board another train. They beg or travel to their destination without a ticket. This is not an exceptional case. Why do you want to waste your money? She will not travel even with a ticket. She may leave if you just give her some money.'

I looked out of the compartment. The train was approaching Wadi Junction and the platform lights were bright. Vendors of tea, juice and food were running towards the train. It was dark. My heart did not accept the collector's advice—and I always listen to my heart. What the collector said might be true but what would I lose—just a few hundred rupees?

'Sir, that's fine. I will pay for her ticket anyway,' I said.

I asked the girl, 'Will you tell me where you want to go?'

The girl looked at me with disbelief. It was at this moment that I noticed her beautiful, dark eyes, which were grief-stricken. She did not say a word.

The collector smiled and said, 'I told you, madam. Experience is the best teacher.'

He turned to the girl and said, 'Get down.'

Then he looked at me and said, 'Madam, if you give her ten rupees, she will be much happier with that than with the ticket.'

I did not listen to him. I told the collector to give me

a ticket to the last destination, Bangalore, so that the girl could get down wherever she wanted.

The collector looked at me again and said, 'But she won't get a berth and you will have to pay a penalty.'

I quietly opened my purse.

The collector continued, 'If you want to pay, then you should pay for the ticket from the train's starting point.'

The train originated from Bombay VT and terminated at Bangalore. I paid up quietly. The collector issued the ticket and left in disdain.

The girl was left standing in the same position. I asked my fellow passengers to move and give the girl some space to sit down because she now held a valid ticket. They moved very reluctantly. Then, I asked the girl to sit on the seat—but she did not. When I insisted, she sat down on the floor.

I did not know where to start the conversation. I ordered a meal for her and when the dinner box came, she held it in her hands but did not eat. I failed to persuade her to eat or talk. Finally, I gave the ticket to her and said, 'Look, I don't know what's on your mind since you refuse to talk to me. So, here's the ticket. You can get down wherever you want to.'

As the night progressed, people started sleeping on the floor and on their berths, but the girl continued to sit.

When I woke up at six o'clock the next morning, she was dozing. That meant that she had not got down anywhere. Her dinner box was empty and I was happy that she had at least eaten something.

As the train approached Bangalore, the compartment started getting empty. Again, I told her to sit on the seat and this time she obliged. Slowly, she started talking. She told me that her name was Chitra. She lived in a village near Bidar. Her father was a coolie and she had lost her mother at birth. Her father had remarried and had two sons with her stepmother. But a few months ago, her father had died. Her stepmother started beating her often and did not give her food. I knew from her torn, bloodstained blouse and the marks on her body that she was telling the truth. She was tired of that life. She did not have anybody to support her so she left home in search of something better.

By this time, the train had reached Bangalore. I said goodbye to Chitra and got down from the train. My driver came and picked up my bags. I felt someone watching me. When I turned back, Chitra was standing there and looking at me with sad eyes. But there was nothing more that I could do.

As I started walking towards my car, I realized that Chitra was following me. I knew that she did not have anybody in the whole world. Now, I was at a loss. I did not know what to do with her. I had paid her ticket out of compassion but I had never thought that she was going to be my responsibility! But from Chitra's perspective, I had been kind to her and she wanted to cling on to me. When I got into the car, she stood outside watching me.

I was scared for a minute. 'What am I doing?' I questioned myself. I was worried about the safety of a girl in Wadi Junction station, but now I was leaving her in a big city like Bangalore—a situation worse than the previous one. Anything could happen to Chitra here. After all, she was a girl. There were many ways in which people could exploit her situation.

I told her to get into my car. My driver looked at the girl curiously. I told him to take us to my friend Ram's place. Ram ran separate shelter homes for boys and girls. We at the Infosys Foundation supported him financially on a regular basis. I thought Chitra could stay there for some time and we could talk about her future after I came back from my tours in a few weeks. There were about ten girls in the shelter and three of them were of Chitra's age. Most of the girls there already knew me.

As soon as I reached the shelter, the lady supervisor came out to talk to me. I explained the situation and handed Chitra over to her. I told Chitra, 'You can stay here for two weeks. Don't worry. These are very good people. I will come and see you after two weeks. Don't run away from here, at least until I come back. Talk to your lady supervisor. You can call her Akka.' (Akka means elder sister in the Kannada language.) I handed over some money to the supervisor and told her to buy some clothes and other necessary things for the girl.

After two weeks, I went back to the shelter. I was not sure if Chitra would even be there. But to my surprise, I saw Chitra looking much happier than before. She was having good food for the first time in her life. She was wearing new clothes and was teaching lessons to the younger children. As soon as she saw me, she stood up eagerly. The supervisor said, 'Chitra is a nice girl. She helps in our kitchen, cleans the shelter and also teaches the younger children. She tells us that she was a good student in her village and wanted to join high school but her family didn't allow her to do so. Here, she is comfortable and wants to study further. What are your plans for her future? Can we keep her here?'

Soon, Ram also joined us. Ram knew the whole story and suggested that Chitra could go to a high school nearby. I immediately agreed and said that I would sponsor her expenses as long as she continued to study.

I left the shelter knowing that Chitra had found a home and a new direction in her life.

I got busier with my work and my visits to the shelter reduced to once a year. But I always inquired about Chitra's well-being over the phone. I knew that she was studying well and that her progress was good.

Years went by. One day, Ram phoned me and said that Chitra had scored 85 per cent in her tenth class. When I went to the shelter to congratulate and talk to her, she was very happy. She was growing up to be a confident young woman. There was brightness in her beautiful, dark eyes.

I offered to sponsor her college studies if she wanted to continue studying. But she said, 'No, Akka. I have talked to my friends and made up my mind. I would like to do my diploma in computer science so that I can immediately get a job after three years.' I tried to persuade her to go to college for a bachelor's degree in engineering but she did not agree. She wanted to become economically independent as soon as possible. Somewhere inside me, I understood where she was coming from.

Three rainy seasons passed. Chitra obtained her diploma with flying colours. She also got a job in a software company as an assistant testing engineer. When she got her first salary, she came to my office with a sari and a box of sweets. I was touched by her gesture. Later, I got to know that she had spent her entire first salary buying something for everyone at the shelter.

Soon enough, Ram called me to discuss a new problem. 'Chitra is now a working girl. So she cannot stay in the shelter since it is only meant for students.' I told Ram that I would talk to Chitra and ask her to pay the shelter a reasonable amount of money per month towards rent. This way she could continue to stay there until she got married. I strongly felt that the shelter was a safe place for an unmarried, orphan girl like Chitra.

Ram asked me, 'Are you going to look for a boy for her?'

This was a new and an even bigger problem. As her informal guardian, I had to find a boy for Chitra or she herself had to find a life partner. This was a great responsibility. No wonder people say I have a penchant for getting into problems! But God also shows me unique ways of getting out of them. I told Ram, 'She is only twenty-one. Let her work for a few years. If you come across a suitable boy, please let me know.'

I called Chitra and gave her my opinion about staying at the shelter, and she happily agreed to stay on and pay rent.

Days rolled by, and months turned into years. One day, when I was in Delhi, I got a call from Chitra. She was very happy. 'Akka, my company is sending me to the USA! I wanted to meet you and take your blessings but you are not here in Bangalore.'

I was ecstatic for Chitra. I said, 'Chitra, you are now going to a different country. Take care of yourself and keep in touch. My blessings are always with you.'

Years passed. Occasionally, I received an email from Chitra. She was doing very well in her career. She was posted across several cities in USA and was enjoying life. I silently prayed that she should always be happy wherever she was.

Years later, I was invited to deliver a lecture in San Francisco for Kannada Koota, an organization where families who speak Kannada meet and organize events. The lecture was in a convention hall of a hotel and I decided to stay at the same hotel. After the lecture, I was planning to leave for the airport. When I checked out of the hotel room and went to the reception counter to pay the bill, the receptionist said, 'Ma'am, you don't need to pay us anything. The lady over there has already settled your bill. She must know you pretty well.'

I turned around and found Chitra there. She was standing with a young white man and wore a beautiful sari. She was looking very pretty with short hair. Her dark eyes were beaming with happiness and pride. As soon as she saw me, she gave me a brilliant smile, hugged me and touched my feet. I was overwhelmed with joy and did not know what to say.

'Chitra, how are you? I have not seen you since ages. What a sweet surprise. How did you know that I will be in this city today?'

'Akka, I live in this city and came to know that you are giving a lecture at the local Kannada Koota. I am also a member there. I wanted to surprise you. It is not difficult to find out about your schedule.'

'Chitra, I have so many questions to ask you. How is work? Have you visited India? And more importantly, have you found Mr Right? And why did you pay my hotel bill?'

'No, Akka. I haven't come to India since I left. If I come to India, how can I return here without meeting you? Akka, I have something to tell you. I know that you were always worried about my marriage. You never asked me about my community. But you always wanted me to settle down. I know it is hard for you to choose a boy for me. Now, I have found my Mr Right. Please meet my colleague, John. We are getting married at the end of the year. You must come for our wedding and bless us.'

I was very happy to see the way things had turned out for Chitra. But I came back to my original question.

'Chitra, why did you pay my hotel bill? That is not right.'

With tears in her eyes and gratitude on her face, she said, 'Akka, if you hadn't helped me, I don't know where I would have been today—maybe a beggar, a prostitute, a runaway child, a servant in someone's house . . . or I may even have committed suicide. You changed my life. I am ever grateful to you.'

'No, Chitra. I am only one step in your ladder of success,' I said. 'There are many steps which led you to where you are today—the shelter which looked after you, the schools which gave you good education, the company which sent you to America and, above all, it is you—the most determined and inspired girl who made your life yourself. One step should never take the credit for the end result.'

'That is your thinking, Akka. I differ with you,' she said.

'Chitra, you are starting a new life and you should save money for your new family. Why did you pay my hotel bill?'

Chitra did not reply but told John to touch my feet. Then, suddenly sobbing, she hugged me and said, 'Because you paid for my ticket from Bombay to Bangalore!'

2

Rahman's Avva

Rahman was a young and soft-spoken employee who worked in a BPO. He was also an active volunteer in our Foundation. He would not talk without reason and would never boast about his achievements.

Rahman was a perfectionist. So any assignment given to him was done exceedingly well. He worked for the Foundation on the weekends and was very kind to the children in the orphanage. He spent his own money and always brought sweets for the children. I really liked him.

Since we worked closely together, he learnt that I am from North Karnataka, from Dharwad district. My language has that area's accent and my love for Dharwad food is very well known. One day, Rahman came and asked me, 'Ma'am, if you are free this Sunday, will you come to my house? My mother and sister are visiting me. Incidentally, my mother is also from Dharwad district. My family has read your columns in Kannada and your books too. When I told them that I am working with you, they expressed their earnest desire to meet you. Is it possible for you to have lunch with us?'

'Will you assure me that I'll get a good Dharwad meal?' I joked.

'I assure you, ma'am. My mother is a great cook.'

'Come on, Rahman. Every boy gives this compliment to his mother, however bad she may be at cooking. It is the mother's love that makes the food great.'

'No, she really is an amazing cook. Even my wife says so.'

'Then she must be really great because no daughter-in-law praises her mother-in-law's cooking without merit,' I smiled. 'By the way, which village in Dharwad district do they come from?'

He told me the name of a village near Ranebennur that I had never heard of. I happily agreed to visit them for lunch.

That Sunday, I took some flowers along. Rahman's newly constructed apartment was on Bannerghatta Road near the zoo. When I entered his home, I met his wife Salma. She was a smart and good-looking girl. She worked as a teacher in the kindergarten nearby.

Then, he called out to his Avva. A mother is usually

referred to as Avva in North Karnataka. An old lady with grey hair came out of the kitchen. Rahman introduced her, 'This is my mother.' I was a bit surprised—she was not quite what I had expected. She was wearing a huge bindi the size of a 25-paise coin and an Ilkal sari with lots of green bangles on both arms. She kept the sari pallu on her head. She had a contented smile on her face and with folded hands she said, 'Namaste.'

Rahman's sister entered from another room. She was so different from Rahman. Rahman was fair and very handsome. His sister was tall and dark. She was wearing a cotton sari with a smaller bindi than her mother and also had two gold bangles on her hands. Rahman said, 'This is my sister Usha. She stays in Hirekerur. Both her husband and she are school teachers.'

I felt confused after meeting Rahman's mother and sister but I did not ask any questions.

After I sat down comfortably, Usha said, 'Madam, we love your stories because we feel connected to them. I teach some of your children's stories at school.'

Salma also joined the conversation. 'Even I like them, but my students are too young to understand.'

Rahman smiled and said, 'You must be surprised to see my mother and sister. I want to share my story with you.'

His mother went back to the kitchen and Usha started cleaning the table. Salma went to help her mother-in-law. Only the two of us remained.

'Ma'am, you must be wondering why my mother and sister are Hindus while I am a Muslim. Only you can understand and appreciate my life story because I have seen you helping people from all religions and communities without bias. I remember your comment to me: we can't choose the community or religion that we are born into—so we should never think that our community is our identity.'

Rahman paused, then continued, 'Ma'am, I believe in that too because I have also been brought up that way. I want to share my life and my perspective with you.'

Rahman started his story.

'Thirty years ago, Kashibai and Datturam lived in the outskirts of our village with their six-month-old daughter Usha. They looked after the ten-acre field of their landlord, Srikant Desai, who lived in Bombay. Srikant only came once a year to collect the revenue. The field was very large and it was too much for Kashibai and Datturam to handle. So, they requested the landlord to get another family to stay with them and help with the field. They also welcomed the thought of having company.

'Srikant contacted his acquaintances and found a

suitable family. Soon, Fatima Bi and Husain Saab came to the village. They occupied one portion of the house and the other portion stayed with Kashibai and Datturam. Husain Saab and Datturam got along very well. However, Kashibai and Fatima Bi didn't see eye to eye at all. It is not that they were bad women but their nature were very different. Kashibai was loud, very frank and hard-working. Fatima Bi was quiet, lazy and an introvert. Inevitably, there was a fight. It all started with a hen. Kashibai's hen would come to Fatima Bi's portion of the house and lay eggs. Fatima Bi wouldn't return the eggs because she thought that her hen had laid them. Kashibai even tried colouring her hen to distinguish it from Fatima Bi's. Both the ladies shared a common well and would fight because both wanted to wash their vessels and clothes almost always at the same time. They also fought about their goats. Fatima Bi's goats came and ate Kashibai's flowers and leaves, which she used for her puja. Sometimes, Kashibai's goats went to Fatima Bi's place and left their droppings behind. Fatima Bi wouldn't return the droppings either.'

'What's so great about droppings?' I interrupted.

'Ma'am, goat droppings are used as manure.'

'Oh, I understand. Please continue,' I urged Rahman.

'The fights continued and sometimes Kashibai felt that she had made a mistake to tell their landlord that they wanted neighbours. She felt that she had been very happy without Fatima Bi. Fatima Bi also wanted to leave the farm and go to some other village but Husain Saab didn't agree. He would say, "You women fight about unnecessary things. This is a good opportunity for us to make money. The land is fertile and there is plenty of water. Our landlord is good and hardly visits. We can easily grow vegetables. Where can I get such work nearby? You should also become active like Kashibai and drop your ego. Try to adjust with her." The same conversation would happen on the other side of the house. Datturam would tell his wife, "Don't be so aggressive. You should mellow down like Fatima. Though she is lazy, she is good-natured."

'But as usual, both women never listened to their husbands.

'As time went by, Kashibai's daughter Usha turned two years old. Fatima Bi loved children and enjoyed seeing Usha play in the field. Fatima Bi liked henna a lot. Every month, she coloured her hand with henna from the plant in the field and Usha always joined her. Usha was fascinated with the beautiful orange colour. She would come home and tell her mother, "Why can't you also colour your hand like Fatima Kaku?" (Kaku is equivalent to 'aunt' in the local language.)

'This comment irritated Kashibai. She said, "Fatima can afford to colour her hands because her husband works and also helps in the kitchen. She sits on the bed and listens to the radio. If I do that, will your father come and work in the kitchen?" Fatima Bi would overhear their conversation but still she continued her friendship with little Usha.

'When Fatima became pregnant, she became even lazier. She eventually reached full term and a distant relative came to help Fatima with her delivery. A few days later, there was a festival in the village and Datturam and his family went to attend it. When they came back, Fatima Bi was not there. She was already in the hospital in critical condition and had delivered a son. The house was in complete silence. But the silence was deafening to Kashibai's ears. She started crying. She was very sad because Fatima Bi was in the hospital in such a serious condition. The next day, they learnt that Fatima Bi was no more.

'Husain Saab was left with his newborn son. The midwife stayed for a month and left. It was an uphill task for Husain Saab to look after a small baby. Neither Husain Saab nor Fatima Bi had any relatives who could take care of the little one. Most of them were coolies and a newborn child would only be a burden to the relatives.

Datturam was very sympathetic and allowed Husain Saab to work less in the field but taking care of a small baby alone is very difficult.

'One night, the child started crying non-stop and Kashibai could not take it. She felt that enough was enough. After all, it was a little baby. A woman is so different from a man when it comes to rearing a child. Her motherly instinct made her go next door and tap on Husain Saab's door without even waiting for her husband. When Husain Saab opened the door, she told him, "Husain Saab, give me the baby. I am a mother. I know how to handle him." She picked up the baby boy, held him in her pallu and brought him to her house holding him tightly to her chest. The baby boy stopped crying immediately. For the first time since the baby was born, Husain Saab slept through the night comfortably.

'The next day, Kashibai told Husain Saab, "I will look after this child until you get married again. Don't worry." She forgot her enmity with Fatima Bi and even felt ashamed. She thought that she should have been nicer to Fatima Bi. Now, Kashibai did not even bother about where the droppings of the goats fell or where the hens laid their eggs. For her, looking after the baby was more important.

'The baby was named Rahman and, to everyone's surprise, Husain Saab did not remarry. Rahman grew up in Kashibai's house and started calling her Avva and Usha became his Akka. Rahman continued to sleep in his father's house but as soon as the sun rose, he ran to Kashibai's house to get ready. While Usha bathed on her own, Kashibai bathed little Rahman. She gave them breakfast, packed their lunches and walked them to school. Though Usha was two years older than Rahman, Kashibai made sure that they studied in the same class. Kashibai worked in the field in the afternoon and brought the children back in the evenings. Husain Saab cooked Rahman's dinner and Rahman would go back and sleep with his father at night. This continued for ten years.

'When Rahman was ten and Usha was twelve years old, Husain Saab fell ill and all his savings were spent on his treatment. Meanwhile, Kashibai purchased two she-buffaloes and started a milk business. She started earning more money than her husband.

'That same year, Husain Saab died of tuberculosis. Rahman was left all alone. There were hardly any people at Husain Saab's burial. A distant uncle came and told the mullah that he would take care of Rahman. But when the time came to take Rahman away, the uncle did not turn up at all. Without a second thought, Datturam and Kashibai took him in. Rahman was happy to stay in Kashibai's house.

'Kashibai was very conscious about Rahman's religion. Every Friday, she sent him for namaaz and on holidays she sent him for Koran class at the local mosque. She told him to participate in all Muslim festivals even though there were very few Muslims in the village. Rahman also took part in the Hindu festivals celebrated in his house. Datturam and Kashibai bought two cycles for both the kids. Rahman and Usha cycled to high school and later they also rode their cycles to the same college.

'Eventually, they graduated and that day Kashibai told Rahman, "Unfortunately, we don't have a picture of your parents. So, turn towards Mecca and pray to Allah. Pray to Fatima Bi and Husain Saab. They will bless you. You are now grown up and independent. Usha is getting married next month. My responsibility to both Usha and you is now over."

'Kashibai's affection and devotion overwhelmed Rahman, who could not remember his own mother's face. He prayed to Allah and his parents and then touched Kashibai's feet. He said, "Avva, you are my Ammi. You are my Mecca."

'Rahman got a job in a BPO in Bangalore and left home. He worked for different firms for a few years, grew in his career and started earning a good salary. He met Salma at a friend's wedding and fell in love with her.

After getting Kashibai and Datturam's approval, he got married to Salma.'

When he finished his story, Rahman was very emotional and in tears.

I was amazed at Kashibai. She was uneducated but far advanced in human values. I was surprised and humbled by the largeness of her heart. Kashibai had raised the boy with his own religion and still loved him like her son.

By this time, lunch was ready and Usha invited me to eat. While having the delicious lunch, I asked Usha, 'What made you decide to visit here?'

'I have holidays at school and I took an extended vacation so I could come for Panchami.'

Panchami is a festival celebrated mostly by girls, particularly married women, who come to their brother's house. It is similar to the Rakhi festival in the north, where a brother acknowledges his sister's love. I recalled our history and remembered that Queen Karunavati had sent a rakhi to Emperor Humayun seeking his protection.

Now, I looked at the wall in the dining room and for the first time I noticed two pictures in Rahman's house, one of Mecca and the other of Krishna, both hanging side by side.

3

Ganga's Ghat

Ganga was a coolie in a tiny village in Karnataka which is infamous for droughts. She was a middle-aged woman who lived in a thatched hut near the rocks; she never locked her hut because there was nothing to steal from it. Her routine was simple. She got up in the morning, went to the fields to work, earned her daily wage and then came back home to fetch water, have a bath, cook her meal, eat and sleep. Her routine was the same on all days except Mondays, which was a village holiday.

Normally, everything was closed in the village on Monday because it is the day of Lord Ishwara and Nandi is his vehicle. So Monday was considered to be a rest day for the bullocks and a holiday for the village.

Water was a big problem in the village because of the rocks around the area. The government had dug borewells, and water was stored in a tank. Everybody had to walk half a kilometre to fetch water from the tank. However, in the summer, it was very hard to get water because there was no electricity and the muddy road would get very hot. Hence, summer was a curse to the people in the village.

Ganga used to feel useless at home. She was very lonely and did not know what to do on the days when she did not have work. During the summer, she did not get much work anyway because of the limited work available in the fields. She felt depressed knowing that she had no aim in life and nothing to live for.

One hot summer evening, she came back from the fields after work and felt very tired. She had her bath and was just about to start cooking when she saw an old beggar standing in front of her hut.

Ganga said, 'Old man, I haven't cooked yet, and I have very little rice today. You can come another day and I will give you some food.'

The old man did not answer. Ganga repeated herself. Then, he said, 'Akka, I do not want rice. Can you give me one bucket of lukewarm water? My body is itchy. Someone said that I should take a bath in lukewarm water. That will reduce the itching. I am unable to sleep at night. In the summer, there is a lot of dust and it is affecting me in this old age.'

Ganga was very upset at his strange request. She said, 'It is not easy to get water in this village. In the hot summer, I have to walk half a kilometre to get water. I can't do this job for you.'

'Akka, I don't have anybody. Neither do I have vessels or firewood. After all, I am a beggar. You are so well-off. You have a hut to stay, vessels, firewood and water. If you don't give me water, I will go away,' he said.

As he turned to leave, Ganga had an indescribable feeling. Nobody had ever told her that she was a rich woman. Nobody had ever called her Akka or asked her for anything. She was always ordered around at work. This was an unusual feeling and she liked it. She changed her mind and called out to the beggar, 'Old man, sit down. I will give you a bucket of lukewarm water.'

When she gave the water, she saw that he was happy. He took a bath on the side of her hut and rubbed his body with a stone instead of soap. He was careful while using the water. After he finished his bath, he changed to another set of torn clothes and said, 'Akka, God bless you.' Then he went away.

The next day, as Ganga was about to start cooking, the beggar came again. Just looking at him irritated her. She thought that once you help a beggar, they never leave you. They know how to get what they want by sheer perseverance.

She was a little rude this time: 'Why have you come again?'

'Akka, I slept very well last night. I have come again to beg you for another bucket of lukewarm water.'

Ganga did not answer. Her mind said no but her heart said yes. What was she going to lose? Just a bucket of water. The old man patiently waited for her answer. She looked at her vessel. There were three buckets of water stored in it. Without saying anything, she heated the water and gave him a bucket. He took a bath, blessed her and went his way.

The following day, she knew that he might come again. So she fetched an extra bucket of water. As usual, he appeared again. Before he could even say anything, Ganga handed him a bucket of lukewarm water and said, 'Don't repeat this again. I can't do this every day.'

'Akka, if you can give me water for a week, I will be very grateful. I am old and can't bring water but I can get dry leaves from the forest for you. They may help you in cooking.' The old man had his bath and left.

As promised, he brought a bundle of dry leaves for Ganga the next day. Ganga knew that he would come for a week. So she always got extra water. Now, every morning, she got up with a purpose. She had to fetch more water. Though it was tiresome, she had a goal. Someone waited for her. Someone blessed her every day. It was a good feeling.

After a week, she thought that the old man might not come again. But on that day, she saw two people coming towards her hut. The old man had brought another old beggar, who was in an equally shabby condition and kept scratching his body. Ganga knew what was coming next. Before they could ask, she said, 'This is not a bathing ghat. You can't bring people here and expect me to keep giving water for their baths.'

Both of them stood silently and did not move. Then the first old man said, 'Please give us some water, Akka. He is really unwell. If you give us one bucket, we will share it somehow.'

Ganga knew that they would not leave unless she gave them water. Grumbling, she gave them one and a half buckets of water. They thanked her profusely and shared the water so carefully that not a drop was wasted. Ganga wanted to tell them, 'Next time, you get your own bucket of water and I will warm it.' But she was unable to say so looking at their condition and old age.

The next day, she was plucking mangoes from the

mango fields at work, and she knew that two people would come to her hut today. She was wondering how she would manage to make an extra trip to the tank to get water.

Her colleague Yamuna asked her, 'Why are you looking so worried, Ganga? The crop is good. We will continue to get work. The coolie rate is also high. You don't have too much expense either. You should be happy.'

Ganga then explained her problem. Yamuna smiled and said, 'Look, if you really want to give them water, I will help you. My eldest son brings water on his cycle. I will request him to give one pot of water to you every day and leave it outside your hut.'

Thus, Ganga's problem was solved.

Now, Ganga started giving two buckets of water to the two old men every day. After ten days, she saw three people in the line. But this time, she did not get upset. She knew that word had spread. People knew that if you want to have a bath, you should go to Ganga's place. She thought, 'What is wrong in giving water? It may be extra work for me, but at least some people benefit from it. What do I do after cooking anyway? I just go to bed. If I work for another half hour, some people might feel better and will even bless me.' This time, without their asking, she gave them three buckets of water.

She was right. Word had spread in the village that Ganga gave free water, warmed, to people for a bath. Some beneficiaries were able-bodied, middle-aged men. They fetched water for her. In the village, some people thought that they themselves could not do this service, so they decided to donate a bucket of water to Ganga every day.

Now, Ganga found that she did not have vessels to store so much water. Almost immediately, a kind-hearted philanthropist gave her a big drum. Also, whoever went to fetch firewood from the forest started dropping a small bundle in front of her hut so that she could use it to heat water.

Ganga never asked anyone why he or she was bringing water to her or keeping firewood on her doorstep. She did her work without talking.

A few months later, women also joined the queue. Ganga made a separate bathing area with walls made out of coconut leaves for the women. She continued her work as a coolie during the day and did this work in the evenings. Now, the number of people gradually increased to thirty and eventually it reached forty.

The season changed. The rains began and it started getting cool. Now, Ganga had to provide hot water for the baths.

Ganga had found her mission in life. She got up in the mornings and went to work. After she came back in the evenings, she checked the quantity of water. If there was not enough water, she fetched some more. Firewood was never a problem and was always in excess.

When I met Ganga, I was taken aback by what she was doing. She never got any public recognition but she was very clear that she did not want to talk to the media. She said, 'I do this because I love it. This gave me an opportunity to serve people like me who don't have anything in life. One needn't have much money to help people. I don't spend any money on this. In a dusty place like this, skin diseases are common. A bath a day keeps the skin doctor away.' And she smiled at her own attempt at humour.

With my overenthusiasm, I said, 'Ganga, I will give you a box of soaps and a hundred cotton towels. You can gift this to everybody. Our medicinal soap might even help them.'

I thought that she would jump for joy but she did not. She said, 'Madam, even today, I don't lock my hut. People are aware of my work and they help me on their own. The moment you give me soap and towels, I will have to keep them under lock and key. Once I distribute the soap, which is perishable, people will ask me for more. Some people may even ask me for a different brand of soap. Once the towel is torn, they will ask me for a new one. If I don't give them, people will think that I hide soaps and towels. I want to do this work within my own limits. If you want to give them soaps and towels, you can give it to the people yourself. I don't have any objection.'

I realized Ganga's philosophy and accepted it wholeheartedly. I knew that she was right. Money comes with expectations and spoils the delicate equilibrium of social work.

Suddenly, I was reminded of the river Ganga. The river flows from the Himalayas and we believe that, if we take a dip in her, it will wash away all our sins and diseases. Hence, the bathing ghats at Varanasi, Hardwar and Rishikesh are famous. I felt peaceful and thought that this Ganga's bathing ghat was no less than the bathing ghats of the river Ganga.

4

The Day I Stopped Drinking Milk

The state of Odisha is beautiful. It has blue mountains known as Niladri, beautiful rivers like Mahanadi, and enchanting forests. It is famous for its historical places like Udayagiri, Dhauli, the largest saltwater lake, Chilka, and the famous Rath Yatra of Jagannath at Puri. Nobody can forget the war of Kalinga, which took place on the banks of Daya River. Even today, when you visit Ashoka's inscription on the rock edict, you realize the greatness of Kalinga, or today's Odisha. But with all these natural resources, there is also a darker side to the state—the poor and tribal people of Odisha.

I was working in a remote village and we were building a school for children there. The area had a beautiful mountain and a lake and there was greenery everywhere. The inaccessible road to the village helped retain its beauty. One day, I was in the village for work and it started raining heavily. When it pours, it is very difficult to get out of the forest and it is impossible to know how long the rains might last. I had a translator with me who knew both Oriya and English and he was helping me in my work. He suggested that we take shelter in a hut nearby until the rain stopped. So we went to the nearest hamlet of huts.

The hut was small and had a thatched roof and mud flooring. As we entered, I noticed that it was a single large room partitioned into two. The first portion doubled as a hall during the day and a bedroom at night. The second portion was the kitchen. The owner of the hut came and welcomed us in. He gave us a mat to sit on. I saw that the pouring rain and the gushing water were joining the lake in front of the hut. It was a riveting moment. Even though I heard my watch ticking, I felt that time was standing still. The owner's baby boy was crying inside and his mother was singing a lullaby to soothe him. After some time, my translator got bored and told me that he was going out and would join me after an hour or so. I asked him where he was planning to go in this pouring rain. He told me that he was going to a small shop near the hut.

My host wanted to give me something to eat or drink. Indian hospitality dictates that if any guest comes to your house, you must offer them something, no matter how poor you are. The Taittiriya Upanishad says, '*Athiti devo bhava.*' This means that God comes home in the form of a guest. Indians believe that you must serve your guest, going out of your way if necessary. This man was no exception.

He did not speak my language, so he asked me in his broken Hindi, 'Tea . . . ?'

I do not drink tea or coffee, so I firmly said, 'No.'

After some time, he hesitantly asked, 'Milk?'

I do not usually take milk either but I didn't want to hurt his feelings by denying everything he offered. So I nodded my head in affirmation.

He went to the other side of the partition and talked to his wife in Oriya. 'Madam has come all the way from a big city. She is helping our village by establishing a school so that our children can study well. This rain may not stop for some time. Please give her a glass of milk because she is our guest.'

I know Sanskrit fairly well since I learnt it at home. As a result, I can understand many Indian languages. I may not be able to speak it fluently but I can certainly understand Oriya to a great extent. My host thought that I did not understand Oriya because I had taken a translator with me. So he felt free to talk about me to his wife in Oriya.

Hearing her husband's words, the wife was very upset. 'The baby is crying continuously. I feel as if the pouring rain and this crying baby are having a jugalbandi!' she said in an irritated tone. 'The lady sitting outside has grey hair but no common sense. We are poor people. We also have to take care of a child. I have only one glass of goat's milk left for the baby. In this village, I have to work hard even to get this milk. If madam wants tea, I can give her a few teaspoons of milk. If she wants to eat fish, I can fetch them from the pond and prepare an excellent fish curry. If she wants to eat *pakhala* [leftover rice and water, an ordinary people's delicacy], it is already there. But she shouldn't ask for an expensive drink such as milk.'

My host requested his wife, 'Please don't be so rude. It doesn't suit you. You are a kind-hearted woman. Fortunately, madam can't understand Oriya. Because of this rain, she has come to our hut. Otherwise, she would have left for Bhubaneswar. She is yet to finish her work for the day. Her translator told me that she is a vegetarian and can't eat fish. She may not be used to eating pakhala either. Unfortunately, she does not drink tea. Offering just water isn't enough. What else can we give her? We only have milk. Is it not true that we should look after our guest well? You can take half of the milk, add water and boil it. Madam can share the milk with the baby.'

Silence fell in the hut. I was shocked hearing the conversation on the other side of the partition.

After some time, the owner brought milk for me in a small tumbler. This was the first time I realized that when a guest demands something, however small it might seem, it might be hard for the host to provide it, especially in a poor country like ours. If the guest has expensive habits, it will definitely hurt the host. In my ignorance and on his insistence, I had agreed to drink milk. But I was not even aware that I was snatching the share of a little baby. I felt ashamed. It was not possible for me to eat fish or drink tea. What should I do?

A few minutes later, my translator returned from the shop chewing the Pan Parag he had gone looking for. I told him, 'Tell my host that I am on fast today as I fast on all Wednesdays. I had forgotten that today is a Wednesday. I don't take anything other than water. So tell him no milk, please.'

My translator was baffled, because he had seen me having milk in the morning for breakfast. But he conveyed to the host what I had told him anyway.

My host asked, 'Nobody fasts on Wednesdays. Usually, people fast on Mondays, Thursdays, Fridays or Saturdays. Why are you fasting today?'

I said, 'I fast on Wednesdays for Buddha.'

Our host felt very sorry that I did not eat or drink anything in his hut but he was happy that he had done his best.

From that day onward, I gave up drinking milk.

5

Changing India

It was 25 April 1979—the first time I went to the USA. My destination was Boston. It was the beginning of summer when I landed at Logan airport. The days were long now so there was still light outside though it was late in the day. I saw that there was still some snow left on the ground—the last vestiges of a long winter.

I was last in the immigration queue. I had had a stopover in Paris and the waiting period for the connecting flight had been long because India was not a frequently travelled to country. So I was tired after the thirty-hour journey.

When my turn came, the stern-faced immigration officer asked me for my passport and started questioning me. 'Lady, why have you come to the United States?'

I handed my passport over to the officer and said, 'My husband is working for Data General Computer

Company and his duration of stay here is eight months. He has already been in Boston for a month and I want to join him. That's why I have come here.'

'How long do you want to stay?'

'A maximum of six months.'

'Are you working in India? If yes, show me your leave certificate and salary slip.'

Expecting these questions, I had brought those certificates with me and I showed them to him.

'How long will you stay in Boston?'

'I will be here for a few months. My brother is in Berkeley and I want to visit him after that.'

'Show me your return ticket and how much money you have brought from your country.'

'I have five hundred dollars.' I showed him the ticket and the money.

He looked at me with disbelief, stamped my visa for three months and gave my passport back to me. Then, he looked at me and said, 'What is that? What are you wearing?'

'I am wearing an Indian traditional sari. It is our national dress.'

'Hmm, you are from India. Where is this country? Is it near Japan? Or in Africa?'

'No, it is a part of Asia.'

'How do you know English?'

'In India, we have many languages. Along with our national language, we also learn English at school.'

His shift was about to end and another officer joined him and asked me, 'What are you wearing on your forehead?'

'This is known as bindi or kumkum. Most Indian women wear it.'

'Is that a caste mark?' he said.

His friend said, 'Oh, I remember learning about India in a documentary. It said that people in your country burn widows. Also, there are only two classes of people there, maharajas and beggars. You play with snakes, and cows are allowed to wander on the highways. Is that true?'

I was taken aback by his rude remarks. 'Burning widows was stopped several hundred years ago. It is not true that every widow in every state was burnt anyway. There are no maharajas left in India. It is a democratic country. In India, you see snakes only in the zoos or in the forests, just like in any other Asian country. Also, cows wander in villages on the road but not on the highways,' I explained patiently.

'Do you own an elephant?'

I laughed and said, 'It is not easy to own an elephant, but I have seen many.'

'That's enough. You can go now.'

I thanked them and went to the customs counter. In those days, customs was very tough on visitors. A customs officer asked me, 'What did you bring from India?'

'Oh, there are very few Indian stores here and we don't have a car. Hence, I have brought some masalas from home.'

The customs officer treated me like I was carrying diseases instead of masalas. He used a stick and asked me to point out and identify the masalas.

When I came out of there, I felt very dejected.

I have always been proud of my country because of our history and five thousand years of civilization. Even today, we continue the practices of the Indus Valley Civilization but other contemporary civilizations of that time have disappeared from the face of the earth. Our contribution to science in the olden days was outstanding and we were very good in astrophysics. We created music and dance forms and wrote books on them. We also generated enormous volumes of literature in the form of poetry, prose and dramas. Our civilization has stored two-thousand-year-old inscriptions that indicate that we knew writing. Our monumental temples show the zenith of architecture but for an outsider we are nothing but a poverty-stricken land of snake charmers and elephants, maharajas and beggars. It was not a good feeling.

Years rolled on. Infosys was formed along with many other companies in Bangalore. In time, Bangalore became the hub of the Indian software industry. The word 'Bangalored' itself became synonymous with outsourcing.

Today, Bangalore International Airport has many flights connecting directly to the USA and the rest of the world. Going abroad is as easy as taking a domestic flight. The next generation has become very confident, well-travelled, tech-savvy and hardworking. The West has finally woken up and taken note of this change.

In 2009, I went to Bogota, the capital of Columbia, in South America. I was visiting Columbia to deliver a talk on 'Lessons in Life'. My experiences at the Infosys Foundation had become very popular and valuable and people wanted to know all about them. I finished my talk and flew from Bogota to Miami, USA.

As always, I was last in the immigration queue. When my turn came, the visa officer was a young, lively African American. He saw me and knew that I was last, so he was quite relaxed and started asking me questions. I was ready to answer the monotonous questions. But this time it was different.

He asked, 'Oh, lady, you are from India?'

As a woman, I talk a lot. As a teacher, I talk a lot. As a trustee, I talk a lot. As an analyst, I talk a lot. I usually talk four times more than the average person. But sometimes, I talk less and listen more.

'Yes, I am from India,' was all I said.

'I know your national dress, the sari. It is really pretty. I like the way you wear it.'

I smiled and said, 'Thank you.' I did not have any other reply.

'Where are you coming from?'

Hesitantly, I said, 'I am coming from a city called Bangalore from the south of India.'

'Oh, I know Bangalore. It is a software hub. Lots of people from Bangalore come to Miami for a holiday. Lady, how long do you want to stay in our country?'

I was flying from Miami to San Francisco and then from San Francisco back to India.

I replied, 'Three days.'

'Why only three days?'

'I have work with Stanford University and after that I will go back home.'

'No, no. You should know that our country has great universities and beautiful states. You can't finish seeing our country in just three days.'

He stamped a six-month visa on my passport and said, 'Can I ask you some questions? Anyway, you have a visa now.'

I nodded my head.

'How is it that you Indians are so good? You are no-nonsense people. Your name is never on the terrorist list. Most of you are very professional.'

I smiled proudly and said, 'We are trained to be that way.' Now, I started asking him questions. 'How do you know so much about India?'

'Oh, it is not difficult. There are lots of Indian restaurants in Miami. On the weekends, I go there and eat.'

'What do you like there?'

'Good Indian food—tandoori chicken, chicken tikka, kebab and biryani.' He finished his work and got up.

I collected my bags and he joined me as I walked to customs. 'You know, lady, I like Bollywood songs,' he said. 'There are also Bollywood dance classes in Miami. By the way, I really like Kajol. She is very talented.'

By then, we had reached customs. 'It was really nice to meet you, lady. Have a good stay.'

As he walked away, I heard him humming 'Suraj hua madhham, chand dhalne laga' from the movie Kabhi Khushi Kabhie Gham in an American accent.

As I walked on, the customs officer did not even look at me. He just waved at me.

I found myself outside the airport with the passport in my hands. I was wondering what had changed in the last thirty years. It is not software alone. It is India in the eyes of the West. India is no longer a poverty-stricken land of snake charmers and elephants. The immigrant Indians in other countries, confident Indians at home who have created wealth, our next generation that has worked hard and competed successfully with the West and our children who are now global citizens have changed India's image in even a small airport like Miami.

I smiled as I looked at my Indian passport.

6

Genes

Anant was an unskilled worker in his early twenties who came to our house one day looking for work. When my grandfather opened the door, Anant requested him, 'Please let me work in your house. Just give me two meals a day. I have no money or family in this world and nowhere to go.'

My grandfather took pity on him and said, 'Boy, you can stay in our house as long as you want. But after some time, you should get married and take care of your family. For that, you will need money. Without skills, one can't earn money. I will teach you to perform pujas and I will pay you a hundred rupees per month as long as you stay with us.'

Anant was taken aback. He never expected to be paid to learn and even get free accommodation. In those days, a hundred rupees was a large sum of money. Anant became the man Friday of our house. All my childhood memories are inevitably linked with Anant.

As man Friday, Anant would perform all tasks without question. My grandmother would call out to him, 'Anant, go and bring vegetables from the market.' My uncle would tell him, 'Anant, go to the post office and get me some postcards. On the way back, get me a newspaper from the bazaar.' My aunt would say, 'Anant, will you pluck flowers from the garden for me? I have to make a garland for God!' I always went with Anant and accompanied him on his errands. Anant never complained and always smiled while he worked. He used to sit with my grandfather every day and learned to perform puja with devotion.

One day, my grandmother lost her gold bangle. It was a wedding gift from her father. Hence, there was a lot of sentimental attachment to it; she started sobbing. Everybody at home scanned the entire house but we did not find it. When night fell, my crying grandmother lit a lamp and told Anant to place it in front of the tulsi plant. When he went there, he saw a shining piece of metal in the mud. When he picked it up, he realized that it was my grandmother's gold bangle and ran back to give it back to her. My grandmother was extremely happy with him. She realized that she must have dropped the bangle while she was watering the plant. Grandfather gave Anant a hundred rupees as a reward and declared, 'Your honesty makes you a role model for all the people in our house.' However, Anant refused to accept the money. He said, 'A reward is for someone who is not family. I consider myself a part of this family. I will not take your money.'

On another occasion, Anant wanted to buy something for himself but he had run out of money. So he took an advance of fifty rupees from my grandfather against his next monthly allowance. At the beginning of next month, my grandfather gave Anant a hundred rupees, forgetting to deduct the advance. Anant immediately said, 'Ajja, please keep fifty rupees with you because you have already given it to me as an advance.' My grandfather was proud of Anant for his honesty and patted his back.

My grandfather told the whole family about this incident and said, 'If Anant had kept the hundred rupees, I wouldn't have known and he would have made a profit of fifty rupees. Even though Anant is in need of money, his honesty and integrity are more important to him. So he will never take money that does not belong to him.'

After a few years, Anant got married to a girl from another village. Her father was the chief priest in their village. Since Anant knew how to perform pujas very well, he decided to move to his wife's village and help her father take care of the local temple. We all cried the day Anant left home and we felt like a beloved daughter was leaving after marriage. Long after he was gone, my grandfather always remembered him and we often talked about him.

All of us children grew up and settled in the city. Time passed by, things changed and Anant faded into the background as a fond memory. Neither our grandparents nor our ancestral house in the village remained.

Several years passed. One day, I was pleasantly surprised to see an unusual visitor in my office. It was Anant. I remembered the time we had spent together wandering in the village and learning many things. Those days were filled with simple and unforgettable moments. I went and touched his feet as a mark of respect. He looked embarrassed. I told him to sit down and made him comfortable. He had brought a young man with him.

Slowly, Anant started talking. 'How is your uncle? Where is your brother? I haven't met you for a long time. Things have changed so much.' He inquired about every member of my family and I replied with all the details.

Finally, Anant introduced the young man sitting next to him, 'This is Hari, my grandson. I have one daughter. He is her son. Hari studied in our village. Then, he went to study in the neighbouring town and has just finished college. He appeared for . . .'

Anant turned to his grandson and asked him, 'What exam have you given? I have forgotten the name.'

Confidently and proudly, Hari said, 'IIT entrance.'

Anant continued, 'He has got admission in Chennai. He has taken a bank loan to pay his college fees because my son-in-law cannot afford the expenses for his education. Hari says that IIT is a very good college in our country. I don't know. But the boy is hell-bent on going there. Can you please help him in any way?'

I replied, 'I can't help you from the Foundation because I know you personally. At the Foundation, we help only those people who don't know anyone and have nowhere else to go. But I will help you with my personal funds.' I saw a sigh of relief on Hari's face and happiness on Anant's.

I thought, 'Here is this bright, young boy who is going to IIT. I am sure that he will get a very good job later and earn lots of money. Why should I give him a scholarship? I would prefer to give him a loan.' I saw Hari's marks and was glad to find out that he had got admission in computer science.

I asked Hari, 'How much money are you short of?'

'Though I have applied for a scholarship and a bank loan, I still need fifty thousand per year to complete the course.'

'Okay, in that case, I will lend you two lakhs now and you can use it for your education. Please remember that it is not a gift. It is a loan without interest. You should return it as soon as you can afford to return it, even if it is a small amount of money per month. This way, I can lend the amount to another bright child like you and the chain can continue. Your grandfather is one of the most honest persons I have ever known. I am sure that the same culture and genes flow in the family.'

'Do I need to sign any document for this loan?' asked Hari.

'No, your word of honour is more than enough. After all, you are Anant's grandson.'

Anant said, 'Please don't worry. Hari will definitely return the money.'

I gave the loan and forgot about the incident.

Years later, I was travelling from Chennai to Bangalore. My flight was delayed and I was waiting at the airport. I saw a well-dressed young man sitting alone and waiting for the same flight. He was engrossed in reading some journals and I noticed his laptop, which was getting charged beside him. He seemed very familiar. After some time, he switched on his laptop and started working on it. When we were called to board the flight, he went to business class. I was left wondering where I had seen him.

That same evening, I went for a speaker series to a college where I was teaching. I sat in the last row because I was late. The goal of the speaker series was to inspire youngsters. I saw that the young man I had seen at the airport was one of the speakers and he spoke very well.

He said, 'I come from a small village and never had money while I was growing up. But I studied in IIT. Today, I am a self-made man. My experience has showed me that we can make life for ourselves. You can achieve whatever you want in life with self-motivation.'

I suddenly realized that he was Anant's grandson, Hari.

I asked my colleague sitting next to me, 'Who is he and why was he invited here by our college?'

'Hari is hardly twenty-eight, but he has become rich by making money in a hedge fund. He is a financial wizard. He comes from a very humble background. So we invited him to be a role model for our students.'

Hari continued his speech and I listened with rapt attention. Then I got an emergency call from my office and I left in the middle of his question and answer session.

I decided to get in touch with him and found his number easily on the Internet. I called Hari the next day. Hari's personal assistant picked up the phone and said, 'What can I do for you?'

I told her my name and said that I wanted to talk to Hari. She consulted Hari and then told me, 'Sir is very busy.'

'Please tell him that I want to talk to him for a minute.'

Hari came on the line. He was courteous and made inquiries about how I was doing. Finally, I asked him, 'How is Anant?'

He said, 'My grandfather passed away a few years ago.' I felt sad and did not know what to say but he ended the conversation and said, 'I'm sorry, I have to go. Thank you for calling.'

I felt the loss of an old friend. But something else was also nagging at me.

I thought, 'Hari never even talked about returning the loan. That money may be a small amount for me, but I know from my experience that he will never return the money. People who intend to return a loan don't end their conversations like this.'

I was very upset that Hari had cheated me. When someone gets cheated, that person gets upset not because they have lost money but because he or she realizes that they have been foolish enough to be tricked by someone. That hurts one's ego and I am no exception. I always thought that I understood people better and could forecast the results of various situations because I have been in the public field for a long time. When I am fooled, I realize that I am still a student.

Soon, I cooled down. I knew that anybody else in my position would have done the same thing. Anant was a man of integrity, so I had trusted both Anant and Hari.

As a teacher, a mother and a woman, I am used to giving sermons without being asked. I picked up the phone and called Hari to give him a piece of my mind. Fortunately, he picked up the phone himself.

I calmly said, 'Hari, I wanted to give you a gentle reminder. I know that Anant would have handed down his values and principles to you. So, if you remember, you have to return the loan of two lakhs.'

With an equally cool voice, Hari replied, 'My grandfather worked in your house for a meagre salary of a hundred rupees for years. He was an assistant to every member of your family. It was nothing but exploitation. In fact, you should pay our family more money. However, to honour my grandfather, I have not asked you for anything.' Then he disconnected the phone.

I realized then that only diseases and not honesty and integrity are passed down to the next generation through genes.

7

Helping the Dead

Vinayak was a college dropout in his early twenties. He came from an economically backward family. Vinayak's father was a timekeeper in a textile mill and his family lived in a chawl. His parents always wanted him to complete his degree and get a job so that he could ease their financial burden. Vinayak got a few interview calls for jobs but he was rejected because his communication skills in English was not good. After the rejections, he went for English classes but his spoken language never improved. His friends Banya, Bapu, Murali and others also lived in the same neighbourhood and had similar backgrounds.

Vinayak was the go-to man of his chawl. He babysat children, brought medicines for old people, got groceries for somebody and fetched water for the house among other things. His favourite of all the tenants was Usha

Tai's mother-in-law, Tunga Bai, who lived on the ground floor. She was old and could barely walk. She always sat outside on a charpoy in front of her *kholi* and counted her prayer beads. Whenever she saw Vinayak she would say, 'Bala, sit down for five minutes. You run around so much. You are a real *paropakari* in the chawl. Have a cup of tea. It is my share of tea, don't worry.'

Vinayak's helpful nature made him quite popular in his chawl but you need money to survive in this world. He always dreamt of becoming a peon in a government office. He applied to many places but there were many aspirants for the same job. Since he did not have any additional qualifications compared to others, he was always rejected. His contacts were also among the same level of people as him and hence the recommendations from them did not help him in getting a job either.

Vinayak always looked forward to the Ganapati festival, which is a big event in Maharashtra. A great political leader, Lokmanya Tilak, started this festival about a century ago. Good dramas and public speeches are showcased during the festival. The idol of Lord Ganapati is kept in a public place and worshipped for nine days. The decoration of the mantap depends upon the creativity of the organizers. Now there are competitions among the mantaps. Usually, there is an organizing committee consisting of men and women of the same age group. This committee plans a month ahead for the festival.

All the events require money and labour. Labour is normally free because many people volunteer but money is usually a problem. The organizers go from door to door to collect money. If the Ganapati is kept in a commercial area, the organizers collect more money. Unfortunately, Vinayak's Ganapati was not in a commercial area. Hence, his collection was moderate.

Sometimes, things happen in unexpected ways. One day, Vinayak and his friends went to a bank in the neighborhood with a receipt book and a donation box to collect money. The bank manager was very upset to see Vinayak and his friends since a lot of people came to the bank asking for donations. But this time, he was even more upset because he had a foreign client sitting in front of him.

It was Jim's first visit to India. He was writing a book about how Indian culture has survived despite foreign rule, various invasions and cultural diversity. Jim had come to the bank to encash his traveller's cheques and asked the bank manager who these kids were.

'Why are you not allowing them to meet you?' asked Jim.

The bank manager casually replied, 'Oh! Don't worry about it. It is very common to ask for donations during the Ganapati festival season.'

Jim had never seen the Ganapati festival and wanted to visit the local mantap. He asked Vinayak, 'Can I come to see and take some photographs for my book?'

Vinayak understood Jim's English and agreed immediately.

Jim came and saw the different activities that were part of the festival. He saw volunteers setting up the pandal, making the stage, decorating it with crêpe paper flowers, stitching colourful curtains and cutting thermocol sheets to make figurines. Amidst all this, the drama rehearsals were also going on in full swing.

While talking to them, he realized that none of them were related to each other and were of different castes. He was amazed to see the total integrity. When he left, he gave a hundred-dollar bill to the Ganapati fund. Vinayak's joy knew no bounds. He immediately ran to the bank and got it encashed. It came to five thousand rupees. This was a big sum from a single donor and was completely unexpected. Vinayak decided not to spend this money unless it was really needed.

Soon, the festival was over with great pomp and show. There was some money left. When the organizers counted the money the next day, it amounted to almost ten thousand rupees. It was a big sum for them. Usually, only two to three thousand would remain every year and the organizing committee would go to a local restaurant and treat themselves to dinner after all their hard work. This was a rare treat since they could not afford to go to such restaurants otherwise.

But this year the money was way too much. Banya said, 'Shall we have beer this year?'

Bapu said, 'How about we go for a picnic and enjoy ourselves?'

Lata said, 'We should buy a microphone set so that we won't need to hire one every year.'

Murali suggested, 'We can keep this money in a bank in a fixed deposit. Then we will get interest and we can use it next year.'

Banya said again, 'Let's just share it so that we can all do whatever we want.'

Vinayak was still thinking about what he had seen that morning. He was in no mood to reply. He was upset because Thunga Bai, who was so dear to him, had died and her body was lying in front of her kholi. That morning he had seen Usha Tai worrying about the cremation. Vinayak knew her precarious financial position. Apart from the sadness of the death, it was the expenses that were making her cry. Her husband, Sakharam, had a weak heart. The rent of the cremation van was too much for them to afford and Usha Tai was afraid that the stress would affect her husband's health. Since it was the end of the month, none of the people in the chawl were able to extend help since they themselves had no money left.

Vinayak took a decision. 'Let us help Usha Tai with the cremation,' he said. 'We are four boys here. We can carry the dead body to the cremation ground and save that expense for Usha Tai. Then we can think about what to do with the money that we have left.'

Everyone was shocked at Vinayak's decision. Banya quietly said, 'We are in a festive mood. Don't spoil it with such work.'

Vinayak did not listen to him. 'If you want, you can support me. Otherwise, I will ask someone else to help me,' he said.

Banya said, 'I don't have any experience carrying dead bodies to the cremation ground. How can I come?'

Vinayak replied, 'Nobody has any experience. There's always a first time.'

Vinayak's parents also raised an objection. 'Oh, my

child! How can you go to the cremation ground when both your parents are alive?'

'But Aai, it is not bad work. One should help. Sooner or later, all of us are going to die right here in this crowded chawl. If we don't help our neighbours, please remember that nobody will be there to help us either.'

His parents pondered over the wisdom in Vinayak's words. After a few moments, his mother said, 'Vinayak, you are absolutely right. You have our blessings. We are proud to have a son like you.'

His friends, however, followed him reluctantly. All of them went to the cremation ground and found that they had to pay some money there. Vinayak took the money from the kitty and paid the required amount.

Suddenly, Vinayak got an idea. He said, 'There must be many people in this city who are very poor and have nobody to help them cremate or bury their dead ones. They could be from any community. Why can't we help some of them? We can donate the remaining money towards that purpose. We won't get into the religious part of the cremation. That is left to the family. I am aware that we may be able to help only a few people, but it is better to spend towards a needy cause than to waste the money having beer. Don't you think that we should help people, particularly at such time when they can't even think straight because their mind is preoccupied with thoughts of losing a loved one?'

Banya and Bapu did not like the idea at all but Lata was very enthusiastic. She said, 'Vinayak, that is brilliant. Everybody does philanthropy in different ways—building schools, providing clothes to the needy, giving books and donating blood—but I really liked your idea. Last year, I went to Rajkot to see my uncle and I told him that I wanted to visit a special place there. He took me to the cremation ground. I was so scared. But it was amazing and beautiful. It was painted well, had nice outer walls—'

'Why should they have walls? Nobody is going to run away from there anyway,' Banya joked.

'Banya, shut up. Let us listen to Lata. She was saying something,' said Vinayak.

Lata continued, 'It had a Shiva temple and a nice garden, shady trees and sheds with benches and water arrangements. The atmosphere soothes and consoles the grieving people to a large extent.'

'We are not rich to make all these arrangements in our city. But the least we can do is help the poorest of the poor in their last journey. If you agree, we can split the remaining amount, but I will use my share for this purpose. I haven't earned this money. It is public money and it should reach the public,' said Vinayak decisively.

Lata immediately said, 'I will give my share too!'

Everybody else looked at each other's faces and said, 'We will also join you.'

Vinayak's hidden leadership now came to the fore. He said, 'Let's make a volunteer group. We'll call ourselves Mukti Sena and we will help poor people.'

'Where will we search for poor people who need help with their dead?' asked Bapu.

'We can start with a government hospital. My friend is a ward boy in one of the hospitals. I am sure that there are many poor people suffering like Usha Tai,' said Vinayak.

Thus, the Mukti Sena's journey began. Soon, they realized that the money they collected was nothing compared to the number of people who needed their help. Some people could not afford to give any money while others gave a few hundred rupees. Now, Vinayak and his team had to think seriously about how long they would be able to continue like this.

The news reached the mill union through Vinayak's father who worked there. The mill union offered to give bundles of free cloth. Still, the Mukti Sena continued to fall short of money in their initial years. Vinayak learnt that economic status is formed like a pyramid. The poor people stay at the bottom but they are also the real users and donors for such causes. Vinayak knew that, over a period of time, they could collect sufficient money for their day-to-day operation.

As Vinayak and his team grew older, they required some money for their livelihood. But Vinayak said, 'We won't take even a rupee from Mukti Sena's fund.'

Once a volunteer becomes a paid worker, there is always a chance of corruption making its way into the organization. So they decided that Mukti Sena would be an all-volunteer organization and people would get other jobs for their livelihood. Almost all the members decided to work on their own. This would give them flexibility and time to contribute to Mukti Sena as well as obtain their own source of income. By this time, the word had spread about Mukti Sena and its honest volunteers. Many people came to help Vinayak and his team set up their individual businesses.

Today, Mukti Sena has thirty volunteers who work day and night. All of them are entrepreneurs who earn a small income to take care of their family. These entrepreneurs run grocery shops, children's nurseries, bicycle lending shops, paper distribution shops and printing shops among others. Whenever a Mukti Sena call comes, these volunteers always have a substitute to look after their shops until they come back. Their business never suffers because of their absence.

Even today, Vinayak says that when a person is dead, caste is never an issue. One's birth only decides how one's body should be disposed of. He says, '*Hindu, Muslim, Sikh, Isaai, sab ko mera salaam.*'

8

Three Ponds

In the olden days, ponds were the only source of water in villages if there were no rivers nearby. Hence, the villagers looked after their pond very well. They cleaned it every year and removed the silt. Each family sent one person to help clean the pond. Nobody was paid any money for this because the pond was an asset of the village. Every year, the villagers worshipped the water in the pond because they considered the water to be like the holy water of the Ganga.

There are different types of ponds: some are used for irrigation, some as a source of drinking water and some are used for both. If the pond was very large and the other shore could not be seen, it was called a *samudra* or ocean, hence the names Shanti Samudra and Vyasa Samudra, among others. Usually, ponds are named after the person who built them, such as kings, queens, rich merchants and powerful commanders.

In my vast experience of travelling in India, I found that every pond is sacred to its village and there is always a story behind the building of the pond. Inevitably, the stories say that Ganga travelled below the earth and appeared in the pond so that people could have water. That is why the water is referred to as holy water or *Gangajal*.

I have seen many ponds in different parts of India but the story of three separate ponds in Karnataka have left a lasting impression on me.

Ammani's Condition

It was the time of the East India Company and the British ruled our land. Ammani was an illiterate woman who lived near Kolar. She kept cows and buffaloes and her job was to deliver milk to the people living nearby. Kolar is a drought-prone area and she regularly saw people struggling to fetch water. Ammani always wanted to do something about this.

One day, she heard that a British camp was being set up near the village. The middleman who knew both English and Kannada came to the village in search of milk, curd, ghee and butter to supply to the British soldiers in the camp. When the news spread, everybody told the middleman that they wanted to sell to the camp.

But Ammani told the middleman, Ramappa, 'I will supply milk to the camp only on one condition. I don't want money.'

Ramappa was surprised. 'You mean you want to supply free to these *firangis*? These white men?'

'When did I say that? After all, I am a poor person.'

'Please make good money now because you are selling in bulk. Make hay while the sun shines. This is a government office. You are guaranteed money, unlike with private parties. If you miss this, you won't get this opportunity again. Be wise,' he advised her.

'Don't get me wrong. I want to sell. But I don't want money every month. It has to be kept with the British officers. You have also just said that they are reliable government people.'

'You mean to say that you will collect the money only at the end? I don't understand this.'

But Ammani insisted that she would provide milk to the British only on this condition. So Ramappa left and decided to talk to the British officers about this strange request.

The next day, Ramappa told officer George, 'There

is a very strange woman in this village. She wants to supply milk, curd and ghee but she does not want to collect money.'

George was curious. 'Bring that woman here. I want to talk to her.'

The next day, Ammani went to meet the officer. In those days, Indians were scared of the firangis. They were always worried that they might be punished without reason. Their colour was different, their language was different and India was a British colony. But Ammani went without fear. She did not know English but she knew what she was going to say.

When she reached the British camp and met George, she said, 'Sir, I am ready to supply whatever you ask for. However, the money should be kept with you. I will take it later.'

The concept of a bank was not there at the time so George thought that Ammani was scared of keeping the money at home. He asked, 'Are you scared of the thieves or relatives who will come and take your money because you are all alone?'

She smiled and said, 'No, sir, that is not the reason.'

'Then what is it?'

'I will tell you later. I am sure that you will respect that.'

Officer George liked Ammani and agreed to her request. Soon after, Ammani started supplying milk, curd and ghee to the camp. The quality of her products was better than other people's and she was very punctual. However, she became a laughing stock of her village because she chose not to take money from the British. Ammani continued to supply to the people living nearby in her village and managed her monthly expenses even though she was not getting any money from the British camp.

Years passed. Everyone in the camp knew Ammani for her honesty and the quality of her products. Over time, Ammani replaced many villagers who were supplying milk and other products. She became the single source of supply to the British camp. All the officers were friendly with her.

One day, officer George came to talk to Ammani. He said, 'Ammani, you should take your money. It is now a huge amount and it is not fair on my part to keep it for such a long time. We might change camps within a year. We really respect your honesty, and we should be honest with you too.'

'Thank you, sir, for informing me in advance. Along with my money, I want help from you and your soldiers.'

'Oh, you want to build a big bungalow?' the officer joked.

'No, sir, I want a pond.'

'What?' The officer was surprised. 'Are you aware that it is not easy to construct a pond in this hard stone area? It requires a lot of manpower. The money itself is not sufficient.'

'Sir, I beg you. That is precisely the reason why I didn't take the money. If I had taken it, I would have spent it all by this time. Since I am a widow, my relatives would have forcibly taken it from me. Sir, you don't understand the difficulties of women in the hot summer. Please do this for me.'

George thought about it. It was a difficult job. He appreciated Ammani's honesty and her concern for people. So he said, 'Let me talk to my boss and see if he can ask our soldiers to do this on a volunteer basis.'

In the end, kind-hearted George and the volunteer soldiers built the pond. The pond became the source of drinking water for the entire village. People did not have to go far to fetch water any more and, today, the pond is still known as Ammani's Pond.

Today, India is independent and Ammani is no more. Still, the pond stands witness to her generous gift to the village.

A Wedding Gift

Let me now tell you the story of the Navalgund pond. Navalgund is a fairly big town in northern Karnataka. Long ago, the village chief was a man named Rame Gowda. He had two lovely daughters, Channamma and Neelamma.

Though Navalgund's land was fertile, it was heavily dependent on rain, and life in Navalgund was very difficult. There was no water or stream nearby. Several wells were dug in search of water but there was not even a drop of water in them. Men and women walked miles to get a few buckets of water. Rame Gowda's family was rich and lived in luxury. They had many servants who fetched water for them in bullock carts. So the family never realized the problem of the poor people.

One day, there was a panchayat meeting headed by Rame Gowda. The poor people came to the meeting and said, 'Sir, please make a pond in this village. We will work hard and help build the pond. We won't even ask for the labour charges.'

Rame Gowda said, 'It is not easy to build a pond. You may say that there are no labour charges. However, we still require a lot of money to build it. Let every rich man in the village contribute something towards the pond.

Then we can think about it and decide.' But no rich man was ready to give money.

In those days, every rich man had plenty of labourers and many of them were bonded labourers. So the rich people in Navalgund never cared to understand the difficulties of fetching water. Neelamma was standing behind the pillar when the conversation was going on. She knew that her father could have funded the construction of the pond because he was the richest man in the village. She also realized that other rich people were waiting for Rame Gowda to contribute some money himself. But nothing happened and the meeting was adjourned.

Neelamma felt very sad. She knew the problems of fetching water because she knew the difficulties of her maid. One day, without informing anyone, Neelamma had walked with the maid to get a bucket of water. It was a Herculean task. But Neelamma knew that her father would never listen to her. So she kept quiet.

A few years went by. Channamma and Neelamma grew up and Rame Gowda found two rich sons-in-law. The weddings were held with great pomp. When Channamma and Neelamma were about to leave their father's home, he asked them, 'Daughters, you are leaving this town. What do you want as a gift?'

Channamma said, 'I want a bullock cart filled with jewellery.'

'Sure, my daughter,' said Rame Gowda.

Neelamma did not say anything.

'Neelamma, what do you want?' her father insisted.

'I don't know whether you will be able to give me what I want,' she said.

That enraged Rame Gowda. 'What do you mean by that? I am the richest man in the village and have only two daughters. Look at your sister. When she asked me for a bullock cart of jewellery, I agreed. Why will I say no to you? Are you going to ask me for something extraordinary?'

Neelamma said, 'I will ask for something that you can definitely give me. But promise me that you will. Only then will I ask you.'

Rame Gowda thought that Neelamma might ask for more jewellery than her sister, or maybe she wanted land. So he said, 'Yes.'

'Father, I don't want a gram of gold or jewellery from your house. I don't even want silk saris. I do not intend to take an inch of your land. But I want a pond to be constructed in the middle of the village so that every poor person can fetch drinking water with ease.'

Rame Gowda was dumbstruck. First, he was very

upset with his daughter. Then he thought of the expense. He knew that he could afford it. He remembered his promise. He smiled and said, 'A promise is a promise. I will build a pond for you.'

Even today, the pond named after Neelamma stands in the middle of Navalgund town. Over a period of time, the pond has been expanded and decorated. But to this day, it is well maintained. Everyone must follow the strict rule of washing his or her feet before entering the pond. There is no way that the people of Navalgund can afford to contaminate the water. Today, Neelamma, Channamma and Rame Gowda are no more but everybody remembers Neelamma's concern for the people of Navalgund.

Bhagirathi

Now, we come to my favourite pond story. If you travel from Hangal to Haveri, you come across a sleepy village known as Kallakere (colloquially known as Kalakeri). There is a beautiful pond with clear water here. There is also a Shiva temple in front of the pond. This pond stands out because of the unusual lotuses and leaves in it. These lotuses look very welcoming. But if you go near the pond, you will feel that the lotuses are moving away from you. It is, after all, Bhagirathi's pond.

Long, long ago, Mallana Gowda was the village headman. He had seven sons and all of them were married. His youngest daughter-in-law was Bhagirathi. She was very beautiful and an extremely good-natured young woman. She was soft-spoken, an introvert who never expressed her feelings in public. Her husband was an officer in the army on active duty. So he was away a lot. Bhagirathi's in-laws looked after her. She was popular with her friends, in-laws and all the people in the village.

Mallana Gowda ordered the building of a pond in the village. A pond was constructed but there was no water in it. He was really worried. If the pond did not have water, people and farmers would continue to suffer. He had spent a lot of money to dig this pond and had performed many pujas but still there was no water.

One day, the elders in the village were discussing something in a very hush-hush manner. Bhagirathi, who was in the garden doing some work, could hear them clearly. Nobody noticed her presence.

Somebody said to Mallana Gowda, 'Sir, there is only one way you can get water in the pond. A married woman should pray for the welfare of the people wholeheartedly and ask God for water. Then, water may come. But . . .' he stopped.

'Oh, what is so tough about that? Every woman in the village can do this,' replied another man.

'But there is a condition. Once the water gushes into the pond, the person who prays may not be able to come out of the water and may eventually drown. Is anyone ready for this?'

Silence fell upon the group. There were many daughters-in-law in the village but no father or father-in-law opened his mouth.

'Is it so difficult to get Bhagirathi?' asked somebody.

Mallana Gowda was very upset. He shouted at him, 'Out of the entire village, why are you only thinking about my daughter-in-law? There are others too.'

'No, sir, I did not mean your daughter-in-law Bhagirathi. I meant Ganga.'

Ganga is also widely known as Bhagirathi. There is a very popular folk story in India. The story goes like this. Ganga was a river that flowed only in heaven. King Bhagiratha prayed for Ganga to come down to earth and help people. He made many penances and begged her. So she came at his request. That is why she is also called Bhagirathi. Even today, we can see the statue of King Bhagiratha in Gangotri, the source of the Ganga.

Bhagirathi heard the conversation and went to her room. She did not sleep that night. She thought to herself,

'My husband is selflessly serving the country in the army. What is the use of my life if I can't make a sacrifice so that everyone can live in peace and harmony?' It was a very difficult situation and her mind was in turmoil.

The next day, she told her father-in-law, 'Father, I want a small favour. I want all of us to perform a small puja at the bottom of the steps of the pond. Who knows, Bhagirathi may come.'

Her father-in-law laughed. 'My child, we have done many pujas but still we have not been able to get water. However, if it is your wish, we will do so next week.'

The next day, Bhagirathi went to her best friend's house and talked to everyone there. While departing, she had tears in her eyes. Her friend consoled her, 'Don't be so sad. Your husband will be back soon. He will be victorious. Be brave.' But Bhagirathi did not say anything.

A day later, she went to her parents' house and they were surprised to see Bhagirathi coming alone to visit them, which she had never done before. She stayed with them for two days. With tears in her eyes, she said goodbye to them. 'Bhagirathi, don't cry. Your husband will be back soon,' they said. Bhagirathi did not reply and came back to her in-laws' house.

The next day, she went and invited the entire village for the puja.

On the day of the ceremony, she dressed like a bride and her family went to perform the puja at the bottom of the pond. Once the puja was completed, everybody started going back.

Bhagirathi climbed a few steps and told her father-in-law, 'Father, I have forgotten my gold plate at the bottom of the pond. All of you please carry on. I will come and join you.' Then she climbed down and stood alone at the bottom of the pond. She folded her hands towards the sky and prayed to River Ganga. 'O Mother Ganga, please come to our village. Please fill this pond with your sweet water and make everyone prosperous. Look after the women, children, old people and animals in this village and give them water. In return, if you want to take my life, it is yours. After all, I am Bhagirathi and am named after you.'

Then she climbed the first step. Suddenly, there was thunder and wind but nobody could see anything. Water started gushing from the sides of the pond and came up to Bhagirathi's ankles. She climbed the second step. Water continued to gush in and came up to her knees. Instantly, Bhagirathi knew what was happening. She was happy and sad at the same time. She climbed the third step. Water came up to her hips. She continued to climb to the fourth step. Water came up to her armpits. She climbed the fifth step. The water reached her neck. She climbed the sixth step. Water came up to her nose. At last, she climbed the seventh step. Water passed over her head and she could not breathe any more. The thunder stopped and the winds calmed.

Mallana Gowda turned back to see what was happening. The pond continued to fill until it was full. The whole village was surprised to see the water in the pond after so many years of praying. After some time, Mallana Gowda realized that his daughter-in-law Bhagirathi was missing. He knew what had happened then. Tears started flowing from his eyes. He sat on the ground and started crying. 'O Bhagirathi my child, you were my responsibility until your husband came back. I loved you like my daughter but I never knew your plan. Is that the reason you visited your parents and friends? Is that why you dressed like a bride today and purposely forgot the gold plate? I did not know that you had heard our conversation last week. Bhagirathi, you gave your life so that others can have water. But how will I face your husband?'

Now the entire village realized that Bhagirathi had sacrificed her life for them. They were unable to enjoy the arrival of Ganga.

The next month, the war ended and Bhagirathi's husband came back victorious. He wanted to talk about his adventures and share his achievements with his wife. He purchased expensive jewellery and saris for Bhagirathi.

When he reached home, he realized that everybody was happy but also sad about something. He could not see a trace of Bhagirathi anywhere. He asked his father, 'Where is Bhagirathi? I want to meet her.'

His father did not have the courage to tell him the truth. He said, 'She has gone to her friend's house.'

Her husband left immediately for her friend's house. Even at her friend's house, the family was in tears but could not tell him the truth. Instead, they said, 'She has gone to her mother's house.'

He immediately left for her parents' house and did not get any reply from them either.

When Bhagirathi's husband was going back home, he became very thirsty. He saw there was a new pond in his village brimming with water. He got down and drank some water. It was very sweet. He looked at the pond and was unable to move. He sat there for a while.

A little boy was taking his cows to graze and stopped there for water. Bhagirathi's husband asked him, 'O my child, I have never seen this lake before. And the water is like nectar. I remember that this was empty with no water. How did this happen?' The innocent child reiterated Bhagirathi's entire story and went away.

Her husband was unable to bear the shock of losing her. He cried for Bhagirathi's sacrifice. He knew that it would be very hard to live without her and told the pond, 'My dear, wherever you are, I will be with you. I don't care whether it is a pond or a house.' And he jumped into the pond.

Even today, when you see this pond, it has unusually large-sized lotuses and leaves. When I visited the village, the lotuses enchanted me. Now there are many borewells in the village, so people do not use the pond for drinking water but it is still used as a washing pond.

I asked a fisherman there to fetch me a lotus flower from the pond. He laughed at my ignorance. He said, 'Madam, you must be an outsider. Don't you know that Bhagirathi and her husband are inside? I have never seen anybody enter this pond and pluck a flower. The flowers appear in couples but the moment you go near them, they drift away from you. The depth of the pond is so deceptive that if you try to pursue the flowers, you might even drown.'

I never knew that such blooming and beautiful flowers would have such a bittersweet story behind them.

9

No Man's Garden

As a child, I went on an excursion to a well-known temple called Someshwara. This temple is located in Lakshmeshwara town. The Someshwara temple is huge and has many beautiful sculptures and pillars. But they did not fascinate me. Instead, there was a particular stone in the courtyard of the temple that touched my heart. The stone is more than a thousand years old and has an inscription and a picture. The picture depicts many cows and buffaloes drinking water from a tank and the water that fills the tank is drawn manually from a well. This is known as 'Dharma Yetha' in Kannada. A philanthropist donates a well, builds a tank, and makes provisions to draw the water. Poor people can at least help draw water from the well and store it in the tank, which can be used by both human beings and animals. Nobody has ownership over the tank or the water. This concept has been etched in my mind ever since I was a child. Normally, when people lend a helping hand, there is always an expectation of getting something in return. But if you are a true philanthropist, the expectation decreases over time. A sense of ownership becomes meaningless in the larger context of life. This selfless helpfulness brings true happiness to a person.

Parappa was an old man in a village. His vision was good, he could hear fairly well, but walking was really hard for him. When he was younger, he could easily walk twenty miles a day. He inherited only five acres of land from his parents but, due to his hard work, he was successful in expanding it to fifty acres of land.

His son Bhimappa told him, 'Father, you have worked very hard in your time. Now the farming methodology has changed. I prefer to use the latest tractors and agricultural machinery. We don't have to come every day to inspect the labourers. Even the numbers of labourers that we need has reduced. If I require your guidance, I will definitely take your advice. You should relax and look after the house.'

So Parappa retired and his son Bhimappa took charge of the land.

Parappa had built a big house that faced the mud boundary of the village tank. This boundary is called *baduvu* in Kannada. In the village, Parappa became known as Baduvina Parappa and the baduvu became his identity. Every evening, Parappa sat in the veranda of the house and his friends joined him to discuss the village news.

Parappa was a prosperous farmer and had many servants. Bhimappa's wife had a maid called Paravva. She came and cleaned the house every day. She was very talkative and brought all the juicy news of the village. It became a regular practice for Parappa to finish his breakfast and sit in the veranda facing the baduvu and talk to Paravva while she worked. Paravva was even better than the local newspaper and gave Parappa the inside stories of the village.

Paravva also told Parappa about her domestic problems. She had a large family—her husband, his parents, two children and a brother-in-law with his three children. Her husband worked in Parappa's farm. But still, life was not easy for them.

One morning, Paravva started her news bulletin. 'There is a new disease in our vegetables. So the price of vegetables in the village has become ten times its usual price. Even the rich people are finding the vegetables expensive and are thinking twice before spending money on vegetables. One kilo of tomatoes is more expensive than two litres of milk. Oh, yesterday I had such a tough time,' she said, sighing.

'What happened?' Parappa asked.

'Yesterday, my sister and her family of five suddenly came to our house. Since they were our guests, I had to give them good food. I made roti, rice and dal but I could not get any vegetables. It was very embarrassing for me.'

'Why didn't you have vegetables?'

'How can I buy vegetables at this price? You know that our village fair is only once a week. Even though I buy vegetables at the fair, I don't have a refrigerator to store them. It is hard to get vegetables in our village any time we want.'

'Didn't you store at least a few pumpkins?' asked Parappa. It was a practice in the village to keep spare pumpkins at home because they did not get spoiled easily and did not need refrigeration.

'I had two pumpkins but I used them a few weeks ago when we had unexpected guests. I wish I had a tiny garden to grow a pumpkin plant to avoid such awkward situations. But I don't have a square inch of land near our hut.' Paravva continued, 'There are many poor people like me in our village. They can't afford to buy or grow vegetables. Vegetables are essential. It is sad that all our political parties promise us rice but not vegetables.' Then she said to herself, 'Today, there is a panchayat meeting in your house. I should keep the hall clean, dust well and prepare some snacks for the meeting.' And she went inside the house to start cleaning the hall.

Parappa started thinking about what she had said. He had never suffered from a lack of vegetables in his diet. Since he was a rich farmer, he always had land to grow some vegetables in his fields. The vegetables were sufficient for his house and he had never needed to buy them. When vegetables were in excess, he distributed them among his workers. But he could not do that all the time. His mother used to say, 'Never keep more flowers, fruits or vegetables than you need because they get spoiled very quickly and should not be wasted. They should be shared with everybody.' His mother's rule was not valid for rice, ragi and jowar grain because they did not get spoiled for months and could be stored easily.

While Parappa was pondering about Paravva's predicament, his dog Bandu started barking. Distracted, Parappa watched Bandu run after another dog. Both the dogs went near the baduvu portion of the tank. There was a lot of congress grass, ordinary grass, cactus and other unknown shrubs there. The two dogs fought and urinated there. They also slept on the grass and relaxed there in the morning sun. Suddenly, a mother pig came along with her piglets. The two dogs barked and chased her away. This was not a new sight. Parappa was used to seeing the same scene every day since the baduvu was no-man's-land and belonged to the village gram panchayat. Nobody ever bothered to clean it. It was the abode of rats, pigs, dogs and other animals.

Parappa got an idea. 'Why can't I use this land to grow vegetables for the poor people?' he asked himself. But the land itself was not flat. It was on a slope. Today, there was a gram panchayat meeting in his house and he decided to submit his proposal there.

Parappa was well respected in the village and everybody called him Ajja. Usually, Parappa did not attend any panchayat meetings since his son Bhimappa was already a member of the panchayat. So Bhimappa was surprised to see him at the meeting. All the members greeted Parappa warmly and started the meeting.

When the meeting was about to come to an end, Parappa stood up and said, 'I have an idea. Many people in our village can't afford vegetables because the prices are very high. It is difficult for them to even store a few pumpkins. The baduvu facing my house is a wasteland. Only unwanted shrubs grow there. If the panchayat allows me, I would like to clean that land, grow some vegetables and distribute it to the poor people of our village.'

Everybody was surprised at his unusual proposal.

'Ajja, I really appreciate your enthusiasm and idea,' said a young member, Suresh. 'But the panchayat office will not pay for the cleaning. It is a waste of money. The dogs and pigs won't let you grow anything there. Who will guard the garden? Who will water it? Have you thought about the details?'

Parappa replied, 'I have thought about it. I don't want the entire baduvu. I am an old man. I can only look after a portion of the land. I will spend my own money to clean it. The panchayat does not need to spend any money on this project. But I want your permission.'

'Whom will you give the vegetables to? Maybe you want to give them to your own servants. But that will be unfair because the slope is not yours,' said Suresh.

'I promise you that none of my servants will get vegetables from this garden. When the vegetables are grown, I will bring the entire harvest to the panchayat office and you can decide on the distribution. Is that acceptable?'

The panchayat members felt that this was not a practical idea but they had a lot of respect for old Parappa. So they agreed to give him a chance.

When the meeting was over, Bhimappa was very upset. 'Why do you want to get into these things at this age?' he told his father. 'Can't you enjoy your old age and relax by going to a temple, watching TV or playing with the kids? If you are unsuccessful, people will make fun of you. If you are successful, we won't benefit anyway. So, no matter what, we will run into losses. In fact, we have to spend money to clean and guard the baduvu and grow the vegetables.'

'Son, think of those people who don't have a square inch of land to call their own. Is it not our duty to help the people who are on the other side of the poverty line? These poor people don't even have a refrigerator and they buy their vegetables only once a week at the fair. I really want to help them. I don't have many expenses. Let me spend some money on this and do some good. Let people say whatever they want about me. It does not matter,' said Parappa.

'I don't know how you will manage. But please don't expect me to help you with this,' said Bhimappa harshly.

This is how Parappa's new project started. He took help of the coolies to identify how much land he needed to grow vegetables. He marked the areas and asked the coolies to clean it. It was full of plastic bags and bottles.

Then he cordoned off the area with thin bamboo woven mats, which served as a barrier that prevented animals from entering. Finally, he sowed pumpkin seeds, cucumber and green vegetables. He knew that water would not be a problem because there was a water tank on the other side of the baduvu and water flowed directly to the garden. He also made a bench near the garden and met people there. People started calling it 'Parappa's garden'.

When the plants grew and flowered, small pumpkins appeared. Parappa was so excited that people thought he was welcoming a new grandchild. When the green vegetables grew and the leaves started appearing in abundance, Parappa felt proud of his plants. But he faced many difficulties. Once, an angry pig almost shattered the bamboo wall. A few weeks later, rats took away a few cucumbers. Some mischievous children even stole a few pumpkins. So Parappa brought a watchdog to protect the garden at night. The farming season ended and a reasonable amount of vegetables had now grown.

One day, his daughter-in-law wanted some cucumbers. Parappa refused to give her any cucumbers even though she offered him money. He said, 'I can't go back on my words to the panchayat.' Paravva, his favourite maid, also made many requests, but he did not give vegetables to her either.

Eventually, he collected all the vegetables that had grown and took them to the panchayat office. He said, 'You can distribute these to anyone you like. But my humble request is that poor people should get the vegetables.'

Parappa went away without even waiting for an answer. The panchayat members were amazed at Parappa's detachment and saluted his spirit. Bhimappa realized what his father had accomplished and he was very proud of him.

Today, Parappa grows vegetables the year round in his garden by the baduvu and continues to give them to the panchayat when they are ready.

Our Parappa's garden of this century is no less than the *Dharma Yetha* of centuries past.

10

Sticky Bottoms

A few years ago, I was going out of town and was about to board a train. From a distance, I saw Venkat on the railway platform. I can never miss Venkat anywhere because he stands out in a crowd. He is tall, thin and always wears white.

The moment I saw him, I immediately got into a train compartment so that he could not see me. I went to my air-conditioned coupé where there were four seats. Three of them were already occupied. I sat on the fourth seat by the window and thought that I should start reading. As I opened my bag to get out the book, I heard, 'Oh, it is you. It is my good luck that you are on this train. I am also travelling by the same train.'

Without lifting my head, I knew that it was Venkat's voice. He was standing in front of me like a coconut tree.

'Yes, yes,' I stammered. As usual, he did not care about what I was saying.

'I thought I saw you on the platform standing next to this train. And then you disappeared so I wasn't sure. I decided to search for you. Your quick disappearance told me that you must be on this train. I was wondering how to start looking for you but, fortunately, I found you in the first compartment I searched. Ha, ha, ha,' he laughed to himself, 'my search is better than your computer search.'

Then he looked around the compartment and said, 'Oh, all the other seats are taken.' He requested the passenger sitting next to me, 'Sir, we are really good friends but we haven't seen each other for a long time. Would you mind exchanging my seat with yours?'

The occupant of the seat was a young man in his mid-twenties with earphones plugged in. He could not hear Venkat properly but understood what was happening and said, 'What is your seat number?' I was praying that he would refuse to move seats but to my misfortune he said yes. Now Venkat became my travelling companion for the next eight hours.

I have known Venkat for more than half a century. He is good-natured and helps everyone in need. But the quirk about Venkat is that he talks too much and does not even realize or care whether the other person is listening to him.

The train left the station and Venkat immediately started chatting about something inconsequential. My mind slipped away and I started recollecting incidents with Venkat over the years.

In school, Venkat was in the debate club. If the time limit for a debate was three minutes, his introduction to the subject itself was at least four minutes. All of us in the class were tired of his incessant talk. Even the teachers regularly told him to be aware and try to talk less but he would say, 'Sir, I have verbal diarrhoea and I can't help myself.' In the end, our class became more patient but Venkat did not change.

Once there was a debate competition in our school. Venkat started his speech. Knowing his nature, our teacher rang the calling bell in two minutes even though the time limit was three minutes. But Venkat continued speaking. The second bell rang warning him that he must stop. He took the calling bell from the teacher's desk, kept it in his pocket and continued talking. After a minute, our department peon came and took away his mike. Then Venkat had to step down. He never ever won a prize for debates.

Nobody in class wanted him as a teammate in any

activity because he talked continuously and gave people a headache. It also took very long to get any work done with him in the team. We all thought that he would end up being the company chairman of either Aspirin or Zandu Balm. He would make an excellent salesperson for these companies.

After we graduated from school, Venkat did not work much because he inherited money and invested it wisely. As a result, he got regular income from his investments.

Soon, our school classmates started getting married one by one and we all wondered who would get married to Venkat. We even had a bet that his wife would run away within a year of marriage—unless, of course, she was deaf. Eventually, Venkat got married to Lata. She was nice, friendly and very quiet.

After a year of marriage, I asked her, 'Lata, how do you handle Venkat's constant chatter?'

She said, 'It is very easy. I pretend that I am listening to a radio.'

'But even a radio can be turned off.'

'Well, I mentally switch off. That's all. Otherwise, Venkat is a fantastic husband. He is very kind to my family and me. He takes care of everything at home. Some people just talk a lot.' She spoke lightly and gently about her husband.

Venkat was very fond of parties and celebrations. When he had his first baby, he called us for a party. I went at the specified time but all his other friends came an hour late because they knew that the later they came the less they would have to hear Venkat's chatter. Unfortunately, I was not as smart. The moment I reached, Venkat started describing Lata's labour pains, the delivery, the baby's vaccinations and its progress through every month until the day of the party. I felt like leaving my gift on his table and running away. I had finally learnt my lesson about spending time with Venkat.

I remembered another incident. One day, Venkat came to my house just to talk. It was hard for me to say no because he is a very kind person. I told him, 'I am in a hurry. Is there anything specific you would like to discuss?'

'Not really,' he replied. 'If you are in a hurry, you go. I will wait here for you.' People at home were terrified because nobody could sit and talk to Venkat for so long.

I told him, 'Okay, in that case, I will talk to you for fifteen minutes and then I have to go.'

Venkat said, 'Sounds fine. I wanted to let you know that I am building a new house.' I knew that he would not stop for the next fifteen minutes. He continued, 'You have already seen the huge house built by my grandfather. He used so much cement that one could have easily built four houses out of it. The kitchen was so huge that it could accommodate a hundred people. We could even perform a small wedding there. The entire site was used to build the three-storey house. You know that my father is the only son of his parents. So he inherited the house and made some foolish changes listening to his expert *vaastu* friend. He removed the door from where people used to enter and shifted it to the side instead. So the side window had to be closed. He changed the beautiful red oxide floor to tiles. He even converted the first floor into an open space for religious discourses. The people who came for these discourses were all quite old. They couldn't even climb to the first floor. So he had to make a lift for them. Then he broke open the bedroom. He spent so much money in renovation that he could have built a new house instead. My mother was very upset about the changes to the ancestral home. So she started pestering me to build a new house on the same site. My wife Lata was very happy living on the second floor of the old house because it is in a very convenient location. It has good schools and shops nearby and is in a good neighbourhood. There is a park in front of our house, which is almost like a private park but it is maintained by Bangalore Corporation. I really feel that it is just like having my own personal park . . .'

I wanted to stop his rambling so I interrupted, 'Tell me, how are you building this new house?'

'Oh, I have to satisfy everyone and keep them happy. In our house, we have five people but fifty opinions. Now my son also participates in the discussions. We are demolishing the old house and building a new one in the same place. I have brought the plan just to show you. Bangalore Corporation may approve of my plan but people at home may not. So, first, I got it approved at home and now I am on my way to the corporation.'

Then he opened his plan. I saw some drawings but I was not really interested. I thought that this was a good opportunity to tell Venkat to leave. 'I think you should rush to the corporation,' I said. 'Their department will close.'

'Oh, don't worry about it. I have an agent. I told him to call me whenever the officer comes. Now it is lunch hour there. So the officer may not come back for some time.'

I was really scared that Venkat might stay for another two hours at my house. With every passing minute, I was getting fed up. But Venkat never realized it. He continued, 'See this plan. Here is the entrance to the house. The first room is a small veranda but not as small as normal verandas. It should be enough to leave the chappals outside. I want to put a few wooden benches so that people can sit down comfortably and remove or wear their slippers. Then we have another veranda where we can greet people formally. So I will keep some sofas and chairs there. You know, everyone enters the living room in our current home. Lata doesn't like that at all and I must obey her instructions because she spends most of her time at home . . .'

Just then, his cellphone rang. He picked it up and said, 'Okay.' I breathed a sigh of relief. Maybe the corporation officer was back. But he finished talking in a few seconds. Then he looked at me and said, 'Well, the corporation engineer is on vacation today. We have plenty of time now. I can explain each room to you.'

'You don't have to, Venkat. These days, you get three-dimensional pictures on the computer that you can walk through.'

'Oh, yes. You are right. I have my laptop also. I can show you.' He opened his laptop. Now I knew that I was his prisoner. I remembered the advertisement: *Fevicol ka jod hai, tootega nahin.*

I decided to be brave and end it. I got up and told Venkat, 'Sorry, Venkat. I have to go somewhere.'

He smiled at me and said, 'Your driver went for lunch a few minutes ago. I saw him leave through the window. You have to wait for him anyway. Until he comes back, I can ask for your suggestions.' Then he asked me, 'Now, where was I?'

'You've been here in front of me forever,' I said sarcastically.

As usual, Venkat did not understand. 'Oh, I thought I was in the veranda of my house,' he continued opening his laptop.

With my new-found bravado, I thought of another way of cutting him off. I got up and walked towards the main door. 'Venkat, let us do this. I will come to your house soon. Lata will also be there. We can sit down and discuss in detail then.' I stepped outside hoping to see my driver.

Now Venkat had to get up and leave.

I was brought back to the present with the sound of the *chaiwala*. I was on the train. Venkat was still chatting away. Remembering these incidents, I did not know if I could listen to him politely for the rest of the journey. The only escape route I had was to use the train toilet. But even I could not sit there for more than five minutes with the level of hygiene they have in there.

Venkat changed the subject and started telling me

about his recent trip to Japan. Now I got ready to hear about Japan—its GDP, its people, and Venkat's journey from the day he went till the day he came back. Venkat continued, 'Japanese people are extremely sensitive. They will never say what's on their minds. They show calmness outside but they are not like that inside. They feel very shy to refuse and consider it bad manners.'

Suddenly, I remembered, 'Hey Venkat, have you heard about sticky bottoms?'

Venkat did not know what it was so he stopped to think for a minute. I told him, 'In Japan, if somebody has a guest and they don't leave for a long time, the host brings a broom and keeps it upside down. They do this when they have a lot of work to do and don't have time to entertain the guest any more. The moment the guest sees the broom upside down, he or she understands. So the guest leaves politely. That person is called a Sticky Bottom.'

'Oh, that is a nice concept. Maybe I should tell Lata. When some people come and never leave our house, she can keep the broom that way.'

'Venkat, nobody in our country will understand because most of us are not that sensitive.'

I was thinking about how I could tell Venkat that he was one of them. By this time, my station had come and

I was very happy. I thought to myself, 'Why is Venkat like this? He is so insensitive and talks too much. Is it because he has a lot of energy and no hobbies, no special responsibilities and no aim in life? Or maybe it is because of anxiety. I do not know. He speaks all the time and spends all his energy.'

As I was getting ready to get down, Venkat suddenly exclaimed, 'Hey, what about my stop? Where is it?'

Then he realized that he had already passed his station.

11

Too Many Questions

At the Foundation, we buy notebooks from a factory in a village located away from Bangalore. Then, we distribute them to needy children annually.

When I went to see this factory, I found that it was in a very congested area. There were two hundred people working in shifts and all of them were poor. I decided to give these men and women a gift because Diwali was approaching.

I called the factory manager and asked him to give me the names of his two hundred employees. He was anxious to know why and when I told him that I wanted to give them gifts for Diwali, I thought that he would be really happy. Instead, he thought for a minute and said quietly, 'I will let you know tomorrow.'

The next day, the manager called me and said, 'Madam, what is the real motive behind this gesture?

Should I reduce their salary by the amount you will spend on the gift?'

'This has nothing to do with their salary,' I said.

'I hope you are not asking for a reduction or a price cut in the notebooks.'

'No, I haven't even thought about it.'

'Did any of my employees suggest that you should give them a gift?'

'No, I haven't met anyone except you from the factory.'

Somehow, he was not convinced that I wanted to give his employees gifts without a valid reason.

He continued with his questions, 'Are you going to give them gifts every year? In that case, please send me a letter stating for how many years you plan to continue giving gifts.'

'I won't give gifts every year. I just felt like giving them this year. I would like to give the gifts to your employees and not through you. Will you give me the list?'

'Sure, madam. I will do that.' And he disconnected the phone.

The manager called me again the next day. 'Madam, what gift are you planning to give my employees?'

'I know a good sari weaver and I don't have much time left now. So I will give a sari to everyone.'

'What about the men?'

'Every man has a woman at home. She could be a mother, wife, sister or daughter. He can give it to her. The sari is of very good quality.'

'Madam, men will be very upset with you. Women can wear your nice saris for the festival but the men won't have anything. I suggest you buy some pants and shirts material for them.'

I was tired of his interference. I said, 'Okay, let me think it over. We will talk later.'

The next day, he called me again. 'Madam, in our factory, there are tall people also. Should I send you the list separately so you can buy extra material for them?'

'Listen, I really don't have time for modifications. I won't be able to do that.'

'What colours are the saris and the material?'

'For the same price range, we will get different colours.'

'Oh, you can't do that. Some people may like the colour of their gift and others may not like it at all. So they may be very upset.'

'In that case, I will give the same colour to everybody.'

'No, madam, don't ever do that. They will think that you are giving them a uniform.'

'Then, what is your suggestion?' I said, exasperated.

'Maybe you can tell me your budget. Instead of you bringing the saris and the required material from Bangalore, I can buy them here in the village so that they can exchange it if they don't like the colour.'

I thought for a minute and said, 'No, that is not my policy.' I was fed up with him.

He continued, 'Okay, fine, madam, that is left to you. After all, you are the donor. Beggars are not choosers. However, I have a question. Who will pay for the stitching charges?'

'I am not paying.' I made it very clear.

'I am not paying either.' He made it even clearer.

He continued politely, 'So, may I suggest something different?'

'What is that?'

'If I give their sizes, you can buy stitched pants and shirts for the men.'

I was at the end of my tether but did not show it. I said, 'Send their measurements.'

My assistant, who had been overhearing the frequent calls said, 'Madam, why are you listening to him and his foolish options? After all, it is a gift.'

I said, 'I am not doing it for his sake. Most of the time, middle-level management do these things because they don't get such benefits or gifts. Ultimately, the poor people will suffer. The gift may not be a big sum for us. But each sari is precious to them. I am sure that they will treasure this sari and wear it for weddings. Unlike them, the manager's wife will buy expensive saris and won't even wear them. At the Foundation, we work for those people in whose life we can make a difference.'

Soon, it was the day to distribute the saris. I got the saris at one-third the price since I got them directly from the weaver. I got the two hundred saris packed and went to the factory. The men and women were standing in a queue happily waiting for their gifts. The manager was standing on one side and looked disapprovingly at me.

Before I gave the saris, I talked to the factory employees. 'My dear friends, I am giving this gift as a token of love and affection. It is coming from my heart. Diwali is an important festival and I want to celebrate it with your family by sharing whatever we have. There is a saying that when you get a gift, don't think of its price because it is the thought that is more important. So please don't worry about its price or colour. If anyone doesn't like the gift, you can return it to me and I will take it back.'

Then I started distributing the saris. I had not bought pants and shirts for anybody. All the men and women took the saris gracefully and happily. I saw that some of them even had tears in their eyes.

After the distribution, a man and a woman came to me and said, 'On behalf of everyone, we want to thank you. We have never seen such a wonderful gift in our twenty years of service. May God bless you. We may not be able to give you any gift but we wish you health and prosperity. Happy Diwali!'

I turned around and saw that there wasn't a single gift left for me to carry back.

12

The Gift of Sacrifice

During my tenure as a professor, Rajiv was one of my computer science students. Before ending each class, I told my students stories related to our country's history. Some students liked to hear them and some did not. Rajiv was not interested in history at all. So I asked him, 'Tell me your concept of history and how your generation thinks.'

He said, 'History is a dead subject of the past that gives us information about dead people and incidents. It is a chronology of events which is of no use today. I really feel that it is a waste of time.'

'Rajiv, when you go abroad for work or education, how do you interact with other people? How do you know what they say and what they mean and vice versa?' I asked.

'Oh, you should know the people with whom you interact.'

'If you want to know people, you should know the history of their land and where they come from. History also tells you about culture and culture is a big part of people's personalities.'

'How do you say that?'

'If you join me for one of my tours, I promise that, at the very least, you will be convinced that you need to keep an open mind.'

During one of my upcoming trips, I was planning to travel to a small town. There was a village near this town. Prakash, one of my ex-students, was now a senior manager in a software company and I knew that he was from that village. When Prakash learnt that I was travelling to the town, he called me up and said, 'Ma'am, instead of staying in the town, why don't you stay in my house in the village? It is only thirty kilometres away. My parents are staying alone there and they will be very happy to see you. Since you are interested in history, they will also take you around.'

I thought of Rajiv and asked him if he would like to come with me. Rajiv agreed and happily accompanied me.

I finished my work in the town and left for Prakash's village.

By the time we reached, it was evening but it was not dark. Prakash's father, Madappa, and mother, Parvati, were waiting for us. They said, 'Please relax at home. Our maid has made nice snacks for you. There is warm water in the bathroom. We will be back in an hour.'

I noticed that they were dressed to go out. They were ready with a thali containing a coconut, a garland, a diya and other small items, and I understood that they were going somewhere to perform a puja. I assumed they were going to a temple and said, 'Oh! If you are going to a temple, please wait a minute. I will change my sari and join you.'

Hesitantly, they said, 'It is not really a temple but it is like a temple to us. It is our family's worship site. Prakash might have told you about it.'

I could not contain my curiosity. 'Yes, Prakash told me that you will take me to a special historical place. Is this the same place?'

When they nodded, Rajiv also got ready and both of us accompanied them.

The worship site was at the outskirts of the village. There were fields all around us and we entered one of them. Green paddy was growing on all sides, but this field had only vegetables. There was a large neem tree in the field. Its shade covered most of the field. Below the tree, there was a large slab of stone standing on the ground. The lower part of the slab was buried deep in the soil.

There were many stone benches all around for people to come and relax here.

I noticed a tap in the corner. Madappa and Parvati washed their feet and face with tap water. With curiosity, Rajiv and I also did the same. Then Madappa took a jug of water and started washing the slab and Parvati got busy lighting a lamp nearby. I started paying attention to the details of the slab. It was approximately five and a half feet tall and two feet wide and the top looked like an arch. The slab had a beautiful border and its five horizontal compartments contained some amazing carvings.

The first compartment contained an inscription.

In the second compartment, on the right side, there was an image of a man with a sword sitting on a horse and, on the left, there was a man on foot who was only carrying a stick. I could see that the man with the stick was wearing a *veeragase*, which is a dress worn in villages. He had shoulder-length hair. He was angry and stood in a ready-to-attack position. There was an image of a cow behind him.

In the third compartment, four women with wings were flying with a palanquin while a man was sitting inside. I noticed the clouds in the background, the smile on the women's faces and their saris with waistbands.

In the fourth compartment, a man was sitting on a

throne. On either side were two women fanning him. The women wore jewellery and had tied their hair in a big bun. I could see the intricate designs of their bangles, chains, anklets and saris.

In the fifth and last compartment, there was an Ishwara Linga with a half-moon on one side and a sun on the other. There was a Nandi or bull in the front and a devotee was sitting with folded hands behind it.

'What is this? Why are you performing puja here?' asked Rajiv.

Madappa replied, 'This is a *veeragallu*, a stone that depicts valour. Gopala Golla, the cowherd, was our forefather. This is his story and his gift to us.'

'I don't understand,' said Rajiv.

Madappa did not talk further and started the puja. After the puja, we all sat on the benches and Madappa started telling us the story.

Gopala Golla was a young cowherd. He was around twenty-five years old and the only child to his parents. He had lost his father when he was very young. Gopala was recently married and his wife was pregnant. He was very happy with his ten cows. He liked to graze them near the hillock and enjoyed his peaceful life. One day, while he was playing the flute and grazing his cows, a soldier came riding on a horse. He stopped and dismounted from the horse. He gave Gopala Golla a silk cover and said, 'There is an urgent message inside. Enemies are following me. If you can go across the river and give this to the captain of our force, you will save the country. The captain is waiting below the neem tree. Since you are not a soldier, nobody will suspect that you are carrying this message.' Without waiting to hear back from Gopala, the solider mounted his horse and galloped away.

Gopala did not know what to do. He was a simple cowherd and did not know anything about how the kingdom was ruled or defended. But he knew one thing. Occasionally, enemy troops came and took away cows from the village. During these incidents, the king's soldiers came to protect the village and fought with the enemy troops. They were normally victorious.

Initially, Gopala thought about ignoring the soldier and doing nothing. He did not want to get into this mess. Then he thought that if he did not deliver the message, the enemy might win and occupy the kingdom. That would be much worse. Everyone would lose their cows and the enemies would burn the village. For the sake of the village and the cows, he decided to do what was necessary.

Gopala heard the sound of horses and immediately hid the silk cover in his lunch bag. A few minutes later, enemy soldiers came riding on horses and asked him, 'Did a soldier on a horse come this way?'

Gopala said, 'A soldier? Here? No, I haven't seen anyone except my cows.'

The enemy soldiers went away. Gopala took his lunch bag and started running towards the river, leaving his cows behind. He was not worried about them. He knew that when the sun went down, the cows would automatically go home.

Gopala's destination was a long distance away and the path was thorny. There was no road and he was worried that someone might follow him.

When he came to the river, he knew that he had to swim across. While he was getting ready to jump in, some enemy soldiers came out of the bushes and attacked him with their swords and javelins. Gopala only had a cowherd's stick, but he fought bravely and was seriously injured. He did not care about his injuries and jumped into the water. He crossed the river somehow and could barely walk once he reached the shore. He limped a short distance and then saw the neem tree. There he saw the captain waiting. Gopala gave the silk cover to him and then he fell to the ground and died.

The message that Gopala delivered was crucial in making an important decision during the battle.

Eventually, the king who ruled Gopala's village won. When the king learnt that a young lad had sacrificed his life without even being a soldier, he considered him to be a great martyr.

The king himself went to Gopala's house and consoled his old mother and pregnant young wife. He told Gopala's wife, 'Your loss is irreparable. Your husband sacrificed his life so that we can live in peace.' And he gave her a large piece of land exactly where Gopala had died.

Madappa paused and continued, 'We are his descendants. Over a period of time, we split the land and some of the descendants sold their portions. This portion has come to our family and I will keep it forever. Once a year, we have a festival in Gopala Golla's remembrance and all his descendants come to the village, no matter where they are. We assemble and conduct a puja for the stone. But Parvati and I come here every day to light a lamp for the great man.'

'Uncle, how did this stone come here and what do these figures mean?' asked Rajiv.

Madappa started explaining. 'This stone tells us Gopala's story. In the first section, it says that on this particular date, a king who ruled this area appreciated Gopala's martyrdom and gave the land as a gift to show respect for his sacrifice. His family will have sole ownership of this land.'

'How old is this inscription?'

'Around seven hundred years. The second section shows Gopala fighting with the soldiers. The third section shows that he died and the angels are taking him to his heavenly abode. The fourth section reveals that he has attained a great place in the court of warriors and is enjoying the luxuries there. Finally, the fifth section says that he is a great devotee of Ishwara. The half-moon and the sun indicate that this glory will last until the sun and moon exist. The stone was erected by the captain of the troop so that Gopala's sacrifice is remembered forever.'

'But who told you the story?' Rajiv asked. 'It is not written on the stone.'

'This story has been passed on from generation to generation in our family. Prakash also knows the story. It is his duty to pass it on to his children. If we didn't know the history of our family, then we would not know the value of this land and would have treated it like a commercial property.'

Now Rajiv looked at me and nodded his head. I knew that he had got his answer.

13

Bad Help

I was visiting the village I grew up in and was awaiting some papers from my office. Since the village was small, there was no courier service and the mail from my office had been sent by registered post. I went to the local post office and noticed that it was a small building with a skeletal staff. The building had not been renovated or painted in years. The fans were also not working because there was no electricity. The post office was hot and dusty. It was old and had very few customers because it had lost its importance due to the increased usage of email and Internet.

While waiting for my papers, I remembered my childhood. In our village, the postman was loved and highly respected. All of us at home waited for him. He was our main link to the outside world. He brought us greeting cards, parcels, money orders and letters. He distributed mail to the entire village. Our house was always his last stop of the day. He gave us our letters and then had lunch with us. During lunch, he told us lots of stories and gave us news from the village. The postman was like our personal news channel and we loved his visits. He also gave us financial advice and told us to buy government bonds and open a post-office savings account.

Today, I do not even go to the post office. I wondered, 'When I was younger, how did I correspond without email?'

I was brought back to reality when the postmaster said, 'It will take some time for us to get your papers. Why don't you go home? I will send the papers to you through my postman in the afternoon or evening.'

I replied, 'Thank you.' And I went home.

After lunch, a postman and a young boy came knocking at the door. The young boy was tall, handsome and reserved but his eyes were bright and shining. I invited them to sit down and offered them lunch. They refused politely.

The postman said, 'Ma'am, we have had lunch. Here are your papers. You need to sign for this. But . . .'

I signed the document and, without looking up, I asked him, 'What is it?'

He said, 'Meet my son, Satish. He is very intelligent. He has just finished his twelfth class with excellent marks. He has got admission in a prestigious engineering college called BITS Pilani . . .' And he stopped.

I looked at the boy. He looked uncomfortable with the conversation. His father continued, 'Ma'am, I can't afford his expenses at Pilani. I have never gone out of Karnataka. In fact, I have never even gone out of Dharwad district. He is my only child. I want him to be educated. You are from our village and you have seen the outside world. Is there any way you can help my boy study at BITS Pilani? With my salary, I can send him to the local engineering college but Satish is very keen to go outside.'

As a trustee of the Foundation, I immediately understood his situation. We come across many intelligent children who have high ambitions but an economically poor background. Most times, we help these children partially and sometimes we completely cover their educational expenses. This was one such case.

In a big city like Bangalore, there are many job opportunities; but in a small village, a postman only depends on his salary. I liked the boy and asked him for his marks card and admission letters. He was well prepared before he came to see me and showed me all the documents.

While browsing through the documents, I noticed that he had an interesting last name. When I asked him about it, Satish said, 'I have taken my last name from the name of my village.'

I told Satish, 'Well, I have everything I need right now. I promise that we will pay your first year's college fees and every year you have to send me your marks card. If you are on the merit list, we will continue paying your tuition until you complete your first degree.'

Satish and his father left the house with smiles on their faces. Every year, Satish's marks card came for our review and we sent money automatically. After four years, the marks card did not come and I knew that he must have completed his degree.

Many years passed and I forgot about Satish because he was one of the thousand recipients who had received help from the Infosys Foundation. We keep records of the recipients and the help we give them but we do not keep records of where they are, nor do they usually inform us.

I have a good friend, Vinita, who is from Maharashtra but lives in Bangalore. Her daughter was a software engineer working in a good company. Typical of an anxious parent, Vinita was searching for a suitable match for her daughter. She registered on bharatmatrimony.com, shaadi.com and many other sites. She also requested me to tell her if I knew someone suitable.

One day, I was visiting her neighbourhood and decided to drop in without calling ahead. It was 4 p.m. on a Sunday and I knew she would be at home. But when I entered, I realized that she had guests in her house. Vinita's daughter was dressed beautifully and she was talking to a young boy. His parents were sitting on a sofa. I understood that a young suitable groom had come to visit their house and talk to the girl.

I told Vinita, 'I am sorry. I should have called. I will come some other time.'

But Vinita did not let me go. She said, 'It doesn't matter. You are just like family. Come, sit down and join us.' So I did.

I looked at the boy's parents. They were fat and took up most of the large sofa. The father was in an expensive safari suit and wore a thick gold chain around his neck and sported a large gold ring. The mother had draped a very pricey Kanjeevaram sari around herself, and almost a quarter kilo of gold adorned her body. She wore a big bindi and plenty of flowers in her hair. I noticed that her hair was decorated with a *moggina male*, a small jasmine bud garland done in gold. She wore diamond *jhumkis*, dangling earrings which were not suitable for her age. The boy was tall and handsome. Despite the hot summer weather, he wore a costly suit, a gold kada and a diamond ring. From where I was sitting, I noticed that a luxurious car was waiting outside for them. I realized that they were extremely rich.

Compared to the boy and his family, Vinita's daughter herself was very simply dressed.

Vinita introduced me, 'Sudha is my old friend from college.' I folded my hands in a namaskara and, even though they reciprocated, I noticed immediately that they were uncomfortable. Before she could introduce them to me, I got a business call and went outside to take it. It turned out to be a long call.

By the time I returned, Vinita's guests were about to leave. The boy looked a bit pale. I smiled and said, 'I wish you all the best.' They left in a hurry.

Vinita and her daughter were very happy. She said, 'These people are very nice and come from a good family. The boy is a senior manager in a good company and owns an apartment in Jayanagar. His only sister is a software engineer. She is married and lives in America. The boy and his parents came last week to our house and liked our daughter. The boy wanted to come one more time. If all goes well, there may be an engagement as soon as next week. After that, the boy is going to America for a project. When he comes back, we will have the wedding. They want a big engagement and wedding—we don't have a problem with that.'

Vinita's husband entered the room. He said, 'Let's not talk about marriage and other details until they officially say yes. If they do so, next Thursday is a good day for the engagement.'

They all felt relaxed and nice about this matrimonial alliance.

I said, 'Sorry I got a call when you were about to introduce them to me. Tell me about this boy and his family.'

Vinita replied, 'We came in contact with them from the matrimonial sites on the Internet. The boy's name is Satish. He has also studied in the US, worked there for a few years and then he came back to India. His parents have been staying in Bangalore for the last five years. We did a background check on his education and job record and everything seems fine. He did his engineering from BITS Pilani. He was so intelligent that the institute even gave him a scholarship.'

BITS Pilani clicked in my mind because Satish was the only one who went to BITS Pilani from the list of people that we had helped through the Foundation. Most of the students that we funded were from Karnataka and went to local colleges.

I asked Vinita, 'What is Satish's last name?'

When Vinita told me his last name, it confirmed my suspicion, but I did not want to say anything to her until I had verified our records. 'When did he complete his education at BITS?' I asked.

Vinita gave me the year and said, 'Right now, he is thirty years old. He finished his degree when he was twenty-two. What did you think of the boy?'

I told her, 'I don't know. I have only met him once. But he looks good.'

Vinita insisted, 'You must come for the engagement.'

I replied, 'Of course. Kindly confirm the date at the earliest.' And I left.

The next day, I went to my office and checked our records. It was indeed the same Satish. I was very happy that he had done well for himself. Now I understood why his parents wore so much gold and showed off their wealth. It was because they came from a deprived background and had recently acquired wealth. So they went overboard buying things that they could never afford before.

I picked up the phone to call Vinita and tell her I

knew the family and that the boy was very intelligent. But something stopped me. I thought, 'Why didn't they recognize me? Why didn't they even acknowledge me? At the Foundation, we do not expect gratitude from everybody but it is normal to at least expect some courtesy.'

As I worked backwards, I realized what might have happened. Satish and his family may not have told Vinita's family about their background. They had probably also hidden the fact that Satish's father was once a postman. They wanted to show Vinita and her family that they had always been rich. I was not sure whether I should tell Vinita. There is nothing wrong in being poor; and if people want to hide their background, it is left to their value system. I should not be judgemental about that.

While my mind was oscillating between whether I should make the phone call or not, the phone rang. It was Vinita. She sounded sad. She said, 'Sorry, there is no engagement. The boy doesn't want to marry our daughter.'

'Why? What happened?' I asked.

'I have no idea. They were so enthusiastic about the wedding until their visit on Sunday. I don't know why they changed their mind.'

I kept quiet. I wanted to be completely sure before I told Vinita anything. 'What is their background? What does the father do?' I asked.

'The father is a landlord. They own properties in a village in North Karnataka and they come from generations of family wealth. You are from the same area. Have you ever heard of them?'

'Yes, Vinita, I know them. I didn't want to say anything until I was absolutely sure. Satish's father was a postman and the boy is very bright. We helped with Satish's education through the Foundation but he has accomplished everything on his own. They must have thought that I recognized them and would tell you the truth. So they backed out of the engagement. That is my reading of the situation.'

I finished the call and kept sitting, busy with my thoughts. I had never thought that getting an economic need based scholarship would bring shame to Satish and his family. That was the reason he had refused to recognize me. For the first time in my life, I understood that if a person is not comfortable with the help given to him, it becomes a lifelong burden for him to carry.

14

Sharing with a Ghost

Two decades ago, I was teaching in a college. The campus was so large that only half the area was occupied by the college, while the other half was taken up by the primary section of a high school. I was chairperson of the prize committee of our college. A philanthropist had left some money to the college for a prize to be given to the student who got the highest marks in the Kannada language. The prize money of one thousand rupees was always given on College Day.

The job of the clerk in the prize committee was to go through all the marks cards of the final-year students and give the list of prizewinners to the committee. In those days, there was no computer scanning, automatic sorting or email. The clerk had to manually prepare the list.

That year, Rohini got eighty-five marks in Kannada. That was the highest in the college. We announced her name as prizewinner on the college noticeboard. The next day, Rohini came to my office. She said, 'Ma'am, there is a mistake. Sunita, who is studying in Section D, has also got eighty-five marks.'

'How do you know?' I asked her.

'Sunita told me to collect her marks card on her behalf. So I came to the office and noticed that she had the same marks as me. But on the noticeboard, only my name was displayed. There must be some error. So I came to tell you.'

I was happy about Rohini's honesty. I immediately called the clerk and asked him about Sunita's marks. Shyly, he said, 'Sorry, madam, I mistook eighty-five for thirty-five, hence the error.'

Firmly, I asked him to get his eyes tested the next day so that this mistake was not repeated. If Rohini had not informed me, the college would have been unfair to a meritorious student.

Rohini happily shared her money with Sunita on College Day.

Sharing reminds me of many other interesting incidents I encountered while at the college.

Once I was interviewing people for a position. My colleague on the interview board said, 'When the merits of the candidates are equal, we should select a person who plays cricket rather than tennis.' I was surprised at this comment. I had always thought that both cricket and tennis were just games. When I looked at him, he explained, 'Cricket teaches us to share success but tennis teaches us individualism.'

One rainy day, I was looking at the primary section of the school from my office. It was drizzling. I saw a young mother with a big umbrella. She had come to pick up her little girl from school. This little girl wanted to share the umbrella with her friend who did not have one. Even though the mother knew that they could share, she told the little girl, 'Look darling, I only have one umbrella. Let her bring her own umbrella. Two of you cannot share one.' I felt that the mother should have encouraged her child to share. It would have been an important lesson in life.

In another incident on Children's Day (14 November), a teacher called me to conduct games in the primary school. We made three groups of ten students each, gave five bananas to each group and asked them to share the fruits among themselves. The results were startling. The first group had five aggressive children. They took a banana each and the remaining five children were left with none. In the second group, three children shared two bananas and seven children shared the remaining three. In the third group, all ten of them shared the five bananas equally. The worst thing was that the mothers of the aggressive children in the first group were extremely happy and congratulated each other, 'Oh, my child is very smart and super-competitive. I am sure that this is the right attitude in the modern age.' I was disillusioned when I realized that the mothers who were supposed to inculcate good moral values in their children had never taught them to share.

In this context, Rohini sharing her prize money made me very happy indeed.

When I was teaching the final-year students, I gave my class an assignment with a time limit of one day. The earliest and first correct submission would get the highest marks. One of my students, Priya, was quite brilliant. I expected her to finish first but she did not. She submitted the assignment with everyone else. I asked Priya to stay back after class and asked her, 'Priya, why did you take so much time? It was not a difficult assignment for a person like you.' With sadness in her voice, she said, 'Ma'am, my assignment was complete and ready last night itself but, when I came to the computer lab, someone had stolen the cable connecting the computer to the common shared printer so I couldn't take a printout. In our college, we don't have individual printers because it is expensive. We use one printer which is shared by all students of the same batch. It reduces our costs and we learn to share. When I came today, the cable was connected. Everybody took printouts and so did I.' I realized that the culprit could have been a jealous classmate who was too lazy to do the assignment early and wanted to delay others by not sharing the printer.

Sharing is an important quality that binds people, and society itself survives on sharing. I always tell the following story to my students in class before I teach management decision-making.

A long, long time ago, an ordinary person was born into a very intellectual family in a village. Everybody looked down upon him because he was not accomplished. He was the black sheep of the family. Unable to bear the insults, he left home and decided to end his life. When he reached the next village, he saw a big abandoned house on the outskirts. He thought that he would spend his last night there.

A passer-by saw him entering the gates of the abandoned house and said, 'Young man, it is getting dark. Are you planning to spend the night there? Are you mad? There is a ghost inside that house. That is why nobody stays there. Take my advice and get out.'

The young man thought that this was perfect. It was

best that the ghost killed him so that he did not even have to plan his death.

Darkness descended as the night drew closer. The young man waited for the ghost.

Suddenly, a voice from somewhere said, 'Young man, why are you here? Are you not scared of me?'

Without getting perturbed, the young man replied, 'I know you are here. Still, I want to stay.'

The ghost was shocked at the reply. Normally, people ran away from him but this man was not scared. So the ghost asked, 'Why have you come here?'

The young man explained his situation.

After listening to the young man, the ghost inquired, 'Are you ready to learn, work hard, do your homework and practise whatever you learn? If so, I will teach you the Sanskrit language including grammar and its great works.'

The young man agreed. So the ghost and the young man started their classes as teacher and student.

Day after day, the young man continued to learn. Months rolled by and years passed. The young man never saw the ghost and only heard his voice. One day, the ghost suddenly appeared in front of him and said, 'Young man, you have now mastered the language. Will you allow me to go to heaven?'

The young man was perplexed, 'When did I stop

you from going to heaven? Who are you? Why did you teach me?'

The ghost sighed and shared his story. 'I was an extremely learned and rich man in this town. This is my mansion. I never shared my knowledge or my money with anyone. I was scared that if I gave away knowledge, then some smart person may become better than me. If I distributed my wealth, I thought that I might become poor. I wanted to remain a learned and powerful man and I died without sharing. When my soul went to heaven, I was thrown back as a ghost to my own mansion with an instruction that until I taught someone, shared my knowledge sincerely and distributed my wealth, I would not attain heaven and would remain a ghost. I could distribute money very easily but not my knowledge. People were so scared of me that they never came and stayed here. I had been waiting for a good and eager student for several years. Then you came here. Whatever I knew, I have taught you. You have helped me attain my salvation. I thank you and now I want to go. Please remember the parting words of your teacher—in life, sharing is important.'

Many years later, this young man became a great critic of the poet Kalidasa. Thanks to him, we have much knowledge about the great poet. The young man's name was Bharavi.

15

Foot in the Mouth

Savitri was a lecturer, a colleague of mine during my teaching days. She was sharp and came from a rich background. She loved to spend her time gossiping about people instead of doing any constructive work. All our colleagues knew about her nature and, as an inside joke, the teachers called her Savitri G, where 'G' stood for 'Gossip'.

People who did not know her realized very soon that she had a knack of creating news out of nothing. After that, they avoided her and, in the end, Savitri was always lonely. So she was always on the lookout for people who would sit with her and gossip.

One day, I accidentally ran into her in the college canteen. Before I could go the other way, she saw me and caught hold of my hand so tightly that even Superman could not have loosened the grip. I did not want to create a scene in front of my students, who consider us role models. So we settled down at a table for a cup of coffee.

Almost immediately, the college bell rang for the next class. I wanted to get out of her clutches, so I lied and said, 'Savitri, I have a class now. I will see you later.'

I got up. She asked, 'Which class are you taking and in which room?'

Lying spontaneously is not my strength and, when we lie, we have to remember the untruths we have fabricated. It is hard work to lie. I said the first thing that came to my mind, 'Room Number 207.'

'Which class?' she asked.

I replied, 'First year MCA students.'

Smiling victoriously, she said, 'Learn how to lie properly. Today, the first year MCA class has gone on a picnic with their class teacher Ganesh.'

I was still trying to escape her clutches and I said, 'Sorry, I meant second year MCA.'

'Keep quiet and sit down. Rooms 201 to 210 have been getting whitewashed since yesterday.'

I knew I was guilty and I had no other option but to sit down again.

Savitri started talking immediately. It felt as if she had been in solitude for months and had found a listener after a long time.

'What is the latest news?'

'Well, there is this latest scam. Also, there is so much traffic in Bangalore.'

Sarcastically, Savitri replied, 'I also read newspapers and see TV, you know. I wasn't talking about that kind of news.' She paused, then continued, 'Have you heard the rumours about Anusuya? I just couldn't believe what I heard.'

Anusuya or Ansi as I called her was a common friend. She was dignified and non-interfering. I was a little worried when Savitri started talking in a hush-hush manner about her. I asked, 'Why? What happened to Ansi?'

'Do you know that there is some problem in her marriage? Ansi and Girish are separated.'

'How do you know that?'

'Whenever I call Ansi, she always says that her husband is abroad or travelling. Tell me, isn't that unusual?'

'No, it isn't. Girish is in a senior position at work and he has to travel a lot. What is wrong in that? And whenever you might have called, he must have been travelling. I met Girish only yesterday.'

'Oh, really? Who was with him?' Savitri shot questions at me like a detective.

'He was at the Taj West End with one of his lady colleagues.'

I saw that Savitri was bubbling with excitement. I regretted the words the moment they came out of my mouth. I did not want to give Savitri any more ammunition.

'Well, don't stop. How old was she?'

'I didn't ask for her birth certificate.' Now I was really annoyed at myself and at her.

'Cool down. Was she in her mid-twenties or in her thirties?'

'I don't know. Girish had a business meeting and there were many people around them. I didn't find anything amiss. Don't you attend seminars with our male colleagues? How would you feel if someone talked about you like that? Savitri, please, let us not gossip.'

But she was not listening to me at all. She continued as if I had not said anything, 'These days, with make-up, even a forty-five-year-old woman looks like she's twenty-five. So maybe that's why you weren't able to guess her age. If I were you, I would have rightly guessed it and immediately informed Ansi to take care of her husband. Cautioning people is also a form of social work. Anyway, you won't understand.'

She changed the topic and without waiting for my answer, she asked, 'Have you met Roma lately?'

Roma was another common friend. She was very

fashionable and had a modern outlook. I knew that Roma was a good woman.

Savitri continued her commentary, 'Money has gone to Roma's head. How can her husband earn so much money in such a short period? They must be doing something illegal. Without working hard, they have made so much money. Look at Roma. She is so fashionable. She wears only designer saris and can be seen in beauty parlours getting expensive facials. She even has a personal fitness trainer. She doesn't help her poor relatives at all but is ready to spend a lot of money on herself.'

'How do you know all this?'

She smiled and said, 'I don't talk without proof. Govind told my driver.'

'Who is Govind?'

'Govind is my driver's friend and Roma's driver's cousin.'

I did not know what Govind had told Savitri's driver and how Savitri had interpreted it. But I knew Roma well. It was true that Roma was fashionable and rich, but that did not mean that she did not help others. Roma had come to our Foundation office many times to give a cheque with a large amount of money as donation. She always requested me not to tell anyone about it. I also knew that all of Roma's relatives had built houses with her help and even bought cars but nobody said it in public because Roma never wanted people to know. She liked to donate anonymously. We should never judge a person from the outside. But there was no point in talking about these things to Savitri, who would just gossip and find a reason to blame others without even knowing the details.

I got irritated with Savitri and was about to get up. Savitri again changed the subject. 'Sumati is a fine lady and very innocent too. I consider innocence and ignorance the same. What do you think?'

Sumati was very calculative, shrewd and not a reliable friend. Sumati's own sisters had told me many stories about her. They said that she pretended to be very simple and behaved as if she was very innocent and principled. She was working in a government department and had been suspended once because she had been caught engaging in malpractice.

Thankfully, the bell rang, and I was glad that this one hour was over.

I got up and firmly said, 'Savitri, don't judge a person by their looks or from rumours. Looks can be deceptive. It is not that all rich people are bad and neither is it true that all simple-looking people are innocent. Ignorance is different from innocence. Ignorance is a lack of knowledge but innocence is about trust and believing other people. A child is always innocent but we adults are ignorant and hardly innocent. Savitri, gossip is bad and spoils many families. When you talk about somebody, remember that someone somewhere is also talking about you. People might like to hear gossip to pass time but everybody dislikes a gossipmonger. Eventually, they want to keep such people at a distance.'

Even as I said the words, I understood that they would not get into Savitri's head. She was now looking at our colleague Kamala, who was settling down with her cup of coffee at a table near us. Without even bidding me goodbye, Savitri got up and moved to Kamala's table. I knew that I would be the next target in her gossip sessions. I had put my foot in my mouth.

16

Miserable Success

Vishnu was a young, bright and ambitious student from the first batch I ever taught at college. So my relationship with him was closer than that with my students from subsequent batches. He was charming, communicative and clear in his thinking.

In college, we used to have long arguments on different issues and we used to agree to disagree on many matters. I used to tell Vishnu, 'Vishnu, I have seen many more seasons than you. With my experience in life, I want to tell you that having good relationships, compassion and peace of mind is much more important than achievements, awards, degrees or money.'

Vishnu would argue back, 'Madam, your stomach is full and you have achieved everything. Hence, you are comfortable in life and can say that. You have received many awards, so you don't care for them and you are not ambitious. You will never understand people like me.' Then, I usually just smiled at him. I liked him for his openness.

Vishnu was also very good at teaching. He completed his degree and got an excellent job in Microsoft in Seattle, USA. He was awaiting his visa to go abroad. I told him to teach at my college while he was waiting. Whenever I could not attend the laboratory sessions, I told him to take charge of the junior lab and be my substitute. He became very popular with the students.

I asked Vishnu, 'You are very good at teaching, why don't you seriously think of becoming a professor?'

He said, 'My monthly salary in the USA is more than a teacher's annual salary here. Why would I want to become a professor?'

'Vishnu, don't be so rude. A teacher is not respected for the salary but for his or her knowledge and teaching. If you don't respect the teaching profession, that is fine but don't make such a comparison.'

Soon, Vishnu left the country on his new assignment.

Many years passed and a decade rolled by. My students, who were once young, were now middle-aged and I had gone from middle age to old age.

One day, my secretary told me that someone called Vishnu wanted to meet me. By this time, I knew many

Vishnus and was not able to place him at once. She said that he was a student from my first batch of students. Now I recognized him instantly and told her to set up an appointment. After all, old wine, old memories and old students are precious in life.

On the day of the appointment, Vishnu walked in right on time. He had less hair than before and some of them were grey. He had put on weight. He was wearing an expensive shirt and there was a platinum diamond ring on his finger. But alas, his face was like a dried tomato. There was not a trace of enthusiasm on it. On the contrary, I could see some lines of worry on his face.

He sat in front of me and I ordered him a cup of tea. Vishnu looked at me and said, 'Madam, you look really old now.'

I smiled and said, 'Time and tide will wait for no one.' But he did not smile back. 'How are you, Vishnu?' I asked. 'I haven't met you for fifteen years. It is very nice of you to remember your old teacher and come to see me. Where are you? What are you doing now? Are you still with Microsoft?'

'No, madam. I left Microsoft after three years,' replied Vishnu.

'No wonder people say that if someone stays in a software company for more than three years, he is a loyal person!'

He did not respond to my joke. 'So where are you now?' I asked again.

'I own a company in Singapore. Two hundred people work for me. We make very good profit.' I felt Vishnu's voice had that pride of achievement, which was very natural.

'So you have settled in Singapore?'

'Not really, I come to India quite often because of work. I have a house in Vasant Vihar in Delhi, a flat in Worli in Mumbai, a bungalow in Raj Mahal Vilas Extension in Bangalore, a farm on Bannerghatta Road . . .'

I stopped him. 'Vishnu, I didn't ask you about your assets. I am not an income tax person. I just wanted to know where you normally stay.' I was pulling his leg, yet he did not smile.

'Vishnu, you have told me enough of your financial assets,' I continued. 'Now tell me about your marital status. Are you married? How many children do you have? What do they do?' Usually, a mother and a teacher get the automatic authority to pose these questions to her children and students. I am no exception. Some people mind my questions because it is their personal life and I get the hint and stop. But most people happily tell me about their life.

'Yes, I am married. I have an eight-year-old daughter,' he said.

Vishnu pulled out his wallet and showed me his family photo. When he was in college, he used to go out with Bhagya, a girl junior to him. But the lady in the photograph was different. She was stunningly beautiful, like a model, and his daughter was cute.

I felt that his life was a picture perfect postcard. He was successful, rich, had a very pretty wife and a daughter. What else can one want in life? With this kind of success, he should be very happy and enthusiastic—but he was not. I did not know the reason, but I knew that he would tell me. I stopped talking and allowed Vishnu to speak.

Slowly, Vishnu opened up. 'Madam, I have a problem. I have come to talk to you.'

'What problem? And why do you think I have the solution? Actually, a successful person like you should help an old teacher like me,' I joked to reduce the tension.

'It is nothing to do with success, madam. For the last few years, I have been feeling very sad. I feel like I am missing something in life. I can't pinpoint exactly what it is,' he said. 'Nothing makes me happy. Nothing even moves me or touches my heart, even if I see a heart-wrenching incident. I feel that I am travelling in a desert without water and the roads are paved with gold and silver . . .'

I asked him directly, 'Have you seen a doctor or a counsellor?'

'Of course I have. They said that a compassionate heart is important to enjoy life. They told me to read books and advised me to try and be happy by doing things such as looking at the sunrise, listening to the birds, taking long walks and exercising regularly.'

'Well, what happened?'

'I lost weight with all the activities but otherwise things didn't improve. I went back to a counsellor again. He told me to go to Somalia on a trip.'

'Why Somalia?' I was surprised. 'I know that there are trips to Europe, Hong Kong and Bangkok. But I have never heard of a trip to Somalia. Tell me, did you go there? What did you do in Somalia?' I was curious.

'Oh, they took us to orphanages, HIV camps and camps of children suffering from malnutrition. But nothing happened. I still didn't feel anything. On the contrary, my mind was busy calculating how Somalia could export to America or other European nations. What would you have done in my place, madam?' he questioned me.

'Don't put me in your shoes. What I would do is left to me and you don't have to do the same thing. Why can't you talk to someone who is very dear to you—maybe a friend or your wife or someone from your age group? They might be able to give you a better solution. After all, there is a generation gap between us.'

He was quiet. Then he said, 'Madam, all my life, I have calculated and made friendships. I have never spent time with people who aren't useful to me in some way. After all, life is a merciless, competitive field. Every move should take me one step higher on the ladder of success.'

I thought to myself, 'Now I know why Bhagya was replaced by the model wife.'

'How much time do you spend with your family?'

'My daughter is friendly but she is nice to me only when she wants something from me. Sometimes, I find it very strange. A child looks beautiful only with innocence but my daughter is more practical. My wife is very busy with the carpet business that she inherited from her father. She doesn't have any time to talk to me and my daughter even though she works from home most of the time.'

He stopped for a second and continued, 'Or maybe I think that way. My wife wants to get all my contacts and clients so that she can expand her business. I am more of a database to her than a companion.'

I understood Vishnu's problem. Sometimes, it is very difficult to talk with your own family. I was touched that he felt safe coming to me. But he was expecting a quick fix from me. I was willing to listen to his problem, but that did not mean that I also knew the solution.

Vishnu continued, 'Madam, tell me, how do I become compassionate? How do I build a strong family? How can I enjoy the sunrise and the moonlight? How much time does it take to get all these qualities? Are there any books or a crash course or people who can teach me? I don't care about the cost but it shouldn't take months together.'

I was shocked by his approach. 'Vishnu, compassion cannot be taught, sold or bought,' I said. 'There is no time limit either. It is one of the characteristics that you have to develop from the beginning. Understand that life is a journey. In that short journey, if you can show compassion to others, show it now. Our ancestors have always talked about the middle path for a reason. That path makes a person stable, happy and content. Vishnu, you are the role model for your children. Children will be what they see. What you have done, your daughter has copied.'

Vishnu sighed and said, 'Yes, madam. I understand what you are saying. I will take my daughter and work with poor people on a regular basis along with her. That will also help us bond. I am hoping that it will make me a better human being and I will be able to feel worthy again. Now I know what brought me to you. I cannot thank you enough.'

Vishnu left my office with hope in his heart and a smile on his face.

17

Shraddha

My father, Dr R.H. Kulkarni, passed away twelve years ago. He was a doctor and a professor of gynaecology in a medical college. He always believed that education for women is essential. So he sent me to an engineering college in 1968. It was a time when most girls' fathers could not even dream of doing that because of societal pressures. My father loved his daughters and son equally and had the same rules for all his children. He even divided his assets equally among all of us.

My father's *shraddha* occurs on 30 October every year. Suresh was my father's favourite nephew and he always performed my father's memorial service. I kept money in a fixed deposit account and the interest accruing from this was used to meet the shraddha expenses in a temple nearby. Every year, our family went to the temple, watched my cousin Suresh perform the shraddha and had lunch together. Then, in the evening, I went to an orphanage and gave fruits to the children. We had been following this routine for the past eleven years.

Last year, however, Suresh was in Paris on work at the end of October and he was not available to perform the shraddha. But, as usual, my family and I went to the temple. I sat on the bench waiting for the manager.

I saw my friend Meera at the temple. She seemed worried. I asked her, 'What's happened?'

'My brother, Murali, has not reached here yet. Today is my mother's shraddha. I want it to be performed here because Murali said that this temple was near his new house.'

I knew Meera's family very well and was surprised by her answer. 'Why has Murali shifted to a new house?' I asked. 'What happened to your old house?'

Meera's mother had been a schoolteacher. She had saved every penny of her salary and pension and built a nice house. She was extremely fond of her home and called it 'Sarthaka' (which means fulfilment). She died a few years ago. Meera had already lost her father when she was a child. Her mother had single-handedly raised Meera and her brother.

With sadness, Meera replied, 'As you know, Murali got into bad company. He had loans to repay, so he sold the house. Now he has rented a house near this temple. Yesterday, I went and begged him to come early to perform our mother's shraddha. I am even paying the entire cost for this ceremony.'

I fell silent and started looking around. There was an older lady sitting near us and she seemed worried as well. She kept looking at her watch and glancing at the door. Casually, I asked her, 'Are you waiting for somebody?'

'Yes, I am waiting for my son. He is a senior manager in a software company. Today is the release date of his project. He said that he would be here by this time. His cellphone is switched off and I don't know what has happened. If he doesn't show up, how will we perform my husband's shraddha? I am very concerned.'

I realized that three women were sitting on a bench waiting to perform shraddha for their loved ones. The temple manager came and asked us for the names of the people for whom we wanted to perform shraddha. All three of us promptly gave the names. Then he said proudly, 'Shraddha is a religious ceremony, which is very important for the family. Today, the deceased, his or her father and forefather, that is, three generations of people, come down to earth in the form of the cow, the sun and God. When a family member gives *til* seeds and water, your remembrance reaches them. Shraddha is a ceremony that must be performed with shraddha or devotion.'

He looked at us and said, 'Where are the male members of your families? Call them now. Tell them to get ready. I will arrange three pundits to help them.'

Then he sat on a chair and started sorting through receipts.

I replied, 'Sir, at this moment, we don't have any male members from our families.'

'Then I will call a helper from the kitchen. He will perform the shraddha on your families' behalf.'

For a second, I stopped. Then, firmly, I said, 'No, sir. I can perform my father's shraddha. I don't need an unknown male to perform shraddha for someone he doesn't even know.'

The manager continued to sort through receipts. He did not even bother to look at me before answering, 'Sorry, madam. No woman can perform shraddha for anyone. This is the rule. If you cannot accept that, then just have lunch here, pray to God and go home.'

'No, sir, I can't accept your decision,' I said. 'After all, this is my father's shraddha. As a daughter, I have the right to remember my father today. It is my duty too. Is there any book that says that a woman can't perform shraddha and that only male members are allowed to do so?'

The manager stopped sorting receipts and looked at me. He was taken aback by my answer. He could not believe what he was hearing. He said, 'It is a tradition.'

'Sorry, sir. Tradition is different from ritual. A tradition passes down values to the next generation but a ritual or ceremony is what you do by practice and habit. For example, performing shraddha is a tradition, but the fact that it is done by a man is a ritual. We shouldn't break traditions but rituals can be changed depending on the circumstances. Rituals are almost always formed based on geographical, economic and social conditions.'

The manager was not happy with my argument. 'Listen, madam,' he said patiently. 'We have never allowed a woman to perform shraddha before. No woman has ever questioned our procedures till now.'

'If it hasn't been done before, you can start today,' I said. 'Every journey starts with a single step. I don't think that it is wise to perform rituals without understanding them. My father used to tell me a story. There was a person who used to perform puja every day and a cat used to trouble him during his puja. So, he told his son, "Tie the cat and give it some milk every day when I do puja." The cat never troubled him again. After a few years, both the man and the cat died. The son took over and started performing the puja. Since the cat had died, he brought the neighbour's cat, tied it and poured milk for the cat every day during puja time. The son had never understood why his father had asked him to give milk to the cat every day. It had become a meaningless ritual. You are doing the same thing.'

By this time, a crowd had formed around us and people were listening to our argument. The manager said, 'But, madam, how can a woman perform shraddha?'

'Why can't she? When I wrote out a cheque for this temple, you accepted it. You never checked whether it came from a man or a woman. In the olden days, there was a division of labour between men and women because large families stayed together. That is why men worked outside the home and women inside. Today, women work equally well in all fields. There is no difference. If you don't allow me to perform shraddha, you are establishing a fact that no daughter can perform her father's shraddha and no wife can perform her husband's shraddha. Just because she is a female, does it mean that a woman has no feelings towards her brother, father or husband? That is unfair. I am going to perform shraddha today, come what may.'

The manager was amused by my insistence and said, 'If that is so, we don't have any pundit who will be willing to help you perform shraddha.'

The crowd stayed silent and nobody took any sides. There were also many young and old pundits listening to us. I looked at them, 'Is there anyone who can help me?'

Some young priests smiled at me but did not step forward. To my surprise, an old man said, 'I will help you perform your father's shraddha.' I knew that this man was the most senior in the temple. Softly, he continued, 'I have seen sons who talk on their phones while performing shraddha. Their mind is never on the ceremony. I have seen men who go out, smoke, come back and continue the ceremony. I have seen men who tell me that they will give me more money if I complete the ceremony in five minutes. Then there are others who do it with love and remembrance. But when men who are not interested can perform shraddha, why should a woman who is sincerely pleading be denied? As per the tradition, we believe that the ancestors come down to earth on the day of the shraddha and they should not go back empty-handed.'

I felt relieved and turned back. I saw that Meera and the older lady wanted to say something. Meera said, 'I also want to perform my mother's shraddha.'

The older lady said, 'I just got a call from my son and he says that he is stuck in a traffic jam. Never mind, I will perform my husband's shraddha too.'

The old man gave each of us a *dharba* ring made of dry straw, black til and water. Then he said, 'Come in. Let us start.'

I am sure my father loved the shraddha that year. I could feel my father, grandfather and great-grandfather smiling down at me proudly.

After the ceremony, I thought to myself, 'With age, I was wondering if I had started accepting a male-dominated society—but now I know that it isn't true. No wonder I wrote that letter to J.R.D. Tata in 1974.'

18

Lazy Portado

Portado was a young, bright, handsome and sweet boy from Goa. We were in BVV College of Engineering at Hubli. He had been my classmate and lab partner throughout our course. So I knew him fairly well.

Portado had peculiar habits. Though he was intelligent, he was extremely lazy. Our theory classes were from eight in the morning till noon and lab was from two to five in the afternoon. Portado never came for the first class at eight. Occasionally, he turned up for the second or third hour but most of the time he only showed up for the last hour. He never missed our lab sessions, however.

In those days, attendance was not compulsory in college and our teachers were very lenient. They requested Portado to come on time but since there was no internal assessment, they couldn't really exercise their authority.

One day, I asked Portado, 'Why are you always late? What do you do at home?'

He laughed and said, 'I have a lot of things to do. I am so busy in the evenings that I can't get up before nine in the morning.'

'What things keep you so busy?' I asked him innocently.

'I meet my friends at night. We have long chats followed by dinner. You know, it takes a lot of time to build friendships. You will not understand. You people are all nerds. You only come to college to study.'

'Portado, you are a student. You should study, get knowledge, learn skills and work hard. Is that not important?'

'Oh, please. You remind me of my mother. Don't give me a sermon. Life is long. We have plenty of time. We should not learn anything in a hurry. We shouldn't be so stingy about time either.'

Then I noticed that he did not even have a watch since, for obvious reasons, he had no need for it.

Portado continued, 'In life, you need connections and networking. That can give you success. You can't network in a day. You have to spend time and money on building a network. Who knows? Some people that I meet now may make it big tomorrow and then that connection will work for me.'

I was a young girl from a middle-class and academic-minded family. I believed only in hard work. I never understood how networking could help.

During our college breaks, Portado proudly told us about his childhood, 'Oh, when I was young, I spent my time in big cities like Bombay, Delhi and Calcutta. In Calcutta, there are so many clubs. It is a matter of prestige to be a member of a club. When I start working, I want to be a member of all the good clubs in the city.' Every now and then, Portado felt that Hubli was a small and boring town. So he regularly went to Belgaum to meet his friends and 'network' with them.

During exams, Portado worked like a donkey. He glass-traced most of my original drawings so that he did not have to think about the solutions to engineering problems himself. His glass trace drawings were definitely better than the originals because they were neater and there were no wrinkles or pencil marks. He always got more than me in drawings. He even kept the question papers of previous years and made his own question papers by process of elimination. Instead of reading textbooks, he read guides to pass the exams. With all this, he always managed to pass in second class.

Once the examiner caught him because in a survey drawing he told the examiner that the mark on his drawing was actually a big tree in the middle of a road. It was a survey of a town near Dharwad. Unfortunately, the examiner happened to be from that town and he knew that there was no tree on that road. He questioned Portado, who said with a serious face, 'Sir, I have done the survey myself. I sat below the tree, had my lunch and then I continued.'

Calmly, the examiner said, 'I can't see this tree in any of your classmates' original drawings. This is only a mosquito between the glass and the drawing that you have tried to cover up.'

Portado just managed to pass the exams that year. But he was not perturbed. He said, 'I am not scared of the exams or the marks. Today's nerds will be tomorrow's mid-level managers. A person with good networking will be their boss.'

Because of his attitude and undisciplined habits, even the college hostel refused to keep him. So he rented a small house near college and lived there like a king.

Once our class planned a picnic trip to Belgaum. Since Portado was familiar with the city, we decided to take his opinion and help. The picnic committee members, including myself, went to his house around eleven on a Sunday morning. We all assumed that Portado would be awake. But to our surprise, he was still in bed. When he opened the door, he said sleepily, 'Oh, why have you come so early on a Sunday?' He was quite annoyed to see us. 'Well, I am awake now, so please come in.'

We went in but there was absolutely no place to sit. His clothes were all over the room and newspapers were scattered on the floor. In the kitchen, the dirty dishes were piled up in the sink and they were stinking. There were fish bones everywhere. There was also a cat and a dog inside the house. They were well fed with Portado's leftovers. The windows were not open either. The bedsheet looked like it had not been changed for a year. I did not have the courage to go see his bathroom.

Portado felt neither perturbed nor guilty. He said, 'Make some space for yourselves and sit down.' Some people moved Portado's undergarments and made some space but I could not do that because I was a girl, so I simply stood. Portado brought a stool for me from his kitchen. It was very sticky. I was even more hesitant to sit on it than on his clothes. I told him, 'It is better that I stand.' Portado offered us tea but none of us had the guts to drink any.

When I asked him about planning the details of the picnic, he said, 'We can start at twelve in the afternoon. My friend owns a lodge so I can take you there. The next day, we can go to Amboli Falls. Then we can also go to

Goa.' Portado made a ten-day programme. But most of us could not afford a ten-day accommodation in a hotel, nor could we skip class for so many days. So the plan fizzled out. We thanked him and left. When I turned back and looked, Portado had closed the door and had probably gone back to bed.

Soon the final year came around. We all passed the examinations and parted ways. Some of us felt sad because we had become a big family in the last four years together. We did not know our destinations and knew that we may not meet again. Of course, as Portado said goodbye he told us, 'If you are ever in Goa, please come to my house.' But I seriously doubted that I would ever run into him again.

Many decades passed. Once I went to Dubai to give a lecture. After the lecture, people came up to talk to me but there was one person who waited until everybody had left. Then he walked over to where I was sitting and smiled. I recognized the smile but I did not remember where I had seen him. The man was bald, fat, had a big paunch and was dressed very ordinarily. I thought that he might be a mid-level manager in a construction company. I meet many people in my field and it is difficult to remember everybody.

I asked him, 'What can I do for you, sir? Are you waiting for me?'

With a cracked voice, he said, 'Yes, I have been waiting for you for a long time.'

'Oh, I'm sorry, I didn't know that you were waiting. Do you have any work with me?' I said.

'Yes, I just wanted to tell you that you were right and I was wrong.'

I was puzzled. What did he mean? I had never even met him before. I hardly came to Dubai since we did not even have an office there.

'I didn't get your name, sir. May I know your name, please?' I asked.

His laugh was bittersweet. He said, 'I am Portado, your classmate.'

I was very happy to see him and shook his hand. 'Oh, Portado, I am seeing you after thirty-five years! It has been so long that I didn't recognize you. Physically, both of us have changed so much. It is nice to meet you. Stay back. If you are here, come for dinner tonight. I want to catch up,' I said.

Sadly, Portado said, 'Sorry, I don't have much time. I am in the night shift. But I can have a cup of tea with you.'

We went to the hotel restaurant and I ordered a cup

of tea for him and juice for myself. I wanted to talk more. I started the conversation with great enthusiasm and could not hold my questions back. 'Portado, where are you working now? How long have you been in Dubai? Are you married? How many children do you have? By the way, how are your networking friends? Do you ever come to India?'

Portado stopped me. 'I know your work involves computers but mine does not. You are too fast for me. Just like a computer. But I am in construction. So bear with me since I am slow. I have been in Dubai for the last five years. Before that, I was in India in several small places in different companies. Of course, I am married. I have two daughters.'

I interrupted him. 'You could have brought them today. I would have liked to meet them.'

'Sorry, I can't bring them because they are not here. I am in the lower level of management. So I cannot afford to bring my family here. My two daughters are studying in India and are doing engineering. I can't even afford their education in this place.'

I did not know what to say. I had never imagined Portado would end up like this.

Now it was his turn to talk. 'Do you remember, when I was in college, I used to make fun of all of you? I spent all my time in networking. After I finished engineering, I didn't get a good job. The reason was very obvious. I did not have the knowledge or the ability to work hard. I looked down upon the two qualities that are the stepping stones to success. I knew that I wanted to go up and reach the top spot in a company but no one can just fly there. I knew what position I should be in but I did not know the route. I thought that a change of job will help, but instead it reduced my value in the market. None of my networking friends helped me. They dropped me like a hot potato. They thought that I was clinging on to them like a parasite. Some of them were like me and also looking for jobs. I always thought that I would come up with someone's help. I never thought that I should take my own help. Now I am old. I am trying to learn new things and make up for lost time. But it is not easy. The market has become extremely competitive. Youngsters in college have more knowledge and quickness. They also have time on their side. I have told my daughters, you should study, get knowledge, learn skills and work hard.'

Portado continued, 'Do you remember who said this to me? It was you.'

He looked at his watch and said, 'My time is up. I must leave.'

I wished him all the best.

He walked a few steps, then came back and said, 'That day, I called you a nerd. Today, I call you smart.'

And he left.

19

Uncle Sam

Our village was thirty kilometres away from the main city. So many people like Keshav lived in our village and commuted to the city, which worked out cheaper. Keshav was our neighbour and he worked for a private company in the city.

Keshav had two sons. One of them went to New York and started working there. The other one became a college lecturer in the city. Keshav was very proud of his son in America. In the sixties and seventies, it was a great achievement to go to America. The possibility of a better future in India was bleak. The jobs offered were either in the government or in public sector companies. Our government strongly discouraged any entrepreneurial activity. The dividends were charged taxes of 98 per cent and imported goods were very expensive. Even now, I clearly remember that when my father booked a Fiat car, the waiting period was seventeen years! Having a telephone at home was also a rich man's affair. The government policies were so strict that it made foreign travel next to impossible, even for wealthy people. In those days, whenever somebody went abroad, even to a place nearby like Bangkok, Hong Kong or Singapore, people would say 'Bon Voyage' in a special section of the local newspaper to spread the word in the city and inform the relatives. When they returned, their picture was printed in the newspaper to announce the successful completion of their tour.

In such an economic situation, Keshav's older son, Mahesh, went on a scholarship to the USA and settled there. The percentage of people who went on a student visa and returned to India was hardly one per cent and Mahesh was no exception to the rule. He was probably the first person from our village to go to the USA. Keshav spoke proudly of him. He fondly referred to him as 'my son in New York' rather than as Mahesh. Whenever anyone went to his house, they saw lots of photographs of Mahesh—in colour, which was rare back then. The different pictures showed Mahesh and his wife standing in front of their car or visiting Niagara Falls or the Statue of Liberty dressed in winter coats with snow all around them.

Whenever Mahesh came to India, he brought two heavy suitcases containing perfumes, cigarette lighters, nylon saris, suit pieces, plastic lunch boxes, cigarettes and many other things. He displayed all of them in his parents' living room. Most people in our village went to meet him to ask about life in America. He talked about life there as if it was a fairyland. 'I stay in a small town near New York. The roads are so clean and neat; there is not an inch of dust there. We don't lock our houses. Nobody comes and steals anything from anyone. When you go to a departmental store there, you get various juices like orange, grape and musambi. They are sold in huge glass jars and we don't have to return the jars. At the billing counter, the items are given in a plastic bag and it is not even charged. You can get everything under one roof, unlike in India. The grocery stores there contain a variety of food which you can't even imagine.' Then Mahesh would show some photographs of the grocery stores.

His brother's wife, Rama, served tea or coffee to the visitors. But Mahesh's wife, Malathi, sat with her husband and continued his speech from where he left off.

'Whenever I wear a sari and go out, people look at me and tell me how beautiful I am. They touch my silk sari and ask me many questions about how I drape it so beautifully. They also look at my bindi and ask many questions. Cooking is a joy there. You get cut and frozen vegetables. If you go to the Indian store, we get the best curry ingredients, and you can't get that quality in India. The best quality is sent there as export. Just the other day, I saw *elaichi* in Rama's kitchen. It was so small. But look at the elaichi that I have brought from there. They are ten times bigger.'

Normally, Mahesh gave a small gift to everybody who visited him—a bottle of perfume, a pack of cigarettes, a sachet of Spanish saffron or cinnamon sticks. It was a custom in our village that when you received a gift, you had to reciprocate. So people requested Mahesh and his family to come to their house for tea or dinner. Mahesh would turn to his wife and ask her, 'Dear, are we free that day? Shall we accept this invite?' Malathi would pull out an appointment diary, make a fuss and say, 'So sorry, we are not free that day.' We had never heard the word 'dear' being used in our village before. We considered it very awkward to call a wife 'dear' in public. But Mahesh would explain, 'That's how a husband and wife address each other in America.'

Mahesh and Malathi had two children—a boy and a girl. They wore beautiful clothes and went around the village wearing imported shoes. Malathi always told her children, 'Don't drink water in anybody's house. Don't eat raw salads here either. Be careful of the mosquito bites and wear a hat so that you don't get sunburnt.'

Rama used to get tired of Malathi's stay in the village. While Keshav and his wife enjoyed the company of 'their son and daughter-in-law from New York', she had to do all the work. Malathi did not like to help because she said that there was so much dirt here. Rama had to boil water and make different dishes every day, according to Mahesh and his family's demands.

Many years passed. Our joint family no longer remained joint. The ancestral home no longer existed. I still referred to our uncles, aunts and cousins as family but the truth was that the relationship was less like one between family members and more like that between acquaintances. Our entire family was spread out in different parts of India and the globe. Physically, there was a distance separating us. In our minds, there was a larger distance between us. And even worse, in our hearts, there was a great chasm that divided us.

The other day, I was surprised to meet Mahesh in the city. Now he looked fit and energetic but somewhere I felt I saw sadness in his eyes. I was very happy to see him after so long. I asked him, 'Do you have time for a cup of tea?'

Without referring to the appointment diary, he

immediately agreed. We went to a nearby cafe and started chatting. 'When did you come here? How is Malathi Akka? How are your children? I heard that they have done very well at studies.'

'I came a few days ago. Malathi has gone to Mount Abu. The children are busy as usual.'

'Is Malathi Akka on a holiday without you?' At the back of my mind, I remembered the word 'dear' which I had heard for the first time when I was a teenager.

'No. She has joined the Brahma Kumaris. They run a successful branch in America. Malathi is in charge of one centre. I find that there is so much change in India.'

'Of course, India has changed a lot in the last two decades.' I asked again, 'Where are your children?'

'My daughter did her MBA from Harvard. She is now in the West Coast, married to a Chinese man and happily settled. My son is pursuing his thesis on "The Difficulties of African Tribes" at New York City and right now he is in Zimbabwe.'

'How is your brother Ramesh? What about his family? I hardly go to the village now. So I don't know how people are doing. After your father's death, we hardly hear about your family.'

'Ramesh is doing exceedingly well. When we were young, he bought a patch of land in the outskirts of the village. We all thought that it was a bad investment and that he should have bought the land adjacent to the highway. But today, there are bridges, underpasses and further expansion of the roads. The government has taken all the land on either side of the highway. Our village is no longer remote. It is an extension of the city. Ramesh has converted his land to a resort and makes good money out of it. His son runs the business and even owns a petrol bunk. Our ancestral home is converted to a shopping mall, and I sold my share of the property to Ramesh for a few thousand rupees in those days. Hmm. There are many things that I shouldn't have done.'

I saw a distinct expression of regret on his face. I was curious to know more but I did not ask. I thought that if he wanted to share, I would let him do so in his own time.

Mahesh continued, 'There is nothing to hide. The Government of India has opened up many opportunities with its new policy in 1991 and hence there are tremendous job prospects in India. I can feel India vibrating with the economic boom and high energy. I find that there is at least one person abroad from each family in our village now. It is no longer a novelty to go to America. Whatever we get there, we can buy in India at a much cheaper price. The land prices have gone up so much that it is more expensive to buy property in India than in the US. Ramesh is the best example of this. I made a mistake.'

'What do you mean?'

'I should not have gone to Uncle Sam's land.'

20

You Should Have Asked Me

I have known Rakesh for a long time. A few years ago, he called me up and said, 'You know that we manufacture school bags in our factory. There are always seconds with small defects. We can probably sell them for half the price depending on the defect. But I thought that it is better to give them to you for free because you can at least distribute them to needy children in rural areas. Will you come once a year and collect the bags from us?'

I was absolutely thrilled by his offer because it is hard to get such donations for rural schools. Most wealthy people live in big cities and if they donate money, it is usually in the city itself. There are a few people who give back to their hometowns but hardly anyone ever gives to rural areas that they are not connected to. Sometimes,

I feel that villages and towns are benefited only if a rich philanthropist originates from that area. Otherwise, thousands of villages go unnoticed without anyone's help and remain totally dependent on the government. I work in such villages where a small donation can make a big difference to its children. Rakesh's offer was like chancing upon a gold mine.

'Rakesh, thank you so much for your help,' I said. 'If you want, I will give you the list of schools where we will distribute your bags. Do you need a letter from us?'

He gave a hearty laugh and said, 'Oh, there is absolutely no formality. You don't have to inform me about anything. I have faith and trust in you. You can come and collect the bags every year in May before the school year starts.'

It is very difficult to earn trust. It takes years to build and it can be destroyed in an instant by one bad deed. Trust requires an enormous amount of integrity and you have to prove every time that you are worthy of it. I am very grateful to our society and community. The Infosys Foundation has built a great reputation for itself and everybody is ready to help us with anything that we might need.

Every year, my assistant went and met the factory manager, and he would bring the bags back with him.

After a few months, my assistant said, 'Ma'am, there is a new manager in the factory.' So I had to explain the whole process to the new manager, which took some time. These days, it is hard to retain employees in any company. So I decided to send an email to the new manager explaining the process and for recordkeeping. The new manager acknowledged my email and the yearly visits to collect the bags went on. In the last ten years, there were four new factory managers but the procedure always remained the same.

Meanwhile, Rakesh grew old. He decided to retire and move back to Delhi. One day, he called me and said, 'I am shifting base to Delhi. Bharat, my son-in-law, will now run this office. I have explained the process to him. So he is aware of the annual donation and you don't have to worry. Nothing is going to change.'

I thanked him and wished him a good retired life.

Bharat joined the factory in April as the new manager. I sent him an email to congratulate him and to explain the usual process. I did not get a reply.

My assistant went to the factory in May that year. All the bags were packed and loaded in the truck. Then Bharat called my assistant and said, 'Please don't load the truck until your chairperson comes and meets me. Kindly unload the truck if you have already loaded it.'

My assistant sent the message to me quickly. As I was the receiver, it was my duty to go meet the donor. I cleared my schedule and went and met Bharat the next day. He said, 'How can you take goods without informing me?'

'Sir, I sent you an email when you joined the factory,' I said. 'Whenever there is a change in management, we have always sent an email explaining the practice. We have had the same procedure for the last ten years. The process was set up by Rakesh. Is there anything wrong?'

'If Rakesh sir started it, I don't have any objections. But I am a new person. Is it not your duty to come and meet me? After all, this is a gift. So it cannot go out without my permission. I haven't received your email at all. It was a shock for me to see your team pack up the seconds and take them away.'

I said, 'That is not true. You can see it in the logs of previous years. We take the seconds once a year in May and also send a thank-you letter to your company.'

'We will send the goods as soon as I receive an email from you,' he said.

I replied, 'But we have already sent an email.'

Bharat argued, 'Maybe, but I haven't received it. You can resend it.'

I came back to my office and was wondering about

the real reason behind this unpleasantness. I checked my email and saw that I had received a read receipt of the email that I had sent Bharat. That meant Bharat had seen my email and was lying to me. Still, I resent the email.

As I sat at my desk, I thought about what had happened. I realized that the email was not the issue. It was Bharat's ego. He was upset because I did not go to meet him as soon as he became the new manager. He thought that the best way to show his importance was to call and tell me that I could not take the seconds without his permission. Now I understood. I was not upset at all. If someone wants me to satisfy their ego by going and standing in front of them in person, I can do so for the sake of the poor children. If I did not go, I would not hurt myself but I would hurt the poor children.

Every human being has an ego. But it is up to us to decide how much we have and how we exercise it. Rakesh's son-in-law was young and had less life experience than Rakesh or me. I could have called Rakesh and told him about what was going on. However, I did not want this to become an issue and cause a fight in the family. But I knew that Bharat would definitely give me the bags in the end.

The next morning, I got a call. 'Madam, I received your email just now. Your assistant can come and collect the bags.' Bharat never used the word 'sorry' even though I was older than him.

'Sorry, Bharat, for the miscommunication,' I said. 'Going forward, every May, we will send you a physical letter. Also, after receiving the school bags, we will send you another letter thanking you. Is that okay? Is there anything else we can do to improve communication? Please let me know. We are ready to make changes.'

There was a pause on the other end. I took another breath and said, 'Can you hear me?'

'Yes, madam. We trust you. We don't need any letters.'

I kept the phone down and smiled. A fire cannot be extinguished with another fire. It is only water that can make a difference.

21

A Mother's Love

Mahanadi is a big river in Odisha and it is breathtaking to see the river in December. But if you want to see her anger, you should take an appointment with her in June, during the rainy season. Her colour is reddish-brown then and the river overflows every year. The poor people who live on the banks have to vacate their homes. The Mahanadi floods have become so common that rehabilitation is a mandatory agenda in Odisha's budget.

We were working in one of these flood-relief areas near Paradweep. The Infosys Foundation supports an orphanage meant for mentally and physically challenged children there.

When I arrived in Bhubaneswar, our Foundation team leader said, 'Let's leave immediately for the spot.'

I said, 'Don't be in a hurry. On the first day of such

a disaster, more than victims, there are people such as newspaper reporters, TV crew, social workers and government officers hanging about. In the middle of this chaos, the progress of the relief work is very slow. There are already people there who are being rescued. We will go tomorrow. By that time, we will know what they have already received and what they really need. We should be prepared to look after ourselves with water and basic amenities and we must also carry vaccinations.'

When we started the next day, I said, 'Let's take a jeep or minivan so that we can bring the children back. Please keep some quilts, biscuits and water bottles ready.'

My new assistant, Varun, asked, 'What do you mean?'

I replied, 'If we find some children, we have to bring them back and put them in the special needs children's school.'

'How do you know that you will get such children?'

'From my experience.'

He was genuinely puzzled. I explained, 'During floods, poor people have to run away in minimum time with the maximum goods that are an asset to them. They take their clothes and money along with their healthy children. If they have challenged children, they leave them behind. So, in the course of relief work, we find such children and put them in the special needs residential school nearby. Sometimes, parents come back and take their children home. But sometimes, they don't.'

'How can you talk like this, madam?' asked Varun, visibly shocked.

'Try to understand the situation, Varun. If they don't have any vehicle and they have to wait for these challenged children to come with them, they will lose everything including their own lives. It is not that they don't love their children, but the extreme economic situation forces them to leave them behind. Be sympathetic to them.'

'I don't agree with you, madam. A mother's love is the highest and most unconditional love in the world. She will sacrifice everything for her children.'

'That may be true often, Varun, but don't generalize about it,' I said.

We all went to work. When we came back that day, we had found four such children.

That night, when we assembled, Varun asked me, 'Madam, I am still confused about a mother's love for her children. You must have worked in many places. Tell me your thoughts about this topic.'

I said, 'Come, sit next to me. I will share a few stories with you.'

I began, 'One day, I read a very funny report about

how a mother chimpanzee behaves in adversity. This experiment was conducted a few years ago. A mother and a baby chimpanzee were kept in a big, empty and transparent glass tank with a closed glass ceiling. They were playing happily. After some time, the researchers started filling the tank with water. As the water level started increasing, the mother chimpanzee became alert, held the baby to her heart and started standing up and howling. She was upset and wanted to break the glass ceiling. Still, the water level continued to rise. She changed her position and kept the baby on one of her shoulders. Then, she kept moving the baby from one shoulder to another. But when the water level came up to her nose, she put the baby below her feet and tried to climb on the baby so that she could breathe. At this point, the researchers drained the water out. This experiment clearly shows that everyone loves his or her life more than anyone else's. I was surprised by how any mother could do this. I reasoned that this may be true only for chimpanzees and may not be true for humans because, after all, we are more social animals and more culturally aware, or at least I hope so.'

Varun said, 'That is so interesting, madam. Tell me more.'

I continued, 'This next story is about Chatrapati Shivaji's era. He was a great warrior, had extraordinary abilities and was a true patriot.

'There was a young married woman called Hirakani who lived in a village near Raigarh, one of Shivaji's forts. She was a milkmaid and supplied milk and milk products to the fort every day. The main door of the fort was known as Simha Dwaram and it was open from sunrise to sunset.

'After some time, Hirakani gave birth to a baby. Every day, she continued to go to Shivaji's fort and supply milk. She returned home before sunset because the gates of the fort closed at sunset and nobody was allowed to enter or leave the fort unless they took permission from the king himself.

'One day, a soldier's wife was in labour inside the fort and Hirakani went to help her. By the time the baby was born, it was night and the doors had been closed. She begged the security guards at the fort gates to open a small slit so that she could go home and take care of her baby who had to be breastfed. There was nobody in the house to take care of the baby. She cried and cried but, even though they felt bad, the guards were afraid to open the doors because it was against the king's orders.

'Then Hirakani thought of an alternative way to reach her baby. The only other way to go home was to climb the hill and jump from there. She knew that she might survive because there was a meadow below with a stream. But she might also die or break her legs. But her motherly instincts did not allow her to sit quietly and do nothing.

'Hirakani prayed to God and, gathering all her courage, she jumped. Luckily, she fell on a treetop and was able to climb down. Then, she went home, bruised but not badly injured.

'The next morning, she carried milk and curd and entered the fort as usual. The guards were surprised to see her. They thought that she was already inside. They asked Hirakani, "How did you reach home safe and sound?"

'She told them the whole episode. Then, she said, "The need of my child is more important than my life. After all, I am a mother. For a mother, the child is an extension of her body. No mother can live in peace when she knows that her child is in danger."

'She walked away as if nothing had happened.

'Soon, news spread that there was a way to escape from the formidable fort, which worried Shivaji. But he knew that even the greatest warrior would think twice before jumping from the hilltop.

'He called Hirakani and honoured her. He told her, "You have a great *matra hridaya*." In her honour, one of the *burjs* of the fort was named Hirakani and it lasts even today.'

I stopped and looked at Varun. 'So, Varun, don't generalize about anything,' I said. 'Decisions are taken depending on the circumstances, but still, I believe that a mother's love is the most unconditional in the world.'

22

Do You Remember?

Dr Raj Reddy, a professor at Carnegie Mellon, won the Alan Turing Award in 1994 for his pioneering efforts in computer science and artificial intelligence. This award is highly coveted and is equivalent to a Nobel Prize in computer science. He was the first person of Asian origin to win this award.

I was very happy that an Indian had received such a prestigious award. I came to know that Dr Reddy was in Bangalore and went to congratulate him.

Went I entered his house, I saw lots of bouquets and gifts scattered around the living room. It was obvious that many people had been visiting him. He was resting in his armchair and wore white cotton pants and a shirt. He was so simply dressed that one could never have guessed that he was such a distinguished person. His wife was busy inside the kitchen preparing snacks.

I thought that Dr Reddy must be really excited about his super success. I said, 'You must be feeling right on top of the world. It is a great milestone to receive this award and it is a big achievement. Don't you feel proud?'

Instead of answering, he smiled at me affectionately. He seemed very calm and peaceful. He said, 'I want to ask you some questions.'

I was so surprised that I almost fell off my chair. I said, 'Sure, sir.'

'Do you remember who got the Nobel Prize in Chemistry last year?'

Though I read the paper every day, I could not recollect the name. 'I don't remember who got the prize for chemistry but I can tell you who got the Nobel Prize for Peace or in Literature in the last two or three years,' I said.

He laughed, 'Peace and literature are often controversial because of their subjective nature. So they are always highlighted in the news. No, I want to know about chemistry.'

I accepted my defeat.

Then he asked me, 'Do you know who was elected Fellow of the Royal Society in London last year?'

Again, I was at a loss.

He asked me another question, 'Do you remember who got the Pulitzer Prize this year?'

'No. But I know the shortlist for the Booker Prize. One of them was Romesh Gunesekera.'

'You remember his name because he is an Asian too.'

'The answer to all your questions can be found on the Internet. I am growing old and I don't remember a lot of things these days,' I defended myself.

He smiled at me again. 'My intention is not to test your memory. It is just to tell you that nobody remembers all the prizewinners all the time. People remember the achievers in their own field or if they are close relatives or friends. The rest of the world reads your name in the newspapers and forgets easily. And that is the right thing to do. So, whenever I get a prize, I always know that only some people will remember this and that too for only a short time. There is nothing great about it. My prize is that I have enjoyed my work. When I win awards, there are some genuine people who share this joy with me. To me, that is the greatest honour.'

His attitude really impressed me. He was not overjoyed when he received an award, nor was he sad when he did not get one. Such people are rare in life. That is the reason I will always respect and remember Dr Raj Reddy.

He asked me in a lighter mood, 'I want to ask you one more thing. Do you remember people who have made a lasting impression on you?'

Within a fraction of a second, I replied, 'Oh, I remember my kindergarten teacher. When my mother left me on the first day at school, I started crying. My teacher came and hugged me and said, "Baby, don't worry. Don't get scared. I am with you." At that age, it was so encouraging that someone was with me in a strange school. I remember my classmate too. I had broken a neighbour's window while playing and was too scared to tell my parents. She said, "Don't worry. I will come with you and tell your parents that we both did it." I also remember one of my cousins. My bus was delayed and I reached her home at midnight. Still, my cousin woke up and cooked an awesome meal for me without an inch of dissatisfaction. I even remember my teacher who scolded me when I didn't do my homework in time. He said, "Time is precious. If you don't do your work on time, it is as good as not doing it." His scolding changed my life forever.'

Dr Raj Reddy smiled and said, 'See, those are the important things in life. Those people might not have achieved anything in the eyes of the world. But they made you secure and confident. They made you feel like a rock star. They gave you strength, courage and values. They are the true prizes in your life and you should always cherish them.'

23

Life's Secret Lessons

It was 1996. I knew that India had twenty-five states and seven union territories and that a majority of us spoke a total of thirty languages. Each state had its own culture, tradition, dress code and folk art. I was aware of the great sages and writers of the land and knew the names of most mountains and rivers of our country.

That was my India as I knew it.

After joining Infosys Foundation that year, I learnt that my perception of India was not India at all. My perception was only a statistical description of India. I realized that there is so much helplessness and poverty here. Poverty does not mean just a lack of money but also a lack of confidence. Money can be earned in life but confidence is easy to lose and very hard to gain back. I learnt lessons that no book could ever teach me and no Internet site could show me, because I had access to real people. Very few people have this privilege.

Still, I usually never know the real opinion of most people I converse with. The reason is that people whom I do not give money to criticize me and people who hope to receive money from me say that I am great. So I have made many enemies and only a few true friends. Now I understand why people at the top are always lonely.

My First Lesson

At times, I feel that only children tell the truth and are the real judges of one's talent. Once I was in Calcutta for the launch of a children's book. Children from various schools came and attended the event. As a part of the book launch, I had to read a few stories from my book. When I started reading, a young boy got up and innocently said, 'Aunty, you write well, but you don't read well.'

I looked at him. He was around twelve years old and had intelligent and sharp eyes. His teacher was about to hush him when I stopped her, 'Please allow him to speak. Children are unbiased and clear in their thinking. They say the truth and the truth alone. Maybe the passage of time changes them. But for now, let him say whatever he wants to say.'

Then I called the boy to me. I asked him, 'Can you read the story for me?'

'Of course, I can read it. I am an actor in my school and I know how to modulate the voice which you don't do.'

'I agree. I am not an actress. I am only a writer.'

The child read the entire story with different modulations and I was quite impressed. I felt that I was meeting a genuine critic of my readings for the first time.

That was my first lesson.

My Second Lesson

As part of my work for the Foundation, I travelled the corners of India, which I would not have done otherwise. Our team worked through five national natural disasters like the earthquake in Gujarat, the tsunami in Tamil Nadu and the Andamans, the drought in Maharashtra and Karnataka, floods in Odisha, Karnataka and Andhra Pradesh and hurricanes in Odisha.

Every disaster taught me my second lesson. I learnt that there is a limitation to human power and achievements, and that even with money you cannot help everyone. You cannot substitute many things in life with money.

My Third Lesson

As I worked with the Foundation, my horizons changed. I met the poorest of the poor, the most talented artists, the victims of natural disasters and the most successful people who climbed the ladder with their hard work. I saw many ungrateful receivers as well. All of them became part of my big canvas. The amazing thing I saw was that, most times, what people presented outside was never how it was inside. The moment you went near, their carefully constructed image started falling apart.

When someone cheated me, I got upset and angry. I usually called that person and scolded him or her. I expressed my anger and disappointment to them. Even now, I remember many experiences of children cheating parents, and vice versa. It was very disillusioning.

A few years ago at the Foundation, we reserved Monday mornings to give money to poor people to buy medicines for cancer treatment. These people usually brought letters from cancer hospitals.

One day, my car was near the entrance gate of our Foundation. I was waiting in the car for an umbrella since it had started raining. I looked around and noticed a car in front of me. A lady was sitting in the backseat of the car. I saw her remove her diamond earrings and then she got down from the car. I did not think much of it at the time. Soon I got my umbrella and went to my office. There I saw the same lady with a letter asking us for some cancer medicine. If the incident had happened ten years ago, I would have given her a piece of my mind. But now, I smiled at her and told her gently, 'Sorry, madam. We can't give money to you. Cancer medicines are much cheaper than diamond earrings. There are many people who require this free medicine more than you.'

Now I look at life differently. Most people do not have the same values when they get money. Money changes a person completely. Very few people can withstand the lure of money and they are difficult to find. I have learnt that wherever there is money, people like to take advantage of the situation and maximize their return.

My Fourth Lesson

I have also received many life lessons from the poorest of the poor.

On one of my trips, I was visiting a village. It was late evening and I stayed with a friend, Neerav, who had a big house. His late grandfather was a well-known local language writer who had achieved great laurels during his lifetime. His grandmother kept talking about him and his awards. Neerav took me aside and said, 'Sorry, my grandmother lives in the past. She does not understand that today many people have forgotten my grandfather even though he was a hero in the old days.'

I asked him, 'Will you show me the room with the awards that your grandmother described?'

He took me upstairs and opened a room full of dust. Of course, there were many awards there, citations and medals. There was also a box full of shawls, and countless dusty volumes. He said, 'When my grandfather was alive, people used to visit him all the time. All his colleagues are dead now. We have hundreds of photographs but we don't recognize a single person in them. We have so many books and grandmother doesn't even want to give them to a library. We don't know what to do with his awards. We can't keep them and neither can we throw them away. I live in Mumbai and have a small two-bedroom apartment. My children occupy one room and we occupy the other. I am the only heir to the family. Grandmother insists that I keep all these things; but I have realized that when a person passes away, what he may have collected materially over a period of time becomes irrelevant to the next generation. I can only keep one photograph of my grandfather. And maybe one of his books, as a memento. My children can't even read and write our native language, even though they can speak it fluently. So his whole library is of no use to me. If my grandmother had allowed me to donate these books immediately after my grandfather's death, at least some people from his generation would have read them. Now these books are useless.'

Suddenly, I realized that this was my next lesson. If we keep collecting material things, it becomes a burden to the next generation. It is better that we reduce our cache while we are alive. This was a great message and I started practising it. Today, I immediately give away what I do not need.

My Fifth Lesson

During one of my train journeys, I met a lady. She hugged me and held my hand tightly. Then she sat next to me and said, 'Oh, don't you remember me? I am your classmate from Hubli. You used to share my lunch with me every day. I have read all your books.'

I was very uncomfortable because I did not remember her and she was not letting go of my hand. But I thought that sometimes it is hard to recognize a person because of changes in external appearance due to age and passage of time.

I told her, 'I am sorry. I don't remember you. However, it is nice to meet you.'

The lady still would not leave me. At the end, she gave me a letter. She said, 'My son is very intelligent and is going abroad for further studies. Can the Foundation help him?'

This behaviour was not an exception because I receive such requests all the time. I have met many people who want to take advantage of the Foundation's name and my position in it. I have learnt that whenever I meet a person, I should expect to get a letter from him or her soon asking for money. All of them remind me that I am like a water tap in a dry area—unthanked if it runs and cursed if it doesn't. I have learnt to be patient and to recognize people's intentions.

My Sixth Lesson

I was attending a music concert and I sat at the back because I thought that I could easily leave if I get bored. There were two well-dressed women wearing big diamond earrings sitting in front of me. Let's call the first lady A and the second one B. I could see that they were from affluent families. They were quite loud in their conversation. So I could clearly hear what they were saying.

A said to B, 'My daughter is quite useless. I want her to work somewhere. Then it will be easy to say in the matrimonial market that she is working. But I don't know who would employ her.'

B replied, 'Oh, don't worry. Get her into teaching.'

A said, 'Oh, she tried. But the school sent her back.'

They must have been best friends or sisters confiding in each other. A was behaving as if she was the student and B was the teacher.

'Then tell her to start an NGO.'

'Isn't it hard to start an NGO and work for it?' asked A with great concern.

B confidently replied, 'It is the easiest job in the world. I will give you an example. Look at Sudha Murty. She doesn't have the brains and is not even talented. So she runs an NGO and has even made a name for herself. When she can run an NGO, anybody can run one.'

I had to interrupt their conversation. So I tapped one of them on the shoulder.

'Do you know Sudha Murty?' I asked.

Confidently, B said, 'Of course.' A seemed baffled but B looked confident. 'Of course, we know her very well.'

'When did you last meet her?'

'This morning—and by the way, who are you?'

Calmly, I replied, 'I am Sudha Murty.'

Without batting an eyelid, B gave me a big smile and said, 'Oh, you have changed so much since morning. I didn't even recognize you.'

'No, I haven't changed,' I said, 'because I never met you in the morning. I want to give you some unsolicited advice, because I really feel that you need it. When a doctor makes a mistake, a person goes six feet below the ground. When a judge makes a mistake, a person is hung six feet above the ground. But when a teacher makes a mistake, the entire batch of students is destroyed. Don't ever look down on teachers. If you had good teachers, you wouldn't be sitting here talking like this today. Don't look down on social work either. Only a person with a compassionate heart and sound judgement can be a philanthropist. When a person in front of you is in need of help, you must decide in a short duration whether you should give money to that person or not, how much you should give and for how long. Understanding human beings is much more difficult than understanding computers. I will accept that I may not be intelligent but, more than that, you should know that you are stupid.'

I walked out feeling brave and happy.

From this incident, I learnt that I must always stand up for myself and follow my heart, even if other people do not always agree with me or like it.

My Seventh Lesson

My son, Rohan, taught me the most important lesson about public speaking.

He said, 'Amma, whenever you are on stage and are giving a speech, please remember that most people are not listening to you. Don't be under the false impression that they have come to listen to you talking about your valuable experiences. They have come to see you because you are a well-known personality, a writer and, more important, it is very hard to meet you in real life. Most of the time you are touring and if you are in office, there are hurdles like security and personal assistants. They won't allow just anyone to come and see you. The Foundation is not run on your personal money. It is corporate money and it's like a honey pot. Wherever there is honey, human beings, ants and honeybees either want to suck it or hoard it for themselves. You are usually not guarded on stage. It is easy for people to give their applications directly to you. That is why they come to see you. Don't let it go to your head.'

I realized the value of this lesson and it has helped in keeping me balanced and grounded.

Usually, I plug my ears when people exaggerate my qualities. I know what I am and I know my shortcomings.

In the twelfth century, there was a famous poetess, Akka Mahadevi, who prayed to God and said, 'Please make me deaf. That way, I won't hear other sounds and can concentrate only on you.' I follow her. So I switch my mind off during introduction sessions.

Once I went to a function as a speaker and there were many important men and women on the stage with me. I mentally switched off as the introductions started. After some time, I heard everyone clapping. I thought that it would be bad manners not to clap and I clapped along with everybody. The person sitting next to me looked at me a bit funnily. I tried to focus on what was being said. The speaker was saying that the lady he was introducing had extraordinary qualities that only Goddess Saraswati could match. He continued praising the lady so I asked the person sitting next to me, 'Do you know who he is talking about? Which of the speakers has these qualities? I don't think I have ever met anyone like her. Have you met her?'

He looked at me kindly and said, 'He is talking about you.'

I was really upset but I knew how to express my discomfort. When it was my turn to speak, I said, 'Please discount my introduction. I am a very ordinary person and I am only here because situations and circumstances have led me here. I am just like any one of you.'

But it did not really matter what I said, because Rohan was right. I still received fifty applications that day.

My Eighth Lesson

In 2005, I was in South Africa. I hired a taxi and decided to see the tourist spots in Cape Town. My cab driver was a friendly white man. He started talking to me as we travelled together.

'Ma'am, my name is John. Are you from India?'

I was more interested in looking outside the window of our moving car. So, I said briefly, 'Yes, I am.'

'Are you enjoying your visit to our country?'

I said, 'Of course. I am a big fan of history and there is so much to be learnt here. I feel like an excited explorer. South Africa is home to famous Nobel laureates such as Nelson Mandela and Desmond Tutu. I am really happy to be here.'

'Ma'am, apart from great laureates, we are also home to other great leaders. There are leaders in South Africa who never won a medal or a prize, but they have left behind a legacy for thousands of years to come. My favourite is Mahatma Gandhi.'

That perked my interest. I was baffled and curious at the same time. Mahatma Gandhi was a leader of my country, not South Africa. How could he say such a thing? I replied, 'John, Mahatma Gandhi is Indian. He is the greatest leader of our country. I don't mean to start a debate here but he is not South African at all. He spent a few years in South Africa during his lifetime but that doesn't make him South African.'

John started smiling. 'Ma'am, when he came here, he was M.K. Gandhi. But he went back as Mahatma Gandhi. He learnt about the non-cooperative movement and the goodness of non-violence here. This became a fundamental tool of freedom struggle in your country. He didn't just transform your country. He changed ours too. He is remembered and highly respected in South Africa. He is a world leader.'

I had to agree. 'You are right, John,' I said. 'I never thought of it that way. I always considered him to be the Father of our Nation. But I know that he never considered himself to be only a part of one nation. He wanted to make a difference to the world.'

I learnt that when a person becomes a compassionate leader like Mahatma Gandhi, Gautam Buddha, Martin Luther King Jr or Abraham Lincoln, they do not just belong to one country. They transcend man-made boundaries and are recognized as leaders of the world.

Scan QR code to access the
Penguin Random House India website

PENGUIN BOOKS

WISE AND OTHERWISE

Sudha Murty was born in 1950, in Shiggaon, North Karnataka. Author, philanthropist, educator, public speaker and engineer, she completed her master's in computer science from IISc, Bangalore. She is the founder of the Infosys Foundation and the chairperson of the Murty Trust. A bestselling author, with more than 300 titles to her acclaim, some of her most famous books include *Three Thousand Stitches*, *Dollar Bahu* and *Wise and Otherwise*. She writes in English and Kannada, and her books have been translated into all major Indian languages and have sold over 60 lakh copies around the country.

Over the years, Sudha Murty has been recognized with many prestigious awards, including the Padma Bhushan and the Padma Shri from the Government of India in 2023 and 2006, respectively; Bal Sahitya Puraskar in 2023; the R.K. Narayan Award for Literature in 2006; the Lal Bahadur Shastri National Award in 2020; and Lokmanya Tilak and Mahatma awards in 2024. She was also awarded the Rajyotsava and Attimabbe Award for excellence in Kannada literature from the Government of Karnataka in 2000 and 2012. Sudha Murty has received nineteen honorary doctorates from various universities across India. Currently, she is also serving as the President-nominated member of Parliament in the Rajya Sabha.

SUDHA MURTY

WISE AND OTHERWISE

A Salute to Life

PENGUIN BOOKS

An imprint of Penguin Random House

PENGUIN BOOKS

Penguin Books is an imprint of the Penguin Random House group of companies
whose addresses can be found at global.penguinrandomhouse.com

Published by Penguin Random House India Pvt. Ltd
4th Floor, Capital Tower 1, MG Road,
Gurugram 122 002, Haryana, India

First published by East West Books (Madras) Pvt. Ltd 2002
Revised edition first published by Penguin Books India 2006
This edition published in Penguin Books by Penguin Random House India 2025

ISBN 9780143062226

Typeset in Sabon by Mantra Virtual Services, New Delhi
Printed at Thomson Press India Ltd, New Delhi

www.penguin.co.in

For the 'shirtless people of India'
who have taught me so much
about my country

CONTENTS

Acknowledgements

I want to thank Mr T.J.S. George, for having kindly consented to write the Foreword. I also thank Penguin India for their long-standing support, especially V.K. Karthika, who showed keen interest in publishing a revised and updated edition of this book.

But readers, ultimately I thank you. You are the best judge and my source of inspiration. Without your support, I cease to be a writer.

Bangalore   Sudha Murty
March 2006

We are heirs to the tradition of seeing human quality as *sattwa*, *rajas* or *tamas*. This is a beautifully Indian way of expressing a metaphysical concept familiar to other civilizations as well: of all God's creations, man alone has a choice between good and evil, and he reaps his rewards according to what he chooses.

Few set out consciously to perform *sattwik* work. Fewer still deliberately desire a life of *tamas*. Some could even start out with *tamas* or *rajas* and elevate themselves to *sattwa*. All this would be attributed to the larger cosmic scheme of karma. Jamshedji Tata appears to have had only a *sattwik* view of life and work—laying an industrial foundation for his country, starting educational and research institutions, and setting up a network of charities when such ideas were unknown. On the other hand, Alfred Nobel spent his genius inventing dynamite and smokeless gunpowder, which would all become agents of mass destruction. Then, perhaps stung by the implications of his life's achievements, he put the fortune he made to *sattwik* use by instituting the Nobel Prizes, as recognition for noble work.

Sudha Murty was not meant to hide her light under a

housewife's bushel. She was born with teacher's blood in her veins, and teaching, she learned early, was a vocation that could help shape the world. But she did not remain just another face in the teaching crowd either. Unseen but clearly felt forces propelled her into unfamiliar territory. For one thing, she married a man with socialist blood in his veins. For another, when the benedictions of capitalism came their way, the instincts of the teacher and the socialist combined to take them into an orbit of public service for public good. While remaining a teacher, wife, mother and very much the woman next door, Sudha Murty turned into an institution.

She has built no edifices. No public announcements accompany her work. No statues or tablets or archways proclaim her presence. She goes into tribal forests, into hamlets ravaged by poverty, into communities devastated by disease. She discovers the deserving on her own. The assistance she supplies meets the demand she sees. Frustrations, obstacles and red tape do not slow her down. Even human greed, a great deal of which she faces in the course of her work, does not dissuade her. Her work is her mission. She does her duty in the style and the spirit of the *karma yogi*.

This book gives a clear account of both her work and her approach to it. An accomplished storyteller in Kannada, Sudha wrote for the first time in English to inaugurate a fortnightly column in the *New Sunday Express*. She focused on her personal experiences, her travels and her encounters with ordinary people with extraordinary minds. The column attracted instant attention because of its freshness and its directness. Evidently, she was writing not with her pen but with her heart. It was clear from the start that these anecdotal insights into human nature merited a format more enduring than journalism could provide.

It would be a pity, though, if the benefits of these stories stop with the pleasure of reading them. Sudha Murty is nothing if not a message. By turning the success of Infosys into an opportunity to serve the less privileged, she has conveyed an idea to others similarly positioned. Corporate championship of social amelioration programmes on the one hand and intellectual creativity on the other is common in advanced countries, but rare in ours. There is nothing in India comparable to the foundations associated with families of great wealth in the West, such as Ford, Rockefeller and Nuffield. The most respected of them, the MacArthur Foundation, gives out what have come to be known as 'genius awards'. No one knows about this because no publicity of any kind is given to it. Yet it quietly identifies people of great talent—like A.K. Ramanujan—and quietly gives them funds to proceed with their chosen work. Thus is excellence, the true worth of a nation, nurtured by society. Sudha Murty's work will be complete only when the tradition of grand foundations rises in India to help the needy, recognize originality, facilitate intellectual inquiry and generally inspire the pursuit of greatness.

T.J.S. George
Editorial Adviser
The New Indian Express

Honesty Comes from the Heart

One bright June morning three years ago, I was reading my Kannada newspaper as usual. It was the day the Secondary School Leaving Certificate results had been published. While columns of roll numbers filled the inside pages, the list of rank holders and their photographs took up almost the entire front page.

I have a great fascination for rank holders. Rank is not merely an index of one's intelligence, it also indicates the hard work and perseverance that students have put in to reach their goal. My background—I was brought up in a professor's family—and my own experience as a teacher have led me to believe this.

Of all the photographs in that morning's newspaper, one boy's snapshot caught my attention. I could not take my eyes off him. He was frail and pale, but there was an endearing sparkle in his eyes. I wanted to know more about him. I read that his name was Hanumanthappa and that he had secured the eighth rank. That was all the information I could gather.

The next day, to my surprise, his photograph was published again, this time with an interview. With growing interest I learned that Hanumanthappa was a coolie's son, the oldest of five children. They belonged to a tribal group.

He was unable to study further, he said in the interview, because he lived in a village and his father, the sole breadwinner, earned only Rs 40 a day.

I felt sorry for this bright boy. Most of us send our children to tuitions and to coaching classes, we buy them reference books and guides, and provide the best possible facilities for them without considering the cost. But it was different for Hanumanthappa of Rampura. He had excelled in spite of being denied some of the basic necessities of life.

While I was thinking about him with the newspaper still in my hands, I gazed at a mango tree in my neighbour's compound. It looked its best with fresh bark, tender green leaves glistening with dewdrops and mangoes that were about to ripen in a few days. Beyond the tree was a small potted plant that, I noticed, had remained almost the same ever since it had been potted. It was a calm morning. The air was cool and fresh. My thoughts were running free. The continuous whistle of our pressure cooker broke the silence, reminding me that half an hour had passed.

Hanumanthappa's postal address was provided in the interview. Without wasting much time, I took a postcard and wrote to him. I wrote only two lines, saying that I was interested in meeting him and asking whether he could come to Bangalore. Just then my father, ever a practical man, returned from his morning walk. He read the postcard and said, 'Where will he have the money to come so far? If you want him to come here, send some money for his bus fare plus a little extra to buy himself a decent set of clothes.'

So I added a third line to say that I would pay for his travel and some clothes. Within four days I received a similar postcard in reply. Two sentences: in the first he thanked me for the letter, in the second he expressed his willingness to come to Bangalore and meet me. Immediately, I sent him some money and details of my office address.

When he finally arrived in our office, he looked like a frightened calf that had lost its way. It must have been his first trip to Bangalore. He was humble. He wore a clean shirt and trousers, and his hair was neatly parted and combed. The sparkle in his eyes was still there.

I got straight to the point. 'We are happy about your academic performance. Do you want to study further? We would like to sponsor you. This means we will pay your fees for any course of study you wish to take up— wherever it may be.'

He did not answer.

My senior colleague, who was in the office with me, interrupted with a smile, 'Don't go at the speed of bits and bytes. Let the boy understand what you are suggesting. He can give us his answer at the end of the day.'

When Hanumanthappa was ready to return home, he said in a low and steady tone, 'Madam, I want to pursue my studies at the Teachers' Training College in Bellary. That is the one nearest to my village.'

I agreed instantly but spoke to him a little more to find out whether there was any other course he preferred. I was trying to make it clear to him that we would pay the fees for any course he might choose. The boy, however, seemed to know exactly what he wanted.

'How much money should I send you per month? Does the college have a hostel facility?' I asked.

He said he would get back to me after collecting the correct details. Two days later, he wrote to us in his beautiful handwriting that he would require approximately Rs 300 per month. He planned to take a room on rent and share it with a friend. The two boys would cook for themselves in order to keep their expenses down.

I sent him Rs 1,800 to cover his expenses for six months. He acknowledged my draft without delay and expressed his gratitude.

Time passed. One day, I suddenly remembered that I had to pay Hanumanthappa for the next six months, so I sent him another draft for Rs 1,800.

This too was duly acknowledged, but I was surprised to find some currency notes in the envelope along with his letter. 'Madam,' he had written, 'it is kind of you to have sent me money for the next six months. But I was not in Bellary for the last two months. One month, our college was closed for holidays and during the next month, there was a strike. So I stayed at home for those two months. My expenditure during these months was less than Rs 300 per month. Therefore, I am sending you the Rs 300 that I have not used for the last two months. Kindly accept this amount.'

I was taken aback. Such poverty and yet such honesty. Hanumanthappa knew I expected no account of the money sent to him for his monthly expenses, yet he had made it a point to return the balance money. Unbelievable but true!

Experience has taught me that honesty is not the mark of any particular class nor is it related to education or wealth. It cannot be taught at any university. In most people, it springs naturally from the heart.

I did not know how to react to this simple village boy's honesty. I just prayed that God would continue to bestow the best on Hanumanthappa and his family.

On Human Foibles

Many years ago, I was working as a Chief System Analyst. The job involved a lot of travelling for project work, sometimes to a small village, sometimes to a neighbouring city. Often, work compelled me to travel on holidays as well.

One particular Friday, I was looking forward to the weekend. The coming Monday was a holiday for some festival and taking advantage of the long weekend, my sisters and I had decided to meet at our grandmother's house in our native Shiggaon. Sunday was a full-moon night and a special moonlight dinner was going to be arranged for us. Moonlight dinners are favourite family occasions for the people of northern Karnataka.

We were all in a hurry to wind up for the day when I heard someone calling out, 'Kulkarni! Can you come to my office?'

My heart sank. It was my boss calling me by my maiden name, and judging by his tone, the matter was urgent. Even though I was on my way out of the office, I stopped to enquire what he wanted.

'Sorry for disturbing you, but your service is required urgently,' he said, handing over a letter for me to read. It said that I had to visit a project site within the next two days.

'No problem at all, sir. I shall attend to it,' I said. I was used to working throughout the week, so cancelling my travel plans didn't bother me. My work gave me more happiness than any celebration or outing.

The next morning, I left for the small town where the project was based. By the time I reached the town it was already noon, but it looked as though the day had just begun there. The shops were just opening and folks were setting out to work.

As I was walking from the bus stand, a young lad hurried towards me and said, 'Sorry I am late, ma'am. I was supposed to receive you at the bus stop.' He was our clients' representative and had come to take me to their office.

We reached the office after a few minutes' walk. It was a small office. Though by no means modern, it was neatly furnished with some old but reconditioned furniture, everything in its right place. They were all waiting for me and I felt comfortable as I sat down. The cool buttermilk they offered me was most refreshing.

Before beginning my work, I was introduced to a neatly dressed young man who was supposed to coordinate with me. He was quite well-mannered and seemed very confident and bright. I was pleasantly surprised to see the good quality of his work. It had a professional touch. I was told that he was the most well-read man in that town.

He had documented his work very well and efficiently. Because of this, our job was completed sooner than expected. I did not forget to compliment him when I was about to leave. He went pink at my appreciation and insisted that I join him for tea at his residence nearby.

His house was also well kept. By teatime his conversation had taken on a personal note. He talked about his parents, his job. He introduced his wife and two-year-old son. He spoke with admiration about his wife's cooking, her beautiful voice, her achievements during her school days. Then he called for his son who immediately came in and stood by my side with folded arms, almost as if he had been trained to do so. As soon as his father asked him to recite a rhyme, he started to do so in his clear, childish voice.

I acknowledged his recitation by nodding my head. The father did not seem satisfied with such nominal recognition of his son's talents. He asked the child to identify all the letters of the alphabet from an old chart hanging on the wall. These are things that children usually hate to do, yet parents continue to force them. Poor kids!

The demonstration in my host's house went on for nearly half an hour until the child began to show signs of restlessness and irritability. The mother, wisely, took him away to the kitchen, hopefully to reward him with a chocolate or a biscuit.

I realized that the father was expecting to hear some compliment from me about his son. 'Your child is very bright for his age,' I said.

'Naturally! I have trained him like that from infancy,' he said with pride. It sounded like he had been training his two-year-old child from the day of his birth!

'So you feel that it is only by training that a child can

become bright like this?' I asked.

'No, no. Heredity and genes also play an important role. My son has taken after me.' His face shone with pride and I was curious to hear more. After all, I had an hour to spare before my bus departed.

'You must have been a good student in your college days?' I probed.

'Yes, I was always a first-ranker in my school and college days,' he replied, clearly appreciative of himself.

'Where did you graduate from?'

'I graduated from BVB Engineering College, Hubli.'

I became alert. I knew Hubli. It was my college. 'Which year?' I asked.

'In 1972, with the first rank.'

'Did you secure the gold medal also?' I persisted.

'Yes, I did obtain the gold medal for that year,' he said, glowing with self satisfaction.

By this time I was able to size him up quite clearly. And what I saw saddened me.

'May I see your gold medal?' I inquired.

Suddenly, the mood in the room changed. 'Why? Don't you believe me?' His voice was uncertain.

'No, I just want to see the gold medal you secured in 1972,' I repeated.

'It is very precious to me and so I have kept it in a bank locker,' he said.

I did not give up. 'Which bank?'

'Why should I give you such details?' he demanded, annoyed with my persistence.

Everything was clear by now. I think it was clear to

him too. The warmth of hospitality was gone. It was time for me to go.

While walking towards the door, I said, 'I don't have to know any of the details about your bank or gold medal. It's none of my business. But I am sure that the medal cannot be with you.'

'How can you say that? And that too so confidently?' He was quite angry by now.

'Because,' I told him sadly, 'I secured that gold medal in 1972 and only one gold medal is awarded each year.'

He was stunned by this revelation and stared blankly at me. I looked at him and asked gently, 'You are bright. You are good in your job. Why do you have to lie? What do you gain from it?'

The click of the front door shutting behind me was the only reply I received.

3

In Sahyadri Hills, A Lesson in Humility

I love travelling. Be it a tiny village, a drought-hit area, a deserted mountain top, a dense forest or even a monument in Egypt or China—I enjoy going to different places.

On one occasion, I went to the Sahyadri Hills, a densely forested region in Karnataka. It had been drizzling the whole day. Though forests are difficult to negotiate during the rains, especially due to the presence of those dreaded leeches, one ought to visit them during the rainy season to get the most out of them. The mild smell of exotic trees, shrubs and flowers; the chirping of different kinds of birds; the gentle whistle of the unpolluted breeze—these are joys that can never be experienced in any town or city.

I was there to visit a tribal village school deep in the forest area. The charitable trust with which I am connected wanted to help improve the school. Thandas (as local groups of tribals are called) are delightful. Normally there is a headman in each Thanda known as the Thandappa. He is the senior-most man of the tribe and is considered the supreme power, almost a living God. All are beholden to him. He practises the customs taught to him in his childhood and everyone follows them.

There was a downpour when I reached the village.

The rain, the glistening leaves and the strong smell of wild flowers made me feel as though I was on a different planet. But I never felt like an intruder. Not even when I reached the school after a long walk and every villager stood by staring at me.

Reaching the school was an adventure in itself. I saw a lady walking with rhythmic grace despite the three pots of water balanced on her head. I stopped her and asked, 'Which way should I go to reach the school?' She made an exclamatory sound, stared at me and walked away. Perhaps she didn't want to talk to a stranger, especially one from a town. Or perhaps she didn't understand my language.

I then approached an old man who was weaving a cane basket while humming a folk song. I knelt in front of him and asked in a loud and clear tone, 'Where is the school?' Curiosity was written all over his face and he seemed anxious to ask me all kinds of questions. But he didn't. He simply said something in his dialect and indicated directions with his hand.

The school was an old thatched building, probably built by the tribals themselves. It was a primary school. I could see a few children playing outside, while others were busy under a shed-like shelter doing something with leaves and straws.

I walked in and found a small room with two chairs, two tables, and a blackboard with a pot of water beside it. There were no electric lights or fans. Instead, a small shutterless opening served as the window. This was the only source of ventilation in the room.

It appeared to be the office room but there was no one there. I did not find any staff around. While I was looking for someone, an elderly man walked up to me and asked what I wanted. I introduced myself and told him that I had come to see what help we could provide the school. His response, however, didn't seem very encouraging. I thought I might be able to communicate better if I first put him at ease, so I started asking him about his life.

It turned out that he was the live-in watchman-cum-peon of the school. He would double as a tour guide sometimes. But he was not a paid employee of either the school or the government. His grandson was studying in the school free of cost in return for the services which the old man rendered. How long had he been living there? 'For many years,' he replied simply. He lived in a small hut in the courtyard of the school.

By now his attitude towards me was slightly more encouraging, so I gently turned the conversation to the affairs of the school. He said that the state government ran the school; there were two teachers and around fifty students who came from far and near. There was no compulsory uniform. I was impressed by the number of children who attended the school. After all, their parents were unschooled themselves and the living conditions were harsh. Yet there was a willingness to educate their children.

'What are the difficulties you face in running this school?'

The old man didn't say much by way of reply. He just took me to a cottage nearby and introduced me to the

Thandappa, who seemed to be more than ninety years old. He was happy to see me.

I asked him the same question: 'What problems do you face in running the school?'

Commuting to school was difficult during the rains, he said. Besides, the school clothes wouldn't dry in the rainy season—the simplest of problems and a familiar one, too. During the course of my work, I have listened to many such problems from many such people.

After acquiring a fair understanding of the people and their lives, I departed, not forgetting to thank them for their cooperation. I decided to return with some umbrellas and clothes for the children.

When I went again, it was winter. The rains were over. Now the scene was transformed. It was paradise. There was no mud and no frogs croaking. Birds were cooing. The sky was clear. Many rare flowers had bloomed. I met the same Thandappa. He recognized me and greeted me with a smile. His eyes seemed to welcome me warmly.

'Please accept these things which I have brought for the children here. Last time, I didn't know what to give them,' I said, handing over a big bag to him.

The Thandappa hesitated. I wondered whether he was feeling embarrassed. I told him, 'You have not asked for any gift from me. I brought this myself. It will help the children during the rains. Please get the clothes stitched according to their size.'

He walked into his hut without saying a word.

'What do you want to learn?' I asked some children who were standing nearby.

No one answered. After a lot of persuasion, a few youngsters came closer, but they were still too shy to talk. I went on coaxing them and ultimately one of them said, 'We've heard about computers but we have not seen them, except on TV. We want to learn about computers. Do you have any book about computers that is written in Kannada?'

Having been brought up in a teacher's family and being a teacher myself, I was delighted to hear what these children had to say. Their ideas were surprisingly fresh and modern despite the fact that they belonged to such a backward region.

I told them that I would look for such books in Bangalore. If I didn't find any, I promised that I would write a book for them myself. They seemed pleased and I was extremely happy. By that time the Thandappa had returned from inside his hut. He held a bottle of red liquid in his hands.

'Amma,' he said, presenting the bottle to me, 'we do not know what you like and what you drink at home. This is a very special drink that we prepare during summer in this forest area. We extract juice from a wild red fruit and store it. It lasts for at least two rainy seasons. Nothing is added to the juice. It is good for health. Add some of this juice to a cup of water and stir it before drinking.'

I was embarrassed. How could I accept a gift from these poor people? They themselves did not seem to have enough to eat and drink. Moreover, I had gone on a mission to give, not to take. I thought it over and politely declined the gift.

The Thandappa then said gravely, 'Amma, then we cannot accept your gift either. Our ancestors have lived in this forest for generations and they have taught us their ways. When you want to give us something, we accept; but only when we can give something to you too. Unless you take our gift, we cannot take the things you have brought for us.'

I was shocked, embarrassed, and humbled. Nothing in my experience had prepared me for this. The usual pattern is for people to express gratitude when a charitable organization provides some assistance. I have come across complaints too. When a group or organization has many problems and we help solve one of them, it is not unusual for the recipients of our help to grumble about what has been left undone rather than show gratitude for what has been accomplished. There have even been cases where recipients have complained about the amount of help given to them. I have taken all this in my stride, finding fulfilment in the giving, not in the responses.

Here in the Sahyadri forest was an old man, a tribal with no schooling, practising a highly principled philosophy of life—give when you take; do not take without giving. This was culture at its best. I smiled and gracefully accepted his gift.

The Thandappa rose even further in my esteem when he remarked with a twinkle, 'There is a grace in accepting also.'

4

DEATH WITHOUT GRIEF

Life has become so busy in a big city like Bangalore that we hardly get to know our neighbours. We are all so busy with our work that often we do not even have the time to think.

Once, I came to know that someone in my neighbours' family had died. I didn't know these neighbours well, but my mother wanted me to visit them to offer our condolences. It is the custom in our society after all, she insisted.

I agreed, but did not find the time to pay a call for several days. Days usually dawned to a rush of busy schedules and night-time was not considered appropriate for such visits. So my condolence visit just got postponed again and again. However, I didn't give up the idea and continued to think that I would find some time to call on our bereaved neighbours.

Ten days passed. I felt so guilty that one Sunday I decided that I would visit my neighbour at any cost. I only knew the man of the family, albeit very casually.

As I walked through their gate, I could hear the loud beat of a popular Kannada film song. There were children playing hide-and-seek in the spacious garden. Some men and women, who seemed to have come from the village, were sitting in the garden and chatting in a carefree way.

For a moment, I thought that I had come to the wrong house. Such mistakes do happen once in a while. Some time ago, for example, I had gone to attend the wedding of my student at the Sagar group of wedding halls near the Ashoka Pillar in Jayanagar. There are four wedding halls in a row. I had forgotten in which hall my student's wedding was to take place. However, I knew that the bride's name was Usha. When I looked at the flower-bedecked welcome arches, which mentioned the names of the couple, I was taken aback. In two of the arches, the bride's name was given as Usha. I could not remember the groom's name. I did not know what to do and just stood between the two halls waiting to see a familiar face.

Here in my neighbour's house, the music and gay atmosphere was so unexpected that I thought of going back home to ascertain the correct address from my mother. Just then, the head of the family came out and saw me. He looked excited as he called out, 'What a surprise! Please come inside. I think you are coming to our house for the first time.'

I had no choice but to go inside. As he went in and called his wife, I observed the big house and the way they had furnished it. The living room was quite large. There was a TV with a VCR in one corner. *Kaho Na Pyar Hai*, a popular Hindi film, was playing on the video. The room was packed with so many youngsters that they managed to occupy a big mat, three sofas and even the entire carpet. All of them were watching the movie with great interest. There was no place for us to sit, but the man of the house managed to move a few kids to the floor and made some room for me to sit down.

The handsome actor Hrithik Roshan was dancing on the television screen. The youngsters around me were all tapping their feet.

A servant arrived bearing a tray of snacks and a cup of tea. I was now faced with a problem. Considering the nature of my visit, I wondered whether it would be appropriate for me to partake of the snacks. My instinct told me that it would not be correct for me to eat, but I also realized that it might seem rude of me to refuse. So I found an acceptable excuse. 'I have not yet had my bath. I cannot eat now,' I said.

That of course did not solve my real problem. The atmosphere in the house had a festive air. There was no trace of grief or mourning at all. How then could I start with my condolences? It looked like my neighbours were having a family get-together for an engagement ceremony or a birthday party. And here I was, bearing a message of condolence.

Just then the lady of the house came in. Both husband and wife sat on a sofa adjacent to my chair. They started the conversation. 'We are very happy about your work. Every day we talk about you. We are proud of it.'

I was puzzled. Why on earth should they talk about me every day? I don't talk about anybody every day. Not even about my husband. What work were they talking about? Was it my writing or my social work?

They noticed my silence but continued talking animatedly. 'How is your husband? He is really a great man.'

I was surprised that my husband should feature in the conversation, considering that this family was supposed to be in mourning.

Both husband and wife were eager to talk. The wife said, 'The other day I saw you. You were wearing a beautiful sari. I thought it was a Patola sari. Was it a Patola or an Orissa sari? Both have similar patterns.'

I really did not remember which sari she was talking about. 'Maybe Orissa,' I said noncommitally.

She beamed and said triumphantly, 'See, I am right. I told Suman the same thing. She does a lot of work in Orissa so she must have purchased that sari from there. What a beautiful colour combination!'

Now, it was the turn of the husband. 'Your company is doing very well. One of the few companies that is independent of the dotcom wave. I suggested to a few of my friends that they should study the trend of IT companies in the last six months.'

This was not related to me. Maybe my husband could comment on the trend, but he was not present.

Now the wife took over. 'What is the admission procedure at your college? Is it possible to get admission with only an 85 per cent score in the tenth standard?'

'Not in SSLC but in ICSE,' the husband clarified hastily, referring to different boards of school education.

'I do not know, I am not on the admission committee,' I replied.

And so it went on. There seemed to be no end to the conversation.

After some time, I found myself wondering who had

died. As far as I remembered, it was the man's mother who had passed away. The old lady had been a friend of my mother's. But I did not know how to raise the topic. Suppose it had been the wife's mother who had died? I had to be careful.

I am sure they noticed my silence, but they were intent on pulling me into the conversation. I was feeling very uncomfortable about the whole thing. By this time I had realized that it was unlikely that I was going to get an opportunity to offer my condolences. But before I left, I wanted to make a last, sincere effort to fulfil the purpose of my visit.

It was only when we neared the gate that I hesitantly raised the topic.

'I heard your mother was not well . . .'

Before the husband could answer, his wife replied, 'Yes. My mother-in-law was not well for a very long time. But we had a lot of problems. She was too old-fashioned and would not adjust. These men go off to work and never understand the difficulties of women at home.'

She continued to complain bitterly about her mother-in-law while the husband looked on guiltily.

'She suffered a lot,' he intervened at one point.

'Actually, we suffered a lot,' the wife interrupted indignantly. 'Of late she was bedridden with a stroke. To look after such people in a place like Bangalore, one requires servants and you know how difficult and expensive it is to get a good servant. I was so tired of looking after her. It was good riddance.' The lady's tone was harsh and cold.

'Death solved the problem for all of us. My mother was finally relieved from all her suffering,' the husband concluded.

I came away saddened and disturbed by my visit.

Have our lives become so busy that grief has become proportionate to the usefulness of the loved one we have lost?

5

When the Mop Count Did Not Tally

My father was a doctor and a very popular professor of obstetrics and gynaecology. He would never bore his class with long lectures. Every now and then he would tell his students stories, usually real-life incidents, in order to liven up his lectures. As a result, his classes were well attended and lively.

I once asked him, 'Why do you tell so many stories in a medical class?'

'Don't you know why the Panchatantra was written?' he asked in reply.

'But the Panchatantra is not relevant,' I insisted. 'It's for young schoolgoing children, not for medical students.'

My father didn't agree. 'If I use stories, then it's easy for my students to understand. Moreover, one cannot hold a student's attention for more than forty-five minutes at a stretch even if the lecture is interesting. So, if I add stories, I can stretch their concentration span for up to two hours.'

The following was one of his stories. My father says that the incident actually took place in England.

The operation theatre is popularly called 'OT' among medical professionals. An OT nurse is considered a very responsible and powerful person in a hospital. She is highly respected by doctors and surgeons. Normally, only senior and experienced nurses are given the post of an OT nurse.

Once, a very popular and senior surgeon was operating on a patient. It happened that the regular OT nurse was on leave that day. The nurse who was posted to the OT in her place was a young girl of twenty-two. She was a greenhorn, just out of nursing school but smart and good at her work.

Before starting an operation, the nurse in charge usually counts the cotton mops. A mop is a piece of sterilized cotton gauze. At the end of the operation, she counts the used and unused mops and totals them. This figure should tally with the number of mops counted at the start of the surgery. This procedure is followed strictly to prevent the possibility of a mop getting left behind in a patient's body through oversight.

The operation was successful and the surgeon was about to sew up and close the abdomen. In keeping with the routine, he asked the OT nurse, 'Sister, is the mop count okay? If it is fine, give me the needle and catgut.'

The young nurse counted the mops and said, 'Sorry doctor, the count is not okay. There is a difference of one mop.'

The surgeon started searching inside the abdomen. He found no mop. 'No, sister, there's nothing inside,' he told her. The nurse searched the OT, but she too could not find the missing mop.

She was quite concerned. If the mop count did not tally, the surgeon could not stitch up the patient's abdomen. The surgeon was concerned too. He insisted that if the missing mop was not found, then there must have been an error in the initial count. But the sister was very confident of her count and was quite firm that she had not gone wrong.

The surgeon became impatient and said, 'Let's not waste any more time. Give me the needle and catgut.'

But the sister would not agree. Politely, but firmly, she said, 'No sir, unless I find that missing mop, I cannot give you the needle and catgut.'

The surgeon contained his rising anger and searched the abdomen once again. Finally, he said in a sharp voice, 'I am the senior person here. I am also responsible. Now, I order you to give me the needle and catgut.'

The nurse was in a dilemma. But she did not change her stance.

The surgeon was really angry by now. 'If you do not obey my instructions, I will dismiss you after the operation,' he warned.

Now the nurse was worried. She was the eldest in her family and the only earning member. It would be terrible if she were to lose her job. She was fully aware of her precarious position, but still she stuck to what she thought was correct. 'Sorry sir, I cannot give you the needle and catgut.'

It was an impossible situation. The inexperienced nurse's apparent defiance had the surgeon fuming. He was so upset that he did not know what to do. He looked down in frustration. To his amazement, he saw the blood-soaked cotton mop lying on the OT floor like a wounded soldier on the battlefield.

He was so relieved that the problem had been sorted out. 'Hey, the mop is here,' he exclaimed. 'Now the count is complete. Give me the—' Before he could complete the sentence, the needle and catgut were in his hands.

After everything was over, the surgeon called the young nurse aside and expressed his appreciation. He told her, 'I am sorry that I put extra pressure on you, sister. However, I am curious to know whether you were scared when I threatened to dismiss you. Did you not believe me when I told you that I was responsible for what happened? Under all this pressure, how could you stand your ground?'

She said hesitantly, 'Sir, I merely obeyed the principle taught to me by my teacher—if the mop count is not correct, then the needle and catgut should not be given to the surgeon. When experienced teachers say something then they must have their reasons. I just followed my teacher's words.'

The surgeon was wonderstruck and immensely pleased.

At the end of a story, my father would say, 'Each patient is precious. Be careful. If a patient dies, it is just one more hospital death for the doctor. But for the unfortunate family, it is a permanent loss.'

6

An Old Man's Ageless Wisdom

Orissa is a state with beautiful thick forests and the famous Chilka Lake. It is well known for its great temples. The Puri Jagannath Temple and the Sun Temple of Konark are among the most remarkable architectural achievements of ancient India. There is also a lot of poverty in Orissa, and around 13,500 NGOs work there to help the poorest of the poor. Many tribal people dwell in remote, inaccessible areas deep in the interior of the state's dense forests. I firmly believe that wherever our company opens a development centre, the services of our Infosys Foundation should also be made available there. Thus Orissa became an area of activity for the Foundation.

Once I had to travel to Kalahandi. It is neither a town nor a city, and it is not known for anything special. It is just another part of another tribal district like Mayur Bhunj or Koraput. They say that before Independence, Kalahandi was ruled by a king. The tribals believed that the king was their caretaker and possessed supreme powers. They are so innocent that, even today, they don't believe that kings no longer exist. If a child is orphaned, it is left at the doorstep of the collector's house. For them the ultimate protector is the raja.

Bhavani Pattanam is the district headquarters of

Kalahandi. It is a small town, quite different from other district headquarters that I know, such as Dharwad, which is my hometown. Frankly, I was surprised that Bhavani Pattanam was such a sleepy place. I had gone there to meet the head of an NGO who had been working tirelessly for the welfare of orphans. Each grey hair on his head told the story of his selfless dedication. In order to serve these children without any distraction, he had chosen to remain unmarried.

While travelling from Bhubaneswar to Kesina, the nearest station, I kept observing the tribal people. They would wait quietly on the platform for their train to arrive. They carried different kinds of fresh produce, such as pineapples, forest bananas and potatoes. The women wore brightly coloured saris—leaf green, bright yellow, dark red—and simply knotted their jet-black hair with flowers tucked in.

I was accompanied by a person who knew the local language and had agreed to be my interpreter. Knowledge of the local language is most essential when one wants to work at the grass-roots level. I had a thousand questions to ask about these tribal people—what civilization meant to them, what their lifestyle was, and so on. Tribals normally live in groups, I was told. They are not too rigid about rituals like we 'civilized' people are. They are direct in their ways. Most importantly, the concept of individual ownership of property is rarely found among them. I was keen to get to know these people. My mission was to provide assistance to them by some means, without threatening their identity.

My interpreter told me that to meet these tribals, I would have to walk two miles, since no car could reach their hamlet. After a long walk, we finally reached a village. I met a woman whose age I could not guess immediately. My interpreter was finding it difficult to translate the lady's words because her dialect was quite different. She was a dark-skinned and dark-haired woman. She must have been around seventy years old but there was no grey in her hair. She obviously could not afford to dye her hair. So what was her secret? The interpreter did not know. But clearly this secret was shared by the entire tribe, because not a single person in that village had a trace of grey hair.

Next, I met an old man. I say old, but again it was virtually impossible to guess his age by simply looking at him. During our conversation, he recalled certain events and occasions and from that we concluded that he was about 104 years old.

I got into a lively conversation with this gentleman. I asked him, 'Who is ruling our country?'

For him 'country' clearly meant Kalahandi. He looked at me and smiled at my ignorance. 'Don't you know?' he said. 'It is company *sarcar* that is ruling our country.' He meant of course the East India Company. The old man was not aware that India had become independent.

I showed him some Indian currency and the emblem of the Ashoka Chakra.

He was not impressed. He said, 'This is just a piece of paper. How can you look at it and tell who is ruling us? It is *goriwali rani* who is ruling us.'

Nothing I said could convince him that the *goriwali rani,* or the 'fair queen' of England, no longer ruled India.

I knew that the barter system was very important to tribal people, so I asked him about that. 'Do you know this small piece of paper can buy firewood, lots of saris, bags of salt, matchsticks, and even a piece of land?'

He looked at me sympathetically and said, 'For this paper, people fight, go away from our ancestral land, leave our forest and go to cities. Have we not led a complete life without that piece of paper? Our ancestors did. We are children of God, settled here happily without this paper. This is God's land. Nobody owns this land. No river is created by us. No mountain is made by us. The wind does not listen to us. The rain does not ask our permission. These are gifts of God. How we can "sell" or "buy" land, I do not understand. When nothing is yours, then how can you make such transactions? This little paper of yours can turn our lives upside down.'

I could find no words to answer him. Until that moment, I had been convinced that I knew more than he did. We know about currency movements, political parties, about the difference between Bill Gates and Bill Clinton. Here was a man who knew nothing of these, yet he was aware of deeper, more eternal truths. He knew that nobody owned the land, the mountains or the wind.

Who is more civilized—this wise old man in the Kalahandi forest or those of us with our fingers on the pulse of the Internet?

7

In India, the Worst of Both Worlds

Monday is the first working day of the week and an extremely busy day in our offices. All emails and papers have to be processed and meetings held. Long lists of appointments inevitably fill up our diaries. In between appointments, unexpected callers invariably turn up. Secretaries sweat it out on Monday mornings. But we have to get past Monday to reach Sunday again.

I recall one such Monday. I was engrossed in checking and replying to my email when my secretary told me that there were two visitors who had come to meet me without an appointment.

I asked her, 'What is special about these visitors that you are letting them in without an appointment?' I have great confidence in my staff and their ways of screening visitors.

She replied in a low tone, 'Ma'am, one is a very old man who looks very pale and the other is a middle-aged person. They say it is very urgent and have been waiting for quite some time.'

'Send them in,' I said.

They came in and sat opposite me. The old man seemed more than seventy years old. He was looking weak, tired and worried. He carried a worn-out bag. He was in a pitiable condition. With him was a middle-aged man who also looked somewhat worried.

I came to the point immediately. 'Tell me, what is the matter?'

The old man did not talk but just looked at the younger man.

The middle-aged man said, 'Madam, I saw this old man sitting near a bus stop. It seems he does not have anybody. He wants some shelter. Unfortunately, he does not have any money.'

This middle-aged man wanted to go on with all kinds of explanations. I often come across people who beat around the bush quite unnecessarily. They never tell you what they want directly. As I am used to such things, I often cut them short even at the risk of sounding curt.

'What do you want me to do?' I asked outright.

'I have read a lot about your work. I want you to help this gentleman.'

'Do you have anybody?' I asked the old man.

Tears welled up in his eyes. In a low voice he said, 'No, I do not have anybody.'

'What about your family?'

'No, I do not have anybody.'

'Where were you working before?'

I asked many questions and he gave reasonably satisfactory replies.

I felt bad for the old man. He had no money and nobody to give him a helping hand. It was a sad case. I thought of an old-age home with which we had regular contact. I called this home and told them that I was sending an old man there and that he should be kept there until we decided what we could do for him. The middle-aged man said, 'Do not worry. I will go with him and leave him there. From there, I will go to my office.'

Then they left my office. Soon, I got lost in my world of work, visitors, vouchers, budgets and so on.

Not that I forgot the old man's case. Once in a while I would call the old-age home and enquire about him. They would tell me that he was fine. I never had time to think more about him. I used to send money every month to the old-age home.

One day, I got a call from the caretaker of the home saying that the old man was very sick and that they had admitted him to a hospital. Could I come in the evening?

I went to see the old man at the hospital that evening. He was really unwell. The doctors felt his condition was critical and that he did not have long to live. I thought there might be somebody he wished to see at a time like this. Maybe not his own children, but perhaps a nephew or a sister or brother, at least a friend? Was there anybody we could inform?

I asked him, 'Do you want to see anybody? We will call whomever you want. Do you have anybody's phone number?'

With a trembling hand, he wrote down a number and gave it to me. We called the number and informed the person at the other end that the old man was critical. After some time, a person came to see him. He looked anxious and worried and he went straight to the old man.

I thought I had seen this man before. I tried to jog my

memory but in vain. I just couldn't remember why the old man's visitor seemed so familiar. Perhaps he resembled someone I had met on my travels.

Meanwhile, the doctor came out and told me that the old man had breathed his last. I felt sad. I neither knew him nor had any contact with him. But somehow I felt very sad.

After a few minutes, the visitor came out. He had tears in his eyes. He sat down quietly on a bench. The whole place was quiet and depressing. The caretaker, this visitor and I sat in the visitors' hall waiting for the formalities to be completed.

The visitor asked, 'Where is the bag he had?'

'What bag?'

'This man came to the old-age home carrying a bag,' he said.

My interest quickened. How did the visitor know that there was a bag?

I sent a peon back to the old-age home to fetch the bag. When it arrived, the visitor was eager to open it, but I did not permit him.

'You may not open the bag unless you identify yourself. What is your relationship with this old man? I want to know how you knew about this bag.'

He seemed very upset with my questions. Maybe he didn't like a woman questioning him. In India, men often get upset when women raise questions that are inconvenient for them. They prefer women who do not question what they do. Fortunately, this trend is disappearing slowly.

'It was I who accompanied him and left him at this home,' said the man.

'Who are you?' I was very curious.

'I am his son.'

You can imagine how shocked I was. Now I remembered—he was the middle-aged man who had come to our office that Monday morning claiming that he had found the old man sitting near a bus stop.

I was very upset. 'Why did you lie to me?'

Of course he had a story to tell. 'I have problems at home,' he said. 'My wife never liked my father. She asked me to choose between her and him. At that time we read about your Foundation. We thought then that our problem could be solved without money.' He said he had no choice but to appease his wife because it was she who owned the house they lived in.

'What a way to solve your problem!' I protested. 'We help people who are orphans, but not orphans with children.'

When the bag was finally opened we found three sets of old clothes in it, some medicines and a passbook. When I opened the passbook, I was astounded. The old man had a bank balance of more than a lakh of rupees. The old man had put down a nominee for the account—his son, the same son who had got rid of him. Here was a son who was heartless enough to pass off his father as destitute in order to admit him in an old-age home. Now, the same son had come to claim his father's money.

Though his son had not wanted to look after him and had made him lie to me that he had nobody in this world, the old man nevertheless had wanted his money to go to his son. It never would have occurred to him to give that money to the old-age home that had sheltered him in his last days.

In Western countries, when old people die in old-age homes, they often will their property to the home or the hospital that cared for them. This is for the benefit of other senior citizens. They do not bequeath their money to their children, nor do the children expect their parents to do so. But in India, we have the worst of both worlds: children neglect aged parents, and parents routinely leave their property to their children.

'It is shameful the way you and your father cooked up this drama for the sake of a few thousand rupees!' I told the man. 'And you are setting a bad example. Next time when a genuinely destitute person seeks help, we will be unwilling to offer it. The memory of people like you will stay on.'

He hung his head in shame.

8

LIVING THROUGH CHANGE

Life and times have changed in truly revolutionary ways. Yet, we seldom feel the impact of change because we live right in the middle of it. Old ways have changed, our festivals have changed, our attitudes have changed, our norms, values and ideas have changed. Two festivals in which I participated recently brought this point home to me fairly dramatically. In both cases, the extent of change that had taken place was conveyed to me through conversation. This added a personal touch and helped underline the fundamental nature of the changes through which we are living. The first event was a Diwali celebration. The second was a music festival.

Diwali is an occasion for great celebration in our country. Everybody buys gifts, prepares sweets and visits friends. Offices remain closed for days. Children buy crackers.

Last Diwali, I saw an advertisement saying that some orphanages were selling sweets prepared by the orphans. I thought that buying these sweets would be the best way to help and encourage the orphanages. I bought a few packets of sweets and went to the house of a close friend.

I expected her to be in a joyous mood, celebrating this great festival with enthusiasm. She was a housewife, hailing from a small town. Her father owned plenty of land in the village. Surprisingly, I found her far from joyous. She didn't seem enthusiastic at all about the festival I had gone to celebrate with her.

'Diwali has lost its real meaning,' she said.

I was frankly surprised to hear this. 'Why do you say that?' I asked her.

She had her reasons. 'In the small town I grew up in, our food pattern was so different from what it is today. Everyone used to have healthy but simple food like roti, rice, dal and vegetables every day, irrespective of the family's income. Sweets were prepared only when there was a festival like Dussera or Diwali. That being so, we children looked forward to the festivals.'

My thoughts went back to my own childhood days. They were similar to hers. We used to eat a healthy and balanced diet like she said.

'But nowadays,' she went on, 'food patterns have changed. One reason is that we have only two children and are keen to give them what they like. We cook accordingly. In case we cannot cook what they want, then in a city like ours we can order it instantly from any restaurant. So children today have no reason to look forward to festivals and sweets like we used to.'

Of course she was right. Food habits have indeed changed. This is particularly true of the middle class and the upper middle class. But I still had a question. Was the availability of sweets throughout the year the only reason for people to lose interest in Diwali?

'No,' said my friend, 'the whole attitude has changed.

People buy whatever clothes they want, whenever they want. They don't wait for any festival. Families are scattered all over India, and sometimes all over the world. Meeting one's relatives is not easy. Even amongst my friends, many of them would like to go to their home town. But getting reservations by rail, air or even by bus, has become so difficult that it is better to stay at home.'

How true! For the trip I would take over Diwali, I had booked my tickets a month in advance.

My friend raised the most fundamental issue when she asked, 'How many of us really know the significance of Diwali? The real meaning of the festival of lights? What our sacred epics say about this festival? The reality is that nobody is bothered. In our country, each state has a special story about this festival. All the stories are from parts of the Mahabharatha and the Krishna legend. But how many know about them?'

I thought that perhaps she was feeling homesick. In such a situation, I told myself, the best thing to do would be to take her out of the house.

'Let us go to Renu's house or Mridula's house,' I suggested. They were old friends and therefore real friends. Nowadays many people refer to me as their friend though I may not know them. Renu and Mridula were different and I thought visiting them would cheer up my depressed friend. But she had news for me.

'No, Renu got bored,' my friend said. 'She works as HRD head in a big firm and she is really tired of having to take care of so many visitors during the Diwali season. So, she has gone to Goa for a holiday. And Mridula is writing a book. She told me not to tell anybody that she is in the company guest house.'

This was something new to me—this method of celebrating Diwali by escaping or hibernating.

My friend had not finished. 'There is one more headache. Some relatives bring gifts, so we have to reciprocate. It has become a racket. I did not unpack last year's gifts hoping that I could give them to somebody this year. I am tired of candle stands and boxes of dry fruits and sweets. We are all getting old. Extra calories and cholesterol-rich sweets are not good for us.'

'So what did you do with them?' I asked.

'I gave them to an orphanage. Let the poor children enjoy themselves.'

I was curious to know to whom she had given the sweets. She named a well-known orphanage. Now I knew what happens to the sweets or candles gifted at Diwali! They are labelled in the name of some charitable organization and sold in the market. What a wonderful way to raise funds! Of course, the little children in the orphanages may still not get to eat any sweets on Diwali.

My music festival experience was quite different but equally illuminating. These days, I am often invited to inaugurate music festivals, philosophy lectures or charity shows. Often, I do not know anything about the subject concerned. But people get offended if I refuse. So, I accept these invitations on the condition that I should not be called to the dais.

I attended one such festival recently. I just wanted to enjoy the music. I went late, so I sat at the back, quite happy that nobody had noticed me. There were retired officers, middle-aged housewives and old ladies, but I could not see any youngsters in the hall. Two middle-aged housewives wearing Dharmavaram saris were sitting right in front of me. They looked elegant with fresh jasmine flowers in their silvery hair. Since the rows were close, I couldn't help but hear what they were talking about. They were discussing the problems of finding grooms for girls these days.

'The software boom has made it difficult to get grooms above twenty-eight years these days,' said one woman profoundly.

The other woman was also interested in the topic. Obviously, the subject of grooms was far more important to them than the music.

The first woman went on to explain, 'Today, when a boy completes his BE, he may be twenty-two years, and he will get a job in one of the software companies. He will work for two years and then he will go abroad for a year. By that time he will be twenty-five and probably would have earned more money than his father, who might have been a bank officer, an honest government employee or a professor. Tell me, why should he not marry and settle down?'

Unaware that someone was eavesdropping, she answered her own question. 'His parents will search for a software engineer girl. Today, I've been told that about 50 per cent of the students in engineering colleges are girls. An engineering college is just like an arts college these days. I am sure the boy's father will get a software girl. The marriage is good for both of them in every sense of the word. He will have someone with him when he works abroad. He will have home-cooked food and there will be somebody to look after him. For the girl also it will be such an advantage. So, at twenty-five, these young men will get married—just like in the old days.'

This woman definitely deserves a medal for her logical and accurate analysis, I told myself. Now it was the turn of the other woman to give her views. She had a different perspective.

'This software boom is really bad in some ways,' she said. 'Look at how it affects others. Nowadays, girls say they do not want to marry electrical engineers, mechanical engineers or even doctors. The chances of these boys going abroad are limited. Their salaries are also not very attractive. Most important of all, they are not respected in the family.'

I was really surprised by this last statement and was eager to hear an explanation for it. I was not disappointed.

'If the boy is abroad,' the lady continued, 'then he will come home for three weeks, bringing gifts with him. Everybody likes him for that. But engineers or doctors don't get the same opportunities to work abroad. Also, if the daughter-in-law stays with her mother-in-law all the time, she is not respected. Today, no girl likes to stay with her mother-in-law. Going abroad is the best solution, but this must be immediately after marriage, not later.'

'Why not later?'

'Later, it is better to be with the in-laws. There will be children and the in-laws will look after them. There will be nothing to worry about. No need to depend on servants. This kind of shuttling between India and the US is possible only in a software job.'

I could not control myself any longer. A whole new window had opened before my eyes and I wanted to know who these women were. They had come to such a beautiful music concert, but preferred to exchange notes on the social aspects of software development. I knew it was bad manners, but I couldn't help interrupting their conversation. 'Excuse me,' I said, 'I am curious to know how you both know so much about software sociology.'

They were startled and turned around to stare at me. I felt that they did not like my question. And I could not blame them. After all, I had broken into what was a private conversation.

'Who are you?' they asked.

I introduced myself and said, 'I have known the software industry for the last two decades but I did not know these social details. I must really compliment both of you on your knowledge.'

My compliment seemed to put them at ease for they smiled as they replied together, 'We are marriage brokers.'

9

WHEN TELEGRAMS WERE BAD

The difference between animals and human beings is communication. If one is good at it, then many misunderstandings can be reduced. Clear thinking and clear communication are therefore essential in everyday life. Indeed, many communication classes are offered nowadays. For those in a hurry, there are crash courses.

Lata and I were close friends right from childhood. In a small town, friendship grows faster and thicker than in big cities. Maybe people from small towns depend on each other more. Or maybe the culture in a small place is different than in a big city. Industrialization has its own impact on human relations. In our small-town environment, Lata and I enjoyed our closeness. I was a frequent visitor to her house and I knew everybody there. It was the same with Lata. She came over to our place often and knew my family very well. In due course, we completed our degrees and the time came for us to go our different ways. We parted with heavy hearts as I took up a job in Pune and went away.

I became involved in my career and used to meet Lata only when I visited my home town. Telephones were the prerogative of the rich in those days—I am talking of the situation some twenty-five years ago—and roadside STD booths were unknown. If anything was urgent, the only channel of communication available was the telegram. The telegram denoted a whole new culture in those days. In villages and small towns, a telegram was a big event, often a harbinger of bad news.

One day, I received a telegram. As usual, it was ominous. 'Father expired. Start immediately,' it said. The sender's name was given as Lata.

I was shocked. My colleagues were very kind to me. One of them called the railway station immediately to book a ticket on the next train to my home town while another applied for leave on my behalf. I just sat still, crying.

My father was more than a friend to me. We used to talk a lot and discuss many things. The previous week, when I had visited him, he had been hale and hearty. He had not shown any signs of illness. What could have happened? Was it a heart attack or an accident? How was my mother? How difficult it would be for her!

One of my colleagues used to get a telegram similar to the one I had just received at least once every year. 'Granny expired. Start immediately,' his telegram would read. He would tell me that this was the best way to get leave.

'Do you have enough leave?' he asked me now, thinking the telegram I had received was one like his. I was very angry with him.

My journey back home was simply unbearable. I thought of my childhood and my college days when my father was a part of everything. At first he was a role model, but later, when I had seen more of the world, he became more of a friend than a hero.

I remember feeling that my childhood had gone forever. My father and I had so many dreams of travelling together, reading many books and discussing things. All my dreams were shattered. I knew life had to go on, but I thought that if he were alive then life would have been so much more enjoyable.

When I reached my home town, I was expecting at least one of my numerous cousins to be at the station to receive me. To my surprise, there was no one from my family. I was a little upset. Then I consoled myself thinking that everybody must be in mourning. And anyhow, how were they to know that I was coming by this particular train, I reasoned. So I took an auto and reached home. As we neared the house, my heart started pounding—the same road, the same house, but today it was without my dear father.

I got down from the auto and noticed that the house was rather quiet. It was calm and there was no sign of people inside. I was surprised. How could that be? My father was a very popular doctor and professor. Surely people would have come to pay their last respects. I couldn't see any of my cousins either. I went in. The house was whitewashed, decorated with flowers and mango leaves. It looked as though it was a happy occasion. I did not know what to do. I stood there still and silent, like a lamp post.

Just then there was a noise coming from my father's room. I turned and I could not believe what I saw. My father was standing there, smiling happily at me. Is it a dream? I asked myself.

My father seemed very happy to see me. He said, 'I knew that you would make it for the engagement somehow. She is your favourite cousin after all.'

'What are you talking about?'

'The engagement. Lata's marriage is fixed. The boy's family wants to hold the engagement this evening itself. He is in Delhi. The marriage is . . .'

I stopped him. 'Who sent the telegram? Why did you write that? Why did you lie to me? You of all people! I never expected you to lie.'

But my father did not understand what I was saying. 'What telegram are you talking about? We had to send a telegram so that you could come.'

'But why this kind of telegram?' I was very upset and agitated as I gave him the telegram I had received. My father was surprised and said that he hadn't sent it. Confusion. Then who had sent it?

Suddenly, he smiled. 'I know what must have happened. Your friend Lata's father passed away yesterday. You know that he was sick. You knew him very well. That may be the reason why Lata sent you a telegram. There was a miscommunication. She should have said, "*My* father passed away".' The word 'my' was missing. What havoc it had caused!

It was now clear to me that the telegram was sent by my friend Lata, and back home it was celebration time for my cousin Lata's engagement. I was left wondering what my colleagues would think when they saw the other telegram, the one actually sent by my family, which read, 'Lata's marriage fixed. Engagement tomorrow.'

10

A Man Too Clever by Half

A few years ago, when the Infosys Foundation was still in its infancy, people were not aware of the kind of work we were trying to do. Our organization worked at the grass-roots level, mainly with village schoolmasters whom we approached voluntarily. Although Infosys, the company, had already made a name for itself in the field of business, the Foundation was housed in two small rooms on the third floor of Infosys Towers; and it still is, even today. Our obscurity was heightened by the fact that there wasn't a single plaque announcing our presence. The security men would confront our staff frequently. Any decent establishment connected to Infosys should have a large signboard with brass lettering, if not a stately banner, they would say.

Right from its inception, the Foundation focused on redressing the grievances of village people, especially children, so that we could help them envision a bright and prosperous future comparable to that of their urban counterparts. It is well known that in our country the rural-urban divide runs deep. The life of village children is devoid of the activities that are taken for granted by our city children. The simple pleasures of modern life— watching a cartoon show on television, listening to a popular Hindi film song, or even reading a book at leisure—are rare luxuries in villages. A lack of basic facilities forces village boys and girls to while away their time uselessly. Having observed this aspect of village life at close quarters, I decided that one of the primary goals of the Foundation should be to launch a project titled 'A library for each village'.

I feel libraries play an important role in the lives of children, the citizens of tomorrow. As I was raised in a middle-class family in a small town, I was well aware of the importance of books and knowledge in the life of a student. In my childhood, I had limited access to books and it was then that I had envisioned starting free libraries offering unlimited access to the world of books. As soon as I had been named trustee of the Foundation, I knew I had to take the first step towards fulfilling my desire to build libraries for village children.

Reading has many advantages. It is not only a useful hobby, but also helps us imbibe better qualities. Keeping this in mind, the trustees planned to establish libraries that contained books in the regional language and not the textbooks that the children were using in school. Simple, illustrated, interesting books that could be read without anybody's help were thus selected for these libraries. In this manner, the Foundation would sow the seeds of a love for reading in the villages of Karnataka.

With sufficient nurturing and caring, the project has grown from a tiny sapling into a huge, wide-reaching banyan tree. More than 4,000 such libraries have been established all over the state. The books have succeeded in putting a smile on the faces of village children who discovered a new world opening up before them.

One hot afternoon, when I was sitting in my room trying to come up with some innovative ideas for the Foundation's projects, I noticed the silhouette of a man standing outside the glass door of my office. He was barely visible among the cartons of books and the jungle of colourful wrapping paper strewn all over the floor. I carried on with my work, which required concentration. It was one of those days when my eagerness to complete the work on hand had made me give up all thoughts of a quick lunch or a midday siesta. Suddenly, I was startled by a loud knock on the door. The stranger walked in, without even a nominal 'May I come in?'

'Is this the Foundation office?' he asked abruptly.

'Yes,' I answered.

'Are you one of the staff members of the Foundation?'

I nodded. He looked puzzled. Perhaps he had expected to see a fancy office with a fancy receptionist. And here was I, wearing the sort of simple cotton sari that did nothing to disclose my identity. When the man arrived, I had been engrossed in dispatching some last-minute packages while also writing an introductory proposal for a new project. A dishevelled person in a tiny cabin amid a maze of paper and piles of books was clearly not his idea of the Infosys Foundation he had come to visit. Without wasting time on introductions, he opened his bag and pulled out two Kannada books that looked like pamphlets.

'These are very good books for children,' he announced. 'I have put in several years and the best of my efforts to publish them. There is a great demand for these books all over Karnataka. You can buy these books for your library project.'

I just listened. Naturally, I wanted to see the books for myself to judge their quality, price and, most importantly, content. Would they prove useful and interesting to children in village schools?

My silence seemed to irritate him. He said, 'I know Sudha Murty and Narayana Murthy very well. Mrs Murty, who is the trustee of the Foundation, asked me to come here. Otherwise I don't do this kind of a salesman's job. It is because of the rapport we share that I have come so far to help her.'

I was amused. 'Have you known Mrs Murty for many years?' I asked.

Without any hesitation, he answered, 'I've known Sudha for a long time. She is my childhood friend.'

This was getting more and more curious—a man I was seeing for the first time claiming to be my childhood friend!

Rather naughtily, I asked, 'But Sudha is from Dharwad and you seem to be from Bangalore. How is it that she is your childhood friend?'

Now he looked quite surprised. 'Do you address your boss by her first name? It is not good etiquette. So what if she is from Dharwad? She used to come to Bangalore quite often to her aunt's house, which is next to ours even now.'

Lord Almighty, I thought. My kith and kin had never crossed the Tungabhadra River, which divides the old Mysore state from northern Karnataka. So, I was indeed surprised to know about this 'aunt' who was his neighbour.

He went on, 'Sudha has always treated me like her elder brother. She doesn't have any brothers, you see. When Murthy wanted to start Infosys, she came to me for advice. Recently she told me she wanted to buy 100 copies of each of my books. She knows my calibre. She told me to give these books here and collect the money. I have to go to the Kannada Sahitya meeting where they are honouring me, so please hurry up.'

I didn't know whether to get upset and shout at him or just carry on with the ruse. I decided to play along with his deception. 'What kind of a person is Mrs Murty?' I asked, perhaps impishly.

He seemed pleased at the opportunity to say more about his friendship. 'Oh! She is a gentle lady, though very quiet by nature,' he said. 'During her MA, nobody even knew about Sudha in the class. It was I who told her not to waste her time at home and do some social work. I also introduced her to Murthy and mediated their marriage.'

'Was it an arranged marriage?'

'Of course. I even got their horoscopes matched. That's why the couple is very fond of me even now and hold me in high regard. After all, it's because of me that she is here today!'

This was too much. He was not even being clever, just careless. Mine was a love marriage. Neither of us was bothered about horoscopes. Moreover, I have always been an extrovert and was much noticed because I happened to be the only girl in class throughout my college days. I am an M.Tech and not an MA. Social service was a cherished idea of Murthy's and mine since the days of our friendship.

I could no longer stand this man's lying. I realized it was time to call his bluff. If I didn't disclose my identity now, who knew what he would be claiming next.

'Mister,' I said very sternly, 'there has to be an end to these lies of yours. I am Sudha Murty, wife of Narayana Murthy. This is the first time that I am meeting you. How dare you talk about Murthy and me in this way? This is outrageous! Even if your books were good in terms of content and language, I would never buy them. Books are meant to reflect the thoughts and personality of the author. By now I know what kind of a person you are. Even if you are willing to offer your books free, I shall not accept them. Remember, only an honest human being can be a good writer.'

He was shocked of course. But before he could think of a suitable response, I had walked out of the office, disgusted, frustrated and amazed at the world we live in.

11

A Bond Betrayed on Rakhi Day

My work at the Infosys Foundation has brought me face to face with many women who have suffered a great deal for no fault of theirs. Most of them are uneducated and victims of exploitation. One of the objectives of our Foundation is to try and help these unlucky women as much as possible.

Those who slip into prostitution are almost always innocent women. Most have been forced into it at a young age and they find it difficult to escape. Many express a desire to leave the profession, but that is next to impossible. Since they have been in this 'trade' from a young age, they have not developed any other special skills. Hence they are not fit for employment and are unable to find alternative means of earning a livelihood. In those rare cases when a woman does manage to extricate herself from this miserable life, our society does not accept her.

In the last few years, I have had some experience in working for these unfortunate women. Initially, they would avoid talking to me. But on repeated visits, they opened up gradually and started speaking with me. The stories they narrated were heartbreaking. At times, I was really at a loss for what to say or how to react. Their agony pained me deeply.

It was on one such visit that I got to know Tara, a middle-aged *gharwali* (commercial sex worker) in a temple. Looking at Tara, I could tell that she had been a very beautiful woman in her younger days. Even now, she came across as someone who was bold and spirited. Tara did not know how to read and write and wanted my help because she thought I was a school teacher. That was fine with me.

'If you know of any other lady teacher, please let me know. I want to learn to read and write,' she told me the first time we met. 'I don't want to call her to my house. I will go wherever the teacher wants me to.'

Her zest for knowledge surprised me. I wanted to know more about her. Once or twice, I tried to broach the subject, but she was reluctant to talk about herself. She always seemed very sad.

It was Rakhi day. In northern Karnataka and the border areas of Maharashtra, this day is called Narali-Poornima, which literally means 'to celebrate the full-moon day with coconuts'. I was in the area for a week, mainly visiting village schools in connection with our library project. There I bumped into Tara again. I still remember it was a bright, sunny day and Tara was buying bangles. I wanted to talk to her. How should I address her, I wondered. Since she was older than me, I decided to call her akka, which means elder sister in Kannada.

Tara was sitting on the steps of the temple, waiting for the crowd to disperse. I went towards her. She looked at me and smiled. I thought she was sad. Or was I sad? I didn't know.

I tried to begin a conversation by returning her smile. 'Tara akka, there is such a crowd because of Narali-Poornima. You will have to wait for a long time to get in.'

Suddenly, I sensed anger. I could see it in her eyes. She began to shout at me. 'Teacher, don't call me akka. I dislike that word. All these relationships, like brother and sister, exist in your world. Not in mine. Don't address me like that. You can call me Tara, Tarabai, but not Tara akka. In my world there is only one relationship, that of a man and a woman.'

Tears rolled down my eyes. I understood the bitter truth behind what she said. One of the volunteers who had accompanied me was very upset. He wanted to tell Tara who I was. I stopped him.

'Tara, I am sorry if I hurt your feelings,' I said politely. 'I used the word akka because you are older than me. I'm sorry if that offended you.'

The atmosphere then changed dramatically. Tara started crying uncontrollably. The pallu of her green Irkal sari became wet with tears. Holding the bangles she had bought from the shop in one hand, she used the other to wipe her tears.

I put my hand on her shoulder. I did not speak. Our silence was much more meaningful than words. After some time, she stopped crying, but she still looked very sad. I sent my volunteer to fetch a cup of tea for her. After a while, Tara calmed down.

She said, 'Teacher, I am sorry I was rude to you. You have not made any mistake. After all, you have shown respect to me by calling me akka. Till this day, no one has ever used such a good word to address me. People call me by different names. I don't want to repeat them to you. Akka brought back childhood memories.'

Tara continued talking. She spoke of her poverty and of losing her parents in an epidemic. A younger brother was all she had. She adored him and though she was only a child herself she found work as a coolie to look after him. But when she was twelve years old and her brother was only eleven, he sold her to an agent in a red light area. He had taken her there on the pretext of visiting the village fair. That was on a Narali-Poornima day.

It was now clear to me what she was going through sitting on the steps of that temple. It was Narali-Poornima day once again and the word akka must have triggered in her mind something she had been desperate to forget all her life. Rakhi is not merely about a sister tying a thread on her brother's wrist. It signifies the bond between a brother and a sister. And Tara, through no fault of hers, was pushed into her dreadful life by her own brother. On a Rakhi day.

12

A Lesson in Life from a Beggar

Meena is a good friend of mine. She is an LIC officer earning a good salary. But there was always something strange about her. She was forever unhappy. Whenever I met her, I would start to feel depressed. It was as though her gloom and cynicism had a way of spreading to others. She never had anything positive to say on any subject or about any person.

For instance, I might say to her, 'Meena, did you know Rakesh has come first in his school?'

Meena's immediate response would be to belittle the achievement. 'Naturally, his father is a school teacher,' she would say.

If I said, 'Meena, Shwetha is a very beautiful girl, isn't she?' Meena would be pessimistic. 'When a pony is young, he looks handsome. It is age that matters. Wait for some time. Shwetha will be uglier than anyone you know.'

'Meena, it's a beautiful day. Let's go for a walk.'

'No, the sun is too hot and I get tired if I walk too much. Besides, who says walking is good for health? There's no proof.'

That was Meena. She stayed alone in an apartment as her parents lived in Delhi. She was an only child and had the habit of complaining about anything and everything.

Naturally, she wasn't very pleasant company and nobody wanted to visit her. Then one day, Meena was transferred to Bombay and soon we all forgot about her.

Many years later, I found myself caught in the rain at Bombay's Flora Fountain. It was pouring and I didn't have an umbrella. I was standing near Akbarallys, a popular department store, waiting for the rain to subside. Suddenly, I spotted Meena. My first reaction was to run, even in that pouring rain. I was anxious to avoid being seen by her, having to listen to her never-ending complaints. However, I couldn't escape. She had already seen me and caught hold of my hand warmly. What's more, she was very cheerful.

'Hey! I am really excited. It's nice to meet old friends. What are you doing here?'

I explained that I was in Bombay on official work.

'Then stay with me tonight,' she said. 'Let's chat. Do you know that old wine, old friends and memories are precious and rare?'

I couldn't believe it. Was this really Meena? I pinched myself hard to be sure it wasn't a dream. But Meena was really standing there, right in front of me, squeezing my hand, smiling, and yes, she did look happy. In the three years she had been in Bangalore, I had never once seen her smiling like that. A few strands of grey in her hair reminded me that years had passed. There were a few wrinkles in her face, but the truth was that she looked more attractive than ever before.

Finally, I managed to say, 'No Meena, I can't stay with you tonight. I have to attend a dinner. Give me your card and I'll keep in touch with you. I promise.'

For a moment, Meena looked disappointed. 'Let's go and have tea at least,' she insisted.

'But Meena, it's pouring.'

'So what? We'll buy an umbrella and then go to the Grand Hotel,' she said.

'We won't get a taxi in this rain,' I grumbled.

'So what? We'll walk.'

I was very surprised. This wasn't the same Meena I had known. Today, she seemed ready to make any number of adjustments.

We reached the Grand Hotel drenched. By then the only thought in my mind was to find out who or what had brought about such a change in the pessimistic Meena I had known. I was quite curious.

'Tell me Meena, is there a Prince Charming who has managed to change you so?'

Meena was surprised by my question. 'No, there isn't anyone like that,' she said.

'Then what's the secret of your energy?' I asked, like Tendulkar does in the ad.

She smiled. 'A beggar changed my life.'

I was absolutely dumbfounded and she could see it.

'Yes, a beggar,' she repeated, as if to reassure me. 'He was old and used to stay in front of my house with his five-year-old granddaughter. As you know, I was a chronic pessimist. I used to give my leftovers to this beggar every day. I never spoke to him. Nor did he speak to me. One monsoon day, I looked out of my bedroom window and started cursing the rain. I don't know why I did that because I wasn't even getting wet. That day I couldn't give the beggar and his granddaughter their daily quota of leftovers. They went hungry, I am sure.

'However, what I saw from my window surprised me. The beggar and the young girl were playing on the road because there was no traffic. They were laughing, clapping and screaming joyously, as if they were in paradise. Hunger and rain did not matter. They were totally drenched and totally happy. I envied their zest for life.

'That scene forced me to look at my own life. I realized I had so many comforts, none of which they had. But they had the most important of all assets, one which I lacked. They knew how to be happy with life as it was. I felt ashamed of myself. I even started to make a list of what I had and what I did not have. I found I had more to be grateful for than most people could imagine. That day, I decided to change my attitude towards life, using the beggar as my role model.'

After a long pause, I asked Meena how long it had taken her to change.

'Once this realization dawned,' she said, 'it took me almost two years to put the change into effect. Now nothing matters. I am always happy. I find happiness in every small thing, in every situation and in every person.'

'Did you give any *gurudakshina* to your guru?' I asked.

'No. Unfortunately, by the time I understood things, he was dead. But I sponsored his granddaughter to a boarding school as a mark of respect to him.'

13

FORGETTING OUR OWN HISTORY

Our country's history is full of martyrs and patriots in whose honour we must bow our heads in perpetual tribute. Their life stories are gloriously inspirational. Particularly inspiring are the stories of our women martyrs. Many of them were not even educated, but they had the courage to face their enemies and fight for their country. Obvavva of Chitradurga district, Kittur Chennamma of northern Karnataka, Belavadi Maamma of Belgaum district—the list is long. Obvavva had nothing but the rice-pounding stick from her kitchen to use against the fully armed enemy soldiers. But how many of our young Indians know about them?

Among history's heroines, few shine as brightly as Rani Laxmibai of Jhansi. A young childless widow, she challenged the might of the British Empire. Such was her courage that she won the admiration of even the enemy. There are many poems written about her. The greatest compliment paid to her courage was the saying that she was the only man in her army. How much do our young people know about her?

Recently, I received the Ojaswini Award from Bhopal. It was presented to me in Delhi. It included a beautiful memento—a statue of Rani Laxmibai of Jhansi riding a horse, sword in hand. It was exquisitely crafted. I returned to Bangalore by air and carried the statue, though rather large, as hand baggage. I feared that it would break if I checked it in. The security personnel at Delhi airport were very kind to me after I explained my situation. They scanned the statue with metal detectors and allowed me to carry it into the aircraft.

The Jet Airways crew were equally nice. I was in economy class and could not keep the statue on my lap. I didn't want to put it under the seat either. Of course, it wouldn't fit into the overhead locker. The air hostess very kindly took away my statue and placed it on an empty seat in business class. Without a doubt, Mardani Rani Laxmibai deserved this deferential treatment.

Quite pleased with the way everyone had helped, I settled down comfortably. I noticed that my fellow passengers were watching these goings-on with interest. After the flight took off, they looked at me with curious eyes. But no one ventured to strike up a conversation.

I have a theory about conversation. You may call it an empirical formula. Quantitatively speaking, 'conversation' is inversely proportional to economic standing. If you are travelling by bus, your fellow passengers will get into conversation with you very quickly and without any reservation. If you are travelling by first class on a train, people will be more reserved. If you are travelling by air, then the likelihood of entering into a conversation is quite small. If you are in first class on an international flight, then you may travel twenty-four hours without exchanging a single word with the person sitting next to you.

There were two teenagers sitting next to me on the Delhi-Bangalore flight, a boy and a girl. They were wearing expensive branded jeans. Both had cut their hair short, making them look similar. The only noticeable difference was that the girl had pierced her ears. They were chewing gum and an MP3 player kept them immersed in their own world. It was evident that they were from an affluent family. It was just as evident that they were in no mood for conversation, even among themselves, let alone others. Music and gum do that to people.

After some time, I decided that I must break the ice and talk to these youngsters. As I teach in a college, I am comfortable with young people. I enjoy talking to them. Normally, at that age they are not manipulative or shrewd. They are spontaneous and less inhibited and often have refreshing views. I engaged them first in small talk and found out that they were studying in a college in Bangalore. They were cousins and had just been to Delhi to visit their grandparents.

The girl asked hesitantly, 'I saw that statue of a black horse and a woman riding on it. It's a nice toy, but is it not available in Bangalore? You seem to have had such a tough time carrying it with you. Is there any special reason for carrying it with you?'

'It's not a toy. It's an award,' I told her.

Now the boy started to ply me with questions. 'Are you very fond of horses?'

I was surprised. 'No, I hardly see horses nowadays.'

'Maybe you are fond of the races!'

I have never gone to a race in my life. I felt a bit uncomfortable. It was getting dark as it was an evening flight, so the young cousins did not see the frown on my face.

The boy asked, 'Is this award for a horse race? There is a lady on the back of that beautiful horse.'

I realized that these young people could only associate my trophy with horses and races. They had absolutely no idea about the woman in battle gear sitting astride the horse. Was I being given an opportunity to tell them?

'Will you go and have a look at the statue and tell me what you think about it?' I asked them.

'We did look at the statue and that's why we are asking these questions,' they replied.

I was taken aback. Being a teacher, I thought it was my duty to tell them about Rani Laxmibai. (I now realize why my son teases me about my habit of viewing every youngster as a potential student and my eagerness to convert every moment available into an opportunity for teaching.)

'Have you heard about the First War of Independence?' I asked the youngsters.

'Yes. It was in 1942, wasn't it?' said the boy vaguely.

The girl added, 'Of course, we've seen the movie *1942– A Love Story*. The war between the Indians and the British. Manisha Koirala was just stunning in that.'

'No, that was the Quit India movement. The First War of Independence was fought a century before that and we lost it.'

They did not reply.

'In 1857 there was a war against the British. The young queen of Jhansi, Rani Laxmibai, led her forces against them. She could have remained passive, accepted a royal pension from the British and led a secure, comfortable life. But she didn't do that. She was a fiery patriot. She fought the war bravely and even her opponents were surprised by her leadership on the battlefield. Since then she has been a symbol of courage and an icon of the Indian people's love of freedom. She died so that we could all live in a free India.'

The two youngsters listened without saying a word. And without chewing.

14

CAUSE, THEN CURE

Travelling opens the doors to knowledge. Without it, education is incomplete. Our country is special in so many ways. It has many states, each with a different language, traditions, customs, flora and fauna. Travelling within India itself gives you the feel and the pleasure of visiting different countries.

If you travel by bus or by second class in a train, then you'll meet people from different backgrounds. It is particularly pleasurable to converse with one's fellow passengers on a bus or a train. I discover this often—like the time I was travelling from Bangalore to Hubli by a day train. Normally in such trains we don't require reservations. We can enjoy the view of nature and also have the pleasure of meeting various kinds of people.

I boarded the train at 2.30 p.m. in Bangalore and was supposed to reach Hubli by 10 p.m. I was alone and was tired after having worked almost continuously on a project for the previous two days. Rest was what I needed most at that time.

I occupied a window seat, stretched my legs and settled down to doze. Just then, someone entered the compartment and sat down beside me. It was a young woman, about twenty-five years old, dressed in a cotton sari. Probably she had come at the eleventh hour and had to run to catch the train, for she was perspiring. She wore no ornaments or any other adornment. She was evidently from an average middle-class family.

She settled down, took out a handkerchief and started wiping her face, looking into the mirror attached to her purse. She drank some water and then looked at me. She reminded me of an enthusiastic, well-prepared student going for an examination. She smiled at me in a friendly way. She seemed ready to start a conversation.

The inevitable opening question came first. 'Where are you going?'

'Hubli,' I said

'Where in Hubli?'

I was hesitant to give her any details, but I found myself replying, 'Vishweshwaranagar. Do you know where that is?'

'Sort of,' she said casually.

'I am going to the Shanti Colony.'

'Where in Shanti Colony?' she wanted to know. 'Because there are two Shanti Colonies.'

I was taken aback by her knowledge of the area. 'Near the railway lines.'

'Both are near railway lines. Is it north or south?'

'North,' I clarified.

I thought I had satisfied her curiosity and that there would be no further questions. Now I looked forward to some rest. I am by nature a friendly and outgoing person, and I love talking to different people, but in the train that day I was tired and wasn't in the mood for conversation.

But the girl did not think the conversation was over.

'Do you work?' she began again.

Expecting further probing, I decided to give her all the details right away. 'Yes, I work in a college and now I have holidays. I belong to Hubli so I am going there.'

If I thought that would satisfy her, I was mistaken. She smiled and said, 'Oh, I see! So you are a professor. What subjects do you teach?'

People who are fond of talking can raise a conversation out of nothing. Introverts, on the other hand, can answer in monosyllables and end a conversation quickly. Some people use conversation to gather a great deal of information about others without divulging any information about themselves. I realized that this young woman belonged to such a category. My sleep and irritation disappeared. I decided to play this game and find out how many questions she could generate.

'I teach computer science at Christ College.'

'Oh, computers! There is no place without a computer nowadays. A day may come when we might be called illiterate if we do not know computers. What do you say?'

I had begun to appreciate her ability to invent questions and pull me into the conversation.

'It depends on how you interpret the concept of literacy,' I answered like a management consultant.

She responded with a comment, 'I strongly believe that there is a great difference between being literate and being educated. Literacy means having the basic knowledge, being educated means understanding what you know. What do you think about this definition?'

I was in a fix to understand this woman. By this time, the train had crossed Bangalore city limits and was heading towards Tumkur. I could see the beautiful landscape passing by. It was just after the monsoon, so the lakes were full and the land was green. The weather was pleasant and no air conditioning or fans were required. Men and women were working in the fields. Cattle were grazing. Hills loomed majestically against the sky. Though it was late afternoon, the sun was not hot.

I thought that if this lady were to go on talking, then it would be impossible to bear the six to seven hours that were left of my journey. One way to save the situation was to tell her politely but firmly that I wanted to rest and would prefer to be left alone. But somehow I was unable to be frank with her. She looked so innocent. She was bubbling with energy. Her face had an open and curious expression. She looked just like one of my eager students in class. As a teacher, I did not have the heart to rebuff her by saying what was on my mind. So, I smiled.

'Smiling is good for health,' the young girl filled the silence promptly. 'When you smile the world smiles with you. But when you weep you have to weep alone. Isn't that true?'

'It's a good quotation,' I said, now resigned to my fate.

'But it's not my statement. This is one of Amitabh Bachchan's dialogues. Do you like Amitabh?'

I thought I would surprise her. 'No, I like Hrithik Roshan.'

'Yes, he is extremely handsome,' she agreed, switching her loyalty from Amitabh to Hrithik in a matter of seconds.

'Hrithik looks handsome because there is a shade of shyness on his face. When there is no shyness on a young boy or girl's face, they look rather bland. Don't you think Akshaye also has a similar shyness?'

'Which Akshay?' All this time, I was answering her questions. Now, I found myself asking a question. I was getting drawn into a conversation without even realizing it. Conversation is like a whirlpool. You can get sucked into it unwittingly.

'Don't you know Akshaye? I mean, Akshaye Khanna, not Akshay Kumar. Akshaye Khanna is the son of Vinod Khanna by his first marriage. He has acted in *Taal* opposite Aishwarya Rai. Akshay Kumar is the one who recently got married to actress Twinkle Khanna.'

Her knowledge of the film industry was extensive.

A slight headache, which I had had since that morning, began to recur now. Was it the incessant talking? If one question from me could bring forth so much by way of an answer, then by the time we reached Hubli, I would be too exhausted to do any work. For a full hour and a half, she had been asking questions or talking nonstop. My headache bore witness to it.

Enough was enough, I thought. I decided to be frank with her and tell her that I wanted to catch up on my sleep. My head was throbbing by now and my hands went instinctively to my forehead to massage it.

'Are you not feeling well?' she asked with concern when she noticed this.

'Well, I had a headache in the morning,' I said. I didn't tell her that it had increased due to her incessant questions.

'Do you have any medicine with you?' she enquired.
'No.'

She opened her handbag and gave me a bottle of balm. 'This is a new product—Neeranjana Balm. It is extremely good for headaches. You will feel fresh and nice after using it. It is scented and also removes all body aches. It is a non-greasy ayurvedic preparation. Less expensive than branded balms but more effective. If you buy it in bulk there is a discount. This is a sample piece.'

Now it was my turn to be curious. 'Where are you working?' I asked.

'I am a salesgirl for Neeranjana Balm,' she smiled.

Yes, smiling is indeed good for one's health.

15

STOVE BURSTS OR DOWRY DEATHS?

We have a saying in Sanskrit: *Ethra naryasthu pujyanthe, ramanthethathra devatha* (God exists where women are respected). In real life, this is not true. Very few women in our country have economic independence or the freedom of choosing their husbands. Most of our women are oppressed. One of the reasons for their misery is the lack of education, which in turn leads to a lack of economic freedom. If a woman is not economically independent, then her life is quite difficult.

Once a doctor friend of mine was discussing the problem of female infanticide. Being a gynaecologist at a government hospital, she had first-hand information on this terrible subject. She asked me, 'Do you want to see the greatest misery a woman can face? Come. Let's go now and I will show you.'

She took me to the burns ward in the hospital. To negatively paraphrase the saying: 'If there is hell on earth, it is this.' The whole atmosphere was deeply depressing. Almost all the patients were female. The majority of them were in the age group of eighteen to twenty-eight years and from fairly poor backgrounds. They were all in agony, suffering from severe burns. All had the same story to tell—I wanted to cook; I lit the stove; the stove burst; the pallu of my nylon sari caught fire; this is my mistake; my husband is very good; the in-laws are like my parents.

In our country, many young married women die every day because of alleged 'stove bursts'. Why is it that nobody sues the stove manufacturer? We all know the answer. These are not stove accidents, but dowry killings. Isn't it sad that in a society where Durga is worshipped and women are called Shakthi, our sisters are burned like brinjals without any mercy? It makes me cry.

In the middle of that hellish ward was a woman who was pregnant. She was in bed number 24 and was supposed to be a 'stove burst' victim. My doctor friend told me that she might not survive. She asked me whether I wished to talk to her. I did not have the courage to face that poor girl writhing in agony. It was a difficult sight to witness. Something urged me to talk, but I did not know what to say. She sensed that I wanted to talk to her. In the middle of her pain, she took the initiative.

'Amma,' she said, 'I do not know how long I will live. But I want to tell you something. If only my parents had educated me, if I had a job, if my parents had fewer children, I would not have come to this position.' She couldn't speak any more. She screamed and flinched as the pain tormented her. Unable to witness her suffering, I came out and sat on the steps of the staircase. I was blank.

After a few minutes, I noticed an old woman crying silently in the corner. She looked tired, harassed and poor. She was all alone. I went to her and asked her what the matter was.

'I am the unfortunate mother of the patient you were

just talking to. I am praying to God that she should not survive.'

Was that mother's pain any less than her daughter's when she begged God to let her daughter die? Silent tears gave way to unabashed weeping. In the hope of calming her, I asked, 'How did the stove burst?'

'There is no stove in their house,' the woman said. 'It is all lies. We have five daughters. She is the eldest. When she was in the ninth class, we stopped her education. She was a good student, but we had no choice. I wanted someone to help me in the kitchen and look after the younger children. So, she had to leave school to take care of her little sisters though she herself was a child. After a couple of years we thought of her marriage. In our neighbourhood, girls get married early. If we do not perform the marriage early enough, what will people say? We gave her a proper dowry and a grand marriage to the best of our ability.'

How typical it all sounded! And, how predictable was what followed!

The hapless mother went on, 'They were not happy. Her husband and mother-in-law would beat her for more money. Then she would come back. We used to tell her to go back to her husband's house even though we knew that they were ill-treating her. We have unmarried daughters. If this daughter came back, what would their future be? Moreover, a girl's place after marriage is in her husband's house, isn't it?'

Who would disagree with that time-honoured principle? I asked her, 'What is your husband's job?'

She said he was a carpenter. 'He believes that we must have a male child. Only a son can make our lives better, he says.' Another light on the notions that govern the lives of many in our country.

Her sorrow seemed to abate a little, but I could see anger in her eyes. Her story continued along predictable lines. 'We thought that when she had children, things would become better. But that didn't happen. When she became pregnant, her mother-in-law came to know that it was a baby girl. Then they decided to kill my daughter. My daughter gave a dying declaration. It said that her sister-in-law had tied her hands in the middle of the night, that her useless husband had poured kerosene over her and that her mother-in-law had lit the match. My doll-like daughter burnt like camphor in no time.'

Inconsolable grief burst forth from that helpless mother, tears flowing like a river. I didn't know what to say. I just mumbled, 'Do not worry. The law will take its course and they will be punished.'

But it turned out that that possibility also had been taken care of. The husband had threatened that if she told the truth, he would harm her sisters and ruin all their hopes of marriage. So she had taken back her dying declaration. Thus the culprits were safe and one more girl was sacrificed on the altar of society's greed. I could now understand the poor girl's words. If she had been educated, she could have taken up a job and left her husband. If her parents had fewer children, then they could have kept and cared for her. Her parents were more worried about how people talked about them than the fate that awaited their daughter.

The case of this pregnant girl would end like any other 'stove burst' story. Her husband would go free. He would marry again. And similar incidents would be repeated. The problem continues because there is no immediate punishment of the offenders. Even when cases are registered, they drag on in courts for years. The greed for material things is growing, so people go for easy dowry money.

Ethra naryasthu pujyanthe, ramanthe . . . Those words came back to me. Without my knowing it, tears welled up in my eyes.

The duty sister came and announced expressionlessly, 'Patient in bed number 24 is dead.'

16

IDEALISTS AT TWENTY, REALISTS AT FORTY

Recently we had a get-together of old friends. We are a group of women who have known each other since the time we were little girls. We began meeting before we were married. We kept up the practice after our marriages and after becoming mothers, and now we meet at our children's weddings. Age, of course, shows its marks on us, but we go on meeting once in a while to exchange notes. Sometimes one of us joins the get-together after a gap of several years, but we quickly take up the thread and connect.

So much has changed in the last twenty-five years. Many of these changes would have been very difficult to imagine before they happened. We had many dreams and very few of them have been realized. My friend Vimla, for example, was a very beautiful girl when we were in college. Everyone used to mistake her for a film star. She was aware of her beauty and quite vain. When we met after twenty-five years, I could not believe that the woman in front of me was Vimla. Where had her long, jet-black hair gone? Where was that perfect complexion? She looked like a barrel with wrinkles all over. Her hair was grey, thin, and cut short. She talked philosophically. Beauty is impermanent. When you are young, you think your beauty will last forever. But beauty is not like intelligence, she said. Intelligent people remain intelligent forever.

My friend Vinutha proved this theory of Vimla's wrong. Vinutha was a very bright girl in our college. She was easily one of the best students. She used to be called a mini-computer. She was gifted in every aspect—she was good-looking, talented and, more importantly, very simple. There were no airs about her. We all used to wonder whom Vinutha would marry. She was so good that it would be difficult to find an equally good match. Vinutha did find a good boy while she was in college. He was very bright. We all felt that Vinutha and Partha would always remain happy and proud of each other's intelligence. How wrong we were!

When I met Vinutha after many years, she looked dull. She had lost her zest for life. When she was in college, she was so full of energy. Be it a college day or cooking competition or math quiz, she would be more involved than anyone else. But now her spirit was dampened by her ever-taunting husband.

'Did you get a rank?' he would needle her. Often he would ask, 'Can you not understand such a simple thing?' Or he would challenge, 'Let us see how much time you take to solve this problem and how much time I take?'

Vinutha began to feel that it was a curse to be so bright. Our society is strange. The woman always enjoys her husband's glory and fame, but the reverse is seldom true. Rarely do men appreciate their wives' talents.

Ratna, on the other hand, was a very ordinary girl in

every sense of the word. The unremarkable sort of person whom people seldom remember. She graduated, married and settled down like most of our middle-class or lower-middle-class people do. Ratna's husband, Raghu, was a clerk and a very timid person.

One year, when Ratna came for our get-together, we were all astounded. She had become so different. She was a leading businesswoman now and had received many awards. She was very fashionable too. So remarkable was the transformation that we just stared at her for a while. Vimla asked Ratna to tell us her story.

'It's the typical rags-to-riches story all right,' said Ratna. 'After marriage, I realized that my husband was an excellent assistant rather than a leader. He always listened to somebody. In the family, my mother-in-law was the boss.'

Psychiatrists say that if parents are very domineering then the child will either become very rebellious and difficult to control or else become timid and docile. Maybe Ratna's Raghu belonged to the latter category.

Ratna continued: 'I realized that I had to make my own decisions, otherwise I would remain forever a slave to my mother-in-law. I decided that I must become economically independent. I was not very talented or skilled, as you know. My academic record was average. With this background, it was difficult to get a job. The one thing I knew was stitching garments. So, I started stitching at home. Initially, I worked with cloth and later with leather. I soon understood the business very well and expanded my work to suit the tastes of my customers.'

'When did you shift to condiments?' we asked.

'Once I was successful with garments, I diversified to home products. Nothing succeeds like success. I always consider the customer as a god. Work for the customer's satisfaction, not for your satisfaction—that principle pays. Life is a great teacher. I learnt everything by experience. By learning something from each of my mistakes, I learnt not to repeat them.'

We were both surprised and delighted at Ratna's courage and the turnaround in her life. We had all thought that Vinutha would be very successful and Ratna would be mediocre. But things turned out totally different. At twenty we were idealists, at forty we had become realists.

17

What is A Red-letter Day? A Holiday

The fifteenth of August is a red-letter day for all of us. That day in 1947 we earned our freedom from long foreign rule, after many people had sacrificed their lives for it. Even children, women and old people had participated in that struggle at great cost to themselves. However, most of them are not remembered today. Their statues are not erected and no poems are written about their sacrifices. They are unsung heroes. They died so that we could live in a free India.

To mark this as a memorable day, our government has declared Independence Day as an important national holiday. On 15 August, we are to remember our martyrs and celebrate our freedom. Normally, lectures and seminars about our independence struggle are arranged in schools and government offices. There are flag hoisting ceremonies at which patriotic songs are sung. Children enjoy and remember this special day.

One Independence Day, I was on one of my week-long tours in a rural area in Karnataka. That year, 15 August fell on a Friday. I thought I would visit some schools and participate in their celebrations. As I was staying in a town, I had to go to the bus stand to travel to a village school seven kilometres away.

At the bus stand, I met the headmaster of one of the schools I wanted to visit. He was very happy to see me and greeted me warmly. He had one of those faces that reflect feelings—a rather rare phenomenon. There are people whose feelings you cannot gauge by looking at their faces. In such cases, it seems like there is no connection between their hearts and their brains. You cannot make out what such people are thinking. This is common in big cities. In smaller places, people are usually more open.

The headmaster seemed to be in a hurry. 'Madam, are you going to Bangalore?' he asked eagerly. Then he followed up his question with an explanation. 'If you are not working on Saturday, this is going to be a long weekend. So, I thought that instead of staying here, you may be going back to Bangalore.'

'No, I am not going to Bangalore,' I said. 'I have a week's work in this area. It is a waste of time to go and come back.'

There was a trace of disappointment on his face and I was curious to know the reason. He explained, 'Oh, I thought I could travel with you. I am leaving for Bangalore.'

Suddenly, I remembered that it was 15 August.

'Wait a minute,' I said, 'today is 15 August. Aren't you celebrating Independence Day in your school? This must be a great event for teachers and students, with flag hoisting, parades and patriotic songs.'

He did not look enthusiastic at all. 'No. This is a ritual every year and a sheer waste of time. The same drill and the same patriotic songs. In my twenty years of service and ten transfers, I have grown bored with these national holidays. We cannot close the school either. As per instructions from the higher education department, we have to conduct all these activities. I wish they would make it a complete holiday like Diwali or Christmas.'

I realized that he was unhappy. So I asked him, 'Why are you going to Bangalore?'

'I want to go and stay there for two days and find out who is concerned with my transfer to the district headquarters. My daughter wants to study computer science. Don't you think it is a good idea to study computer science and get a job? If a girl is a graduate in computer science, then getting a groom will be easy.'

Perhaps he was more of a father than a headmaster. What he was talking about did not really register with me because I was still thinking about Independence Day. 'Who will conduct today's functions in your school?' I asked.

He looked at me with pity. 'What is there in a function? I have told my assistant master to conduct this ritual. I prepared speeches for this day twenty years ago. Nothing has changed. So he can read the same speech. I have not even gone to the school. The students are not interested in the speeches or in these celebrations. There is a new film in the tent near our village. They would like to go there. Nobody is bothered about Independence Day.'

I was immersed in my thoughts. Then the bus came. There was a rush and the headmaster ran to get a seat. He waved to me and got in. The bus left in a cloud of dust.

I returned to Bangalore the following week. I went to a friend's house for dinner. She is also a teacher, so we have many things in common. Both of us are so immersed in work that we hardly meet, even though we live in the same city. We have found that the best way to meet once in a while is to have dinner together.

I asked her, 'How did you and your school celebrate 15 August?'

She looked sad. 'It was horrible. We teachers went to the school early in the morning for the flag hoisting. We had invited a senior government official to be the chief guest. Poor chap! He had prepared a long speech and come on time. But . . .' she stopped.

The memory of my meeting with the headmaster of the village school a week earlier was still fresh in my mind. 'Was there any problem with the headmistress? Did she come?' I asked.

'Yes, our headmistress is a nice person. She was on time although she was suffering from high fever. It was our students who didn't come. Though our school has more than a thousand students, only about fifty of them turned up that day.'

'Why?'

'It happened to be a long weekend. Parents took their children away on holiday. Many students who stayed in Bangalore were seen at the theatres. Apparently, there was heavy rush at video shops as well that day. It was a bad show in front of our chief guest.'

'Wasn't attendance mandatory?'

'Yes, we sent notices stating that children must be

brought to school that day. But what is the use? They will just produce false medical certificates. At times, I feel we should just not have a holiday on 15 August or 26 January. We should have regular school and one or two periods can be used for the function. Today, it has become a holiday only to make merry, not a day to remember the saga of our leaders. What do you think?'

I didn't know what to say.

18

Once Upon A Time, Life was Simple

I was born and brought up in a village in northern Karnataka. Things were very simple in those days. If you didn't like a person, you could just tell him to his face why you were upset with him. If somebody helped you, you could show your gratitude without any reservation. If somebody did wrong, we asked for justice. There was no hide-and-seek when it came to feelings. Maybe it was not civilized or polished behaviour, but it was definitely a straightforward society and a simple life.

I do not know how societies in villages function today. In my childhood, village societies functioned smoothly and fairly. I still remember vividly the day our cow was lost. We came to know that it was tied up in Gopal's cowshed. Immediately, he was called by the elders of the panchayat. Gopal owned a piece of land where he used to grow vegetables. Selling them on market day was his only source of income. Our cow had run away and gone into Gopal's garden where it had eaten up all the fresh vegetables. Naturally, Gopal was very upset and had tied up the cow. We felt genuinely sorry and offered to compensate Gopal's loss. He agreed immediately and released the cow. No legal code was referred to and no lawyer was called. The panchayat made the decision, calculated the loss and solved the problem amicably. There were no ill feelings between the parties concerned.

I remember another incident. In our neighbour's family, a girl was having problems with her mother-in-law. Mothers-in-law harassing daughters-in-law is an age-old problem in all communities, irrespective of language or culture. An old Chinese proverb says: 'Is it ever possible for a mouse and a cat to be friends?' There are, of course, exceptions, but these only prove the general rule.

The young daughter-in-law from our neighbour's house used to come to the village pond to fetch water. She was hardly twenty years old, delicate and sensitive. At the pond, she would usually be alone and she would sit on the steps and cry. Evidently, she was going through a rough time at home.

My old grandmother saw the girl crying. She understood the problem. Immediately, she went to the neighbour's house, called the mother-in-law outside and told her, 'Don't be harsh to your daughter-in-law. Please remember that your daughter is also a daughter-in-law in another house. I have seen you as a young bride. There is always a court above and you have to answer for all your deeds.'

My grandmother never felt that it was none of her business to get involved in somebody else's family matter. For her, injustice to a lonely young girl was more than a 'personal matter'. After some time, our neighbour mended her ways. More importantly, she never held a grudge against my grandmother. She knew, as people of that generation always did, that it was important to listen to one's elders. A sense of fairness and respect for elders were fundamental values in those times. Common sense reigned. Rules and legalities were secondary to plain and simple common sense.

My father passed away recently. There was a cooking gas connection in his name. I thought it would be illegal to keep the connection after his death, so I submitted an application for transferring the connection to my name, along with his death certificate and my ration card. One day, I was called to the gas agency.

'Your application is incomplete,' the manager told me. 'Though your father has left a will stating that you should inherit his gas connection, there is no legal document on paper in which your brothers and sisters tell us that they will not claim this gas. In the absence of that document, it is illegal to transfer the connection to your name.'

I told him that my sister and brother were American citizens living abroad, and that they were not interested in this gas connection. But he was an official with an official mind. Common sense was of no value to him. Rules alone mattered.

He said, 'You should get a notary certificate from America regarding this connection.'

I was taken aback by the sudden complication in what I had thought would be a simple procedure in light of my father's will.

When I mentioned this, the manager turned even more uncooperative. 'Madam, nobody is above the law. So what if they are American citizens? They must follow the rules. I don't want to get into any problems for this later.'

It is difficult to get notary authorization in America for such a small thing. You have to take half a day's leave for this kind of work. Of course, the manager didn't accept any of my arguments. I left the gas office dejected. After a month, when I wanted to refill the gas, the manager stuck to his rule book. 'Your father is no more. You cannot take a cylinder in his name.'

It struck me that if I had not informed him about my father's death, things would have been simpler. Many of us try to do what is lawful and proper, only to realize that our system is not made for such behaviour.

There is a woman working as a sweeper on my road whom I have known for a long time. The other day I saw her crying. I felt bad for her. The reason for her unhappiness was her husband, who often got drunk and beat her. I could not resist the urge to go and advise her husband. Perhaps the influence of my grandmother was working on me. My neighbours saw her crying too but did not bother about it or care to talk to her husband. Maybe they were wiser. For when I talked to her husband, he turned around and said, 'Madam, it is none of your business to interfere in our personal life. This is a matter between a husband and wife. If I cause any problems, then my wife can go to a lawyer. She need not come to you.'

I did not know how to respond. When he talked about law, I wondered what law meant to us. Laws are made to create a strong society that will protect the common people. But when laws become difficult to follow, their very purpose is lost. When they are interpreted narrowly by over-zealous officials, their purpose is lost too.

What can ordinary people do about this? We have to deal with a range of ordinary problems, from gas connections to drunken husbands. Can some learned lawyers suggest solutions to these day-to-day problems?

19

Powerful Politicians and Unsung Donors

Honours are quite often bestowed upon people in power. Whether they deserve the honour or not is immaterial. What matters is the power they wield. Those who bestow the honour have some expectations from those honoured. Sometimes, I feel that there should be no honours at all because beneath every shawl and garland there is an application.

The Infosys Foundation built an annexe to an existing government hospital in one of the states where we work. The hospital was in a small town and our Foundation had no interest there other than helping the poor. It was a very backward area. The inaugural function was held on the hospital premises. The chief guest was the health minister of the state. I had requested the function coordinator to arrange it in the morning because if things got delayed, I would still be able to drive back safely. I do not like the idea of travelling alone by road at night. But the coordinator could not oblige. A morning function was not convenient for the chief guest, so the inauguration was fixed for seven in the evening.

The dais was arranged with quite a number of chairs. There were a dozen or more garlands of jasmine, sandalwood and marigold, varieties of shawls and baskets full of colourful fruit kept on the dais for distribution. There was also a silk sari in a box, probably an expensive one. They clearly had spent a great deal of money on all these things.

In the kind of welfare work I am engaged in, we don't expect much from the beneficiaries. When they say a few good words about our work, we feel a sense of satisfaction. Often these words are the inspiration for our next job. It also means that the beneficiaries appreciate our donation. I sat there thinking about how grateful the people were, how they were honouring us because we built a hospital for them and how graceful their culture was.

The breeze was cool and the crowd kept getting bigger. The minister arrived an hour late and the people rushed to touch his feet. Some people came running with applications. Soon it was like a mini-durbar.

The function finally started. I was given a corner seat on the dais. There were plenty of speeches describing how efficient the minister was, how great his leadership was and how fond he was of his fellow men. Under his able leadership, a new hospital building had been added by a donor. In all those speeches, there was not a single mention of the donor's identity or even the hospital. It was all about the minister and the government.

The minister then rose to inaugurate the building. He said he had great faith in democracy and that he cared for his people immensely. He wanted this annexe to the hospital because he was concerned about the people's health. He said that he was still not happy because the hospital required more facilities. Then he turned to look at me and said, 'Madam, we expect fans, beds, cupboards, linen, drinking water facility and so on for the entire hospital. I am sure you people will be able to provide these. I assure you that our people will make the best use of these.'

I did not answer.

Then came the most important part of the ceremony, that of honouring the people who had helped to build the hospital. It was followed by the national anthem. Then the function was over. The minister rushed back to his car and everyone ran behind him. Soon the whole area was deserted. Crushed flowers were strewn around the dais. Except for the pandal area, it was pitch-dark outside. I stood there with a faded garland and my handbag. I was all alone, like a goalpost after the match.

In front of me was the illuminated new building erected by our Foundation. I was by no means the only one who had put in hard work. There were architects, artisans, trustees and several others. None of their names had been mentioned. There was no time for them or for our Foundation. I was clearly an unwanted guest and had been called only for formality's sake.

I was feeling quite depressed about the whole evening. I wondered why they did not even have the simple courtesy of caring for a lady, especially one who had come from far away and represented a charitable organization. Look at these people, I said to myself. This health minister had in no way contributed time, money or resources for building this annexe. He was not even aware that it was being built. But he saw to it that he was honoured and praised like a hero. He was garlanded the most. Was it just politics or was it moral corruption?

I reminded myself that the ultimate aim of our work was not to please ministers, politicians, rich people or people in power. Every effort of ours was aimed at improving the lot of suffering people. Not the minister, but the poor people were the ones who mattered.

My depression did not last long. An old lady in tattered clothes came up to me and said, 'Amma, someone told me that your company has built this building. We are very grateful to you. Many people like us never get admission in the main hospital because of lack of space. But you have given us a common space, with no special wards. Special rooms will always be used by people with connections. For people like us, common halls are better.'

Then she took a step closer to me and said, 'I don't have anything to give you. I am just a flower vendor. I cannot afford a shawl or a sari. But I can give you this string of jasmine flowers with love and affection. I pray to God that many people like you should be born in our country.'

That string of jasmine was more precious than all the shawls and fruit baskets.

Leprosy. Just the word scares most people. There is an international convention that discourages the use of the word 'leper' because of its terrible connotations. The moment we think of a person afflicted with leprosy we think of a beggar or a person who has lost some fingers or toes. People suffering from leprosy are often ostracized by society. There are many myths regarding this dreaded disease—that it is contagious, that it is hereditary, and so on. These are just myths. In fact, not all cases of leprosy are contagious. If proper treatment is taken at an early stage, leprosy can be cured completely, leaving behind none of the telltale physical disfigurement that sometimes accompanies the disease. Normally, the treatment period is long. It requires a lot of patience and family support. Due to ignorance, however, people neglect early symptoms. Detection in the initial stages often does not take place, though the media carries advertisements about how to recognize the symptoms. Most people just don't bother. We always think that leprosy is a problem that affects other people, not us. We forget that disease knows no social hierarchy; it does not distinguish between rich or poor, man or woman. And leprosy is a disease that has been with mankind for many centuries.

One of the programmes of the organization with which I am associated is to help people suffering from leprosy. There are different theories in this field. Some people think that the patients should stay with their families, while others believe they should be kept in an isolated colony. I was working in a remote area where there was a separate colony for leprosy patients. It was a hot summer and temperatures were difficult to bear. The scene at the colony was depressing. Most of the inmates were clearly disgusted with the disease and their sufferings. They were all poor and helpless. They required psychological as well as material help. Even soothing words like, 'Don't worry, we're here with you,' were important to them.

Our project's aim was not to show pity or to hand out money. We planned to rehabilitate the patients economically. If they could handle even some limited work and earn their own livelihood, then we were ready to finance them. We figured it was the best way to make them feel confident. For when a person feels confident, he can face society. Acceptance by society and a reasonable measure of economic independence can change the lives of these people.

There were many huts in the colony, with a family staying in each hut. In every family, at least one person was afflicted by the disease. The weather was harsh but I had to do my duty and go from hut to hut. The women kept telling me their difficulties. Perhaps the most frustrating of these was their inability to get jobs even as housemaids because of the disease. Some of them had resigned themselves to their fate. Youngsters were sleeping even though it was only mid-morning. Children were playing in the dirt. The older people were in a pathetic state. When the infirmities of age are added to the ravages of a disease like leprosy and the consequent social ostracism, people can be driven to suicide.

There was a small hut with a thatched roof, clay walls and the bare semblance of a bamboo door. A woman lived there, the oldest in the colony. Her name was Veeramma. I called out to her and asked her to come out. She did not. I thought she might be partially deaf and that it would be better if I went in to talk to her. I knocked carefully at what passed for a door, lest it fall down. She still did not respond or come out. I pushed the door open and went in.

There was hardly anything in the hut. Holes in the roof let in some air and light. There were two or three earthen pots and one earthen plate. Three stones made up a stove. There was a torn mat, two or three onions on the ground and a pot of water. I still could not see Veeramma inside the hut, but I could hear the sound of breathing. As I had entered the hut from the bright sunlight outside, it took my eyes a while to adjust to the darkness inside.

I called out to her softly once more, 'Veeramma, I want to talk to you. Where are you?'

Then she answered, 'Amma, I am here. But don't come near me.'

Now I could see the frail form of a woman in the corner of the room, all her hairy grey skin shrunk, no flesh on the body. She was just a skeleton covered with skin. She was sitting in a corner holding her hands against her chest, her legs also drawn towards her chest.

'Amma,' she mumbled, 'I know you called me several times, but I could not come out to talk to you. I am a woman. Irrespective of my age, how can I come out in front of other people without any clothes?'

It was then that I realized that she was almost naked.

I have seen poverty-stricken areas in the course of my work and I have met a lot of poor people, but nowhere had I seen a woman like this. This was a picture of dehumanizing poverty in our own country after fifty years of independence. An old woman could not even cover her body. Still she had no complaints about anything. I felt guilty wearing a six-yard sari.

For a minute, I felt too ashamed to talk. The shock of what I saw made me forget our policy of simply not handing out money and material. This was a situation that cried out for immediate remedy. I sent my driver to get 100 saris to be given to all the women in that colony. Whether they are rehabilitated or not, the minimum need of covering a woman's body could not wait. A gesture like this may not change a great deal in their lives. But the sight of abject misery often prods us into action, even if it is just an impulse. Those of us who have a generous share of God's blessings must do what we can to help the poorest of the poor who are wretched through no fault of theirs.

India does not always mean technology, fashion, films or beauty contests. The real India is in the dark, neglected interiors of our country. Helpless and miserably poor people live beyond the reach of any government departments. To serve our country means to serve such people.

After that visit to the colony of leprosy patients, I make it a point to carry at least ten saris with me whenever I go on my rounds.

SALAAM NAMASTE

I used to buy books for the Bangalore slum schools we supported from Sheikh Mohammed's tiny shop. He had a shop selling stationery near our office and we would buy the books in bulk from him. We would pick up the books from the shop and let him know when the cheque was ready. He would then come to the office and collect it.

Once, when he came to the office to get his cheque, we were celebrating something and sweets were being handed out to everyone. Sheikh was offered some as well. He took a couple and put them away carefully in his pocket. Seeing him do that, I asked, 'What's the matter, Sheikh? Why aren't you eating the sweets? Are you a diabetic?'

Sheikh was a shy, taciturn man and I knew little about him and his family, so I was pleasantly surprised to hear his explanation: 'No, madam. I'm going to take them home and give them to the kids. They love these sweets.'

'How many children do you have?' I had noticed he had picked up only a couple of pieces.

'I have one daughter, but my niece also stays with us, so there are two children in the house.'

'Why does your niece stay with you?'

'She is my sister Zubeida's daughter. She is a widow

and both stay with us.'

I realized it must be tough for Sheikh to manage a fairly large household with only the income from his little shop. So I asked, 'Does Zubeida work?'

'Yes, she is a very good tailor. She and my wife do tailoring at home. With their income and the money I earn from the shop we get by quite well. We are contented.'

I was touched by his story. 'Contented' is a word rarely heard these days. A few months passed and one day I suddenly got a call from Sheikh. He wanted me to give him his cheque a few days earlier than usual. 'Why, Sheikh? Is anything the matter?' I asked.

'Yes, madam. We discovered some time back that Zubeida is suffering from cancer. The operation is tomorrow and we need the money desperately.'

I instructed the cheque be sent to him immediately, but I also realized that it would probably not be enough. Such operations are expensive and I was sure he was struggling to raise the money. Yet he had asked me only for what was due to him and nothing more.

I have learnt many lessons in life ever since we started helping people monetarily through the Infosys Foundation. I have seen women hiding their diamond studs in their purses and asking for funds for the poor. I have seen well-off parents declaring their children orphans and applying for scholarships. I even know some men who presented their parents as destitutes so they could get help from us.

I called up Sheikh. 'Sheikh, tell me, have you managed to get all the money you need for the operation?'

'I have sold all of Zubeida's and my wife's jewellery. I

have also taken a loan from the bank.'

'Sheikh, why didn't you ask us?'

'Madam, at least I can afford this much. You should be helping those who are poorer and cannot even afford this. They require your help more than I do.'

I was touched. I asked him to get the papers and meet me as quickly as he could. He came the next morning and showed me all the documents. I took a look and handed him a cheque for fifty thousand rupees.

Surprised and hesitant, he said, 'This is a lot of money. I never expected such help to come from the blue. May you be blessed forever.'

A few days passed and Sheikh sent a message saying the operation had gone well. For a long time after that we did not hear anything from him. Then one day as I walked into the office I found him sitting in the reception, a little girl of about four by his side. She was wearing an ordinary cotton dress decorated with laces and buttons. Her hair, neatly oiled, was pulled up into a ponytail.

'How are you, Sheikh?' I asked him. 'How is Zubeida?'

Sheikh's face was lined with grief. 'Zubeida passed away a fortnight back. In spite of all our efforts and your help she did not survive. It was Allah's wish. I wanted you to meet her daughter Tabassum.'

I looked at Tabassum. She was scared and ill at ease in this strange office where people bustled about busily. Just to make her feel comfortable, I offered her some biscuits. She took one and then asked me in a shy voice, 'Can I take another one? For Ameena?'

Ameena was her cousin. I smiled and said, 'Of course.'

I looked sadly at the girl, orphaned so young. Then her uncle said, '*Beti, Ammi ne bola than na? Inko salaam karo.*' Putting down the biscuits, the little girl said in a clear voice, 'Madam, *Ammi ka salaam.*'

I was at a loss for words. Sheikh wiped his tears and pulled out an envelope from his bag. He handed it to me saying, 'This is yours. I am sorry, I am a bit late with this.'

I opened it. There were three thousand rupees in it. I looked at Sheikh in confusion. 'Out of the fifty thousand you gave us, we used only forty-seven thousand for Zubeida's treatment. When we came home and she knew she was dying, Zubeida made me promise that I would return the remaining money to you. "Don't waste this on me," she said. "Tell madam to give it to some other sick person." She had wanted so much to meet you and give you her salaam, but Allah took her away. I promised her I would carry out this last wish.'

I sat there in stunned silence. I had never met Zubeida, but the largeness of her heart even on her deathbed left me speechless. In spite of her own pain and poverty, she had thought about someone who might be in greater need of help. Her story was a lesson in compassion. She wanted to thank me, and when she knew she would not make it, she sent her daughter. Through the act of sending Tabassum she was perhaps passing on her positive attitude to the child. I was sure Tabassum would grow up to be a fine human being. I looked at the envelope. 'This is for Tabassum. May Allah be kind to her. Let her study well. If you need any more help for her, let me know. And always tell her about her mother. Our earth is enriched by people like Zubeida.'

Tabassum sat quietly, her big eyes puzzled. One day she would understand and perhaps emulate her mother's courage.

22

A WEDDING TO REMEMBER

As a trustee of the Infosys Foundation, I get stacks of letters. We help people financially for various reasons. Naturally, both needy and not-so-needy people write to us. The most difficult aspect of this job is to tell the difference between both kinds of people.

One typical Monday morning, letters poured in. I was going through the letters. My secretary told me, 'Ma'am, there is a wedding invitation card with a personal note attached to it. Will you be attending?'

As a teacher in a college, I get many wedding invitations from my students, so I assumed the card was from one of my students. But when I read the card, I was unable to remember either of the persons getting married. I wondered who could have sent me an invitation with a hand-written note stating, 'Madam, if you do not attend our marriage, we will consider it unfortunate.'

I was still not able to place the girl's or the boy's name, but I decided to attend the wedding out of curiosity. It was the rainy season and the venue was at the other end of the city. I wondered if attending some unknown person's wedding was worth the trouble.

It was a typical middle-class wedding with a stage decorated profusely with flowers. Film music, which nobody was listening to, was blaring over the speakers. Because of the rain, the numerous children in attendance were not able to play outside and were playing hide-and-seek in the hall. Women were wearing Bangalore silk saris and Mysore crepes.

I looked at the couple standing on the dais. I still was unable to remember either of them. I thought that perhaps one or both of them might have been my students. Standing in the middle of the crowd, without knowing anybody, I didn't know what to do.

Just then, an elderly man approached me and asked politely, 'Would you like to meet the couple and greet them?'

I followed him to the dais, introduced myself and wished the couple a happy married life. They seemed very happy. The groom asked the elderly man to look after me. Still the question nagged me: who were these people and why had they sent a note to me?

The man took me to the dining hall and brought me something to eat. Enough is enough, I thought to myself. I can't eat without knowing who these people are.

Sensing my doubts, the elderly gentleman smiled and said, 'Madam, I am the groom's father. My son fell in love with Malati, the bride, and we arranged the wedding. After the engagement, Malati developed leucoderma. My son backed out of the marriage. We all felt very sad. I asked him what he would have done if Malati had got leucoderma after marriage, but he would not listen. Her family was worried about her future. There was so much unpleasantness. To escape from the tension at home, my son began to go to the library often. After about a month, he came back and told me that he was ready to marry Malati. We were all pleasantly surprised and were truly happy. Today is the marriage.'

I still did not have an answer to my question. How on earth was I involved in this? The groom's father provided the answer.

'Madam, later we came to know that he read your novel, *Mahashweta*,' he said. 'The situation of my son was similar. It seems he read this novel at least ten times and understood the plight of the girl. He took a month and decided he did not want to be like the man in your novel, who shed his responsibilities only to regret it later. Your novel changed his thinking.'

Now I could put the pieces together! Then the groom's father brought a packet and insisted that I accept the gift. When I hesitated, he pressed it into my hands and said, 'Malati has purchased this sari for you. She will talk to you later.'

The rain grew heavier and water splashed into the hall. Raindrops were falling on my face; my silk sari was getting wet. But nothing mattered. I felt so happy. Never in my wildest dreams had I thought that an ordinary person like myself would change somebody's life. Whenever I wear that sari, I think of the happy face of Malati and the cover page of *Mahashweta*. It's the most precious sari I own.

23

INSENSITIVITY INDEX

February is usually a season of house-warming functions, thread ceremonies and quick weddings, particularly for software engineers who come back from the USA on short visits. It is also the time for students to prepare for their examinations.

My friend Suma had purchased a house and was keen that her close friends attend the house-warming ceremony. For us, it was an occasion to get together after a long time. The traditional ceremony was going on when I reached her house at an early hour. The other friends had not yet come. I found a place to sit and watch the puja while waiting for my friends. Though the house was quite a big one, the puja was being performed in a small hall and just two carpets had been spread for the guests to sit on. Suma was busy doing the puja. She was wearing a beautiful silk sari and the flowers in her hair added to her grace. As usual, the majority of the guests had nothing to do and were thus engrossed in chatting about a variety of topics—the problems of teenagers, the Prime Minister, gossip about Madhuri Dixit, Miss India, the best beauty parlours, the latest fashion jewellery . . . the list was endless. However, it was the subject of in-laws that received the maximum attention and active participation from many.

Though I was listening to the conversation, there was an altogether different thought at the back of my mind. It had been hardly a week since the Gujarat earthquake and almost all the TV channels had been telecasting the latest information. Although I did not know the victims personally, just the thought of their plight sent a shiver through my body and tears welled up in my eyes. All this was on my mind constantly.

Though I was not taking part in the conversation, I could not help but hear what some of the guests were saying.

'Look at Suma, lucky person. She got such a beautiful house at a good price.' There was a tinge of envy in the woman's tone.

'How much did she pay?'

'Hardly fifty lakhs. It was a distress sale. I know the man who owned the house.'

'Why was there a distress sale?'

'He owned a factory and the recession hit his business badly. So he had to close the factory and sell the house.'

'This house is so beautiful—all marble flooring and attached bathrooms with fitted tubs. It's a steal for this price.'

'By the way, how are the preparations for your daughter's wedding getting along?'

'I thought it is better to go to Kanchipuram and buy all the saris there. It works out cheaper and the choice of colour combinations is better.'

'What about silverware?'

'That is no problem. I know a person in Chickpet. He

is our silversmith. I've told him to make one hundred silver *kumkum bharanis* and one hundred small silver bowls. The *bharanis* will be given to distant relatives and the bowls to the closer people.'

'Have you thought of the catering?'

'Am I a fool not to think about catering? I have discussed with my children and husband in detail. We have decided to have pani puri, bhel and chat stalls on one side and south Indian snacks on the other side. Cool drinks and sweets are also included. We all love Gujarati sweets, but our cook has gone to Gujarat. He has lost his family. I wouldn't want him to come to the wedding because it is inauspicious.'

'By the way, how much did you contribute to the earthquake relief fund?'

'They were collecting money in my office. But I told them that I had given money elsewhere and did not participate. Our country is always facing one problem or another. There is no end to the problems. So why pay? Anyway, I don't have any relatives in that area.'

I wondered what our so-called upper-middle-class people were doing for Gujarat. Is it not a part of our country? I do agree that life is larger than death. One cannot go on mourning forever. But is our life full of only silver *kumkum bharanis*, Kanchipuram saris and wedding menus? Our children learn from watching us. If we all behave in this way, our next generation will also have the same insensitive minds.

I remembered the story of a young prince with a beautiful wife and child. When he saw a sick person, an old person and a dead body, he renounced the world, became an ascetic and preached in our land. What would his social sensitivity index have been? How much have we learnt from him?

24

To Sir with Love

Asha and I were shopping on MG Road when we saw an old man walking slowly towards us. He might have been around sixty, with silver-grey hair and a few wrinkles on his face, but he still looked fit. He looked at Asha and smiled. She did not show any sign of recognition. The man stood in front of us for a second and then walked away.

After he left, I asked her, 'Asha, don't you think that man knows you? He smiled at you. Do you remember him?'

'Of course I know him. He was my maths teacher in school. He taught us very badly and ruined my interest in maths. He was a terror, unapproachable and stern. He hardly taught us.' There was anger and frustration in Asha's voice. She might have exaggerated.

It is true that school teachers, more than college teachers, build your fundamentals. It is easy to teach at graduate and postgraduate levels, but difficult to do so at the school level. Teachers—good ones at least—must have an enormous amount of love for their students. Knowledge is not the only criterion to judge a teacher.

I thought of my own maths teacher. I wondered how I would have reacted had he met me on the road. What would he have done and how would he have greeted me? He probably would have said, 'Why are you wasting your time on MG Road? Go back to office or work at home. Don't teach without preparation.'

Without a second thought, I would have said, 'Yes sir.' Then, hesitantly, I would have asked, 'Where are you staying? Can I come and see you some time later?'

He would have patted me on my shoulder with the same affection and concern that he showed me as a student and both of us would have laughed.

My teacher, Raghavendra Varnekar, was an extraordinary man in every sense of the word. He was from my home town, Hubli. He lived a very humble life and did not receive any recognition or awards. He excelled in his profession even though he was not a graduate. He taught mathematics so well that we never felt it was a difficult subject.

He would refer to mathematics as the 'queen of science'. 'Let us go and meet the queen,' he would say as he led us into the wonderland of mathematics. There were numerous riders in geometry, hundreds of problems in algebra. He would teach them enthusiastically and say, 'I am here for students who believe they are not good in maths. Good and bad are concepts of the mind. If you are hard-working and honestly want to understand the subject, then you can have an audience with the queen.' He attracted students to his class the way a snake charmer attracts snakes with his music.

In his last days, he was unwell and I went to meet him with a small gift. In spite of his financial difficulties, he did not accept it. He told me, 'The duty of a teacher is to make a student confident to face life. Life poses unknown examinations. The greatest joy to a teacher is to produce students better than him. I have done my duty very well. My students are so famous today that it gives me great joy and pride to be recognized as their teacher.'

I was surprised to hear this simple philosophy, which is very difficult to practise. Had he been in a bigger city and working in a bigger school, he would have made money by taking tuitions or by starting a school himself. He did not do that. He believed in his principle and his life was an example of it. He reminds me of a burning candle—giving light to everybody while burning itself out.

Today, when I stand on a dais and speak confidently or face any kind of difficulty in life, I think of my teacher. He taught me this lesson, which no amount of money can buy, no difficulties can dilute and no university can grant.

25

Pay or I'll Commit Suicide

At the Infosys Foundation we get approximately 10,000 letters annually. It is a Herculean task for my secretaries to sort them, read them and send replies. Some letters are eye-openers and some are funny and crazy. One day I received a letter that seemed like an SOS. It was a five-page letter from a woman. The first two pages described the vagaries of the stock market. She explained how she had lost her money by choosing the wrong stocks. The actual message was in the last few sentences. She asked me to pay all the loans she had incurred due to her foolishness. 'It is not a big amount. It is a mere five crores,' she concluded. I didn't know who this woman was and marvelled at her audacity in writing a letter like this. I didn't reply.

The very next week there was another letter from her, again five pages long, but this time describing her domestic difficulties and how important it was for me to help her. She also wrote that she would commit suicide if I did not send her the money, and that she would hold me responsible. What could I reply to such a letter? I didn't write back. After two weeks, a third letter came, saying that I had a heart of stone, that I didn't have any love and sympathy for fellow human beings. She wondered how a person like me could be involved in philanthropic work.

Such letters hurt me at times. I really cannot understand this kind of philosophy. If you fail to give money when asked, you are immediately treated with hostility. Relatives often behave in the same way. They comment, 'What is the use of relatives when you do not give money to your own people? How can you help others?'

Help is a word whose real meaning very few people understand. It is essential that we help our people and our country, but giving money to a well-to-do person should not be considered help. Giving money to buy a second house, expensive jewellery or for a holiday abroad is not help. If somebody loses money on the stock market in his greed to become rich quickly, then why should anyone feel obliged to help him?

If somebody honours me with a shawl, there is usually an application that comes with it. If a person praises me, most of the time there is a request at the end. I have decided to help only people who do not have anything, people who may perish without support. These are my people. They are my relatives. I work for them, regardless of their caste, community, gender, language or political affiliation, provided that we have funds. I don't expect anything from them, not even a bouquet of flowers. The happiness in their eyes is the real reward.

After the woman's suicide threat, I asked my secretary to discard such letters without showing them to me. As a result, I have fewer letters to read these days.

26

Not All's Wrong with the Next Generation

Recently, I visited Egypt. I wanted to see the oldest pyramid in the country. It is not in Giza but in Sakkara, 24 km from Cairo. It is a five-step pyramid built for the Pharaoh Zosheyer. The architect was Imenhotep, the most intelligent and wise man at that time. While I was travelling, I was accompanied by a guide who also happened to be a well-read student of Egyptology. He was describing the writings on some of the pyramids. Pointing to some inscriptions, he translated aloud, 'The children of the next generation will be spendthrifts, will not think much and will not know much about life. We do not know what their future will be. Only the sun god Ra can save them.'

While this was being read out to me, I remembered the oft-heard complaints about the next generation in our own country—that youngsters do not respect our ideas, that they are rude, that they don't read much. It struck me that every generation has the same complaints about the next one. This has been going on from generation to generation, all over the world, for at least the last 5000 years.

Today's children have far more knowledge and far less

patience compared to our generation. I casually asked my teenage son the other day, 'Tell me the three most important revolutions or ideas of the twentieth century.'

He looked at me for a while and said, 'You behave like a teacher even at home. The most important revolutions and ideas of the century, according to me, are the principle of non-violence, the effect of violence and the impact of the communication media.'

'I will explain it to you,' he went on, noticing my surprise. 'When India was enslaved for centuries, when we did not have any power to make our decisions, a thin little man started a new kind of movement without bloodshed. No weapons, no money, but a message to the rulers: "We will not cooperate with you, come what may." He won freedom for India with this new thinking. He really deserved the Nobel Prize for peace. He was Mohandas Karamchand Gandhi, the father of our nation. His revolutionary idea influenced leaders like Martin Luther King Jr, Nelson Mandela and Aung San Suu Kyi, in gaining freedom for their people.

'The second idea was almost during the same period, but in the reverse direction. This man believed in the idea of hatred. He thought he could rule people with weapons and violence. He killed people like flies. He never understood the meaning of love and kindness. He could not bring peace by his method and became the cause for World War II. Millions of people suffered because of him and his policies. His life is the best example of war, intolerance and prejudice. He was Adolf Hitler.'

I thought that my son had a point, but I still felt that

the computer was the most important invention of the twentieth century. The young teenager did not agree.

'Today the world has shrunk because of mass media. In a matter of seconds, we come to know what is happening anywhere in the world. Television and the Internet are part of it. This has cut the cost of communication and barriers are disappearing. You can see its effect in the business world as well as in social life. That doesn't mean we're losing our old culture, but I can say we're exposed to other cultures also.'

I was surprised with my son, whom long ago I had taught how to hold a pencil. Now he was talking like an experienced adult about global subjects like peace, violence and communication. I am sure that many parents will often have the same thoughts. They might have also experienced how their little ones have become wiser than themselves. Our scriptures say, 'The one who acquires knowledge should be respected, irrespective of age, gender or class.'

My son wants to study abroad and I always wondered if this little boy of mine could manage alone. After this conversation with him, I realized that this young bird's wings have become strong and healthy. The time has come for him to fly on his own and see the world.

27

THINK POSITIVE, BE HAPPY

My mother had a cook called Girija who came from a poor family. She never spoke about her personal life. She was always cheerful and neatly dressed in a cotton sari and wore flowers in her well-combed hair. She looked smart and contented. While working in the kitchen she would hum songs and comply to our requests with a smile. I never saw her sad or grumbling. The only thing we knew about her was that her husband had abandoned her and their son. With very little formal education, the opportunities in a small town were limited, so she opted to be a cook.

Vasant, a family friend of ours, was an executive with a multinational company and he used to visit us often. He was always complaining about something or the other and after each visit of his, the whole atmosphere would become gloomy.

'My son is not studying well in his 12th class,' he complained.

I knew that his son was a very bright and hardworking boy. Why was his father complaining about him?

'I want my son to get into IIT.'

In today's competitive world, there are lakhs of children trying to get admission into one of the prestigious

Indian Institutes of Technology. If a child loses even five marks in the entrance examination because of stress, his rank comes down considerably. We can tell our children to study hard, but we should not put pressure on them to get ranks ahead of others.

The next time Vasant visited us, he was unhappy for a different reason. 'I purchased a plot about five years ago. Now that I want to sell it, the price is drastically lower,' he grumbled. 'There's a slump in the market. I invested in real estate, but it has failed.'

This was a countrywide phenomenon. The housing market was going through a recession and all those who had invested in it had lost money. He was no exception. But he made it sound as though he was the sole victim of recession and that he alone was suffering.

Several days later, Vasant paid us another visit. He looked exhausted. 'Bangalore is no longer what it was,' he complained. 'Twenty years back, the summers were so beautiful that it felt like a hill station. Today we require air-conditioners or need to get away to hill stations.'

Global warming is a worldwide phenomenon. Bangalore is no special place. But still our friend would complain.

One day, when Girija and I were alone at home, I casually asked her, 'Tell me Girija, where is your husband? Do you meet him?'

She looked at me in silence and said, 'He is here with another woman and works for your neighbour as a driver.'

I was taken aback. She saw her husband every day

and that too with another woman!

'Are you not mad at him?' I asked her.

'Initially, I used to be. But now, I think I am lucky because I have only one child to support. My son is bright and obedient. Because his father deserted us, my son is more concerned about me. If I was all alone or if I had many children or if my child was irresponsible, then I would have had serious problems. God has been kind enough to me that I don't have any such problems.'

'Are you not worried about your future?'

'Why should I worry? Can worrying solve any problem? Your mother has given us a quarter to stay. I work sincerely. All of you are happy. If I need anything, I can always ask you people. For that matter, demands are never-ending. When my son grows up, he will not be like his father, because he has seen me suffer. Amma, I have not learnt much in school, but life has taught me one thing: always look at life in a positive way. You feel nice and so do the people around you.'

Immediately, I thought of Vasant. He had made his life miserable by thinking about what he did not have, whereas this uneducated woman, Girija, had learnt to see the positive side of every difficulty and to enjoy life.

28

LIGHT AS MANY CANDLES AS POSSIBLE

I was travelling with my father in the interior parts of Karnataka, in the areas bordering Maharashtra. My father, a retired professor and doctor, used to guide my work and was my favourite companion on my travels. We were in a village where there was a famous temple dedicated to a goddess. It was a Friday, the auspicious day of the week for women all over India. Many women had come with offerings of fruit and flowers for the goddess. They had formed a long queue, but I was not part of it.

Having come to study the destitute in the area, I sat separately, talking to people. There were fruitsellers, bangle sellers and other vendors. I learned a lot from these people on the street. They had faced the harsh realities of caste, money, politics, old beliefs and much more. Their opinions and suggestions at times educated me better than any Ph.D thesis or seminar on poverty.

Once, I met a retired *gharwali* (commercial sex worker) along with a beautiful girl of sixteen who had long hair, a pretty face, beautiful eyes and a smooth complexion. Innocence added radiance to her face. She was wearing a green sari, green bangles and plenty of jasmine in her hair. The older woman claimed she was the young girl's aunt.

Though I was talking to the aunt, my eyes were fixed on the young girl. During the course of our discussion, I learned that this young girl had just become a *devadasi* (woman dedicated to the temple). There is a ban on converting women to *devadasis*, but many things happen illegally in our country.

I looked at the aunt. She was a *devadasi* too. She smelled strongly and had black teeth stained from chewing tobacco, a big paunch and red eyes. Her face bore a harsh, greedy expression. She was wearing a silk sari, gold bangles and a necklace. But no amount of gold could make her beautiful.

This young girl was going to be a gold mine for the old hag. I imagined that this girl of sixteen would probably become like her aunt after thirty years or so. Then she would also catch hold of some innocent girl, make her a *devadasi* and exploit her as a source of income. What a pity—the girl was not even aware of where she was heading.

Tears filled my eyes and suddenly I started sobbing uncontrollably. People standing around stared at me, wondering what had gone wrong. They probably thought that I had lost something. For the first time in my life, words failed to express my feelings. But my father immediately understood what was troubling me. He said, 'Tears cannot solve age-old problems. We can only try to reduce them. You cannot change the life of every single person. If you can rehabilitate ten such people in your lifetime, I will be a proud father. Proud that I have given birth to a daughter who could change the lives of ten helpless women.'

Everybody should know her own capacity and strength. One should also know one's own limitations. It is more difficult to recognize our weaknesses than our strengths. Don't aim for the sky. Keep your feet firmly on the ground and work around you. There is so much misery and gloom, but it is better to light a single candle than to remain in darkness. Try to light as many candles possible.

29

Woman with A Mind

My friend Nalini is a professor at a college in Bangalore. A Ph.D in history, she is a good teacher and an excellent wife. I had not met her for a long time, so one day I decided to visit her. She was excited to see me. She was cooking a special meal for her only son, who had returned from school. While her son was preparing for the 12th standard exams, her husband, Satish, an engineer in a multinational company, was away at work. So there was enough space and time for us to talk.

'I haven't seen you around at all, Nalini. What's new in life?'

'Nothing. I have been busy because Sameer is in the twelfth standard.'

'Come on, Nalini. You are not appearing for the exam. What you can do is help him at home, but that does not mean cutting yourself off from the world.'

Nalini did not agree. She was tense and worried.

'Nalini, what is the problem? Have you finished with the construction of your house?'

'Satish is looking after that.'

'You were planning to buy a new vehicle. What happened?'

'Yes. Satish is planning to buy a scooter rather than a car.'

I soon realized that all the decisions were Satish's. 'Nalini, don't you have any preferences?'

'Satish is better than me in all things. He knows the outside world and has lots of contacts. So his decisions will always be correct.'

I was surprised by her answer. Usually, educated, working women are more confident and independent, and they like to make their own decisions.

The next day, I was travelling to a village by bus. For a change, the bus was not crowded. A village woman, Yellamma, got into the bus along with me. I knew her because whenever I was in her village she would bring me fresh vegetables and refuse to accept money. Yellamma was around thirty-five, healthy and cheerful. Her well-oiled hair was tied in a knot and a thick black-bead *mangalsutra* rested on her neck. She also wore heavy gold ear studs, a big nose ring and more than a dozen green glass bangles on each wrist. No cosmetics and no pretence. Her pleasant smile added radiance to her glowing reddish-brown complexion. Yellamma and her husband, Rudrappa, owned a small garden in the village and that was their biggest asset. They grew and sold seasonal vegetables for a living.

'Amma, I have to rush back to my garden today,' she said.

'Why are you in such a hurry? Isn't your husband in the garden?' I asked.

'Yes. But still I must go because I have to take an important decision today. I have to sow the seeds ideal for the next three months.'

'Surely your husband can do that,' I suggested.

'No, I have to make my own decision. Rudrappa is also very good and experienced, but I should also give my views because not all seeds can be sown in the rainy season.'

I liked her confidence.

'Initially, when I gave my opinions, everyone used to laugh at me. I realized, however, that unless I became assertive, they would not give me any chance to make decisions. Without making decisions, I would not gain experience. So I started sowing vegetable seeds in one corner of the garden. Neither my mother-in-law nor my husband knew that place and I experimented. The first few times, they failed, but I didn't give up. Eventually I learnt which vegetables grew in which season. Today they respect my ideas and ask me to decide. This year, I want to plant carrots and cauliflower. I am sure that the yield will be good and fetch good money.'

Though uneducated and untrained, Yellamma was so different from Nalini.

My friend Swapna had been unwell for three weeks, but I had come to know about her illness only after many days. After office one day, I thought of visiting her, though it was late afternoon. I wanted to take some fruit and flowers, but I was wondering where to buy them. Normally, my mother and sister do the shopping. I called my assistant, Ramesh, and asked him to show me where I could get good fruit and flowers. He knew of a shop that was on the way to Swapna's house and we decided to stop there to make my purchases.

It was one of those hot afternoons. I was nearly drenched in sweat and my cotton sari was crumpled. As I was going to meet a good friend, I wanted to choose the flowers myself, instead of leaving the choice to Ramesh.

At the shopping complex, the ice-cream stall appeared to be doing brisk business. I could see the rush of excited children and their worried mothers. Being holiday time, the children seemed totally unconcerned about their mothers' threats and warnings. It reminded me of the times when my children used to do the same and I felt sorry that those childhood days were gone.

I was now standing in front of the flower shop, which also sold fruit. The bright, colourful and fragrant flowers were arranged so well that it was hard to take my eyes off them. There were fragrant white rajnigandhas, bright red roses, gladioli in half bloom and many other kinds of flowers. They seemed to have just arrived from the garden, as their stems were still being trimmed and dipped in water.

On the other side were mounds of neatly arranged fruit: mangoes from Mumbai, grapes from Bijapur, guavas from Allahabad, oranges from Nagpur. They all looked so tempting that I was confused about what to buy. I asked the shopkeeper how much a bunch of pink roses would cost. They hadn't bloomed fully and looked very beautiful. Though he had heard me, he did not bother to answer. I repeated my question.

Disdainfully he answered, 'Each rose will cost Rs 3.50 and there are twenty roses to a bunch. That makes it Rs 70.'

I was taken aback. I had become like Rip Van Winkle. Unaware of the prevailing rates, I could recall only the old prices and felt that everything had become very expensive. I decided to enquire about the price of mangoes as well. I pointed to some Ratnagiri Alphonsos and asked him the cost of a dozen.

The irritable vendor answered, 'Rs 150 a dozen.' Then, speaking in Tamil, thinking I wouldn't understand, he remarked sarcastically to his friend, 'These people cannot afford anything but come shopping anyway. They are only window-shopping. I get tired of answering their questions. People who really want to buy don't ask the price.'

By this time, Ramesh had completed his shopping and came to the flower shop. Smart and well dressed at all times, he was wearing a T-shirt with the company logo and his employee card dangled around his neck. Now it was his turn to enquire about the price of the roses and the mangoes.

Looking at him or probably at his T-shirt, the shopkeeper replied politely, 'Sir, a bunch of those roses will cost you Rs 100. Only five rupees per flower. The actual price is Rs 150 but for you, I will give it at Rs 100. See these mangoes. They will cost only Rs 200.'

Ramesh didn't say anything, but I couldn't keep quiet.

'How can you demand such a price? Two minutes ago you were telling me that the roses and mangoes cost Rs 70 and Rs 150. Now you have increased the price. How can you do such a thing?'

The shopkeeper got angry. 'If you can't afford to buy, then keep quiet. Here is a man who is working for a big company. Can't you see his badge and company shirt? He is in a software company. They can afford any price and they don't bargain. People like you cause only headaches to us.'

Ramesh was about to reply, but I stopped him. It was a matter of great interest to me. I have heard many people, including real estate brokers, marriage brokers, landlords and job consultants, classify our company as a software company or an IT company. But this was more than all that.

'Is it really true that people working in IT companies have to pay different rates compared to ordinary people like us?' I asked.

'Yes. I am from Mangalore. I have seen that the moment

a man is working in an IT company, the dowry rises by at least two lakhs. After all, they do earn so much. What is wrong if I increase my price by just fifty rupees?'

Back in the car, I reflected on the digital divide-and-rule policy in operation for IT and non-IT workers, even in everyday life.

Where There's A Will . . .

Recently, I was invited to inaugurate a college auditorium. Though not large, the auditorium was well planned. After the inauguration, I was shown around the place. To my surprise, there was not even an inch of vacant space anywhere. All the walls were decorated with granite slabs and on every slab was inscribed the donors' names and the amounts they had donated. There was also a series of photographs on the wall. It all seemed a little odd.

The organizer noticed my expression and explained, 'Madam, we appealed to our donors for help in this work. Very few people came forward. Then we thought it over and decided to advertise that whoever donated more than Rs 1000 would have their name engraved on a granite slab on the wall. Whoever donated Rs 5000 and above would have their photos displayed on the wall.'

'What about those people who pay more than Rs 10,000?' I asked.

'Their names would be engraved on a separate marble stone and displayed at the entrance itself,' he replied. 'Just as we expected, we collected enough money to complete this project. There were even some strange donors who donated Rs 1000 four times so that their names could appear on four slabs on the wall!'

Yes, it is important to remember the person who has donated his hard-earned money, but not to this extent. My mind went back to a great personality who was far ahead of his time: Mariappa, a wealthy merchant from Bangalore, who first thought of doing philanthropic work in 1914. Though he was not educated, he was a great benefactor of poor students. He would provide them with food at his house and also take care of their fees.

He died on 12 March 1914, having written his will barely eight days earlier. In it, he bequeathed a monthly pension of Rs 60 to his wife till her death. The couple did not have children. He also arranged to supply oil and perform pujas in four temples in the city. He then specified that among the needy Hindu students, fifteen Nagaratha Lingayats, fifteen Brahmins and fifteen Hindus from other castes should be provided the facility of free boarding and lodging in Bangalore.

Not much is known about Mariappa's personal life. Probably, great philanthropists are introverted. They don't wish the whole world to know about their deeds. On the contrary, they believe that the *dana* given by the right hand should not be known even to the left hand.

It took almost seven years to liquidate Mariappa's assets. The money obtained was approximately Rs 1.45 lakh, which was a huge sum in those days. Half the money was spent on buying some land and constructing a hostel on it, while the remainder was kept as a corpus fund in the then newly started Mysore Bank. B.K. Mariappa Hostel, located on Chamarajapet, III Main, Bangalore, officially started on 1 July 1921 with forty-five poor and needy students from different castes. The Trust had six honorary trustees who were recognized as eminent people in public life.

Recently, the Mariappa Hostel celebrated its eightieth anniversary and also the 120th birth anniversary of its founder. This great philanthropist has helped educate many eminent people who have gone on to become famous in different walks of life. Without the gesture of this generous person, they probably would have faced great difficulty in completing their education.

CRISIS OF CONFIDENCE

Charu was one of my students who used to excel in her studies. She got a job in a bank, married an engineer and settled down happily. I used to meet her once in a while. Initially, she looked happy and radiant, but later, as time passed, she looked as though she carried a big burden. One morning, she came to my office. It surprised me because she would never disturb me in the mornings. I was sure something was wrong when she burst into tears on seeing me.

'Ma'am, I thought I could live happily once I chose my husband,' she said.

Apparently things hadn't turned out that way. After the first few days of love and care, Charu's husband and his mother began harassing her, forcing her to do all the housework in addition to her job at the bank. She had to hand over her entire salary to her husband and when she required any money—even ten rupees—she would have to ask him for it.

'As this marriage was against the wishes of my mother-in-law, she finds fault with everything I do,' said Charu. 'My husband, Suresh, is always a mother's son first, but never Charu's husband. I try to please them by doing whatever they tell me to do. But still they are unhappy with me.'

There are millions of Charus in our country who are well educated and hold good jobs. Once they are married, they have one problem or the other and they suffer throughout their lives. If providing education to women is empowerment, then why are so many women still crying? If economic independence is real independence, then why are they still suffering? This question always puzzles me. All these women are, by any standard, competent individuals. If such women suffer and shed tears, then what will happen to those young girls in the villages who are uneducated, economically dependent and who do not have any say about any aspect of their lives, be it buying clothes or choosing a husband? What could be the extent of their suffering?

As a teacher, I feel that apart from academics, it is very important to teach students the basic code of life. Many a time, my female students discuss marriage, money and careers. I always try to encourage the idea of self-reliance and confidence. It is important, particularly for the girls in our country, to have self-confidence. After all, getting married and raising children is not the ultimate aim of a woman. Education can, no doubt, fetch you good jobs. But more than that, one should be able to face life and its realities, and understand society.

Charu should have discussed her problems openly with her husband and mother-in-law and should have asserted her rights, but she was always submissive and wanted to please them. If you try to please everyone, you will please no one. It is impossible to lead your life for others' happiness. In any permanent relationship, it is wiser to put all your cards on the table, show how much you can change and how much you cannot.

Recently, I was invited to a function in Delhi. Its main theme was the empowerment of women and it was also an occasion where a few awards were being given away. One of the speakers was Kiran Bedi. I have always had a special appreciation and regard for Kiran because she symbolizes women with inner strength. It shows on her face also. Speaking extempore from her heart, forceful and sincere, she narrated the following incident.

A girl with a master's degree in business administration fell in love with her classmate and ran away to get married in a temple. There was no proof of their wedding other than a *mangalsutra* round her neck. No registration, no photo. After living together for a few days, the man abandoned her and this girl had to run from pillar to post for help.

Blaming the girl for being ignorant and finding the runaway husband were secondary to Kiran's fundamental question: what kind of education had this girl actually received? What was the use of all those years she had spent studying in school and college? A girl who was educated, who could lead an economically independent life but was now crying for help, was not a thing to be brushed aside, Kiran Bedi pointed out.

Education means more than scoring good marks in exams or receiving certificates. Life is an exam where the syllabus is unknown and question papers are not set. Nor are there model answer papers. There are various types of questions that can come from any direction, but one shouldn't run away. Education and financial independence are tools that can help us face difficulties, but confidence must be developed throughout life.

THE PRICE OF JEALOUSY

Life is a mixture of many kinds of people. I have seen some people always talking ill of others. Not that I am against people giving one another feedback. But such feedback should be constructive and help to improve oneself. Unfortunately, people can be remarkably insensitive and make comments that are in poor taste when they offer criticism.

Recently, a social worker received the Padmashree. He is a dedicated person and works selflessly; he truly deserved the award. But the comment that my friend Parvati made about him was horrible: 'Oh! He is a rich man. He must have spent a lot of money to buy the award. What else can he do with all his money? He donates some money and the Padmashree is awarded. If I had that kind of money, I would have got it much earlier. Besides, there is nothing great about a Padmashree. Can anybody remember who got it last year? Every year, hundreds of people get it; this year he got it.'

I have known Parvati for many years. Whenever somebody achieves something, her first reaction is negative. The reason is jealousy. She is so self-centred and insensitive that she is not bothered about what others think.

Manish, another friend's son, got the first rank in his degree examination. Naturally, his mother was thrilled. At the party, a gloomy-faced Parvati took me aside and said, 'Manish was not such a great student compared to my daughter, Mala. There must have been something wrong in the paper evaluation. What do you think, as a teacher?'

'You're wrong. Both Manish and Mala are good students. There is nothing wrong in the evaluation. He must have worked harder,' I said.

I met Parvati recently in the market.

'Who is your ghost writer?' she asked.

I was taken aback. 'Why should anybody write for me? I can write myself.'

'No, you hardly get any time, so I assumed that you must be hiring a writer, just as you hire a cook,' she said.

I was upset. How on earth could she talk like that? How could she assume such things? Without being in the least perturbed about having upset me, she delivered her parting shot before she walked away, 'Normally people do things like that, so I asked you.'

Parvati is an example of educated people who always comment on others. Their energy is spent in criticizing others. They always think that there is foul play in everything. We dream of so many things in life, but we may not be able to achieve them. Achievement is the product of many factors and not of hard work alone. One requires the right opportunity, the right people to work with and the right timing. Maybe there is an element of luck too.

An achiever has to work hard and have faith in his work. Often people work hard but do not achieve much. That doesn't mean they are any less than others who are more successful. If I am unable to realize my dream and somebody else does, it is better for me to feel happy for the other person than to feel sorry for myself. The best culture is one in which we rejoice in each other's success.

Today, nobody likes Parvati. She hardly has any friends. She feels that good things should happen to her alone, that she alone deserves the best in the world. Her world consists only of her family—her daughter, her son and her husband. Others do not exist for her.

What do such people achieve in life? No genuine friendship, no affection, no sharing. Is life worth living with this kind of jealousy?

When women in India won the right to vote, it was seen as a sign of equality and freedom. But, in reality, their social status is not good. That is why we see plenty of bride burnings, female infanticides and other atrocities committed against women.

Recently, I attended a seminar on women's issues. During the talks, something very interesting was read out. It was a list of countries where women enjoy freedom in all respects—economically, socially and politically. The countries where women were more emancipated featured at the top of the list while countries which lagged behind in empowering women came lower in the list. I assumed that India would feature somewhere in the middle of the list. In fact, it was the second-last country to be named. It came as a total surprise to me and, of course, a bitter one.

I was curious to know which were the first three countries. I expected England or America to be at the top of the list. I was wrong again. The top three countries were all Scandinavian: Sweden, Norway and Denmark. Most of us at the seminar were taken aback. We were surprised that such small countries lying in a corner of Europe were the countries that respect their women the most.

Once, on a visit to Stockholm, I was late in returning to my hotel one night. As I was quite far from the hotel, I had to take a taxi. The fare to the hotel was 40 kronor, but thinking that the taxi driver would charge at least double considering the late hour, I gave him 100 kronor and waited for the change. He returned 80 kronor.

When I asked why, he said, 'You are a lady travelling at this hour of the night, so we take only half of the actual fare.'

I was really impressed. Back home in my country, I would not even dare to travel after dark. Even if I did, the taxi driver would surely charge me multiples of the actual fare.

We talk endlessly on the podium. We worship goddesses. We are proud to say that women have the same rights as men in our constitution. The Ardhanareeshwara form of Lord Shiva shows that he too had consented to this equality. Our scriptures and our history tell of women with extraordinary qualities. But, in reality, do our women really feel secure? Do they actually enjoy freedom? Do they enjoy equal rights in society? Maybe a few do.

Women are usually identified in relation to men—as a daughter, a wife or a mother. Often, Indian women do not have a say even in personal matters. Their services are not rewarded nor is their efficiency appreciated. They have to live in a male-dominated society. It is ridiculous that often those of their own gender are their worst enemies. It is a different matter, a matter of pride, that the Indian woman has learnt to live and excel in such an environment.

In contrast, women are respected in the three Scandinavian countries. We just talk, but they practise. The saying, 'Where women are happy, the goddess dwells,' holds true only in such places.

Not all that glitters is gold. Not all that is white is milk. Not all people who wear saffron clothes are sages. These age-old sayings hold true even now, especially the last one. We see a lot of people wearing saffron clothes, but not all of them are *sanyasis* in the true sense of the word. A *sanyasi* is one who guides his followers on the right path.

Recently, I attended the inaugural function of a home for destitute women in Mysore. In most cases, the women were there because they were either harassed by their in-laws or tortured by drunken husbands. Owing to their socio-economic conditions, even the parents of the victims were unable to take them in and care for their hapless children. There had also been instances when young girls, lured by romance, had run away from their homes and had been deserted by their lovers after the honeymoon. These girls usually did not dare return to their parents.

The saying that 'success has many fathers, but failure has none' is true indeed. We get to see only the distressed women and their children, while the main cause of their problems remains hidden in the background. So the victims cannot be blamed altogether. Often it is circumstances that force them into such drudgery. These women and girls need to be psychologically strong and determined to face difficulties with courage and go on with their lives. The more unfortunate ones may get caught in the ugly network of commercial sex or other unlawful activities, either knowingly or unknowingly.

It is nice to respect or reward people who work for such women. More importantly, it is also necessary to lend a helping hand to those who have stumbled or lost their way. Do we have such a system? There are very few institutions where such people are given shelter and efforts made to rehabilitate them. In such institutions, women are taught how to earn a livelihood so that they can live with dignity.

In Mysore, the first person who came up with the idea to open such an institution was not someone who had political powers or wanted fame. He is the head of the Suttur *math*. The swamiji is well read and felt the need to help the downtrodden and destitute, having truly understood the meaning of compassion.

He could have led a quiet life, performing his religious duties and looking after his own *math*, but he thought of something different. The swamiji gave a donation worth Rs 1 crore in the form of one-and-a-half acres of land belonging to his *math*. He showed the true nature of a leader, exemplary in his behaviour. It is a matter to be highlighted that he did all this without any expectation of a return. *Acharya devo bhava,* say our ancestors, implying that the guru or the teacher is equal to God. How truly the actions of the swamiji of the Suttur *math* reflect this saying!

36

On Column Writing

Whenever I write a column, I give my email address to enable readers to express their views on the article. I also add a sentence reminding them that their emails should be regarding the column only. However, I do get plenty of emails about things other than the column. Some emails appreciate the contents of the column, but some of them are sarcastic.

The column 'Last Word', which I have been writing for a while, is my personal opinion and is naturally highly subjective. As far as possible, I try to convey to the readers what is on my mind. It is very easy to narrate the horrors of dowry death, the causes of corruption or moralize on the virtue of honesty and so on. Anyone can preach, for that matter. But most of the readers ask me to narrate something personal that happened to me or to someone in my circle of friends. As a teacher, I am always aware that analogies and examples make the subject clearer. So, when I write I narrate some of my experiences. The incidents might have happened in my own family or among my friends. But it is not to highlight what my son said or how my friend spoke. I write only to share those few everyday moments, something that my readers can identify with. But I have come across many readers who misunderstand this and waste their time sending some critical and hurtful emails.

I got a letter after I wrote 'Not all's wrong with the next generation'. I was describing a conversation with my son. The purpose of the article was not to glorify either my son or myself. It was a conversation between two generations, my son representing the next generation and I, my own generation. I could have written the conversation more impersonally as one which took place between Mister A and Mrs B or just as an objective essay making generalizations on the generation gap. But I felt it was better to write about something that had really happened. However, the response I got for this was the accusation, 'You write about your son.'

Once, I wrote about social insensitivity. My aim was to tell others how much we are insulated in our own world, with no time at all to know or care about what is happening around us. We must definitely care for our families and I don't deny that. Family is important and one should not become a philanthropist at the cost of one's family. My concern was that we should at least think of other people. I did not mean it was necessary to offer financial help or give money. I gave a small example from my experience. But some readers were critical about my narrating a story and praising Buddha. Lord Buddha, in my article, symbolized the ultimate sacrifice of a sensitive person who went on to help others. Everyone cannot be Buddha, but at least we can think and learn from such great people.

When my articles end on a positive note, they are

popular with readers. But the moment an article ends on a negative note, I get letters saying, 'We never expected such a thing from you,' or 'You should always write good things.' In real life, no human being has all good qualities, no human being has been successful in every aspect of life, no system is without its negatives. In reality, life is a mixture of plus and minus, joy and sorrow, ups and downs. It is the duty of a writer to portray that the negative is also a part of life and that we should accept it as such while also thinking positively.

The same incident can be viewed from two different angles by two different people. In my column, I try my level best to show my sincere feeling towards issues of common concern. My aim is not to show off or describe anything personal. I just want to narrate an incident and let readers think about it in relation to their own lives. Unbiased inputs from the readers help me to think and improve myself in my personal column.

Neither the money I earn from writing nor the desire for fame makes me write. I just have the urge to share my vast experience of meeting people, trying to understand them and realizing what life is all about. Many times, people act impulsively due to emotions like greed or jealousy. That doesn't mean they are bad. These are also the qualities of a human being. That's why I believe that readers are the source of my inspiration.

37

THE NOBEL PRIZE

Recently, I wrote a column about the century's greatest idea—the idea of non-violence, conceived by our own leader, Mahatma Gandhi. By following the ideal of non-violence, three people were awarded the Nobel Prize for peace. They were Martin Luther King Jr, Nelson Mandela and Aung San Suu Kyi of Myanmar. Martin Luther King, in particular, when he received the Nobel Prize at Oslo in Norway, described and praised Mahatma Gandhi and declared that he would follow the path of non-violence in the violent country of America. Ironically, Gandhi himself never received the Nobel Prize.

When I wrote this article, one of the readers sarcastically wrote, 'It was good that Mr M.K. Gandhi did not get the Nobel Prize because after all it was instituted by the Dynamite King.'

What a wrong way to think of Alfred Nobel! He probably was the first philanthropist who thought of the entire globe as his own village. He was truly an international man, as early as a century ago. In 1896, when he wrote his will, he probably would never have dreamt that he was creating a new idea of philanthropy. The recipients of his award are international. Incidentally, seven hundred Nobel Prizes have been given in the last one hundred years. Nobel never gave away any of these prizes in his lifetime. Though the will was written in 1896, the first prizes were given only in 1901. Very few Swedes have received the Nobel Prize. But the people who receive them are, by and large, respected throughout the world.

A reader's question, 'What's great about Nobel?' prompted me to write about the Nobel Prize. Why did Nobel give away all his property, approximately three million dollars in those days, to charity? He could have given his vast estates to his relatives or to a religious society or to his countrymen. What made him institute prizes for literature, peace, physics, chemistry and medicine? He might have earned money from dynamite, but that doesn't mean he was fond of war.

A knife is very essential in the kitchen, but it can also be a horrible weapon that can take life. It depends on who wields it. Western Europe and America are very grateful to Nobel because he invented dynamite. Dynamite helped build the railways by cutting through mountains and making tunnels. Railways connect people. But if somebody used the railways for war, it was not Nobel's fault.

It seems Nobel never liked propaganda or any publicity. Very few photographs of him can be seen in the Nobel Museum. He was a great achiever. Whatever he did, he did well, be it business or philanthropy. Nobel, as a person, was shy and a peace lover. This is evident in his will. He clearly writes, 'Anything for the betterment of the human race should be respected and awarded, so that the person will not have any financial difficulties in achieving his goals.'

It is very interesting to note that very few women have been awarded the Nobel Prize, particularly in science. The reason is that very few countries encourage women's education. Most of the time, Americans and Europeans have won the award. The reason is the expensive infrastructure for research in science that exists in these countries.

It is not necessary that the Nobel Prize be awarded in the specified field every year. If the Nobel Committee does not find the right candidate one year, then the Nobel Prize in that field is not awarded. Jean Paul Sartre, a famous French writer, rejected the Nobel Prize. Madame Curie was awarded it twice; her daughter, Irine, received it once in chemistry and another daughter, Eva, representing UNESCO, also received this award. Probably this is the only case in history where all members of the same family received the award.

Nobel sowed the seed of 'helping mankind'. Then in the early part of 1910, Rockefeller and later Ford started their foundations. Today, there are many prizes all over the world for various activities. But Nobel remains as strong as the Himalaya in his deed and symbolizes the love for peace and mankind.

38

Unwed Mothers

A few years ago, I was a counsellor to students. That was the time when I came to know about the problems faced by teenagers, particularly girls. Normally, girls are shy and parents expect 100 per cent obedience from them. One of my students, Kusuma, had become pregnant before marriage. The boy was her classmate, but he was not brave enough to marry her. When her parents came to know about it, they were very upset. When they met me, the first thing they said was, 'What will others think? How will we face society?' The boy's parents were not prepared for this marriage. Ultimately, the girl committed suicide.

I felt extremely sad and helpless. For the first time, I recognized the problems of unwed mothers in our society. In real life, the pressure on the girl and the family is enormous.

Recently, I visited Norway. A Norwegian friend, Martha, took me to her house for a meal. Hers was a simple middle-class family. Martha was an only daughter and both her parents were teachers. She was also a teacher in a high school.

It was summer and around 8 p.m. The sun was shining like it was 2 p.m. in the afternoon. Isn't that the reason

Norway is called the land of the midnight sun? The house was simple and sparkling. Everyone at dinner knew English, which was of great help to me. Simple vegetarian fare was served at the table. A little boy of five came running in and hugged Martha. He was very naughty and yet innocent and lovable. He sat next to me in a high chair.

After some time, Martha's cousin, Mary, joined us for dinner. The conversation was casual. Mary was a postgraduate student in political science. While I was talking to her about the political conditions in Norway, the little boy pulled Mary's skirt and said, 'Mom, I want more bread.'

I was surprised to hear that. Mary was a young girl of about twenty-four; she seemed too young to have such a grown-up son. During the conversation, I asked Mary where her husband was working. Without any guilt or shyness she replied, 'I am not married. But John is my son. I am an unwed mother.'

I could not believe this. Here was a woman who had a son out of wedlock and announced it without hesitation. And he was accepted by the family, too.

After dinner, Martha came to drop me. I could not resist the temptation and asked her, 'Tell me, Martha, if you don't mind, is Mary happy? What do her parents feel? Where is the boy's father? I just want to know because of my student back home.'

I explained Kusuma's story to her. Martha was distressed to hear the sad story and replied, 'Mary met Daniel at a summer camp when they were both just eighteen years old. He used to come and visit us often. They fell in love and she became pregnant by mistake. Sex education is given to us at school, but mistakes still happen. When Mary got pregnant, Daniel did not want to marry her because he was also in college. Moreover, they figured that their temperaments were too different. Even if they had married, it would have ended in divorce. They decided to separate. Mary felt that she could continue with her pregnancy. She never wanted to have an abortion, so she gave birth to the baby. She nursed him for a year and now is back at college. She may marry her new boyfriend next year.'

For me, there were thousands of questions to ask. What was the reaction of Mary's parents? Did John know his father? Where was Daniel? And so on.

Martha probably sensed my curiosity and explained, 'My uncle and aunt did not worry because it was Mary's decision and there are many unwed mothers in our country. Daniel has a good job and visits John twice a year. He pays money for the child's maintenance and he too may marry his new girlfriend in the new year. John knows about it. Mary is not upset with Daniel.' My thoughts drifted back to my student, Kusuma, and her death. Same situation, probably at a similar age, but the outcome was so different. Mary looks confident and happy whereas poor Kusuma is dead.

39

ALLIANCES INVITED

Time and tide wait for no one. This is really true. A quarter of a century ago, we used to attend our friends' weddings. Now we attend their children's weddings.

I attended Vani's marriage. Her mother Vanita is a friend of mine. I distinctly remember Vanita's own wedding. Her marriage was finalized through an advertisement placed by her father in the matrimonial column of the *Hindu*, thirty years ago. Matrimonial advertisements were something new in those days. Normally, matches were made through personal contacts. Advertising in a paper was the last resort. Vanita was a tall girl. Finding a boy taller than her in our small circle was not easy, so her father had to resort to advertising.

I still remember the advertisement. 'Alliance invited for a tall, 24-year, from a traditional family, Smarta, Athreya Gothra, Ashwini Nakshatra Prathama Charana girl, a commerce graduate, bank employee. Knows all household work, excellent in a joint family, ready to work or stay at home after marriage. Knows good embroidery and knitting. Tall grooms aged 29 yrs to 34 yrs, above 5.8", from the same community, with horoscope, through their parents, from good family, should apply. Groom should be at least a graduate. Working in Bank/Govt/ Public sector is preferable. A good wedding is assured. Apply to Box No. xxx.'

Vanita got a husband who was working as an engineer in a public-sector company. He was from a joint family and belonged to the same community. Her father-in-law demanded twenty sovereigns of gold, five silk saris, a suit for the boy, to-and-fro bus charges for the entire marriage party and a good three-day wedding. Though it was difficult for them, Vanita's family agreed.

The wedding preparations were enormous and time-consuming. As she was the first girl in our group to get married, we too were involved in the preparations. We accompanied her to select saris and jewellery. Elders at home were busy arranging for cooks and varieties of sweets.

Now, years later, at the wedding lunch of Vanita's daughter, I saw the new couple, Vani and her husband, happily chatting away as if they had known each other for a long time. Caterers were very busy arranging different kinds of food. Tired but happy, Vanita came and sat next to me.

My mind went back to the days of Vanita's wedding. Because I knew all the details of her marriage and because her daughter's marriage had happened so suddenly, I asked for details.

Vanita smiled and replied, 'Oh! It was just like mine. An advertisement in the *Hindu* matrimonial column. But the kind of ad was different.'

It was a hot May day. Wiping the perspiration with

her silk sari, Vanita opened her purse and showed me the paper cutting. She said, 'I am going to attach this to Vani's wedding album.'

I read the ad. 'Alliance invited for a smart, slim, fair, 22-yr-old software engineer, from a modern family, preferring to stay overseas. The girl is convent educated and prefers nuclear family. Outgoing and Karate Black Belt. Enjoys Western music and travelling. Handsome boys between 22-25 yrs, well connected, well settled, preferably a software/MNC, small family, can apply directly. Horoscope not needed. Caste no bar.'

Vanita then explained how her daughter's marriage had been fixed in a week's time, without hassle or tension. Vani received about one hundred applications from all over, but only five were short-listed. She met all the five boys separately; two did not approve of her and she did not like another two. Thus, the final choice was made. This boy was working in the US as a software engineer. Vani's passport had been readied when she was in her final year. She had got a job in a software company. She knew that she had to marry soon so she learnt driving, swimming, aerobics, nutrition and diet.

'Does she know cooking?' I asked, since Vani was going to live abroad.

'Not needed. But she knows how to make pasta, soup, noodles and pizzas. Anyway the market is flooded with ready-to-use mixes. She can manage the kitchen with all these things.'

'Did you buy a lot of jewellery and saris?'

'No. Nowadays the in-laws don't demand jewellery or

a dowry. Instead, they want the first-time airfare to the US for the bride. My daughter does not want to buy many saris either. She hardly wears them and feels it will be a waste. So she bought just two saris, six salwar kameez sets and ten sets of Western clothes, which are more useful to her. And we made lightweight jewellery.'

I was amazed at how times have changed. Traditional matrimonial columns show the change even in arranged marriages. Change is very essential in life. Depending on the circumstances, rituals and people change. Is it not true that nothing is constant in life except change?

Recently, I was in a selection committee to recruit a software engineer for a small firm. There were many young girls and boys anxiously awaiting their turn. They were all in the age group of twenty-one to twenty-four. It was probably the first interview for many of them and they looked tense. They were all computer science graduates, so I was sure that their technical knowledge would be sound.

It was the turn of a young boy. He was well mannered and as soon as he entered the room, he produced his certificates. The topmost one attested to his knowledge of Java, GW Basic, C++, etc.

I casually asked him how much time he would require to learn a new computer language.

'Not more than six months,' he replied.

Suddenly, my mind flashed back to a quarter-century earlier. I had met a young man of the same age as this boy in a similar situation and had asked him a similar question. But the answer I had received was so different. The young boy then had answered with confidence: 'I don't know anything about computers or their language. But give me four months' time. I will try to understand computers and I will come back to tell you how much time I require to learn the language.'

I was bowled over by his confidence and his straightforwardness. I still remember the whole scene vividly.

That was in Bombay. I was on an overview panel and this young man, who was basically a civil engineer, had come for the interview. It was for the post of a software engineer. Many people had done well in the interview. He was the last candidate to appear. He entered the interview room with a very clear mind and was very frank. He was given a logic test, not related to computers, and he solved it quickly. He made it clear that he had no computer background but that he was ready to learn and if found good, hoped to be given the job.

He got the job, worked relentlessly and came back saying, 'Give me any language. I will learn it in ten days. I will master it. Computer language is just a tool. The essence of programming is logic. One requires good logic, and that I have mastered.'

Over a period of time he did master many languages and became one of the most successful programmers I know. Though he was a junior, most of his seniors, including me, would ask for his opinion. He would do a lot more homework on the desk than on the system and once he started programming there would never be a single bug.

Whenever a youngster talks about computers, I am reminded of this young man with his admirable willingness to learn and frankness in accepting things. I pray that all our colleges produce more students like him.

41

SORRY, THE LINE IS BUSY

Rakesh and I had been classmates from school to college. He had become a part of our family and I of his. Later on, as we grew older, we chose different professions, parted and settled. He had his family and I had my own and we were immersed in our own worlds. In spite of being in the same city, we hardly met, though we really would have liked to meet often.

I thought of Rakesh on his birthday and wanted to greet him, but his telephone lines were busy from morning. Maybe, since it was his birthday, everybody wanted to wish him, so I decided to call him later in the day. Still, I had no luck. His lines remained busy. Now I thought his phones were off the hook. Even when I called him late at night, I could not get through. His lines must be out of order, I concluded.

After a month I met Rakesh at a party. He commented ironically that I was too busy to call a friend on his birthday. I defended myself saying that I had called him but his lines were perpetually busy. He was taken aback.

'Telephones are so unreliable. Always some repair or the other and lines are always out of order.'

Tara, Rakesh's very sensible wife, interrupted our conversation. 'Don't blame the telephone department. The problem lies in our house.'

I was surprised by her comment. 'Is there anything wrong at home?'

'Yes! I have two teenage children. And at any point of time when we want to use the telephone, those two are keeping both lines busy.'

'Surely not for the whole day!'

'Yes, for the whole day. They have parallel lines in their rooms. Material affluence has spoiled our normal living.'

I could make out that she was quite upset.

'All of us have one or two children and we pamper them,' she continued. 'Look at my daughters. They have separate rooms. There are two telephones and these girls use the telephones like we use water.'

'What are your telephone bills like?' My math-oriented mind thought of that.

'Who is worried about bills? Telephone bills are paid by the company. The children know that it's a perk given by all corporate houses. And cost is also not an important factor for them. My worry is about the constant conversation with friends. They solve their maths problems on the telephone. They share jokes on the telephone. They read books on the telephone.'

'Really? I have never heard of that!' Rakesh showed his ignorance of what went on in his house.

'Yes,' Tara went on. 'Normally they talk loudly, but when they are on the telephone their voices are almost like a whisper. One has to make an effort to hear what they're saying.'

'What happens if you lock up the telephone?' I suggested.

'It's of no use. Their friends will call our house and the telephone lines will be just as busy.'

'What do they do at night?'

'This computer chat takes up the remaining time. They connect to the Internet and that's it. Whatever you say, they do not understand.'

'Too much is too bad,' Tara continued. 'Telephones are used for communication, but when we do not get to use it even in an emergency, I feel frustrated. Today's children abuse the resources available to them. They do not know how to control their wants and desires,' concluded Tara, sighing with unhappiness.

I'm sure there are many Taras among us. Times have changed, but what Tara says is valid. The next generation will not understand that their elders advise them from experience. Probably these children will only realize the value of good advice when they become parents themselves and their children do not listen to them.

42

BE FAIR TO OTHERS

Once my aunt took me to her ladies' club to preside over a function. There was a delay due to some miscommunication among the organizers, so I was made to wait in the antechamber, where I couldn't do anything but observe the people around. I often feel that studying people's behaviour is more interesting than reading a book.

The ladies' club is in a posh area of Bangalore and is considered an elite institution. The members are mostly from the upper middle-class and most of them are well settled and well travelled. They were busy conversing about all the topics under the sun, from silk saris to the most recent English film in the town. My aunt was talking to her friend, Shanta, and they were engrossed in conversation. My aunt's voice was a little loud and though I was seated at a distance I could hear her conversation quite clearly.

'It is really wrong on your daughter-in-law's part,' my aunt declared like a Supreme Court judge. She was confident that her judgement was perfect, but she dragged me into the conversation anyway, just to get my opinion. 'Be fair. Is it correct on her part to behave like that?'

'Who is she?'

'Shanta's daughter-in-law, Rashmi. She wants an easy

life and loves to relax in far-off places during the school holidays.'

I looked so confused that my aunt decided to give me a brief history of the problem. 'Rashmi's in-laws, that is Shanta's family, are rich. They earned their wealth through hard work. Rashmi hails from an ordinary middle-class family and she loves to enjoy the money that she never earned. She wants to buy new clothes every month. As soon as her husband comes home, she wants to go out for a film or somewhere else. She gets up late in the morning . . .' The list of complaints was never-ending.

I suddenly thought of Radhika, my cousin, the daughter of the same aunt. Radhika too was married into a wealthy business family. Radhika was a schoolteacher and quite used to working very hard. After her marriage, I had met her at my place once. I could not believe what I saw. She had bloated up like a balloon. She was dressed in an expensive sari and decked with ornaments.

Radhika explained her daily routine to me. 'I get up in the morning around nine.'

'Why so late?'

'We have plenty of servants at home. They do all the work. Why should I get up so early? I worked a lot before marriage. Mahesh is very busy so I wait for his arrival from office. As soon as he comes, I want to go out for a film or a walk. I have not seen much of the world and managing two kids for the whole year is tiring. I've told Mahesh that we should go abroad for every holiday. Let it be Nepal or Sri Lanka, but I want to travel abroad during the school holidays.'

Thinking of what Radhika had said, I interrupted my aunt's complaints to ask, 'How is Radhika?'

'She's fine. Poor child. Her mother-in-law is a nagging type. She comments on everything. She is lucky to have a daughter-in-law like Radhika. If her mother-in-law had a daughter-in-law like Rashmi, then she would appreciate my daughter's worth.'

I felt depressed. These elderly women, despite being educated, were behaving like kindergarten children. What one's daughter does is all right but when a daughter-in-law does the same thing, then everything is wrong. The yardsticks are different because one is your daughter and the other is somebody else's daughter.

All this time I had been wondering what I should talk about to the gathering. At times, I feel at a loss because I don't know what topic will be of interest to the audience. Now I had decided—I would speak on the topic 'Be fair to others'.

43

Bonded by Bisleri

The 26 January horror of Kutch in Gujarat is well known. Without any warning, Mother Earth opened her mouth and engulfed the people and their belongings. Overnight, rich people were reduced to the streets. But the spirit of the Kutchi people is admirable. They faced this disaster bravely and are still fighting to restore life to normalcy.

The media has to be congratulated for its role in the relief efforts. Within hours of the tragedy, all newspapers and television channels had zoomed in to cover the disaster and broadcast it all over the world. Along with India, the rest of the world participated in helping these unfortunate people. After all the rush of the TV crews and media people, hordes of NGOs and government officials landed up in Kutch. People started picking up their life from where they had left it. Life started to return to normal at a slow pace.

I went to visit these areas after some time, when the dust of propaganda had settled down, in order to see actual life. After all, the emotions had drained off and reality had become the priority.

Several small villages deep inside Kutch, away from the main road connecting Ahmedabad and Bhuj, had been badly affected by the earthquake. I was visiting these remote places in the deep interior when one of the tyres of my jeep went flat. Getting it fixed would take some time. My driver went to get this done.

I was alone and bored. I saw a few tents nearby. They were temporary sheds covered with blue plastic sheets. They were the temporary houses, schools and health centres for the people residing in that area. Later, I heard that there were tent hotels as well.

Life was busy and people were getting on with their chores. As it was monsoon season, men and women were busy in the fields. It was very strange. For many years there had not been much rain in Kutch, but that year it had rained abundantly. Farmers were having a bumper crop. I suppose nature has its own method of justice. On the one hand she takes away something and on the other she gives something in return. Small children were playing in the dust happily.

I peeped into one of the nearby tents. A young girl, about fourteen years old, was cleaning grains and preparing to cook a meal. When she saw me, she rose with a smile and said, 'Please come in and sit down.'

As I wanted to see how they lived, I entered the shed. She gave me a charpoy to sit on. Inside the tent it was clean and neat. There was a thin partition made of an old sari. I understood from her conversation that her family was not from Kutch.

The girl offered me a glass of water. Though it was the monsoon season, the sun was hot, but I was a little hesitant to drink the water. Many thoughts flashed across my mind. If the water was not sterile, then I was at risk of contracting diseases like dysentery, hepatitis B and jaundice. If I refused to accept the water, however, I knew I would hurt the girl's feelings. So I took the glass but did not drink the water.

The girl had a younger sister who might have been around twelve years old. There was a little boy sleeping in a home-made cradle. Outside, there was a temporary open kitchen where *sabzi* was being cooked. The elder one was making a dough of wheat flour.

'It seems from your language that you are not Gujaratis. Where are you from?' I asked.

Smiling, the younger sister answered, 'We're not from Gujarat, we're from Mumbai.'

'Have you come here to visit your relatives?'

'No, we don't have any relatives here. This is our house. We have come here with our parents.'

I was very surprised by this answer because, normally, people flee areas afflicted by calamities, whereas these people had moved in. 'What is your father doing here?'

Both girls were eager to give me information. The elder one replied, 'My father used to beg in Mumbai at Mahim Creek, near the church. My mother used to sell candles at the church entrance.'

'What made you come here?'

'One day, we saw the news on TV and we came to know that there had been an earthquake here. It was shown every hour on TV in the corner shop. My father said "Let's go" and we came here.'

'Who paid for your train tickets?'

'Nobody. We came here without tickets. The whole

train was full of people. There were many people like us who have come. The entire station was heavily crowded. There was no ticket collector.'

'How did you come from the train station?'

'We didn't know anyone. But there were plenty of buses running between the station and Bhuj. There were many foreign volunteers. The buses were jam-packed. We also got into one of the buses and landed on the main road.'

'How did you come to this particular area?'

'There were many jeeps going from the main roads to all interior villages. On the main road, there was a convoy of trucks full of different relief materials. They used to unload materials on either side of the road. People who did not have anything would pick them up from the roadside. We also picked up some.'

'What were the materials on the roadside?'

'There were food articles, apples, biscuit packets, clothes, blankets and many more items. My father told each one of us to pick up what we could and we collected a lot. We have never seen so much in our life in Mumbai. Everything was in plenty.'

Children are innocent and they always tell the truth until they become adults and lies creep into their lives. One lies to boast, to show what he is not. But children are so confident. They never pretend to be what they're not. Naturally, the Mumbai beggar's daughters described the whole scenario as if it was a very memorable event.

The elder one said much more than that. 'There were people crying, some of them in pain. Some had lost their children or parents. It was very sad to see. But there **were** plenty of people to help also. There were doctors working overnight. There were swamijis working like common men, distributing medicines. There were army people digging to build houses. There was no difference between day and night, the rich and the poor.

'Our position was better. We did not lose anybody, nor did we lose any material, because we never had anything to begin with. People who have something have to fear losing it, but people who don't have anything to lose have no such fear. My mother and father helped people and someone said that inside the villages there was nobody to help. There were jeeps constantly travelling between the villages and the main road. So we got into one of the jeeps and landed in this village. Some organization was giving bamboo, camping materials like tents, and other roofing materials, free to all those people who had lost their houses. As we had no home, we also got all the materials. Sometimes we got double because my mother was in one queue and my father in another.'

'What all have you got?'

'Plenty of food. We have been eating to our hearts' content every day and we have also been giving some to people who were unable to stand in the queue. We know what it is to be hungry.'

'Why did you settle here then?'

'My father had asthma in Mumbai. He was unable to breathe and on many days we would go hungry. Someone said it was due to the pollution. It might be true, because after we came here, he has been normal, because there's no pollution here. Anyway, we had also built our own house, so we decided to settle down.'

'What job does your father do here? Does he continue to beg?'

'No. We are self-sufficient now. He is working as a coolie in a nearby field. He earns Rs 100 a day. Our mother also does the same thing, so the income is doubled. We're comfortable. The earthquake has come like a boon to us.'

She asked her sister to get some tea and biscuits. She inquired, 'Which biscuits do you want?'

'Do you have a variety?' I asked, surprised.

She pulled the curtain aside and I was amazed to see the varieties of biscuit packets, cartons of Bisleri mineral water, utensils, steel trunks and other things.

'From the day of earthquake, most of us here have been drinking only Bisleri water. It seems some foreign country has sent a shipful of it. What I have given you is also mineral water.'

I drank the water with contentment.

44

BAHUT KUCH HOTA HAI

One Sunday morning I had an unusual visitor. He was a close friend from my childhood days and had also been our neighbour then. We had not met in thirty-five years. Suddenly, he appeared with his son, without any prior notice. Thirty-five years is a long time and much had happened since we last met. The young, handsome teenager I had known then now looked short, tired, with a bald head and a paunch. The confident, talkative person had become a little diffident, anxious and hesitant. I wonder how I appeared to him.

I was very happy to see him. We had great times as children. At the back of my mind, I remembered those carefree days. No wonder the words of the beautiful ghazal sung by Chitra and Jagjeet Singh, *'woh kagaz ki kashti woh baarish ka paani . . .'* bring tears to our eyes at times.

My friend introduced his son to me. He was a young man of twenty-two years with a bachelor's degree in electrical engineering. He looked indifferent and was not interested in our talk. I casually asked him what he was doing.

He perked up. 'I want to join a software company and then go to America. I want to stay there for five years and come back and start my own company and become big. I know that with ten thousand rupees one can build an empire. Is it not true, Aunty?'

I didn't know what to answer, because starting a company means a lot of struggle and hard work, and success is unpredictable. 'Where are you working now?'

'I am not working anywhere. I am waiting to join a good software company.'

'Do you have a background in programming or any experience?'

'No, I don't, but I'm sure that I will learn fast. I don't want to take up any other job now. If I take up a non-software job, I will get a salary of only five or six thousand rupees and I will have to be on the site too. It's not at all big money, so I haven't taken up anything.'

Now I understood the anxiety on my friend's pale face. He was about to retire and here was his son, unemployed and dreaming big. Dreaming is always good, but turning the dream into reality is more important. I remembered the words of TISCO chairman, J.J. Irani: 'Vision without action is merely a dream; action without vision is merely passing time; but vision and action together can change the world.'

As a teacher, I am used to giving advice. So, whether he liked it or not and whether he had asked for it or not, I gave him a piece of my mind. When he left with his father, his face was glum.

I could not help recalling the laziness and conceit of this young man when I met a boy with a totally different attitude some time later, on a beach in Orissa. Because

Orissa is blessed with both nature's beauty and magnificent examples of our nation's cultural heritage, most of us know only of the state's famous tourist attractions. There is a place, however, that is not as well known yet extremely beautiful. It is a small sleepy town of fishermen known as Chandipur, facing the Bay of Bengal. It is approximately 200 km from Bhubaneswar by road. It has a small guesthouse, but few visitors come here. Those who do make it this far are treated to a game of hide-and-seek with the sea. The unusual phenomenon is that at low tide the sea retreats a good five kilometres and the water disappears completely, revealing a stretch of flat land. One can walk, play or even drive a jeep on this temporary land. After a few hours, the sea comes back in full swing, as if nothing has happened. Visitors wait on the seashore to see this wonder. It's an amazing sight.

Once I was waiting on the seashore for the sea to recede in order to walk on the tidal plain. The sea was retreating slowly, but it hadn't receded far enough to walk. There were many fisherfolk on the shore, busy with their work. Whenever the sea starts to ebb, red crabs come out on the sand. Older children were busy collecting them and younger ones were collecting shells. The lean, dark and rugged fisherwomen, dressed in saris, were spreading their nets to catch fish. Then I saw a young boy of maybe twelve helping his mother to hold the net. When she became tired, he would help her, and when she did not need him, he would collect crabs. His actions showed that he was enthusiastic and happy. When he came to the shore, he approached me and offered me fresh crabs, perhaps thinking I was a prospective buyer. I said that I didn't eat crabs but that I wanted to talk to him.

He came and sat with me on some steps specially made for visitors. I looked at him carefully. He was thin and dark, but his eyes were like diamonds sparkling at night. He was wearing only shorts and his body was completely wet, but he did not seem uncomfortable or self-conscious. He was as natural as a fresh flower. His smile and enthusiasm were contagious.

I asked about his family. I came to know that his father was a rickshaw driver, earning fifty rupees a day. His mother supplemented the family income by catching fish and crabs. The boy, whose name was Javed, was studying in school and always stood first. He also had a little sister at home. I was curious to know how much Javed earned every day and also his schedule.

He said, 'In the morning, when the sea goes back, I hunt for crabs, help my mother and then go home, take a bath and do a little kitchen work to reduce my mother's burden. Then I go to school. Evenings, I do my homework and in the night, when the sea goes back, I go crab hunting again. Allah is very kind to our land. I heard that this is the only place in our country where the sea disappears and we can get crabs twice a day without much difficulty.' He probably earned five or ten rupees a day.

I was unhappy that he earned so little for such hard work. I asked him, 'Only five or ten rupees, Javed? What will you get with that? And to earn that, you wake up at 5 a.m. and you don't go to sleep till 11 p.m.'

The boy's enthusiasm did not fade with this question. Smiling, he said, 'Madam, is five rupees not a big sum compared to nothing? *Panch rupay se bahut kuch hota hai!* We can buy salt; we can buy chillies. If we sit idle, we cannot buy even that. Nobody gives us money in hundreds and thousands. Every drop makes an ocean.'

I was amazed at Javed's answer. A poor fisherboy had reminded me of the famous saying, 'It is better to light a candle than to curse the darkness.'

Then I remembered my friend's son wasting his time as he waited for a lucrative software job.

45

Oh Teacher, I Salute Thee

Once upon a time a teacher was more powerful than a ruler. He loved his students immensely and punished them when they were wrong. They would stay with him for ten to twelve years, helping him in all his work. He treated them like his own children. When these children grew up, they would remember the teacher and his wife and respect them throughout life. There was an unwritten rule that they had to give back to their teachers a part of their earnings later in life. The teacher felt proud of his students' progress. He never amassed wealth; his wealth was his students. Every teacher used to pray to God that his own students should overtake him in acquiring knowledge. That would be the greatest joy to him. *'Shishyad ichchet parajayam'*—the student should be better than the teacher. That system was known as Gurukula.

When I was young, we used to participate in district or state-level competitions. For this purpose, we used to travel from our home town to different places. Our teacher used to accompany us. We never stayed at hotels. He would take us to his sister's house and our entire team stayed there. Our teacher never gained any profit from the whole exercise, but he thought of us as his own family.

His sister would house and feed us without expecting anything. Now, when I look back, I feel that our system was great.

There is a very nice story of how students once held their teachers in great esteem. A mighty emperor was asked, 'You are a powerful emperor with so much of wealth, a vast kingdom and a mighty army. Your teacher is poor and does not own even a piece of land. But still when you meet him, why do you bow down and touch his dusty feet? Why do you sit below him and listen so earnestly? Why don't you summon him to the court?'

The emperor smiled and said, 'What a fool you are! My teacher is one of the richest men. The land that you talk about can be gained or lost in a war. The might of an emperor lasts only as long as he is young and healthy. The money he has can be spent, looted or destroyed. In no way is an emperor a great man. Look at the teacher. He has knowledge and, every year, he gives it to his students. The more he gives, the more he prospers. Nobody can loot his wisdom or his knowledge. No one can take it away by force or violence. He flourishes every year with more and more knowledge. Is he not a great man? All his students are like his own children and when children prosper, is not the father a wealthy man?'

This story shows the respect for the teacher and the teacher's great attachment both to knowledge and to his students. That is the reason we Indians place the teacher in the third-highest position in the social hierarchy, after the mother and the father.

Today, the Gurukula system neither exists nor is it

practical. Our government has taken enough pains and invested considerable resources to establish modern education in villages and cities. It has appointed several thousand teachers who have been trained to teach different subjects and the values of life. Their main objective is to produce better citizens for tomorrow.

Recently, I was in Orissa on work. In October 1999, there had been a great cyclone in Orissa, which nobody expected. The cyclone uprooted trees, took away roofs and destroyed buildings. The state also suffers from chronic floods. Every year, many people lose their mud houses, their cattle and other property. Statistics show that there is a rise in the number of orphans, the physically handicapped and the mentally retarded after every disaster. Orphanages thus become overcrowded. Many a time, parents simply abandon their physically handicapped and mentally retarded children. They consider them an additional burden in their poverty. Due to waterborne diseases in the aftermath of natural disasters, government hospital wards fill up with three times more patients than they can handle. Doctors, NGOs and government officials work hard, but the disasters are often too much to handle.

No government can repair schools every year. It is a Herculean task. So our Foundation decided that some of the schools we planned to build near a river should be built at an elevation, so that they could also act as a shelter during floods. We involved schoolteachers in this work and they were very proud to help us because, after all, it was their school. The system worked well with us because of the teachers' participation.

I went to inaugurate one of the shelter-cum-school complexes in an interior part of Orissa. It was early in the morning. The whole atmosphere was quite festive. The teacher who had helped us to build the school had been transferred to a neighbouring village, but he still came for the occasion.

Before the inauguration, I felt like talking to the students. When I went to one of the classes I was surprised to see that the classroom was very crowded with students. Most of the children were sitting on the floor. Only a few benches were available. I looked in the next room. It was the same. Outside, a class was being taught in the shade of a neem tree. Clearly, there was a dearth of classrooms.

I was there a little earlier than scheduled. The new principal of the school came and met me with apologies. She was a middle-aged woman, but looked quite fit. She appeared very strict, but looks are often deceptive. She said that she was very busy with the day's function. While talking to her, I saw another structure in one corner of the compound. In front of that building, a sari and a few other wet clothes had been hung out to dry.

Having been a teacher, I know that we tend to talk a lot, so I cut her short. Pointing to the sari, I asked who was staying in that building.

She was taken aback and fumbled, 'Oh, that building is a relief shelter.'

'Why is there a relief shelter in the school premises?'

'Just like yours. When there is a natural calamity, it serves as a shelter. Otherwise it is a school.'

'What is the natural calamity now?'

'There was a cyclone.'

'But that was two years back. Are people still staying here?'

She changed her tone and said, 'No, but people affected by the floods are staying there.'

That was also not true, because the floods had receded by that time. The headmistress insisted that we should not waste any more time on this matter because it was getting late for the inauguration. But I was adamant to know who was staying there. She was helpless and accompanied me.

It was a good building with several benches inside that had been arranged as a cot. There were utensils and trunks. Firewood was piled in a corner, indicating that someone was cooking here.

'Who lives here?' I asked again.

She was a little irritated but tried not to show it. 'Some adivasi students. This is used as their hostel.'

Again, this was a blatant lie because this was a boys' school while the clothes were all women's clothes. Besides, it didn't look like a dorm. When I expressed my opinion, the headmistress said nothing. She then told me, 'This building is not very good. Many of our teachers are very poor and they have to come from a great distance. So I have given them a place to stay temporarily.'

I didn't believe her.

'The teachers are paid well and also get a house rent allowance. Why would they stay in the school premises?'

I could hear a murmur behind me. Young children with

eyes wide open were looking at me. Children are the best spokespersons. They tell the truth and won't lie to please anybody. So I called a young boy and asked, '*Beta,* who is staying there?'

The boy pointed his finger at the headmistress. She bowed her head in shame.

I went to her and said, 'Why did you lie to me, that too four times, giving four different reasons? If you lie, the children learn from you and do the same. You should be a model to them. You should lead by example. You are a woman and the essential quality of a woman is compassion. When your students are crowded like animals in the classroom, how can you convert their classroom into your house? It is their building. Can't you just think like a mother? If your child had been in the same class, would you not feel bad? You are also a teacher. Is it not true that the essential quality of a teacher is to care and love the students? I am also a teacher. We should worry about our students' benefit, not ours. This is not a business house. This is a training house for the future generation. How could you use their place to save your house rent, just because these children cannot speak out against this injustice? How can you tolerate their suffering? No government official comes to this godforsaken place and checks. When these children grow up, how will they remember you? Is this not the land of great teachers?'

There was no reply.

46

TREAT ME AS HUMAN

Recently, I had to attend the birthday party of a one-year-old baby. It was arranged lavishly at a five-star hotel. I went with my friend. I didn't know what gift to give such a young child. Nowadays, giving and accepting gifts has become big business. A new equation seems to have arisen: your present should be proportional to your prosperity. The very meaning of a gift symbolizing love and affection has been lost.

There is a very beautiful saying in Gujarati: 'hishob kavadi ma, bakshees laakhma'. It means, 'Whenever you are settling the account, you should settle up to the last paisa. But when you are giving a gift to somebody, think not of the price of the gift, but the affection behind it.' One may give a very expensive gift, but there may not be any affection behind it. On the other hand, a small gift may carry a tremendous amount of love with it.

For a one-year-old child, the only gift I could think of was a food bowl and a spoon with which he could eat. When I picked it up from the store, my friend laughed and said, 'You'll get into trouble. People will expect a bigger gift from you. Think about it before you buy.'

I repeated the Gujarati proverb and went ahead with my purchase.

We went to the hotel. Everybody who was somebody in the city had been invited. There were children, adults and old people. There were society ladies and businessmen. Kanchipurams, patolas, chiffons and matching diamonds could be seen everywhere. The total amount of gold worn at the party must have exceeded what is stocked in Tribhuvandas Bhimji Javeri, the most famous jewellery shop in Mumbai!

The usual rituals were performed—parents cutting the cake, father blowing out the first candle, mother feeding the cake to the baby, video recording of the event, bursting of balloons and singing 'Happy Birthday'. Then people started giving the gifts. This was followed by dinner.

Suited and booted men were thinking of new contacts and women were exchanging news of the latest fashions. Young teenage girls and boys were busy listening to Metallica and heading for the dance floor. Old people were complaining and talking nostalgically about the past days, or exchanging news about their illnesses and treatments. Young mothers were busy feeding their kids. The birthday boy was crying. His uncomfortable clothes were hurting him; so were the gold ornaments he had been made to wear. The bright, unfamiliar lights were scaring him. I saw the gifts given to the baby. Expensive silverware, gold chains, cash, even a laptop computer!

Many people whom I did not know came to me and started narrating the difficulties in their organizations. Everybody had the same question: 'When you are free, shall I come and meet you? We don't want money, but we want your guidance.' Experience has taught me that nobody asks for money at the first meeting; most people ask for guidance in various matters that are totally unrelated to me, like finding a suitable match for their daughter or a job for their son. They ask for various types of assistance, in cash or kind, for their social organizations. If nothing else, they want me to address some gathering. At such times, I often feel like shouting, 'Don't treat me as a machine that can be used for your benefit, treat me as human!'

Some time later I was in Ahmedabad for some work. The Law Garden Road there is popularly known as the Love Garden area. There are small shops that open only in the evenings and remain open till 11 p.m. There are open-air restaurants with chairs and tables placed on the road. It reminds me of Paris, a tourist paradise. Normally young tourists visit this place late in the evenings.

The shops are small but extremely colourful. They sell handicrafts of Gujarat. Gujarat is famous for its embroidery, such as kutch work, *chaniya cholis,* bed sheets and pillow covers. There are shops selling inexpensive silver pendants and other silver ornaments of rural design. These are enchantingly beautiful. When one sees such attractive wares, one feels tempted to buy something, unmindful of whether the items purchased will ever be worn or used.

One evening I had gone to this area to window-shop with my friends. While I was walking on the streets aimlessly, a beautiful purse embroidered in mirror work caught my eye. I liked it and asked the shopkeeper its price. The owners were a young couple probably married only two or three years earlier. The girl was charming and healthy and had a beautiful smile. She was wearing a simple cotton sari; other than a black bead chain and glass bangles, she wore no other ornaments. If a woman is healthy and smiling, she appears beautiful even without ornaments. Her husband was a little older, maybe around twenty-five, lean and tall. He said that the price of the purse was Rs 100.

My friend from Ahmedabad felt that it was too costly. She wanted to bargain. Just then, I noticed a baby, probably a year old, lying in a cradle, close to the footpath near the shop. He was dressed in a simple cotton outfit, playing with a wooden toy. The baby was healthy and cheerful. I did not see his parents around, so I asked the girl about it.

She said proudly, 'He's our baby.' Her warm smile made me want to converse with her.

'Why do you bring the baby to the market? Can't you leave him with someone at home, or with a neighbour?'

She replied hesitantly, 'I don't have anyone at home and all my neighbours are in different shops here, doing the same business.'

I always like to converse with these women and try to understand their way of living. The beautiful kutchi purse disappeared from my mind and thoughts about this baby crept in.

'How do you manage with your baby and work?'

'I wake up early in the morning and do all the embroidery work and household chores. My husband looks after the baby. In the afternoon he does the embroidery and I look after the baby. In the evening both of us look after the shop and the baby together.'

'Do you read the newspaper? Or watch TV?' These questions were quite irrelevant, but I wanted to know.

'We don't have a TV. Once in a while, we go to our neighbour's house to see it. In our *basti*, we get only one Gujarati paper, which my husband reads and tells me the news. Anyway, there is no great news every day. Some political party rules the country, somebody is murdered or there is some natural calamity. Our life will not be affected by any of these. It is the same, ever since I was a small girl. My father in Kutch used to do the same thing that my husband does now.'

'Can you read? Have you gone to a school?'

'No, I never went to school. I had a stepmother who never sent us to school. We're from Kutch. When we were children, from the very beginning, we had to learn embroidery rather than attend school. My husband has studied up to the fourth class, enough to read a Gujarati newspaper.'

'How old is your child?'

'One year. Today is his birthday. We've decided not to have any more children. Though we may not be educated, let him study and we shall work hard for him.'

By this time, the bargaining was over. The shopkeeper would not reduce the price, so my friend didn't buy the purse and we were about to move. I looked at the child again—a happy, healthy child. It was his birthday, so I suddenly remembered the birthday party at the five-star hotel. Being born in a wealthy family is merely a matter of chance. This child had been born here. I felt like giving him a gift. I opened my purse and placed a hundred rupee note in his plump hands and started walking away.

Immediately, his mother came running after me. 'Please take your money back. We're not beggars. We don't know you. Why should you give us money?'

I could see the anger on her face. I said, 'It's not for you. Today is his birthday and we have a custom: whenever a child completes a year, we give him a small gift. I talked to you for the past five minutes, so I do know you a little. I'm giving this money to the child as a blessing. Don't refuse.'

By this time, her anger had cooled. Her eyes brightened and her smile came back. I turned and was about to walk on. She caught my right hand and gave me the purse. I was shocked. I resisted accepting it.

'Are you returning what I've given the baby as a gift?'

'No *ben*, I am really amazed about the whole thing. Many customers come to our shop, but it is always about business. They ask the price and then they bargain. After they give the money, they take the packet, don't even turn back and go away. Not even once has anybody talked to us like a human being. They always treat us like business people. Nobody asks how we live, what we do. They see exactly what you saw today. You are the first person who has treated us like any other human being. That's a nice feeling. Do not get upset that I am giving you this. My child is giving you this. It felt so nice that someone who is not from my place, who does not know our language, who is unknown to us, is blessing my baby on his first birthday. Is it not our duty to respect such a lady within our capacity? God has not given me enough money to fill this empty purse, but I pray that God will shower enough fortune on you to fill up many purses.'

I could identify totally with her desire to be treated as a human being and not as some faceless machine. I accepted the gift happily. The child was still smiling and playing with his toy, oblivious to us.

47

An Unknown Benefactor from Chennai

The concept of fund-raising is extremely popular in the USA. There are separate departments in universities and charitable organizations for this activity. They catch the right fish by different methods so that donors give money to the organization or university concerned. This notion is now catching on in India too.

My friend Mythili works for an NGO. She is a fund-raiser, smart and talkative, hailing from a middle-class family. One morning, she called up asking me to accompany her to the house of a very affluent person, a lady who was well known in the city. Mythili had been approaching this woman for a donation. At last, the lady had agreed to meet Mythili in her farmhouse forty kilometres away from the city. Mythili was a little hesitant to go alone and so she asked me to accompany her.

We reached the palatial house. It was built on a huge twenty-five acre plot and was surrounded by a beautiful garden. The house was built in the traditional cottage model. There was strict security and we were asked a number of questions. Only after confirming our appointment over the intercom did the guard let us in.

Though it had a rustic look from the outside, the house was gorgeous and modern inside. All the walls were painted in pastel shades. There was a pond with a fountain sprinkling scented water. It seemed to bring nature into that big hall. The wooden floor and antique objects added to the charm. There was also a terrace garden.

The lady of the house was sitting on a swing hung by shining chains. She looked gorgeous in a chiffon sari and platinum ornaments. From a distance, she made a gesture telling us to sit down. Though in her mid-fifties, she looked much younger. There was the aroma of sandalwood all around. Fresh flowers were kept in vases. Two smart-looking secretaries were next to her. Both Mythili and I felt very uncomfortable because the most important things in life—the smile and warmth—were missing here. I have always observed that it is not the food, nor the ornaments, nor the house, but a host's genuine warmth that puts guests at ease and opens the gateway to friendship, irrespective of status, age, gender and language.

Mythili talked about her NGO, of course everything in superlative terms as befitted her mission. Ultimately, she has to sell her ideas. The lady listened patiently, not showing any reaction. When people don't show any reaction, the person on the other side of the table often becomes tongue-tied. Shrewd people never allow anyone to read their mind. Simple-minded people talk a lot, open their heart and reveal what they are, which is exactly what Mythili did. The other lady revealed nothing at all.

After an unbearable silence, she said, 'Give your papers to my secretary. I will go through them and get back to you.'

Our balloon of enthusiasm was pricked by that answer. After all, she could have said this over the phone. We drove back all the way, having wasted half a day's work.

I met Mythili a month later at a school opening ceremony where the same would-be donor was the chief guest. I asked Mythili about the donation.

Mythili took me aside and told me in hushed tones, 'It's very difficult to get money out of her. She is ready to spend any amount of money on herself, but she thinks ten thousand times before giving to a charity. You know, after I wooed her for a month she finally agreed to give Rs 10,000 on the condition that we invite her for this function as the chief guest, put her photo in the paper and give a press release about her.'

'You shouldn't have asked her for such a small amount.'

'Please remember that raising funds for an NGO is very difficult. You don't have the same experience. Every rupee counts. Is it not true that every drop of water makes an ocean? Nobody donates money without expecting something in return. This is the lesson I've learnt in fund-raising.'

Since I had no experience in fund-raising, I had to accept what Mythili said.

Some time later I returned to work after having been on leave for a week. I dreaded coming back to my office because of the number of letters and emails that would have piled up while I was away. I was busy sorting out letters when my secretary took out a small envelope. There was an expression of surprise on her face.

'What is so surprising in that envelope?'

She showed me a small handwritten note. It said, 'I know that you do not know me. I read about your work in the newspapers. I read your articles as well. When a writer really experiences life, only then can he or she write about it. Language is just a tool but in no way can good language alone make a readable article. It is the personal experience along with suitable language that makes an article interesting to read. By reading your experiences, I have realized what kind of work you do and how passionately you do it . . .'

I was busy so I handed the note back to my secretary and said impatiently, 'This is just one of those exaggerated letters of appreciation. Just file it. You don't need to show me such things. Morning time is very precious in the office.'

'Ma'am, did you read it completely? This is something different.'

I took the note back and continued reading. 'I am old and cannot travel like you. I have saved some money. I would like to give it to you so that you can use it in your work. You may have much more, but this is my contribution to your work. I will not ask to whom you give it or how you use it. I have confidence in you.'

A draft for Rs 4,00,000 was attached to the note.

Now I was even more surprised than my secretary. In my public life, I have received hundreds of applications asking for money and many letters telling me that the money I have donated is insufficient. But here was a person spontaneously giving me money for my work. There was not a single demand. I held up the draft. It was like a star shining in the dark blue sky.

I asked my secretary whether she knew the person who had written the note and donated such a large sum, but she did not. The donor had neither written anything about himself nor given any contact details. From the postmark we knew that the letter was from Chennai.

I bow to this unknown donor from Chennai with great respect. I remembered the poem about Abu Ben Adam and prayed, 'May his tribe increase.'

My mind went back to the rich lady whom Mythili had approached. How different the two donors were!

48

LIFE IS AN EXAMINATION

Sumitra and Suresh were my classmates. Sumitra was bright and sharp in her youth. She was dynamic and pushy. She used to top the class in her studies. Suresh was not as bright as Sumitra, but he was a very nice person. They fell in love and got married. Suresh earned lots of money through business. Sumitra lent a helping hand in managing the business. Even though they were well off, Sumitra would never spend money unnecessarily. She knew the value of money and hard work.

I used to meet them once in a while, maybe at a get-together at their place. They were perfect hosts. We would all sit on their lawn remembering our golden days. Outwardly, they looked happy, the perfect couple, made for each other. But there was always a trace of sadness. They had no children, and they had decided not to adopt a child for reasons of their own.

One day Sumitra called me with an invitation. 'Can you come over for dinner in the evening?'

I thought that it was one of their usual parties, but when I entered their house I felt tension. They were both looking tired and worried and not at all themselves.

As soon as Sumitra saw me she broke down. 'Today I went for a medical check-up. It was a routine check-up, that's what I thought. But my doctor says there is a problem with my kidney. I'm really worried.'

Death, a five-letter word, scares everyone. The person may be a king, a billionaire, a pauper or a beggar. But there is nobody who can escape death. I could easily understand Sumitra's and Suresh's worries. The previous year Suresh had had a heart attack. They were entirely dependent on each other. Now the time had come when they did not know how long they would survive. In life, nothing can be equated with health. Good health is the greatest asset. Money can buy medicine and comfort, but not happiness. They wanted me to listen to their worries and I did so wholeheartedly.

Suresh was very practical. 'Look, now we must think of how we should spend money in the remaining years. We should write our will so that later on there won't be any problem among the relatives. No relative helped us in our difficult period, so I don't want to give anything to any of them.'

Suresh was right. When a person earns money through hard work, his personality is different, whereas if he inherits money without hard work, he will not be strong. But Sumitra had a different opinion. It was the first time that I saw Sumitra opposing her husband. Though it was a cool night, their heated arguments raised the temperature in the room. I did not interfere in their discussion. It was their personal matter and their money. How could an outsider like me get involved? I thought it better not even to witness such things, so I decided to leave.

Sumitra stopped me and said, 'We called you for

suggestions. You've been dear and impartial to us. Don't consider yourself an outsider.'

So I had to stay and listen to both their arguments.

'I have never spent money on myself. I don't know how long I will live. Let me enjoy life the way I want.' This was Sumitra's argument.

No conclusion was drawn on that day.

Days passed. I could see a rift between the couple. I used to see and hear about Sumitra more than I did of Suresh. She started buying very fashionable clothes regardless of whether they suited her or not. I saw her photos in the society pages.

Once, when I was returning from a trip, I ran into her at the Mumbai airport. I could not believe my eyes. Was she the same Sumitra, the Sumitra of long hair and cotton saris? Now she was dressed in transparent Western clothes, dripping diamonds all over—bracelets, earrings, rings and chains. Her face had half an inch of make-up and she was drenched in perfume.

She explained why she was in Mumbai. 'I was here for a horse race. I had never seen a horse race before, so I thought, let me have that experience. From here I'm flying to Chennai to attend the wedding of a film producer's daughter.'

'Since when have you started moving in the same circles as film producers?'

'Of late, I've started financing movies. It's a great field. I was not even aware of it. I spent all my life without enjoying so many things. Now I'm busier than before.'

'How is Suresh?'

She was unhappy with my question. 'He is, as usual, immersed in his business.'

Now I realized that both of them were leading their lives independently. Suresh called me a few times to ask about certain educational institutions. Because of my experience, I gave him my sincere opinion.

After a few days, Suresh's lawyer called me up. 'Suresh has made his final will and he wants you to be the executor. Is this acceptable to you?'

I was surprised about Suresh's decision. Neither was I his relative nor did I have any business association with him. I thought that I should go and meet him. One of the most important responsibilities in life is to handle somebody else's money. You can afford to lose your own money, but if you are a trustee of any organization then your responsibilities are a thousand times greater. Trust is one of the most precious qualities you can find in this world.

I met Suresh at his home. Sumitra was away in Delhi. He was alone and cheerful, talking to his lawyer. When I read the will, I was surprised. He wanted to fund scholarships and make donations to educational institutes, libraries and computer centres. But nowhere did he want his name to be mentioned. All donations were in Sumitra's name.

I raised my eyebrows.

'Yes,' he explained. 'We may differ in our ideas. But without her help, I would not have built my business. She has her own opinions, but this is the way I look at it.'

'Is Sumitra aware of this will?'

'No. Please don't tell her about this.'

After a week's time, I came to know that Sumitra's condition was very serious. She was dead before I could reach the hospital. I also came to know that her bank balance was nil. Suresh seemed to take his dear wife's death very well. They had been married for a very long time, so I imagined how hard it must be for him to live without her. After a year, Suresh's lawyer called me and informed me that he had passed away in his sleep.

Thus the lives of two of my great friends, two individuals, ended within the span of one year. Whenever I look at the Sumitra Memorial Prize, I am faced with a question: is life not strange? Both of them knew that they would die, but chose two different paths. Sumitra was brighter than Suresh, but did not understand life the way Suresh understood it. She opted to enjoy life, whereas Suresh opted for philanthropic deeds. The same set of circumstances brought two different results from two different individuals.

49

My Money, Your Money

I always feel that I am young at heart, irrespective of my age. The reason is that I am a teacher, so I mix with the younger generation. Their energy is contagious. They share their secrets with me. They are my inspiration. I teach in a college and I meet many students in each batch. Over a period of time I might not remember their names, but they remember me. Many a time they have helped me in critical situations, such as in an airport or in a hotel when I don't have reservations. They remember that I was their teacher and do their best to help me. It gives me enormous happiness to meet and talk to my old students. No wonder old wine, old memories and old students are so precious and rare.

About a decade ago, I was teaching computer science to postgraduate students. In that batch there were many bright students and among them were Ashok and Anitha. I liked them a lot. They were very sincere and hard-working. One day, after their graduation, both of them came and met me. They wanted to take up teaching as a career. They asked my opinion.

'If you love teaching and have a passion for it, only then take it up. Today, in the software industry, both of you can earn high salaries, which no college can match.

However, money won't give you the same satisfaction you get in teaching. If you don't like teaching and take it up, it will be an unwise move. If a teacher makes a mistake, an entire class is affected and so is the future of all those students.'

Anitha and Ashok still opted for teaching. When they were married, I went to their wedding and blessed them wholeheartedly. Now they were teachers like me.

Time passed and they had a baby girl. Ashok bought a scooter. They were a small, happy family settled in a rented two-bedroom house, like any educated middle-class family. Ashok's widowed mother stayed with them. Overall, their life looked serene, filled with happiness and laughter.

Though Anitha and I were colleagues now, we met rarely since our timings were different. One day, I met her in the computer lab. She looked worried and unhappy. 'Ma'am, our owner wants the house back. I feel the story may repeat itself in any rented house. It's better if we have our own house. My daughter has grown up now. I have to register her at the toddler's play school. I cannot drop her by scooter because of the clash of timings. My mother-in-law is old and has arthritis. We require a maid to help her. There are so many financial demands.'

I understood her problem and nodded. After all, I too had undergone the whole cycle and much more in my younger days.

She continued, 'I have decided to take up a job in a software company that will pay more. Ashok says he's very happy teaching and doesn't want to shift, but I feel that one of us has to take a better-paying job. What does it matter who takes up the job? There is no difference between Ashok and me. Together we make a unit. It doesn't matter who earns what. Ashok is a very supportive and understanding husband, and my mother-in-law is a great lady. I have started applying for jobs in software companies. Can I give your name as a reference?'

She was logical and practical. I agreed that she could give my name as a reference. As soon as she got a job, she called up and thanked me.

After three years, I received an email from her inviting me to her house-warming ceremony. I was happy for her and went to the function. It was a compact three-bedroom house with all the modern amenities. She was looking very confident and happy. I was the last guest to leave, so she had some time to talk to me.

'Ma'am, this is the result of my hard work. I saved every single rupee for this house. Today, I have built the house and I feel nobody can remove us from here.'

'How is your job?'

'It's great. Very demanding, but I enjoy it. In three years, I have been made the group leader and five people report to me. I work long hours. The company has sent me to the USA twice, each time for a period of three months.'

'How do you manage all these things, with your child?'

'My mother-in-law and the maid manage my daughter. My maid is extremely efficient. Of course, Ashok is also there to supervise.'

Some time later, I saw her in a new Opel Astra car in

Jayanagar with her 'extremely efficient' maid. The maid was well dressed and was holding the hand of Anitha's five-year-old child. Anitha was happy to meet me, but I was surprised by her appearance. She looked different. She wore an expensive sari, shining diamond droplets and nearly a dozen gold bangles. And, beneath her make-up, her face showed some arrogance. Was it over-confidence or a shade of rudeness? I couldn't tell.

Anitha was excited. 'Ma'am, I got employee stock option shares from my company. I cashed part of it and bought a car. I took my family, along with the maid, to Singapore for a holiday. I've told Ashok to come with me, along with the child, when I next visit the USA. Anyway the company pays for the dependents. Isn't it great?'

Yes. It was great. But something was missing.

'How's Ashok?'

In a tone tinged with a little unhappiness she replied, 'He's still in college, teaching the same old stuff. He got a promotion recently, a small hike of just five hundred rupees. Ma'am, you should tell Ashok that he's wasting his time in a college. He can get a better job than mine. He's brighter than I am. But he won't listen to me. Maybe the academic field has made him too soft.'

'Anitha, everyone is grown up and they know what they want.'

She didn't like my answer.

Later, I happened to meet Ashok at a teachers' workshop. It was lunch break and we had some free time.

'Sorry to barge in on you with my personal problems,

but you're the only person whom Anitha and I have known fairly well for a long time. You have seen us as students and as colleagues. Your advice and your opinion matter a lot to me.'

'Did Anitha ask you to talk to me?' I inquired, remembering my earlier meeting with Anitha.

'No. I'm extremely unhappy with my marriage. Many a time, I wonder whether I should stay married or separate.'

'Ashok, don't be silly. There are always differences of opinion in a couple, particularly when they're young. Those who say there's no difference of opinion are not really husband and wife,' I joked. I wanted to release the tension and ease the problem with humour.

Ashok was not affected by my humour. 'No, ma'am. Anitha now feels her job is better and she acts superior. She looks down upon other people. Everything is just "me" for her now. Like, "I bought this house with my money," and "with my ESOP shares, I bought a car". She behaves as though she can buy everything with the money she earned by selling her shares. The share price of the IT company she works for keeps rising, so no wonder ESOP is a boon to employees. But it's bringing unhappiness in our family. She doesn't respect my old mother as she used to do before.'

'Why?' I asked foolishly.

'Because she can be replaced by an efficient maid. Anitha feels she can get what I earn for the entire year simply by selling a few of her shares. She keeps telling me all the time that she's better than I am. I cannot live with a wife who's got such an attitude.'

'But Ashok, suppose you were in her position. Wouldn't there be any problems then? Can you not accept your wife earning more than you? Maybe it's hurting your ego.'

Ashok thought for a while and replied, 'To some extent you may be right, ma'am. More than that, if the roles had been reversed and I went on harping about "my money", then definitely she would have felt bad. Between husband and wife there shouldn't be any difference. One shouldn't respect the other partner just because he or she earns more. But what hurts me is that she ignores my support. If people get a lot of money in a short time, they act the way Anitha is acting now. Money should come slowly over a period of time. Then only does one respect it. Whether it's a man or a woman, earning too much money in too short a period is as bad as excess liquor.'

I didn't have an answer. I was lost in an ocean of thoughts. Money is a double-edged knife that can be used to cut a fruit and also to kill a person. It's important to earn money, but how you handle it is much more important. If Anitha had been mature, she would have thanked the people around her who cooperated with her. She would have said 'we' instead of 'I'. She would have said, 'With my husband's support, I have built this house.'

50

IS LIFE FAIR?

When a person suffers physically, people sympathize with him or her. When someone is mentally ill, on the other hand, people in our country think differently. Mental disease is a taboo subject in our society. We never consider that mental health is as important or even more important than physical health.

I was working with a psychiatrist who specializes in treating mental diseases. I was helping her rehabilitate patients. Treatment alone is not enough; it is equally important to rehabilitate these patients. Normally people presume that a mentally ill patient will always remain mentally ill. A mentally ill patient is often considered a mad person in our society.

My doctor friend, Kusuma, tells me of many such instances. These true stories are heart-rending and, at times, also amusing. It seems that once at a party, Kusuma met a woman who was well known in society. A few years earlier, Kusuma had treated this lady for depression and cured her completely. Kusuma was happy to see her and went to greet her. But as soon as this woman saw Kusuma, she walked away. Kusuma was taken aback, having expected a warm welcome. After some time, the host introduced Kusuma to all the guests. This lady behaved as if she didn't know Kusuma at all.

After the party was over, she came and apologized. 'Doctor, you should excuse me for seeming indifferent towards you. You have given me a new life, but I didn't want to recognize you in the presence of so many people. Everybody knows you are a psychiatrist. They will guess that I was once your patient and may think I am still mad.'

She left in tears as Kusuma looked on helplessly.

Once, I wanted to discuss some low-technology projects that could employ patients and give them a source of income, so I went to Kusuma's clinic. The receptionist asked me to wait as there was a patient inside. In the waiting room, I saw an old couple sitting next to me. There were no smiles on their faces. They looked very worried. Their clothes showed that they were affluent. The patient was probably their daughter. I then thought that children's mental health brings much more happiness to parents than money.

After some time, the patient came out and I entered Kusuma's chamber. I forgot my ideas of rehabilitation as thoughts about this couple troubled me. I wondered what their problem was and asked Kusuma, but she wouldn't tell me as it would have been a breach of trust. However, she did narrate a few incidents about patients whose identity she did not disclose.

'One of my patients, Maya, came from a cultured background. She was married into a highly educated but less cultured family. It was an arranged marriage where the groom's job was more important than cultural compatibility. She was married to Jagadish, and his sisters and mother were always cruel to her. It was surprising that Jagadish, who was in a good position, was scared of his mother and extremely obedient. The mother took advantage of the situation and would always trouble the innocent daughter-in-law. Jagadish was more his mother's boy than Maya's husband.'

'Kusuma, this is the story in most homes. How many women have suffered in the same way!'

'That's true. Social pressures are high. Many a time, films and TV serials give too much importance to marriage and finding a husband.'

'How did Maya react?'

'Maya tried her level best, like any other Indian woman, to adjust to her in-laws. She worked hard to establish a good relationship. She always felt that one day or the other, her in-laws would change. But when she became convinced that her husband would never take her side, she went into depression. A woman wants her husband to love her. For that, she will be ready to face anything. But once she knows that she will not get this love, she feels utterly disappointed.'

I imagined the young and sensitive Maya going through all these trials. It takes time to recover from mental agony. She might have come and cried many times to Kusuma.

'What treatment did you give Maya?'

'I called Jagadish and his mother, explained to them that what Maya needed was tender love and care, not money. They never understood. He is the principal of a college, but does not understand the simple philosophy of love. He is acclaimed as a great teacher on paper, but his wife is a mental patient. I called Maya's parents and told them there seemed to be no hope that Jagadish would care for their daughter. Maya should realize that and start to live her own life without depending on her husband's love. It was very hard for them to accept this, but as a doctor it was my duty to tell the truth.'

'What happened to Maya?'

'I treated Maya for a long time, over several counselling sessions, many anti-depression tablets, and now she's all right. She is back with her parents.'

'Kusuma, isn't it unfair? Jagadish is the bad person but poor Maya had to undergo the treatment? The person causing the problem is happy and through no fault of hers, Maya suffers. What is worse is that society will blame Maya for leaving her husband.'

'Yes, who says life is fair? Life is always unfair. If you want, you can make it fair.'

51

THREE BRIGHT YOUNG MEN

Many years ago, I was the chief guest at a function. This was held in a hostel for poor students that had been built by a philanthropist. Food and shelter were free, but students had to bear other expenses like tuition and clothing.

In my younger days, I have come across many families who would look after students who were economically backward but otherwise bright. They used to help them with their fees or clothing and often with their food as well. In those days, most colleges were located in larger towns. Many poor students who came to study in these towns used to stay with these families and would be treated as part of the family. The woman of the house considered this a good deed and helped the poor students wholeheartedly. Today, the situation is different. Even smaller towns have schools and colleges, so this custom has disappeared.

While I was sitting on the dais, I remembered the past and congratulated the person who had built the hostel. It was a good deed and of great help to many students. The hostel secretary told me about some of the students in the hostel who had secured ranks but had a problem paying their tuition fees.

He said, 'Madam, this year we have three students from different disciplines who have secured ranks. All of them are from extremely poor families. They have one more year to complete their degrees.'

'What are they studying?'

'One is in medicine, the second in engineering and the third in commerce.'

'Can I meet them after the function?'

The function went on as usual. Often, at such functions, too much praise is lavished on the chief guest. Sometimes, they even make exaggerated and false claims about the chief guest. I feel this unnecessary praising is the highest form of corruption where people are easily fooled, and it encourages those who are praised to develop an inflated opinion of themselves. That's why in the twelfth century, in Karnataka, the great revolutionary leader Basaveshwara warned in his teaching that praise is like golden gallows.

After the function, I met the three poor bright boys whom the secretary had told me about. They were a little puzzled, shy and nervous. All of them had the same story: father in a small job unable to make ends meet, a large family back in the village, no land or any other asset. Only sheer determination to excel in studies had brought them here against all odds.

I felt sorry for them. There are many parents who struggle to give their children the best of education with tuitions, coaching and plenty of books. But here were these eager, hard-working students who were struggling to pay their fees. Perhaps Saraswati, the goddess of learning, liked them.

'Please call on me in June. I will help you with your fees,' I promised.

They did not expect this and I could see the happiness on their faces.

As promised, I paid their fees and forgot about the whole incident. Some years later I was going abroad and wanted to buy a sari for a friend who lived there. I remembered it on the way to the airport and stopped at a sari shop on the way. It was lunchtime, so hardly anybody was in the shop. It was very quiet. I was in a hurry, so I quickly selected a sari that was on display and asked one of the salesmen to pack a similar one and get me the bill.

Suddenly, a young gentleman appeared from the back of the shop. He was well dressed, charming and sophisticated. He smiled at me and invited me to sit in his office. I didn't know who he was. I thought he might be one of my ex-students. Many a time I cannot remember their names, particularly if they were in undergraduate classes.

I stepped into his office. It was well furnished—fresh-cut flowers, marble flooring, latest modern artwork on the walls, electronic gadgets and the whole works. In a nutshell, it was an affluent office.

'I'm in a hurry to go to the airport. I want the packet immediately,' I told him. I opened my purse and gave the money for the sari. I didn't sit down and insisted that I must leave immediately.

The young man smiled and said, 'Please sit down, ma'am. Your packet will be ready any moment.'

I wondered when this young man had passed out of

our college. 'Which year did I teach you?' I asked, trying to place him in a batch I had taught.

'No, ma'am, I was not your student.'

'But you know me?'

'Yes, I met you a few years ago in the student hostel.'

I was unable to remember him.

'You had come there as a chief guest,' he reminded me. 'I met you with two of my friends. You paid my final year B.Com fees.'

Now I did remember him. He had been one of those bright-eyed and nervous young boys, so different from what I saw today.

I felt happy. 'What are you doing now?'

'Ma'am, I am manager and partner in this sari shop. God is very kind. We are doing good business.'

'Where is your family?'

'I am married and settled here. My two brothers are students and live with me. My two sisters are married. My parents are very happy.'

By then my packet had been delivered to me and I got up to leave. He came right up to the car to say goodbye. It was getting late so I rushed and just made it to the aircraft. As the flight took off, I wanted to ensure the sari was good and opened the bag. I was surprised. There were two saris. I had wanted to buy only one and had paid for only one. And the packet contained not only two saris, but also the money that I had paid, along with a small note.

'Ma'am,' the note read, 'it was very kind that you paid for my fees without knowing me. Many times, I have wondered why you did that. I was a total stranger and not related to you at all. You never expected anything from me. Now, I have made it a point to help people who are not related to me, without any expectation. This is my small gift to you. It may not be a big thing, but I would like to give it with affection and gratitude. You have changed my life.'

I was touched by his words and tears filled my eyes.

I reached Mumbai. My international flight was delayed due to a technical problem, so I thought I would go and buy some snacks at the Santa Cruz market. While walking on the footpath with a friend, I stumbled and fell down. My foot swelled up. I was worried that it might be fractured. My friend lived in Mumbai, so she took me to a doctor close by. She assured me that though he was a little expensive, he was very good.

We went to this doctor in Khar. The clinic was modern, the receptionist was smart and professional. She asked whether I had an appointment and when I said no, she asked me to wait. She talked to the doctor and then sent us in. The doctor was young and very confident. I felt at ease. He made me comfortable with his smile. While he was examining my leg, he started a conversation.

'Ma'am, I have met you before. You look older now.'

'Where have you met me before?'

'I was in a student hostel. You had come there as a chief guest. After the function, I met you with my two other friends.'

I guessed who he was but wanted to reconfirm. 'Where are your friends now?'

'One is in Bangalore, a partner in a sari shop, and the other is in the US. How come you are here?'

I explained the reason. By that time, he knew what was wrong with my leg.

'Don't worry. It's not a fracture, just a torn ligament. You'll be all right with medicine.'

I was happy that this boy was doing well and was also relieved that there was no fracture.

While I was about to leave, I asked him, 'Are you married?'

With the same confident smile he replied, 'Yes. My wife is also a doctor and we have settled here.' Then he called the next patient in.

When I came out, the telephone on the receptionist's desk buzzed. Probably the doctor was talking to the receptionist. Maybe he was telling her not to collect any fees, but I wanted to pay. He had just started a clinic in such a posh area and was also married. I wanted to encourage him.

I opened my purse. The receptionist said, 'It's Rs 300.'

'Isn't that a bit too much?' I was surprised and my hand was still inside the purse.

'No. The doctor himself told me the amount. Yours was not a confirmed appointment.'

I paid the bill and left.

I had helped three people at the same time without expecting anything in return, but their attitudes were so different. One person felt grateful for my help and wanted to help others in a similar manner. The other didn't even mention the help he had received from me and felt neither grateful for it nor obliged to me. He treated me exactly as he would have treated a perfect stranger. When people with different ideas face the same situation, they act differently.

I have yet to meet the third one who is in the USA.

Scan QR code to access the
Penguin Random House India website

PENGUIN BOOKS

HERE, THERE AND EVERYWHERE

Sudha Murty was born in 1950, in Shiggaon, North Karnataka. Author, philanthropist, educator, public speaker and engineer, she completed her master's in computer science from IISc, Bangalore. She is the founder of the Infosys Foundation and the chairperson of the Murty Trust. A bestselling author, with more than 300 titles to her acclaim, some of her most famous books include *Three Thousand Stitches*, *Dollar Bahu* and *Wise and Otherwise*. She writes in English and Kannada, and her books have been translated into all major Indian languages and have sold over 60 lakh copies around the country.

Over the years, Sudha Murty has been recognized with many prestigious awards, including the Padma Bhushan and the Padma Shri from the Government of India in 2023 and 2006, respectively; Bal Sahitya Puraskar in 2023; the R.K. Narayan Award for Literature in 2006; the Lal Bahadur Shastri National Award in 2020; and Lokmanya Tilak and Mahatma awards in 2024. She was also awarded the Rajyotsava and Attimabbe Award for excellence in Kannada literature from the Government of Karnataka in 2000 and 2012. Sudha Murty has received nineteen honorary doctorates from various universities across India. Currently, she is also serving as the President-nominated member of Parliament in the Rajya Sabha.

ALSO BY THE SAME AUTHOR

FICTION

Mahashweta
Gently Falls the Bakula
House of Cards
Dollar Bahu
The Mother I Never Knew
The Circle of Life

NON-FICTION

Wise and Otherwise
The Old Man and His God
The Day I Stopped Drinking Milk
Something Happened on the Way to Heaven (Ed.)
Three Thousand Stitches
Common Yet Uncommon

CHILDREN'S

Grandma's Bag of Stories
Grandpa's Bag of Stories
Grandparents' Bag of Stories
How I Taught My Grandmother to Read and Other Stories
How the Onion Got its Layers
How the Mango Got its Magic
How the Bamboo Got its Bounty
How the Sea Became Salty
How the Earth Got its Beauty
The Bird with Golden Wings
The Serpent's Revenge
The Man from the Egg
The Daughter from a Wishing Tree
The Upside-Down King
The Sage with Two Horns
The Magic Drum and Other Favourite Stories
The Magic of the Lost Temple
The Magic of the Lost Story

Here, There and Everywhere

Best-Loved Stories of Sudha Murty

PENGUIN BOOKS

An imprint of Penguin Random House

PENGUIN BOOKS

Penguin Books is an imprint of the Penguin Random House group of companies whose addresses can be found at global.penguinrandomhouse.com

Published by Penguin Random House India Pvt. Ltd
4th Floor, Capital Tower 1, MG Road,
Gurugram 122 002, Haryana, India

First published in Penguin Books by Penguin Random House India 2018
This edition published in Penguin Books by Penguin Random House India 2025

Copyright © Sudha Murty 2018

ISBN 9780143444343

Typeset in Dante MT Std by Manipal Digital Systems, Manipal
Printed at Thomson Press India Ltd, New Delhi

www.penguin.co.in

To Shini,
You are my reflection in thoughts,
in deeds and in appearance

Contents

Introduction

Often, I sense that there is a lot of myself in my stories, whether it is my friends or family or the people I meet. However, the experiences that I write about are mine. I cannot disassociate from myself while writing about them. This book contains some of my most cherished experiences that are like beautiful flowers to me and have been put together here as if to complete a garland. While most of the experiences are from previously published books, there are two new flowers: one that highlights my literary journey and the other that elaborates on the true meaning of philanthropy.

This book is dedicated to my brother Shrinivas. Writing about him is easy enough and yet so difficult. I look like him, think like him, read like him and eat like him. I have enjoyed his company since he was born—I was the second child and he was the fourth. I can spend hours with him without any boredom setting in.

Today, he is a renowned astrophysicist who has innumerable awards and distinguished accomplishments to his credit. His work is all Greek to me, just like mine is to him. I think he is extremely focused and absolutely impractical—he doesn't care much about his appearance, social appropriateness, what others think of him, or even food for that matter. I am much more practical in my approach. In my journey, I have been an integral part of the administration of many organizations. But despite what may appear to be major differences, we are the best of friends.

When Shrinivas and I were children, we had decided to memorize a dictionary each during the summer holidays. Shrinivas was part of the first batch of a recently formed English-medium school in our locality. That school was Kendriya Vidyalaya. So, he chose to learn the English dictionary while I defaulted to the one in Kannada. At that time, the children in the family had been assigned the task of walking the family dog. At times, both of us did not want to take him out individually because we wanted to use that time to learn a few more words. After some thought, we decided to walk the dog together in an effort to recite the new words we had learnt and to avoid monotony. During our walks, we did more than what we had planned. I educated myself about *madhyama* yoga that my brother was learning in Sanskrit, and I spoke to him about trigonometry. I was surprised at the speed with which he learnt its concepts despite the fact that he was younger than me and that it was not even part of his syllabus at school. Other times, we loved to debate about our difference in opinion on various topics.

From the time that I can remember, Shrinivas has loved his three sisters equally. When he was sixteen, he had gone to Nagpur for a debate and won a cash prize. With that money, he bought one sari. He brought it back and gave it to the three of us, saying, 'This is all that I could afford, and I want all of you to share this sari.'

Time has passed and our lives have changed. Still, the four of us are there for each other when things get rough and when happiness abounds.

My brother has been living in a different country for the past forty years, and we meet only annually. But we remain strongly connected and he continues to occupy a very special place in my heart. He is caring but not very expressive and lives in his bubble of science and astrophysics, along with stars, brown dwarfs, black holes and other entities. The only gift that I can really and truly give him is this book: a dear and precious part of me.

1

A Tale of Many Tales

Every person's life is a unique story. Usually, the story becomes famous only after a person receives recognition in ways that matter to the world. If you peep into what lies deep inside, it is the changes he or she has gone through—subtle changes that the world may never understand.

Most people undertake an arduous journey full of highs and lows that helps them modify and create new perspectives, thus forming a better understanding of the world and realizing the fact that real passion is much more beautiful than the pinnacle of their accomplishments. Ironically, life appears to be barren and aimless to some achievers even after they reach a big goal.

Recently, I received the Lifetime Achievement Award from Crossword Books at Mumbai's Royal Opera House. The categories were unravelled on stage one by one: fiction, non-fiction and children's, among others. The jury members gave insights into their strategies and opinions, and my mind went back to the beginning of my literary journey.

I am not a student of literature; I did not pursue a degree in the subject. But literature has always fascinated me. I belong to a family of teachers where books are treasured and I was inclined towards books at a very young age.

I grew up in a village where the medium of communication was the local language—Kannada. Mine was a Kannada-medium school. Sometimes, a makeshift theatre under a tent would showcase Kannada movies. There were barely any radio stations either. After we finally did get a radio at home, it was monitored closely by the older members of the family who limited its use to Kannada programmes only. But as kids, we all have our ways. When the elders weren't at home, I would listen to Radio Ceylon and one of its popular shows called *Binaca Geetmala*. I even recall Sri Lanka's national anthem, *Namo Namo Mata*, which often played on that station. Other than that, there was no trace of English in my childhood but there was plenty of time to figure out my creative outlets.

My family frequently went for small day trips: temple visits, wedding-related events, picnics or a visit to a historical site.

As soon as we would return home and settle for the evening, my mother would insist, 'Now sit and write about your day. You may not remember tomorrow what you have seen today, and writing is a wonderful exercise for your tiny fingers and young minds.'

I almost always resisted her instructions. Sitting in one place after an exciting day didn't sound like a lot of fun. So, I would respond, 'I will write tomorrow.'

'That's fine. You can also have your dinner tomorrow then,' my mother would say.

This is how I was forced to sit and write.

Once I began writing, I slowly but surely began to find it fun. I could play with combinations of the fifty-two letters in the Kannada alphabet and create meaningful words to express my feelings: joy, sadness, excitement and anything else that I felt. Before long, writing became a fond habit.

For many, many years, I wrote down my daily thoughts—at least twenty-five lines a day for two decades, not realizing that the process was inadvertently improving my expression and adding clarity to my ideas. For this, I owe gratitude to my first teacher, my mother.

As a teenager, I began writing with a tinge of seriousness, a lot of adventure and perhaps even a shade of romance. Modernity was the best thing there was, or so I thought.

I wrote about Mozart and submitted the article to a local newspaper. When it appeared on a Sunday, I was ecstatic. I took the newspaper to school and shared the article with my teachers and classmates. My friends looked at me with awe and I felt like I had really achieved something! It was very rare for women to get published in those days and, in that instant, I realized that I was possibly the only girl in school whose article had been picked up by a newspaper.

Later, I wrote a romantic story and sent it to the same newspaper. Days passed but I did not receive a reply. So, I sent a reminder to the editor with a prepaid stamped envelope, hoping that it would encourage him to reply. Still, there was nothing. Finally, I gathered all the courage that I could muster and went to meet the editor. As expected, it was a man since women editors and journalists were absolutely unheard of then. The editor looked at me and spoke gently, 'My child, we cannot publish this article. A good piece of literature must use the right mix of reality and imagination. Experience, observation, introspection: these senses must be developed consciously. So don't give up, but think about the feedback that I have given you today.'

As I sat and brooded over this, I understood that imagination in itself was only a shining thread and not a piece of beautiful cloth, that writing simply about facts or real issues could be dry and writing without creativity would be akin to reporting. The editor was right—a good mix of both aspects makes for interesting and impactful writing. It was a lesson that I have never forgotten and one that I practise even today!

My mother encouraged me. She said, 'Don't worry about getting published. Even if you don't, don't stop writing. I can promise you that when you look back and read your articles again after ten years, you will see the improvement in your expression.'

Motivated, I kept writing.

Later, when I submitted my articles to a local newspaper, some of them began to be published occasionally—like a pleasant shower during the summer. There was no financial compensation for these articles, and I didn't expect any either. Getting my writing published felt like the biggest compensation!

The years flew by. I completed the tenth grade from my Kannada-medium school and joined an English-medium college.

In the old days, nobody cared about the plight of the teenagers who were switching from Kannada to English as a medium of instruction. There were many like me in the same rocky boat. To make it worse, it was the critical year where my academic performance would become the greatest factor in deciding whether I got admission to engineering or medical courses or not. Some of my peers were so aghast at the change in language that they changed their courses to study the arts—not because they really wanted to change their subjects, but because science was known to be tough and the arts course was thought to be easy, giving them a chance to do well while accommodating the change in language.

I was fifteen years old then and unable to write a single paragraph in English. Confused, I approached my mother. She said, 'You love Kannada and writing in it, don't you?'

I nodded.

'Then don't get scared now. English is just another language. You simply have to read more in English and start writing in it too until you get comfortable with the language.'

From that day on, I concentrated on reading English books and found it very challenging. But I persevered, unwilling to give up, and wrote at least one paragraph in English every day. My grandfather gifted me an English–Kannada dictionary for my birthday that year, which became my constant companion for years after that.

Luckily for me, mathematics, physics and chemistry do not require extensive English. I managed to do well and get admission to an engineering college. For a brief period, I stopped writing because of my schedule. Apart from the regular coursework, the engineering drawings were tough and the experiments tedious. Not to mention that I had to manage everything alone. There was barely any time to write.

The years flew by and I wrote less and less, but I read more and more. My inclination towards reading was augmented by my husband's love for it. Since the day we met, he has been gifting me books and continues to do so even today. There is always a brief message on the first page of each gift: 'To You, From Me'. We read some books together, especially biographies and humour. But I was also interested in other subjects such as history, technology and anthropology while Murthy was more motivated towards reading about communism and coding.

There was an inherent shortage of money but the desire to read more books remained as strong as ever. So, Murthy and I decided to set aside a budget of three hundred rupees a month to purchase books from the once-iconic Strand Book Stall. That was all that we could afford back then, and we would save this money by cutting down on expenses in other areas—we would travel only in crowded buses and local trains and cook and clean at home. That helped us save the money we needed for the books. But even then, this budget wasn't enough for me. During those days, shopkeepers would frown at customers who spent a lot of time simply browsing through books. 'Please don't touch the books if you don't intend to buy them because then they will start looking used and old and a potential customer will not want to buy them,' they would say. So, I would stand at a distance and stare at the books with greedy eyes.

In 1979, I had very little money but a lot of spirit. So, off I went to America all alone with a backpack. One late evening in New York, two policemen flagged me down suspecting that I was carrying drugs in my obviously heavy bag. When they scanned my bag, all they found was what I was truly addicted to—curd rice! They were so surprised at their finding that I had to explain where I was from and the significance of curd rice in south India.

Many more of such daring incidents marked my journey. When I came back to India, I wrote about my adventures in Kannada, titled my writing 'From beyond the Atlantic', and kept it aside. The thought of publishing it never crossed my mind.

More than a year later, I was speaking to my father about my adventures and my writing when he suggested, 'Why don't you go ahead and publish this as a book? You already know how rare it is for young girls from our area to go backpacking to an unknown land. It is sure to be a unique book for that reason alone.'

I wasn't prepared for that thought. Me: an author? When I thought of the word, I was usually reminded of people like Jerome K. Jerome, P.G. Wodehouse, V.S. Naipaul, Jean-Paul Sartre and Kannada writers such as Triveni and Bhyrappa. An author must be of that calibre, or so I thought. I felt silly and strange just at the thought that someone as ordinary as me was thinking of becoming an author.

I brooded over it for a few days until the feeling settled. Then I wondered: 'Is there anything wrong in sending my manuscript to a publisher? The worst that could happen is that they would reject my work. But I am used to rejection, am I not?'

With bravado in my heart, I approached a popular Kannada publishing house called Manohara Grantha Mala, whose legendary founder G.B. Joshi was known for giving newcomers a break. Among the authors who had started out this way were Girish Karnad and M.K. Indira. I spoke hesitantly to Mr Joshi and gave him my manuscript, who said that he would contact me within two days. Forty-eight hours later, I was impatient and tense. My feelings at that time were somewhat similar to going through labour during a pregnancy. Finally, he informed me that he would publish my manuscript. He never spoke of royalty and I did not ask for it. That day, my family and I celebrated as if I had become a prominent author already. Nevertheless, it was a first. I was the first author in my family of seventy-five first and second cousins, aunts and uncles.

Much like a pregnancy, the book took ten months to reach the market. When I heard of this development, I took a bus from Hubli to Dharwad to accept my first brainchild from the publisher and received the first twenty copies with great affection. I was thrilled!

I wondered how I would distribute these copies among my big family. In the end, I gave a few copies to my parents-in-law, a few more to my friends and kept three with myself. The remaining copies were exhausted quickly. Some friends congratulated me and brought boxes of sweets. Others said with pride, 'We had no clue that an engineer could turn into a writer too! We are very happy!' A few remarked, 'Even we would have written a book had we gone to America and returned. You need money to travel and write a book.'

The first book finally gave me the title of being an author and made me want more.

In 1979, when I was in Jamshedpur, then in Bihar, for two months, I found myself all alone in the company guest house. It was then that I conceived the idea for my next book. I came from a middle-class background and was quite fascinated by how rich women led their lives, especially those whose husbands were perpetually busy with business. I decided to use this fascination and some of my imagination for this novel.

I returned to Mumbai with the idea still lingering in my mind. When I ran the idea past Mr Murthy, he gave me a blank stare. 'I can't help you there, I'm afraid. I am neither rich nor am I a lady.'

So, that was that. After some thought, I made some inquiries with various colleagues at work and observed the 'rich' women that I could see on Juhu beach, in tow with their children and ayahs.

The result of the imagination and research led to my first novel, *Athirikthe*, in Kannada. As I wrote it, I allowed myself to enter the lead character's mind and feel the joy and pain of her circumstances. At the end, I had to make an effort to exit from the character's life and return to my own. Thus began my journey in Kannada literature. This time, I went through another publisher who was located in Mysore.

I continued to write. My subsequent novels, however, were rejected. I figured that if I wanted to grab more eyeballs, I must try my hand at writing a series for a newspaper. To my surprise, even these were rejected. Some papers did not respond at all while others said that my writing wasn't series material.

Years passed, and I continued to read avidly.

One day, I went to a wedding where I saw a young girl with leucoderma sitting in front of me, having a meal. Just then, someone from the family came and said to her, 'You cannot sit here with the others. You have leucoderma. Please get up.'

Humiliated, the girl cried and left immediately.

This behaviour hurt me. I am the daughter of a doctor and I know that unlike leprosy, leucoderma is only a cosmetic disease. It is not contagious and not proven to be hereditary either. Then why do people behave this way with fellow beings?

The incident provoked me into undertaking some research. As I spoke to people, I realized that many engagements were broken and marriages called off, especially in cases where one or more of the bride's relatives had the disease but she did not. I had long chats with dermatologists and rebelled strongly against this heinous treatment which does nothing but kill confidence.

For the first time in my life, I thought of writing about this to create awareness, but in the form of a story. This is how my novel *Mahashweta* was born.

Many, many years later, I was at another wedding. To my pleasant surprise, the groom came up to me and said, 'I have read *Mahashweta* and today I am marrying a girl who has leucoderma. The book completely changed my perspective.'

It was the day that I realized that perhaps I could make a difference if I continued to write about issues I was passionate about.

In the seventies and the eighties, going to America was an outstanding achievement. India wasn't close to liberalization yet and the number of job opportunities was very low in the country. The American dollar, however, was a magic wand— one dollar equalled ten rupees. People who settled there and came back to India for a vacation almost always looked down upon those here. Even the local families differentiated between the children and grandchildren who were in the US and those who stayed here. It was but natural that the wives and daughters who lived in America got much more attention and importance.

But I knew by then that life in America wasn't as green as it was made out to be. Living there wasn't devoid of struggles.

So, I wrote *Dollar Bahu* (or *Dollar Sose*) in Kannada. The manuscript first became a series in a newspaper, then a book and then a television series. It was even translated into Italian along with other Indian languages. Today, it is still widely available in bookshops.

My journey with Kannada continued, and the thought of writing in English didn't even cross my mind.

The year 1998 marked my very first book launch with the novel *Yashasvi*. The event was held at Mythic Society in

Bangalore. To me, it was like a small wedding signifying the marriage of my book to the publisher. I invited many people. All kith and kin fond of literature came for the launch, including some of my wonderful friends who couldn't even read Kannada. But they loved me and were proud of the fact that I was an author. One of them gifted me a silver idol of Saraswati, the goddess and symbol of knowledge. For the first time, and what I thought may also be the last, I stood on stage, spoke to my readers and expressed my love for books and Kannada. Little did I know that this would be the first of many public events.

One day, T.J.S. George, the editor of the *New Indian Express*, sent word that I should write my columns in English. He simply said, 'A language is but a vehicle. It's the person inside who's weaving the story that's more important. You are a storyteller. So, just get on with your story and the language will fall into place.'

With his kind words and encouragement, I began writing in English. My columns, named 'Episodes', started to appear in the *New Indian Express* on 12 November 2000. I was in Shimoga the day I heard someone in a hotel say, 'Sudha Murty has written a column in English.' Instantly, I was elevated to being an English writer by a stranger. It took me some time to believe that people wanted to read my columns. This journey continued with other avenues like the *Times of India*, *The Hindu* and the *Week*.

One advantage of writing in English was that it led me to form friendships with people from different states and walks of life. One of those turned out to be the late

President A.P.J. Abdul Kalam. This was 2001, and he wasn't our President yet. He was a scientist at the Defence Research and Development Organization (DRDO). He happened to read one of my columns in the *Week*, an Indian news magazine, and said that the humour in my writing was nice and the message strong. He asked how I had learnt the art of ending an article with a gist of the story and expressed interest in meeting me.

A year later, my first book in English came out as a collection of my columns thanks to George, who introduced me to East West Books Pvt. Ltd in Chennai. George, with his genuine encouragement, wrote the foreword for the book and gave it an enchanting title: *Wise and Otherwise.*

I realized that when a book is released in English, it is read by more people and translations into regional languages happen more easily. Today, my books have been translated into all major Indian languages and are read in most states of India.

As the years passed, the Infosys Foundation's work provided me with experiences that enlarged my canvas even as the writing continued. I approached many publishers who rejected my manuscripts. They said, 'Your language is too simple. It is not flowery or sophisticated and comes across as too simple and even naive. Our opinion is that people will not appreciate it.' A few suggested, 'You tell your story to someone who has a good command over the English language. They will rewrite it and, together, you both can co-author.'

But I didn't agree. I wanted to keep my style distinctive and portray it exactly the way I am.

Along the way, I realized the importance of a good editor—someone who can take the book to greater heights. I have learnt that a great editor must be a reflection of the author, someone who understands the author. I am extremely lucky to have found these qualities in my young and bright editor Shrutkeerti Khurana, who is a talented engineer and a management graduate with an immense love for the English language. I have known Shrutee since the day she was born because I was friends with her parents even then. I have seen her growing up, she has seen me getting old, and our bond has deepened with each passing day over the years. She reads my mind, tells me frankly where I am wrong, where she is getting bored with my writing and edits as required. In addition to work, we both love reading and discuss countless things—things that are here, there and everywhere.

I also want to thank my wonderful family who knew of my love for writing and understood it and allowed me to prioritize it over their needs.

In time, Penguin Random House became my sole English publisher. I was also fortunate enough to get interest from publishers who worked in regional languages, and I have remained with them since the beginning. For the Marathi language, there is Mehta Publishing House in Pune, R.R. Sheth in Ahmedabad for Gujarati, Prabhat Prakashan in Delhi for Hindi translations, DC Books in Kottayam for Malayalam and Alakananda Prachuranalu in Vijayawada for Telugu translations, among others.

One day, I received an email from a Gujarati reader who asked, 'Sudha Ben, you look like a Gujarati and you even eat like one. Your books are really wonderful. I am very curious: how did you get married to a south Indian?'

The email made me smile. I responded to the reader that I was a south Indian myself and that the quality of the translations in Gujarati was so good that she thought that I belonged to her land.

During one of my international trips, I was pleasantly surprised to come across my books in New Jersey. As I beamed and picked one of them up, the Gujarati shopkeeper looked at me and commented, 'Take it. *Saras che.*' He meant that the book was nice and that I should buy it.

Happily, I nodded.

As I heard my name being called on stage again for the Lifetime Achievement Award, my mind returned to the present and I slowly climbed the steps leading up to the stage. Each step was a reminder of the journey that has lasted over forty years. It was a journey filled with rejections, negative comments and disapprovals, along with appreciation, a lot of love and affection. I hope that I have somehow been the voice for people who remain shy, hidden, unknown and yearn for an outlet of their expression.

I have lost count of the number of times people have said to me, 'I can't write. But I want to share my story. Will you write it and share it with the world?'

Some of my students have frequently remarked, 'Madam, each of us has faltered and made mistakes during the course of our lives. We don't want the next generation to go through trying times that can be avoided with just a little bit of advice and wisdom. Will you tell our stories in your book?'

I am always hesitant. I don't want to take anyone's privacy for granted or share anything without his or her permission and faith. But powerful stories, no matter where they come from, are meant to be told. So, I fancy myself as only a carrier.

My vast experience with the truly underprivileged in India, my publishers who had unwavering faith in me, my excellent editor and my readers have made me what I am today. So, my journey is not mine alone. It is also about the people around me. There's a part of me that realizes that my writing emanates from Saraswati, the goddess of knowledge, learning and writing, and that I am only her scribe. Without her assent and blessing, I can't write even one line.

Today, I have a résumé of twenty-nine books and am a bilingual writer in both English and Kannada with writings across categories such as novels, non-fiction, fiction, children's books, travelogues and technical books. My books have been translated into twenty languages and one Braille system. This book is my 200th title. As many as 2.6 million copies of my books have been sold, of which 1.5 million are in English alone.

But I have also learnt the hard way that nothing succeeds like success. The proof, I've been told, lies in the sales and the number of reprints sold in the last decade and more. Despite the numbers, I know that I am not an author for the English elite and that I cannot spin words like the books from the West or some Indian authors. But English is no longer a language meant only for the elite, as it was in the days before.

Somehow, the common people of India have found a way to welcome English into their daily lives, and that includes me too. I can only tell stories from the heart and in a simple manner. That's all I really know, and that is also the only thing in the world that is truly mine.

2

'Amma, What Is Your Duty?'

At that time, my daughter, Akshata, was a teenager. By nature she was very sensitive. On her own, she started reading for blind children at Ramana Maharishi Academy for the Blind at Bangalore. She was a scribe too. She used to come home and tell me about the world of blind people. Later she wrote an essay on them, called 'I Saw the World through the Blind Eyes of Mary'. Mary was a student at the academy who was about to appear for the pre-university exam. Once, Akshata took Mary to Lalbagh for a change. The conversation between them was quite unusual.

'Mary, there are different types of red roses in this park,' Akshata told her.

Mary was surprised. 'Akshata, what do you mean by red?'

Akshata did not know how to explain what was red. She took a rose and a jasmine, and gave them to Mary.

'Mary, smell these two flowers in your hand. They have different smells. The first one is a rose. It is red in colour. The second one is jasmine. It is white. Mary, it is difficult to explain what is red and what is white. But I can tell you that in this world there are many colours, which can be seen and differentiated only through the eyes and not by touch. I am sorry.'

After that incident Akshata told me, 'Amma, never talk about colours when you talk to blind people. They feel frustrated. I felt so helpless when I was trying to explain to Mary. Now I always describe the world to them by describing smells and sounds which they understand easily.'

Akshata also used to help a blind boy called Anand Sharma at this school. He was the only child of a schoolteacher from Bihar. He was bright and jolly. He was about to appear for his second pre-university exam.

One day, I was heading for an examination committee meeting. At that time, I was head of the department of computer science at a local college. It was almost the end of February. Winter was slowly ending and there was a trace of summer setting in. Bangalore is blessed with beautiful weather. The many trees lining the roads were flowering and the city was swathed in different shades of violet, yellow and red.

I was busy getting ready to attend the meeting, hence I was collecting old syllabi, question papers and reference books. Akshata came upstairs to my room. She looked worried and tired. She was then studying in class ten. I thought she was tired preparing for her exams. As a mother, I have never insisted my children study too much. My parents never did that. They always believed the child has to be responsible. A responsible child will sit down to study on his or her own.

I told Akshata, 'Don't worry about the exams. Trying is in your hands. The results are not with you.' She was annoyed and irritated by my advice. 'Amma, I didn't talk about any examination. Why are you reminding me of that?'

I was surprised at her irritation. But I was also busy gathering old question papers so I did not say anything. Absently, I looked at her face. Was there a trace of sadness on it? Or was it my imagination?

'Amma, you know Anand Sharma. He came to our house once. He is a bright boy. I am confident that he will do very well in his final examination. He is also confident about it. He wants to study further.'

She stopped. By this time I had found the old question papers I had been looking for, but not the syllabus. My search was on. Akshata stood facing me and continued, 'Amma, he wants to study at St Stephen's in Delhi. He does not have anybody. He is poor. It is an expensive place. What should he do? Who will support him? I am worried.'

It was getting late for my meeting so I casually remarked, 'Akshata, why don't you support him?'

'Amma, where do I have the money to support a boy in a Delhi hostel?'

My search was still on.

'You can forfeit your birthday party and save money and sponsor him.'

At home, even now both our children do not get pocket money. Whenever they want to buy anything they ask me and I give the money. We don't have big birthday parties.

Akshata's birthday party would mean calling a few of her friends to the house and ordering food from the nearby fast-food joint, Shanthi Sagar.

'Amma, when an educated person like you, well travelled, well read and without love for money does not help poor people, then don't expect anyone else to do. Is it not your duty to give back to those unfortunate people? What are you looking for in life? Are you looking for glamour or fame? You are the daughter of a doctor, granddaughter of a schoolteacher and come from a distinguished teaching family. If you cannot help poor people then don't expect anyone else to do it.'

Her words made me abandon my search. I turned around and looked at my daughter. I saw a sensitive young girl pleading for the future of a poor blind boy. Or was she someone reminding me of my duty towards society? I had received so much from that society and country but in what way was I giving back? For a minute I was frozen. Then I realized I was holding the syllabus I was looking for in my hand and it was getting late for the meeting.

Akshata went away with anger and sadness in her eyes. I too left for college in a confused state of mind.

When I reached, I saw that as usual the meeting was delayed. Now I was all alone. I settled down in my chair in one of the lofty rooms of the college. There is a difference between loneliness and solitude. Loneliness is boring, whereas in solitude you can inspect and examine your deeds and your thoughts.

I sat and recollected what had happened that afternoon. Akshata's words were still ringing in my mind.

I was forty-five years old. What was my duty at this age? What was I looking for in life?

I did not start out in life with a lot of money. A great deal of hard work had been put in to get to where we were today. What had I learnt from the hard journey that was my life? Did I work for money, fame or glamour? No, I did not work for those; they came accidentally to me. Initially I worked for myself, excelling in studies. After that I was devoted to Infosys and my family. Should not the remaining part of my life be used to help those people who were suffering for no fault of theirs? Was that not my duty? Suddenly I remembered JRD's parting advice to me: 'Give back to society.'

I decided that was what I was going to do for the rest of my life. I felt relieved and years younger.

I firmly believe no decision should be taken emotionally. It should be taken with a cool mind and when you are aware of the consequences. After a week, I wrote my resignation letter as head of the department and opted only for a teacher's post.

I am ever grateful to Akshata for helping to bring this happiness and satisfaction to my work and life. It means more to me than the good ranks I got in school, and my wealth.

When I see hope in the eyes of a destitute person, see the warm smile on the faces of once helpless people, I feel so satisfied. They tell me that I am making a difference.

I joined the Infosys Foundation as a founder trustee. The foundation took up a number of philanthropic projects for the benefit of the poor in different states of India.

I received many awards on various occasions. One of them was the Economic Times Award given to the Infosys Foundation. As a trustee I was invited to receive this award. At that time I remembered my guru. Now she was a student in the US. I told her, 'At least for one day you must come for this award ceremony in Mumbai. If you had not woken me up at the right time, I would not have been receiving it today. I want you to be present.'

I will remain indebted to Akshata forever for the way she made me change my life and the lesson she taught me.

3

Honesty Comes from the Heart

One bright June morning three years ago, I was reading my Kannada newspaper as usual. It was the day the Secondary School Leaving Certificate results had been published. While columns of roll numbers filled the inside pages, the list of rank holders and their photographs took up almost the entire front page.

I have a great fascination for rank holders. Rank is not merely an index of one's intelligence, it also indicates the hard work and perseverance that students have put in to reach their goal. My background—I was brought up in a professor's family—and my own experience as a teacher have led me to believe this.

Of all the photographs in that morning's newspaper, one boy's snapshot caught my attention. I could not take my eyes off him. He was frail and pale, but there was an endearing sparkle in his eyes. I wanted to know more about him. I read that his name was Hanumanthappa and that he had secured the eighth rank. That was all the information I could gather.

The next day, to my surprise, his photograph was published again, this time with an interview. With growing interest I learnt that Hanumanthappa was a coolie's son, the oldest of five children. They belonged to a tribal group. He was unable to study further, he said in the interview, because he lived in a village and his father, the sole breadwinner, earned only Rs 40 a day.

I felt sorry for this bright boy. Most of us send our children to tuitions and to coaching classes, we buy them reference books and guides, and provide the best possible facilities for them without considering the cost. But it was different for Hanumanthappa of Rampura. He had excelled in spite of being denied some of the basic necessities of life.

While I was thinking about him with the newspaper still in my hands, I gazed at a mango tree in my neighbour's compound. It looked its best with a fresh bark, tender green leaves glistening with dewdrops and mangoes that were about to ripen in a few days. Beyond the tree was a small potted plant that, I noticed, had remained almost the same ever since it had been potted. It was a calm morning. The air was cool and fresh. My thoughts were running free. The continuous whistle of our pressure cooker broke the silence, reminding me that half an hour had passed.

Hanumanthappa's postal address was provided in the interview. Without wasting much time, I took a postcard and wrote to him. I wrote only two lines, saying that I was interested in meeting him and asking whether he could come to Bangalore. Just then my father, ever a practical man, returned from his morning walk. He read the postcard and said, 'Where will he have the money to come so far? If you want him to come here, send some money for his bus fare plus a little extra to buy himself a decent set of clothes.'

So I added a third line to say that I would pay for his travel and some clothes. Within four days I received a similar postcard in reply. Two sentences: in the first he thanked me for the letter, in the second he expressed his willingness to come to Bangalore and meet me. Immediately, I sent him some money and details of my office address.

When he finally arrived in our office, he looked like a frightened calf that had lost its way. It must have been his first trip to Bangalore. He was humble. He wore a clean shirt and trousers, and his hair was neatly parted and combed. The sparkle in his eyes was still there.

I got straight to the point. 'We are happy about your academic performance. Do you want to study further? We would like to sponsor you. This means we will pay your fees for any course of study you wish to take up—wherever it may be.'

He did not answer.

My senior colleague, who was in the office with me, interrupted with a smile, 'Don't go at the speed of bits and bytes. Let the boy understand what you are suggesting. He can give us his answer at the end of the day.'

When Hanumanthappa was ready to return home, he said in a low and steady tone, 'Madam, I want to pursue my studies at the Teachers' Training College in Bellary. That is the one nearest to my village.'

I agreed instantly but spoke to him a little more to find out whether there was any other course he preferred. I was trying to make it clear to him that we would pay the fees for any course he might choose. The boy, however, seemed to know exactly what he wanted.

'How much money should I send you per month? Does the college have a hostel facility?' I asked.

He said he would get back to me after collecting the correct details. Two days later, he wrote to us in his beautiful handwriting that he would require approximately Rs 300 per month. He planned to take a room on rent and share it with a friend. The two boys would cook for themselves in order to keep their expenses down.

I sent him Rs 1800 to cover his expenses for six months. He acknowledged my draft without delay and expressed his gratitude.

Time passed. One day, I suddenly remembered that I had to pay Hanumanthappa for the next six months, so I sent him another draft for Rs 1800.

This too was duly acknowledged, but I was surprised to find some currency notes in the envelope along with his letter. 'Madam,' he had written, 'it is kind of you to have sent me money for the next six months. But I was not in Bellary for the last two months. One month, our college was closed for holidays and during the next month, there was a strike. So I stayed at home for those two months. My expenditure during these months was less than Rs 300 per month. Therefore, I am sending you the Rs 300 that I have not used for the last two months. Kindly accept this amount.'

I was taken aback. Such poverty and yet such honesty. Hanumanthappa knew I expected no account of the money sent to him for his monthly expenses, yet he had made it a point to return the balance amount. Unbelievable but true!

Experience has taught me that honesty is not the mark of any particular class nor is it related to education or wealth. It cannot be taught at any university. In most people, it springs naturally from the heart.

I did not know how to react to this simple village boy's honesty. I just prayed that God would continue to bestow the best on Hanumanthappa and his family.

4

The Red Rice Granary

Every year, our country has to face natural disasters in some form. It may be an earthquake in Gujarat, floods in Orissa or a drought in Karnataka. In a poor country, these calamities cause havoc.

In the course of my work, I have found that after such calamities, many people like to donate money or materials to relief funds. We assume that most donations come from rich people, but that is not true. On the contrary, people from the middle class and the lower middle class help more. Rarely do rich people participate wholeheartedly.

A few years back, I was invited to a reputed company in Bangalore to deliver a lecture on corporate social responsibility. Giving a speech is easy. But I was not sure how many people in the audience would really understand the speech and change themselves.

After my talk was over, I met many young girls and boys. It was an affluent company and the employees were well off and well dressed. They were all very emotional after the lecture.

'Madam, we buy so many clothes every month. Can we donate our old clothes to those people who are affected by the earthquake? Can you coordinate and send these to them?'

Some of them offered other things.

'We have grown-up children, we would like to give their old toys and some vessels.'

I was very pleased at the reaction. It reminded me of the incident in the Ramayana where, during the construction of the bridge between India and Lanka, every squirrel helped Sri Rama by bringing a handful of sand.

'Please send your bags to my office. I will see that they reach the right persons.'

Within a week, my office was flooded with hundreds of bags. I was proud that my lecture had proven so effective.

One Sunday, along with my assistants, I opened the bags. What we saw left us amazed and shocked. The bags were brimming with all kinds of junk! Piles of high-heeled slippers (some of them without the pair), torn undergarments, unwashed shirts, cheap, transparent saris, toys which had neither shape nor colour, unusable bed sheets, aluminium vessels and broken cassettes were soon piled in front of us like a mountain. There were only a few good shirts, saris and usable materials. It was apparent that instead of sending the material to a garbage dump or the *kabariwala*, these people had transferred them to my office in the name of donation. The men and women I had met that day were bright, well-travelled, well-off people. If educated people like them behaved like this, what would uneducated people do?

But then I was reminded of an incident from my childhood. I was born and brought up in a village called Shiggaon in Karnataka's Haveri district. My grandfather was a retired schoolteacher and my grandmother, Krishtakka, never went to school. Both of them hardly travelled and had never stepped out of Karnataka. Yet, they were hard-working people, who did their work wholeheartedly without expecting anything from anybody in their life. Their photographs never appeared in any paper, nor did they go up on stage to receive a prize for the work they did. They lived like flowers with fragrance in the forest, enchanting everyone around them, but hardly noticed by the outside world.

In the village we had paddy fields and we used to store the paddy in granaries. There were two granaries. One was in the front and the other at the back of our house. The better-quality rice, which was white, was always stored in the front granary and the inferior quality, which was a little thick and red, was stored in the granary at the back.

In those days, there was no communal divide in the village. People from different communities lived together in peace. Many would come to our house to ask for alms. There were Muslim fakirs, Hindu dasaiahs who roamed the countryside singing devotional songs, Yellamma Jogathis who appeared holding the image of Goddess Yellamma over their heads, poor students and invalid people.

We never had too much cash in the house and the only help my grandfather could give these people was in the form of rice. People who receive help do not talk too much. They would receive the rice, smile and raise their right hand to bless us. Irrespective of their religion, the blessing was always 'May God bless you.' My grandfather always looked happy after giving them alms.

I was a little girl then and not too tall. Since the entrance to the front granary was low, it was difficult for grown-ups to enter. So I would be given a small bucket and sent inside. There I used to fill up the bucket with rice and give it to them. They would tell me how many measures they wanted.

In the evening, my grandmother used to cook for everybody. That time she would send me to the granary at the back of the house where the red rice was stored. I would again fill up the bucket with as much rice as she wanted and get it for her to cook our dinner.

This went on for many years. When I was a little older, I asked my grandparents a question that had been bothering me for long.

'Why should we eat the red rice always at night when it is not so good, and give those poor people the better-quality rice?'

My grandmother smiled and told me something I will never forget in my life.

'Child, whenever you want to give something to somebody, give the best in you, never the second best. That is what I have learnt from life. God is not there in the temple, mosque or church. He is with the people. If you serve them with whatever you have, you have served God.'

My grandfather answered my question in a different way.

'Our ancestors have taught us in the Vedas that one should:

'Donate with kind words.

'Donate with happiness.

'Donate with sincerity.

'Donate only to the needy.

'Donate without expectation because it is not a gift. It is a duty.

'Donate with your wife's consent.

'Donate to other people without making your dependants helpless.

'Donate without caring for caste, creed and religion.

'Donate so that the receiver prospers.'

This lesson from my grandparents, told to me when I was just a little girl, has stayed with me ever since. If at all I am helping anyone today, it is because of the teachings of those simple souls. I did not learn them in any school or college.

5

Lazy Portado

Portado was a young, bright, handsome and sweet boy from Goa. We were in B.V.B. College of Engineering at Hubli. He had been my classmate and lab partner throughout our course. So I knew him fairly well.

Portado had peculiar habits. Though he was intelligent, he was extremely lazy. Our theory classes were from eight in the morning till noon and lab was from two to five in the afternoon. Portado never came for the first class at eight. Occasionally, he turned up for the second or third hour but most of the time he only showed up for the last hour. He never missed our lab sessions, however.

In those days, attendance was not compulsory in college and our teachers were very lenient. They requested Portado to come on time but since there was no internal assessment, they couldn't really exercise their authority.

One day, I asked Portado, 'Why are you always late? What do you do at home?'

He laughed and said, 'I have a lot of things to do. I am so busy in the evenings that I can't get up before nine in the morning.'

'What things keep you so busy?'' I asked him innocently.

'I meet my friends at night. We have long chats followed by dinner. You know, it takes a lot of time to build friendships. You will not understand. You people are all nerds. You only come to college to study.'

'Portado, you are a student. You should study, get knowledge, learn skills and work hard. Is that not important?'

'Oh, please. You remind me of my mother. Don't give me a sermon. Life is long. We have plenty of time. We should not learn anything in a hurry. We shouldn't be so stingy about time either.'

Then I noticed that he did not even have a watch since, for obvious reasons, he had no need for it.

Portado continued, 'In life, you need connections and networking. That can give you success. You can't network in a day. You have to spend time and money on building a network. Who knows? Some people that I meet now may make it big tomorrow and then that connection will work for me.'

I was a young girl from a middle-class and academic-minded family. I believed only in hard work. I never understood how networking could help.

During our college breaks, Portado would proudly tell us about his childhood: 'Oh, when I was young, I spent my time in big cities like Bombay, Delhi and Calcutta. In Calcutta, there are so many clubs. It is a matter of prestige to be a member of a club. When I start working, I want to be a member of all the good clubs in the city.' Every now and then, Portado felt that Hubli was a small and boring town. So he regularly went to Belgaum to meet his friends and 'network' with them.

During exams, Portado worked like a donkey. He glass-traced most of my original drawings so that he did not have to think about the solutions to engineering problems himself. His glass-trace drawings were definitely better than the originals because they were neater and there were no wrinkles or pencil marks. He always got more than me in drawings. He even kept the question papers of previous years and made his own question papers by process of elimination. Instead of reading textbooks, he read guides to pass the exams. With all this, he always managed to pass in second class.

Once, the examiner caught him because in a survey drawing he told the examiner that the mark on his drawing was actually a big tree in the middle of a road. It was a survey of a town near Dharwad. Unfortunately, the examiner happened to be from that town and he knew that there was no tree on that road. He questioned Portado, who said with a serious face, 'Sir, I have done the survey myself. I sat below the tree, had my lunch and then I continued.'

Calmly, the examiner said, 'I can't see this tree in any of your classmates' original drawings. This is only a mosquito between the glass and the drawing that you have tried to cover up.'

Portado just managed to pass the exams that year. But he was not perturbed. He said, 'I am not scared of the exams or the marks. Today's nerds will be tomorrow's mid-level managers. A person with good networking will be their boss.'

Because of his attitude and undisciplined habits, even the college hostel refused to keep him. So he rented a small house near college and lived there like a king.

Once, our class planned a picnic trip to Belgaum. Since Portado was familiar with the city, we decided to take his opinion and help. The picnic committee members, including myself, went to his house around eleven on a Sunday morning. We all assumed that Portado would be awake. But to our surprise, he was still in bed. When he opened the door, he said sleepily, 'Oh, why have you come so early on a Sunday?' He was quite annoyed to see us. 'Well, I am awake now, so please come in.'

We went in but there was absolutely no place to sit. His clothes were all over the room and newspapers were scattered on the floor. In the kitchen, dirty dishes were piled up in the sink and they were stinking. There were fish bones everywhere. There was also a cat and a dog inside the house. They were well fed with Portado's leftovers. The windows were not open either. The bed sheet looked like it had not been changed for a year. I did not have the courage to go see his bathroom.

Portado felt neither perturbed nor guilty. He said, 'Make some space for yourselves and sit down.' Some people moved Portado's undergarments and made some space but I could not do that because I was a girl, so I simply stood. Portado brought a stool for me from his kitchen. It was very sticky. I was even more hesitant to sit on it than on his clothes. I told him, 'It is better that I stand.' Portado offered us tea but none of us had the guts to drink any.

When I asked him about planning the details of the picnic, he said, 'We can start at twelve in the afternoon. My friend owns a lodge so I can take you there. The next day, we can go to Amboli Falls. Then we can also go to Goa.' Portado made a ten-day programme. But most of us could not afford a ten-day accommodation in a hotel, nor could we skip class for so many days. So the plan fizzled out. We thanked him and left. When I turned back and looked, Portado had closed the door and probably gone back to bed.

Soon the final year came around. We all passed the examinations and parted ways. Some of us felt sad because we had become a big family in the last four years together. We did not know our destinations and knew that we may not meet again. Of course, as Portado said goodbye he told us, 'If you are ever in Goa, please come to my house.' But I seriously doubted that I would ever run into him again.

Many decades passed. Once, I went to Dubai to give a lecture. After the lecture, people came up to talk to me but there was one person who waited until everybody had left. Then he walked over to where I was sitting and smiled. I recognized the smile but I did not remember where I had seen him. The man was bald, fat, had a big paunch and was dressed very ordinarily. I thought that he might be a mid-level manager in a construction company. I meet many people in my field and it is difficult to remember everybody.

I asked him, 'What can I do for you, sir? Are you waiting for me?'

With a cracked voice, he said, 'Yes, I have been waiting for you for a long time.'

'Oh, I'm sorry, I didn't know that you were waiting. Do you have any work with me?' I said.

'Yes, I just wanted to tell you that you were right and I was wrong.'

I was puzzled. What did he mean? I had never even met him before. I hardly came to Dubai since we did not even have an office there.

'I didn't get your name, sir. May I know your name, please?' I asked.

His laugh was bittersweet. He said, 'I am Portado, your classmate.'

I was very happy to see him and shook his hand. 'Oh, Portado, I am seeing you after thirty-five years! It has been so long that I didn't recognize you. Physically, both of us have changed so much. It is nice to meet you. Stay back. If you are here, come for dinner tonight. I want to catch up,' I said.

Sadly, Portado said, 'Sorry, I don't have much time. I am in the night shift. But I can have a cup of tea with you.'

We went to the hotel restaurant and I ordered a cup of tea for him and juice for myself. I wanted to talk more. I started the conversation with great enthusiasm and could not hold my questions back. 'Portado, where are you working now? How long have you been in Dubai? Are you married? How many children do you have? By the way, how are your networking friends? Do you ever come to India?'

Portado stopped me. 'I know your work involves computers but mine does not. You are too fast for me. Just like a computer. But I am in construction. So bear with me since I am slow. I have been in Dubai for the last five years. Before that, I was in India in several small places in different companies. Of course, I am married. I have two daughters.'

I interrupted him. 'You could have brought them today. I would have liked to meet them.'

'Sorry, I can't bring them because they are not here. I am in the lower level of management. So I cannot afford to bring my family here. My two daughters are studying in India and are doing engineering. I can't even afford their education in this place.'

I did not know what to say. I had never imagined Portado would end up like this.

Now it was his turn to talk. 'Do you remember, when I was in college, I used to make fun of all of you? I spent all my time in networking. After I finished engineering, I didn't get a good job. The reason was very obvious. I did not have the knowledge or the ability to work hard. I looked down upon the two qualities that are the stepping stones to success. I knew that I wanted to go up and reach the top spot in a company but no one can just fly there. I knew what position I should be in but I did not know the route. I thought that a change of job would help, but instead it reduced my value in the market. None of my networking friends helped me. They dropped me like a hot potato. They thought that I was clinging on to them like a parasite. Some of them were like me and also looking for jobs. I always thought that I would come up with someone's help. I never thought that I should take my own help. Now I am old. I am trying to learn new things and make up for lost time. But it is not easy. The market has become extremely competitive. Youngsters in college have more knowledge and quickness. They also have time on their side. I have told my daughters, you should study, get knowledge, learn skills and work hard.'

Portado continued, 'Do you remember who said this to me? It was you.'

He looked at his watch and said, 'My time is up. I must leave.'

I wished him all the best.

He walked a few steps, then came back and said, 'That day, I called you a nerd. Today, I call you smart.'

And he left.

6

A Life Unwritten

It was the year 1943. My father was a young medical doctor posted at a small dispensary in a village known as Chandagad, located on the border of the two states of Maharashtra and Karnataka. It rained continuously for eight months there and the only activity during the remaining four months was tree cutting. It was a lesser-known and thinly populated village surrounded by a thick and enormous forest. Since British officers came to hunt in the jungle, a small clinic was set up there for their convenience. None of the villagers went there because they preferred using the local medicines and plants. So there was nobody in the clinic except my father.

Within a week of his transfer there, my father started getting bored. He was uprooted from the lively city of Pune to this slow and silent village where there seemed to be no people at all! He had no contact with the outside world—his only companion was the calendar on the wall. Sometimes, he would go for a walk outside but when he heard the roar of the tigers in the jungle nearby, he would get scared and walk back to the clinic as fast as he could. It was no wonder then that he was too afraid to step out at night because of the snakes that were often seen slithering on the ground.

One winter morning, he heard heavy breathing outside his main door and bravely decided to peep through the window. He saw a tigress stretching and yawning in the veranda with her cubs by her side. Paralysed with fear, my father did not open the door the entire day. On another day, he opened the window only to find snakes hanging from the roof in front of his house—almost like ropes.

My father wondered if he was transferred to the village as a form of punishment for something he may have done. But there was nothing that he could do to change the situation.

One night, he finished an early dinner and began reading a book by the light of a kerosene lamp. It was raining heavily outside.

Suddenly, he heard a knock on the door. 'Who could it be?' he wondered.

When he opened it, he saw four men wrapped in woollen rugs with sticks in their hands. They said to him in Marathi, 'Doctor Sahib, take your bag and come with us immediately.'

My father barely understood their rustic Marathi. He protested. 'But the clinic is closed, and look at the time!'

The men were in no mood to listen—they pushed him and loudly demanded that he accompany them. Quietly, my father picked up his bag and followed them like a lamb to the bullock cart waiting for them. The pouring rain and the moonless night disoriented him and while he didn't know where they were taking him, he sensed that the drive might take some time.

Using all the courage he had left, he asked, 'Where are you taking me?'

There was no reply.

It was a few hours before they reached their destination and the bullock cart came to a complete halt. By the light of a kerosene lamp, somebody escorted them. My father noticed the paddy fields around him and in the middle of it all, he saw a house. The minute he set foot in the house, a female voice said, 'Come, come. The patient is here in this room.'

For the first time since he had come to the village, my father felt that he could finally put his medical expertise to good use. The patient was a young girl, approximately sixteen years old. An old lady was standing near the girl who was obviously in labour. My father turned pale. He went back to the other room and told her family, 'Look, I haven't been trained in delivering a baby and I am a male doctor. You must call someone else.'

But the family refused to listen. 'That's not an option. You must do what needs to be done and we will pay you handsomely,' they insisted. 'The baby may be delivered alive or dead but the girl must be saved.'

My father pleaded with them. 'Please, I am not interested in the money. Let me go now.'

The men came close, shoved him inside the patient's room and locked the door from outside. My father became afraid. He knew he had no choice. He had observed and assisted in a few deliveries under the guidance of his medical college professors, but nothing more. Nervously, he started recalling his limited past experience and theoretical knowledge as his medical instincts kicked in.

There was no table in the room. So he signalled the old lady, who appeared to be deaf and dumb, to help him set up a makeshift table with the sacks of paddy grains around them. Then my father extracted a rubber sheet from his bag and laid it out neatly on top of the sacks.

He asked the girl to lie down on it and instructed the old lady to boil water and sterilize his instruments. By then, the contraction had passed. The girl was sweating profusely and the doctor even more. She looked at him with big, innocent, teary eyes and slowly began, 'Don't save me. I don't want to make it through the night.'

'Who are you?'

'I am the daughter of a big zamindar here,' she said in a soft voice. The rain outside made it hard for him to hear her. 'Since there was no high school in our village, my parents let me study in a distant town. There, I fell in love with one of my classmates. At first, I didn't know that I was pregnant, but once I found out, I told the baby's father who immediately ran away. By the time my parents learnt of what had happened, it was too late to do anything. That's why they sent me here to this godforsaken place where nobody would find out.'

She stopped as a strong contraction hit her.

After a few minutes, she said, 'Doctor, I am sure that once the baby is born, my family will kill the child and beat me violently.' Then she grabbed my father's arms as more tears gathered in her eyes. 'Please don't try to save the baby or me. Just leave me alone here and let me die. That's all I want.'

At first, my father didn't know how to respond. Then he said to her as gently as he could, 'I am a doctor and I can't let a patient die when I know that I can do something to save him or her. You mustn't discourage me from doing my duty.'

The girl fell silent.

The labour was hard, scary and long and finally, my father managed to deliver the baby successfully with the assistance of the old lady. The young girl was exhausted and sweaty at the end of the ordeal. She closed her eyes in despair and didn't even ask to see the baby. Hesitantly, she asked, 'Is it a boy or a girl?'

'It's a girl,' replied my father, while trying to check the baby's vitals.

'Oh my God! It's a girl!' she cried. 'Her life will be just like mine—under the cruel pressure of the men in the family. And she doesn't even have a father!' She began sobbing loudly.

But my father was busy with the baby and barely heard her.

Suddenly, the girl realized that something was wrong, 'Doctor, why isn't the baby crying?' When she didn't get a reply, she continued, 'I will be happy if she doesn't survive. She will be spared from a cursed life.'

My father held the baby upside down, gently slapped her and, instantly, the baby's strong cries filled the room. When the men outside heard the baby cry, they opened the door and instructed him, 'Doctor, get ready to leave. We will drop you back.'

My father cleaned up his patient, gathered his instruments and packed his bag. The old lady began cleaning the room. He looked at the troubled young girl and said, 'Take the baby and run away from this place if you can find it in your heart to do so. Go to Pune and look for Pune Nursing School. Find a clerk there called Gokhale and tell him that RH has sent you. He will help you get admission in a nursing course. In time, you will become a nurse and lead an independent life, with the ability to take care of your own needs. Raise your daughter with pride. Don't you dare leave her behind or else she will end up suffering like you. That's my most sincere advice for you.'

'But, doctor, how will I go to Pune? I don't even know where it is!'

'Go to the nearest city of Belgaum and then from there, you can take a bus to Pune.'

My father said goodbye to her and came out of the room.

An old man handed him one hundred rupees. 'Doctor, this is your fee for helping the girl with the delivery. I warn you—don't say a word about what happened here today. If you do, I will learn of it and your head will no longer be attached to the rest of your body.'

My father nodded, suddenly overtaken by a sense of calm. 'I'm sorry,' he said. 'I think I forgot my scissors in the room. I will need it tomorrow at the clinic.'

He turned around and went back inside and saw the young girl gazing at the sleeping newborn with tears in her eyes. When the old lady's back was turned towards him, my father handed over the money to the girl. 'This is all I have with me right now,' he said. 'Use it and do what I have told you.'

'Doctor, what is your name?' she asked.

'My name is Dr R.H. Kulkarni, but almost everyone calls me RH. Be brave, child. Goodbye and good luck.'

My father left the room and the house. The return journey was equally rough and he finally reached home at dawn. He was dead tired and soon, sleep took over. The next morning, his mind wandered back to his first patient in the village and his first earning. He became aware of his shortcomings and wished he was better qualified in gynaecology. However, his current shortage of funds made him postpone the dream for another day.

A few months later, he got married and shared his dream of becoming a gynaecologist with his wife.

Time passed quickly. He was transferred to different places in Maharashtra and Karnataka and had four children along the way. By the time he turned forty-two, the couple had carefully saved enough money for further education and my father decided to pursue his desire. So he left his family in Hubli and joined Egmore Medical College in Chennai, and fulfilled his dream of becoming a gynaecologist surgeon. He was one of the rare male gynaecologists at the time.

He went back to Hubli and started working at the Karnataka Medical College as a professor. His sympathetic manner towards the underprivileged and his genuine concern for the women and girls he treated made him quite popular—both as a doctor and as a teacher. The same concern reflected in his liberal attitude towards his daughters and he allowed them to pursue their chosen fields of education, which was unheard of in those days.

My father was an atheist. 'God doesn't reside in a church, mosque or temple,' he would often say. 'I see him in all my patients. If a woman dies during childbirth, then it is the loss of one patient for a doctor but for that child, it is the lifelong loss of a mother. And tell me, who can replace a mother?'

Despite his retirement, my father's love for learning did not diminish and he remained active.

One day, he went for a medical conference to another city. There, he met a young woman in her thirties. She was presenting cases from her experience in the rural areas. My father found her work interesting and went to tell her so after the presentation. 'Doctor, your research is excellent. I am quite impressed by your work,' he said.

'Thank you,' she said.

Just then, someone called out to my father, 'RH, we are waiting for you to grab some lunch. Will you take long?'

The young woman asked, 'What is your name, doctor?'

'Dr R.H. Kulkarni, or RH.'

After a moment of silence, she asked, 'Were you in Chandagad in 1943?'

'Yes.'

'Doctor, I live in a village around forty kilometres away from here. May I request you to come home right now for a brief visit?'

My father was unprepared for such an invitation. Why was she calling him to her house?

'Maybe some other time, doctor,' he replied, hoping to end the matter.

But the woman was persistent. 'You must come. Please. Think of this as a request from someone who has been waiting for you for years now.'

My father was puzzled by her enigmatic answer and still refused, but she pleaded with him. There was something in her eyes—something so desperate—that in the end, he gave in and accompanied her to the village.

On the way to the village, both of them exchanged ideas and she spoke animatedly about her work and her findings. As the two of them approached her residence, my father realized that the house was also a nursing home. He walked in through the front door and saw a lady in her fifties standing in the living room.

The young woman next to him said, 'Ma, this is Dr RH. Is he the one you have been waiting for all these years?'

The woman came forward, bent down and touched her forehead to my father's feet. He felt his feet getting wet from her tears. It was strange. Who were these women? My father didn't know what to do. He quickly bent forward, placed his hands on the older woman's shoulders and pulled her up.

'Doctor, you may not remember me but I can never forget you. Mine must have been your first delivery.'

Still, my father couldn't recognize her.

'A long time ago, you lived in a village on the border of Maharashtra and Karnataka. One night, there was a heavy downpour and you helped me—a young, unmarried girl then—through childbirth. There was no delivery table in the room, so you converted stacks of paddy sacks into a makeshift table. Many hours later, I gave birth to a daughter.'

In a flash, the memories came flooding back and my father recollected that night. 'Of course I remember you!' he said. 'It was the middle of the night and I urged you to go to Pune with your newborn. I think I was as scared as you!'

'You gave me a hundred rupees, which is what my family paid you for the delivery. It was a big amount in those days and still, you handed it all over to me.'

'Yes, my monthly salary was seventy-five rupees then!' added my father with a smile.

'You told me your last name but I couldn't hear it because of the deafening sound of the rain. I took your advice, went to Pune, found your friend Gokhale and became a nurse. It was very, very hard, but I was able to raise my daughter on my own. After such a terrible experience, I wanted my daughter to become a gynaecologist. Luckily, she shared my dream too. Today, she is a doctor and is also married to one and they practise here. At one point, I spent months searching for you but with no luck. Then we heard that you had moved to Karnataka after the reorganization of the state departments in 1956. Meanwhile, Gokhale also passed away and I lost all hope of ever finding you. I prayed to God to give me a chance to meet you and thank you for showing me the right path at the right time.'

My father felt like he was in a Bollywood movie and was enchanted by the unexplained mystery of life. A few kind words and encouragement had changed a young girl's life.

She clasped her hands together. 'We are so grateful to you, doctor. My daughter wanted to call you for the inauguration of the nursing home here and we were very disappointed at not being able to reach you then. Time has passed and now the nursing home is doing very well.'

My father wiped his moist eyes and looked around to see the name of the nursing home. He looked to the right and found himself staring at it—R.H. Diagnostic.

7

The Line of Separation

During my trip to Pakistan, I was part of a large group. Each person in the group was keen to visit one place or the other in that country. Some wanted to see Takshila, others Lahore, Islamabad or Karachi. One day, we were having a discussion about this and everyone was voicing his or her opinion loudly. I noticed only Mrs Roopa Kapoor was sitting quietly. She was a seventy-five-year-old lady from Chennai and did not speak much unless spoken to. So I asked if there was any place she wanted to visit.

Without any hesitation, she said, 'I have to visit Pindi.'

'Where is Pindi? Is it some small town or village? I don't think we will have the time to make a detour like that from our packed itinerary.' Roopa smiled at my ignorance and said, 'I meant Rawalpindi. It is called Pindi for short by those who stay there.' I was intrigued. 'How do you know? Have you ever stayed there?'

'I was born and brought up there,' she replied, and then slowly she told me the story of her life.

She had stayed in Rawalpindi till the age of nineteen, when she got married and settled down in Chennai. Now Chennai was her home and she could speak Tamil and make excellent Tamil dishes, like puliyogare and rasam, as well as any natural-born Tamilian. But she had always yearned to come back and see her childhood home if she ever got the chance.

Soon we reached Islamabad and I was surprised to find it surrounded by mountains, as cool as a hill station. Roopa saw my surprise and said, 'Islamabad is a new city. Rawalpindi is a sister city, but it is older. Islamabad was built after the Partition with wide roads, shopping centres and rose gardens. Pindi is only twenty-odd kilometres away from Islamabad.' By now the soft-spoken, introverted Mrs Kapoor had become quite garrulous. There was a spark in her eyes and she spoke non-stop. Many of us wanted to see Islamabad first, but she insisted on going on to Rawalpindi.

She needed a companion for the trip and I volunteered to go with her. She was now quite excited, and told me, 'I want to see the house I left fifty-seven years ago.'

'That's a good idea,' I said. Then I remembered the lovely bouquet of flowers I had been presented on landing at Islamabad which I was still carrying. 'I will present this to whoever is staying in your house now.'

She was touched.

As the car left Islamabad airport behind, Mrs Kapoor started pointing out the sights to me like a tour guide. She showed me an old building on the left side of the road in a crowded area and said, 'That used to be an electrical goods manufacturing factory. Its owner, Kewal Ram Sahani, was my father's friend. My friends and I would come to this house for Lakshmi puja during Diwali.'

I told the driver to slow down a little so that she could cherish the journey. The car passed Sadar Bazar and looking at an old building with many shops, she said, 'Here my father's cousin Ratan Sethi owned a jewellery shop along with his partner Maqbool Khan. It was known as Khan and Sethi. My wedding jewellery was made here.'

She continued pointing out various buildings, each holding some fond memory for her. But many a time the buildings she was looking for had changed to new skyscrapers and she got disoriented. Suddenly the car stopped. A tyre was punctured, and the driver said it would take him a while to fix it. Roopa was restless. She did not want to wait even a minute more than required. So she said, 'You change the tyre. In the meantime I will go and visit some of the old places. We will join you at the next main road. To go to the main road, you take a left turn and the first right turn. You wait for us there.'

She behaved as if she knew every inch of that area and I followed her quietly. We walked into a small lane. She explained, 'I have been here many times with my friends Fatima and Noor. This used to be known as Tailor's Road. My neighbour Mehboob Khan's wife Mehrunnisa Chachi was an expert in designing new embroidery patterns. We used to come and give the designs. Come, we will take a shortcut . . . That is where my uncle lived.'

By now she was talking more to herself and making her way with ease through the narrow lanes. We went to the next road. There were old houses on the road and she went into the first huge bungalow. She said, 'This was my uncle Motiram Rai's house and the next house was that of Allah Baksh. They were great friends and loved each other. I still remember whenever Allah Baksh Chacha planted a tree in his house, my uncle would plant the same. This mango tree here was planted on a Basant Panchami day. There was so much of joy in both houses. My grandmother prepared kheer and sent me to Allah Baksh's house with a jug full of it. While I was carrying that jug, I bumped into a young man and the hot kheer fell on his feet. I was so scared and embarrassed.'

'Did you know him?'

'Not then but later. I married him!'

She then looked up at the tree and said, 'This has become so old now.'

We walked in through the gate. There was no one around and I was afraid we would be stopped by someone for trespassing. But Roopa was least bothered. It was as if she was in a world of her own. She walked to the backyard while I stood hesitating in the front. A couple walked in and were visibly surprised to see a stranger standing in their garden, that too in a sari. It was also just then that I noticed a board hanging in front of the door. It said 'Dr Salim and Dr Salma: Dentist'.

I started apologizing and explained the situation to them. Their faces lost the look of suspicion as soon as I finished my story. Roopa was still looking at all the trees and remembering her childhood. The couple welcomed us courteously. 'Please sit down. Do join us for a cup of tea.' They pulled up two chairs.

By now I was feeling very awkward, disturbing them in the morning. But Dr Salim said, 'Please sit. We are glad you came. Our grandparents too were from Surat in Gujarat. They emigrated to Pakistan and I was born and brought up here. My parents talk with great nostalgia about Surati farsan, Parsi dhansak and khakra.'

Just to make conversation I said, 'It must be difficult maintaining such a large bungalow now.'

Dr Salim replied, 'We moved to this house some years back. You see, this house happens to resemble the one my parents lived in in Surat, and they made me promise that I would not break it and make apartments as long as I stayed here. Allah has been kind to us and we don't need the money. Our neighbour Allah Baksh's children sold their property long back and now there is a commercial complex.'

By then Roopa had finished wandering in the garden and I formally introduced her to the couple. She asked if she could see the house from the inside. Dr Salim agreed happily. 'After we purchased this house ten years ago we made very few modifications. It is perhaps in the same state as you last saw it,' he said.

I walked in with Roopa. She looked into the main room and said, 'This was where my grandfather used to sit and control the house.' Then she pointed to a coloured glass door and said Allah Baksh's wife had painted it for them. 'That was the window through which she would send dry fruits to my aunt', 'That was where we used to fly kites.' Every brick, every wall held a memory for her. Finally I reminded her that it was time we left. We walked back to the garden and said our goodbyes to the couple. Dr Salim handed us a packet. 'There is no time for you to eat, but I cannot send two elders away without offering anything. Please take this and if God is willing we will meet again.'

We came out of the house and when we reached the main road the car was there, having followed Roopa's directions. Now she wanted to see her own house.

She told the driver, 'Take a right turn from the *chauraha*. I know the way. The first building on the right side is Al-Ameen School for girls and a little farther there is a Jesus and Mary convent. A little ahead on the left side, there is a government boys' school. Next to that is the Idgah maidan. Next to that is a lane with five huge bungalows. Each plot is an acre in size. The first one belonged to Kewal Ram. Second to Mia Mehboob Khan and the third one to Sardar Supreet Singh. Fourth one to Rai Sahib and the fifth was ours . . .'

She talked on and the driver followed her directions. She was mostly right. Yes, the red brick building on the right was the Al-Ameen School for girls. The Jesus and Mary convent was now a Loyola College and the government boys' school had become a degree college. But the Idgah maidan was not there. Instead there was a shopping complex. The five beautiful bungalows she described were also missing. Instead there was a mass of shops, hotels and video libraries piled next to each other. Roopa became upset.

'Madam, are you sure it is the same road?' the driver asked politely.

'Of course I am sure. I was born here. I spent nineteen years here. You were not even born then. How can I make a mistake?'

She told him to stop the car and got off to search. She was sure the house was still there behind the new buildings. She was possessed, as if searching for a lost child, or a precious jewel.

'My house was yellow in colour and there were two storeys. It had an entrance from the right side. From my house I could see the Idgah maidan. Two years back a friend of mine who also stayed here came to see the place and she told me the house was still very much here.'

She turned to me and continued, 'You know, once I had unknowingly walked on the wet cement floor near the entrance of the house and my footmark stayed there forever. My father wanted to keep it as a reminder of me after I got married and went away. I can recognize my house without any trouble.' But there was no house of that description in that area, with the footmark in the entrance. I knew by this time that the house was not there. But Roopa was reluctant to accept it.

We stood in front of the building where she said her house used to be. It was a hotel and a chowkidar was sitting at the entrance.

I asked him, 'How old is this hotel?'

He got up and replied, 'It is only a year old.'

'How long have you been working here?'

'Ever since the old building was demolished and the construction started.'

Roopa was quiet now.

'Was there a two-storeyed yellow building here with the entrance on the right and footprints along the portico?'

'Yes. There was a building like that but I don't remember the footprints.'

Now I knew that Roopa's house had been demolished to make way for this hotel. I looked at the chowkidar and told him, 'That was my friend's house.'

'Oh, please come inside. So what if your house is not there? The hotel stands on the same land. I am sure my owner will be happy to receive you. Have a cup of tea and a samosa.'

I looked at Roopa but she was not listening to our conversation.

She took a handful of soil from the little patch of garden in front of the hotel and said, 'This is my land. This is my soil. My ancestors made this their home. They were born and burnt here. The land, the trees, the air, the water, everything was ours. We knew the customs, the culture and the food. One day, some person drew a line and created two nations. And suddenly we became foreigners in our own land. We had to leave and adopt some other place whose language, food and culture were alien to us. A single line made me a stranger to my own land. People who have been uprooted feel a special pain which no one else can understand.'

I was quiet. I could only imagine her agony. I held her hand and suddenly realized that the bouquet of flowers I had meant to give to the owners of her old house was lying on the front seat of the car, withering slowly in the December sunshine.

8

India, the Holy Land

Maya was a simple young lady who lived in the Tibetan settlement on the outskirts of Mundugod, near Hubli in north Karnataka. She used to teach the Tibetan language to the children in the camp, so they would not forget their roots. She was smart and hard-working.

My father was a doctor working in Hubli and he occasionally visited that settlement. If any of the Tibetans wanted further treatment, they would visit my father at the Government Hospital in Hubli. Maya too started visiting my father when she was expecting her first child.

Over the months she became quite friendly with all of us. Whenever she came to the hospital she would pay us a visit too. My mother would invite her for a meal and we would spend some time chatting.

In the beginning, we would be in awe of her and stare at her almost-white skin, dove eyes, the little flat nose and her two long, thin plaits. Slowly we accepted her as a friend and she graduated to become my knitting teacher. Her visits were sessions of knitting, chatting and talking about her life in the camp and back in her country for which she still yearned. Maya would describe her homeland to us with great affection, nostalgia and, at times, with tears in her eyes.

'Tibetans are simple people. We are all Buddhists but our Buddhism is of a different kind. It is called Vajrayana. There's been a lot of influence from India, particularly Bengal, on our country and religious practices. Even our script resembles Bengali.'

Her words filled me with a sense of wonder about this exotic land called Tibet and I would pester her to tell me more about that country. One day we started talking about the Dalai Lama.

'What is the meaning of Dalai Lama?' I asked.

'It means "ocean of knowledge". Ours is a unique country where religious heads have ruled for 500 years. We believe in rebirth and that each Dalai Lama is an incarnation of the previous one. The present Dalai Lama is the fourteenth . . . You know, India is the holy land of Buddha. Historically, we have always respected India. There is a nice story about how Buddhism came to Tibet through India . . .'

I could not wait to hear about this!

'Long ago there was a king in Tibet who was kidnapped by his enemies. They demanded a ransom of gold, equal to the weight of the king. When the imprisoned king heard this, he somehow sent word to his son: "Don't waste any gold to get me back. Instead, spend that money to bring good learned Buddhist monks from India. With their help, open many schools and monasteries so that our people can live in peace and gain knowledge."'

Months passed and Maya delivered a baby. After that our meetings became less frequent. But she succeeded in awakening within me a curiosity about Tibet and a great respect for Buddhism.

Recently I got a chance to visit Tibet and memories of Maya filled my mind. I knew I would be seeing a Tibet filled with the Chinese but nevertheless I was keen to go. Among the places I wanted to see was a Buddha temple in Yarlung Valley that she had described to me.

When I finally reached the valley, it was past midday. There was a cold wind blowing though the sun was shining brightly. The Brahmaputra was flowing like a stream here, nothing like the raging torrent in Assam. Snow-capped mountains circled the valley and there was absolute silence all around.

The monastery at Yarlung is supposed to be a famous pilgrimage spot, but I could see only a handful of people in the entire place. After seeing everything inside I sat down on the steps and observed the serene beauty of the place.

I noticed an old woman accompanied by a young man walking into the monastery. The woman was very old, her face was wrinkled and she walked slowly and weakly. She was wearing the traditional Tibetan dress and her hair was plaited. The young man on the other hand was dressed in the usual modern manner, in tight jeans and a body-hugging T-shirt. The woman started circumambulating the monastery using her stick for support while the man sat down on the steps like me.

When she finished, I realized the old lady was staring at me. Then she said something to the young man in Tibetan.

She looked tired by the end of her ritual and sat down on the steps. She said something to her companion again but he took little notice of her. So she slowly picked up her stick and came towards me. She sat down near me, took my hands and, saying something, gently raised them to her eyes and kissed them. Before I could say anything, she got up and started to walk away. But I noticed she was smiling, as if she had achieved a long-held desire. I realized there was a wetness where her eyes had touched my hand.

Now the young boy reluctantly came up to me and apologized. 'Please forgive my grandmother,' he said. 'She is from a village in the interior part of Tibet. She has never ventured out of her village. This is the first time she has come to Yarlung. I beg your pardon for her behaviour.'

He was talking to me in English with an Indian accent.

'How come you speak English like us?' I asked in surprise.

'My name is KeTsang. I was in India for five years. I studied at Loyola College in Chennai. Now I run a restaurant in Lhasa. People here like Indian food and movies. I accompanied my grandmother for her pilgrimage. She was thanking you.'

'But for what? I have not done anything for her!'

'That is true, but your country has. It has sheltered our Dalai Lama for so many years. He is a living god to us, particularly to the older generation. We all respect the Dalai Lama, but due to political reasons, we cannot express it in public. You might have seen that there isn't a single photo of his in any public place in the whole of Lhasa. He is the fourteenth, but we have paintings, statues and pictures only up to the thirteenth.'

I still did not understand the old lady's gesture. The grandson explained, 'She said, "I am an old lady and don't know how long I will live. If I don't thank you before I die, I will never attain peace. Let anyone punish me for this, it does not matter. It is a gift that I met an Indian today and was able to thank you for sheltering our Dalai Lama. Yours is truly a compassionate land."'

Her words eerily echoed Maya's from many years back. I could only look down at the wet spot on my hand and smile.

9

Bonded by Bisleri

The 26 January horror of Kutch in Gujarat is well known. Without any warning, Mother Earth opened her mouth and engulfed the people and their belongings. Overnight, rich people were reduced to the streets. But the spirit of the Kutchi people is admirable. They faced this disaster bravely and are still fighting to restore normalcy.

The media has to be congratulated for its role in the relief efforts. Within hours of the tragedy, all newspapers and television channels had zoomed in to cover the disaster and broadcast it all over the world. Along with India, the rest of the world participated in helping these unfortunate people. After all the rush of the TV crews and media people, hordes of NGOs and government officials landed up in Kutch. People started picking up their life from where they had left it. Life started to return to normal at a slow pace.

I went to visit these areas after some time, when the dust of propaganda had settled down, in order to see actual life. After all, the emotions had drained off and reality had become the priority.

Several small villages deep inside Kutch, away from the main road connecting Ahmedabad and Bhuj, had been badly affected by the earthquake. I was visiting these remote places in the deep interior when one of the tyres of my jeep went flat. Getting it fixed would take some time. My driver went to get this done.

I was alone and bored. I saw a few tents nearby. They were temporary sheds covered with blue plastic sheets. They were temporary houses, schools and health centres for the people residing in that area. Later, I heard that there were tent hotels as well.

Life was busy and people were getting on with their chores. As it was monsoon season, men and women were busy in the fields. It was very strange. For many years there had not been much rain in Kutch, but that year it had rained abundantly. Farmers were having a bumper crop. I suppose nature has its own method of justice. On the one hand she takes away something and on the other she gives something in return. Small children were playing in the dust happily.

I peeped into one of the nearby tents. A young girl, about fourteen years old, was cleaning grains and preparing to cook a meal. When she saw me, she rose with a smile and said, 'Please come in and sit down.'

As I wanted to see how they lived, I entered the shed. She gave me a charpoy to sit on. Inside the tent it was clean and neat. There was a thin partition made of an old sari. I understood from her conversation that her family was not from Kutch.

The girl offered me a glass of water. Though it was the monsoon season, the sun was hot, but I was a little hesitant to drink the water. Many thoughts flashed across my mind. If the water was not sterile, then I was at risk of contracting diseases like dysentery and jaundice. If I refused to accept the water, however, I knew I would hurt the girl's feelings. So I took the glass but did not drink the water.

The girl had a younger sister who might have been around twelve years old. There was a little boy sleeping in a home-made cradle. Outside, there was a temporary open kitchen where sabzi was being cooked. The elder one was making dough from wheat flour.

'It seems from your language that you are not Gujaratis. Where are you from?' I asked.

Smiling, the younger sister answered, 'We're not from Gujarat, we're from Mumbai.'

'Have you come here to visit your relatives?'

'No, we don't have any relatives here. This is our house. We have come here with our parents.'

I was very surprised by this answer because, normally, people flee areas afflicted by calamities, whereas these people had moved in. 'What is your father doing here?'

Both girls were eager to give me information. The elder one replied, 'My father used to beg in Mumbai at Mahim Creek, near the church. My mother used to sell candles at the church entrance.'

'What made you come here?'

'One day, we saw the news on TV and came to know that there had been an earthquake here. It was shown every hour on TV in the corner shop. My father said "Let's go" and we came here.'

'Who paid for your train tickets?'

'Nobody. We came here without tickets. The whole train was full of people. There were many people like us who have come. The entire station was heavily crowded. There was no ticket collector.'

'How did you come from the train station?'

'We didn't know anyone. But there were plenty of buses running between the station and Bhuj. There were many foreign volunteers. The buses were jam-packed. We also got into one of the buses and landed on the main road.'

'How did you come to this particular area?'

'There were many jeeps going from the main roads to all interior villages. On the main road, there was a convoy of trucks full of different relief materials. They used to unload materials on either side of the road. People who did not have anything would pick them up from the roadside. We also picked up some.'

'What were the materials on the roadside?'

'There were food articles, apples, biscuit packets, clothes, blankets and many more items. My father told each one of us to pick up what we could and we collected a lot. We had never seen so much in our life in Mumbai. Everything was in plenty.'

Children are innocent and they always tell the truth until they become adults and lies creep into their lives. One lies to boast, to show what he is not. But children are so confident. They never pretend to be what they're not. Naturally, the

Mumbai beggar's daughters described the whole scenario as if it was a very memorable event.

The elder one said much more than that. 'There were people crying, some of them in pain. Some had lost their children or parents. It was very sad to see. But there were plenty of people to help also. There were doctors working overnight. There were swamijis working like common men, distributing medicines. There were army people digging to build houses. There was no difference between day and night, the rich and the poor.

'Our position was better. We did not lose anybody, nor did we lose any material, because we never had anything to begin with. People who have something have to fear losing it, but people who don't have anything to lose have no such fear. My mother and father helped people and someone said that inside the villages there was nobody to help. There were jeeps constantly travelling between the villages and the main road. So we got into one of the jeeps and landed in this village. Some organization was giving bamboo, camping materials like tents, and other roofing materials, free to all those people who had lost their houses. As we had no home, we also got all the materials. Sometimes we got double because my mother was in one queue and my father in another.'

'What all have you got?'

'Plenty of food. We have been eating to our hearts' content every day and we have also been giving some to people who were unable to stand in the queue. We know what it is to be hungry.'

'Why did you settle here then?'

'My father had asthma in Mumbai. He was unable to breathe and on many days we would go hungry. Someone said it was due to the pollution. It might be true, because after we came here, he has been normal, because there's no pollution here. Anyway, we had also built our own house, so we decided to settle down.'

'What job does your father do here? Does he continue to beg?'

'No. We are self-sufficient now. He is working as a coolie in a nearby field. He earns Rs 100 a day. Our mother also does the same thing, so the income is doubled. We're comfortable. The earthquake has come like a boon to us.'

She asked her sister to get some tea and biscuits. She inquired, 'Which biscuits do you want?'

'Do you have a variety?' I asked, surprised.

She pulled the curtain aside and I was amazed to see the varieties of biscuit packets, cartons of Bisleri mineral water, utensils, steel trunks and other things.

'From the day of the earthquake, most of us here have been drinking only Bisleri water. It seems some foreign country has sent a shipful of it. What I have given you is also mineral water.'

I took the glass of water and immediately gulped it down.

10

In India, the Worst of Both Worlds

Monday is the first working day of the week and an extremely busy day in our offices. All emails and papers have to be processed and meetings held. Long lists of appointments inevitably fill up our diaries. In between appointments, unexpected callers invariably turn up. Secretaries sweat it out on Monday mornings. But we have to get past Monday to reach Sunday again.

I recall one such Monday. I was engrossed in checking and replying to my email when my secretary told me that there were two visitors who had come to meet me without an appointment.

I asked her, 'What is special about these visitors that you are letting them in without an appointment?' I have great confidence in my staff and their ways of screening visitors.

She replied in a low tone, 'Madam, one is a very old man who looks very pale and the other is a middle-aged person. They say it is very urgent and have been waiting for quite some time.'

'Send them in,' I said.

They came in and sat opposite me. The old man seemed more than seventy years old. He was looking weak, tired and worried. He carried a worn-out bag. He was in a pitiable condition. With him was a middle-aged man who also looked somewhat worried.

I came to the point immediately. 'Tell me, what is the matter?'

The old man did not talk but just looked at the younger man.

The middle-aged man said, 'Madam, I saw this old man sitting near a bus stop. It seems he does not have anybody. He wants some shelter. Unfortunately, he does not have any money.'

This middle-aged man wanted to go on with all kinds of explanations. I often come across people who beat around the bush quite unnecessarily. They never tell you what they want directly. As I am used to such things, I often cut them short even at the risk of sounding curt.

'What do you want me to do?' I asked outright.

'I have read a lot about your work. I want you to help this gentleman.'

'Do you have anybody?' I asked the old man.

Tears welled up in his eyes. In a low voice he said, 'No, I do not have anybody.'

'What about your family?'

'No, I do not have anybody.'

'Where were you working before?'

I asked many questions and he gave reasonably satisfactory replies.

I felt bad for the old man. He had no money and nobody to give him a helping hand. It was a sad case. I thought of an old-age home with which we had regular contact. I called this home and told them that I was sending an old man there and that he should be kept there until we decided what we could do for him. The middle-aged man said, 'Do not worry. I will go with him and leave him there. From there, I will go to my office.'

Then they left my office. Soon, I got lost in my world of work, visitors, vouchers, budgets and so on.

Not that I forgot the old man's case. Once in a while I would call the old-age home and inquire about him. They would tell me that he was fine. I never had time to think more about him. I used to send money every month to the old-age home.

One day, I got a call from the caretaker of the home saying that the old man was very sick and that they had admitted him to a hospital. Could I come in the evening?

I went to see the old man at the hospital that evening.

He was really unwell. The doctors felt his condition was critical and that he did not have long to live. I thought there might be somebody he wished to see at a time like this. Maybe not his own children, but perhaps a nephew or a sister or brother, at least a friend? Was there anybody we could inform?

I asked him, 'Do you want to see anybody? We will call whomever you want. Do you have anybody's phone number?'

With a trembling hand, he wrote down a number and gave it to me. We called the number and informed the person at the other end that the old man was critical. After some time, a person came to see him. He looked anxious and worried and went straight to the old man.

I thought I had seen this man before. I tried to jog my memory but in vain. I just couldn't remember why the old man's visitor seemed so familiar. Perhaps he resembled someone I had met on my travels.

Meanwhile, the doctor came out and told me that the old man had breathed his last. I felt sad. I neither knew him nor had any contact with him. But somehow I felt very sad.

After a few minutes, the visitor came out. He had tears in his eyes. He sat down quietly on a bench. The whole place was quiet and depressing. The caretaker, this visitor and I sat in the visitors' hall, waiting for the formalities to be completed.

The visitor asked, 'Where is the bag he had?'

'What bag?'

'This man came to the old-age home carrying a bag,' he said.

My interest quickened. How did the visitor know that there was a bag?

I sent a peon back to the old-age home to fetch the bag. When it arrived, the visitor was eager to open it, but I did not permit him.

'You may not open the bag unless you identify yourself. What is your relationship with this old man? I want to know how you knew about this bag.'

He seemed very upset with my questions. Maybe he didn't like a woman questioning him. In India, men often get upset when women raise questions that are inconvenient for them. They prefer women who do not question what they do. Fortunately, this trend is disappearing slowly.

'It was I who accompanied him and left him at this home,' said the man.

'Who are you?' I was very curious.

'I am his son.'

You can imagine how shocked I was. Now I remembered— he was the middle-aged man who had come to our office that Monday morning claiming that he had found the old man sitting near a bus stop.

I was very upset. 'Why did you lie to me?'

Of course he had a story to tell. 'I have problems at home,' he said. 'My wife never liked my father. She asked me to choose between her and him. At that time we read about your foundation. We thought then that our problem could be solved without money.' He said he had no choice but to appease his wife because it was she who owned the house they lived in.

'What a way to solve your problem!' I protested. 'We help people who are orphans, but not orphans with children.'

When the bag was finally opened we found three sets of old clothes in it, some medicines and a passbook. When I opened the passbook, I was astounded. The old man had a bank balance of more than a lakh of rupees. The old man had put down a nominee for the account—his son, the same son who had got rid of him. Here was a son who was heartless enough to pass off his father as destitute in order to admit him in an old-age home. Now, the same son had come to claim his father's money.

Though his son had not wanted to look after him and had made him lie to me that he had nobody in this world, the old man nevertheless had wanted his money to go to his son. It never would have occurred to him to give that money to the old-age home that had sheltered him in his last days.

In Western countries, when old people die in old-age homes, they often will their property to the home or the hospital that cared for them. This is for the benefit of other senior citizens. They do not bequeath their money to their children, nor do the children expect their parents to do so. But in India, we have the worst of both worlds: children neglect aged parents, and parents routinely leave their property to their children.

'It is shameful the way you and your father cooked up this drama for the sake of a few thousand rupees!' I told the man. 'And you are setting a bad example. Next time when a genuinely destitute person seeks help, we will be unwilling to offer it. The memory of people like you will stay on.'

He hung his head in shame.

11

How I Taught
My Grandmother to Read

When I was a girl of about twelve, I used to stay in a village in north Karnataka with my grandparents. Those days, the transport system was not very good, so we used to get the morning paper only in the afternoon. The weekly magazine used to come one day late. All of us would wait eagerly for the bus, which used to come with the papers, weekly magazines and the post.

At that time, Triveni was a very popular writer in the Kannada language. She was a wonderful writer. Her style was easy to read and very convincing. Her stories usually dealt with complex psychological problems in the lives of ordinary people and were always very interesting. Unfortunately for Kannada literature, she died very young. Even now, after forty years, people continue to appreciate her novels.

One of her novels, called *Kashi Yatre*, was appearing as a serial in the Kannada weekly *Karmaveera* then. It is the story of an old lady and her ardent desire to go to Kashi or Varanasi. Most Hindus believe that going to Kashi and worshipping

Lord Vishweshwara is the ultimate *punya*. This old lady also believed in this, and her struggle to go there was described in that novel. In the story there was also a young orphan girl who falls in love but there was no money for the wedding. In the end, the old lady gives away all her savings to help the girl, without going to Kashi. She says, 'The happiness of this orphan girl is more important than worshipping Lord Vishweshwara at Kashi.'

My grandmother, Krishtakka, never went to school so she could not read. Every Wednesday, the magazine would come and I would read the next episode of this story to her. During that time she would forget all her work and listen with the greatest concentration. Later, she could repeat the entire text by heart. My grandmother too never went to Kashi, and she identified herself with the novel's protagonist. So more than anybody else she was the one most interested in knowing what happened next in the story and used to insist that I read the serial out to her.

After hearing what happened next in *Kashi Yatre*, she would join her friends at the temple courtyard, where we children would also gather to play hide-and-seek. She would discuss the latest episode with her friends. At that time, I never understood why there was so much debate about the story.

Once I went for a wedding with my cousins to the neighbouring village. In those days, a wedding was a great event. We children enjoyed ourselves thoroughly. We would eat and play endlessly, savouring the freedom because all the elders were busy. I went for a couple of days but ended up staying there for a week.

When I came back to my village, I saw my grandmother in tears. I was surprised, for I had never seen her cry even in the most difficult situations.

What had happened? I was worried.

'Avva, is everything all right? Are you OK?'

I used to call her 'Avva', which means 'mother' in the Kannada spoken in north Karnataka.

She nodded but did not reply. I did not understand and forgot about it. In the night, after dinner, we were sleeping on the open terrace of the house. It was a summer night and there was a full moon. Avva came and sat next to me. Her affectionate hands touched my forehead. I realized she wanted to speak. I asked her, 'What is the matter?'

'When I was a young girl I lost my mother. There was nobody to look after and guide me. My father was a busy man and got married again. In those days people did not consider education essential for girls, so I never went to school. I got married very young and had children. I became very busy. Later I had grandchildren and always felt so much happiness in cooking and feeding all of you. At times I used to regret not going to school, so I made sure that my children and grandchildren studied well . . .'

I could not understand why my sixty-two-year-old grandmother was telling me, a twelve-year-old, the story of her life in the middle of the night. But I knew I loved her immensely and there had to be some reason why she was talking to me. I looked at her face. It was unhappy and her eyes were filled with tears. She was a good-looking lady who was usually always smiling. Even today I cannot forget the worried expression on her face. I leant forward and held her hand.

'Avva, don't cry. What is the matter? Can I help you in any way?'

'Yes, I need your help. You know when you were away, *Karmaveera* came as usual. I opened the magazine. I saw the picture that accompanies the story of *Kashi Yatre* and I could not understand anything that was written. Many times I rubbed my hands over the pages wishing they could understand what was written. But I knew it was not possible.

'If only I was educated enough. I waited eagerly for you to return. I felt you would come early and read for me. I even thought of going to the village and asking you to read for me. I could have asked somebody in this village but I was too embarrassed to do so. I felt so dependent and helpless. We are well off, but what use is money when I cannot be independent?'

I did not know what to answer. Avva continued.

'I have decided I want to learn the Kannada alphabet from tomorrow. I will work very hard. I will keep Saraswati Puja day during Dasara as the deadline. That day I should be able to read a novel on my own. I want to be independent.'

I saw the determination on her face. Yet I laughed at her.

'Avva, at this age of sixty-two you want to learn the alphabet? All your hair is grey, your hands are wrinkled, you wear spectacles and you work so much in the kitchen . . .' Childishly I made fun of the old lady. But she just smiled.

'For a good cause if you are determined, you can overcome any obstacle. I will work harder than anybody, but I will do it. For learning there is no age bar.'

The next day onwards I started my tuition. Avva was a wonderful student. The amount of homework she did was amazing. She would read, repeat, write and recite. I was her only teacher and she was my first student. Little did I know then that one day I would become a teacher in computer science and teach hundreds of students.

The Dasara festival came as usual. Secretly I bought *Kashi Yatre* which had been published as a novel by that time. My grandmother called me to the puja place and made me sit down on a stool. She gave me the gift of a dress material. Then she did something unusual. She bent down and touched my feet. I was surprised and taken aback. Elders never touch the feet of youngsters. We have always touched the feet of God, elders and teachers. We consider that as a mark of respect. It is a great tradition but today the reverse had happened. It was not correct.

She said, 'I am touching the feet of a teacher, not my granddaughter; a teacher who taught me so well, with so much affection that I can read any novel confidently after such a short period. Now I am independent. It is my duty to respect a teacher. Is it not written in our scriptures that a teacher should be respected, irrespective of gender and age?'

I did return namaskara to her by touching her feet and gave my gift to my first student. She opened it and read immediately the title *Kashi Yatre* by Triveni and the publisher's name. I knew then that my student had passed with flying colours.

12

Rahman's Avva

Rahman was a young and soft-spoken employee who worked in a BPO. He was also an active volunteer in our Foundation. He would not talk without reason and would never boast about his achievements.

Rahman was a perfectionist. So any assignment given to him was done exceedingly well. He worked for the Foundation on the weekends and was very kind to the children in the orphanage. He spent his own money and always brought sweets for the children. I really liked him.

Since we worked closely together, he learnt that I am from north Karnataka, from Dharwad district. My language has that area's accent and my love for Dharwad food is very well known. One day, Rahman came and asked me, 'Madam, if you are free this Sunday, will you come to my house? My mother and sister are visiting me. Incidentally, my mother is also from Dharwad district. My family has read your columns in Kannada and your books too. When I told them that I am working with you, they expressed their earnest desire to meet you. Is it possible for you to have lunch with us?'

'Will you assure me that I'll get a good Dharwad meal?'
I joked.

'I assure you, madam. My mother is a great cook.'

'Come on, Rahman. Every boy gives this compliment
to his mother, however bad she may be at cooking. It is the
mother's love that makes the food great.'

'No, she really is an amazing cook. Even my wife says so.'

'Then she must be really great because no daughter-
in-law praises her mother-in-law's cooking without merit.'
I smiled. 'By the way, which village in Dharwad district do
they come from?'

He told me the name of a village near Ranebennur that
I had never heard of. I happily agreed to visit them for lunch.

That Sunday, I took some flowers along. Rahman's newly
constructed apartment was on Bannerghatta Road near the
zoo. When I entered his home, I met his wife, Salma. She was
a smart and good-looking girl. She worked as a teacher in the
kindergarten nearby.

Then, he called out to his avva. A mother is usually
referred to as 'avva' in north Karnataka. An old lady with
grey hair came out of the kitchen. Rahman introduced her,
'This is my mother.' I was a bit surprised—she was not quite
what I had expected. She was wearing a huge bindi the size
of a 25-paisa coin and an Ilkal sari with lots of green bangles
on both arms. She kept the sari *pallu* on her head. She had a
contented smile on her face and with folded hands she said,
'Namaste.'

Rahman's sister entered from another room. She was so
different from Rahman. Rahman was fair and very handsome.

His sister was tall and dark. She was wearing a cotton sari with a smaller bindi than her mother and also had two gold bangles on her hands. Rahman said, 'This is my sister Usha. She stays in Hirekerur. Both her husband and she are schoolteachers.'

I felt confused after meeting Rahman's mother and sister but I did not ask any questions.

After I sat down comfortably, Usha said, 'Madam, we love your stories because we feel connected to them. I teach some of your children's stories at school.'

Salma also joined the conversation. 'Even I like them, but my students are too young to understand.'

Rahman smiled and said, 'You must be surprised to see my mother and sister. I want to share my story with you.'

His mother went back to the kitchen and Usha started cleaning the table. Salma went to help her mother-in-law. Only the two of us remained.

'Madam, you must be wondering why my mother and sister are Hindus while I am a Muslim. Only you can understand and appreciate my life story because I have seen you helping people from all religions and communities without bias. I remember your comment to me: we can't choose the community or religion that we are born into, so we should never think that our community is our identity.'

Rahman paused, then continued, 'Madam, I believe in that too because I have also been brought up that way. I want to share my life and my perspective with you.'

Rahman started his story.

'Thirty years ago, Kashibai and Datturam lived on the outskirts of our village with their six-month-old daughter,

Usha. They looked after the ten-acre field of their landlord, Srikant Desai, who lived in Bombay. Srikant only came once a year to collect the revenue. The field was very large and it was too much for Kashibai and Datturam to handle. So, they requested the landlord to get another family to stay with them and help with the field. They also welcomed the thought of having company.

'Srikant contacted his acquaintances and found a suitable family. Soon, Fatima Bi and Husain Saab came to the village. They occupied one portion of the house and the other portion stayed with Kashibai and Datturam. Husain Saab and Datturam got along very well. However, Kashibai and Fatima Bi didn't see eye to eye at all. It is not that they were bad women but their natures were very different. Kashibai was loud, very frank and hard-working. Fatima Bi was quiet, lazy and an introvert. Inevitably; there was a fight. It all started with a hen. Kashibai's hen would come to Fatima Bi's portion of the house and lay eggs. Fatima Bi wouldn't return the eggs because she thought that her hen had laid them. Kashibai even tried colouring her hen to distinguish it from Fatima Bi's. Both the ladies shared a common well and would fight because both wanted to wash their vessels and clothes almost always at the same time. They also fought about their goats. Fatima Bi's goats came and ate Kashibai's flowers and leaves, which she used for her puja. Sometimes, Kashibai's goats went to Fatima Bi's place and left their droppings behind. Fatima Bi wouldn't return the droppings either.'

'What's so great about droppings?' I interrupted.

'Madam, goat droppings are used as manure.'

'Oh, I understand. Please continue,' I urged Rahman.

'The fights continued and sometimes Kashibai felt that she had made a mistake to tell their landlord that they wanted neighbours. She felt that she had been very happy without Fatima Bi. Fatima Bi also wanted to leave the farm and go to some other village but Husain Saab didn't agree. He would say, "You women fight about unnecessary things. This is a good opportunity for us to make money. The land is fertile and there is plenty of water. Our landlord is good and hardly visits. We can easily grow vegetables. Where can I get such work nearby? You should also become active like Kashibai and drop your ego. Try to adjust with her." The same conversation would happen on the other side of the house. Datturam would tell his wife, "Don't be so aggressive. You should mellow down like Fatima. Though she is lazy, she is good-natured."

'But as usual, both women never listened to their husbands.

'As time went by, Kashibai's daughter Usha turned two years old. Fatima Bi loved children and enjoyed watching Usha play in the field. Fatima Bi liked henna a lot. Every month, she coloured her hands with henna from the plant in the field and Usha always joined her. Usha was fascinated with the beautiful orange colour. She would come home and tell her mother, "Why can't you also colour your hands like Fatima Kaku?" (Kaku is equivalent to 'aunt' in the local language.)

'This comment irritated Kashibai. She said, "Fatima can afford to colour her hands because her husband works and also helps in the kitchen. She sits on the bed and listens to the radio. If I do that, will your father come and work in the kitchen?" Fatima Bi would overhear their conversation but still she continued her friendship with little Usha.

'When Fatima became pregnant, she became even lazier. She eventually reached full term and a distant relative came to help her with her delivery. A few days later, there was a festival in the village and Datturam and his family went to attend it. When they came back, Fatima Bi was not there. She was already in the hospital in critical condition and had delivered a son. The house was in complete silence. But the silence was deafening to Kashibai's ears. She started crying. She was very sad because Fatima Bi was in the hospital in such a serious condition. The next day, they learnt that Fatima Bi was no more.

'Husain Saab was left with his newborn son. The midwife stayed for a month and left. It was an uphill task for Husain Saab to look after a small baby. Neither Husain Saab nor Fatima Bi had any relatives who could take care of the little one. Most of them were coolies and a newborn child would only be a burden to the relatives. Datturam was very sympathetic and allowed Husain Saab to work less in the field but taking care of a small baby alone is very difficult.

'One night, the child started crying non-stop and Kashibai could not take it. She felt that enough was enough. After all, it was a little baby. A woman is so different from a man when it comes to rearing a child. Her motherly instinct made her go next door and tap on Husain Saab's door without even waiting for her husband. When Husain Saab opened the door, she told him, "Husain Saab, give me the baby. I am a mother. I know how to handle him." She picked up the baby boy, held him in her pallu and brought him to her house, holding him tightly to her chest. The baby boy stopped crying immediately. For the first time since the baby was born, Husain Saab slept through the night comfortably.

'The next day, Kashibai told Husain Saab, "I will look after this child until you get married again. Don't worry." She forgot her enmity with Fatima Bi and even felt ashamed. She thought that she should have been nicer to Fatima Bi. Now, Kashibai did not even bother about where the droppings of the goats fell or where the hens laid their eggs. For her, looking after the baby was more important. The baby was named Rahman and, to everyone's surprise, Husain Saab did not remarry. Rahman grew up in Kashibai's house and started calling her Avva and Usha became his akka. Rahman continued to sleep in his father's house but as soon as the sun rose, he ran to Kashibai's house to get ready. While Usha bathed on her own, Kashibai bathed little Rahman. She gave them breakfast, packed their lunches and walked them to school. Though Usha was two years older than Rahman, Kashibai made sure that they studied in the same class. Kashibai worked in the field in the afternoon and brought the children back in the evenings. Husain Saab cooked Rahman's dinner and Rahman would go back and sleep with his father at night. This continued for ten years.

'When Rahman was ten and Usha was twelve years old, Husain Saab fell ill and all his savings were spent on his treatment. Meanwhile, Kashibai purchased two she-buffaloes and started a milk business. She started earning more money than her husband.

'That same year, Husain Saab died of tuberculosis. Rahman was left all alone. There were hardly any people at Husain Saab's burial. A distant uncle came and told the mullah that he would take care of Rahman. But when the time came to take Rahman away, the uncle did not turn up at all. Without a second thought, Datturam and Kashibai took him in. Rahman was happy to stay in Kashibai's house.

'Kashibai was very conscious about Rahman's religion. Every Friday, she sent him for namaz and on holidays she sent him for Koran class at the local mosque. She told him to participate in all Muslim festivals even though there were very few Muslims in the village. Rahman also took part in the Hindu festivals celebrated in his house. Datturam and Kashibai bought two cycles for both the kids. Rahman and Usha cycled to high school and later they also rode their cycles to the same college.

'Eventually, they graduated and that day Kashibai told Rahman, "Unfortunately, we don't have a picture of your parents. So, turn towards Mecca and pray to Allah. Pray to Fatima Bi and Husain Saab. They will bless you. You are now grown up and independent. Usha is getting married next month. My responsibility to both Usha and you is now over."

'Kashibai's affection and devotion overwhelmed Rahman, who could not remember his own mother's face. He prayed to Allah and his parents and then touched Kashibai's feet. He said, "Avva, you are my ammi. You are my Mecca."

'Rahman got a job in a BPO in Bangalore and left home. He worked for different firms for a few years, saw growth in his career and started earning a good salary. He met Salma at a friend's wedding and fell in love with her.

'After getting Kashibai and Datturam's approval, he got married to Salma.'

When he finished his story, Rahman was very emotional and in tears.

I was amazed at Kashibai. She was uneducated but very advanced in human values. I was surprised and humbled by the largeness of her heart. Kashibai had raised the boy with his own religion and still loved him like her son.

By this time, lunch was ready and Usha invited me to eat. While having the delicious lunch, I asked Usha, 'What made you decide to visit here?'

'I have holidays at school and I took an extended vacation so I could come for Panchami.'

Panchami is a festival celebrated mostly by girls, particularly married women, who come to their brother's house. It is similar to the Rakhi festival in the north, where a brother acknowledges his sister's love. I recalled our history and remembered that Queen Karunavati had sent a rakhi to Emperor Humayun, seeking his protection.

Now, I looked at the wall in the dining room and for the first time I noticed two pictures in Rahman's house, one of Mecca and the other of Krishna, both hanging side by side.

13

Cattle Class

Last year, I was at the Heathrow Airport in London, about to board a flight. Usually, I wear a sari even when I am abroad, but I prefer wearing a salwar-kameez while travelling. So there I was—a senior citizen dressed in typical Indian apparel at the terminal gate.

Since the boarding hadn't started, I sat down and began to observe my surroundings. The flight was bound for Bengaluru and so I could hear people around me chatting in Kannada. I saw many old married couples of my age—they were most likely coming back from the US or UK after helping their children either through childbirth or a new home. I saw some British business executives talking to each other about India's progress. Some teenagers were busy with the gadgets in their hands while the younger children were crying or running about the gate.

After a few minutes, the boarding announcement was made and I joined the queue. The woman in front of me was a well-groomed lady in an Indo-Western silk outfit, a Gucci handbag and high heels. Every single strand of her hair was in place and a friend stood next to her in an expensive silk sari, pearl necklace, matching earrings and delicate diamond bangles.

I looked at the vending machine nearby and wondered if I should leave the queue to get some water.

Suddenly, the woman in front of me turned sideways and looked at me with what seemed like pity in her eyes. Extending her hand, she asked, 'May I see your boarding pass, please?'

I was about to hand over my pass to her, but since she didn't seem like an airline employee, I asked, 'Why?'

'Well, this line is meant for business-class travellers only,' she said confidently and pointed her finger towards the economy-class queue. 'You should go and stand there,' she said.

I was about to tell her that I had a business-class ticket but, on second thoughts, held back. I wanted to know why she had thought that I wasn't worthy of being in the business class. So I repeated, 'Why should I stand there?'

She sighed. 'Let me explain. There is a big difference in the price of an economy- and a business-class ticket. The latter costs almost two and a half times more than . . .'

'I think it is three times more,' her friend interrupted.

'Exactly,' said the woman. 'So there are certain privileges that are associated with a business-class ticket.'

'Really?' I decided to be mischievous and pretended not to know. 'What kind of privileges are you talking about?'

She seemed annoyed. 'We are allowed to bring two bags but you can only take one. We can board the flight from another, less-crowded queue. We are given better meals and seats. We can extend the seats and lie down flat on them. We always have television screens and there are four washrooms for a small number of passengers.'

Her friend added, 'A priority check-in facility is available for our bags, which means they will come first upon arrival and we get more frequent-flyer miles for the same flight.'

'Now that you know the difference, you can go to the economy line,' insisted the woman.

'But I don't want to go there.' I was firm.

The lady turned to her friend. 'It is hard to argue with these cattle-class people. Let the staff come and instruct her where to go. She isn't going to listen to us.'

I didn't get angry. The word 'cattle class' was like a blast from the past and reminded me of another incident.

One day, I had gone to an upscale dinner party in my home city of Bengaluru. Plenty of local celebrities and socialites were in attendance. I was speaking to some guests in Kannada, when a man came to me and said very slowly and clearly in English, 'May I introduce myself ? I am . . .'

It was obvious that he thought that I might have a problem understanding the language.

I smiled. 'You can speak to me in English.'

'Oh,' he said, slightly flabbergasted. 'I'm sorry. I thought you weren't comfortable with English because I heard you speaking in Kannada.'

'There's nothing shameful in knowing one's native language. It is, in fact, my right and my privilege. I only speak in English when somebody can't understand Kannada.'

The line in front of me at the airport began moving forward and I came out of my reverie. The two women ahead were whispering among themselves. 'Now she will be sent to the other line. It is so long now! We tried to tell her but she refused to listen to us.'

When it was my turn to show my boarding pass to the attendant, I saw them stop and wait a short distance away, waiting to see what would happen. The attendant took my boarding pass and said brightly, 'Welcome back! We met last week, didn't we?'

'Yes,' I replied.

She smiled and moved on to the next traveller.

I walked a few steps ahead of the women intending to let this go, but then I changed my mind and came back. 'Please tell me—what made you think that I couldn't afford a business-class ticket? Even if I didn't have one, was it really your prerogative to tell me where I should stand? Did I ask you for help?'

The women stared at me in silence.

'You refer to the term "cattle class". Class does not mean possession of a huge amount of money,' I continued, unable to stop myself from giving them a piece of my mind. 'There are plenty of wrong ways to earn money in this world. You may be rich enough to buy comfort and luxuries, but the same money doesn't define class or give you the ability to purchase it. Mother Teresa was a classy woman. So is Manjul Bhargava, a great mathematician of Indian origin. The concept that you automatically gain class by acquiring money is outdated.'

I left without waiting for a reply.

Approximately eight hours later, I reached my destination. It was a weekday and I rushed to office as soon as I could only to learn that my day was going to be spent in multiple meetings. A few hours later, I requested my program director to handle the last meeting of the day by herself as I was already starting to feel tired and jet-lagged.

'I am really sorry, but your presence is essential for that discussion,' she replied. 'Our meeting is with the organization's CEO and she is keen to meet you in person. She has been following up with me for a few months now and though I have communicated our decision, she feels that a discussion with you will change the outcome. I have already informed her that the decision will not be reversed irrespective of whom she meets, but she refuses to take me at my word. I urge you to meet her and close this chapter.'

I wasn't new to this situation and reluctantly agreed.

Time went by quickly and soon, I had to go in for the last meeting of the day. Just then, I received an emergency call.

'Go ahead with the meeting,' I said to the program director. 'I will join you later.'

When I entered the conference room after fifteen minutes, I saw the same women from the airport in the middle of a presentation. To my surprise, they were simply dressed—one was wearing a simple khadi sari while the other wore an unglamorous salwar-kameez. The clothes were a reminder of the stereotype that is still rampant today. Just like one is expected to wear the finest of silks for a wedding, social workers must present themselves in a plain and uninteresting manner. When they saw me, there was an awkward pause that lasted for only a few seconds before one of them acknowledged my presence and continued the presentation as if nothing had happened.

'My coffee estate is in this village. All the estate workers' children go to a government school nearby. Many are sharp and intelligent but the school has no facilities. The building doesn't even have a roof or clean drinking water. There are no benches, toilets or library. You can see children in the school . . .'

'But no teachers,' I completed the sentence.

She nodded and smiled. 'We request the foundation to be generous and provide the school with proper facilities, including an auditorium, so that the poor kids can enjoy the essentials of a big school.'

My program director opened her mouth to say something, but I signalled her to stop.

'How many children are there in the school?' I asked.

'Around 250.'

'How many of them are the children of the estate workers?'

'All of them. My father got the school sanctioned when he was the MLA,' she said proudly.

'Our foundation helps those who don't have any godfathers or godmothers. Think of the homeless man on the road or the daily-wage worker. Most of them have no one they can run to in times of crisis. We help the children of such people. The estate workers help your business prosper and in return, you can afford to help them. In fact, it is your duty to do so. Helping them also helps you in the long run, but it is the foundation's internal policy to work for the disadvantaged in projects where all the benefits go directly and solely to the underprivileged alone. Maybe this concept is beyond the understanding of the cattle class.'

Both the women looked at each other, unsure of how to respond.

I looked at my program director and said, 'Hey, I want to tell you a story.'

I could see from her face that she was feeling awkward. A story in the middle of a serious meeting?

I began, 'George Bernard Shaw was a great thinker of his times. One day, a dinner was arranged at a British club in his honour. The rules of the club mandated that the men wear a suit and a tie. It was probably the definition of class in those days.

'Bernard Shaw, being who he was, walked into the club in his usual casual attire. The doorman looked at him and said very politely, "Sorry, sir, I cannot allow you to enter the premises."

'"Why not?"

'"You aren't following the dress code of the club, sir."

'"Well, today's dinner is in my honour, so it is my words that matter, not what I wear," replied Bernard, perfectly reasonable in his explanation.

'"Sir, whatever it may be, I can't allow you inside in these clothes."

'Shaw tried to convince the doorman but he wouldn't budge from his stance. So he walked all the way back to his house, changed into appropriate clothes and entered the club.

'A short while later, the room was full, with people sitting in anticipation of his speech. He stood up to address the audience, but first removed his coat and tie and placed it on a chair. "I am not going to talk today," he announced.

'There were surprised murmurs in the audience. Those who knew him personally asked him about the reason for his out-of-character behaviour.

'Shaw narrated the incident that happened a while ago and said, "When I wore a coat and tie, I was allowed to come inside. My mind is in no way affected by the clothes I wear.

'"This means that to all of you who patronize the club, the clothes are more important than my brain. So let the coat and the tie take my place instead."

'Saying thus, he walked out of the room.'

I stood up. 'The meeting is over,' I said. We exchanged cursory goodbyes and I walked back to my room.

My program director followed me. 'Your decision regarding the school was right. But what was that other story all about? And why now? What is this cattle-class business? I didn't understand a thing!'

I smiled at her obvious confusion. 'Only the cattle-class folks will understand what happened back there. You don't worry about it.'

14

The Old Man and His God

The Old Man and His God

A few years back, I was travelling in Thanjavur district of Tamil Nadu. It was getting dark, and due to a depression over the Bay of Bengal, it was raining heavily. The roads were overflowing with water and my driver stopped the car near a village. 'There is no way we can proceed further in this rain,' said the driver. 'Why don't you look for shelter somewhere nearby rather than sit in the car?'

Stranded in an unknown place among unknown people, I was a bit worried. Nevertheless, I retrieved my umbrella and marched out into the pelting rain. I started walking towards the tiny village, whose name I cannot recall now. There was no electricity and it was a trial walking in the darkness and the rain. In the distance I could just make out the shape of a small temple. I decided it would be an ideal place to take shelter, so I made my way to it. Halfway there, the rain started coming down even more fiercely and the strong wind blew my umbrella away, leaving me completely drenched. I reached the temple soaking wet. As soon as I entered, I heard an elderly person's voice calling out to me. Though

I cannot speak Tamil, I could make out the concern in the voice. In the course of my travels, I have come to realize that voices from the heart can be understood irrespective of the language they speak.

I peered into the darkness of the temple and saw an old man of about eighty. Standing next to him was an equally old lady in a traditional nine-yard cotton sari. She said something to him and then approached me with a worn but clean towel in her hand. As I wiped my face and head I noticed that the man was blind. It was obvious from their surroundings that they were very poor. The Shiva temple, where I now stood, was simple with the minimum of ostentation in its decorations. The Shivalinga was bare except for a bilwa leaf on top. The only light came from a single oil lamp. In that flickering light, a sense of calm overcame me and I felt myself closer to God than ever before.

In halting Tamil, I asked the man to perform the evening *mangalarati*, which he did with love and dedication. When he finished, I gave him a hundred-rupee note as the *dakshina*.

He touched the note and pulled away his hand, looking uncomfortable. Politely he said, 'Amma, I can make out that the note is not for ten rupees, the most we usually receive. Whoever you may be, in a temple, your devotion is important, not your money. Even our ancestors have said that a devotee should give as much as he or she can afford to. To me you are a devotee of Shiva, like everyone else who comes here. Please take back this money.'

I was taken aback. I did not know how to react. I looked at the man's wife expecting her to argue with him and urge him to take the money, but she just stood quietly. Often, in many households, a wife encourages the man's greediness. Here, it was the opposite. She was endorsing her husband's views. So I sat down with them, and with the wind and rain whipping up a frenzy outside, we talked about our lives. I asked them about themselves, their life in the village temple and whether they had anyone to look after them.

Finally I said, 'Both of you are old. You don't have any children to look after your everyday needs. In old age one requires more medicines than groceries. This village is far from any of the towns in the district. Can I suggest something to you?'

At that time, we had started an old-age pension scheme and I thought, looking at their worn-out but clean clothes, they would be the ideal candidates for it.

This time the wife spoke up, 'Please do tell, child.'

'I will send you some money. Keep it in a nationalized bank or post office. The interest on that can be used for your monthly needs. If there is a medical emergency you can use the capital.'

The old man smiled on hearing my words and his face lit up brighter than the lamp.

'You sound much younger than us. You are still foolish. Why do I need money in this great old age? Lord Shiva is also known as Vaidyanathan. He is the Mahavaidya, or great doctor. This village we live in has many kind people. I perform the puja and they give me rice in return. If either of us is unwell, the local doctor gives us medicines. Our wants are very few. Why would I accept money from an unknown person? If I keep this money in the bank, like you are telling me to, someone will come to know and may harass us. Why should I take on these worries? You are a kind person to offer help to two unknown old people. But we are content; let us live as we always have. We don't need anything more.'

Just then the electricity came back and a bright light lit up the temple. For the first time I saw the couple properly. I could clearly see the peace and happiness on their faces. They were the first people I met who refused help in spite of their obvious need. I did not agree with everything he had just said, but it was clear to me that his contentment had brought him peace. Such an attitude may not let you progress fast, but after a certain period in life it is required. Perhaps this world with its many stresses and strains has much to learn from an old couple in a forgettable corner of India.

15

A Lesson in Life from a Beggar

15

A Lesson in Life from a Beggar

Meena is a good friend of mine. She is an LIC officer earning a good salary. But there was always something strange about her. She was forever unhappy. Whenever I met her, I would start to feel depressed. It was as though her gloom and cynicism had a way of spreading to others. She never had anything positive to say on any subject or about any person.

For instance, I might say to her, 'Meena, did you know Rakesh has come first in his school?'

Meena's immediate response would be to belittle the achievement. 'Naturally, his father is a schoolteacher,' she would say.

If I said, 'Meena, Shwetha is a very beautiful girl, isn't she?' Meena would be pessimistic. 'When a pony is young, he looks handsome. It is age that matters. Wait for some time. Shwetha will be uglier than anyone you know.'

'Meena, it's a beautiful day. Let's go for a walk.'

'No, the sun is too hot and I get tired if I walk too much. Besides, who says walking is good for health? There's no proof.'

That was Meena. She stayed alone in an apartment as her parents lived in Delhi. She was an only child and had the habit of complaining about anything and everything. Naturally, she wasn't very pleasant company and nobody wanted to visit her. Then one day, Meena was transferred to Bombay and soon we all forgot about her.

Many years later, I found myself caught in the rain at Bombay's Flora Fountain. It was pouring and I didn't have an umbrella. I was standing near Akbarallys, a popular department store, waiting for the rain to subside. Suddenly, I spotted Meena. My first reaction was to run, even in that pouring rain. I was anxious to avoid being seen by her, having to listen to her never-ending complaints. However, I couldn't escape. She had already seen me and caught hold of my hand warmly. What's more, she was very cheerful.

'Hey! I am really excited. It's nice to meet old friends. What are you doing here?'

I explained that I was in Bombay on official work.

'Then stay with me tonight,' she said. 'Let's chat. Do you know that old wine, old friends and memories are precious and rare?'

I couldn't believe it. Was this really Meena? I pinched myself hard to be sure it wasn't a dream. But Meena was really standing there, right in front of me, squeezing my hand, smiling, and yes, she did look happy. In the three years she had been in Bangalore, I had never once seen her smiling like that. A few strands of grey in her hair reminded me that years had passed. There were a few wrinkles on her face, but the truth was that she looked more attractive than ever before.

Finally, I managed to say, 'No, Meena, I can't stay with you tonight. I have to attend a dinner. Give me your card and I'll keep in touch with you. I promise.'

For a moment, Meena looked disappointed. 'Let's go and have tea at least,' she insisted.

'But Meena, it's pouring.'

'So what? We'll buy an umbrella and then go to the Grand Hotel,' she said.

'We won't get a taxi in this rain,' I grumbled.

'So what? We'll walk.'

I was very surprised. This wasn't the same Meena I had known. Today, she seemed ready to make any number of adjustments.

We reached the Grand Hotel drenched. By then the only thought in my mind was to find out who or what had brought about such a change in the pessimistic Meena I had known. I was quite curious.

'Tell me, Meena, is there a Prince Charming who has managed to change you so?'

Meena was surprised by my question. 'No, there isn't anyone like that,' she said.

'Then what's the secret of your energy?' I asked, like Tendulkar does in the ad.

She smiled. 'A beggar changed my life.'

I was absolutely dumbfounded and she could see it.

'Yes, a beggar,' she repeated, as if to reassure me. 'He was old and used to stay in front of my house with his five-year-old granddaughter. As you know, I was a chronic pessimist. I used to give my leftovers to this beggar every day. I never spoke to him. Nor did he speak to me. One monsoon day, I looked out of my bedroom window and started cursing the rain. I don't know why I did that because I wasn't even getting wet. That day I couldn't give the beggar and his granddaughter their daily quota of leftovers. They went hungry, I am sure.

'However, what I saw from my window surprised me. The beggar and the young girl were playing on the road because there was no traffic. They were laughing, clapping and screaming joyously, as if they were in paradise. Hunger and rain did not matter. They were totally drenched and totally happy. I envied their zest for life.

'That scene forced me to look at my own life. I realized I had so many comforts, none of which they had. But they had the most important of all assets, one which I lacked. They knew how to be happy with life as it was. I felt ashamed of myself. I even started to make a list of what I had and what I did not have. I found I had more to be grateful for than most people could imagine. That day, I decided to change my attitude towards life, using the beggar as my role model.'

After a long pause, I asked Meena how long it had taken her to change.

'Once this realization dawned,' she said, 'it took me almost two years to put the change into effect. Now nothing matters. I am always happy. I find happiness in every small thing, in every situation and in every person.'

'Did you give any gurudakshina to your guru?' I asked.

'No. Unfortunately, by the time I understood things, he was dead. But I sponsored his granddaughter to a boarding school as a mark of respect to him.'

16

May You Be the
Mother of a Hundred Children

I was on my way to the railway station. I had the nine o'clock Bangalore–Hubli Kittur Express to catch. Halfway to the station our car stopped. There was a huge traffic jam. There was no way we could either move forward or reverse the car. I sat and watched helplessly as a few two-wheelers scraped past the car through a narrow gap. Finally I asked my driver what the matter was. Traffic jams are not uncommon but this was something unusual. He got out of the car and said the road ahead was blocked by some people holding a communal harmony meet. I now realized it was perhaps impossible to get to the station. The papers had reported about the meeting and had warned that the roads would be blocked for some time. The car was moved into a bylane and seeing there was no way I could try and make my way back home, I decided to join the crowd and listen to the speeches.

From a distance, I could see the dais. There were various religious heads sitting on a row of chairs on the stage. An elderly gentleman stood next to me and commented loudly,

'All this is just a drama. In India, everything is decided on the basis of caste and community. Even our elections are dictated by them. Whoever comes to power thinks only of the betterment of his community. It is easy to give speeches but in practical life they forget everything.'

Just then a middle-aged lady started speaking into the mike. From the way she was speaking, so confidently, it was apparent that she was used to giving speeches and had the gift of the gab. Her analogies were quite convincing. 'When you eat a meal, do you eat only chapattis or rice? No, you also need a vegetable, a dal and some curd. The tastes of the dishes vary, but only when they are put together do you get a wholesome meal. Similarly different communities need to live together in harmony and build a strong country . . .' etc.

'It is a nice speech but who follows all this in real life?' the gentleman next to me commented.

'Why do you say that?' I had to ask finally.

He looked at me, surprised at my unexpected question, then answered, 'Because my family has suffered a lot. My son did not get a job as he was not from the right community, my daughter was transferred as her boss wanted to replace her with someone from his own community. It is everywhere. Wherever you go, the first thing people want to know is which caste or religion you belong to.'

The woman was still talking on the podium. 'What is her name?' I asked.

'She is Ambabhavani, a gifted speaker from Tamil Nadu.'

Her name rang a bell somewhere in my mind and suddenly I was transported away from the jostling crowds and the loud speeches. I was in a time long past, with my paternal grandmother, Amba Bai.

Amba Bai was affectionately called Ambakka or Ambakka Aai by everyone in the village. She spent her whole life in one little village, Savalagi, near Bijapur in north Karnataka. Like most other women of her generation she had never stepped into a school. She was married early and spent her life fulfilling the responsibilities of looking after a large family. She was widowed early and I always remember seeing her with a shaven head, wearing a red sari, the pallu covering her head always, as was the tradition in the then orthodox Brahmin society. She lived till she was eighty-nine and in her whole life she knew only the worlds of her ten children, forty grandchildren, her village and the fields.

Since we were farmers she owned large mud-houses with cows, horses and buffaloes. There was a large granary and big trees that cooled the house during the hot summers. There were rows of cacti planted just outside the house. They kept out the mosquitoes, we were told. Ajji (that's what we called Amba Bai) looked after the fields and the farmers with a passion. In fact, I don't recall her ever spending too much time in the kitchen making pickles or sweets like other grandmothers. She would be up early and after her bath spend some time doing her daily puja. She would make some jowar chapattis and a vegetable, and then head out to the fields. She would spend time there talking to the farmers about the seeds they had got, the state of the well or the health of their cattle. Her other passion in life was to help the women of the village deliver their babies.

Though I did not realize this till I was a teenager, Ajji was most unlike an orthodox Brahmin widow. She was very much for women's education, family planning and had much to say about the way society treated widows.

Those days there were few facilities available to the villages. There were a handful of medical colleges and not every taluk had a government hospital. In this scenario women who had borne children were the only help to others during childbirth. My grandmother was one of them. She was very proud of the fact that she had delivered ten perfectly healthy children, all of whom survived. And in turn, she would help others during their delivery, irrespective of caste or community. She always had a word of advice or a handy tip for the pregnant women of the village.

I would often hear such nuggets of wisdom from her.

'Savitri, be careful. Don't lift heavy articles. Eat well and drink more milk.'

'Peerambi, you have had two miscarriages. Be careful this time. Eat lots of vegetables and fruits. You should be careful but don't sit idle. Pregnancy is not a disease. You should be active. Do some light work. Send your husband Hussain to my house. I will give some sambar powder. My daughter-in-law prepares it very well.'

Of course, not everyone appreciated her advising them. One such person was Shakuntala Desai, who had stayed in the city for some time and had gone to school. 'What does Ambakka know about these things?' she would comment loudly. 'Has she ever gone to school or read a medical book? She is not a doctor.'

But Ajji would be least bothered by these comments. She would only laugh and say, 'Let that Shakuntala get pregnant. I will deliver the baby. My four decades of experience is better than any book!'

My father's job took us to various towns to live in, but we always came to Ajji's village during the holidays. They were joyous days and we would enjoy ourselves thoroughly.

Once, when we were at the village, there was a wedding in the neighbouring village. Ajji always refused to attend these social gatherings. That time, I too decided to stay back with her and one night there was only Ajji, me and our helper Dyamappa in that large house.

It was an unusually cold, moonless winter night in December. It was pitch dark outside. Ajji and I were sleeping together. Dyamappa had spread his bed on the front veranda and was fast asleep. For the first time that night, I saw Ajji remove her pallu from her head and the wisps of grey hair on her head. She touched them and said, 'Society has such cruel customs. Would you believe that I once had thick long plaits hanging down my back? How I loved my hair and what a source of envy it was for the other girls! But the day your grandfather died, no one even asked my permission before chopping off that beautiful hair. I cried as much for my hair as for my husband. No one understood my grief. Tell me, if a wife dies, does the widower keep his head shaved for the rest of his life? No, within no time he is ready to be a groom again and bring home another bride!'

At that age, I could not understand her pain, but now, when I recall her words, I realize how helpless she must have felt.

After some time she changed her topic. 'Our Peerambi is due any time. I think it will be tonight. It is a moonless night after all. Peerambi is good and pious, but she is so shy, I am sure she will not say anything to anyone till the pain becomes unbearable. I have been praying for her safe delivery to our family deity Kallolli Venkatesha and also at the Peer Saab Darga in Bijapur. Everyone wants sons, but I do hope there is a girl this time. Daughters care for parents wherever they are. Any woman can do a man's job but a man cannot do a woman's job. After your Ajja's death, am I not looking after the entire farming? Akkavva, always remember women have more patience and common sense. If only men realized that . . .'

Ajji had so many grandchildren she found it hard to remember all their names. So she would call all her granddaughters 'Akkavva' and grandsons 'Bala'.

As Ajji rambled on into the night, there was a knock on the door. Instinctively Ajji said, 'That must be Hussain.' And indeed it was. Ajji covered her head again and forgetting her griefs about widowhood, she asked quickly, 'Is Peerambi in labour?'

'Yes, she has had the pains since this evening.'

'And you are telling me now? You don't understand how precious time is when a woman is in labour. Let us go now. Don't waste any more time.'

She started giving instructions to Hussain and Dyamappa simultaneously.

'Hussain, cut the cactus, take a few sprigs of neem. Dyamappa, you light two big lanterns . . .

'Akkavva, you stay at home. Dyamappa will be with you. I have to hurry now.'

She was gathering some things from her room and putting them into her wooden carry-box. By that time, the huge Dyamappa, with his large white turban on his head and massive moustaches appeared at the door bearing two lanterns. In the pitch darkness he made a terrifying picture and immediately brought to my mind the Ravana in the Ramayana play I had seen recently. There was no way I was going to stay alone in the house with him! I insisted I wanted to go with Ajji.

Ajji was impatient. 'Akkavva, don't be adamant. After all, you are a teenage girl now. You should not see these things. I will leave you at your friend Girija's house.' But like any other teenager, I was adamant and would not budge from my decision.

Finally Ajji gave up. She went to the puja room, said a quick prayer and locked the house behind her. The four of us set off in pitch darkness to Hussain's house. Hussain lead the way with a lantern, Ajji, with me clutching on to her hand, followed, and Dyamappa brought up the rear, carrying the other lantern.

We made our way across the village. Ajji walked with ease while I stumbled beside her. It was cold and I did not know the way. All the time Ajji kept up a constant stream of instructions for Hussain and Dyamappa.

'Hussain, when we reach, fill the large drums with water. Dyamappa will help you. Boil some water. Burn some coal. Put all the chickens and lambs in the shed. See that they don't come wandering around . . .'

Finally we reached Hussain's house. Peerambi's cries of pain could be heard coming from inside.

Hussain and Peerambi lived alone. They were poor farm labourers who worked on daily wages. Their neighbour Mehboob Bi was there, attending to Peerambi.

Seeing Ajji, she looked relieved. 'Now there is nothing to worry. Ambakka Aai has come.'

Ajji washed her feet and hands and went inside the room with her paraphernalia, slamming the doors and windows shut behind her. Outside on the wooden bench, Hussain and Dyamappa sat awaiting further instructions from Ajji. I was curious to find out what would happen next.

Inside, I could hear Ajji speaking affectionately to Peerambi. 'Don't worry. Delivery is not an impossible thing. I have given birth to ten children. Just cooperate and I will help you. Pray to God to give you strength. Don't lose courage . . .' In between, she opened the window partly and told Hussain, 'I want some turmeric powder. I can't search in your house. Get it from Mehboob Bi's house. Dyamappa, give me one more big bowl of boiling water. Hussain, take a new cane tray, clean it with turmeric water and pass it inside. Dyamappa, I want some more burning coal . . .'

The pious, gentle Ajji was a dictator now!

The next few hours were punctuated by Peerambi's anguished cries and Ajji's patient, consoling words, while Hussain sat outside tense and Dyamappa nonchalantly smoked a bidi. The night got dark and then it started getting lighter and lighter. The cock, locked in its coop, crowed and with the rising sun we heard the sounds of a baby's crying.

Ajji opened one windowpane and announced, 'Hussain, you are blessed with a son. He looks just like your father, Mohammed Saab. Peerambi had a tough time but God is kind. Mother and child are both safe and healthy.'

S-l-a-a-m . . . the door shut again. But this time outside we grinned at each other in joy. Hussain knelt down and said a prayer of thanks. Then he jumped up and knocked on the door, wanting to see the baby. It remained shut. Ajji was not entertaining any visitors till she was done.

'Your clothes are dirty,' she shouted from inside. 'First have a bath, wear clean clothes and then come in, otherwise you will infect the baby and mother.'

Hussain rushed to the bathroom, which was just a thatched partition and poured buckets of clean water from the well on to himself.

Even after he rushed in, I could hear only Ajji's voice. 'Peerambi, my work is over. I have to rush home. Today is my husband's death ceremony. There are many rituals to be completed. The priests will arrive any time and I have to help them. I will leave now and if you want anything, send word through Hussain.

'Peerambi, to a woman, delivering a baby is like going to the deathbed and waking up again. Be careful. Mehboob Bi, please keep Peerambi's room clean. Don't put any new clothes on the baby. They will hurt him. Wrap him in an old clean dhoti. Don't kiss the baby on his lips. Don't show the baby to everybody. Don't keep touching him. Boil the drinking water and immerse an iron ladle in that. Peerambi should drink only that water. I will send a pot of home-made ghee and soft rice and rasam for Peerambi to eat . . . Now I have to go. Bheemappa is supposed to come and clean the garden today. If I am late, he will run away . . .'

By now she had allowed the window to be opened. I peeped in and saw the tired but joyous face of Peerambi and a tiny, chubby version of Mohammed Saab, Hussain's father, asleep on the cane tray. The neem leaves were hanging, the cactus was kept in a corner and the fragrance of the *lobana* had filled the entire room. Ajji also looked tired and there was sweat on her forehead. But she was cleaning her accessories vigorously in the hot water and wiping them before placing them carefully back in her wooden box.

Just as we were about to leave, Hussain bent down and touched Ajji's feet. In a choked voice he said, 'Ambakka Aai, I do not know how to thank you. We are poor and cannot give you anything. But I can thank you sincerely from the bottom of my heart. You are a mother of a hundred children. You have blessed my son by bringing him into this world. He will never stray from the correct path.'

Ajji touched him on his shoulder and pulled him up. There were tears in her eyes too. She wiped them and said, 'Hussain, God only wants us to help each other in difficult times. Peerambi is after all like another Akkavva to me.'

By now the sun was up and I followed Ajji back home without stumbling. Dyamappa was strolling lazily far behind us. One doubt was worrying me and I had to clear it. 'Ajji, you have given birth only to ten children. Why did Hussain say you are a mother of hundred?'

Ajji smiled and adjusting the pallu that was slipping off her head because of her brisk walk, she said, 'Yes. I have given birth only to ten children but these hands have brought out a hundred children in our village. Akkavva, I will pray that you become the mother of a hundred children, irrespective of the number you yourself give birth to.'

17

Food for Thought

Rekha is a very dear friend and our families have known each other for generations. Since I hadn't seen her for a long time, I decided to visit her. I picked up the phone and dialled her number.

Her father, Rao, who is like a father to me, picked up the phone. 'Hello?'

We exchanged greetings and I said, 'Uncle, I am coming to your house for lunch tomorrow.'

Her father, a botanist, was very happy. 'Please do. Tomorrow is a Sunday and we can relax a little bit. Don't run off quickly!' he replied.

In a city such as Bengaluru, going from Jayanagar to Malleswaram on a weekday usually takes a minimum of two hours. Travelling on a Sunday is much easier because it takes only half the time. When I reached her home the next day, I could smell that lunch was almost ready, and yet the aromas wafting in from the kitchen indicated to me that the day's menu would somehow be different. None of the typical

Karnataka dishes were laid out on the table, and the cuisine was, in fact, quite bland for my taste.

'I may wear a simple sari but I am a foodie, Rekha! Is the lunch specially arranged so that I don't come again?' I joked, as one can with an old friend who will not misunderstand and take offence.

Rekha's father laughed heartily. 'Well.' He sighed. 'Today is my mother's *shraddha* or death anniversary. On this day, we always prepare a meal from indigenous vegetables.'

'What do you mean by indigenous?' I was perplexed. 'Aren't all the vegetables available in our country indigenous, except perhaps ones like cauliflower, cabbage and potato?'

'Oh my God! You have just brought up the wrong topic on the wrong day with the wrong person!' exclaimed Rekha in mock dismay. 'After lunch, I think I should just leave you with my father and join you both later in the evening. This will take at least four hours of your time.'

I knew that Rekha's father was a botanist, but it was then that I realized that he was passionate about this subject. Though I had known him for a really long time, I had never seen this facet of his personality before. Probably, he had been too busy during his working years while we had been too busy playing and fooling around.

'Is this really true, Uncle?' I asked.

He nodded.

Since I come from a farmer's family on my paternal side, I have always had a fascination for vegetables. I knew vaguely about the things we could grow, the seasons to grow them in and the ones that we could not grow, including the reasons why. However, whenever I broached the subject with friends interested in agriculture and farming, I never really received a proper answer. Finally, here was a man more than willing to share his knowledge with me! I couldn't resist.

'You know, Rekha,' I said, 'it is difficult to get knowledgeable people to spend time explaining their subject matter to others. Today, Google is like my grandmother. I log on to the website any time I require an explanation of something I don't understand or want to learn about.'

'Right now, you are logging on to an encyclopedia,' Rekha smiled and glanced at her father affectionately.

The conversation drifted to other subjects as we ate lunch. The meal constituted of rice, sambar without chillies, dal with black pepper and not chillies, gorikayi (cluster beans), methi saag, cucumber raita and rice payasam. It was accompanied by udin vada with black pepper. There was pickle and some plain yogurt on the side too. After we had eaten this lunch, well-suited for someone recovering in a hospital, Rekha's father said, 'Come, let's go to the garden.'

Rekha's family owned an old house on the corner of a street. Her grandfather had been in the British railways and was lucky enough to buy the corner plot at a low price and had built a small home with a large garden there. In a city like Bengaluru, filled with apartments and small spaces, the garden was something of a privilege and a luxury.

Uncle and I walked to the garden while Rekha took a nap. He settled himself on a bench, while I looked around. It was a miniature forest with a large kitchen garden of carrots, okra, fenugreek and spinach—each segregated neatly into sections. A few sugar-cane stalks shone brightly in front of us while a dwarf papaya tree heavy with fruit stood in a corner. On the other end was a line of maize as well as flowering trees such as the parijata (the Indian coral tree), and roses of varying colours.

'Uncle and Aunty must be spending a lot of time here making this place beautiful,' I thought. 'All the trees and plants seem healthy—almost as if they are happy to be here!'

'Do you think that all the vegetables we have around us are from India? Or are they from other countries?' he asked out of the blue.

I felt as if I was back in school in front of my teacher. But I wasn't scared. Even if I gave him a wrong answer, it wasn't going to affect my progress report. 'Of course, Uncle! India has the largest population of vegetarians. So, in time, we have learnt to make different kinds of vegetarian dishes. Even people who eat meat avoid it during traditional events such as festivals, weddings, death anniversaries and the month of Shravana.'

'I agree with your assessment of everything, except that most vegetables are grown in India. The truth is that the majority of our vegetables are not ours at all. They have come from different countries.'

I stared at him in disbelief.

He pointed to a tomato plant—a creeper with multiple fruits, tied to a firm bamboo stick. 'Look at this! Is this an Indian vegetable?'

I thought of tomato soup, tomato rasam, tomato bhat (tomato-flavoured rice), sandwiches and chutney. 'Of course it is. We use it every single day. It is an integral part of Indian cuisine.'

Uncle smiled. 'Well, the tomato did not originate in India, but in Mexico. It made its way to Europe in 1554. Since nobody ate tomatoes over there at the time, they became ornamental plants because of the beautiful deep-red colour. At some point, there was a belief in Europe that it was good for curing infertility, while some thought that it was poisonous. The contradicting perspectives made it difficult for this fruit to be incorporated into the local diet for a long time. Its lack of value must have been a real push for initiating Spain's tomato festival, where millions of tomatoes are used every year to this day. A story goes that one business-savvy European surrounded his tomato plants with a sturdy, thick fence to show his neighbours that the fruits were not poisonous, but rather valuable and thus desirable. Gradually, the fruits reached India and began to be used as a commercial crop, thanks to its tempting colour and taste. It must have come to us during the reign of the British. But today, we cannot think of cooking without tomatoes.'

'Wow!' I thought. Out loud, I said, 'Uncle, tell me about an essential item that is used in our cooking but isn't ours.'

'Come on, try and guess. We simply cannot cook without this particular vegetable.'

I closed my eyes and thought of sambar, that essential south Indian dish, and the mutter-paneer typical of the north Indian cuisine. It took me a while to think of a common ingredient—the chilli. I brushed my thought away. 'No, there's no way that the chilli can be an imported vegetable. There can be no Indian food without it,' I thought.

Uncle looked at me. 'You are right. It is the chilli!' he exclaimed almost as if he had read my mind.

'How did you know?'

'Because people never fail to be shocked when they think of the possibility that chilli could be from another country. I can see it clearly on their faces when the wheels turn inside their head.'

My disbelief was obvious. How could we cook without chillies? It is as important as salt in Indian cooking.

'There are many stories and multiple theories about chillies,' Uncle said. 'When Vasco da Gama came to India, he came from Portugal via Brazil and brought many seeds with him. Later, Marco Polo and the British came to India. Thus, many more plant seeds arrived. The truth is that what we call "indigenous" isn't really ours. Think of chillies, capsicum, corn, groundnut, cashews, beans, potato, papaya, pineapple, custard apple, guava and sapodilla—they are all from South America. Over time, we indigenized them and learnt how to cook them. Some say that the chilli came from the country of the same name, while some others say it came from Mexico. According to a theory, black pepper was the ingredient traditionally used in India to make our food hot and spicy. Some scholars believe that the sole goal of the East India Company was to acquire a monopoly over India's pepper trade, which later ended in India's colonization. But when we began using chillies, we found that it tasted better than black pepper. To give you an example, we refer to black pepper as *kalu menasu* in Kannada. We gave a similar name to the chilli and called it *menasin kai*. In Hindi, it is frequently referred to as *mirchi*. In the war between black pepper and chilli, the former lost and chilli established itself as the new prince and continues to rule the Indian food industry even today. North Karnataka is famous for its red chillies now.'

'That much I do know, Uncle!' I closed my eyes and had a vision of my younger days. 'I remember seeing acres and acres of red-chilli plants during my childhood. The harvest used to take place during the Diwali season. I remember that Badgi district was dedicated to the sale of chillies. I had gone with my uncle one day and was amazed by the mountains of red-chillies I saw there.'

'Oh yes, you are right! Those red chillies are bright red in colour but they aren't really hot or spicy. On the contrary, chillies that grow in the state of Andhra Pradesh in the area of Guntur are extremely spicy. They are a little rounded in shape, not as deep red in colour and are called Guntur chillies. A good cook uses a combination of different kinds of chillies to make the dish delicious and attractive. Now that's what I call indigenous.'

'There were also two other kinds of chillies in our farm—one was a chilli called Gandhar or Ravana chilli that grows upside down and the other one, of course, was capsicum.'

Uncle nodded. 'Capsicum in India is nothing but green or red bell pepper in the West. But if you eat one tiny Ravana chilli, you will have to sit in the bathroom with your backside in pain and drink many bottles of water for a long, long time!

Or you will have to eat five hundred grams of candies, sweets or chocolates.'

We both laughed.

Hearing the laughter, Rekha's mother came and joined us. 'Are you folks joking about today's menu? I'm sorry that there wasn't much variety. When I heard that you were coming for lunch, I told Uncle to inform you that today's food was going to be bland and that you could come another Sunday, but he said that you are like family and wouldn't mind at all,' she said to me.

That sparked my interest. 'Tell me the reason for the bland food, Aunty!'

'We have a method to the madness, I guess. During death anniversaries, we do not use vegetables or spices that have come from other countries. Hence, we use ingredients like fenugreek, black pepper and cucumber, among others. Our ancestors were scared of using new vegetables and named these imports Vishwamitra *srishti*.'

This was the first time that I had heard of such a thing. 'What does that mean?'

Aunty settled into a makeshift chair under the guava tree. 'The story goes that there was a king called Trishanku who wanted to go to heaven along with his physical body. With his strong penance and powers, the sage Vishwamitra was able to send him to heaven, but the gods pushed him back because they were worried that it would set a precedent for people to come in with their physical bodies. That was not to be allowed. Vishwamitra tried to push Trishanku upwards but the gods pushed him down, like a game of tug of war. In the end, Vishwamitra created a new world for Trishanku and called it Trishanku Swarga. He even created vegetables that belonged neither to the earth nor heaven. So vegetables like eggplant and cauliflower are the creations of Vishwamitra, which must not be used at a time such as a dear one's death anniversary.'

Silence fell between us and I pondered over Aunty's story. After a few minutes, I saw Rekha coming towards us with some bananas and oranges and a box of what seemed to be dessert.

'Come,' she said to me, 'have something. The banana is from our garden and the dessert is made from home-grown ingredients too! You must be . . .'

Uncle interrupted, 'Do you know that we make so many desserts in India that aren't original to our country?'

'Appa, tell her the story of the guava and the banana. I really like that one,' Rekha said. She smiled as she handed me a banana.

Uncle grinned, pleased to impart some more knowledge. 'The seeds of guava came from Goa,' he said. 'So some people say that's how it was named. In Kannada, we call it *perala hannu* because we believe that it originated in Peru, South America. Let me tell you a story.

'Durvasa was a famed short-tempered sage in our ancient epics. He cursed anyone who dared to rouse his anger. The sage was married to a woman named Kandali. One day, she said to him, "O sage, people are terribly afraid of you while I have lived with you for such a long time. Don't you think I deserve a great boon from you?"

'Though Durvasa was upset at her words, he did not curse her. He thought seriously about what she had said and decided that she was right. "I will give you a boon. But only one. So think carefully," he said.

'After some thought, she replied, "Create a fruit for me that is unique and blessed with beautiful colours. The tree should grow not in heaven but on earth. It should have the ability to grow easily everywhere in our country. It must give fruits in bunches and for the whole year. The fruit must not have any seeds and must not create a mess when we eat it. When it is not ripe, we should be able to use it as a vegetable and once it is ripe, we should use it while performing pujas. We must be able to use all parts of the tree."

'Durvasa was surprised and impressed at the number of specifications his wife was giving him. He was used to giving curses in anger and then figuring out their solutions once he had calmed down, but this seemingly simple request was a test of his intelligence. "No wonder women are cleverer. Men like me get upset quickly and act before fully thinking of the consequences," he thought.

'The sage prayed to Goddess Saraswati to give him the knowledge with which he could satisfy his wife's demand. After a few minutes, he realized that he would be able to fulfil his wife's desire. Thus he created the banana tree, which is found all over India today. Every part of the tree— the leaf, the bark, the stem, the flowers and its fruits are used daily. Raw banana can be cooked while the ripe banana can be eaten easily by peeling off its skin. It is also an essential part of worship to the gods. The fruit is seedless and presents itself as a bunch. A mature tree lives for a year and smaller saplings are found around it.

'Kandali was ecstatic and named the plant *kandari*. She announced, "Whoever eats this fruit will not get upset, despite the fact that it was created by my short-tempered husband."

'Over a period of time, people started using the banana extensively and loved it. Slowly the name kandari changed to *kadali* and the banana came to be known as *kadali phala* in Sanskrit.' Uncle took a deep breath at the end of his story.

I smiled, amused at the story that seemed to result from fertile imagination. I had a strong urge to grab a banana and took one from the plate in front of me. 'You may have given me bland food today,' I said, 'but I really want some dessert.'

Rekha opened the box. It was filled with different varieties of sweets. I saw gulab jamuns, jhangri (a deep-fried flour-based dessert) and gulkand (a rose petal–based preserve). I can't resist gulab jamuns, so I immediately picked one up and popped it into my drooling mouth. It was soft and sweet. 'What a dessert!' I remarked, amazed at how delicious it was! 'Nobody can beat us Indians when it comes to desserts. I don't know how people can live in other countries without gulab jamuns.'

'Wait a minute, don't make such sweeping statements,' said Rekha. 'Gulab jamun is not from India.'

'Yeah, right,' I said, not convinced at all. Before she could stop me, I grabbed another gulab jamun and gulped it down.

'I'm serious. A language scholar once came to speak in our college. He told us that apart from English, we use multiple Persian, Arabic and Portuguese words that we aren't even aware of. Gulab jamun is a Persian word and is a dish prepared in Iran. It became popular in India during the Mughal reign because the court language was Persian. The same is true for jhangri, which is a kind of ornament worn on the wrist and the jhangri design resembles it.'

'You will now tell me that even gulkand is from somewhere else!' I complained loudly.

She grinned. 'You aren't wrong! Gulkand is a Persian word too—*gul* is nothing but rose and *kand* means sweet. Gul, in fact, originates from the word *gulab*, meaning rose.'

My brain was thoroughly exhausted with all this information. When I saw the oranges, I said with pride, 'I will not call this an orange now, but its Kannada name *narangi*.'

Uncle cleared his throat. 'Narangi is an Indian word but it does not originate in Karnataka. It is made up of two words—*naar*, which means orange or colour of the sun, and *rangi*, meaning colour.'

The conversation was making me feel truly lost.

'When people stay in one place for some time,' he continued, 'they unknowingly absorb the culture around them, including the regional food and language. At times, we adopt the changes into our local cuisine and make it our own. That's exactly what happened with the foods we have discussed.'

I glanced at my watch. It was time for me to leave. I thanked them profusely, especially Uncle, for enlightening me in a way that even Google could not.

There was a huge traffic jam despite it being a Sunday evening as I set out for home, but I wasn't bored on the way.

In fact, I was happy to recollect Uncle's words and perhaps, as a result, suddenly remembered an incident.

My mother had two sisters. Though all three sisters were married to men from the same state, their husbands' jobs were in different areas—one lived in south Karnataka in the old Mysore state, my parents lived in Maharashtra and the third stayed in the flatlands in a remote corner of Karnataka.

After their husbands retired, the three sisters lived in Hubli in the same area. It was fun to meet my cousins every day and eat meals together. We celebrated festivals as a family and the food was cooked in one house, though everybody brought home-cooked desserts from their own houses.

During one particular Diwali, we had a host of delicacies. My mother made puri and shrikhand (a popular dish in Maharashtra made from strained yogurt and sugar). My aunt from Mysore made kishmish kheer and a rice-based main course called bisi bele anna, while the other aunt made groundnut-based sweets such as jaggery-based sticky chikki and ball-shaped laddus.

As children, my cousins and I had plenty of fun eating them but in the car, I realized for the first time that all the sisters had absorbed something from the area that they had lived in. Despite their physical proximity, the food in each household was so diverse. I couldn't help but wonder how exciting the food really must be in the different regions of India.

I thought of paneer pizzas, cheese dosas and the Indian 'Chinese' food. They must have originated the same way. Who really said that India is a country? It is a continent—culturally vibrant, diverse in food and yet, distinctly Indian at heart.

18

Bombay to Bangalore

It was the beginning of summer. I was boarding the Udyan Express at Gulbarga railway station. My destination was Bangalore. As I boarded the train, I saw that the second-class compartment was jam-packed with people. Though the compartment was reserved, there were many unauthorized people in it. This side of Karnataka is popularly known as Hyderabad Karnataka since the Nizam of Hyderabad once ruled this area. There is scarcity of water here, which makes the land dry, and the farmers cannot grow anything during summer. Hence, many poor farmers and landless labourers from Hyderabad Karnataka immigrate to Bangalore and other big cities during the summer for jobs in construction. They return to their homes in the rainy season to cultivate their lands. This was April, so the train compartment was particularly crowded.

I sat down and was pushed to the corner of the berth. Though it was meant for three people, there were already six of us sitting on it. I looked around and saw students who were eager to come to Bangalore and explore different options to enhance their careers. There were merchants who were talking about what goods to order from Bangalore. Some government officers, though, were criticizing Gulbarga. 'What a place! Staying here is impossible because of the heat. No wonder people call this a punishment transfer!'

The ticket collector came in and started checking people's tickets and reservations. It was difficult to guess who had a ticket and who had a reservation. Some people had tickets but no reservation. This was an overnight train and people needed sleeper berths, but they were limited in number. People who did not have a reserved berth were begging the ticket collector to accommodate them 'somehow'. It was next to impossible for him to listen to everyone.

With his eagle eye, he easily located people who did not have a ticket. People without tickets were pleading, 'Sir, the previous train was cancelled. We had a reservation on that train. It is not our fault. We don't want to pay for this ticket again.' Another person was begging him: 'Sir, I was late to the station and there was a big queue. I didn't have time to buy a ticket. So, I got into this compartment.' The collector must have read the Bhagavad Gita thoroughly; he remained calm while listening to their stories and kept issuing new tickets for ticketless passengers.

Suddenly, he looked in my direction and asked, 'What about your ticket?'

'I have already shown my ticket to you,' I said.

'Not you, madam, the girl hiding below your berth. Hey, come out, where is your ticket?'

I realized that someone was sitting below my berth. When the collector yelled at her, the girl came out of hiding. She was thin, dark, scared and looked like she had been crying profusely. She must have been about thirteen or fourteen years old. She had uncombed hair and was dressed in a torn skirt and blouse. She was trembling and folded both her hands.

The collector asked again, 'Who are you? From which station did you get on? Where are you going? I can issue a full ticket for you with a fine.'

The girl did not reply. The collector was getting very angry since he had been dealing with countless ticketless passengers. He took out his anger on this little girl. 'I know all you runaways,' he shouted. 'You take a free ride in trains and cause tremendous problems. You neither reply to my questions nor pay for your ticket. I have to answer to my bosses . . .'

The girl still did not say anything. The people around the girl were not bothered at all and went about their business. Some were counting the money for their ticket and some were getting ready to get down at Wadi Junction, the next stop. People on the top berth were preparing to sleep and others were busy with their dinner. This was something unusual for me, because I had never seen such a situation in my vast experience of social work.

The girl stood quietly as if she had not heard anything. The collector caught hold of her arms and told her to get down at the next station. 'I will hand you over to the police myself. They will put you in an orphanage,' he said. 'It is not my headache. Get down at Wadi.'

The girl did not move. The collector started forcibly pulling her out from the compartment. Suddenly, I had a strange feeling. I stood up and called out to the collector. 'Sir, I will pay for her ticket,' I said. 'It is getting dark. I don't want a young girl on the platform at this time.'

The collector raised his eyebrows and looked at me. He smiled and said, 'Madam, it is very kind of you to offer to buy her a ticket. But I have seen many children like her. They get in at one station, then get off at the next and board another train. They beg or travel to their destination without a ticket. This is not an exceptional case. Why do you want to waste your money? She will not travel even with a ticket. She may leave if you just give her some money.'

I looked out of the compartment. The train was approaching Wadi Junction and the platform lights were bright. Vendors of tea, juice and food were running towards the train. It was dark. My heart did not accept the collector's advice—and I always listen to my heart. What the collector said might be true but what would I lose—just a few hundred rupees?

'Sir, that's fine. I will pay for her ticket anyway,' I said.

I asked the girl, 'Will you tell me where you want to go?'

The girl looked at me with disbelief. It was at this moment that I noticed her beautiful, dark eyes, which were grief-stricken. She did not say a word.

The collector smiled and said, 'I told you, madam. Experience is the best teacher.'

He turned to the girl and said, 'Get down.'

Then he looked at me and said, 'Madam, if you give her ten rupees, she will be much happier with that than with the ticket.'

I did not listen to him. I told the collector to give me a ticket to the last destination, Bangalore, so that the girl could get down wherever she wanted.

The collector looked at me again and said, 'But she won't get a berth and you will have to pay a penalty.'

I quietly opened my purse.

The collector continued, 'If you want to pay, then you should pay for the ticket from the train's starting point.'

The train originated from Bombay VT and terminated at Bangalore. I paid up quietly. The collector issued the ticket and left in disdain.

The girl was left standing in the same position. I asked my fellow passengers to move and give the girl some space to sit down because she now held a valid ticket. They moved very reluctantly. Then, I asked the girl to sit on the seat—but she did not. When I insisted, she sat down on the floor.

I did not know where to start the conversation. I ordered a meal for her and when the dinner box came, she held it in her hands but did not eat. I failed to persuade her to eat or talk. Finally, I gave the ticket to her and said, 'Look, I don't know what's on your mind since you refuse to talk to me. So, here's the ticket. You can get down wherever you want to.'

As the night progressed, people started sleeping on the floor and on their berths, but the girl continued to sit.

When I woke up at six o'clock the next morning, she was dozing. That meant that she had not got down anywhere.

Her dinner box was empty and I was happy that she had at least eaten something.

As the train approached Bangalore, the compartment started getting empty. Again, I told her to sit on the seat and this time she obliged. Slowly, she started talking. She told me that her name was Chitra. She lived in a village near Bidar. Her father was a coolie and she had lost her mother at birth. Her father had remarried and had two sons with her stepmother. But a few months ago, her father had died. Her stepmother started beating her often and did not give her food. I knew from her torn, bloodstained blouse and the marks on her body that she was telling the truth. She was tired of that life. She did not have anybody to support her so she left home in search of something better.

By this time, the train had reached Bangalore. I said goodbye to Chitra and got down from the train. My driver came and picked up my bags. I felt someone watching me. When I turned back, Chitra was standing there and looking at me with sad eyes. But there was nothing more that I could do.

As I started walking towards my car, I realized that Chitra was following me. I knew that she did not have anybody in the whole world. Now, I was at a loss. I did not know what to do with her. I had paid her ticket out of compassion but I had never thought that she was going to be my responsibility! But from Chitra's perspective, I had been kind to her and she wanted to cling on to me. When I got into the car, she stood outside watching me.

I was scared for a minute. 'What am I doing?' I questioned myself. I was worried about the safety of a girl in Wadi Junction station, but now I was leaving her in a big city like Bangalore—a situation worse than the previous one. Anything could happen to Chitra here. After all, she was a girl. There were many ways in which people could exploit her situation.

I told her to get into my car. My driver looked at the girl curiously. I told him to take us to my friend Ram's place. Ram ran separate shelter homes for boys and girls. We at the Infosys Foundation supported him financially on a regular basis. I thought Chitra could stay there for some time and we could talk about her future after I came back from my tours in a few weeks. There were about ten girls in the shelter and three of them were of Chitra's age. Most of the girls there already knew me.

As soon as I reached the shelter, the lady supervisor came out to talk to me. I explained the situation and handed Chitra over to her. I told Chitra, 'You can stay here for two weeks. Don't worry. These are very good people. I will come and see you after two weeks. Don't run away from here, at least until I come back. Talk to your lady supervisor. You can call her Akka.' (Akka means elder sister in the Kannada language.) I handed over some money to the supervisor and told her to buy some clothes and other necessary things for the girl.

After two weeks, I went back to the shelter. I was not sure if Chitra would even be there. But to my surprise, I saw Chitra looking much happier than before. She was having good food for the first time in her life. She was wearing new clothes and was teaching lessons to the younger children.

As soon as she saw me, she stood up eagerly. The supervisor said, 'Chitra is a nice girl. She helps in our kitchen, cleans the shelter and also teaches the younger children. She tells us that she was a good student in her village and wanted to join high school but her family didn't allow her to do so. Here, she is comfortable and wants to study further. What are your plans for her future? Can we keep her here?'

Soon, Ram also joined us. Ram knew the whole story and suggested that Chitra could go to a high school nearby. I immediately agreed and said that I would sponsor her expenses as long as she continued to study. I left the shelter knowing that Chitra had found a home and a new direction in her life.

I got busier with my work and my visits to the shelter reduced to once a year. But I always inquired about Chitra's well-being over the phone. I knew that she was studying well and that her progress was good.

Years went by. One day, Ram phoned me and said that Chitra had scored 85 per cent in her tenth class. When I went to the shelter to congratulate and talk to her, she was very happy. She was growing up to be a confident young woman. There was brightness in her beautiful, dark eyes.

I offered to sponsor her college studies if she wanted to continue studying. But she said, 'No, Akka. I have talked to my friends and made up my mind. I would like to do my diploma in computer science so that I can immediately get a job after three years.' I tried to persuade her to go to college for a bachelor's degree in engineering but she did not agree. She wanted to become economically independent as soon as possible. Somewhere inside me, I understood where she was coming from.

Three rainy seasons passed. Chitra obtained her diploma with flying colours. She also got a job in a software company as an assistant testing engineer. When she got her first salary, she came to my office with a sari and a box of sweets. I was touched by her gesture. Later, I got to know that she had spent her entire first salary buying something for everyone at the shelter.

Soon enough, Ram called me to discuss a new problem. 'Chitra is now a working girl. So she cannot stay in the shelter since it is only meant for students.' I told Ram that I would talk to Chitra and ask her to pay the shelter a reasonable amount of money per month towards rent. This way she could continue to stay there until she got married. I strongly felt that the shelter was a safe place for an unmarried, orphan girl like Chitra.

Ram asked me, 'Are you going to look for a boy for her?'

This was a new and an even bigger problem. As her informal guardian, I had to find a boy for Chitra or she herself had to find a life partner. This was a great responsibility. No wonder people say I have a penchant for getting into problems! But God also shows me unique ways of getting out of them. I told Ram, 'She is only twenty-one. Let her work for a few years. If you come across a suitable boy, please let me know.'

I called Chitra and gave her my opinion about her staying at the shelter, and she happily agreed to stay on and pay rent.

Days rolled by, and months turned into years. One day, when I was in Delhi, I got a call from Chitra. She was very happy. 'Akka, my company is sending me to the US! I wanted to meet you and take your blessings but you are not here in Bangalore.'

I was ecstatic for Chitra. I said, 'Chitra, you are now going to a different country. Take care of yourself and keep in touch. My blessings are always with you.'

Years passed. Occasionally, I received an email from Chitra. She was doing very well in her career. She was posted across several cities in the US and was enjoying life. I silently prayed that she should always be happy wherever she was.

Years later, I was invited to deliver a lecture in San Francisco for Kannada Koota, an organization where families who speak Kannada meet and organize events. The lecture was in a convention hall of a hotel and I decided to stay at the same hotel. After the lecture, I was planning to leave for the airport. When I checked out of the hotel room and went to the reception counter to pay the bill, the receptionist said, 'Madam, you don't need to pay us anything. The lady over there has already settled your bill. She must know you pretty well.'

I turned around and found Chitra there. She was standing with a young white man and wore a beautiful sari. She was looking very pretty with short hair. Her dark eyes were beaming with happiness and pride. As soon as she saw me, she gave me a brilliant smile, hugged me and touched my feet. I was overwhelmed with joy and did not know what to say.

'Chitra, how are you? I have not seen you for ages. What a sweet surprise. How did you know that I will be in this city today?'

'Akka, I live in this city and came to know that you are giving a lecture at the local Kannada Koota. I am also a member there. I wanted to surprise you. It is not difficult to find out about your schedule.'

'Chitra, I have so many questions to ask you. How is work? Have you visited India? And more importantly, have you found Mr Right? And why did you pay my hotel bill?'

'No, Akka. I haven't come to India since I left. If I come to India, how can I return without meeting you? Akka, I have something to tell you. I know that you were always worried about my marriage. You never asked me about my community. But you always wanted me to settle down. I know it is hard for you to choose a boy for me. Now, I have found my Mr Right. Please meet my colleague, John. We are getting married at the end of the year. You must come for our wedding and bless us.'

I was very happy to see the way things had turned out for Chitra. But I came back to my original question. 'Chitra, why did you pay my hotel bill? That is not right.'

With tears in her eyes and gratitude on her face, she said, 'Akka, if you hadn't helped me, I don't know where I would have been today—maybe a beggar, a prostitute, a runaway child, a servant in someone's house . . . or I may even have committed suicide. You changed my life. I am ever grateful to you.'

'No, Chitra. I am only one step in your ladder of success,' I said. 'There are many steps which led you to where you are today—the shelter which looked after you, the schools which gave you good education, the company which sent you to

America and, above all, it is you—a determined and inspired girl who made your life yourself. One step should never be given all the credit for the end result.'

'That is your thinking, Akka. I differ with you,' she said.

'Chitra, you are starting a new life and you should save money for your new family. Why did you pay my hotel bill?'

Chitra did not reply but told John to touch my feet. Then, suddenly sobbing, she hugged me and said, 'Because you paid for my ticket from Bombay to Bangalore!'

19

Miserable Success

Vishnu was a young, bright and ambitious student from the first batch I ever taught at college. So my relationship with him was closer than that with my students from subsequent batches. He was charming, communicative and clear in his thinking.

In college, we used to have long arguments on different issues and we used to agree to disagree on many matters. I used to tell him, 'Vishnu, I have seen many more seasons than you. With my experience in life, I want to tell you that having good relationships, compassion and peace of mind is much more important than achievements, awards, degrees or money.'

Vishnu would argue back: 'Madam, your stomach is full and you have achieved everything. Hence, you are comfortable in life and can say that. You have received many awards, so you don't care for them and you are not ambitious. You will never understand people like me.' Then, I usually just smiled at him. I liked him for his openness.

Vishnu was also very good at teaching. He completed his degree and got an excellent job in Microsoft in Seattle, USA. He was awaiting his visa to go abroad. I told him to teach at my college while he was waiting. Whenever I could not attend the laboratory sessions, I told him to take charge of the junior lab and be my substitute. He became very popular with the students.

I asked Vishnu, 'You are very good at teaching. Why don't you seriously think of becoming a professor?'

He said, 'My monthly salary in the US is more than a teacher's annual salary here. Why would I want to become a professor?'

'Vishnu, don't be so rude. A teacher is not respected for the salary but for his or her knowledge and teaching. If you don't respect the teaching profession, that is fine, but don't make such a comparison.'

Soon, Vishnu left the country on his new assignment.

Many years passed and a decade rolled by. My students, who were once young, were now middle-aged and I had gone from middle age to old age.

One day, my secretary told me that someone called Vishnu wanted to meet me. By this time, I knew many Vishnus and was not able to place him at once. She said that he was a student from my first batch of students. Now I recognized him instantly and told her to set up an appointment. After all, old wine, old memories and old students are precious in life.

On the day of the appointment, Vishnu walked in right on time. He had less hair than before and some of them were grey. He had put on weight. He was wearing an expensive shirt and there was a platinum diamond ring on his finger. But alas, his face was like a dried tomato. There was not a trace of enthusiasm on it. On the contrary, I could see some lines of worry on his face.

He sat in front of me and I ordered him a cup of tea. Vishnu looked at me and said, 'Madam, you look really old now.'

I smiled and said, 'Time and tide will wait for no one.' But he did not smile back. 'How are you, Vishnu?' I asked. 'I haven't met you for fifteen years. It is very nice of you to remember your old teacher and come to see me. Where are you? What are you doing now? Are you still with Microsoft?'

'No, madam. I left Microsoft after three years,' replied Vishnu.

'No wonder people say that if someone stays in a software company for more than three years, he is a loyal person!'

He did not respond to my joke. 'So where are you now?' I asked again.

'I own a company in Singapore. Two hundred people work for me. We make very good profit.' I felt Vishnu's voice had that pride of achievement, which was very natural.

'So you have settled in Singapore?'

'Not really, I come to India quite often because of work. I have a house in Vasant Vihar in Delhi, a flat in Worli in Mumbai, a bungalow in Raj Mahal Vilas Extension in Bangalore, a farm on Bannerghatta Road . . .'

I stopped him. 'Vishnu, I didn't ask you about your assets. I am not an income-tax person. I just wanted to know where you normally stay.' I was pulling his leg, yet he did not smile.

'Vishnu, you have told me enough about your financial assets,' I continued. 'Now tell me about your marital status. Are you married? How many children do you have? What do they do?' Usually, a mother and a teacher get the automatic authority to pose these questions to her children and students. I am no exception. Some people mind my questions because it is their personal life and I get the hint and stop. But most people happily tell me about their life.

'Yes, I am married. I have an eight-year-old daughter,' he said.

Vishnu pulled out his wallet and showed me his family photo. When he was in college, he used to go out with Bhagya, a girl junior to him. But the lady in the photograph was different. She was stunningly beautiful, like a model, and his daughter was cute.

I felt that his life was a picture-perfect postcard. He was successful, rich, had a very pretty wife and a daughter. What else can one want in life? With this kind of success, he should be very happy and enthusiastic—but he was not. I did not know the reason, but I knew that he would tell me. I stopped talking and allowed Vishnu to speak.

Slowly, Vishnu opened up. 'Madam, I have a problem. I have come to talk to you.'

'What problem? And why do you think I have the solution? Actually, a successful person like you should help an old teacher like me,' I joked to reduce the tension.

'It is nothing to do with success, madam. For the last few years, I have been feeling very sad. I feel like I am missing something in life. I can't pinpoint exactly what it is,' he said. 'Nothing makes me happy. Nothing even moves me or touches my heart, even if I see a heart-wrenching incident. I feel that I am travelling in a desert without water and the roads are paved with gold and silver . . .'

I asked him directly, 'Have you seen a doctor or a counsellor?'

'Of course I have. They said that a compassionate heart is important to enjoy life. They told me to read books and advised me to try and be happy by doing things such as looking at the sunrise, listening to the birds, taking long walks and exercising regularly.'

'Well, what happened?'

'I lost weight with all the activities but otherwise things didn't improve. I went back to a counsellor again. He told me to go to Somalia on a trip.'

'Why Somalia?' I was surprised. 'I know that there are trips to Europe, Hong Kong and Bangkok. But I have never heard of a trip to Somalia. Tell me, did you go there? What did you do in Somalia?' I was curious.

'Oh, they took us to orphanages, HIV camps and camps of children suffering from malnutrition. But nothing happened. I still didn't feel anything. On the contrary, my mind was busy calculating how Somalia could export to America or other European nations. What would you have done in my place, madam?' he questioned me.

'Don't put me in your shoes. What I would do is left to me and you don't have to do the same thing. Why can't you talk to someone who is very dear to you—maybe a friend or your wife or someone from your age group? They might be able to give you a better solution. After all, there is a generation gap between us.'

He was quiet. Then he said, 'Madam, all my life, I have calculated and made friendships. I have never spent time with people who aren't useful to me in some way. After all, life is a merciless, competitive field. Every move should take me one step higher on the ladder of success.'

I thought to myself, 'Now I know why Bhagya was replaced by the model wife.'

'How much time do you spend with your family?'

'My daughter is friendly but she is nice to me only when she wants something from me. Sometimes, I find it very strange. A child looks beautiful only with innocence but my daughter is more practical. My wife is very busy with the carpet business that she inherited from her father. She doesn't have any time to talk to me and my daughter, even though she works from home most of the time.'

He stopped for a second and continued, 'Or maybe I think that way. My wife wants to get all my contacts and clients so that she can expand her business. I am more of a database to her than a companion.'

I understood Vishnu's problem. Sometimes, it is very difficult to talk with your own family. I was touched that he felt safe coming to me. But he was expecting a quick fix from me. I was willing to listen to his problem, but that did not mean that I also had the solution.

Vishnu continued, 'Madam, tell me, how do I become compassionate? How do I build a strong family? How can I enjoy the sunrise and the moonlight? How much time does it take to get all these qualities? Are there any books or a crash course or people who can teach me? I don't care about the cost but it shouldn't take months together.'

I was shocked by his approach. 'Vishnu, compassion cannot be taught, sold or bought,' I said. 'There is no time limit either. It is one of the characteristics that you have to develop from the beginning. Understand that life is a journey. In that short journey, if you can show compassion to others, show it now. Our ancestors have always talked about the middle path for a reason. That path makes a person stable, happy and content. Vishnu, you are the role model for your children. Children will be what they see. What you have done, your daughter has copied.'

Vishnu sighed and said, 'Yes, madam. I understand what you are saying. I will take my daughter and work with poor people on a regular basis along with her. That will also help us bond. I am hoping that it will make me a better human being and I will be able to feel worthy again. Now I know what brought me to you. I cannot thank you enough.'

Vishnu left my office with hope in his heart and a smile on his face.

20

How to Beat the Boys

Recently, when I visited the US, I had to speak to a crowd of both students and highly successful people. I always prefer interacting with the audience, so I opened the floor to questions.

After several questions were asked, a middle-aged man stood up to speak. 'Madam, you are very confident and clear in communicating your thoughts. You are absolutely at ease while talking to us . . . '

I was direct. 'Please don't praise me. Ask me your question.'

'I think you must have studied abroad or done your MBA from a university in the West. Is that what gives you such confidence?' he asked.

Without wasting a second, I replied, 'It comes from my B.V.B.'

He seemed puzzled. 'What do you mean—my B.V.B.?'

I smiled. 'I'm talking about the Basappa Veerappa Bhoomaraddi College of Engineering and Technology in Hubli, a medium-sized town in the state of Karnataka in

India. I have never studied outside of India. The only reason I stand here before you is because of that college.'

In a lighter vein, I continued, 'I'm sure that the young people in the software industry who are present here today will appreciate the contribution of Infosys to India and to the US. Infosys has made Bengaluru, Karnataka and India proud. Had I not been in B.V.B., I would not have become an engineer. If I wasn't an engineer, then I wouldn't have been able to support my husband. And if my husband didn't have his family's backing, he may or may not have had the chance to establish Infosys at all! In that case, all of you wouldn't have gathered here today to hear me speak.'

Everyone clapped and laughed, but I really meant what I said. After the session got over and the crowd left, I felt tired and chose to sit alone on a couch nearby.

My mind went back to 1968. I was a seventeen-year-old girl with an abundance of courage, confidence and the dream to become an engineer. I came from an educated, though middle-class, conservative Brahmin family. My father was a professor of obstetrics and gynaecology at the Karnataka Medical College at Hubli, while my mother was a schoolteacher before she got married.

I finished my pre-university exams with excellent marks and told my family that I wanted to pursue engineering. I had always been fascinated with science, even more so with its application. Engineering was one of those branches of science that would allow me to utilize my creativity, especially in design. But it was as if I had dropped a bomb inside our house.

The immediate reaction was of shock. Engineering was clearly an all-male domain and hence considered a taboo for girls in those days. There was no questioning the status quo, wherein girls were expected to be in the company of other female students in a medical or science college. The idea of a woman entering the engineering field had possibly never popped up in anyone's mind. It was akin to expecting pigs to fly.

I was my grandmother's favourite granddaughter, but even she looked at me with disdain and said, 'If you go ahead and do this, no man from north Karnataka will marry you. Who wants to marry a woman engineer? I am so disappointed in you.' My grandmother never thought that I would do anything she disapproved of. However, she also didn't know that in the city of Mysore, across the river of Tungabhadra, lived a man named Narayana Murthy who would later want to marry me.

My grandfather, a history teacher and my first guru who taught me reading and writing, only mildly opposed it. 'My child, you are wonderful at history. Why can't you do something in this field? You could be a great scholar one day. Don't chase a dry subject like engineering.'

My mother, who was extremely proficient in mathematics, said, 'You are good at maths. Why don't you complete your post-graduation in mathematics and get a job as a professor? You can easily work in a college after you get married instead of being a hardcore engineer struggling to balance family and work.'

My father, a liberal man who believed in education for women, thought for a moment and said, 'I think that you should pursue medicine. You are excellent with people and languages. To tell you the truth, I don't know much about engineering. We don't have a single engineer in our family. It is a male-dominated industry and you may not find another girl in your class. What if you have to spend four years without a real friend to talk to? Think about it. However, the decision is yours and I will support you.'

Many of my aunts also thought that no one would marry me if I chose engineering. This would possibly entail my marrying somebody from another community, an absolutely unheard-of thing in those days.

However, I didn't care. As a student of history, I had read Hiuen Tsang's book *Si-Yu-Ki*. Before Tsang's travel to India, everybody discouraged him from making the journey on foot, but he refused to listen and decided to go. In time, he became famous for his seventeen-year-long journey to India. Taking courage from Tsang, I told my family, 'I want to do engineering. Come what may, I am ready for the consequences of my actions.'

I filled out the application form for B.V.B. College of Engineering and Technology, submitted it and soon received the news that I had been selected on the basis of my marks. I was ecstatic, but little did I know that the college staff was discomfited by this development.

The principal at the time was B.C. Khanapure, who happened to know my father. They both met at a barber shop one day and the principal expressed his genuine anguish at what he perceived to be an awkward situation. He told my father, 'Doctor Sahib, I know that your daughter is very intelligent and that she has been given admission only because of merit, but I'm afraid we have some problems. She will be the only girl in college. It is going to be difficult for her. First, we don't have a ladies' toilet on campus. We don't have a ladies' room for her to relax either. Second, our boys are young with raging hormones and I am sure that they will trouble her. They may not do anything in front of the staff but they will definitely do something later. They may not cooperate with her or help her because they are not used to talking to girls. As a father of four daughters, I am concerned about yours too. Can you tell her to change her mind for her own sake?'

My father replied, 'I agree with you, Professor Sahib. I know you mean well, but my daughter is hell-bent on pursuing engineering. Frankly, she's not doing anything wrong. So I have decided to let her pursue it.'

'In that case, Doctor Sahib, I have a small request. Please ask her to wear a sari to college as it is a man's world out there and the sari will be an appropriate dress for the environment she will be in. She should not talk to the boys unnecessarily because that will give rise to rumours and that's never good for a girl in our society. Also, tell her to avoid going to the college canteen and spending time there with the boys.'

My father came back and told me about this conversation. I readily agreed to all of the requests since I had no intention of changing my mind.

Eventually, I would become friendly with some of the boys, but I always knew where to draw the line. The truth is that it was these same boys who would teach me some of life's lessons later, such as the value of keeping a sense of perspective, the importance of taking it easy every now and then and being a good sport. Many of the boys, who are now older gentlemen, are like my brothers even after fifty years! Finally, it was the lack of ladies' toilets on campus that made me understand the difficulty faced by many women in India due to the insufficiency or sheer absence of toilets. Eventually, this would lead me to build more than 13,000 toilets in Karnataka alone!

Meanwhile, my mother chose an auspicious day for me to pay the tuition fee. It was a Thursday and happened to be the end of the month. My mother nagged me to pay the fee of Rs 400 that day although my father only had Rs 300 left. He told her, 'Wait for a few days. I will get my salary and then Sudha can pay her fees.'

My mother refused to budge. 'Our daughter is going to college. It is a big deal. We must pay the fees today—it will be good for her studies.'

While they were still going back and forth, my father's assistant, Dr S.S. Hiremath, came along with his father-in-law, Patil, who was the headman of Baad village near Shiggaon, the town where I was born. Patil curiously asked what was going on and my father explained the situation to him. He then took out his wallet and gave my father a hundred rupees. He said, 'Doctor Sahib, please accept this money. I want to gift it to this girl who is doing something path-breaking. I have seen parents take loans and sell their houses or farms to pay their sons' fees so that they can become engineers. In fact, sometimes, they don't even know whether their child will study properly or not. Look at your daughter. She desperately wants to do this and I think she is right.'

'No, Mr Patil,' my father refused. 'I can't take such an expensive gift. I will accept this as a loan and return it to you next month after I receive my salary.'

Patil continued as though he hadn't heard my father, 'The most important thing is for your daughter to do her best and complete her course and become a model for other girls.' Then he turned to me and said, 'Sudha, promise me that you will always be ethical, impartial and hard-working and that you will bring a good name to your family and society.'

I nodded meekly, suddenly humbled.

My first day of college arrived a month later. I wore a white sari for the first time, touched the feet of all the elders at home and prayed to Goddess Saraswati who had been very kind to me. I then made my way to the college.

As soon as I reached, the principal called me and gave me a key. He said, 'Here, Ms Kulkarni, take this. This is the key of a tiny room in the corner of the electrical engineering department on the second floor. You can use this room whenever you want.'

I thanked him profusely, took the key and immediately went to see the room. I opened the door excitedly, but alas! The room had two broken desks and there was no sign of a toilet. It was so dusty that I could not even consider entering it. Seeing me there, a cleaner came running with a broom in his hand. Without looking at me, he said, 'I'm so sorry. Principal Sahib told me yesterday that a girl student was going to join the college today, but I thought that he was joking. So I didn't clean the room. Anyway, I will do it right now.'

After he had finished cleaning, I still felt that the room was dusty. Calmly, I told him, 'Leave the broom here and give me a wet cloth, please. I will clean the room myself.'

After cleaning the room to my satisfaction, I brushed off the dust on my clothes and went to class.

When I entered the room on the ground floor, there were 149 pairs of eyes staring at me as though I were some kind of an exotic animal. It was true though. I was the 150th animal in this zoo! I knew that some of them wanted to whistle but I kept a straight face and looked around for a place to sit. The first bench was empty. As I was about to sit there, I saw that someone had spilt blue ink right in the middle of the seat. This was obviously meant for me. I felt tears threatening to spill over, but I blinked them away. Making use of the newspaper in my hand, I wiped the seat clean and sat on a corner of the bench.

I could hear the boys whispering behind me. One grumbled, 'Why the hell did you put ink on the seat? Now she may go and complain to the principal.'

Another boy replied, 'How can she prove that I have done it? There are 149 of us here.'

Despite feeling hurt, I did not go to the principal to complain. He had already warned my father that if I complained, these boys might persist in troubling me further and I may eventually have to leave the college. So, I decided to keep quiet no matter how much these boys tried to harass me.

The truth was that I was afraid of being so troubled by the boys' activities that I would quit engineering altogether. I thought of ways to stay strong—physically and mentally. It would be my *tapas*, or penance. In that instant, I resolved that for the next four years, I would neither miss any class nor ask anyone for help with class notes. In an effort to teach myself self-restraint and self-control, I decided that until I completed my engineering degree, I would wear only white saris, refrain from sweets, sleep on a mat and take baths with cold water. I aimed to become self-sufficient; I would be my best friend and my worst enemy. I didn't know then that such a quote already existed in the Bhagavad Gita where Krishna says, '*Atma aiva hi atmano bandhu aatma aiva ripu atmanah*'.

We really don't need such penance to do well in our studies, but I was young and determined and wanted to do all I could to survive engineering.

I had good teachers who were considerate and sought to look out for me in class. They would occasionally ask, 'Ms Kulkarni, is everything okay with you?'

Even our college principal, Professor Khanapure, went out of his way to inquire about my welfare and if any boys were troubling me.

However, I can't say the same about my classmates.

One day, they brought a small bunch of flowers and stuck it in my plaited hair without my knowledge when the teacher was not around. I heard someone shout from the back—'Ms Flowerpot!' I quietly ran my fingers through my hair, found the flowers and threw them away. I did not say anything.

At times, they would throw paper airplanes at my back. On unfolding the papers, I would find comments such as, 'A woman's place is in the kitchen or in medical science or as a professor, definitely not in an engineering college.'

Others would read, 'We really pity you. Why are you performing penance like Goddess Parvati? At least Parvati had a reason for it. She wanted to marry Shiva. Who is your Shiva?' I would keep the paper planes and refrain from replying.

There was a famous student-friendly activity in our college known as 'fishpond'. Rather than an actual fishpond, it was a fishbowl that carried a collection of anonymous notes, or the 'fish'. Anybody from the college could write a comment or an opinion that would be read out later on our college annual day. All the students would eagerly wait to hear what funny and witty remarks had been selected that year. The designated host would stand on the stage in the college quadrangle and read the notes out loud. Every year, most of the notes were about me. I was often the target of Kannada limericks, one of which I can still remember vividly:

Avva avva genasa,
Kari seeri udisa,
Gandana manege kalisa.

This literally translates to:

> Mom, Mom, there is a sweet potato,
> Please give me a black sari and send me to my husband's
>   house,
> This is because I'm always wearing a white sari.

Some of the romantic north Indian boys would modify the lyrics of songs from movies like *Teesri Kasam*:

> *Sajan re jhoot math bolo*
> *Sudha ke pass jaana hai*
> *Na haathi hai na ghoda hai*
> *Vahan paidal jaana hai.*

This can be translated as:

> Dear, come on, don't lie
> I want to go to Sudha
> I neither have an elephant nor a horse
> But I will go walking (to her).

All the boys would then sneak a glance at me to see my reaction, but I would simply hold back my tears and try my hardest to smile.

I knew that my classmates were acting out for a reason. It was not that they wanted to bully or harass me with deliberate intention as is the norm these days. It was just that they were unprepared—both mentally and physically—to deal with a person of the opposite sex studying with them. Our conservative society discouraged the mingling of boys and girls even as friends, and so, I was as interesting as an alien to them. My mind justified the reason for the boys' behaviour and helped me cope. And yet, the remarks, the pranks and the sarcasm continued to hurt.

My only outlet in college was my actual education. I enjoyed the engineering subjects and did very well in my exams. I found that I performed better than the boys, even in hardcore engineering subjects such as smithy, filing, carpentry and welding. The boys wore blue overalls and I wore a blue apron over my sari. I knew that I looked quite funny, but it was a small price to pay for the education I was getting.

When the exam results were announced, everyone else knew my marks before I did. Almost every semester, my classmates and seniors would make a singular effort to find out my marks and display them on the noticeboard for everyone to see. I had absolutely no privacy.

Over the course of my studies, I realized that the belief 'engineering is a man's domain' is a complete myth. Not only was I just as capable as them, I also scored higher than all my classmates. This gave me additional confidence and I continued to not miss a single day or a single class. I persisted in studying hard, determined to top the subsequent examinations. In time, I became unfazed that my marks were displayed on the noticeboard. On the contrary, I was proud that I was beating all the boys at their own game as I kept bagging the first rank in the university.

My ability to be self-sufficient made me strong and the boys eventually started to respect me, became dependent on me for surveys and drawings and asked me for the answers to the assignments. I began to make friends and even today, my good friends include Ramesh Jangal from the civil department, my lab partner Sunil Kulkarni, and Fakeer Gowda, M.M. Kulkarni, Hire Gowda, Anand Uthuri, Gajanan Thakur, Prakash Padaki, H.P. Sudarshan and Ramesh Lodaya.

I will never forget my teachers: L.J. Noronha from the electrical engineering department, Yoga Narasimha, a gifted teacher from Bangalore, Prof. Mallapur from the chemistry department, Prof. Kulkarni from hydraulics and many more. Between my classes, I also spent much time in the library and the librarian became very fond of me over time, eventually giving me extra books.

I also spoke frequently to the gardener about the trees that should be planted in front of the college, and during my four years there, I had him plant coconut trees. Whenever I go to B.V.B. now, I look at the coconut trees and fondly remember my golden days on the campus.

The four years passed quickly and the day came when I finally had to leave. I felt sad. I had come as a scared teenager and was leaving as a confident and bright young engineer! College had taught me the resilience to face any situation, the flexibility to adjust as needed, the importance of building good and healthy relationships with others, sharing notes with classmates and collaborating with others instead of staying by myself. Thus, when I speak of friends, I don't usually think of women but rather of men because I really grew up with them. When I later entered the corporate world, it was again dominated by men. It was only natural for my colleagues or friends to be men and only sometimes would there be women, whom I would get to know over many years.

College is not just a building made up of walls, benches and desks. It is much more intangible than that. The right education should make you a confident person and that is what B.V.B. did for me.

I later completed my master's programme from the Indian Institute of Science, Bangalore. Yet, B.V.B. continues to have a special place in my heart.

When my father passed away due to old age, I decided to do something in his memory. He had allowed me to go ahead and become an engineer, despite all odds and grievances he had heard from our family and society. Thus, I built a lecture hall in his memory in our college campus.

Whenever I go abroad to deliver a speech, at least five people of different ages come and tell me that they are from B.V.B. too. I connect with them immediately and can't help but smile and ask, 'Which year did you graduate? Who were your teachers? How many girls studied in your class?'

Now, whenever I go back to the college, it is like a celebration, like a daughter coming home. Towards the end of the visit, I almost always stand alone in the inner quadrangle of the stage. My memories take me back to the numerous occasions when I received awards for academic excellence. I then spend a few minutes in front of the noticeboard and walk up to the small room on the second floor of the electrical engineering department that was 'Kulkarni's Room', but no longer dusty. I remember the bench on which I sat and prepared for my exams. My heart feels a familiar ache when I recall some of my teachers and classmates who are no longer in this world today.

And then, as I walk down the stairs, I come across groups of girls—chatting away happily and wearing jeans, skirts or traditional salwar-kameez. There are almost as many girls as there are boys in the college. When they see me, they lovingly surround me for autographs. In the midst of the crowd and the signings, I think of my parents and my journey of fifty years and my eyes get misty.

May God bless our college, B.V.B.!

21

Three Thousand Stitches

We set up the Infosys Foundation in 1996. Unfortunately, I knew precious little about how things worked in a non-profit organization. I knew more about software, management, programming and tackling software bugs. Examinations, mark sheets and deadlines occupied most of my days. The concept behind the foundation was that it must make a difference to the common man—*bahujan hitaya, bahujan sukhaya*—it must provide compassionate aid regardless of caste, creed, language or religion.

As we pondered over the issues before us—malnutrition, education, rural development, self-sufficiency, access to medicine, cultural activities and the revival of the arts, among others—there was one issue that occupied my uppermost thoughts: the devadasi tradition that was pervasive throughout India.

The word devadasi means 'servant of the Lord'.

Traditionally, devadasis were musicians and dancers who practised their craft in temples to please the gods. They had a high status in society. We can see evidence of this in the caves of Badami, as well as in stories like that of the devadasi Vinapodi, who was very dear to the ruling king of the Chalukya dynasty between the sixth and seventh century in northern Karnataka. The king donated enormous sums of money to temples. However, as time went by, the temples were destroyed and the tradition of the devadasis fell into ruin. Young girls were initially dedicated to the worship and service of a deity or a temple in good faith, but eventually, the word 'devadasi' became synonymous with 'sex worker'. Some were born into the life, while others were 'sacrificed' to the temples by their parents due to various reasons, or simply because they caught a hair infection like the ringworm of the scalp, assumed to be indicative that the girl was destined to be a devadasi.

As I thought about their plight, I recalled my visit to the Yellamma Gudda (or Renuka temple) in Belgaum district of Karnataka years ago. I remembered their green saris and bangles, the smears of yellow *bhandara* (a coarse turmeric powder) and their thick, long hair as they entered the temple with goddess masks, coconuts, neem leaves and a *kalash* (a metal pot). 'Why can't I tackle this problem?' I wondered.

I didn't realize then that I was choosing one of the most difficult tasks for our very first project.

With innocence and bubbling enthusiasm, I chose a place in northern Karnataka where the practice was rampant and prostitution was carried on in the name of religion. My plan was to talk to the devadasis and write down their concerns to help me understand their predicament, followed by organizing a few discussions targeted towards solving their problems within a few months.

On my first day in the district, I armed myself with a notebook and pen and set out. I dressed simply, with no jewellery or bindi. I wore a pair of jeans, T-shirt and a cap. After some time, I found a group of devadasis sitting below a tree near a temple. They were chatting and removing lice from each other's hair.

Without thinking, I went up to them, interrupting their conversation. 'Namaskaram, Amma. I've come here to help you. Tell me your problems and I'll write them down.'

They must have been discussing something important because the women gave me a dirty look. They lobbed questions at me with increasing ferocity.

'Who are you? Did we invite you here?'

'Have you come to write about us? In that case, we don't want to talk to you.'

'Are you an officer? Or a minister? If we tell you our problems, how will you solve them?'

'Go away. Go back to where you came from.'

I did not move. In fact, I persisted. 'I want to help you. Please listen to me. Are you aware that there is a dangerous illness called AIDS that you could be exposed to? There is no cure for . . .'

'Just go,' one of them snapped. I glanced at their faces. They were furious.

But I did not leave. 'Maybe they need a little convincing,' I thought.

Without warning, one of them stood up, took off her chappal and threw it at me. 'Can't you understand simple Kannada? Just get lost.'

Insulted and humiliated, I felt my tears threatening to spill over. I turned back and fled.

Upon returning home, with the insult fresh on my mind, I told myself, 'I won't go there again.'

However, a few days later, it occurred to me that the women were probably upset about something else and that maybe I had simply chosen the wrong time and date to visit them.

So after another week, I went there again. This visit took place during the tomato harvest. The devadasi women were happily distributing small oval-shaped bright-red tomatoes to each other from the baskets kept near them. I approached them and smiled pleasantly. 'Hello, I've come to meet you again! Please hear me out. I really, really want to help you.'

They laughed at me. 'We don't need your help. But would you like to buy some tomatoes?'

'No, I am not very fond of tomatoes.'

'What kind of a woman are you? Who doesn't like tomatoes?'

I attempted to engage them once more. 'Have you heard of AIDS? You must know that the government is spending a lot of money on increasing awareness about it.'

'Are you a government agent? Or maybe you belong to a political party. How much commission are you getting to do this? Come on, tell us! We don't even have a proper hospital in this area and here you are, trying to educate us about a scary disease. We don't need your help. Our goddess will help us in difficult times.'

I stood dumbfounded, struggling to find words.

One of the women said decisively, 'This lady must be a journalist. That's why she has a pen and paper. She'll write about us and make money by exploiting us.' Upon hearing this, the others started throwing tomatoes at me.

This time, my emotions overpowered me and I started to cry. Sobbing, I fled from there once again.

I was in despair. 'Why should I work on this project? Why do they keep insulting me? Where else do the beneficiaries humiliate the person working for their well-being? I am not a good fit for this field. Yes, I should resign and go back to my academic career. The foundation can choose a different trustee.'

When I reached home, I sat down to compose a resignation letter.

My father came down the stairs and seeing me busy, with my head bent close to the paper, he asked, 'What are you writing so frantically?'

I narrated the entire episode to him.

To my amazement, rather than sympathizing with me, my father chuckled and said, 'I didn't know that you were so impractical.'

I stared at him in anger.

He took out an ice cream from the fridge and forced me to sit down and eat it. 'It'll cool your head,' he said and smiled.

After a few minutes, he said, 'Please remember. Prostitution has existed in society since ancient times and has become an integral part of life. It is one of the root problems of all civilizations. Many kings and saints have tried to eliminate it but no law or punishment has been successful in bringing it down to zero. Not one nation in the world is free of this. Then how can you change the entire system by yourself? You're just an ordinary woman! What you should do is reduce your expectations and lower your goal. For instance, try to help ten devadasis leave their profession. Rehabilitate them and show them what it means to lead a normal life. This will guarantee that their children will not follow in their footsteps. Make that your aim, and the day you accomplish it, I will feel very proud knowing that I gave birth to a daughter who helped ten helpless women make the most difficult transition from being sex workers to independent women.'

'But they threw chappals and tomatoes at me, Kaka,' I whined petulantly. I always called my father 'Kaka'.

'Actually, you got a promotion today—from chappals to tomatoes. If you pursue this and go there a third time, maybe you'll get something even better!' His joke brought a reluctant smile to my face.

'They won't even talk to me. Then how can I work for them?'

'Look at yourself,' my father said, dragging me in front of the nearest mirror. 'You are casually dressed in a T-shirt, a pair of jeans and a cap. This may be your style, but the common man and a rural Indian woman like the devadasi will never connect or identify with you. If you wear a sari, a *mangalsutra* [a married woman's holy necklace], put on a bindi and tie your hair, I'm sure that they will receive you much better than before. I'll also come with you. An old man like me will be of great help to you in such an adventure.'

I protested, 'I don't want to alter my appearance for their sake. I don't believe in such superficial changes.'

'Well, if you want to change them, then you have to change yourself first. Change your attitude. Of course, it's your decision in the end.'

He left me in front of the mirror and walked away.

My parents had never thrust their choices or beliefs on me or any of my siblings, whether it was about education, profession or marriage. They always gave their advice and helped us if we wanted, but we made all the choices.

For a few days, I was confused. I thought about the skills needed for social work. There was no glamour or money in this profession and I could not behave like an executive in a corporate house. I required language skills, of which English may not be needed at all! I had to be able to sit down on the floor and eat the local food, no matter where I travelled to for work. I had to listen patiently, and most of all, I should love the work I did. What would give me higher satisfaction—keeping my external appearance the way it was or the work that I would do?

After some introspection, I decided to change my appearance and concentrate completely on the work.

Before my next visit, I pulled my hair back, tied it and adorned it with flowers. I wore a two-hundred-rupee sari, a big bindi, a mangalsutra and glass bangles. I transformed myself into a *bharatiya nari*, the stereotypical traditional

Indian woman, and took my father along with me to meet the devadasis.

This time, when we went there, upon seeing my aged father, they said, 'Namaste.'

My father introduced me. 'This is my daughter and she is a teacher. She has come here on a holiday. I told her how difficult your lives are. Your children are the reason for your existence and you want to educate them irrespective of what happens to your health, am I right?'

They replied in unison, 'Yes, sir!'

'Since my daughter is a teacher, she can guide you with your children's education and help them find better jobs. She'll give you information about some scholarships which you may not be aware of and help your kids apply so that your financial burden may be reduced. Is that okay with you? If not, it's all right. She'll go to some other village and try to help the people there. Please don't feel pressured. Think about it and get back to us. We'll be back in ten minutes.'

Grasping my hand tightly, he pulled me a short distance away.

'Why did you say all that?' I asked. 'You should have first told them about things like the dangers of AIDS.'

'Don't be foolish. We will tell them about it some other time. If you start with something negative, then nobody will like it. The first introduction should always be positive and bring real hope to the beneficiary. And just like I've promised them, you must help their children get scholarships first. Work on AIDS later.'

'And why did you tell them I'm a teacher, Kaka?' I demanded. 'You could have said I was a social worker.'

My father offered a calm rebuttal. 'They consider teaching to be one of the most respectable jobs and you are a professor, aren't you?'

I nodded reluctantly, still unsure of his strategy.

When we went back, the women were ready to listen. They called me 'akka'.

So I started working with them to help their children secure the promised scholarships. Some of these children even started going to college within a year. Only after this happened did I bring up the subject of AIDS, and this time, they heard me out. Months went by. It took me almost three years to establish a relationship with them. I was their darling akka and eventually, they trusted me enough to share their heart-rending stories and the trials they had endured.

Innocent girls had been sold into the trade by their husbands, brothers, fathers, boyfriends, uncles or other relatives. Some entered the sex trade on their own, hoping to earn some money for their families and help future generations escape poverty. Still others were lured into it with the promise of a real job, only to find themselves tricked into sex work. Hearing their stories, there were moments when I couldn't hide my tears, yet they were the ones who held my hand and consoled me! Each story was different but the end was the same—they all suffered at the hands of a society that exploited them and filled them with guilt and shame as a final insult.

I realized that simply donating money would not bolster their confidence or build their self-esteem. The best solution I could think of was to unite them towards a common goal by helping them build their own organization. The state government of Karnataka had many good policies that encouraged housing, marriage schemes and scholarships, but if we started an association or a union exclusively for the devadasis, they could address each other's problems. In time, they would become bold and independent, learning to organize themselves in the process.

Thus, an organization for the devadasis was formed. I believe that God cannot be present everywhere at once and, instead, he sends people to do his work. Abhay Kumar, a kind-hearted and idealistic young man from Delhi, joined us unexpectedly. He wanted to work with me and so I decided to give him the toughest job in order to test his passion for social work. I told Abhay, 'If you work with the devadasis for eight months and survive, I'll think about absorbing you into the project full-time.'

As promised, he did not show up for eight months, and then one day, he confidently strolled into my office, a little thinner, but grinning from ear to ear.

I said, 'Abhay, now you know how hard social work is. It takes extreme commitment and persistence to keep going.

'You can go back to Delhi with the satisfaction of having made a difference to so many lives. You are a good human being and I'm sure that this little experience will stay with you and help you later.'

He smiled and replied in impeccable Kannada, 'Who said that I wanted to go back to Delhi? I've decided to stay in Karnataka and complete this project.'

'Abhay, this is serious work. You are young and that's a great disadvantage in this line of work and . . .' My voice faded away. I didn't know what else to say!

'Don't worry about that, madam! You gave me the best job I could possibly have. I thought that you might give me a desk job. I never imagined that you'd give me fieldwork, that too the privilege of working with the devadasis. This past year has made me realize their agony and unbearable hardships. Knowing that, how can I ever work anywhere apart from here?'

I was astonished at such sincerity and compassion in one so young. I offered him a stipend to help with his expenses but he stopped me with a show of his hand, 'I don't need that much. I already have a scooter and a few sets of clothes. I just need two meals a day, a roof over my head and a little money for petrol. That's it.'

I gazed at him fondly and knew that I was seeing a man who had found his purpose in life. He bade goodbye and left my office with determined strides.

Obviously, Abhay became the project lead, and I supported him wholeheartedly, taking care to converse with him regularly about the project's progress.

One day, I met with the devadasis and inquired about the welfare of their children.

'Our greatest difficulty is supporting our children's education,' they said. 'Most of the time, we can't afford their school fees and then we have to go back to what we know to get quick money.'

'We will take care of all your children's educational expenses, irrespective of which class they are in. But that means that you must not continue being a devadasi, no matter what,' I replied firmly.

The women agreed without hesitation. They had come to trust Abhay and me and knew that we would keep our word.

Hundreds of children were enrolled in the project—some went on to do professional courses while others went on to complete their primary-, middle- or high-school classes.

We held camps on AIDS awareness and prevention and sponsored street art and plays to educate the women and children on various medical issues—including the simple fact that infected hair is not an indication that one must become a devadasi. Rather, it is a simple curable disease that causes the hair to stick together and become matted over time. The women got themselves treated and some of them even had their heads shaved.

Eventually, we were able to get them loans by becoming their guarantors. Often, the women would tell me, 'Akka, please help us get a loan. If we can't repay it, then it is as good as cheating you and you know that we'll never do that.'

By this time I knew in my heart that a rich man might cheat me but our devadasis never would. They had great faith in me and I in them.

On the other hand, life became more dangerous for Abhay and me. We received death threats from pimps, local goons and others through phone calls, letters and messages. I was scared more for Abhay than myself. Though I asked for police protection, Abhay flatly refused and said, 'Our devadasis will protect me. Don't worry about me.'

A few weeks later, some pimps threw acid on three devadasis who had left their profession for good. But we all still refused to give up. The plastic surgery the victims underwent helped to bring back their confidence. They would not be intimidated. Our strength came from these women who were collectively trying to leave this hated profession. Though the government supplemented their income, many also started rearing goats, cows and buffaloes.

Over time, we established small schools that offered night classes which the devadasis could attend. It was an uphill battle that took years of effort from everybody involved.

After twelve years, some of the women met me to discuss a particular issue.

'Akka, we want to start a bank, but we are afraid to do it on our own.'

'What do you think happens in a bank?' I asked.

'Well, you need a lot of money to start a bank or even have an account. You must wear expensive clothes. We've seen that bankers usually wear suits and ties and sit in air-conditioned offices, but we don't have money for such things, Akka.'

After they brought this problem to our attention, Abhay and I sat down with the women and explained the basics of banking to them. A few professionals were consulted, and under their guidance, they started a bank of their own, with the exception of a few legal and administrative services that we provided. However, we insisted that the bank employees and shareholders should be restricted only to the devadasi community. So finally, the women were able to save money through fixed deposits and obtain low-interest loans. All profits had to be shared with the bank members. Eventually, the bank grew and the women themselves became its directors and took over its running.

Less than three years later, the bank had Rs 80 lakh in deposits and provided employment to former devadasis, but its most important achievement was that almost 3000 women were out of the devadasi system.

On their third anniversary, I received a letter from the bank.

We are very happy to share that three years have passed since the bank was started. Now, the bank is of sound financial health and none of us practise or make any money through the devadasi tradition. We have each paid a hundred rupees and have three lakhs saved for a big celebration. We have rented out a hall and arranged lunch for everyone. Please come and join us for our big day. Akka, you are very dear to us and we want you to be our chief guest for the occasion. You have travelled hundreds of times at your own cost and spent endless money for our sake even though we are strangers. This time, we want to book a round-trip air-conditioned Volvo bus ticket, a good hotel and an all-expenses-paid trip for you. Our money has been earned legally, ethically and morally. We are sure that you won't refuse our humble and earnest request.

Tears welled up in my eyes. Seventeen years ago, chappals were my reward, but now, they wanted to pay for my travel to the best of their ability. I knew how much the comfort of an air-conditioned Volvo bus and a hotel meant to them.

I decided to attend the function at my expense.

On the day of the function, I found that there were no politicians or garlands or long speeches as was typical. It was a simple event. At first, some women sang a song of agony written by the devadasis. Then another group came and described their experiences on their journey to independence. Their children, many of whom had become doctors, nurses, lawyers, clerks, government employees, teachers, railway employees and bank officers came and thanked their mothers and the organization for supporting their education.

And then it was my turn to speak.

I stood there, and words suddenly failed me. My mind went blank, and then, distantly, I remembered my father's words: 'I will feel very proud knowing that I gave birth to a daughter who helped ten helpless women make the most difficult transition from being sex workers to independent women.'

I am usually a spontaneous speaker but on that day, I was too choked with emotion. I didn't know where to begin. For the first time in my life, I felt that the day I meet God, I will be able to stand up straight and say confidently, 'You've given me a lot in this lifetime, and I hope that I have returned at least something. I've served 3000 of your children in the best way I could, relieving them of the meaningless and cruel devadasi system. Your children are your flowers and I am returning them to you.'

Then my eyes fell on the women. They were so eager to listen to me. They wanted to hear what I had to say. Abhay was there too, looking overwhelmed by everything they had done for us.

I quoted a Sanskrit sloka my grandfather had taught me when I was six years old: 'O God, I don't need a kingdom nor do I desire to be an emperor. I don't want rebirth or the golden vessels or heaven. I don't need anything from you. O Lord, if you want to give me something, then give me a soft heart and hard hands, so that I can wipe the tears of others.'

Silently, I came back to my chair. I didn't know what the women must be thinking or feeling at that moment.

An old devadasi climbed up on to the stage and stood there proudly. With a firm voice, she said, 'We want to give our akka a special gift. It is an embroidered bedspread and each of us has stitched some portion of it. So there are three thousand stitches. It may not look beautiful but we all wanted to be present in this bedspread.' Then she looked straight at me and continued, 'This is from our hearts to yours. This will keep you cool in the summer and warm in the winter—just like our affection towards you. You were by our side during our difficult times, and we want to be with you too.'

It is the best gift I have ever received.

22

The Meaning of Philanthropy

One day, I attended a wedding in the family and met my friends and relatives after a long time. Since we were guests and not part of the organizing committee, there was plenty of time for us to chat. Everybody was giving updates about their lives as we sat in a group when the conversation moved to the topic of giving back to our country and society.

One of the women opined, 'Philanthropy needs a lot of time. Also, a woman must be financially strong and have fewer responsibilities at home. Assuming that there are no other hobbies that she is passionate about, it is possible to pay attention to charitable work.'

'I think it is all to do with unpaid debts,' remarked a cousin. 'If a person has taken assistance from someone in a previous lifetime and they haven't repaid that debt, be it financially or physically, then the person must repay the debt in this lifetime. So, all it means is that philanthropists have taken a lot of help in their last birth and are simply repaying those debts now.'

Another woman said, 'You don't need talent when it comes to distributing money for charity. It is nothing but a way to pass time.' Then she looked at me with a friendly smile and asked, 'You are from the industry. What do you think?'

I knew that the intentions of my family and friends weren't bad at all. So, I did not get hurt or feel upset. With time, I have become insensitive to unhelpful comments and more sensitive to causes. I explained to them as best as I could. 'In my long journey of philanthropy,' I said, 'I have met many people who have helped others, irrespective of their circumstances. For instance, some of them did not have any money, some had a little, while there were others who had more than they would ever need. The only thing you really need to be a philanthropist is the attitude and determination to assist others.'

'Give me an example,' said one of them.

'Of course I will. That is the best way to convince you. You must have travelled at least once from the Badami railway station to the town. There are huge neem trees on either side of the road. The story goes that there once lived a lame man who wanted to make a difference. So, he planted neem saplings all by himself on both sides of the road. In the old days, there was sufficient rain and not much global warming. So the plants grew into trees. Today, however, no one remembers his name and all that remains is a story of an unknown lame man who provided shade to all the future travellers on that road. Tell me, isn't that an act of charity?'

There were 'oohs' and 'aahs' from the women sitting around me.

'Tell us more,' a few chorused. I noticed more people joining our group.

'Well, there is a well-known urologist in Bangalore named Dr Sridhar. He lived and worked abroad before making a decision to come back to the country. He could easily have decided otherwise and worked for a private hospital in a foreign land and earned much more money. Instead this doctor lives with his family in a two-bedroom rented home for the last thirty-one years and works every day towards fulfilling his dream of providing a professional opinion and helping people, with complete disregard to financial consideration. He has found a way to do this by making a clear demarcation in the way he works. He sees patients in the morning and charges his usual fees. However, in the evening, between 4 p.m. and 6 p.m., he sees each patient for free, irrespective of the income of the patients. Thus, he balances both parts of his life with sincerity.

'When I asked him the secret behind his noble deed, he said, "I have a very understanding and supportive wife and encouraging children, who have allowed me to go down this road. I wouldn't have been able to do so without them." That's when it hit me that even in philanthropy, great things cannot be achieved without family support.'

I saw a few nods in the group.

I continued. 'Recently, I was in Jaipur for work. While I was travelling in the city, my driver stopped to go to a dhaba and have tea. While waiting, I saw a beautiful farm surrounded by a boundary wall. There was a patch of green vegetables between the boundary wall and the road, and I saw a gardener working there. Curious, I went up to him and started a conversation. "Why are you working outside the boundary? Who does this patch belong to?" Just then, a big and strong man came out of the farm and headed towards the patch. When I asked him the same question, he invited me to come inside and have a look. I went in and immediately realized that the land belonged to a rich family. When I threw some more questions at the man, he said, "This is my ancestral land. I realize deeply that there are others who do not have land and are not as fortunate as I am. So, I decided to grow a few simple vegetables like coriander, spinach, fenugreek and other green leafy ones in the patch outside. The gardener has been instructed to take care of it in the same way that he takes care of the rest of my land. I have also told him to let anyone take the vegetables from there without question. He must only do his work with sincerity."

'I was surprised. "Who takes the vegetables?" I asked.

"There are many labourers who work around here. They come and pick some up."

"What happens if a person who isn't poor takes it?"

"Then I feel nothing but pity for him or her, but we don't say anything. I have been doing this for many years now, and everyone in this area knows that poor people get free vegetables from this garden." I was amazed at his quiet benevolence.'

I looked around and saw everyone listening with rapt attention. A cousin smiled and asked me to continue with a show of her hand.

'Let me tell you of another incident. In Rajasthan, people believe that giving free water to people is a pious act, especially in the summer. I saw mud pots on the side of the road that were almost always filled with water for passers-by. One day,

I saw a man taking away the mud pot. Unable to contain my inquisitiveness, I asked him, "Why are you carrying this? This must always be kept filled and on the side of the road."

'The man gave me a slight smile. He said, "Behenji, people happily fill water in the pots, but what they fail to realize is that the same pot can become a source of infectious diseases if nobody cares to clean it. So, once the pot is empty, my job is to thoroughly clean it and only then fill it with drinking water."'

'Ah!' The crowd around me chorused.

A friend remarked, 'I know many autorickshaw drivers in the city who drive old and sick people and pregnant women free of charge once a week.'

'Yes, that's exactly what philanthropy is about. Philanthropy is a Greek word where *philos* means loving and *anthropos* means man. Just like the autorickshaw drivers, the people I spoke about were not rich. Some were middle-class and some were poor. So, it isn't about how much a person has but their attitude towards fellow beings. It is compassion, a kind word, a warm hug and a little sharing that makes us better human beings. If we are lucky enough to be rich, then we can help more people. If a person can be a leader with compassion and a good attitude, then he or she can make a definite change in society. Don't you think?'

A murmur of agreement and hopeful sighs went through the group, even as someone announced that it was time for us to head to the next room for the wedding meal. Quickly, the group split into smaller clusters as we headed towards some well-deserved lunch.

Scan QR code to access the
Penguin Random House India website